BREAKING THE TONGUE

Language, Education, and Power in
Soviet Ukraine, 1923–1934

In the 1920s and early 1930s, the Communist Party embraced a policy to promote national consciousness among the Soviet Union's many national minorities as a means of Sovietizing them. In Ukraine, Ukrainian-language schooling, coupled with pedagogical innovation, was expected to serve as the lynchpin of this social transformation for the republic's children.

The first detailed archival study of the local implications of Soviet nationalities policy, *Breaking the Tongue* examines the implementation of the Ukrainization of schools and children's organizations. Matthew D. Pauly demonstrates that Ukrainization faltered because of local resistance, a lack of resources, and Communist Party anxieties about nationalism and a weakening of Soviet power – a process that culminated in mass arrests, repression, and a fundamental adjustment in policy.

MATTHEW D. PAULY is an associate professor in the Department of History at Michigan State University.

Breaking the Tongue

*Language, Education, and Power
in Soviet Ukraine, 1923–1934*

MATTHEW D. PAULY

UNIVERSITY OF TORONTO PRESS
Toronto Buffalo London

© University of Toronto Press 2014
Toronto Buffalo London
utorontopress.com

Reprinted in paperback 2022

ISBN 978-1-4426-4893-7 (cloth)
ISBN 978-1-4875-4806-3 (paper)
ISBN 978-1-4426-1906-7 (EPUB)
ISBN 978-1-4426-1905-0 (PDF)

Publication cataloguing information is available from Library and Archives Canada.

 This publication was made possible by the financial support of the Shevchenko Scientific Society, USA, from the Ivan and Elizabeta Khlopetsky Fund.

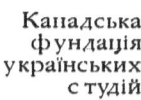  Canadian Foundation for Ukrainian Studies
Fondation canadienne des études ukrainiennes

Канадська фундація українських студій

This publication was made possible by the financial support of the Canadian Foundation for Ukrainian Studies.

We wish to acknowledge the land on which the University of Toronto Press operates. This land is the traditional territory of the Wendat, the Anishnaabeg, the Haudenosaunee, the Métis, and the Mississaugas of the Credit First Nation.

University of Toronto Press acknowledges the financial support of the Government of Canada, the Canada Council for the Arts, and the Ontario Arts Council, an agency of the Government of Ontario, for its publishing activities.

 Canada Council for the Arts / Conseil des Arts du Canada

 ONTARIO ARTS COUNCIL
CONSEIL DES ARTS DE L'ONTARIO
an Ontario government agency
un organisme du gouvernement de l'Ontario

 Funded by the Government of Canada / Financé par le gouvernement du Canada

For Amelia and Nadia

Contents

List of Illustrations ix

Acknowledgments xi

List of Terms xv

A Note on Transliteration xvii

A Note on Administrative Divisions in Soviet Ukraine xix

Introduction 3
1 Primary Lessons 15
2 Adapting to Place 42
3 The Conversion 63
4 Treading Carefully 85
5 Learning the New Language of Pedagogy 104
6 Limited Urgency 131
7 The Question of the Working Class 152
8 Children as Salvation: The Young Pioneers and Komsomol 174
9 Ukrainization in a Non-Ukrainian City 200
10 The Correction 235
11 Children Corrupted and Exalted 281
12 The Path Ahead 301
Conclusion 340
Biographical and Informational Sketches 349

Notes 359

Bibliography 413

Index 431

Illustrations

Map   Ukrainian Soviet Socialist Republic (UkrSSR) in 1927.   34
- 2.1   Teachers and second-grade pupils of the Taras Shevchenko Kyiv Labour School No. 1.   59
- 3.1   A demonstration to celebrate the opening of a four-year school in the village of Romanivka, Artemivsk region, 1928.   72
- 4.1   A demonstration of labour-school pupils in Kyiv, 1924.   98
- 5.1   Delegates from the Kharkiv province at the First All-Ukrainian Teachers' Congress, January 1925.   111
- 6.1   Mykola Skrypnyk, Narkomos commissar, speaks at a meeting of the Young Pioneers in Kharkiv, 1930.   150
- 7.1   A cartoon of a teacher resisting Ukrainization.   166
- 8.1   A group of Young Pioneers at a rally in the city of Kyiv, 1930s.   177
- 9.1   Lenin Street in central Odesa, 1934.   206
- 10.1   An overhead view of the courtroom in the Kharkiv opera house during the trial of the SVU, 1930.   259
- 11.1   Young Pioneer girls conducting a public reading of Ukrainian-language newspapers, 1933.   291
- 12.1   A group of schoolteachers in the village of Huliaipole in the Kyiv oblast, 1934–5.   306

Acknowledgments

Late into a recent research trip, I found myself buying a camera in one of the shopping malls off Deribasivska in central Odesa. I began the exchange, as I often did, in Ukrainian. "Are you from Galicia?" the young saleswoman asked me. This was the first time in my years of travel that I had ever been mistaken for a Ukrainian and I was proud, but perplexed. Was Galicia in western Ukraine the one place in an Odesan's imagination that the Ukrainian language lived as something more than the rhetoric of public ceremony? I knew that this could not be the case. It was probably just that my accent was off, that my Ukrainian was "too Polish." Indeed, I found through many further interactions that there was a vibrant, Ukrainian-speaking community in the predominantly Russophone city. Yet, the short conversation served as a reminder of what intrigued me about this project when I began. In a different time, how did officials try to make a language, which was unfamiliar to key communities in Soviet Ukraine, familiar?

Research for this book was enabled by grants from the International Research and Exchange Boards (IREX); American Councils for International Education; the College of Social Sciences and Department of History at Michigan State University; and the Graduate School, Russian and East European Institute, and Department of History at Indiana University. I am especially grateful for publishing grants from the Canadian Foundation for Ukrainian Studies and the John and Elisabeth Chlopecky Fund of the Shevchenko Scientific Society in the United States. Publication of this book would not have been possible without this generous aid. At the University of Toronto Press, I am extremely grateful to Richard Ratzlaff, who acquired this book, gave me encouragement, and ably guided me through the process of completing revisions, and to Frances Mundy, who saw the manuscript to publication. The suggestions of Michael Moser and two other anonymous reviewers made the manuscript better and much more precise and thoughtful.

While any shortcomings of this work are my own entirely, I have been privileged to work in a lively, supportive community at Michigan State University; this project has been considerably advanced from conversations with faculty in the Department of History, Center for European, Russian, and Eurasian Studies, and James Madison College. I have also benefited from the commentary of countless colleagues at the meetings of the Association for Slavic, East European, and Eurasian Studies; Association for the Study of Nationalities; History of Education Society; and the International Standing Committee for History of Education and Society for the History of Children and Youth. The Midwest Russian History Workshop has offered a special space for stimulation and fellowship when I have been able to attend. I am particularly thankful for the observations, questions, and contextualization offered by Lewis Siegelbaum, Francine Hirsch, Peter Blitstein, Christine Ruane, Lisa Kirschenbaum, Donald Raleigh, James Andrews, Matthias Neumann, Serhy Yeklechyk, William Risch, Mayhill Fowler, Serhii Polkhii, David Marples, Roman Senkus, Yaroslav Bilinsky, Joshua First, and Iveta Kestere. Steven Seegel, Susan Smith, and Heather DeHaan provided valuable advice on portions of material on "local studies" in the primary school that first appeared in article form, and Olga Bertelsen generously shared archival notes and her own perspective on the role and fate of the Ukrainian intelligentsia in the 1920s and 1930s. I enjoyed exceptional training at Indiana University and early guidance on this project from Hiroaki Kuromiya, as well as Toivo Raun, William Fierman, Alexander Rabinowitch, David Ransel, and Ben Eklof. I shared an intellectual kinship and camaraderie with Lynn Sargent, Mara Lazda, Kara Brown, Martin Blackwell, David Fisher, and Jude Richter in Bloomington, along with my many classmates at SWSEEL, the Harvard Ukrainian Summer Institute and the University of Kansas's Language Institute at Lviv State University.

On repeated trips to Kyiv, I relied considerably on the counsel of Yuri Shapoval, Stanislav Kulchitsky, and Valerii Vasyliev to navigate the archives and gain familiarity with recent Ukrainian scholarship. I would have been lost without their aid. Furthermore, this book would considerably less accurate without the intervention of Oksana Yurkova, who helped track down the full names of many of the personages in this study when I was working on revisions in East Lansing. Viktor Kuzio, my good friend in Lviv, helped immensely in formulating petitions and establishing initial telephone contact with archival administrators. My knowledge of Ukrainian was vastly improved by the tutelage of Svitlana Diachenko at Taras Shevchenko Kyiv National State University, and I am forever in the debt of her and her family for the warm hospitality they showed me on many trips to Ukraine and my first long winter. Petro Bekh, Liliia Tovstolis, Oksana Musiienko, Natalia Musiienko, Anton Strutynsky, and Jonathan Frais gave encouragement in my years as a graduate student; Aleksandr Gogun was a great apartment mate on a subsequent trip and convinced me of the importance of strong tea during the writing process. I continued work on this project during my short but engaging time at the US Embassy in Kyiv and benefited from the comradeship and intellectual curiosity of Jason Hyland, Jason Grubb, and Amy Mason. Robert and Tanya Peacock always opened their home to me when I returned to Kyiv and my long friendship with them has offered much comfort. In Odesa, I enjoyed warm and critical support from Anatolii Mysechko, Yevhen Stepanchenko, and Leonid Fursenko, and an unforgettable evening dinner hosted by Taras Maksymiuk in his garden. The archivists and librarians in Ukraine who aided me in my research are far too numerous to detail, but it goes without saying that I could not have completed this book without their assistance. The staff at the Vernadsky National Library, Sukhomlynsky State Scientific-Pedagogical Library, and Maksysmovych Scientific Library provided me with early support. Ivan Nitochko and Liliia Bilousova at the Odesa State Oblast Archive deserve special mention for their openness, keen interest, and backing of this project. Tetiana Kryshevych, the caretaker of a depository of the National Parliamentary Library, on the outskirts of central Kyiv, came to my rescue when I was on a search of an early Soviet pedagogical journal article that could be accessed nowhere else. Lastly, I am indebted to Tamara Rzhondovska, the head of the reading room at the Pshenychny Central State Kinofotofon Archive, for the kindness and aid she extended me in my pursuit of photographic illustrations.

My deepest thanks go to my family, to my mother, father, brother, and sister, all of whom came to visit me in Ukraine, to investigate what drew me there and share in the vibrancy and beauty of the country. Two amazing daughters, Amelia and Nadia, were born after research for this book began. Both have spent their formative years wondering when it would end. Ukraine, to them, represents a land of never-ending presents and mystery, and I hope they are able to discover it for themselves someday. I remember my oldest daughter meeting two dancers from Odesa at the Grand Rapids Ballet and listening in awe as we chatted away in a language that she knew first from bedtime storybooks. I extend my final and most abiding gratitude to my wife, Mindy, who is a remarkable scholar of language and education in her own right, and who put up with my numerous research trips to Ukraine and summers devoted to writing. She bravely read several versions of the manuscript, sometimes in very rough form, and has been an unparalleled source of opinion, support, and affection. As I have striven to balance the demands of an academic life with the adventures of parenthood, I am eternally grateful that I am doing it together with Mindy.

List of Terms

Agitprop	Central Committee propaganda department
Borotbist	Member of the left wing of the Ukrainian Party of Social Revolutionaries
DVU	State Publishing House of Ukraine
FZU school	Factory-Apprenticeship School (literally, School of Factory and Plant Apprenticeship)
GPU (DPU)	State Political Directorate, the Soviet security police
guberniia (huberniia)	large administrative area (province)
Gymnasium	Pre-Soviet preparatory secondary school
Holovsotsvykh	Main Administration for Social Upbringing, later Uprsotsvykh and Sektor sotsvykhu
INO	Institute of People's Education, Soviet post-secondary school
katsap	Ukrainian derogatory term for an ethnic Russian
KDR	Communist Children's Movement – Young Pioneers
KP(b)U	Communist Party (Bolshevik) of Ukraine
KPZU	Communist Party of Western Ukraine
Komsomol	Communist Youth League
korenizatsiia	indigenization, the policy promoting non-Russian cadres and languages
kraieznavstvo	local studies
Narkomos	People's Commissariat of Education, UkrSSR
Narkompros	People's Commissariat of Education, RSFSR
NEP	New Economic Policy
oblast	administrative area (territory), larger than *okruha*
okruha	administrative area (region) smaller than *guberniia*
perevirka	examination, used to test teachers' Ukrainian knowledge

politosvita	political education (for adults)
poradnyk	Narkomos guide to instructional methodology
profshkola	vocational school
Radnarkom	Council of People's Commissars, UkrSSR
raion	smaller administrative area (district) in an *okruha* or oblast
Robos	Ukrainian branch of the Union of Educational Workers
RSFSR	Russian Soviet Federated Socialist Republic
RSI	Workers' and Peasants' Inspectorate
ShKM	School for Collective Farm Youth
smychka	union or alliance (between city and village); in Ukrainian – *zmychka*
sotsvykh	social upbringing (pre-school and primary school education)
SUM	Union of Ukrainian Youth
SVU	Union for the Liberation of Ukraine
tekhnikum	technical college
TsB	Central Bureau of the KDR
TsK	Central Committee of the KP(b)U, VKP(b), or Komsomol
Ukrius	Ukrainian Communist Workers' Youth Union
Ukrliknep	All-Ukrainian Special Commission for the Struggle with Illiteracy under Narkomos
UkrSSR	Ukrainian Soviet Socialist Republic
UNR	Ukrainian People's Republic
USSR	Union of Soviet Socialist Republics
VKP(b)	All-Union Communist Party (of Bolsheviks)
VUAN	All-Ukrainian Academy of Sciences
VUK	All-Ukrainian Committee of Robos
VUTsVK	All-Ukrainian Central Executive Committee
Young Pioneers	Communist organization for children, overseen by Komsomol

A Note on Transliteration

Historians who conduct research with Ukrainian and Russian sources, but present their findings in English, must make accommodations that ensure precision as well as readability. In this study, I use a modified Library of Congress system for transliteration of Ukrainian and Russian names and terms introduced in the text: I have suppressed soft signs for proper names in the text and rendered -yi (Ukrainian) and -ii (Russian) personal name endings as -y, and the initial Ia-, Ie-, Io, or Iu- in personal names as Ya-, Ye-, Yo-, or Yu-. However, for the sake of accuracy, I have transliterated Ukrainian and Russian sources in the notes and bibliography in accordance with the unadjusted Library of Congress system. Additionally, I have favoured Ukrainian abbreviations for republican branches of government, but transliterated the names of Communist Party and security police units (e.g., Agitprop, Orgbiuro, GPU) from Russian because these variants are more familiar to English-language readers. I have also relied on transliteration from Russian for names of ethnic Russians and leading non-Ukrainian party leaders. Finally, I have transliterated the names of cities and administrative divisions in the UkrSSR from Ukrainian (e.g., Kyiv, Odesa, Kharkiv) and have generally used Ukrainian variants for the names of minor non-Russian figures.

A Note on Administrative Divisions in Soviet Ukraine

The history of administrative divisions of the Ukrainian SSR (UkrSSR) can be confusing. The republic went through three, major, administrative changes during the period under study. Soviet authorities initially preserved the tsarist-era *gubernii* (provinces; generally known by its Russian spelling, it is transliterated from Ukrainian as *hubernii*), increasing their number to twelve in 1920. From 1923 to 1925, the republican government began to abolish the *gubernii* and replace them with smaller *okruhy* (regions) and to create *raiony* (districts) through the merger and repartition of tsarist-era *volosti* (counties). However, the institution of this shift was not immediate and sometimes *gubernii* co-existed with the smaller *okruhy* until the former's final abolition. Initially, there were fifty-three *okruhy* in Soviet Ukraine, but this number declined to forty-one through division and the transfer of territory to the Russian SFSR. Within the territory of the UkrSSR, Soviet officials also created the Moldovan Autonomous Soviet Socialist Republic (ASSR) along its southwestern border and national *raiony* for ethnic minorities, including Russians. By 1931, there were twenty-five national *raiony*. Beginning in 1930, the *okruhy* were abolished and, by 1932, had been replaced by seven large oblasts that were further subdivided into *raiony*. In 1934, the capital of the UkrSSR was transferred from Kharkiv to Kyiv; the number of oblasts increased through the 1930s to a total of fifteen oblasts (with the addition of the Moldovan ASSR) by the beginning of the Second World War.[1]

Throughout 1923 to 1939, the territory and names of *raiony* shifted; some had a short life, and it is difficult to find a discussion of them beyond their mention in a source document. Names of cities also changed, as did the Ukrainian spelling of these names after the creation of a new, unified, Ukrainian orthography in 1928 (known sometimes as the Kharkiv orthography) and its formal adoption by the Soviet Ukrainian Academy of Sciences in March 1929. To make matters even more complicated, this orthography was subsequently reformed in 1933 because of its alleged embrace of "nationalist deviation." Of course, there were Russian variants for names of cities and administrative divisions as well.

With the intent of simplifying reading for the non-specialist and specialist alike, I use English-language translations for the UkrSSR's administrative divisions with the exception of "oblast," a term that is widely used in English-language literature and reflects the current administrative division of Ukraine. I provide consistent English-language translation at each mention of the equivalent Ukrainian administrative division, so that *guberniia (huberniia)*=province, *okruha*=region, and *raion*=district. Where there is a possibility of confusion, the Ukrainian-language variant is parenthetically offered. I also employ the pre-Kharkiv orthography spelling of Ukrainian cities (e.g., Stalino, not Staline) because contemporary Ukrainian historical scholarship favours this spelling and the Kharkiv orthography had a relatively short existence. Lastly, as noted already, I generally transliterate place names from the Ukrainian variant, the one exception being the formal name of the republic because an English-language equivalent is commonly accepted: the Ukrainian SSR (abbreviated as UkrSSR).

BREAKING THE TONGUE

Language, Education, and Power in
Soviet Ukraine, 1923–1934

Introduction

Now we issue a call for Ukrainization, for a rebirth of national culture for social reasons, in the name of a living historical current which takes us through the vast mouth of a river to the sea of a new social life.

P. Sapukhin, *Narodnii uchytel'*, 1925

Teachers in Soviet Ukraine who read their professional newspaper regularly confronted reminders such as this that their responsibilities in the new Soviet republic were great. They were to assume a vanguard position in the "third front" of the socialist revolution, education, by transforming their teaching and the learning objectives for their young charges, while carrying socialism to their community as public educators and political activists. The young Communist state focused on the nation for conveyance of these campaigns. "National culture" would push the "living historical current" along, providing it with substance and energy. This effort would result in the consolidation of a "new social life," but it would be a form of socialism enabled, for the foreseeable future, by acceptance and promotion of national identity. The public's embrace of this truth would be a critical determinant of the success of socialism.

The effort to use the Ukrainian nation for this construction of socialism was known as Ukrainization. Scholars have devoted considerable attention to high-level political debates over early Soviet nationalities policy, labelled *korenizatsiia* (literally, "rooting" or indigenization) for its application in the Soviet Union generally. Their studies have provided valuable information regarding the general character of korenizatsiia and its significance, but the picture is incomplete. The full impact of this policy can be understood only by an investigation into how Soviet nationalities policy was experienced and interpreted by the individuals who were most immediately entrusted with the policy's execution and success, especially at the local level.¹ This work suggests that primary schools in Ukraine provide the most productive arena in which to investigate this concern, since political authorities gave education administrators, inspectors, and teachers critical responsibility in the implementation of nationalities policy, and Ukrainian schools were the sites of the policy's most rapid achievements. On paper, the percentage of Ukrainian-language schools rose from 50.7 per cent at the beginning of 1923 to 88.1 per cent in the 1932–3 academic year, in excess of the ethnic-Ukrainian proportion of the republic's population.² Ukrainian People's Commissariat of Education (*Narodnii komisariat osvity* – *Narkomos*) records, party communications, pedagogical journals, and the teachers' newspaper chronicle not only the development of Ukrainization, but also how educators understood and employed directives. What emerges from these documents is not simply an account of the development of Ukrainian-language instruction, but the reimagining of the entire school curriculum. The Communist Party intended schools to be the training ground for a new generation of skilled, politically conscious, and economically informed Soviet citizens, and Ukrainization was seen as the primary means to this end. It was through the national language, promoted by schoolteachers, that the Soviet ideal was to be realized. The campaign translated Soviet notions of governance to the Ukrainian-speaking population as well as defined much of the character and authority of Soviet power in the republic as a whole.

But, as the archival and published material illustrates, Ukrainization in the schools was by no means easily accomplished. The success of the linguistic aspect of Ukrainization relied on educators who would not only teach children in Ukrainian, but also instruct government bureaucrats, party officials, and rank-and-file workers in the language. In addition, they had an immense amount of responsibility within the classroom itself. Teachers had to use, and in many cases learn, not only a new language of instruction ("to break their tongues"), but also a radical form of pedagogy. Furthermore, despite proclamations regarding the importance of education, the reality was that the Communist Party's support of the new education system and its trust in teachers to perform correctly under this system was limited. Central and republican party authorities and the republican security service targeted a group of leading teachers and intellectuals because of their suspicion of the educators' management of everyday Ukrainization as well as qualms about their leadership of progressive education and their patronage of youth. These anxieties did not stem from an actual threat, but rather from the concern of the Soviet political leadership about programs that had the potential to become unmanageable or go awry. The arrest and denunciation of prominent non-party Ukrainizers[3] foreshadowed not the absolute abandonment of Ukrainization, but a critical alteration in the form of social transformation that these educators had supported. What ultimately becomes apparent through an investigation of Ukrainization on the local level is that language policy and the fate and direction of the schoolhouse were inextricably linked.[4]

Objectives of Soviet Nationalities Policy in Ukraine

The Communist Party meant Ukrainization as a means of integrating the bulk of the rural population into the Soviet order. It recognized the concerted resistance of the Ukrainian peasantry to the imposition of Soviet power during the civil war. Peasant anarchist armies made short-term alliances with the Red Army, but primarily to protect their own parochial interests.[5] Few Ukrainian peasants saw themselves as nationalists or were nationally minded. But they recognized the Soviets as fundamentally alien. Ukrainization was then meant to win this large population over to the Soviet cause. It recognized the reality of a majority-Ukrainian-speaking population in the countryside and feared the potential for nationalism resulting from a growing feeling of alienation from a government that aspired towards a wholesale transformation of rural life. The Communist Party was highly suspicious of peasants, but in Ukraine, there was little option but to engage them, and it viewed the national divide between the city and village as particularly troubling.[6] Ukrainization offered a means to ensure that the Soviet authority possessed the tools to administer the village (and control any threats stemming from it), as well as to alter the linguistic environment of the city so that a peasant-centred workforce could more easily acculturate. This suggested not a victory of the village over the city, but rather the alignment of the village to the interests of the city.[7] Ukrainian culture would become identifiable with the urban and modern, and Ukrainian-speaking peasants would seek to mimic its new form and use it for their own social mobility.[8] Schools were instrumental to this effort to bridge the rural and the urban because of the concerted attempts by Narkomos to orient the curriculum of all schools towards a recognition of the city's leadership status, and to link rural and urban schools.

Elements in the KP(b)U – the Ukrainian branch of the Communist Party – viewed Ukrainization as an erroneous strategy that privileged a backward, rural culture. As the high-ranking secretary of the KP(b)U TsK (Central Committee), Dmitrii Lebed, had insisted in a published 1923 theory labelled a "Battle of Two Cultures," it was the urban-based Russian culture that was rightly dominant in the Ukrainian context and would inevitably triumph in the long term. Expansive support for the Ukrainian language was a "reactionary," wasteful cost that did not benefit the interests of the working class and the socialist state.[9]

Resistance to Ukrainization persisted in republican and all-Union party organizations and state institutions, but this opposition must be seen along a graduated scale. A member might believe that funding for Ukrainian-language use should be minimized relative to other expenditures, that publication should be correlated with levels of Ukrainian literacy, or that all-Union organizations (including educational institutions) should operate exclusively in Russian. Such views were not necessarily provoked by a prejudice against Ukrainian culture, but rather a conviction that state authorities even in Ukraine needed to most efficiently communicate with the population that mattered most: the Russian-speaking industrial working class. The establishment of a Ukrainian-language education system was meant to break this reality. It was the linkage by Narkomos of the Ukrainian primary school to a ladder of educational institutions extending to the university, and support for authoritative Ukrainian primary schools in the urban setting, that undermined the position of Lebed and his supporters and confirmed the party's abandonment of a principle of "neutrality" in nationalities policy.[10]

While the initial articulation of a Ukrainization strategy in 1923 might be seen as arising from the political requirements of an unstable post-war Ukraine, the 1925 acceleration of the campaign appeared to be a genuine (if sometimes constrained) effort at the transformation of the linguistic culture of the Ukrainian republic. Joseph Stalin remained through the later 1920s and into the early 1930s a consistent supporter of Ukrainization generally, even while signalling a need for a correction. The fundamental questions were what the targets of Ukrainization should be, who should lead the policy, and, from the perspective of some, what dangers might arise from its pursuit. These were issues for debate, but they did not mean the party formulation of Ukrainization or korenizatsiia in general was insincere.[11] This study seeks to remind readers of the practical as well as political limitations on the success of Ukrainization in education, in particular, primary schooling, while advancing the proposition that few engaged in the process of Ukrainization fully understood what constraints would be imposed.[12] If the state police in Ukraine long viewed the activities of bourgeois Ukrainizers with trepidation, the Ukrainizers did not anticipate the full scale of the repression that the State Political Directorate (GPU) would impose or the restrictions on Ukrainization that their actions would set.

The parameters of Ukrainization, in short, were not readily discernible or predictable, especially to educators. To argue that the party (or the security police) would inevitably move to rid itself of the participation of these bourgeois intellectuals minimizes activity that resulted from the fusion of party and national interests, the legacy this activity had on future nationalities policy, and further exploration of the motivations for the KP(b)U's initial alteration of Ukrainization in 1930 and definitive shift in 1934. Furthermore, not all in the KP(b)U or even the VKP(b) – the All-Union Communist Party – expected or believed in such a full-scale jettisoning of bourgeois specialists, and the republican and local state administrations were considerably invested in their participation in Ukrainization. Despite criticism directed at individual Ukrainizers, or non-party educators and teachers as a whole, Narkomos and provincial or municipal soviets widely acknowledged that Ukrainization could not succeed without this collaboration.[13] In other words, for multiple parties, Ukrainization was not a cynical or short-term measure. Stalin, First Secretary of the KP(b)U Lazar Kaganovich, Ukrainian commissars of education Oleksandr Shumsky and Mykola Skrypnyk, and less notable personages all believed that Ukrainization should succeed, but their understanding of the objectives of success differed.

This study contends that Ukrainization was a highly decentralized process, that its course was fundamentally determined by non-party educators, and that, in spite of penalties for non-involvement, its success hinged on willing cooperation. Francine Hirsch's comments regarding the role of ethnographers in Soviet nation building generally are helpful in this context: "To be sure the party-state was the locus of political power. But the party-state did not have a monopoly on knowledge; on the contrary, it depended to a significant degree on the information about the population that experts and local elites provided."[14] Similarly, Ukrainian educational theorists and linguists supplied knowledge necessary for Ukrainization and entrusted local education sections and teachers to carry out their instructions. This reliance created opportunity for significant progress in Ukrainian-language instruction, while allowing for a modification of the initial intent of central authorities.[15]

Assessing Ukrainization in the Context of Progressive Education

By choosing to focus on the daily implementation of Ukrainization, this study parts with previous works largely concerned with high-level discussions of nationalities policy.[16] This work's close reading of the daily implementation of Ukrainization points to an important conclusion underemphasized by other scholars: the formal, linguistic Ukrainization of institutions did not mean a qualitative improvement in their use of Ukrainian and an uncontested expansion of the Ukrainian-speaking environment. This phenomenon is particularly problematic regarding schooling, an area frequently cited as evidence of the policy's greatest success. George Liber argues a Ukrainian environment had developed beyond its rural core due to the campaign of the KP(b)U for the promotion of Ukrainian culture, literature, and press and advancement of Ukrainian cadres. Terry Martin, in his authoritative work *The Affirmative Action Empire*, maintains that an urban linguistic predominance of Ukrainian never existed in any prevailing fashion.[17] However, he views language transformation in the schools as largely untroubled, a finding that this study disputes.

While the goal of Narkomos and its people's education sections (*viddily narodnoi osvity*)[18] was for the transition to Ukrainian schooling to be "natural," it was not in reality "routine."[19] Furthermore, these efforts did not result in an immediate conversion of the wider language climate. Teachers did not make the transition easily; they continued to use Russian or a mixture of the two languages that few Ukrainian speakers could recognize. Most Young Pioneer youth groups continued to use Russian exclusively, and urban children fell into Russian outside the classroom. By 1926, Soviet republican leaders labelled the formal Ukrainization of primary schools "complete." However, this meant only that educational authorities had succeeded in grouping ethnic-Ukrainian schoolchildren together in single schools or groups and that the proportion of Ukrainian-language schools was equivalent to the proportion of ethnic Ukrainians: 80 per cent in the UkrSSR.[20] Furthermore, the process was not automatic. It met resistance from both educators and parents who opposed or passively resisted a shift in the language of instruction. Narkomos considered Ukrainization unfinished until there had been both a significant improvement in language instruction and universal enrolment of school-age Ukrainian children.[21] At the beginning of the 1925 school year, only 34.8 per cent of all eight- to fifteen-year-old children in the republic were enrolled. If the account is limited to children eight to eleven years old, 63.0 per cent of this subgroup was enrolled. Significantly, school enrolment of eight- to eleven-year-old children was worse in the largely ethnic-Ukrainian countryside relative to the city: 59.0 per cent compared to 79.0 per cent.[22] Although the proportion of children attending school increased throughout the 1920s, rural areas would continue to lag behind. In 1926, ethnic Ukrainians constituted 87.5 per cent of the rural population in the republic as a whole; the lower enrolment of rural children disproportionately affected the ethnic-Ukrainian population and it remained a concern for Narkomos's Ukrainizers.[23]

While it is true that teachers often exhibited apathy and hostility towards Ukrainization, the documentary record illustrates that this was not universally the case. The fact that teachers were publishing critical articles in the teachers' newspaper *Narodnii uchytel* (People's Teacher),[24] exhorting their colleagues to build socialism in the manner advocated by the party (e.g., in a child's "native" language), meant that some had taken up the charge. This study highlights a number of the problems associated with Ukrainization, but it should not be forgotten that there was a cohort of committed Ukrainizers, most of whom were teachers and educators. Without them, the policy would have died an early death. Furthermore, there is evidence that if teachers gave children time and proper instruction and enjoyed parental support, children adopted or expanded Ukrainian-language use with relatively little effort. A confident Ukrainian-speaking generation might have developed throughout the republic if the prevailing climate had been different.[25]

This project was integrally linked to a program of progressive educational reform that promised the liberation of children's abilities and training for their future participation in the Soviet society and economy. What is often lost in the existing scholarship on nationalities policy is that the Soviet development of national culture took place within the context of larger educational and cultural projects of reform. The Narkomos and its local sections pushed Ukrainian-language schooling (and native-language schooling for non-Ukrainians) concurrently with a program for progressive education. Its administrators believed that a program of progressive education – that is, a child-centred education that integrated disciplinary learning around specific themes – would be successful only if schools embraced native-language instruction. Native-language schooling would ensure that students would engage "naturally" with one another and their environment. Initially, progressive educators expected that children would discover their own innate capacity to work collectively and a curiosity for labour culture.

As education administrators modified their expectations and introduced greater structure to progressive education (the introduction of some disciplinary lessons, inclusion of direct political content, and a mandate for limited teacher-directed instruction), Narkomos officials continued to insist that schooling in the Ukrainian language afforded Ukrainian students the best opportunity to gain the skills necessary for active participation in the building of a socialist economy and state. The progressive vision of student participation in an integrated education remained. It was this education that would give students an introduction to the labour values of the socialist state, a prerequisite for entry directly into the workforce as conscious workers or matriculation to a particular Ukrainian institution, the vocational school (*profshkola*). It was not until this secondary school was eliminated as the result of the unification of the Ukrainian education system with the Russian, or arguably not until the turn to conservative pedagogy after the tumult of the cultural revolution (a shift in activist attitudes towards the production and form of cultural and intellectual expression in the Soviet Union generally from 1927 to 1931, initially sanctioned and supported by the Communist Party leadership under Stalin), that this orientation fundamentally changed. Education inspectors regularly complained about the absence of Ukrainian-language textbooks, but since the complex system favoured by progressive educators relied on content provided by students and teachers, there was less reason for concern.

Levels of Perspective: Privileging the Local

In the discussion that follows, the hand of the party leadership (in Moscow and in Kharkiv) is often absent, with the exception of key, wider junctures: the First All-Union Party Meeting on Education in 1920, the promulgation of Ukrainization in 1923, the KP(b)U's repeated rejection of "forced" Ukrainization of ethnic Russians in 1926, its censure and ousting of Commissar of Education Oleksandr Shumsky in 1926–7, its growing suspicion of nationalism among educators and sanction of a trial of the Ukrainian intelligentsia in 1930, and the Second All-Union Party Meeting on Education's decision to eliminate a separate Ukrainian education system. This is not because central and republican party authorities did not care about the direction of educational policy, but rather because they entrusted daily management of its course to a state organ, Narkomos, and intervened most directly when they perceived a need for a correction. Narkomos had considerable freedom to design educational policy in the interim. Apart from the Shumsky affair, less is said here about central party interference because Stalin's views regarding Ukrainization generally coincided with those of the principal republican leaders tasked with overseeing the campaign: Lazar Kaganovich and Mykola Skrypnyk. Ultimately, the party leadership in Moscow determined the direction of nationalities policy, and its instructions to the Ukrainian branch of the Communist Party, the KP(b)U, were instrumental in designing the campaign against non-party educators in 1930. However, the KP(b)U also reported internally about a supposed growth in nationalism and was independently concerned with maintaining party control over Ukrainization throughout the period under study.

This study dwells on the republican level because of its concern for a local history of nationalities policy and education. The question of schooling in Ukraine rose to the union level only on occasion, when an issue seemed most intractable or most heated and was generally linked to wider disputes about the overall scope of Ukrainization. There was no all-Union commissariat of education and only two all-Union conferences on education for the period under study. This is not to say that Moscow did not matter; Stalin signalled his support for the continuation but correction of Ukrainization, and these decisions impacted the field of education. Of critical importance to schooling was Stalin's authorization of repression against Ukrainian educational theorists and teachers, alleged to be members in a fictional nationalist organization, the SVU (*Spilka vyzvolennia Ukrainy*, Union for Liberation of Ukraine). On one level, schools were subject to the general sweep of the cultural revolution and the party's increasing disdain for non-party specialists and intellectuals during the First Five-Year Plan. An awareness of this context provides greater insight into the reasons for a shift in nationalities policy, but it cannot wholly explain the particular targets, the fabricated character of political terror, and the special focus on youth and schools. For these questions, the republican and local-level context must be considered. The all-Union presence was at its greatest at the time when Soviet authorities in Russia and Ukraine were considering the unification of the education systems. There was clear pressure from Moscow to standardize the educational experience for children and move away from local content. But even at this juncture, debates over the question of unification indicate a local embrace of the Ukrainian educational model that could be lost by focusing purely on the outcome, however predictable it may have been.

It was republican and local Narkomos institutions that defined much of what happened in regard to Ukrainization. Ukrainization commissions under the KP(b)U TsK and Radnarkom (the Ukrainian Council of People's Commissars, the leading institution of government) were responsible for political and administrative oversight, but much of the responsibility for implementation rested with the commissariat. Its adult literacy department, Ukrliknep (literally, the *Vseukrainska nadzvychaina komisiia z borotby iz nepismennostiu pry Narkomosi* – All-Ukrainian Special Commission for the Struggle with Illiteracy under Narkomos) created Ukrainization courses for all employees of Soviet institutions, including teachers, and teachers were employed as instructors in these courses as well. It was local Ukrainization commissions (formed at the regional and district level) that exercised the greatest influence in everyday Ukrainization, and a Narkomos representative was almost always a member. In short, the state and party set up multiple layers of oversight to ensure proper compliance with Ukrainization decrees, but lower-level organizations met the first instances of resistance, passivity, and approval on the part of Soviet employees and members of the public.[26] In specific regard to the Ukrainization of schools, local education sections decided which schools would be Ukrainized, its inspectors investigated failures of teachers to comply, and its methodology commissions (and teachers themselves) produced Ukrainian-language instructional literature to fill in for regular shortages and to ensure localized content.[27]

What is remarkable is that a process of nation building was so intimately tied to local and non-party institutions. The republican "centre" received complaints about lack of progress in Ukrainization or perceived coercion, but ultimately for schools, the most fundamental unit in Soviet nationalities policy, this was a highly localized process. Local education sections hired and fired teachers, and communities paid for teachers' salaries and maintenance of the school. Costs for the recruitment and relocation of teachers fell to the local education sections. In addition, because parents were financially invested in schools, they reacted even more negatively to Ukrainization of instruction against their will, or positively, if they saw benefit. Local conditions were thus critical to the pursuit of nationalities policy and, by extension, to the contours of national identity.

The character of the Ukrainization campaign specifically varied according to the rural–urban relationship and the concentration of national groups in a region. Ukrainization tended to reinforce the predominance of the city in the campaign and the political structure. The best assets for Ukrainization (teachers, literature, pedagogical literature, seven-year schools) went to the cities, although the highest numbers of Ukrainian speakers were accumulated in the countryside. In fact, the most revealing information about Ukrainization tends to come from the reports of urban Narkomos sections, or about urban schools. Ukrainization was not uncontested in the countryside, but here, the primary questions were the quality of instruction and language standardization and not high teacher or parent resistance: what language were teachers in fact teaching in, and how well did they know Ukrainian, if at all? Unsatisfactory teacher performance on Ukrainian-studies tests in rural areas put into question the whole purpose of Ukrainization. City schools were supposed to lead the campaign, but they faced substantial opposition. Rural schools lacked qualified personnel and tools to function effectively as pressure points on the city.

Regional context also determined the character of Ukrainization. If Russian history was often written from the perspective of two capitals, then Ukrainian history can also be imagined as such. Kharkiv was the political capital of the Ukrainian republic, chosen because of its perceived loyalty to the Bolsheviks over that of Kyiv. It was the symbolic centre of Ukrainization, the home of Narkomos, and (especially important for teachers) the residence of its institute for correspondence courses in Ukrainian studies. Figuratively speaking, teachers' heads turned towards Kharkiv. The city also represented modern Ukraine, what the Ukrainization campaign invoked and claimed. In Kharkiv, Soviet authorities believed, a clean break could be made from a romantic Ukrainian historicism or folklorism. The fact that the GPU did not choose to fabricate a SVU cell for the city indicates that the KP(b)U had a certain level of trust in Ukrainization in the capital. Kharkiv also represented the industrial East where Ukrainization was supposed to be centred, especially after 1930, when the cultural revolution refocused the attention of the party and Narkomos on economic areas critical to the First Five-Year Plan.

Kyiv was the former political capital of the civil war-era Ukrainian national governments, such as the Central Rada, General Secretariat, and Directory of the Ukrainian People's Republic (UNR), as well as the historical centre of the pre-revolutionary Ukrainian national movement and the alleged headquarters of the fabricated SVU. It was also home to the All-Ukrainian Academy of Sciences (*Vseukrainska akademiia nauk* – VUAN) and, for this reason, remained the intellectual heart of the Ukrainian republic.[28] As a consequence, Ukrainization in Kyiv should have been a comparatively easy matter. The fact that Narkomos reported problems regarding teachers' ability to teach in Ukrainian and parental resistance to a shift in language of instruction is an indication of the challenges Narkomos faced. But in Kyiv, KP(b)U cell reports warned of nationalist sentiment among teachers in the school. In the city and region of Kyiv, the paradox of Ukrainization was apparent: not enough was being done and too much was being done. As the SVU case would make plain, in Kyiv and other central (and "western") Ukrainian cities, Narkomos policy makers and educators had to walk a fine line in the campaign. Teachers presumably benefited from an association with teachers who were highly qualified instructors as well as authorities on Ukrainian studies, to say nothing of an overwhelmingly Ukrainian-speaking countryside. For children, proximity to historical places in Kyiv associated with Ukrainian nationhood must have bolstered the campaign, but these were aspects of an historical memory that Narkomos and the party needed to regulate and sometimes contest. In Kyiv, Ukrainization was always messier and its concern for the modern less apparent. Kyiv was a place of history, a nexus of peasant trade, and a former fulcrum in the Ukrainian national movement. As a consequence, it was less visibly Soviet.

This study also focuses in specific on the main city and region in Ukraine's heterogeneous south, Odesa. Unlike eastern Ukraine, the region did not border the Russian republic, and ongoing migration from Russia was less than in eastern Ukraine. Thus, the dynamic of Ukrainization was not equated solely with de-Russification,[29] but it was a considerably more complex process. In this environment, Ukrainization made progress because it offered yet another alternate identity, but now one that was considerably more attractive. Parts of the population of this port region, long accustomed to ethnic diversity, proved themselves adaptable. The Ukrainian-speaking intelligentsia and their supporters in Narkomos were determined to push the policy through, and they found the tide might have been shifting in their favour by the end of the 1920s. The GPU's creation of an SVU cell for the city is at least indicative of the security service's anxiety regarding non-party leadership of Ukrainization in the city, if not some appreciation of the Ukrainizers' tentative success.

To some extent, Ukraine was an aggregate of these local experiences. This acknowledgment does not, however, invalidate Ukraine's reality as a nation. In the final analysis, this story is in part about the development of national sensibility and the Soviet contribution to this awareness. People can conceive national identity in multiple ways, and Ukraine offers a conceptually provocative case of an experiment in nation building that was sincere, but contradictory. This study seeks to explore this tension from the ground up, and explore ways in which the local connected to the national and made this concept tangible and safe for a time to political authorities, even if teachers and parents occasionally contested the use of the "national" language in the classroom.

Chapter One

Primary Lessons

This study presumes the intrinsic power of educational institutions. It maintains that education set the barometer for the Soviet political agenda because it was education officials, instructors, and teachers who determined campaign objectives and the bar for success in nationalities policy. This chapter outlines the place of the schoolhouse not as the object of language planning, but as the agent of language change. Drawing on existing scholarship on the relationship between education and political authority, it argues that the shift in language of education pursued by the Soviets represented a powerful dictum. Schooling in Ukrainian was meant to upturn the existing arrangement of language authority, and interrupt and refract the consequences of schooled literacy. A new school of literacy would work as a corrective to the perceived exploitative functions of Russian dominance and standards.

The intersection between language and education is, in short, critical and reveals more than studies focused solely on Soviet education can highlight. Nearly all scholars who examine the subject of Soviet education stress the ambition of Soviet authorities to alter youth habits through the tutelage of the young. The linguistic component of this study suggests an even more revolutionary potential. However, it was also one fitting with established pedagogical trends. What education officials aspired to in Ukraine, other reformers in the United States and Europe sought: a curricular environment attuned to children's abilities that liberated their potential and allowed an investment in democratic citizenship. The difference in Ukraine was that progressive education was a component of a state-directed program and its objectives were more stridently political. Soviet authorities had high ambitions for the children's acculturation to a socialist labour culture through progressive education. Their general concern for a state role in the upbringing of children was motivated in part by a large population of at-risk children and specific Ukrainian concern for the early vocational training of youth. An embrace of progressive education meant entrusting lower-level teachers and educators with provision of curricular content. A tension inevitably existed between the state's lofty expectations and the system it implemented in order to attain them, as well as the state's discomfort with unpredictable outcomes. The additional requirement for teachers to transfer the language of instruction presented a dual burden, but one that the state remained adamantly committed to throughout the period under study.

Ukrainian nation building then took place in this unconventional, decentralized educational format. This is a story about the dissemination of new political values in concert with national culture. Language is at the centre of the discussion, but not a debate over language standardization or purism. Soviet efforts to promote the Ukrainian language and correlate it with a Ukrainian ethnic identity furthered the acceptance of a Ukrainian ethnic category, which in turn informed a republican identity. However, just who was Ukrainian and should be principally targeted by Ukrainization was in dispute. This study confronts the problematic category of Russified Ukrainians and the related question of a prohibition against the forced Ukrainization of the working class. The Ukrainization of the children of Russian-speaking Ukrainians was a run around this prohibition, and it also required some creativity in the ethnic identification of Ukrainian. The policy of Ukrainization had no future without a shift in the language of the workers and the city more generally. The repression of urban-based Ukrainizers and the scaling back of the objectives of educational institutions put limits on the policy generally.

A key component of urban Ukrainization was the delegation to the Leninist Young Communist League of Ukraine (LKSMU – *Leninska komunistychna spilka molodi Ukrainy*) or the Komsomol and its subsidiary organization, the Young Pioneers, of the task of converting the linguistic sensibilities of urban youth. Progress in the Komsomol and Young Pioneers was a barometer of the success of Soviet nationalities policy generally. The campaign to implement the correct Soviet nationalities policy raised questions about the loyalty and corruption of youth and the impact of place (rural and urban) on Soviet nationalities policy. Of critical importance to Soviet nationalities policy was the relationship of the policy to the cultural revolution. The cultural revolution was intimately linked to the promotion of youth, in which the Komsomol and Young Pioneers played a critical part. The flexibility of Ukrainian education created suspicion on the part of the Communist Party of the potential of schools to lead children and youth down an unsanctioned path. Fears of nationalism provided a script for an attack on education, and yet the demands of the cultural revolution required an acceleration of education. Schooling had to be placed in the right hands and directed towards new, shifting objectives, but the school was still the answer. Educators responsible for the schoolhouse in the 1920s believed this all along and worked towards this end, even if they did not anticipate the shift ahead.

Redeeming the Importance of "Soft-Line" Ukrainization: Education and Language Instruction

This study stresses the importance of a discussion of "soft-line" Ukrainization and contests the assumption that activities in this area had little meaning. According to Martin, hard-line Ukrainization had two components: first, the party, Central Control Commission, and Council of People's Commissars would assume responsibility for Ukrainization and apply it to economic and political institutions; second, it would use force to ensure compliance.[1] By contrast, Martin places education and so-called "culture building" in a category of soft-line Ukrainization, characterized by Narkomos oversight and persuasion. Since Narkomos's activities did not control party administration, Martin minimizes their significance. This division seems overdrawn. Success in Ukrainization did rely on the party's authority, but it was Narkomos agents and "soft-line" Ukrainizers who decided what officials in "hard-line" institutions needed to know. It was their yardstick that determined whether progress had been achieved. Narkomos had considerably less power to enforce agreement, but education officials acted against troublemakers in organs directly under their control and could draw attention to problems elsewhere. Lastly, perceived problems in soft-line areas, such as education, occasioned direct party interest.

While the KP(b)U assigned the field of education few funds, in time it came to fear the potential influence educators might have. The party's own lack of attention, in the end, became the liability it identified most. Martin suggests that the central and republican party leadership instituted a campaign of repression against prominent members of the intelligentsia and educators because it had always viewed them as opportunistic collaborators and saw the beginning of the First Five-Year Plan as an auspicious time to get rid of them. This conviction is certainly part of the reason for the intelligentsia's repression. Yet, party authorities also grew fearful because non-party educators defined and instituted Ukrainization on a daily basis. Soft-line Ukrainization was not innocuous. The party believed that the consequences of its going amiss were considerable and acted to correct its course. For republican leaders like the Old Bolshevik and the Ukrainian commissar of education from 1927 to 1933, Mykola Skrypnyk, who were actively involved in Ukrainization's promotion and alteration, the repression of the campaign's non-party activists was a damaging act even though, as will be discussed, Skrypnyk's own actions contributed to this course.

Scholars have underscored the role of education as a component of korenizatsiia, although, generally, native-language instruction at the primary school level is assumed to have been an accomplished fact. Clearly, the potential of education to influence the wider language environment was critical. For example, in Turkic regions of the Soviet Union, educational authorities promoted "selected patterns of linguistic and ethnic separation already in place."[2] In doing so, they codified and raised linguistic categories, thereby fostering the predominance of specified identities perpetuated in cultural institutions such as the schools. Similarly, the Soviets hoped a move towards latinization of Turkic languages would break the authority of Arabist clerics and the old intelligentsia, who had historically dominated the educational space, as well as increase literacy in newly defined vernaculars for Turkic speakers and Europeans alike.[3] The effect of these measures was not immediate in the schools, due to low enrolment by non-European children. This study seeks to move beyond a discussion of language planning to an investigation into its use as an instrument of political and social management through the schools.

Decisions made in defining the course of language policy can have profound social and political consequences. Speaking on the standardization of French during the first French Revolution, sociologist Pierre Bourdieu argues that "the conflict between the French of the revolutionary intelligentsia and the dialects of patois was a struggle for symbolic power in which what was at stake was the formation and re-formation of mental structures."[4] This intelligentsia sought not just to facilitate communication, but assert a "new language of authority" that incorporated a political vocabulary that peasant dialects could not express. Similarly, the Narkomos hoped to disseminate a standardized Ukrainian through the schools, not only to supplant Russian as the dominant language and enable efficient communication between regions, but also to alter peasant and urban attitudes. Although there was disagreement within the central party leadership regarding the former task, most authorities aligned themselves with the latter. In the years following the civil war, Narkomos believed that an urban–rural union (*smychka* – Russian; *zmychka* – Ukrainian) was a necessary prerequisite to the building of socialism.[5] Socialism would falter if cities could not effectively administer rural communities and procure the agricultural goods necessary to feed a workforce for industrialization. The peasantry had to see familiarity in the city to accept its leadership. Furthermore, a common linguistic (and symbolic) culture would enable peasant migrants to the city to work effectively upon arrival. As Michael Smith puts it, for Soviet authorities, language was "a fundamental tool of political power, economic production, and social management."[6] It intended language to assert control over Russians and non-Russians alike.

Schools played a critical part in this campaign. To return to Bourdieu, an education system is essential "in the process which leads to the construction, legitimation, and imposition of an official language."[7] Groups fight for control over education because the rewards are high. An education system has a monopoly on the creation of producers and consumers of language because it assigns "a social value to linguistic competence." If schools legitimized Ukrainian and made proficiency in standardized Ukrainian a requirement for educational advancement, speakers would act to protect and perpetuate this "linguistic capital." As will be discussed below, VUAN worked through the 1920s to define accepted rules for grammar and syntax, but Narkomos relied on teachers to inculcate standardized Ukrainian in children. This represented the kind of purposeful act described by Bourdieu: "Through its grammarians, who fix and codify legitimate usage, and its teachers who impose and inculcate it … the education system tends, in this area as elsewhere, to produce the need for its own services and its own products."[8] At least, this was what Narkomos intended. An education system had the capacity not just to transfer knowledge, but also to shape the habits of language speakers and the general language environment. As such, it had intrinsic power.

Ukrainizers were fully aware that literacy was not "context free." They appreciated that, as James Collins writes, "schooling produces consequences that seem like literacy but are the function of the institutions," and that these functions could be exploitative.[9] From the perspective of "national communists" and non-party educators, tsarist-era Russian schooling had accomplished this. It had deflated Ukrainian national self-esteem and denigrated the Ukrainian language. Schools were already deeply flawed, even if lessons in Russian nationalism, monarchism, and religion were not as direct or effective as Soviet authorities charged. Ukrainizers hoped that "schooled literacy," defined and promoted by Soviet authorities, would replace pre-existing literacies, including "backward" systems of knowledge developed in the home or church, as well as schooled literacies promoted or condoned by the old regime. The purpose of the new "schooled literacy" was to eliminate Russian-dominated literacy and dialectical variance in Ukrainian, as well as what the Soviets viewed as the romanticism or provincialism of existing Ukrainian literature. The Ukrainian language was generally associated with peasant life, the village priest, and the "bourgeois" Ukrainian general educational society known as "Prosvita."[10] The Soviets intended to alter this dynamic. If, as Collins claims, "schooling reflects and reproduces a stratified social system," the Soviets sought to undo or upset this consequence by using schooling to define and privilege a new Ukrainian labour culture.[11] To be Soviet in Ukraine meant knowledge of Ukrainian. However, part of the tension in the campaign was that the initial fodder and human capital needed for Ukrainization was derived from non-Soviet experts. Schooled literacy is certainly a "hegemonic project," but it is never as single-minded or totalizing as language planners expect or Collins suggests. The case of Soviet Ukraine offers an intriguing place in which to take up Collins's challenge, to study not just literacy, but study the "dynamic social formulations that these literacies enable."[12] In socialist Ukraine, this question is decidedly complex. Part of the aim of this book is to sort out the difference between what different stakeholders in the Ukrainization of schooling desired and what was produced.

Importantly, Ukrainian educators saw Soviet schools as different from the "institutions of discipline and order for the laboring poor" that Collins describes.[13] Soviet Ukrainian schools were supposed to provide the tools necessary for social uplift and, at least initially, concepts of discipline were absent. Children were to learn in an environment that privileged their interests and not those of an intrusive educational bureaucracy. The state subjected teachers to disciplinary constraint through the measurement and assessment of their Ukrainian knowledge, but this act was supposed to be undertaken in the interests of children, assumed native speakers of Ukrainian. In regard to curriculum for children, disciplinary methods (e.g., dissemination of a stringently codified reading list) were initially absent. Knowledge of Ukrainian did, however, matter. Collins writes that grouping in schools is a "primary form of literacy and power" because it enforces "rigid categories of legitimate knowledge" through the division of students according to their acceptance and use of this knowledge.[14] The Ukrainian education system's acceptance of progressive educational values worked against testing in the classroom and separation of children by achievement. Education officials, however, divided children by ethnicity, which was correlated to a perceived innate ability to learn a "native tongue." All children, regardless of ethnicity, were obliged to learn Ukrainian, but this sort of grouping meant that Ukrainian children had privileged access to a new form of "legitimate knowledge." This was a knowledge ridiculed by some, but promoted by the Soviet Ukrainian republic as the basis for modern (socialist) citizenship. In time, some ethnic-Ukrainian parents who had resisted an embrace of the knowledge came to accept its value and legitimize this grouping. By choosing to honour native-language instruction in an absolute sense (formal language equality), republican officials reworked the hierarchy of legitimate knowledge and set up the conditions for prioritization of the Ukrainian "grouping." This, in fact, never occurred; the Ukrainian-language environment grew, but it did not supersede Russian. Still, the perceived consequence of this policy was at the heart of tensions in Soviet nationality and educational policy. Where would this campaign end? Would equality of languages result in the dominance of Ukrainian in the republic (a dynamic that might weaken the tie to the centre), a cacophony of languages, or the basis for democratic citizenship?

The Intersection of Education and Language

As the proceeding section suggested, the revolution offered an opportunity for substantial reform in what and how schools taught. With the exception of Stepan Siropolko's 1934 classic, no comprehensive work on the early years of Soviet

Ukrainian schooling has been published outside of Ukraine.[15] This study attempts to address the gap in our knowledge of what occurred at the level of the primary-school classroom by examining the understudied intersection between the two overriding demands the school faced: Ukrainization and pedagogical reform. Narkomos conceived of the two objectives as fundamentally compatible strategies, and any history of schooling in this period must consider both Narkomos's rationale for this correlation and how the policies actually interplayed.[16] This study works towards the closure of the gap Thomas E. Ewing has identified in the existing literature, which does not examine "the range of experience contained within so-called national education, the tensions between policies decreed by the centre and the practices within classrooms, or the agency of those involved in schools."[17]

While research on non-Russian schooling has generally focused solely on the language aspect of educational policy, Sheila Fitzpatrick and Larry Holmes have addressed the other side of the equation: structural reform, educational advantage, and methodological innovation in the early Soviet school, but almost wholly in the Russian context. Both Fitzpatrick and Holmes emphasize that leaders of the RSFSR (Russian Soviet Federated Socialist Republic) People's Commissariat of Education (Narkompros) expected primary schools would function as a conversional mechanism. Fitzpatrick writes that once teachers had adopted a progressive curriculum, "it was hoped that they would automatically develop a Marxist world-view and pass it on to their pupils."[18] Similarly, Larry Holmes argues, "Narkompros wanted nothing less than a world of fundamentally-altered structures and values."[19] Catriona Kelly argues that Soviet schooling had at its beginning "a repressive edge," but concedes that "in the earliest days, the mood was one of iconoclastic euphoria combined with democratic utopianism."[20] In the 1920s, the question, Kelly suggests, was how much "the will of the 'collective'" (teachers and peers) could harness this impulse to produce the ideological indoctrination that the Soviet state desired. In the Ukrainian republic, this aspiration took on an added transformative aspect along the lines Bourdieu suggests. Not only would Ukrainian schools use new pedagogy for this "reformation of mental structures," they would empower a new "language of authority": Ukrainian. In its discussion of methodology, this study has perhaps most benefited from William Partlett's publications on the pedagogical experimentation of Stanislav Shatskii.[21] Partlett emphasizes that Shatskii's experimentation was fundamentally a strategy for rural schooling.[22] This study emphasizes the use of progressive pedagogy to bridge the divide between the rural and urban, which in Ukraine had an added ethnic dimension, given the generally Ukrainian character of the countryside and Russian character of the city. "Becoming Bolshevik," for much of the 1920s, was about breaking this separation or, at the very least, about orienting the village towards the city, now recast as Ukrainian.

This study investigates an understudied aspect of the history of education and European cultural and social history. Ukrainian educators borrowed freely from the experience of western European and American educational theorists, and Soviet educational journals frequently published the studies and commentaries of foreign educators. The Ukrainian education system had advocates in the Komsomol and trade unions in Russia because of its intention to provide students early on with an orientation towards labour and applied skills. To educators of the time, the Soviet Union offered an opportunity to witness what resulted from state support for progressive pedagogy.[23] In its initial ideal, schooling in the Ukrainian republic promised a participatory, democratized education and the training of students attuned to the world outside the classroom and committed to its betterment. Teachers were to design lessons from an evaluation of students' innate talents and a faith in the power of "local studies" to stimulate interest. Although the state did not adequately fund or intercede in daily instruction, political authorities in Ukraine had a defined interest in the achievements of these teachers and the types of students they graduated. Furthermore, in spite of Narkomos's protests that its schools were not offering trade training, there was an expectation that its education system would produce students capable of entering the workforce at an earlier age. There was, explicit or not, a functional goal. Lastly, while Narkomos meant Ukrainization as a liberal, remedial measure to correct tsarist repression of the Ukrainian culture, satisfy national frustration, and redirect national culture to the building of a socialist state, its basic assumption that all ethnic-Ukrainian children should attend Ukrainian schools required state intercession in parental choice.

Thus, the irony of the Ukrainian education system was that it suggested flexible instruction, where teachers and students collaborated in learning, after receiving initial guidelines from Narkomos. It claimed and aspired to this principle; but it was also a system that operated even at its inception with the potential for significant political intervention. This potential increased over time and was most apparent during the purges of the teaching ranks in the early 1930s. This story has important implications, then, regarding the tension between a state's liberal impulse and propensity to control.[24] The Ukrainian case offers an illustrative example of a dilemma of modern governance that was not particular to the socialist state: how was it possible to liberate human potential without creating conditions in which citizens might question the legitimacy of the state? Narkomos hoped that graduates of Ukrainian schools would see their own futures tied to the progress of socialism, but did not wholly trust children (or the teachers who taught them) to reach this conviction without intercession.

In addition, this study offers an important perspective on the relationship between nation building and education, a linkage that scholars of nationalism have long posited. What is most intriguing in the Ukrainian case was that the education system that the Soviet republican state designed to bolster a Ukrainian sense of national identity was flexible at its heart, as outlined above. Scholars who have worked on the subject of national schools in other contexts have assumed a centralized system of education that would assure the hoped-for reproduction of lessons in nationhood.[25] In the Ukrainian case, Narkomos believed that a localized curriculum, whose content would partly be determined by teachers and students, would allow schools to "telescope out" to Ukrainian-inflected studies while preserving a grounding in familiar labour culture.[26] Part of the intent of this expansion was to link the city and village in the minds of schoolchildren, but it also served to reify a notion of a Ukrainian territorial homeland, a touted benefit for Ukrainians in Poland and Czechoslovakia as well as the other Soviet republics. Narkomos hoped that schools would function as a base for local studies (*kraieznavstvo*) for the communities in which they were situated and encourage study of the republic. It placed heavy emphasis on a public analysis of the economic potential and labour culture of the UkrSSR, and sought to motivate citizens to contribute to their further development. An attention to labour in the classroom presumably limited the risk of lessons adopting the wrong kind of nationalism. However, it was the very flexibility of the lessons that invited the suspicion of the KP(b)U regarding nationalism. It did not (and, practically, could not) have daily control of the content of Ukrainian studies in the classroom, and interceded when it believed the risks of something going awry were most high. Thus, the history of Ukrainization in the schools offers a complex counter-example to conventional histories of nation building through education: a decentralized system would teach a nuanced sense of national identity that promised to not be separatist but, because of the absence of centralized oversight, was perceived as such.

The Ukrainian educational experience was exceptional in that it was born in the highly stressed environment of a civil war that significantly affected Ukraine's juvenile population. Thousands of children were orphaned, homeless, or part of families that were fractured, poor, and hungry. Narkomos set up an education system designed initially to care for these children's physical and developmental well-being as well as their intellect. It established children's homes and whole "children's villages" in order to concentrate staff, supplies, and services. Through this effort, the state assumed the role of parent, building upon an established Bolshevik suspicion of the harmful influence of the family.[27] The party hoped to liberate mothers from what it viewed as the drudgery of housework, rationalize child rearing, and free children from the selfish desires it believed the family cultivated alongside religion, superstition, and inattention to hygiene. As the social fabric stabilized in Ukraine, children's homes remained for the youngest children in diminished numbers, but local sections of Narkomos increasingly directed older children to schools. The state simply lacked the capacity or authority to fully supplant the family, and the immediate social and health crises for children had faded. However, the state's impulse to assume a directed role in the lives of children remained and inevitably influenced its approach to schooling. The RSFSR Narkompros embraced this same inclination, but it had not worked with as clean a slate as the Ukrainian commissariat in terms of sheer numbers of children at risk, and had arguably encountered greater resistance in its efforts to reorient the character and objectives of primary schooling.

Reality, however, did not always match the ideal. This study corroborates Holmes's findings regarding the difficulties Soviet authorities had in implementing a bold educational plan.[28] Teachers lacked the experience to understand what was expected of them, let alone innovate in the manner that Narkomos advised. They taught with little pay, instruction, or support. As their attempts to implement instruction by the complex method faltered, so did the academic achievement of their students. Parents, and even some educational authorities, demanded a return to instruction in the basic skills of reading, writing, and arithmetic. In Ukraine, teachers confronted the added burden of abiding by and enforcing Ukrainization. Some complained that the Ukrainization campaign, put in place ostensibly to aid teaching, was complicating their best efforts to institute the new pedagogy. Narkomos's solution was better Ukrainization: an improvement in teachers' use of Ukrainian and the complete transfer of all instruction to Ukrainian in designated schools. Language and Ukrainian studies were fundamental components of the drive for educational innovation.

The key structural difference between the Ukrainian and Russian systems was the Ukrainian truncation of primary schooling to seven years and creation of a two-year vocational secondary school. Narkomos insisted that these schools were not purely vocational because they continued to offer elements of a general education.[29] Nevertheless, the curriculum of each vocational school included practical training in some field of the economy (identified in the name of the secondary school), and Narkomos designed these schools to graduate students to the workforce at an earlier age. While the secondary vocational school is not the central subject of this study, its embrace of work skills affected lessons in Ukrainian primary schools, which emphasized a student appreciation for the value of labour, even if there was not a clear link under the progressive methodology of the 1920s to a specific economic goal. Because of the unification of the Russian and Ukrainian education systems in 1930, Ukrainian schools functioned similarly to their Russian counterparts. There were distinctions, however. The famine of 1932–3, centred in the Ukrainian republic, inevitably affected the operation of rural schools, and, as this study argues, the SVU arrests and mounting anxiety about Ukrainian nationalism influenced the tenor of the purges of teachers, the

Komsomol, and Young Pioneer organizations and the cultural revolution in the schools generally.

Language Standardization and Soviet Ukrainian Identity

When Ukrainization was begun in 1923, linguists had not yet definitively agreed on syntactical and orthographic norms for the language. A modern literary Ukrainian existed, but pre-revolutionary publications still displayed dialectal variation. Progress had been hampered in the Russian Empire's Ukrainian lands due to the nineteenth-century restrictions on Ukrainian-language use. The problem of linguistic standardization was complicated by the existence of two principal literary variants, one based on the Kyiv–Poltava vernacular and another on a Western Ukrainian form, chiefly a Galician dialect. Furthermore, the Ukrainian-speaking community remained divided by a political boundary in the interwar era between the UkrSSR and Ukrainians concentrated in Poland (Galicia, western Volhynia, the Kholm region), Czechoslovakia (Subcarpathian Ruthenia), and Romania (Bukovina).

Under Habsburg rule, Ukrainians had enjoyed considerable national cultural and educational rights. Ukrainian journals and newspapers, Ukrainian schools, and Ukrainian educational, scientific, and cultural societies were established by the turn of the twentieth century, most notably in Galicia. However, although Galician scholars published several school textbooks and grammars, none achieved universal authority.[30] In the early Polish republic, Galician scholars debated whether to promote the Lviv dialect in spelling and terminology or to incorporate elements of the Kyiv–Poltava dialect. Both sides to this dispute criticized spelling rules published by the Shevchenko Scientific Society, the main Ukrainian academic institution in Lwów (Lviv), in 1922. No side won out because there was no governmental body under Polish rule willing or sanctioned to recognize them as standard. As George Shevelov writes: "the spelling rules were rarely applied consistently, and usages in publications continued to differ."[31]

The principal work on language standardization took place in the UkrSSR because Soviet Ukrainian authorities intentionally sponsored this effort, Polish authorities increasingly placed restrictions on Ukrainian academic, cultural, and educational activity in Galicia (and even more so in Volhynia, Polissia, and Kholm), and the Ukrainian national movement was relatively weaker in Transcarpathia and Bukovina.[32] In the pre-Ukrainization period, progress was slow. The VUAN set up an orthography division, headed partly by Volodymyr Durdukivsky, the director of the first pre-Soviet Ukrainian secondary school in Dnipro Ukraine, the Taras Shevchenko Gymnasium (later Kyiv Labour School No. 1).[33] In 1921, with the sanction of the then commissar of education for the UkrSSR, Hryhorii Hrynko, it published a sixteen-page booklet of orthographic norms modified slightly from rules compiled under Hetman Pavlo Skoropadsky's short-lived government.[34] The academy also established a commission under philologist Agatangel Krymsky to compile a dictionary of the "living" (*zhyva*) Ukrainian language. In 1924, it published the first volume of a Russian-Ukrainian dictionary (*Rossiisko-ukrainskyi slovnyk*) for letters A–Zh. Ethnographic researchers recorded lexical material on stacks of cards that served as the basis for the dictionary's entries. Linguist George Shevelov writes that the dictionary's "vacillations between standard and dialectal, urban, and rural (often folkloric), made it somewhat eclectic and the effort to represent the standard language often collided with a desire to introduce the richest material possible."[35] By casting its net as widely as possible, the commission complicated the task of promoting a universalized language.

As the Ukrainization campaign accelerated, so did work on language standardization. Literature specialist Serhii Yefremov took over the chairmanship of the VUAN dictionary commission and published five more volumes of the *Rossiisko-ukrainskyi slovnyk*. Under the directorship of Hryhoryi Kholodny, the Institute of the Ukrainian Scientific Language had all but ceased work in the early Soviet period due to lack of funds, but, after 1925, it gradually began to increase its activity, publishing over two dozen terminological dictionaries after that year.[36] Furthermore, its researchers took a leading role in the publication of textbooks and self-study guides. Language planners regularly debated the question of how closely the literary (and, by extension, academic and technical) language should reflect dialectal forms. Paul Wexler divides what he calls "regulators" into two camps: a purist, ethnographic group that prioritized unique Ukrainian features over breadth and frequency of use; and a modified ethnographic group that allowed for the incorporation of some non-native characteristics in the interest of promoting a language that could be widely recognized and used.[37] By the mid-1920s, the latter approach assumed greater importance. Yefremov minimized the *Rossiisko-ukrainskyi slovnyk*'s emphasis on local forms, and it became "a representative, reliable, and fairly complete collection of Ukrainian words and idioms."[38]

The work that had the greatest impact on how Ukrainian was used on a daily basis was undertaken by a special orthographic commission, appointed by a Radnarkom (the Ukrainian Council of People's Commissars) decree of July 23, 1925. Formally, two successive commissars of education headed the commission: Oleksandr Shumsky and Mykola Skrypnyk. An orthographic conference, held from May 25 to June 6, 1927, in Kharkiv under Skrypnyk's auspices, began the most concerted work on standardization. The most contentious issue at this conference was how to render loan words. The presidium of the orthographic commission later decided on a compromise that allowed for a distinction between words of Greek origin and those of modern European origin. In reality, this decision simply reflected a variation in the central and eastern Ukrainian tradition of borrowing words through Russian and the Western Ukrainian practice of borrowing through Polish.[39] Skrypnyk confirmed the orthographic rules on 6 September 1929, and required their use in all schools and publications. This compromise was to ultimately break down in the mid-1930s after Skrypnyk's fall in 1933, but the conference represented an important attempt at bridging the gap between competing literary traditions. Skrypnyk invited three Galician scholars to attend the 1927 conference, and their input was critical in forcing the presidium to consider an agreement that would satisfy the wider speaking community and ensure the UkrSSR's status as the "Piedmont" of Ukrainian national culture.[40] From this perspective, the 1929 "Kharkiv orthography" was a critical moment in the standardization of the language, even if it later became the subject of political attack. It was flexible enough to incorporate the two leading conventions in Ukrainian orthography and yet it significantly reduced dialectal variations as a whole.

By the end of the 1920s, then, Ukrainian scholars, writers, and publicists could still debate aspects of what was "proper" Ukrainian, but the number of questions open for dispute was much smaller. When education officials or the press criticized teachers for failing to use Ukrainian well, they already had a clear idea of what constituted a significant departure from a "standard" literary Ukrainian. To be sure, some teachers still relied on dialectal forms in the classroom and had difficulty procuring guides on correct terminology and the evolving orthographic rules. Nevertheless, the chief culprits of "language abuse" had little sense of literary Ukrainian at all, and used a Ukrainian based wholly on Russian cognates or interspersed with Russian words. National communities throughout the former Russian empire were dealing with many of the same questions regarding linguistic standardization, although Ukrainian's linguistic "proximity" to Russian heightened questions about language purism. The "normalization" of Ukrainian, like that for other languages, was neither inevitable nor immediate.[41] It required the active intervention of government and scholarly authorities. Yet, even before Ukrainization had begun, there was widespread agreement among the Ukrainian national intelligentsia and the literate population regarding the corpus of literary Ukrainian, and language planners had made significant progress during the 1920s towards a consensus for standardization. They intended teachers to inculcate these language norms among the next generation.

The connection between language and identity can be problematic to define. This study highlights incidents of those who doubted the distinctiveness of a Ukrainian language or identity, or sought to denigrate it and limit its spread, partly because local education inspectors had an obligation to report on tension. Incidents of conflict enter the archival and published record. However, the mere creation of Ukrainian-specific schools and assignment of children by national affiliation served to strengthen this perception of a Ukrainian national category, even if not all individuals who self-identified as Ukrainian (or were recognized as such by the state) took up daily speech in Ukrainian. The work of teachers and Narkomos officials, together with directives from the party, helped consolidate national identification. This work builds upon Hirsch's discussion of the way in which tsarist-era ethnographers aided the Bolsheviks in this "conceptual conquest," merging and dismantling previous loyalties, ascribing nationally specific traits, and using the 1926 census to marshal popular participation in nationally delineated notions of citizenship and administrative governance. It accepts the Soviet faith in "state-sponsored evolutionism," the idea that national awareness was a prerequisite to a weakening of kinship ties, modernity, and the construction of an internationalist, socialist state. The growing Ukrainian national movement, the resistance of successive "nationalist" Ukrainian governments to Soviet rule, and the Bolsheviks' own accommodation with nationally oriented, leftist forces in Ukraine (and pledges of support for national self-determination) all contributed to the party's commitment to a Ukrainian identity and aversion to automatic acceptance of a "Little Russian"/Russified Ukrainian category.[42]

That said, even if the population of the republic came to recognize a Ukrainian identity, language, and culture, just who was Ukrainian remained a subject of dispute. Commissar of Education Mykola Skrypnyk regularly claimed that the true language of Russified Ukrainians was a form of Ukrainian that had simply been corrupted over time. Thus, in his mind, there was no question of their Ukrainian identity. This dispute is, however, central to this study. Narkomos used census data as a guideline for Ukrainization and a measurement of Ukrainization's progress, to set and evaluate goals for the number of Ukrainian schools in proportion to regional population. However, urban residents may have identified themselves to census takers as Ukrainian and specified their "native" language as Ukrainian, but this did not mean that they spoke Ukrainian well or, more importantly, that this was the language they preferred to use in their daily speech or in which to have their children schooled.[43, 44]

What made "Russified Ukrainians" Ukrainian? Why not simply call them Russian? The two questions of identity and language choice (and choice of language of instruction) should be considered separately. Soviet citizens may have been "unconsciously" identified as Ukrainian by census takers (without their own specification), but a great number must have self-identified as Ukrainian. Thus, whether they chose to speak Ukrainian or not, they saw themselves as Ukrainian, a choice conceivably based on any number of factors; presumably, for some, a remaining or remembered link to a Ukrainian-speaking village or provincial town. Narkomos saw such identification as a green light for the Ukrainization of these communities. None of the protests or doubts regarding a school's Ukrainization identified in this study questioned a student's identification as Ukrainian, although some claimed that a student body as a whole was multi-ethnic. Educators, officials, and parents were less concerned with "forced" national alignment (although it undoubtedly occurred), but occasionally debated situations in which Russian, Jewish, Polish, German, or even Ukrainian children found themselves "trapped" in a Ukrainizing school. By law, ethnic minorities could study in their own national schools, but in the case of urban schools, such study sometimes required their transfer away from a school with an established authority in the community. For non-Russian ethnic minorities in smaller population centres, such schools may not have existed. Urban Jews, like Ukrainians, constituted another Russified population that protested its forced linguistic "indigenization" – Yiddishization – although there is little doubt that they saw themselves as Jews.[45] There are significant distinctions to the Ukrainian case, to be sure; nevertheless, the resistance of assimilated Jews to Soviet nationalities policy speaks to the cultural prestige of Russian and the authority of the existing language hierarchy for all non-Russians.[46]

It is not surprising, then, that some Ukrainians, like ethnic minorities in the republic, showed little interest in using the Ukrainian language, but continued to identify themselves as Ukrainian. Narkomos's Ukrainizers hoped to change the linguistic habits of the children of this population and reorient the sympathies of the parents. The early period of Soviet rule reinforced a Ukrainian identity through the creation of a Ukrainian republic, promotion of the census, standardization of Ukrainian, and the creation of a network of formal Ukrainian schools. Whether ethnic Ukrainian or not, Ukrainian-speaking or not, most residents of the UkrSSR recognized a form of a republican Ukrainian identity.[47] Whatever Ukraine was, it was not Russia. What was at play was just how inflected republican culture was with the language and history of ethnic Ukrainians.[48]

Part of the issue with Russification was connected to the question of standardization of the Ukrainian language. Where did Russian end and Ukrainian begin? This question assumes that Russian was standardized and Ukrainian was not, or presupposes that Ukrainian was less developed. In fact, Russian was undergoing language reform as well; there was debate within the RSFSR Narkompros about what form of Russian should be taught in the classroom, and Ukrainian writers had already conceded a core form of a literary Ukrainian before comprehensive standardization began. The parallel processes of standardization serve as a reminder that all languages are, in fact, in flux, that some areas of contestation remain, and that the early twentieth century was a promising arena for a language like Ukrainian in which to expand. That said, language standardizers faced some specific challenges for Ukrainian. It lacked a deeply expansive literary tradition, a history of institutional support, a long-standing press, and a vocabulary for certain areas of science. Furthermore, divergent historical traditions and a political border that divided a Ukrainian-speaking community complicated regional dialectal variance. Russian and Ukrainian are proximate to one another, and assimilation to Russian in urban environments happened as a matter of course for Ukrainian speakers, but it is difficult to judge how easy the conversion to Russian was or what "full" assimilation constituted. What matters is that peasant migrants to Russian-speaking cities, including some of the parents featured in this study, perceived a difference in the languages. To argue that the two were interchangeable is incorrect and in a way anachronistic. The divide between the two speech communities was real and went beyond a debate regarding linguistic differentiation.

Of course, sorting out what was a "foreign" borrowing in Ukrainian presented a challenge, and it was one that preoccupied Narkomos administrators, education inspectors, and teachers in Ukrainizing schools, and most immediately the Narkomos commission tasked with developing a new orthography. Like this commission, Ukrainizing schools employed teachers from Galicia in an effort to ensure, not a commitment to dialectal variation, but rather genuine and authoritative language instruction. One of the particular concerns of this study is an issue expressed by education inspectors and commentators in the pedagogical press that teachers did not know Ukrainian well enough to teach in it, but also that when required to use the language, they "corrupted" their instruction by failing to use standard literary Ukrainian. To be fair, this was a language in the midst of a deeper standardization, but a specific objective of the Ukrainian training that the state provided teachers, and that teachers were supposed to pursue on their own, was the use throughout the republic of already accepted syntactical and orthographic conventions.

The peculiar quality of Ukrainian was that it was a language whose speaking base was in rural communities, and yet it had to become an urban-centred, modern language under the auspices of a political authority (the Communist Party) whose members overwhelmingly favoured Russian. A gauge of the success of the language standardization was how much republican authorities turned this language practice on end: made the city the centre of the Ukrainian-speaking community and positioned it to define language norms for the village and the republic as a whole. The best teachers went to the city partly because of practical considerations: state publishing houses printed Ukrainian literature in the city, Narkomos and urban communities paid teachers better, and teachers enjoyed access to better resources for their own professionalization. But the state concentrated these assets in the city to ensure the command of the city over Ukrainian. Gone, at least for a time, was an emphasis on folkloric tropes to define national culture. In distinction from nation-building experiences elsewhere, Ukrainization was not the raising of lower culture to high, but rather a fundamental reworking of the high with greatly distilled elements of the low. The SVU affair weakened the urban link in Ukrainian culture by its attack on an urban-based intelligentsia. Although Ukrainization continued, it had lost part of its shoring. Ukrainization's future, before and after 1930, was in the city.

With the exception of Martin's sweeping study of "affirmative action" for non-Russians, the emphasis of recent English-language work on Soviet education has been on the Russian experience, particularly in the 1930s or later.[49] Peter Blitstein deals most directly with the question of non-Russian education, and his argument that obligatory Russian instruction introduced in 1938 did not signal a public campaign for "Russification" of schooling is convincing.[50] However, by this time, the cultural values associated with language knowledge in the Soviet Union had shifted (or stabilized), as Laada Bilaniuk makes clear, and mastery of Russian was a privileged asset for professional advancement. The parents and officials from non-Russian areas who campaigned for early Russian-language instruction, as identified by Blitstein, did so precisely because they understood this reality, even if there was no official push for the "Russification" of education. What is perhaps more important, then, is what Soviet authorities did not do. Beyond the preservation of native-language schooling and the writing of Russian textbooks gauged to the abilities of specific language communities, an energetic program of nation building appears absent.

Recent scholarship has emphasized the persistence of the Soviet commitment to the national idea without investigating in detail how this pursuit was qualitatively different. Soviet authorities removed or intimidated the core of educators dedicated to Ukrainization in 1930. This invites the questions, then: who implemented the campaign post-1930, when the archival record clearly indicates that Ukrainization, even in schooling (considered by other scholars to be the most successful arena for Ukrainization), was far from complete? How did its content change? The number of Ukrainian schools continued to grow, but this says little about the daily use of Ukrainian and the quality of instruction. Urban environments remained largely Russian-speaking, post-secondary schools privileged instruction in Russian, and non-Ukrainians did not aspire towards Ukrainian fluency. Ukrainian primary schools thus represented rungs in a broken-off ladder. To say this is not to deny the Soviet role in fostering a Ukrainian identity and promotion of Ukrainian ethnic elites, but it was a substantively different form of national culture in the republic from that imagined by Ukrainizers first in the 1920s.

While accepting Yuri Slezkine's proposal that the Soviet Union maintained, relied upon, and, in some cases, accelerated national constructs,[51] this study contends that the repression against local elites that took public form in the late 1920s (the culmination of an extended campaign of security police surveillance) marked a substantive shift in the actual implementation of Soviet nationalities policy. Scholarship on Soviet nationalities policy in Central Asia has pointed to this fact, while still stressing the continuities inherent in the Soviet commitment to the national idea. Thus, Adeeb Khalid argues that the "centralizing impulses of the new period" motivated Soviet leaders to abandon their alliance with Jadids, a group of progressive Muslim reformers and surrogate nation builders.[52] Edgar locates a similar disjuncture in Soviet nationalities policy in Turkmenistan: "If the linguistic debates of the 1920s had symbolically represented Turkmen attempts to define their place in the world, the silencing of those voices symbolized not just a loss of linguistic autonomy, but a curtailing of the role of the indigenous intellectuals in debating and defining Turkmen identity."[53]

This work maintains that a parallel shift occurred in Soviet Ukraine, and suggests that it undermined the effectiveness of Ukrainization during its perceived "high point" and made the definitive adjustment (although not wholesale abandonment) of Ukrainization in 1933–4 possible. It does not seek to minimize the gains made in Ukrainization, but rather to emphasize that it was a process responsive to the external political environment and far from automatic.

A Ukrainian identity coalesced by the mid-1930s, but it was one that did not require daily and expanded use of Ukrainian, and parents ceased to view knowledge of Ukrainian as a prerequisite for the advancement of their children. The Ukrainizers had not generally sought to force non-Ukrainians to use the language outside employment in public institutions, but they did favour supplanting Russian by the increased use of ethnic-minority languages. If schools taught a republican identity to Ukrainian and non-Ukrainian schoolchildren alike, it was an identity that asked all students to learn a basic level of "Ukrainian studies," slanted towards a history and culture of Ukrainians as the titular population of the republic. Formally, lessons promoted ties between the diverse populations of the republic, partly through common knowledge of Ukrainian-studies subjects, but also through their common social and political acculturation. More than anything, Ukrainizers hoped that schoolchildren and their parents internalized a reversal of cultural prejudices against Ukrainian and for Russian. If citizens were to choose an "interethnic" language of communication, it should be Ukrainian. The repression of the 1930s extinguished this aspiration, although promotion of the republic as "Ukrainian" persisted, demonstrating the continuance of the state's aversion to national indifference.

The Working Class, Young Pioneers, and
Political Authority over Children

A central question this study deals with is the Ukrainization of the "proletariat," the working class. This was a highly contested issue that had a significant impact on the debate over schooling in Ukraine. The KP(b)U had repeatedly prohibited the forced Ukrainization of the working class. In a way, this ban was misleading. Members of the KP(b)U, Komsomol, or trade union leadership, regardless of class background, were expected to demonstrate proficiency in the Ukrainian language and Ukrainian studies in examinations. Failure meant in theory that they might face censure or dismissal. However, the forced Ukrainization of the rank-and-file workers could not take place. Workers were encouraged to join Ukrainian reading circles, amateur theatre groups, or choral societies as a way of inciting an interest in the Ukrainian language, culture, and history, but they could not be compelled to do so. The question of requiring working-class children to attend Ukrainian schools was, however, decidedly more complex. In response to concerns provoked by local reports, the KP(b)U TsK clearly proscribed the enrolment of ethnic-Russian children in Ukrainian schools. However, local authorities were still allowed to assign children of "Russified" Ukrainians to Ukrainian schools and to dissuade parents from protesting their children's enrolment. Narkomos capitalized on the ambiguity surrounding what made a "Russified" Ukrainian and what made a Russian in order to implement what amounted to a run around the party's prohibition on the Ukrainization of workers. The working class would become Ukrainian-speaking gradually through maturation or influence of children educated in Ukrainian. In reality, the Ukrainizers had little choice. In the absence of a clearly "Ukrainian" proletariat, children would become a surrogate. To permit children of workers to choose Russian schools would undermine the authority of the policy because it would appear that that class most aligned with the interests of the party had rejected it.

This study would not be complete without an investigation of the impact of nationalities and educational policy on the primary political units responsible for oversight over schools and children: the Komsomol and Young Pioneers. The Communist Youth League, the Komsomol, had oversight over youth aged fourteen to twenty-eight and administered the Young Pioneers for children aged ten to fourteen. Both the Komsomol and Young Pioneers had an established interest in the affairs of primary schools regardless of the age of children among their membership, because lessons in the schools had a wide-ranging influence on all children and youth, and dropouts from primary schools often ended up in educational institutions for older youth tied to the Komsomol. Although the Young Pioneer membership was small in the period under study and largely drawn from

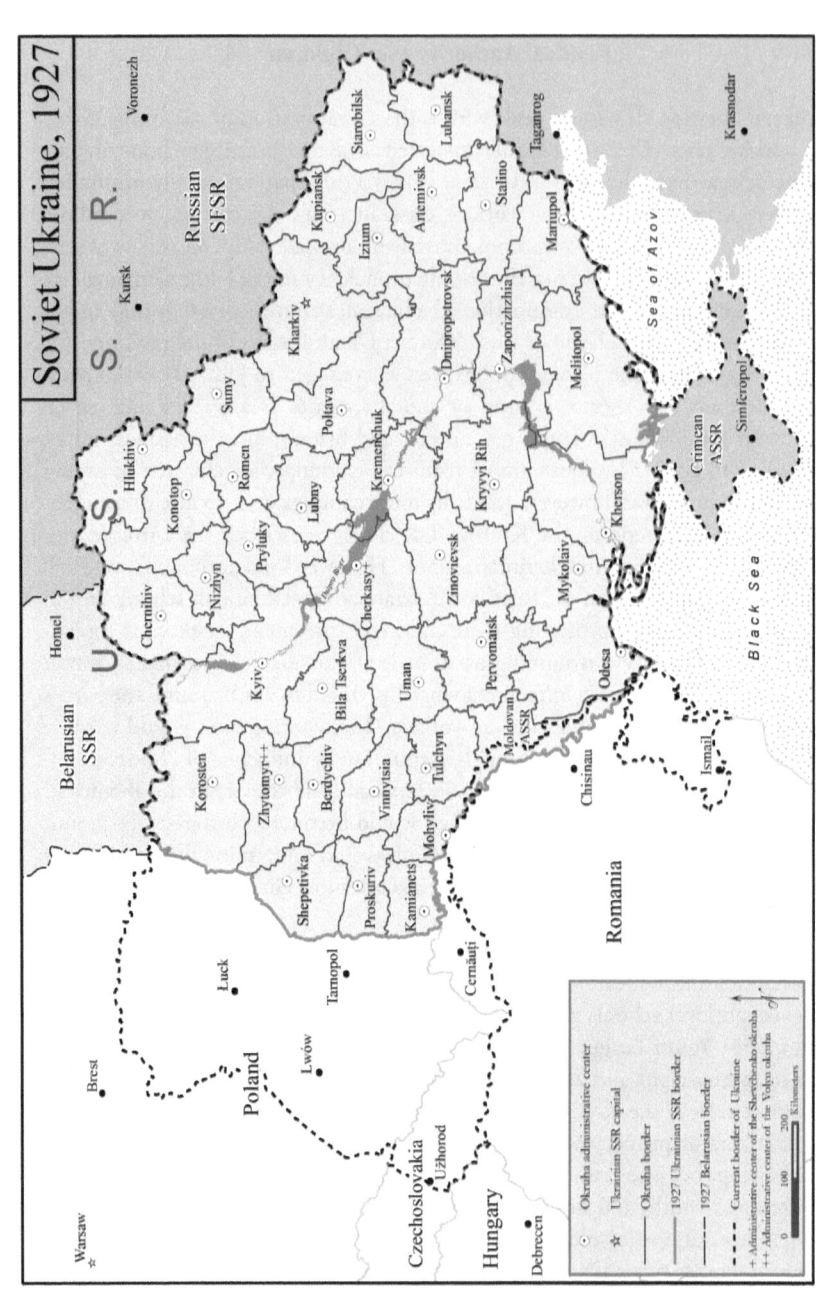

Ukrainian Soviet Socialist Republic (UkrSSR) in 1927. Map created by RS&GIS at Michigan State University (2013).

urban children, the attitudes of even these members had an impact far beyond their numbers. The Young Pioneers was the most familiar face of political authority, and even for children and population centres where no detachment existed, news of Young Pioneer activities that appeared in the popular press reinforced notions of generational cohesion and suggested normative behaviour. If the Young Pioneers acted in a particular manner (or were reported to have), other children were expected to model their actions accordingly. Thus, Narkomos, the KP(b)U, and the Komsomol saw Young Pioneer resistance to Ukrainization and public work linked to school instruction as suspect. As the social tensions increased during the midst of the Five-Year Plan, the Komsomol leadership saw local Komsomol organizations and Young Pioneer detachments as key agents of the party line, especially in largely Ukrainophone rural areas, and direct competitors with "class enemies" for influence over youth. Komsomol and party organizations notified the public about the treachery of supposed Ukrainian nationalists through their own publications, partly because these forces were allegedly infiltrating the schools and ranks of Komsomol teachers and Young Pioneer students, especially in the village.

Ultimately, Ukrainization of the working class and the wider urban environment was meant to ensure that the city remained in a position of leadership over the countryside. Lack of knowledge of Ukrainian would limit the capacity of urban-based state employees and workers to administer rural parts of the republic. Furthermore, it would be more difficult to integrate Ukrainian-speaking labour from the countryside into the "foreign" city. Urban Ukrainization was also meant to capitalize on the resources the city had: a Ukrainian intelligentsia that had its roots in the pre-revolutionary national movement, but also a young, Soviet, national intelligentsia produced in the city's transformed educational institutions; the best and most motivated Ukrainian teachers; a concentration of full primary schools (often in the space of former gymnasia); theatres; exhibition spaces; and a relatively more literate population and newspaper readership. Ukrainization in the countryside was assumed to be a much more straightforward matter. It was in the republic's villages and provincial towns that the Ukrainian-speaking population was concentrated. The question of "forced" Ukrainization was less relevant, although, in the drive to create new Ukrainian schools, Jews, Poles, Germans, Bulgarians, and other ethnic minorities occasionally got swept up in enrolment campaigns. In areas where the number of any one single ethnic minority was too small, local education officials faced a dilemma, but in most cases they made an effort to create ethnic-minority schools whether the non-Ukrainians liked it or not.

On paper, Narkomos converted rural schools quickly to Ukrainian instruction – but, as the archival record makes clear, local officials confronted a whole series of problems regarding Ukrainization: dialectal variance; unqualified teachers; lack of parental support for education; substandard buildings; shortages in paper, ink, and fuel; and limited supplies of Ukrainian-language textbooks, literature, and newspapers. Urban schools all confronted these challenges, but to a lesser degree. The irony of Ukrainization in schooling is that the state's best resources for the campaign went to population centres where there were comparatively fewer Ukrainians, and the central archival records, at least regarding conversion of language of instruction, are concentrated on challenges in urban schools. This study utilizes provincial archival material from Kyiv and Odesa and reports in the pedagogical press to reference the rural side of this dynamic and to fill in the gap of the central archival records.

Political terror had a discernible impact on matters of education throughout the republic, but especially in the countryside. The files of the teachers' union (Robos), KP(b)U, and the Komsomol all reference purges of teachers, some of whom were labelled nationalists in the aftermath of the SVU show trial. Peasants allegedly attacked activist teachers, schoolchildren, and Young Pioneers for their work on exposure of the "class enemy" in and beyond the schoolhouse. Educators and children thus were expected to participate in the exclusion of those deemed "foreign" by the party. A direct discussion of the 1932–3 famine's impact on schooling is beyond the scope of this study. Narkomos's files on the early 1930s are limited, concentrated largely on reports on the challenges and successes of carrying out party decrees on universal enrolment.[54] It is inconceivable that such a calamitous event would not have had an effect on the lives of children, teachers, and the school. The famine and rural violence are present in this study. The study discusses in some detail increased party and Komsomol concern regarding the need for teachers and Young Pioneers to participate in grain-requisition campaigns (including those allegedly motivated by nationalist convictions) and gives some sense of the struggle of individual teachers, but a full account is difficult to compose from the perspective of Narkomos. What can be reasonably assumed is that matters of Ukrainization and pedagogical reform were much less important than questions of survival in areas devastated by hunger.

The Cultural Revolution and National Education

Narkomos was pursuing an experiment that called for considerable tact. It advocated a methodology that required individual creativity on the part of teachers, asking only that they conform to broadly outlined standards. Although they were teaching the values of socialism in Ukrainian and through distinctly Ukrainian subjects, party authorities in Ukraine began to worry about what information teachers were actually passing to their students. Ernest Gellner has argued that states institute "universal, standardized, and generic" education systems in order to equip society for economic development.[55] These education systems enable members of a community to speak with each other not only in the same language, also but on the basis of the same experience in the "universalized" national culture introduced in the schools. In fact, the Ukrainian education system was not universal, standardized, or generic, but the Communist Party leadership had developed its own innate Gellnerian sense of the potential capacity of schools to teach an orientation it did not control. It was concerned that the ties among schools, or at least influential ones, were strong enough to enable a common transmission of a mentality that diverged from Soviet aims. The education system's mixture of flexibility in implementation but coordination in strategy is what made Soviet leaders fear its combustibility. The progressive education system that Narkomos had created relied too greatly on teachers' individual initiative. It was possible they would use the classroom for subversive instruction.

In the end, the party did not wholly trust educators. Part of this was a result of a long-standing suspicion that the cooperation of non-party elements with Soviet authorities was temporary, as Martin argues.[56] However, this distrust was also a consequence of the lack of the KP(b)U's command over Ukrainization. The course of Ukrainization could not be neatly set. Michael Smith writes: "We should not underestimate the dynamism and treacherousness of language. It was conducive and valent in ways which Soviet leaders were able to control, and in ways that they never could."[57] In pursuing Ukrainization, the KP(b)U conceded a dependence on national elites and simultaneously created "political and cultural spaces" in which the Ukrainizers moved without strict restraint. This did not mean that teachers, as executors of Ukrainization, acted against Soviet power, just that they were not always passive executors of the party's intent.

A key ambition of this study is to demonstrate the central role that the show trial of the Union for Liberation of Ukraine (*Spilka vyzvolennia Ukrainy* – SVU) – a nationalist organization fabricated by the Soviet security police (DPU – Ukrainian; GPU – Russian) – played in determining the future of Ukrainization. The KP(b)U's identification in November 1933 of "local Ukrainian nationalism" as the pre-eminent danger to Soviet power in the republic is seen by some scholars to be the definitive marker of an end to Ukrainization. Others argue that the aims of korenizatsiia were altered in Ukraine and elsewhere, but the policy, broadly considered, never ended.[58] This study questions whether any progress could have been achieved in the field of education after 1930, despite statistical evidence of "complete" Ukrainization in schooling. Responding to central and republican party concerns about growing nationalism in the Ukrainian cultural field, the GPU sent a critical signal to would-be activist Ukrainizers with the SVU affair: it arrested some of the most prominent Ukrainizing educators, claimed that teachers throughout the republic were involved in counter-revolutionary nationalist activities directed by the SVU, and suggested that one of the organization's chief activities was the indoctrination and recruitment of the young into a parallel youth organization. In the climate of fear that followed the trial, teachers had every reason to shirk the task of Ukrainization, and evidence from the early 1930s demonstrates that many had already taken this course. Schools were formally Ukrainized, but teachers did little to improve their quality of instruction.

The SVU show trial coincided with moves towards the abandonment of the complex system and the subordination of the Ukrainian school system. The indictment of leading Ukrainizers, who were simultaneously well-known educational innovators, permitted republican authorities to blame what they now identified as the disorder of the complex method on nationalist saboteurs. As this study will argue, the perception of a wayward education system offered a rationale for the centralization of education under stricter all-Union control. The same suspicion of independent teachers and scholars that had led to the fabrication of the SVU motivated these moves towards a regimentation of the methodology and structure of education. Narkomos had looked at progressive pedagogy as a way of shaping the next generation, but the potential errant development of this group became a lurking political fear. The commissariat had intended Ukrainization to enable educational progressivism. The damage that the SVU show trial did to Ukrainization created an opportunity for the eventual rejection of this task.

On one level, as will be discussed in greater detail below, the documentary records suggest the cultural revolution accelerated Ukrainization. Narkomos, under People's Commissar Mykola Skrypnyk from 1927 to 1933, called for an expansion of Ukrainian in areas deemed to be most vital to the First Five-Year Plan: the industrial eastern portion of the republic and educational institutes engaged in the training of new Soviet technical specialists. After sweeping aside the bourgeois national intelligentsia, republican authorities faced an even greater imperative to produce a new Ukrainian-speaking and loyal elite. This effort began at the primary-school level, especially in parts of the republic where the Ukrainizers had met resistance for much of the 1920s, and took place alongside a campaign to complete and perfect the Ukrainization of post-secondary education that had never really taken off. Skrypnyk turned to formerly disgraced and now reformed Ukrainizers such as Mykola Khvylovy to stimulate a new interest in the study of Ukrainian. The problem was that the incentives for a renewed campaign for Ukrainization remained few, and those who took up the charge risked being condemned as nationalists, like those who came before them.

The cultural revolution prioritized the youth's role in politics, in upturning cultural and educational institutions where pre-revolutionary intellectuals still exercised considerable sway. The emphasis of the campaigns promoted by young activists was a turn towards programs driven by ideological content and, as this study makes clear, this mandate affected primary schooling as well. Narkomos required teachers to transform their teaching outside the classroom, to ensure that each activity they planned for their students had an ideological purpose and clear contribution to the state's economic and political goals. In the case of Ukraine, this focus on activity-centred learning drew from an established effort to connect the classroom with the "building of socialism" in the 1920s. In a way, the shift was simply a reapplication of an existing trend. Yet, there were also signs of a pedagogically more conservative tack to come. It was during the period of the cultural revolution that Skrypnyk oversaw the unification of the Ukrainian and Russian education systems.

The basic reform was structural; it did away with the Ukrainian republic's distinctive seven-year primary school and two-year vocational secondary school, and established a nine-year expanded primary school and standardized curricular expectations. However, the reform's significance was deeper. It meant an abandonment of the Ukrainian educational alternative, which still had advocates in Ukraine and elsewhere in the Soviet Union, although Skrypnyk was publicly supportive of the shift. This suggested some limitation on the Ukrainian republic's autonomy in the cultural field, but more importantly, it required an eventual conceptual shift away from Narkomos's early orientation of children to the practice of labour. Although children were to remain engaged with economic activity, the curriculum became much more generalized in spite of Narkomos's emphasis on "polytechnization." The state's deployment of schoolchildren to specific tasks of the First Five-Year Plan (e.g., collectivization) retained elements of the applied aspects of the complex method, but this activity was discrete and more crudely political, divorced from a larger pedagogical vision of a practice-centred education. By the end of the cultural revolution, the commissariat mandated greater use of standard textbooks and the achievement of formal knowledge alongside the full enrolment of children. The cultural revolution's radicalism paved the way for the emergence of an education system that was more conventional in instructional approach than what preceded it. The fact that it was the Old Bolshevik Skrypnyk who saw this transformation through speaks, perhaps, to the continuities inherent in the cultural revolution in Ukraine before a definitive shift towards educational conservatism.

In the end, the cultural revolution was symbolically about the promise of youth. Youth would transform culture, overturn conventions in education, lead the charge of the state's "great turn," and build the socialist future. The cultural revolution's lasting legacy must be this preoccupation with youth. It is not surprising, then, that the vulnerability the KP(b)U chose to expose regarding Ukrainization at this time had to do with youth. The cultural revolution's demonstration that the future of Soviet power lay in the hands of the young provoked anxiety. To repeat, the party had delegated responsibility for implementing Ukrainization (and evaluating its progress) largely to non-party intellectuals, some of whom had occupied prominent roles in the Ukrainian national movement. The purging impulse of the cultural revolution demanded their removal, but elements within the KP(b)U had resented the independence of these non-party intellectuals, and the GPU harboured greater suspicions of counter-revolutionary activity, well before the cultural revolution. The cultural revolution offered an opportunity to act upon these suspicions, and concerns about national management of Ukrainian-language schools provided a script. In the effort to redefine Ukrainization, the party and the GPU structured the task as a battle for the hearts and minds of children and youth. The GPU created a "school group" for the fabricated SVU, implicating some of the most authoritative individuals responsible for the Ukrainization of schooling, and invented a youth organization (SUM) for recent graduates of Ukrainized schools, to parallel the SVU. Instead of being saviours of the revolution, youth were the targets of the counter-revolution and were vulnerable to corruption.

This was the paradox of the cultural revolution in the context of Ukrainization: youth and children were not burdened by a tie to the tsarist era and thus could be strong leaders of the transformation called for by the cultural revolution, while, at the same time, the KP(b)U and the GPU viewed them as particularly weak in the face of a nationalist threat. Although the party leadership continued to insist on the essential value of Ukrainization, they also argued that Ukrainization had given "class enemies" opportunity. The party had to eliminate this enemy not only because of who they were (irreconcilable class enemies, from the perspective of the party), but because of what they could be doing in the classroom beyond the eyes of the party; the party did not need to structure the attack on the Ukrainian intelligentsia in the way that it did, if it did not hold this concern. The existence of a separatist, nationalist grouping was an absurdity, but what was true was that the party was deeply dependent on non-party members for Ukrainization, and some intellectuals such Serhii Yefremov had very ambiguous views towards Soviet power. The party's anxiety was not irrational, but if it acted to remove prominent non-party intellectuals, educators, and teachers, who, then, would lead Ukrainization? As has been argued, the lesson the SVU affair taught educators as a whole was that it was best not to be strident in their embrace of the policy, whatever Narkomos's exhortations were, and this study contends that the case critically weakened further efforts towards Ukrainization. At the same time, regardless of party and Komsomol discomfort with NEP-era (New Economic Policy) concessions to accommodation with the petite bourgeoisie, there was no certainty at the start of Ukrainization that the party leadership would sanction a move against the national intelligentsia. Ukrainizers in the 1920s were not cognizant of a shift in the offing and acted earnestly to fulfill the agenda that they believed was in agreement with party aims and their own convictions: the training of children and youth for the fulfillment of socialism and flourishing of Ukrainian national culture. Schools were the answer for all.

Chapter Two

Adapting to Place

The Ukrainian education system drew inspiration from Western pedagogical experience. Revolution in the Russian Empire meant a reconsideration of the way in which teaching was done. For long-time advocates of progressive education, the altered political environment meant freedom to act upon a faith in the liberating power of schooling. The short-lived Ukrainian national governments that formed in the intervening time between the collapse of the tsarist government and lasting Bolshevik military victory in Ukraine aspired towards the creation of a network of schools under state administration. But it was the Bolshevik embrace of progressive pedagogy that motivated a fundamental shift in classroom activity. The new methodology was not strictly Bolshevik or even socialist. It was modelled on educational theories developed by John Dewey and others that emphasized an interconnected relationship between learning and real-life experience, acquired through independent discovery. The Ukrainian commissariat actively sought to collect and publish the writing of foreign progressive educators and found ready correspondents.

Ukrainian educators enjoyed what Western educators did not: broad state support for a progressive education system, even if underfinanced. The Ukrainian commissariat further aspired towards an interventionist role in education because of the particular dilemma it faced: large numbers of children left orphaned, semi-orphaned, and homeless by the civil war in Ukraine and the after-effects of famine. It saw these children as the core population towards which the state could direct its transformative agenda. Although Ukrainian education administrators lacked the funding to carry out the campaign fully, their administration of "children's homes" in the immediate post-revolutionary period shaped the mentality of these children.

The progressive method favoured by commissariat authorities (if not all authority) suggested a certain trust that teachers and children would develop an innate socialist sensibility through their own elaboration and exercise, but the initial requirements and guidance were set by the state. A participatory, collectivist education would prepare primary-school students for secondary vocational school, the peculiarly Ukrainian answer to a desperate need for labour to propel the republic's devastated economy forward. Progressive education in Ukraine thus emphasized an awareness of labour culture through the application of the complex method, an instructional method derived from a Soviet understanding of Western pedagogical theory in which all disciplinary exercises would be regrouped around thematic "complexes." Teachers were unprepared and resisted this shift, and it did not enjoy universal political support (partly because of concerns regarding teachers' ideological loyalties), but Narkomos administrators believed the complex system offered the best opportunity to wipe the slate clean. Narkomos instructed teachers to orient their complexes around economic and labour activity, and stressed the locally derived nature of material for the compilation of the complexes.

In short, complexes needed to be generated from a concern for "contemporary" local studies, or *kraieznavstvo*. Unlike local studies by middle-class intelligentsia in the past, which privileged folkloric tradition, Soviet local studies emphasized active engagement with the present and daily. It was through a concern for the local that Narkomos administrators believed teachers would have their greatest success, because learning was derived from what was already familiar to students. The expectation was that children would see greater meaning and applicability in their study. From the Soviet perspective, urban children enjoyed the advantage in the application of local studies because of their proximity to industry, and Narkomos administrators encouraged rural teachers to develop links to urban schools as an extension of their local studies program, an exercise that fostered the children's awareness of connections beyond an insular community to a Ukrainian republic.

Locally oriented material encouraged an aversion to textbooks. Under the conditions of Ukrainization, Ukrainian-language literature was in short supply anyhow. Teachers adapted tsarist-era publications, Russian literature, and academic works for classroom use, but Narkomos ordered the creation of regional and district commissions to develop locally centred texts and, most importantly, encouraged teachers and students to compile their own classroom material. Experimental schools provided the testing ground to work out local variants of centrally defined themes. The concern for the local linked to the region and to the wider Ukrainian republic, as well as an emphasis on Ukrainian themes and the intersection between ethnic-Ukrainian communities in the countryside and city, meant that kraieznavstvo generally and as realized in the schools was a critical element in Ukrainian studies. This chapter highlights the experience of three model teachers and their students, as published in the pedagogical press. These teachers envisioned local studies as a way to stimulate community civic participation; children's active learning and engagement with the tasks of socialism; and the selective teaching of the Ukrainian revolutionary past, the Ukrainian national category, and republican identity. The tasks of a socialist and national education were fused in pursuit of the complex method that was politically driven but freed of strict doctrinaire instruction.

Scholars have often placed education at the heart of their discussions of nation-building projects. However, Celia Applegate has emphasized that modernization arguments regarding national identity, such that of Gellner, are incomplete.[1] In her investigation of how provincial Germans in the border region of Pfalz understood and used the concept of homeland (*Heimat*), Applegate seeks to provide an answer to how individuals experienced this feeling of national belonging. This study accepts Applegate's claim that local studies projects facilitated national identity construction.[2] However, local studies in Soviet Ukrainian schools explored this association in a fundamentally different manner. Like Heimat campaigns in Germany, kraieznavstvo offered a way to think about national belonging. However, the type of national identification this effort embraced was necessarily shaped by the particular challenges of defining a national culture for an historically rural nation in the world's first Communist state. An examination of the case of Soviet Ukraine provides a reminder of the unpredictable nature of nation-building campaigns accomplished through local studies education and of the limits of state support for such efforts.[3]

Theoretical Foundations

Russia's October Revolution set off a period of violence and disorder, but it also created opportunity for significant intellectual, scientific, and artistic experimentation. A progressive stratum of the former empire's educated elite welcomed the chance to do away with hated practices of the old, and the pedagogical world was no exception. Revolution inspired discussion throughout the former empire regarding the task of building a radical "new school." Educators debated numerous options, but their overwhelming concern was a disassociation from the classical education of the tsarist gymnasia and promotion of pedagogical innovation.

In Soviet Ukraine, the campaign for a transformation of pedagogy led to the development of a highly progressive and distinctive education system that lasted until the late 1920s. The founders of this system argued that the republic required schools attuned to its economic and social particularities, particularities that were, in their view, a result of the devastation of the civil war and centuries of tsarist oppression and economic exploitation. Ukrainian educational planners recognized the critical importance of linguistic Ukrainization to the creation of the "new school," and progressive pedagogy created opportunities for Ukrainian national exploration and expression. However, these were means to an end. For the Ukrainian Soviet government, the intent of the "new school" was the creation of a new Soviet generation and the transformation of society.

In the early years of the Soviet state, educational theorists and Narkomos did not rely exclusively upon Marxist theory for inspiration, but rather turned to the wealth of pedagogical theory developed in the West. Commissar of Education Hrynko publicly argued in an article entitled "Our Path to the West" that "spontaneous-revolutionary pedagogical activity" unleashed in Ukraine could be grounded in ties with the West.[4] Narkomos representatives travelled to Germany, Austria, and Czechoslovakia to secure material and solicit ideas for creating new schools in Ukraine. From 1922 to 1927, a permanent representative of Narkomos resided in Berlin in order to facilitate ties with German educators, collect publications on the subject of educational reform, and see to the publication of Ukrainian textbooks abroad. Foreign educational theorists regularly contributed publications to the Ukrainian educational journal *Shliakh osvity* (literally, Path of education), a periodical that became well known abroad for its promotion of educational change. According to one count by education historian Olha Sukhomlynska, *Shliakh osvity* published 458 articles regarding problems in foreign pedagogy and education, and maintained ties with 113 organizations and individuals abroad.[5]

Drawing upon this contact with the West and research published in pre-revolutionary Russia, Ukrainian educational theorists sought to develop an education system tailored to a child's aptitude for learning. Several prominent, Ukrainian, pre-revolutionary pedagogues such as Yakiv Chepiha helped formulate pedagogy for the new education system. One theory that gained particular favour among educational progressives was reflexology, elaborated by pre-revolutionary Russian researchers such as Ivan Pavlov and Vladimir Bekhterev. According to Bekhterev, "the essence of reflexology is that all the behaviour of a person begins with elementary organized reactions and ends with deep acts of creation, which come together in reflexes."[6] Ukrainian educational theorists believed that an instructive methodology that accounted for these reflexes and directed them towards a prescribed educational goal would achieve the most effective results in the classroom.

Ukrainian progressives coupled reflexology with an interest in the ideas of American educational theorist John Dewey, who emphasized the necessity of connecting instruction with real life and allowing children to solve problems through independent application. Furthermore, his arguments for the merger of math and humanities and against the textbook as the central instructional device proved attractive to Ukrainian educators searching for ways to offer effective education with scant resources. Yet another approach that appealed to Ukrainian educational planners reluctant to mimic their tsarist predecessors and impose an obligatory and universal curriculum was the so-called Dalton Plan. Designed by American Ellen Parkhurst for a Massachusetts high school, it allowed for individualized instruction based on a child's knowledge. Parkhurst's students entered into contracts with teachers and then joined small laboratory groups. Teachers and students decided the course of instruction collectively.[7]

The Ukrainian Variant

In a broad assessment of the Ukrainian education system, written on the occasion of the tenth anniversary of the October Revolution, People's Deputy Commissar of Education Jan Riappo maintained that Ukraine had developed an educational "path" distinct from the Russian Soviet Federated Socialist Republic (RSFSR), which better satisfied the republic's needs.[8] In designing its education system, Riappo wrote, Ukraine benefited from the fact that civil war prevented establishment of a network of schools in the newly formed UkrSSR until 1920, under the then commissar of education, Volodymyr Zatonsky. Russia already had two years of experience by this time, and planners made liberal use of Russian debates over the intent and form of education.[9]

Initially, Ukraine did not concern itself with implementation of progressive pedagogy in the schoolhouse. Narkomos's pre-eminent worry was the civil war's legacy of millions of homeless children. Their numbers grew even higher as the result of a 1921–2 famine in the Volga basin, which stretched into southern Ukraine and brought countless refugees to the republic.[10] Narkomos's first duty, then, was to organize, protect, and provide for these children. Unlike its Russian counterpart, Riappo argued, Narkomos was forced to fully realize the child-rearing aspect of its directive. The principal institution for this task was the children's building, described by Riappo as a "lighthouse" (*maiak*) for Ukraine's neglected children.[11] In 1923, at their high point, 1,928 children's buildings in Ukraine cared for 114,000 homeless and neglected children.

As the economy in Ukraine stabilized to some degree and starvation no longer posed an immediate danger, the number of children's buildings steadily declined. However, the ideology of "social upbringing" that motivated the formation of children's buildings did not diminish. Zatonsky's successor as the UkrSSR commissar of education, Hryhorii Hrynko, argued for children's buildings to take charge of all children, claiming that a school's pedagogical and organizational influence on a child left in the care of the "individualistic" family will be lost "in a night."[12] Although this idea was abandoned as both impractical and fiscally impossible, the state's desire to ensure instruction by the "social collective" persisted and influenced Narkomos's preference for a progressive pedagogy that emphasized the centrality of the school, shared projects, and civic activity. Narkomos labelled this approach "social upbringing" (*sotsiialne vykhovannia – sotsvykh*)

With the gradual decline of the children's building, Narkomos turned to the schools as the basis of the Ukrainian education system. The commissariat's leadership outlined the structure of a separate Ukrainian variant at the First All-Ukrainian Meeting on Education in Kharkiv (March 1920).[13] Whereas the RSFSR People's Commissariat of Education (Narkompros) retained a four-year primary school followed by a five-year general secondary school, the Ukrainian Narkomos opted for a seven-year extended primary school followed by a two-year vocational secondary school. The vocational schools offered training in a specified field of employment to students as early as age fifteen. The Ukrainian Commissariat saw them not only as models for proletarian schooling, but also as the answer to Ukraine's desperate need for qualified workers.[14] Hrynko was a strong advocate for this type of applied instruction and a critic of the duplicative general-education function of the Russian secondary school. Although, in comments he made to the Collegium of the RSFSR People's Commissariat of Education in September 1920, he insisted it was not Ukraine's initial intent to pursue a separate path, he added he would not permit "any slave-like copying" of the Russian education system.[15] Hrynko believed that not only was a technical–vocational orientation better suited to the needs of Ukraine, but also that this orientation should form the basis for a united educational policy for the Soviet Union.

The differences between the Russian and Ukrainian systems were most striking at the secondary level. Historians such as Sheila Fitzpatrick and Larry Holmes have referenced these distinctions, particularly in regard to the discussions held at the First All-Union Party Meeting on Education in Moscow (December 31, 1920, to January 4, 1921).[16] Riappo and Hrynko's promotion of vocational schools at this meeting elicited support from Komsomol, Vesenkha (Supreme Economic Council), and labour union representatives, and the meeting passed a resolution criticizing Russian moves away from vocational training. In instructions to the VKP(b) Central Committee and in a February 1921 *Pravda* article, Vladimir Lenin also proposed early vocational training as a "temporary and practical expedient."[17] The Komsomol continued to press the case, and the Russian Commissariat did permit several types of vocational schools, the most widespread being the FZU school (*shkola fabrichno-zavodskoho uchnivstva* – factory-apprenticeship school; literally, school of factory and plant apprenticeship), to operate parallel to its general secondary schools. However, the Komsomol maintained its pre-existing suspicion of junior trade schools as "circles of hell" for the poor, which stifled their cultural liberation and restricted their advancement.[18] While it allowed for the FZU school, it insisted on its inclusion of a general educational curriculum even in this institution.

The Ukrainian preference for early vocational training at the secondary level inevitably influenced the character of its extended primary school, the chief concern here. The continuing battle for the expansion of vocational training in Russia detailed by Fitzpatrick and, to a lesser extent, Holmes, was absent in Ukraine because the republic had already committed itself to this path. Emboldened by the party meeting's decision, the Ukrainian Commissariat insisted on an education system oriented towards vocational training.[19] The curriculum of Ukraine's primary schools reflected their mandate to prepare and matriculate students into vocational secondary schools. Although both the Russian and Ukrainian education systems embraced the principle of a "united labour school," the Ukrainians insisted that their institutions truly embraced labour-oriented methodology and successfully integrated a general educational foundation with technical preparation. Graduates of the Ukrainian seven-year primary school, Riappo maintained, were far more ready to undergo this training than the many Russian youths who sought admission to a FZU school or other alternative vocational-type school with only four years of completed primary schooling.[20] The reality, of course, was that probably an equivalent proportion of Ukrainians left school before completion of their seven-year degree, but, on paper, the Ukrainian system did offer the opportunity for uninterrupted study leading to vocational schooling. The Russian route towards this end was indirect and one that enjoyed little institutional support by the Russian Narkompros.

The Complex Method

The principal medium for a labour approach at the primary-school level was not a uniquely Ukrainian solution. Labelled the "complex method," it was a system of instruction derived by Russian and Ukrainian Soviet educators alike from the progressive pedagogy embodied in Dewey's writings and the Dalton Plan. Ukraine's annual teaching guide, the *Poradnyk sotsiialnoho vykhovannia* (Handbook for social upbringing), had embraced child-centred instruction early on, arguing that education should be tailored to the natural development of children and to children's surroundings. An explicit shift to complex instruction was a natural consequence of this approach, and Ukrainian educational planners looked first to the 1922–3 program of the Russian State Academic Council for a model on how to proceed.[21] The program mandated instruction around a set theme or complex placed under one of three broad headings: Nature, Society, and Labour. All traditional disciplines (such as mathematics, science, history, and language) would be subordinated to this complex. The children's talents and interest played a significant part in the selection of a complex, which often called for the study of children's immediate surroundings through the performance of various practical tasks.[22]

Hrynko's course of education reform caused unease for some in the KP(b)U Politburo, and Zatonsky returned to the post of commissar in October 1922. However, it was under Zatonsky's administration that Narkomos officials first began promoting the complex methodology in earnest (with Hrynko's structural reforms left intact). By the time of Oleksandr Shumsky's appointment to the position in September 1924, the complex method was the undisputed preferred form of instruction. As Mykola Vyhovsky notes, apart from changes in the position of people's commissar, the central staff of Narkomos did not fluctuate greatly through much of the 1920s.[23] More permanent mid-level administrators, such as Deputy Commissar Riappo, who served in this position from 1921 to 1928, oversaw curriculum matters; however, final responsibility for the complex method rested with local education authorities.

Primary schoolteachers in Ukraine were far from enamoured with the complex method. When implemented in Russia, educational planners had attributed near "mystical" powers to the method and offered few details on how it should be employed.[24] The Ukrainian Narkomos was little better in supplying instructions. Narkomos set the structure of complexes in the annual *poradnyk* (guide) and published them in the pedagogical press, and purportedly distributed the guide to all schools. (In fact, local education sections were lucky to receive it.) The guide was simply that, a guide: short on details, but filled with tables of possible complexes and the type of material that teachers should cover. It provided grand abstract models, but stopped short of offering a comprehensive and universal program. Narkomos administrators believed that the actual content of work in the schools must have a local character and relied on local institutions to work out specifics.[25] Teachers remained confused. Having never encountered, let alone been trained in, this method of instruction, teachers were understandably skeptical about the method's benefits and at a loss on how to innovate.

A 1923 report by the Kharkiv Provincial Education Section stated that schools in the city of Kharkiv were transferring to instruction by the complex system, but in the countryside, old methods of teaching persisted. It argued that rural teachers lacked instructions and basic educational material to carry out this task.[26] After a 1924–5 push by Narkomos, one school director at a regional (*okruha*) meeting of the heads of district labour schools in Kyiv noted that although schools were moving to complex instruction, teachers often worked strictly according to the guides with entirely abstract material, and were unable to integrate them with material that students could readily understand. These were the better teachers.

Others abandoned the method altogether: "Often instruction by the complexes has turned into idle chatter and has entirely ignored technical skills and mastery of material on their reproduction."[27] Even when local education sections took it upon themselves to provide additional material on the complex method, perhaps in an attempt to outdo the central planners, the guides remained theoretical and served only to baffle teachers more.[28]

Those who did not accede to complex instruction were, in practice, forced to employ it: a 1925 internal order from the Narkomos Collegium stressed that its primary school program, which formally endorsed the complex method, should be mandatory and any other approach was impermissible.[29] However, it also called for "attentive checks" on the work carried out as part of this program. Narkomos was anxious to demonstrate that instruction by the complex method could supply required skills. In particular, it ordered that local education sections monitor not just the general development of children, but also their skill level in reading, writing, and arithmetic (*lichba*). As will be discussed in more detail below, teachers who remained unable or unwilling to implement complex instruction sometimes abandoned a methodology altogether, fearing being accused of defending the old school.[30] The result was a lack of any sort of discipline in the classroom and a high incidence of academic failure.

To be sure, the challenge for teachers was immense. Their own material situation was often desperate. Dependent upon local authorities for their salaries, rural teachers went unpaid for months and subsisted on a minimum ration.[31] Some fled to urban posts or quit the profession entirely. Schools closed down due to lack of financing or limped along as best they could without fuel, light, or paper. Teachers, inspectors, and local education sections alike decried the lack of Ukrainian-language textbooks, noting that even when new ones finally became available, they remained either too expensive or impossible to acquire.

Narkomos leaders also had lingering questions about teachers' political commitment to the new Soviet school. They continued to rely largely on teachers who had received their education before the revolution, due to a shortage of Soviet-trained staff. Oleksandr Shumsky (Commissar of Education from 1924 to 1927) conceded that rural teachers had fallen in with the agrarian Ukrainian Party of Socialist Revolutionaries (SRs) during the civil war because of their "weak tie to the city" and peasant origins.[32] He argued that after Soviet power came to the countryside, "the public teacher honestly and openly returned to the working masses, the truant is catching up and with his efforts Soviet power will be victorious on this third front."[33] Teachers, he insisted, were not the same as the intelligentsia because they had "returned" to the working population. Just in case, he recommended continued Komsomol oversight.

Narkomos was determined to implement instruction by the complex method regardless. It conceded that textbooks were in short supply, and not until 1924 was literature available in the Ukrainian language that corresponded to Ukrainian conditions and to the requirements of the new Soviet school.[34] Until then, pre-revolutionary textbooks were simply translated from Russian. From the perspective of Narkomos and progressive educators, however, textbooks remained an auxiliary device, to be used to stimulate class activity and, in the particular circumstances of linguistic Ukrainization, to provide Ukrainian-language vocabulary for class discussion. Salvation, however, was to be found in the new methodology, not in the book alone. One presenter at the 1925 Kyiv regional conference of school directors noted that teachers remained entirely too reliant on textbooks when attempting to teach by the complex method, and were failing to incorporate "concrete material" into their lesson plans or engage in true interactive activity with their students.[35] Another delegate claimed that teachers had taken educational authorities' concern with the quality of instruction to mean an abandonment of the complex method. In fact, "the system of complexes, which the programs provide, gives the only means to implement the whole structure of Soviet schools. It is impossible to do away with them, it is rather necessary to manage the transfer to them by the schools."[36] Narkomos and progressive educators were concerned with perfecting complex instruction, not rejecting it. They stuck stubbornly to this course until the late 1920s.

An Introduction to Kraieznavstvo in the Schools

If the *profshkoly* were to offer hands-on vocational training at the secondary level, it was the responsibility of the seven-year primary school to prepare students with the proper proletarian mentality. The complex method, however imperfectly applied, was the means Narkomos chose to purge schools of the didactic teaching of the past and instruct students in the value of labour and the promise of the revolutionary future. In 1927, Riappo argued that because of Ukraine's early adoption of the complex method, "the life of the school began to adapt to the demands of the children's Communist society and the program to the productive tasks of a Soviet country."[37] Although the Russian Narkompros also adopted the complex method, it constantly battled for its continued use and scaled back its expectations. As Holmes demonstrates, it ultimately was forced to reintroduce traditional instruction by subjects in its 1926 and 1927 curricula.[38] Because the object of the Ukrainian education system as a whole was the vocational training of its youth, the Ukrainian Narkomos continued to advance the preparatory value of the complex method for the cultivation of future labourers.

Narkomos's most successful application of the complex method was in the field of kraieznavstvo. Strictly speaking, this term means "local studies," but its definition shifted. In the early 1920s, kraieznavstvo denoted a general, often folkloric, study of a region surrounding a school and the larger Ukrainian republic.[39] In the commissariat's 1920–1 instructional plan, courses on Ukrainian studies had formed a significant part of the school's curriculum. Through the third grade, general courses labelled "kraieznavstvo" predominated, and in the fourth through seventh grades, more specific courses on civics history (*istoriia z hromadianoznavstvo*) and geography covered Ukrainian studies. According to one calculation, out of an aggregate of 173 instruction hours per week, the program devoted 79 hours to subjects that were considered to be Ukrainian studies.[40] These included courses on kraieznavstvo, native-language instruction, civics, geography, and singing. However, the 1920–1 plan and subsequent plans did not explicitly detail the content and form of kraieznavstvo. For this reason, schools interpreted kraieznavstvo and related subjects differently and developed variant plans.

In the 1924–5 academic year, when Narkomos mandated a full-scale transfer to education by the complex method, kraieznavstvo proved agreeable to this shift because of its early emphasis on self-discovery of a region's features and places of interest. The year 1925 saw the publication of several articles in the Soviet Ukrainian pedagogical journal *Radianska osvita* (Soviet Education) on the subject of teaching kraieznavstvo, using in particular the complex method. One author, Lazaris, pointed to a lack of ideological and organizational leadership in kraieznavstvo prior to 1924 to explain confusion over its teaching.[41] According to Lazaris, initial efforts to tie kraieznavstvo to practical work were insufficient and its instruction had little to do with concerns of real life. Now, "proletarian students" had taken over leadership of kraieznavstvo and directed its application to present concerns. A 1924 All-Union Congress on Local Studies set the defining agenda for all future kraieznavstvo work. Kraieznavstvo could no longer devote time to the study of customs and tradition, but should rather concentrate on an examination of the "productive forces and general growth of planned economic construction."[42] Although the congress placed primary schools at the centre of kraieznavstvo work, it called upon "a wide circle of workers" to involve themselves in the development of this work.

Ukrainian scholarship on kraieznavstvo in the 1920s has generally been concerned with the activities and eventual repression of individual scholars and groups.[43] Teachers staffed several civic- and state-sponsored local studies groups, including subject-specific commissions that operated under VUAN, but a detailed investigation of their role is still needed.[44] Until the 1925 creation of a Ukrainian Committee for Local Studies under Holovnauka (the Main Administration for

Science – a subsidiary organ of Narkomos), commissions in Kyiv, Kharkiv, and Odesa managed regional coordination of activity.[45] It fell to regional methodological committees of Narkomos and individual educators to develop municipal and regional curricular material for the schools.[46]

Chapter 5 will explore in detail the challenges teachers faced in attempting to implement a kraieznavstvo curriculum. I. Haliun, a contributor to *Radianska osvita*, described the ideal in an article on experimental work with children. He and other progressives believed that kraieznavstvo should form the basis of instruction for all disciplines, rather than be set aside as a separate subject of study. They argued for the "unification" of all schoolwork to the study of real life.[47] It was their concern for this goal that motivated them to promote instruction by the complex method. Kraieznavstvo could not be studied from textbooks, Haliun wrote, but should be tied to "living, passionate feelings towards life and toiling people, who with the sweat and blood of struggle have built their labour life and culture." The complex method was favoured because it organized schoolwork towards this end, but the primary concern with kraieznavstvo advocates was instruction integrated with "productive" life.

Kraieznavstvo's new emphasis on active engagement with the community promised greater localization of its application. Teachers were encouraged to favour the study of the immediate surroundings of the school first and foremost. Urban children had the advantage in the study of kraieznavstvo because of the great variety of "productive forces" in their place of residence. Haliun argued that constant change in a child's urban environment produces a "type of existence that is more developed, with a sharpened interest to everything that surrounds him."[48] He further insisted that schools must develop courses suited to this particular "psychology" of the urban child, with the ultimate goal of producing a "future, conscious worker" for socialism. Kraieznavstvo in the cities should also encompass the surrounding region's topography, natural world, and material culture. Haliun recommended that urban teachers collect "living folklore," including common sayings and songs, as well as "living memories," such as personal accounts of the revolution and histories of specific enterprises.

Narkomos adjusted the complex system to meet its educational objectives in rural schools. Kraieznavstvo determined the content of complexes in rural schools just as it did in cities. However, rural students were to focus primarily on agricultural activity, as well as some folklore, local customs, and events. Although Haliun lauded the presence of expressions of the "victorious new" in the villages, he conceded that folklore derived from the past should form a large basis for the study of kraieznavstvo in the rural school. Material such as fairytales, fables (*baiky*), legends, and customs had an effect on rural children at birth and could be used to inspire an interest in the everyday life of the village and its "productive forces."[49]

Haliun lamented the fate of children in rural schools, "now completely torn from city schools" and from the city in general. Rural schools must strengthen their ties to urban schools so that the student does not act like a "wild beast" when he encounters the city.

A common instructional emphasis on production would facilitate interaction between the urban and rural school. Narkomos plans obligated rural students to learn about cities. Thus, not only were a school's immediate surroundings important, but also wider Ukraine. Urban students studied Ukraine's rural resources as well, but the emphasis of broader Ukrainian studies was on the proletarian city and industrial production. The 1927–8 Narkomos program recommended that rural students make excursions to the cities and that those who lived in isolated locations learn from illustrated journals. The program argued that "it is necessary to inculcate in children an awareness that a person can do everything when he is armed with knowledge and organization and that the culture of the village depends on the culture of the city."[50] The most valued form of knowledge, then, was to be found in the cities. The oft-cited cultural union (*smychka*) between the village and the city was not entirely false, but it was unequal. Narkomos intended educated rural youth to either join the proletariat or contribute to the agricultural production necessary for its strength. The new Ukraine was unequivocally proletarian, and Ukrainian studies in the schools reflected this aspiration.

Furthermore, for both urban and rural children, lessons in kraieznavstvo work were not confined to the limits of the classroom. Children made trips in their region (and sometimes beyond) to visit farms, factories, architectural sites, and other points of interest. However, children were not to just passively observe the places they visited. I. Kopyl, a teacher from the Zolotonosha region, described the experience of his sixth-grade group in *Radianska osvita*.[51] For this group's kraieznavstvo work, Kopyl assigned students the task of examining village soviets in the district. The students designed a form (*anketa*) in order to plan questions for their observation of the village and interviews with residents and members of the soviet. They included questions not only on the village's economy and production, but also on its social structure, party membership, civic activism, and cultural achievements (in particular, literacy levels). One group went even so far as to judge the number of dogs and cats, information, Kopyl stressed, that was not easy to acquire. Kopyl noted that the students planned to compile the group's more important findings into a directory of the district (*raion*), together with maps, and send it to the district executive committee and other local governmental and cultural institutions. The students also hoped to host a workshop with schools of the neighbouring district and collaborate on a comparative economic study of the larger area.

Such interactive excursions served a number of purposes, according to Kopyl. First, they satisfied a public need. Although Kopyl conceded that the students' work may not have been entirely accurate, the students still helped inform the executive committee and "improve their parents' and neighbors' economic management."[52] Notwithstanding the students' inexperience, the report may well have been less biased than other official reports of the time because the children posed questions with few inhibitions. Second, Kopyl argued that the students' work in the region had the potential to increase the school's authority among the population, "an authority, by the way, that many schools do not have." Through their engagement of local officials and residents, students demonstrated the utility of schooling to a rural society that, when confronted with the daily challenge of survival, had not historically valued it. Lastly, because the students were required to conduct their research independently, they took greater pride in the realization of the project. This, in the end, was the chief merit of instruction by the complex method coupled with kraieznavstvo. Since the students were investigating something already familiar to them, they accomplished their tasks with greater alacrity and effect.

Narkomos did attempt to provide some institutional oversight to the kraieznavstvo movement. The All-Union Congress on Kraieznavstvo was the first comprehensive attempt to define an agenda for the entire country. In 1925, the VUAN Commission of Kraieznavstvo assumed responsibility for the coordination of work throughout the republic. There were two further regional centres, the commission's branch in Odesa (Odessa) and the Commission for Kraieznavstvo of Slobidska Ukraine,[53] overseen by the Kharkiv Institute of People's Education (*Instytut narodnoi osvity* – INO, the Soviet post-secondary institution that replaced the university). More regional bureaus were to be set up under regional planning commissions. Narkomos called upon all members of society, but particularly representatives of science, education, professional trade unions, and student organizations, to attend periodical plenums on kraieznavstvo and coordinate their work.

Some standardization of instructional content in the classroom, Narkomos officials concluded, was also beneficial. Due to the nearly complete absence of appropriate school texts, teachers initially attempted to adapt more technical works to classroom needs. Matvii Yavorsky's *Korotka istoriia Ukraini* (Short history of Ukraine) and a Ukrainian translation of Miron Volfson's *Ocherki obshchestvovedeniia* (Essays on social studies) were the most widely used textbooks in Ukrainian schools in the latter half of the twenties.[54] As one of Ukraine's leading Marxist historians, Yavorsky played a significant part in the design of kraieznavstvo material. His *Korotka istoriia* represented the first attempt to provide a party-centred and class approach to Ukrainian history for the general public. Following the return to Ukraine of pre-eminent Ukrainian historian

Mykhailo Hrushevsky in 1924, both he and Yavorsky worked on the promotion of kraieznavstvo. Hrushevsky formed a VUAN commission to encourage the development of regional histories.[55] Yavorsky and Stepan Rudnytsky, the author of several geography textbooks, directed the work of the VUAN Main Committee for Kraieznavstvo. Both bodies relied on the work and participation of teachers at the local level for the success of their work.

Publishers included illustrations in *Korotka istoriia* and Matvii Yavorsky's 1925 publication, *Revoliutsiia na Ukraini* (Revolution in Ukraine), to make the books more accessible to children. Yavorsky also incorporated material from Ukrainian history, essays on intervention in Ukraine, the constitution of the UkrSSR, and Soviet nationalities policy in the Ukrainian translation of Volfson's *Ocherki obshchestvovedeniia* so that it might be more readily used in Ukrainian schools. Teachers used Oleksandr Sukhov's *Ekonomichna heohrafiia Ukrainy* (Economic geography of Ukraine), due to the absence of any suitable textbooks on geography. However, it was difficult for children to understand, and teachers also employed Konstantin Vobly's 1922 publication, *Ekonomichna heohrafiia Ukrainy* (Economic geography of Ukraine), which included illustrations, tables, questions, and recommended further reading for students.[56] In 1925, Sukhov published a revised version of his geography designed for use in the schools.

Although local education sections were responsible for defining specific methodological plans for their schools, the annual poradnyk held that no other program was permissible for the design of curricular planning. In order to ensure reproduction of the poradnyk's ideal principles, Narkomos ordered regional sections to issue supplementary guides and instructed district labour schools to offer models for their implementation. Speakers at one meeting of Kyiv regional school directors labelled the district labour school a "laboratory."[57] Located in the district seat, the district labour school was often the only full seven-year school in the area and was the first institution to try out the region's variant for the poradnyk plan, collect and anticipate the concerns of other schools in the district, and disseminate the plan further. The Narkomos division responsible for administering primary schooling in Ukraine, the Main Administration for Social Upbringing (*Holovne upravlinnia sotsiialnoho vykhovannia – Holovsotsvykh*), also set up a number of experimental institutions and assumed direct budgetary and administrative control over these institutions, unlike local *trudshkoly* (labour schools). For the 1925–6 academic year, there were at least five such schools in Kharkiv, Kyiv, Odesa, Luhansk (Lugansk), and Katerynoslav (Ekaterinoslav), enrolling nearly 1,500 students.[58] Similarly, these central schools were to give local schools "models of normal work," so that these schools might "exactly carry out the directives of the centre."[59] They were to lead by example, testing the new progressive methodology and disseminating a script for innovation.

To spread progressive methodology throughout the republic, Narkomos also advocated the publication and use of books that emphasized regional models of centrally defined themes. The Second All-Union Conference on Kraieznavstvo (1924) emphasized the need for textbooks with guides to local areas and statistical information. In Ukraine, several such textbooks were published for regions throughout the republic. Local (*okruzhni*) methodological committees of Narkomos further argued for kraieznavstvo textbooks that provided a detailed plan for localized programs.[60] These methodological committees supported the publication of several municipal and regional textbooks. Student elaboration on themes articulated in the textbooks further broadened the type of material available for classroom use. Independent schoolwork like that described by Kopyl was published in supplementary form alongside textbooks such as *Korotka istoriia Ukrainy* and disseminated to other schools.[61] Local educators and students also sought to fill the gaps left by a shortage in official printed guides. A teacher-supervised student committee in the Myronivka District Labour School, for example, put out its own journal entitled *Promin* (Ray of light) and a wall newspaper, *Chervonyi shkoliar* (Red pupil).[62] The question of problems associated with general textbook distribution will be explored further in chapter 5. Here, it is enough to say that local education officials relied on teachers to supplement whatever published literature they received from central authorities in Kharkiv.

Teachers also took a leading role in coordinating kraieznavstvo work beyond the school. These "directors and providers of culture," Haliun argued, had to take a leading role and convince workers to consider the relationship between their way of life and all that surrounded them, even the remnants of the failed past.[63] Under the teachers' leadership, educators believed that schools could become the centres for kraieznavstvo work. Teachers sought to unite their own senior pupils and the "conscious young" of the surrounding population in such study circles. In rural locations, these school centres assumed even greater importance, due to the lack of other institutional support. They provided the foundation for the public's study of its environment and maintained ties to urban research establishments. Teachers were encouraged to establish kraieznavstvo museums under the schools or coordinate their activities with stand-alone museums in the district centres. Ultimately, the aim of the teachers' efforts was to bridge the peasant-worker divide, to create a "new labour intelligentsia" drawn from both elements that would recognize that "for them kraieznavstvo will be life with the great, true school and furthermore, through the school, a tie between this life and the conscious life."[64] Schools functioned as the foci of cultural activity at the local level, and it was through schools that Narkomos hoped the Soviet Ukrainian public would be linked.

The Kobzar

Narkomos also allowed for the possibility of expanding kraieznavstvo to its broadest extent, the study of Ukraine. Narkomos formalized Ukrainian studies, *ukrainoznavstvo*, as a separate course in ethnic-minority schools, and encouraged a variety of Ukrainian-related subjects, even as it moved to instruction by the complex method. The shift to the complex method meant classes in separate traditional areas such as history, literature, and language had to give way to the complex. However, educational planners had begun to promote a generalized discipline of social studies (*suspilnoznavstvo*) as a mechanism for the creation of new complexes. The commissariat's promotion of social studies enabled schools to orient their curriculum around revolutionary themes, without having to formally emphasize any one "productive force" in the immediate region. Some Ukrainian-language schools sought to use Narkomos's promotion of social studies to make a link directly with ukrainoznavstvo. All knowledge began with a local experience, starting with a child's village or district, but then connecting to an awareness of the region and the republic. Accordingly, kraieznavstvo was a vital prerequisite of Ukrainization and Ukrainian studies, as Narkomos encouraged schools to privilege "Ukrainian" material.

Narkomos and Ukrainian educators drew on numerous aspects of Ukraine's past to develop social studies complexes, including the lives and works of pre-revolutionary and revolutionary heroes. The paradigmatic figure of Ukrainian Soviet values was the Ukrainian national poet and hero Taras Shevchenko. After Shevchenko was raised to an exalted level by the Ukrainian national movement, the young Soviet state co-opted and reworked the mythology surrounding him. Ukrainian literary specialist George Grabowicz places Shevechenko on the level of Pushkin or Mickiewicz: "he is Bard and Prophet, the inspired voice of the people, and the spiritual father of the reborn nation."[65] One school that responded to the Soviet authorities' promotion of the Shevchenko myth was a former Kyiv gymnasium, renamed the Taras Shevchenko Kyiv Labour School No. 1. Volodymyr Durdukivsky, a well-known pedagogue, headed the school. Under his leadership, the school gained a reputation as a centre of pedagogical innovation and Ukrainian cultural advancement.

Durdukivsky emphasized his school's advancement of social studies to Soviet authorities. Ostensibly due to his school's largely middle-class student body, Durdukivsky maintained to Narkomos that an industrial or agricultural orientation was impossible.[66] In a 1924 article published in the Soviet pedagogical journal *Radianska osvita*, Durdukivsky further outlined his school's development and use of a "Shevchenko complex."[67] In designing the complex, the school did not seek

Teachers and second-grade pupils of the Taras Shevchenko Kyiv Labour School No. 1. In the second row from the bottom are the teacher Oleksandr Hrebenetsky and the school's director Volodymyr Durdukivsky (from left to right), 1925–6. Courtesy TsDKFFAU.

to provide the conventional kraieznavstvo study in production, but rather sought to "light in children, with Shevchenko's fiery words, disgust of all despotism, tyranny, and exploitation and to educate in them a class proletarian consciousness, a revolutionary fuse and capacity for struggle." Lessons on Shevchenko therefore pertained to the country at large, Ukraine. Durdukivsky believed that by encouraging children to engage with the life of Shevchenko, to learn his poetry and write works inspired by him, these children would spread Shevchenko's legacy and his message of "social truth." Although Durdukivsky noted Shevchenko's importance as a figure for national liberation, Shevchenko was most importantly an "inflexible revolutionary" and "prophet for a joyous socialist future."[68] Durdukivsky claimed that instructors placed primary significance on this role in their development of lessons for the complex.

Durdukivsky also addressed another fundamental part of instruction by the complex method: exercises that encouraged independent study. In his school, children kept journals of their thoughts on Shevchenko's works and illustrated their favourite images described by the poet. Durdukivsky suggested that because such assignments were attuned to a child's "psychology," they were more engaging. Independent, "non-mechanistic" study, he argued, stimulated a desire for greater learning and elaboration by the "young researchers." Progressive educators like Durdukivsky believed instruction by the complex method to be a more effective means to train the young. The complex method, when properly applied, would encourage schoolchildren to readily participate in the design and goals of their education.

The Shevchenko complex also afforded an opportunity for civic training. One second-grade teacher at the Kyiv Labour School No.1, who published under the initials Yu. T. (probably the teacher Yurii Trezvynsky, who, like Durdukivsky, was tried for being a member of the SVU in 1930), described how his students planned and agreed upon assignments for the complex.[69] The process mimics the formulaic proceedings of a village or city soviet. The teacher convened a meeting at the school; the children proposed several projects that were then debated. The teacher reserved the right to support or reject proposals on the basis of their practicality. The results of the debate were drawn up in a plan, entitled protocol No. 10, that was voted on and approved by the class as a whole. Furthermore, even at this early age, the children were encouraged to perform a public function. The school arranged for the children to perform a skit on Shevchenko at the district theatre and participate in celebrations honouring Shevchenko's birth at a workers' theatre and club.[70] Even the children's journals and drawings were put on display at the school museum for the whole school and the public to see. Information regarding Shevchenko was collected and retransmitted by these little *kobzari* (bards, a moniker usually applied to Shevchenko),[71] as Durdukivsky called them, to the Soviet public at large.

It should be stressed that because of the less formalistic nature of the complex approach, the kind and character of information acquired by children were not strictly regulated. Teachers, in fact, encouraged children to use all sources open to them to collect information on Shevchenko. The children of Kyiv Labour School No. 1 invited the school caretaker, the son of a contemporary of Taras Shevchenko, to tell them about his father's acquaintance with the famous poet. His story was subsequently published in the school newspaper. Furthermore, Yu. T. asked the children to compare their childhood and their "region of the world" to that Shevchenko's. They solicited material at home and retold their stories the next day. Yu. T. did not describe in detail what they related, but emphasized that all work was done independently. The children were thus permitted to make their own judgment regarding the progress made in Ukraine since Shevchenko's time. These children, born in the midst of the civil war, adopted Shevchenko's words for their poster art: "struggle, [and you shall] overcome." In the poverty of 1925 Kyiv, it was the promise of the revolution, repeatedly cited by Yu. T., and not its immediate accomplishment, that must have had the greatest resonance. As Durdukivsky conceded, "Shevchenko's convictions are close, native to our contemporary life."[72]

The children would be taught about the history of the revolution in Ukraine in other complexes. It is perhaps significant, however, that this personage from the past, and not a contemporary figure, was chosen as the pre-eminent revolutionary for Ukraine. Durdukivsky argued that "every year we must unite not only the children of our school but of all schools in Ukraine" in the study of Shevchenko. It was Shevchenko's life that further provided material for the study of Ukraine, in turn. Children learned of Ukraine outside Kyiv through Shevchenko's works and by tracing Shevchenko's life and journeys on a map. A study of Shevchenko, then, defined territorial Ukraine, told of the oppression of its people, and invoked its revolutionary spirit. Neither Durdukivsky nor Yu. T. explicitly mentioned the role of the Communist Party in this struggle, and lessons in Marxism were conspicuously absent from the complex. They placed Shevchenko at the fore of contemporary revolutionary struggle and called upon the children to connect their own experiences to this movement. Yu. T. concluded that at the end of the complex, his students sang with greater awareness the Ukrainian version of the "Internationale" (and, at the time, the Soviet state anthem): "oppressed and hungry workers of all countries rise up!" Shevchenko was in the lead.

Narkomos thus embraced and held up a progressive methodology for its promise of transformation. Borrowing from liberal educational theorists such as John Dewey, it advocated the complex method to rid the school of traditional teaching and supply students in its extended primary school with the proletarian mindset needed for future vocational training. Even when confronted with resistance from teachers who were not able or not willing to teach with complexes, Narkomos and progressive educators insisted on perfecting their use. Lessons based on the productive capacities of the students' immediate environment, Narkomos believed, would make the instruction that much more effective and had the added benefit of public outreach. Children equipped with an understanding of the value of industry and agriculture could readily embrace the physical task of "building socialism." An awareness of Ukraine's past suffering would provide some with the proper spirit.

Some exceptional instructors, like Kopyl, were able to implement instruction by the complex system. Most likely, the majority of teachers did not. Because of the importance Narkomos attached to the complex method for its formative value in future vocational training, it did not abandon the technique until the height of the cultural revolution in 1930. Even then, schools pursued progressive methods, such as the student involvement in collaborative projects, but now largely to demonstrate their participation in the First Five-Year Plan campaigns for collectivization and industrialization. Progressive advocates of Ukrainian studies, such as Durdukivsky and Hryhorii Ivanytsia, a co-editor of *Radianska osvita* and secretary of VUAN's historical–philological division, were implicated early on in the 1930 SVU public show trial. The GPU arrested the party historian Yavorsky in 1931, following the SVU trial. Progressive pedagogy, as a whole, fell widely out of favour. Ultimately, education by the complex method proved to be a dangerous proposition that provided too much freedom for non-party interpretations and too much opportunity for critics to claim academic failure.

Chapter Three

The Conversion

Education could not be a tool for political and social transformation if children could not comprehend and quickly internalize its message. Education administrators saw conversion to Ukrainian-language instruction for the republic's majority ethnic-Ukrainian population, as well as well as the provision of Ukrainian-language training for ethnic minorities, as absolute priorities. The Ukrainian republican government mandated the quick study of Ukrainian and conversion to work in the language by its civil servants, but Narkomos's timeline was even more truncated. Efforts for the transfer of schools and educational administration to Ukrainian in fact preceded government-wide decrees. Narkomos occupied the leading position in Soviet nationalities policy in the republic, and believed that schools were the linchpins in the unification of the working populations of the predominantly Ukrainian-speaking countryside and the city.

Local sections of Narkomos, individual schools, and teachers faced the immediate task of fulfilling what appeared on paper. Narkomos administrators envisioned some flexibility for more multi-ethnic and relatively more Russian-speaking areas of Ukraine, but even there, local officials' overly ambitious central demands failed to account for the lack of knowledge of existing teachers and the time and resources needed for teachers to shift. Narkomos set initial targets for the conversion of schools by a count of ethnic-Ukrainian children. Quantitative goals mattered more than real assistance on how to effect qualitative change.

The paradox of Ukrainization was that what was a critical aspect of Soviet policy by any measure – the transformation of the language and symbolic hierarchy of power – was entrusted by political authorities to a category of public servants whom they did not trust: teachers. The teachers' union, Robos, insisted that teachers were reliable executors of Soviet power, that the building of socialism through national culture offered a new defining mission, and that the union served as a guarantor of teachers' commitment. Robos gave teachers a new collective identity that could rally formerly disaffected teachers and new personnel around this common cause. The task of using national culture to accelerate the advent of socialism required, however, well-trained pedagogues. Narkomos recognized that the number of teachers skilled in Ukrainian instruction was small, and its administrators left it largely to local education sections to search for the talent needed to fulfill this critical task, intervening only occasionally to relocate teachers to much more "Russified" eastern Ukraine. Ukrainization, in spite of its proclaimed importance to Soviet power in the republic, remained a decentralized campaign.

Still, education officials equated resistance to Ukrainization to pedagogical conservatism, and sought to push Ukrainian-language instruction as a measure to upturn education and to promote the regime's political and social goals. Education officials remained concerned about students' real and potential academic failings, but saw the use of Ukrainian in concert with the complex method as a definitive remedy. They blamed shortcomings in student knowledge on the incomplete or incorrect use of the complex system and flawed instruction in Ukrainian. For Ukrainizing educators who published in Robos's newspaper, the fluent use of Ukrainian in teaching superseded any other concern. They placed language study at the centre of planning complexes while also viewing language as the principal facilitator of instruction in disciplinary knowledge tied to a complex. The Communist Party shared a belief in the link between language and educational radicalism as a determinant of the orientation of children and the future of socialism.

Setting the Timeline

If Narkomos and the circle of progressive educators who supported it were to be successful in their ambition to radically transform the education system in Ukraine and, as a consequence, the skills and mentality of its graduates, it would have to teach students in a language they understood. For nearly three-quarters of the juvenile population of Ukraine, this meant instruction in Ukrainian. Although this may have sounded like a simple proposition, it was not. Throughout the pre-revolutionary period, schools had educated Ukrainian children in Russian. Teachers, regardless of their ethnicity, were trained and accustomed to teaching in Russian. Pre-revolutionary publications, still widely used in Soviet schools, and even the early Soviet primers were overwhelmingly written in Russian. Ukrainian national leaders had made an attempt to set up a network of Ukrainian-language schools after the February Revolution, but their efforts were disrupted by the chaos of civil war and the falls of successive governments.

On August 1, 1923, the VUTsVK (All-Ukrainian Central Executive Committee) passed a decree ordering the linguistic Ukrainization of all levels of government and requiring Ukrainian-language instruction in primary and secondary schools according to the republic's proportion of ethnic Ukrainians. This decree was the culmination of a long battle within central and republican party organs over nationalities policy in Ukraine. Early party orders regarding the need for internal Ukrainization had done little. A February 1920 VUTsVK resolution establishing the equality of Ukrainian to Russian was similarly ineffectual. Thus, immediately after the promulgation of the 1923 decree, KP(b)U First Secretary Emanuel Kviring released an editorial confirming that the party leadership meant to do more than recognize a "formal equality of nations." Narkomos set its own accelerated calendar plan for the proactive Ukrainization of its own apparat on August 28.[1] In provincial sections, staffed almost entirely by Ukrainians, the switch to use of the Ukrainian language could begin immediately. Sections with a large proportion of Ukrainians were given three months to transfer and sections that employed a significant number of non-Ukrainians and serviced a high proportion of non-Ukrainians were allowed six months. Narkomos also set six months as a goal for the Ukrainization of its central apparat.

Educational institutions that operated under the jurisdiction of these provincial sections were to follow a similar phased schedule of Ukrainization. Teachers who did not know Ukrainian, but wished to continue working in primary-school institutions designated for Ukrainization, were to learn Ukrainian also over the course of the next six months.[2] Holovsotsvykh, the Narkomos organ responsible for primary schooling, understood, however, that full institutional Ukrainization would come about slowly. Not only would many teachers have to learn Ukrainian, but Ukrainian- and non-Ukrainian-speaking teachers alike would have to learn how to teach in Ukrainian, and local education sections needed to translate their lessons plans, acquire Ukrainian literature, and group Ukrainian children in ethnic-homogeneous schools. In the eastern and southern regions of Ukraine, where non-Ukrainians constituted a significant minority, Narkomos recognized that complete Ukrainization would necessarily proceed more slowly. Plans for Ukrainization of primary schools in the Kharkiv, Odesa, Katerynoslav (later Dnipropetrovsk), and Donets provinces (*gubernii*) allotted a two-year time period for a complete transfer.[3] However, pedagogical courses in these regions were to be immediately Ukrainized in 1923 so that their graduates would be ready to teach in Ukrainian for the 1924–5 academic year. As will be discussed below, few teachers whom Narkomos rushed through Ukrainian-language courses were able to reliably teach in the language. While Holovsotsvykh initially recognized a measured pace for Ukrainization, teachers and prospective teachers immediately felt the effects of the new policy. It would take some time for a Ukrainian-language environment to develop in the schools. In order for this to be accomplished, teachers had to teach in Ukrainian or quickly learn how to do so.

Rationale and Intent: Unifying a Rural Republic

The party provided a definitive rationale for Ukrainization. The Soviet republican government had to conduct its affairs in Ukrainian if it was to justly serve the interests of the predominantly Ukrainian-speaking population. Furthermore, the party regularly claimed it sought to correct an historical wrong. Tsarist authorities had forbidden the publication of Ukrainian literature and effectively stigmatized the language as a peasant dialect. While some in the party's central and even Ukrainian leadership held a similar disregard for the Ukrainian language, Lenin had succeeded early on in affirming a party line that recognized the equality of all languages, required republican and local governments to communicate in the language of the resident population, and strongly condemned Russian chauvinism.

The Ukrainian branch of the Communist Party, the KP(b)U, took its lead, then, from the all-Union party's position. However, in Ukraine, nationalities policy was inexorably linked to the general Soviet strategy of *smychka*. Derived from the Russian word for "linking," it called for an alliance between the urban proletariat and the toiling peasantry. In most non-Russian areas, there was a deep divide between the largely Russian-speaking city and the countryside. In Ukraine's case, this separation was considerable. With the exception of an industrialized, mineral-rich East, the republic was overwhelmingly rural and its rural population was overwhelmingly Ukrainian.

The Ukrainian peasantry remained deeply suspicious of urban-centred authority. It took the Red Army three tries to establish lasting control over this population. While a Ukrainian national movement was growing, it remained too weak to enlist the support needed to secure an independent state. The Greens, armies made up of peasants frustrated by the persistent demands of invading armies and their empty promises of land redistribution, proved to be a greater challenge to the Bolsheviks. Led by charismatic commanders such as Nestor Makhno, the Greens brokered a number of loose alliances with the Red Army, only to break them when their interests diverged. While peasants may not have universally identified themselves as "Ukrainian," most viewed the largely Russian-speaking Bolsheviks as foreign.

The young Soviet Ukrainian government drew a number of lessons from the civil war. First, it recognized that the Ukrainian national movement had garnered significant, if not sufficient, support. Second, it concluded that the Ukrainian disenchantment might only grow stronger if the population continued to view Soviet power as something entirely alien. In a largely rural republic, such as Ukraine, peasant sentiment was critical. A campaign to "win over" the peasantry offered a solution to the dilemma. Ukrainization was a critical component of this approach.

The Soviet government saw Ukrainization of primary schooling as an effective means to both cultivate a new generation of loyal citizens and gain the support of a suspicious peasantry. In a 1923 document, entitled in Russian "Project: The Smychka of the City with the Village, According to the Social Upbringing Line," the deputy head of Holovsotsvykh, Vasyl Arnautov, argued that all local Narkomos sections had to re-evaluate which children's institutions should be Ukrainized, according to the proportion of ethnic Ukrainians residing in a given location.[4] Arnautov insisted that Narkomos had to develop a network of Ukrainian schools, not only in the countryside but throughout the republic. He stressed that the Donets, Kharkiv, Katerynoslav, and Odesa provinces should give special attention to the question of setting up Ukrainian-language schools and that all schools, regardless of the general language of instruction, should include courses in the Ukrainian language and Ukrainian studies.

This document represents one of the earliest formulations of a Ukrainization policy for education following the 1923 VUTsVK decree. Here, Arnautov sees Ukrainization as part and parcel with the smychka strategy. Ukrainian-language schooling would function as a critical link between the city and the village. Urban schools and rural schools alike would offer instruction for ethnic Ukrainians in the same language, a language the majority of Ukraine's peasant population could most readily understand.

While it is true that many Communists viewed peasants with distrust and cared little about their self-articulated interests, the party needed the peasantry. The peasantry not only fed the proletarian cities, but also provided the workforce for industrialization. Until the party made its final decision for collectivization of the countryside, it alternated between coercion and persuasion in its relations with the peasantry.[5] The Soviet Ukrainian government regarded Ukrainization as a means not only to legitimize Soviet rule among the rural population and regulate peasant demands, but also to facilitate a peasant's interaction with, and, perhaps, ultimate entry into, the urban population.

Nuts and Bolts: Appraisal and Implementation

Early Ukrainian Soviet officials, particularly those in Narkomos, then often spoke of Ukrainization in reference to socialist construction. The party proclaimed that Ukrainization held the promise for cultural advancement, but this goal was not an end in itself. Instruction in, and the promotion of, the Ukrainian language would lead most effectively to the development of a literate and educated population in the republic. Ultimately, the party planned, this population would be a skilled and active participant in the Soviet political order and expansion of the republic's economic base. Like the shift towards progressive pedagogy, a concerted program of

Ukrainization was begun under Zatonsky's second tenure as UkrSSR commissar of education from 1922 to 1924. During his first term, Zatonsky spoke in favour of the "equality of languages" and advocated the study of Ukrainian as a separate subject in Russian schools, but he did little to alter the language of instruction in existing educational establishments. The Ukrainization policy initiated in 1923 was more transformative, and Zatonsky supported its pursuit, even if he believed its final purpose was the closening of Ukrainian culture with "international, that is Russian, culture."[6] Although Ukrainization of schooling enjoyed the greatest encouragement under Commissar Shumsky beginning in 1924, it was still up to Narkomos's more permanent staff to carry out the policy.[7] A debate regarding the limits of Ukrainization, in which both Zatonsky and Shumsky would take part, was yet to come, but in the early years of the policy's implementation, there was little distinction in the daily work of successive commissariats of education that embraced the program's modernizing mission.

The Soviet Ukrainian government as a whole viewed the Ukrainization of educational institutions and of the Narkomos apparat as absolute priorities. A Radnarkom decree of July 27, 1923, to Narkomos and its local organs was, in fact, the first order to set definite requirements for Ukrainization, correlating a targeted number of Ukrainian-language schools with the proportion of local ethnic-Ukrainian populations.[8] The August VUTsVK decree essentially affirmed this policy and, most importantly, expanded its scope to the Ukrainization of all government departments.

Ukrainization of schooling had already begun prior to these pronouncements, but progress had been slow. As noted above, a succession of short-lived, independent, Ukrainian governments had begun work on the establishment of a network of Ukrainian-language schools during the civil-war period. These governments, however, could accomplish little while their very existence was threatened. If the nationalist governments were more motivated to ensure the protection and preservation of the Ukrainian language through schooling, their Soviet successors saw Ukrainian-language schooling as a key to the republic's cultural and future economic development. In early 1923, Holovsotsvykh drafted a plan for the expanded use of the Ukrainian language that foreshadowed the later Radnarkom and VUTsVK Ukrainization decrees by identifying the chief obstacles to expanded instruction in Ukrainian.

According to the plan, at the end of the 1922–3 school year, perhaps 60.0 per cent of the republic's primary schools had transferred to Ukrainian-language instruction.[9] The ethnic-Ukrainian population, however, then stood at 72.6 per cent. This meant that significant numbers of Ukrainian children were studying in Russian. Holovsotsvykh blamed the gap on two chief causes: the absence of trained Ukrainian-language teachers, and insufficient or non-existent Ukrainian instructional literature in some areas of study. It argued that some provincial education sections had exaggerated their previous counts of Ukrainian-language schools. For example, the Donets province had reported that it had fifty such schools in May 1923 when there were only ten, and the Katerynoslav province had made a similar overestimate.[10] Holovsotsvykh maintained that teachers in most villages knew Ukrainian, but that local inspectors needed to work with these teachers and the local population to encourage the transfer of schoolwork to Ukrainian. Its plan viewed the expanded use of Ukrainian as a republic-wide strategy. Village schools in the Donets, Katerynoslav, Kharkiv, and Odesa provinces were desperate for Ukrainian-language teachers. The situation was even worse in the cities. One education inspector cited in the report noted that children's buildings in the city of Katerynoslav often lacked a single teacher who understood Ukrainian, "the language of the children." While this is an overstatement (even exclusive Russian speakers could comprehend a little Ukrainian), some teachers in predominantly Russian-language environments, such as Katerynoslav, likely viewed the Ukrainian of peasant migrants as a coarse dialect of Russian and made little attempt to understand, and thereby sanction, the language of their Ukrainian students.

Training had to begin, Holovsotsvykh argued, with teachers who already had some practical knowledge of Ukrainian in order to meet the immediate needs of ethnic-Ukrainian children. Some provincial education sections recognized that some measure of pressure would need to be brought to bear on both teachers and its own employees if instruction in Ukrainian was to be expanded. The Podillia Provincial Education Section ordered its employees to transfer to use of Ukrainian beginning July 6, some three weeks prior to the VUTsVK decree.[11] They were given two months to study Ukrainian and had to demonstrate their knowledge in a September 1, 1923, exam. The section allowed teachers under its jurisdiction six months to display their mastery of the language, but their challenge was greater. They not only had to prove their ability to converse and write, but demonstrate they could teach a variety of subjects in Ukrainian. The provincial section's rationale for this early emphasis on Ukrainization is informative. Its employees needed to learn Ukrainian in order to communicate with not only its peasant clients, but also its district sections, staffed primarily with civil servants of peasant origin. Children of Ukrainian peasants also were the majority of schoolchildren in the province.[12] Local officials therefore prioritized the task of Ukrainization and, on paper, accomplished it quickly.

Generally, however, the Holovsotsvykh plan set overly ambitious targets for Ukrainization over the course of the 1923–4 academic year. It designated specific numbers of Ukrainian teachers whom its provincial sections needed to train, focusing specifically on the eastern and southern regions of Ukraine: 500 for Donets,

300 for Katerynoslav, 300 for Odesa, and 300 for Kharkiv.[13] In keeping with its comprehensive strategy for Ukrainization of the republic, it also called for the preparation of Ukrainian-language teachers for schools of non-Ukrainian instruction (Russian, Jewish, Polish, and German). All teachers were to demonstrate knowledge of the Ukrainian language, literature, geography, and history. Provincial sections had to meet the basic numerical targets for Ukrainian-language teachers over the summer. Similarly, Holovsotsvykh insisted that the need for educational literature in Ukrainian be satisfied by the beginning of the 1923–4 year and called upon Radnarkom to set aside specific funds for publication. It maintained that each school be provided with 100 books out of this fund (an unrealistic but laudatory goal) at a cost of 30 kopecks per book, a total of 331,710 gold rubles.[14]

Although the Narkomos Collegium issued both the initial marching orders for Ukrainization and stern reprimands for the cases of failure that inevitably followed, responsibility for the policy's implementation was localized. Narkomos ordered local sections either to set up short-term Ukrainian-language courses or require employees themselves to form self-study groups.[15] Central organs, such as Holovsotsvykh, were permitted to organize classes with workers of other commissariats and optimistically estimated mobilizing up to fifty teachers in the province of the republican capital, Kharkiv, to lead study circles.[16] Other provincial branches did not have this option, and the costs for such training were considerable: 120 rubles for two and half months' training of a single group, according to a Holovsotsvykh estimate.[17] Narkomos also entrusted the chief of the local section to form a Ukrainization commission to ensure that Narkomos bodies and the educational institutions under their jurisdiction transferred to use of Ukrainian. The formal penalties for non-compliance were severe. Employees who did not study and master Ukrainian in the allotted time were to be dismissed or transferred. As will be discussed below, sections did initiate cases of dismissal, although bureaucratic obstacles often stood in their way.

The governmental decrees mandated that local education sections tally the number of Ukrainian schools already operating in their areas and the number of Ukrainian-speaking teachers available to staff new groups. Once again, Narkomos's attention turned to the eastern and southern regions of Ukraine. A May 1923 account had revealed a striking gap between the number of ethnic-Ukrainian children in these regions and the number enrolled in Ukrainian-language schools. In the Kharkiv province, there were some 1,916,000 ethnic-Ukrainian children ages four to fifteen, according to the 1920 census, but only 32,000 pupils enrolled in Ukrainian-language schools out of a total of 127,986 pupils overall in the province for the 1922–3 school year.[18] Large numbers of Ukrainian children were not enrolling in school at all, and the majority of those enrolled were attending Russian-language schools or schools of mixed-language instruction. Even these figures were inflated, as later counts corrected the number of Ukrainian-language schools reported for 1922 and placed the number slightly lower for Kharkiv (from 360 to 345) and substantially lower for Katerynoslav, Odesa, and Donets provinces.[19] Data for the 1923–4 academic year varied so greatly that Holovsotsvykh ordered its provincial sections to compile a new report by 15 January 1924.[20]

Strictly speaking, the government had legislated that children had the right to study in their native language. This often meant local education sections correlated students' language of instruction with their nationality. Of course, Ukrainian students continued to attend Russian-language schools. Ultimately, however, Narkomos expected students to be divided by nationality, with little planned regard to children's preference. The "forced" enrolment of Russified Ukrainian children in Ukrainian-language schools became the subject of a bitter debate in 1926. In 1923, however, data regarding the nationality of students informed Narkomos educational policy and targets.

Local education sections therefore set as their optimal goal the grouping of students according to national designation. Success in meeting this objective again varied by region. In the central regions, an overwhelming majority of ethnic-Ukrainian schoolchildren attended Ukrainian-language schools of instruction. In the Kyiv province, 92.5 per cent of all schools were Ukrainized to correspond to the proportion of ethnic-Ukrainian children.[21] The Podillia and Volyn provinces reported similarly that almost all Ukrainian children in the first concentration of primary school were being taught in Ukrainian and that the transfer of older concentrations of children to Ukrainian-language instruction was proceeding apace. By contrast, education sections in the South and East pursued a piecemeal approach to Ukrainization. Many Ukrainian children in the Katerynoslav and Kharkiv provinces continued to study in schools of mixed Ukrainian- and Russian-language instruction. In practice, teachers in these schools largely taught in Russian, although Narkomos's ultimate ambition was the transfer of all lessons within a single school to Ukrainian. Odesa pleaded with Narkomos for patience, citing local "conditions."[22] Local officials claimed these areas would need at least two more years before all Ukrainian children would enjoy instruction in their native language.

In reality, even this prognosis was overly optimistic. As Narkomos officials throughout Ukraine continued to stress, a successful transfer to Ukrainian-language instruction depended on the reliable staffing of schools by teachers trained to teach in Ukrainian. Narkomos's initial decrees provided a formula for the quantitative reporting of successes in Ukrainization, but the commissariat did not yet offer substantial help to improve the quality of instruction. Ukrainian teachers in the central regions taught according to their own dialectal inventory, and teachers in more Russified regions switched regularly between Russian and a Ukrainian heavily reliant on Russian borrowings.

A demonstration to celebrate the opening of a four-year school in the village of Romanivka, Artemivsk region, 1928. Courtesy TsDKFFAU.

Assessing Teachers

Whereas some Ukrainian teachers before and during the revolution embraced a message of social and economic liberation in explicitly nationalistic terms, after the Bolshevik victory, educators as a whole struggled to redefine their mission. Teachers who had sided "wrongly" during the civil war adapted partly out of a realization of the political reality of Bolshevik victory, but also because the Soviet state's imperatives coincided with their collectivist vision of broad social betterment *and* national liberation achieved through public work. Teachers' preparations in a series of 1924 local conferences for the First All-Union Teachers Congress, to be held in Moscow in January 1925, testify to this effort to reorient their professional objectives and status. At a December Kyiv regional meeting, the head of Robos (*Profspilka robitnykiv osvity* – Professional Union of Workers of Education), Mykhailo Baran, argued that "at the beginning of the revolution, since all classes of Ukrainians were suffering under the national yoke by tsarism, everyone believed that Ukrainian society was an unbroken mass, in which there was no class struggle and we called ourselves socialists, confusing national chauvinism with the revolution." Teachers were afraid to own up to their "mistake" because they feared that "the proletariat wanted to destroy the independence [*samostiinist*] of Ukraine." Only after Soviet victory, Baran argued, did teachers realize that the working class could secure "economic-national rebirth in society"; Ukrainian teachers "changed ideologically, began to merge with the proletariat and the Communist party and our task now is to strengthen the new communist ideology of the teachers and make room for all active forces of revolutionary teachers."[23]

In his explanation, Baran offered a interpretation of the flawed collective that was the object of teachers' loyalties and "socialist" zeal – a Ukrainian nation undivided by class – and mandated a new, legitimate one, a merger of "revolutionary teachers" and labouring elements of society. Baran specifically cited the switch to Ukrainian-language instruction of schools as a key element of the collectivist effort to "draw national forces" – that is, Ukrainian-speaking teachers – to "state construction." A report given in the same year by Yefremov, the head of the Kyiv Regional Education Section, at the Makariv district conference of teachers, insisted that teachers were revolutionary by nature anyhow; during tsarist times, the government sought to limit teachers' wages for fear that it would only be backing the forces of its own overthrow. He made no mention of teachers' past errors, arguing, "During the time of the revolution, the teachers internally crossed over to all [Bolshevik] revolutionary ideas and accepted them." For him, what was key was teachers' innate revolutionary élan. They were inherently supporters of the Soviet regime because of their opposition to the old regime and old social order. In place of the self-interested concerns of bourgeois intellectuals, teachers were dedicated to the "grandiose tasks" of building a socialist state and "the internal impulse of this work comes from the lower ranks."[24]

Just as peasants could be divided between pro-Soviet poor and middle peasants and *kulaks* (anti-Soviet rich peasants),[25] speakers at these early local teachers' conferences divided up the Ukrainian intellectual community in an effort to counter assumptions about teachers' loyalty to Soviet goals. Loboda, a speaker at a Chornobyl district teachers' congress (Kyiv region), conceded that the old intelligentsia was educated in "obsolete literature," while the new literature that formed the basis for Soviet teacher training had nothing in common with this previous orientation towards the "camps of [the former head of the UNR Directory, Symon] Petliura and [monarchist White general, Anton] Denikin." Mekhets, another speaker, stressed that whereas teachers in the past, particularly during the time of the revolution, had been led astray due to their political immaturity, "now teachers are organized into a union under the leadership of the Communist party and will continue to implement the great idea of communism." The union, Robos, offered teachers a new collective – professional identity – and also served as the mediator by which they were instructed in their new mission and liberated from nationalist ideology. In its final statement, the congress declared that "we teachers consciously broke all ties with the intelligentsia and stood for the building of a new socialist life in cooperation with the proletariat and poor peasantry."[26] Teachers constituted a distinct, labouring intelligentsia whose purpose was to educate children and the general public in the task of the young socialist state.

The proceedings of nearly all these local conferences credit Soviet nationalities policy with reducing national frustration and giving "nationally conscious" teachers an opportunity to redirect their efforts and to use the "nation" as a tool to accomplish Soviet goals. Yakymenko, a teacher at the Pervomaisk regional teachers' congress (Odesa province) in December 1924, argued that "banditry" in the area had been eliminated only in 1923, after Soviet power had undermined its base by "resolving" the national question. Teachers could now play a critical role in refining and directing national culture for the service of the Soviet state: "The renewal of national culture is the result of our work in many areas and without this we would not have raised the standing of Soviet power so soon."[27] In other words, instruction in national culture expedited transmission of Soviet goals.

An explicit aspect of this renewal was the conversion of four-year primary schools to Ukrainian instruction and the establishment of full (seven-year) primary schools that would serve the largely rural Ukrainian-speaking community, either by moving some of these schools out of the city to the village or setting up boarding schools for rural children in the towns to ensure that they too gained the knowledge necessary for a secondary education.[28] Teachers were to use Ukrainian schools to ensure that Soviet culture extended to the village; that children were integrated into the task of "building socialism"; and that retarding influences of rural life were halted by following the example of the city's leadership. Nesterenko, a teacher at the Odesa regional teachers' conference, noted that teachers regularly turned to his city school for Ukrainian literature, presumably to support their instruction. Even though rural communities, especially around the city of Odesa, were much more Ukrainian-speaking, teachers in city schools had the greatest access to guidance issued by Narkomos on Ukrainization. And, perhaps because the policy was often contested, urban teachers' understanding of what was needed to correctly accomplish a transfer in the language of instruction was more developed: "Here Ukrainization is often talked about." He called for each city school to tie itself to one or two village schools and to require its pupils to participate in this association.[29] His school, for example, had set up an Office for Ties with the Village. Continual oversight by the city would prevent a repeat of teachers' civil war-era failings.

What was primary was that schools taught children to actively participate in the achievement of Soviet goals. According to a resolution of the Bila Tserkva regional meeting (Kyiv province), Robos's foremost objective was to ensure that "the preparation and education of the young generation in the village and city follows the path of the creation of schooling, tied to publicly useful work, of pointed communist ideals, and organically tied to the needs of our economy."[30] The best way to ensure that city and urban schools were united in this task was to foster a relationship between the two. Ukrainization offered a common enterprise, but it was more importantly the means by which "publicly useful work" would be accomplished, especially in the rural setting. Urban oversight provided greater assurance that such work did not go awry. As the Bila Tserkva teachers specified, "helping the peasantry to rise to a high cultural level is a part of general state building."[31] It was now part of the wider agenda of state-sponsored and teacher-driven collectivism: participation by peasants and workers alike in the building of socialism. At the specific level of the classroom, another speaker, Pokhylevych, argued that use of Ukrainian-centred subject matter was necessary for tasks beyond the immediate community to be understood and ideological imperatives promoted. An understanding of "the most familiar national culture" was the first step on "the path to liberation."[32]

Local teachers' conferences repeatedly emphasized that the development of national culture in the Soviet context would not undermine internationalism, but would reinforce it. At the Kyiv provincial conference, a delegate from Berdychiv pointed to national conflict in Poland, whose border lay a short eighty kilometres away from his home city, and argued that in the congress itself was proof of Soviet success: teachers of different nationalities were working together towards a common aim. He concluded, "National forms of the cultural renaissance do not delay class consciousness, but on the contrary [they] should be the path for the development of a conscious solidarity between workers."[33] Similarly, a resolution of the Cherkasy congress maintained that "the national question has been faithfully solved by Soviet power and this makes the free and thorough growth of national culture possible, bringing the working masses closer to socialism."[34] Teachers were instrumental to this campaign because of their work in schools and among the general public to improve literacy in Ukrainian and ethnic-minority languages, and to provide a comprehensive education in Ukrainian-centred subject material tied to the task of socialism.

Ukrainization from the Bottom Up: The Hiring of Teachers

At this early stage, Narkomos central authorities saw their chief responsibility in the issuance of marching orders for Ukrainization, not the day-to-day administration of the policy. In fact, at the same time Holovsotsvykh was demanding rapid transfer to Ukrainian-language instruction, it requested information from its provincial sections about measures they had taken on their own and about which resources they believed were needed for the policy to be a success.[35] Holovsotsvykh entrusted its provincial sections with the formulation of their own plans, rather than seeking to define and necessitate a universal arrangement. This delegation of authority is apparent in its query to the provincial sections. Among the questions Holovsotsvykh asked was: "How many teachers are needed to carry out Ukrainization and teach Ukrainian and ukrainoznavstvo as a subject in non-Ukrainian schools?"[36] Holovsotsvykh was taking stock of progress achieved, but it refrained from setting an explicit teacher–pupil ratio for all Ukrainian schools.

Narkomos also recognized that Ukrainian-speaking teachers might have to move to more multi-ethnic provinces to staff Ukrainian schools. However, again, it largely left it to local authorities to recruit and hire these teachers. In the same Holovsotsvykh query, educational authorities asked the provinces how many Ukrainian-speaking teachers could be transferred to other institutions in the province or beyond its borders.[37] A Narkomos report in early 1924 confirmed that Katerynoslav authorities had transferred teachers who volunteered for new posts, although it did not provide exact numbers. The practice, however, was not uncommon.

Occasionally, Narkomos intervened and facilitated the relocation of teachers, especially to the industrial East, where it viewed Ukrainization as an absolute political priority. In September 1923, Pavlo Stodolia, a teacher in the city of Lokhvytsia (Poltava province), petitioned Narkomos for a transfer to Kharkiv or the Donbas, where "a worker is needed in connection with Ukrainization."[38] In his letter, he emphasized his political credentials. According to his account, tsarist authorities had imprisoned him in 1903 for "revolutionary activities" and Denikin's army had persecuted him during the civil war. However, Stodolia also stressed his educational and cultural experience, including a list of his own publications on Ukrainian ethnography and literature and a description of his work in language studies and in the fight against illiteracy. He maintained that he had received a fraction of his monthly salary of 20 rubles a month and could not afford bed linen, underwear, or even such a staple as milk. In the Donbas, if Narkomos supported him financially, he could put his talents to good use as an instructor, journal editor, book distributor, or cultural organizer. Apparently, Stodolia succeeded in convincing Narkomos that his skills were valuable enough to warrant its involvement. Oleksandr Mizernytsky, the then assistant head of Holovsotsvykh, replied that his agency had arranged for Stodolia's appointment as an instructor at a Narkomos experimental children's building near Kharkiv.[39] Mizernytsky stressed that the institution was supported by expenses from the centre and the educators received their wages on time.

More often, Narkomos told teachers to seek employment by contacting local authorities directly. Stodolia's ostensibly favourable political background and experience may have helped him obtain a position. Ivan Horozhynsky, a former official under the pro-Soviet Galician Revolutionary Committee installed in eastern Galicia (during the Soviet–Polish War of 1920), who was now working as a labourer in the Podillia province, made a similar request for a teaching job in July 1923.[40] He had less teaching experience, having worked only as an instructor for the provincial agricultural cooperative office. However, he also underscored his Galician origins, suggesting to Narkomos that they "ask any Galician about me; everyone knows me and can vouch for me." Narkomos may not have held any overt bias against employing Western Ukrainians as teachers at this time, but Horozhynsky's Galician background meant that authorities could find out less about him.[41] Thus, he may have been viewed as less politically reliable. His professional fall might have also raised suspicions. By contrast, the Holovsotsvykh main education inspectorate sanctioned the request of Stepan Hohol, a teacher of "proletarian" origin, originally from Bukovyna but then living in Kharkiv.[42] After an initial query to Narkomos, he wrote directly to the regional education section in Stalino (now Donetsk), likely upon the advice of someone at Holovsotsvykh. Hohol gave Holovsotsvykh as his return address and a recommendation for him was attached to the bottom of his request, signed by a secretary of the main inspectorate section.[43] Proper professional and political qualifications may have aided his plea.

The need, of course, for Ukrainian-language teachers was great in the East, especially after the issuance of the VUTsVK and Radnarkom decrees. Narkomos recognized this, even if it was unwilling to make specific arrangements for teachers. In September 1923, Holovsotsvykh had to reprimand its own Donets Provincial Education Section for its failure to hire reliable Galician teachers, whom it listed by name, for vacancies for Ukrainian-language instruction.[44] Arnautov, the deputy head of Holovsotsvykh, advised Horozhynsky in September to turn directly to the Donets or Katerynoslav provinces, noting that "in regard to the Ukrainization of schools in the specified province, workers who know the Ukrainian language are needed."[45] However, he refrained from issuing an order directly to these sections. When the sections erred, Narkomos might correct them, but they had the responsibility of making hires and filling the gaps in needed resources.

Ethnic Ukrainians living in the Russian Soviet Federated Socialist Republic (RSFSR) also soon learned of Ukraine's need for Ukrainian-language instructors. A preschool instructor from the Chernihiv province, Mykola Osmolovsky – who had claimed to have been arrested for anti-government propaganda in 1906, imprisoned for three years, and then fled to Siberia in fear of the Russian nationalist Black Hundreds[46] – wrote to Narkomos in October 1923 requesting a teaching job in his "homeland" for him and his wife: "in my time, I knew theoretically and practically the Ukrainian language and I hope to be useful in my native Ukraine in a field of my specialty."[47] He emphasized his academic qualifications, including his publication of a children's alphabet book published by the Siberian education section. The Siberian education section issued a letter of introduction for him to Narkomos and announced that it did not oppose his transfer. There is no record of any action taken by Narkomos, but also in the fall of 1923 it informed another ethnic Ukrainian residing in Siberia who sought to obtain teacher training in Ukraine that it had no funds to facilitate his travel.[48] This petitioner, a Galician named Kapko, also invoked a sense of duty to Ukraine, claiming it was his desire to train to work "amongst my beloved Ukrainian people."

Clearly, Ukrainians abroad knew Ukrainian-language skills were in demand, but the localized nature of educational policy meant that they were rarely successful in landing a job. Narkomos may have wanted to employ them, but it lacked the funding and perhaps the daring to recruit teachers with ill-defined political baggage and uncertain professional abilities. The most Narkomos did for these applicants abroad was to direct them to local authorities, as it did for Zanozovsky, a Ukrainian teacher who had taught in the Podillia province but was now working near Krasnodar.[49] He too emphasized his educational qualifications (completion of a teacher's seminar and ten years' experience in a Ukrainian school [*uchylyshche*]) and fluency in Ukrainian, but to little avail. His own case may have been hampered by his insistence on a position in the city of Kyiv, where Ukrainian-language teachers were more plentiful.

Narkomos appears to have found it easier to intervene in the transfer of a teacher already in its employment. Furthermore, as Ukrainization picked up pace, it judged the need for teachers in the East to be more acute. In early 1924, the main Holovsotsvykh inspector sent a memorandum to the central Ukrainian provincial education sections, asking for information regarding Ukrainian teachers willing to move to the Donets province.[50] A December 1924 report by the Donets provincial inspector had pointed to a gap between the number of teachers needed for Ukrainization in the province (2,791 persons) and those who spoke Ukrainian (523). The inspector allowed for the possibility of transferring teachers from elsewhere in Ukraine, but admitted he had little idea of how many would be available.[51] The main inspectorate undoubtedly viewed this disparity in the Donets province with concern.

Although Narkomos referred individual Ukrainian-speaking teachers to the Donets province, the number of its referrals appears to have been small, and it left its provincial sections the task of investigating further details regarding the teachers' qualifications and eligibility for transfer. In fact, when the Podillia Provincial Education Section responded that some of its teachers were interested in a transfer and wished to know the terms of employment, Narkomos simply forwarded its query on to Donets provincial authorities and recommended that they correspond directly with the Podillia province.[52] It is surprising that, given the desperate shortage of Ukrainian-language instructors, Narkomos did little to provide incentives for those willing to take up the arduous task of teaching, particularly in the changing industrial East.

Regardless, teachers from central Ukraine were clearly interested in being transferred. They hoped that reassignment to Donets province would offer them the financial security that eluded most provincial teachers. The Podillia section's questions to Donets officials sought specific material guarantees: payment for the costs of a transfer; the monthly wage of a teacher by position; class loads; and prices for foodstuffs, lodging, and fuel.[53] The Donets Provincial Education Section promised reimbursement of a train ticket and a monthly wage of 24 rubles for teachers in rural schools and 33 for teachers in "city schools organized by the proletariat." However, educational authorities in each region (*okruha*) were responsible for working out all other details. The Donets section noted that officials could offer lodging only to heads of schools, and then only to those who worked in schools "which served the organized proletariat." It asked interested teachers to travel to regional seats to receive their appointments.[54] Only the most desperate or the most enterprising would have accepted the risk associated with such a move and, even then, they would have had to pay for the initial cost of a ticket. The Donets section did not specify which regions may have been in the most need of Ukrainian-language teachers. The choice for point of arrival was left entirely to the teacher.

Identifying Opposition: Chauvinism and Pedagogical Conservatism

In addition to training existing teachers in Ukrainian and recruiting new ones, some local educational authorities moved early on to rid schools of teachers opposed to Ukrainization. In the case of T. Ivanov, a teacher in the Cherkasy region, officials sought to explicitly link resistance to teaching in Ukrainian with anti-Soviet, backward-looking, pedagogical methodology.

Ivanov worked as a teacher in the Matusivka Sugar Refinery Labour School. Local educators began to Ukrainize this school in early 1922, well in advance of the VUTsVK decree on Ukrainization. According to a petition sent by Ivanov to Narkomos, the Cherkasy education section removed him and four other teachers from their posts for "Russification and other misdeeds."[55] Ivanov immediately protested this action and sent a letter of complaint to Narkomos, along with the minutes of a meeting of the school's students and the factory's cultural committee (composed of the students' parents) held in support of the ousted teachers. Ivanov insisted on his right to teach in Russian and demanded his reinstatement. This complaint and a second petition to Radnarkom apparently went unanswered.

Holovsotsvykh ordered an inquiry into the dismissal after having received a third letter from Ivanov. As a result, Ivan Vovchenko, the Cherkasy regional education inspector, organized a commission to investigate the affair in August 1923. Vovchenko reported the commission found that Ivanov had refused to use Ukrainian in a school with Ukrainian children.[56] Furthermore, the commission judged that "Ivanov's outlook is of a conservative type, unworthy of being a Soviet teacher and [the committee] therefore concludes that it is impossible to allow Ivanov to work in sotsvykh institutions [children's buildings and primary schools]." Furthermore, Vovchenko added that, on the basis of information he learned from Ivanov's estranged wife, "Ivanov appears to be the type of teacher-bureaucrat of the olden days ... self-confident and insolent, he 'tolerantly' regards Soviet power, but he cannot bear the Ukrainian language."

Clearly, Vovchenko and the commission members were concerned that Ivanov and his compatriots were hostile to the teaching of Ukrainian. He noted that other Russian teachers, other than those who were dismissed, held similar views, but continued to work in Ukrainian schools. However, Vovchenko did not use the accepted language of chauvinism to describe the antagonism of these teachers, but rather termed their attitude "anti-Soviet." For him, they were "foreigners [*chuzhi*], regardless of nationality, to Soviet power and education."[57] The commission allowed that Ivanov might be permitted to teach in a Russian-language secondary school. But Vovchenko believed Ivanov and others like him could not be employed in primary schools, where Narkomos sought to begin the fashioning of a new Soviet generation. He criticized the provincial education section for lack of guidance in managing this affair. Implicit in his firm defence of the region's actions was a belief that instruction in Ukrainian was the most effective way for the Soviet state to meet its educational goals among the Ukrainian population.

Ukrainization as Key to Academic Success

Although Narkomos authorities did not intervene in Ivanov's case, they generally shared the opinion that only instruction in the Ukrainian language could ensure academic success for ethnic-Ukrainian children. Consequently, they sought to link progress in Ukrainization with educational accomplishment. In May 1924, Holovsotsvykh demanded that the Donets province immediately implement measures to fully Ukrainize and "raise the cultural achievement" of children's institutions in the Luhansk region (*okruha*).[58] Rudova, the senior Donets primary-school inspector, proposed "to separate the remaining [children's buildings] into individual groups, having created for them more satisfactory conditions for work, and during the summer to bring the cultural level of the children's buildings up to the level of schoolchildren."[59] His inclusion of information on the slow pace of Ukrainization suggests that this grouping of children was to be done according to ethnicity. The province was set to begin a campaign for full Ukrainization according to a plan worked out by the head of the Donets education section.[60] It would reorganize schools under the terms of this mandate.

Donets authorities then placed hope for educational success on the rapid expansion of the Ukrainian language. However, realities on the ground level frustrated this hope. The Luhansk regional inspector argued to the Donets Provincial Education Section that while schools were being Ukrainized, they lacked textbooks to truly conduct instruction in Ukrainian.[61] He claimed that an early credit of 5,000 rubles for books had already been used up, and further Ukrainization would depend on the extension of another credit. Even where authorities accomplished Ukrainization on paper, the language of the classroom changed little without substantive support from the centre. Most students, if they learned anything, had to acquire knowledge from Russian-language texts. Those in rural schools, who had little exposure to a Russian-speaking environment, would have found this prospect particularly challenging.

Some indication of educational shortcomings in Ukrainized schools is provided by the head of Luhansk Children's Building No. 3 in a May 1924 account to the Donets Provincial Education Section of a recent visit of the VUTsVK representative Hryhorii Petrovsky. The children's building was one of eighteen schools Ukrainized in the region. The second-grade children of this school were unable to correctly answer a question posed to them by Petrovsky: "Who is Trotsky?"[62] Petrovsky stressed they had to know the details of the life of Lenin and the revolutionary leaders of Ukraine. The Luhansk regional inspector warned the provincial section not to generalize on the basis of this one school, but it passed on this information to Holovsotsvykh anyhow, together with its plan for Ukrainization.

Although the province had not blamed this children's building for shortcomings in Ukrainian-language instruction, Holovsotsvykh responded by coupling the two problems of Ukrainization and academic failings together, and tasked the province with finding a solution to both concurrently. Similarly, the Kharkiv Provincial Inspectorate found that low levels of expenditure had led to a qualitative decline in primary school education and teacher training in the Okhtyrka region, and demanded the subordinate regional organ include a detailed proposal for the completion of Ukrainization in its operative plan for academic improvement.[63] For education authorities at various levels, Ukrainian-language schooling was a necessary part of any proposal for progress.

The push towards Ukrainization placed pressure on teachers to use Ukrainian even when they were not prepared to do so. Narkomos viewed the improper use of

Ukrainian as equal to the failure to use Ukrainian at all. A report by the Kharkiv Provincial Education Section noted that although some teachers knew Ukrainian, they lacked scholarly training and could be teaching flawed grammar.[64] The Russian-language environment inevitably had an effect on the quality of instruction in Ukrainian. It pointed to a shortage of Ukrainian-language schools in the city of Kharkiv and demanded the full Ukrainization of two schools that had kept the instruction of their older grades in Russian. Teachers had other problems with which to contend. In the cities of the Kharkiv province, the constant transfer of students had led to overcrowding. In rural areas, teachers lacked books, guidance, and even minimum pay.[65] Both urban and rural teachers, then, saw little incentive to shift their methods of instruction, let alone their language of instruction. When they did use Ukrainian, those who did not know it well did so half-heartedly.

For true believers in Ukrainization, no other task took higher priority than the perfection of Ukrainian-language instruction. P. Sapukhin, one Ukrainization advocate writing in the teachers' newspaper *Narodnii uchytel*, claimed that retraining teachers to use the Ukrainian language correctly was more important than preparation of new instructional systems, such as the complex method, because "language is 'our primary tool' for school work."[66] In an article entitled "Ukrainization: 'Ichthyosaurs' of the Modern School," Sapukhin cited the reminder RSFSR Commissar of Education Lunacharsky gave to the All-Union Congress of Teachers in 1925: pedagogues must not ignore simple literacy when developing complexes. In Sapukhin's estimation, such misplaced attention posed an even greater danger to Ukrainian than Russian. He pointed to the deleterious "cross influence" bilingual culture had on Ukrainian and claimed that the overwhelming majority of ethnic-Ukrainian teachers were functionally illiterate in the language. Even so-called experts failed to understand the most elementary and popular rules of Ukrainian. Teachers were "crippled at both knees" and needed real training. Otherwise, Sapukhin insisted, "there will be no complex, no formal training, no respect or faith in the school and teachers."

An educator writing in the pedagogical journal *Radianska osvita*, O. Polubotko, insisted that improvements in language training would facilitate the promotion of a progressive pedagogy. Narkomos had to confront those teachers who sought to place language in the "second tier of subjects studied."[67] Polubotko argued that language was both a means for deepening knowledge and "a tool, our weapon in the class struggle." Therefore, its study must be at the centre of any school's curriculum. Because so many disciplines required students to write, Polubotko insisted that language study was particularly well suited to the complex system's approach of uniting subjects of study, and must form its foundation. Language teachers should examine all essays composed in the school, so that students would understand the need to always write well, not just for "language class." As discussed in chapter 2, the demands of the "new school" meant that students would study on the basis of real-life experience. The Dalton Plan, touted widely by progressive pedagogues of the time, recommended that teachers take their students on excursions so they could make direct observations and present their conclusions in written form. Teachers could link these observations to formal subjects of study (such as mathematics, natural sciences, etc.), but writing would be the basis for all future work.

Under the complex system, the teacher was to be a supplementary guide, with students performing mostly independent work. Parents and some teachers worried that the promotion of this method might lead to the neglect of instruction in formal knowledge. Polubotko argued, to the contrary, that complexes could and should be designed so that children would know all they needed to know when they left school: they would understand "working life."[68] However, with properly designed complexes, students could obtain formal skills, such as reading and writing, largely on their own. Self-motivated study might be a necessity for language preparation, anyhow. Due to a shortage of books, Polubotko recommended that children copy excerpts of Ukrainian literature and compile a collection of works they liked.

The orientation of complex work was varied, but the goal of all work, explicitly or implicitly expressed, was the development of responsible future Soviet citizens. Supporters of Ukrainization like Polubotko believed native-language instruction – and, in particular, native-language literacy – had to form the core of the complexes. Written work offered students very concrete knowledge, coupled with lessons in civic obligation. For example, a common complex recommended by Narkomos concerned preventative health care. Polubotko proposed integrating language instruction even here, encouraging to students to write their own works on the subject or repeat poetry with passages such as "Dirty boy – wash up quickly. Shake out your clothes girl. Untidiness is the enemy. Be afraid. Do not bring us an epidemic [*poshest*]."[69]

Similarly, language was a fundamental part of a school's transfer of political ideology. Complexes dedicated to the October Revolution, Lenin Days, Shevchenko Days, and May 1 were not to be simply opportunities for celebration, but "culminating points of struggle and life" expressed in written form. Polubotko gave a number of examples of such work. The complex on the October Revolution might include an essay comparing differences in form and ideology of works written before and after the revolution. A complex for a rural school could include a reading of Arkhyp Teslenko's story "Shkoliar" (The pupil), in which the main character, a peasant boy, dies from hunger in pre-revolutionary Ukraine. Polubotko proposed asking students why this happened and why such "capable children of proletarians" will not needlessly die in today's Ukraine. In short, complexes offered teachers a chance to have children shape their own civic education: "They obtain that which they still have to obtain, that which they need to know for life and not for a diploma certification."[70]

The KP(b)U official line saw the complex system and Ukrainian studies as complementary parts of its campaign to educate Ukrainian children and retool Ukrainian national culture. In a February 1925 memorandum to Narkomos, Radnarkom, and the Komsomol, KP(b)U First Secretary Emanuel Kviring repeated a party directive for broadening the network of the republic's primary schools. For this to happen, however, Kviring emphasized that teachers needed to continue their requalification: "It is necessary to concentrate all efforts on the development of methodological approaches of school work, while remaining oriented to the new complex programs and children's Communist movement."[71] New methodology meant both the promotion of a civic education through progressive pedagogy in the classroom and its continuation in Young Pioneer groups once the school day was over. Kviring emphasized that in order for teachers to have any chance of successfully implementing this program, more native-language literature must be published and supplied to the schools for Ukrainians and non-Russian ethnic minorities. He further ordered the Narkomos academic committee to define specific textbooks for city and rural schools. This distinction will be examined later. For now, it is enough to say that Ukrainian textbooks would not conform to an all-Union norm. They would reflect the particularities of the republic and individual localities. In considering innovation in education, the larger agenda of Ukrainization informed the tactics pursued. Ukrainian-language literacy and knowledge of Ukrainian-area studies were essential parts of the new pedagogy.

Chapter Four

Treading Carefully

The Ukrainization of primary schools was supposed to be automatic. Narkomos administrators stressed it would be. They set short-term goals for a process they believed had begun with the assumption of Bolshevik power and needed only a determined push. Yet, Narkomos administrators, inspectors, and the pedagogical press reported early on (and throughout the period of this study) on obstacles that hindered the fulfillment of a process that was expected to be routine. Much of the initial concern was for the lack of Ukrainian-language literature and trained teachers. These shortages were a persistent problem in the relatively more Russian-speaking East and South, but even in the central regions around Kyiv, local education officials worried that existing teachers were not up to the task of teaching proficiently in Ukrainian. Such practical impediments were ongoing, significant concerns, but an equal and more fundamental problem was Narkomos anxiety about the lack of authority for the Ukrainian language generally in the urban environment and as a tool for political training. Russian continued to be a privileged language for political authority in spite of the decrees on Ukrainization.

For Ukrainizing educators, the shift to Ukrainian-language instruction was about the alteration of this language hierarchy; it was not a program simply for de-Russification. They imagined the saturation by Ukrainian of the public environment, that knowledge of things deemed to be central to Ukrainian studies should inform future citizens and public servants of the republic, and thus its governance. They saw expertise in teaching in Ukrainian and Ukrainian studies as a high civic duty. Without teachers' acquisition of this knowledge, the policy would fail as a whole because the state looked to teachers to train children as well as the public. A key means for ensuring teacher competence in Ukrainian was an examination, or *perevirka*, of their knowledge. Teachers viewed such examinations with trepidation, but they were a necessary requirement to ensure that the campaign was not retarded.

Yet, the initial steps towards Ukrainization of primary schools were tentative. Local education officials judged Ukrainization to be easiest where the Ukrainian-speaking population was most concentrated and where a shift in language instruction would not meet resistance from groups invested in the continued high cultural value associated with Russian-language schooling (most critically, parents of children enrolled in urban, centrally located, primary schools). Local education sections decided which schools to target for conversion (or, more rarely, new establishment or construction) on the basis of centrally approved census figures, and often it was easier to pursue a selective course of little dispute. This sort of policy, however, was not in keeping with the wide-ranging plans envisioned by central Ukrainizers and the expectations of a perevirka, and arguably allowed some educators to feel immune from Ukrainization until they encountered an increased role for the language in the public space. Russian-speaking party members, state employees, and parents of schoolchildren saw less reason to shift.

Ukrainizing educational authorities believed that the wider linguistic environment had to change for parents to make different choices. This meant that the overall predominance of Russian had to decline. In keeping with a correlation between ethnicity and language, Narkomos believed that children of each ethnic group in Ukraine should gain their education in their own "national language." This strategy would reduce the influence of Russian overall, as schools throughout the republic would continue to promote a program of basic Ukrainian studies for children, regardless of ethnicity. Narkomos officials often equated preference by parents of ethnic minorities (Jews, Poles, Germans, etc.) for continued education in Russian with class interests; that is, a bourgeois faith in the cultural superiority of Russian. In this way, the Ukrainian language was imagined as a language befitting the new political order, at least within the Ukrainian republic. It would become the new language of "inter-ethnic communication," and Narkomos asserted its new Soviet character because it was the language of the formerly oppressed. Education in the national languages would provide access into the revolutionized cultural world and developing form of republican identity. To be sure, many within the Ukrainian branch of the Communist Party, and certainly within the larger party, did not share this essential suspicion of Russian, but a diminished space for Russian was the understood result of Narkomos's efforts. Narkomos also backed the interests of ethnic-Ukrainian schoolchildren living outside the UkrSSR, symbolically tying this population to the fate of Ukrainization within, and strengthening Narkomos's advocacy of the principle of native-language instruction generally.

Although the central republican government and the KP(b)U assumed leading roles in oversight over the process of Ukrainization, Narkomos remained the critical institution entrusted with the direct and daily implementation of the policy. It was a Narkomos unit, Ukrliknep, that designed Ukrainian-studies courses for state employees and administered the testing of their knowledge. Importantly, Narkomos recruited teachers to staff these courses, and teachers solicited employment. The state asked teachers to fulfill multiple roles: educator of children, political guide, and public Ukrainizer. Narkomos set the bar for what constituted proficiency in Ukrainian and thus defined the agenda for the policy as a whole. Educators, including primary-school teachers, were a critical part of this effort.

Taking Stock

If Ukrainization was necessary to the success of Narkomos's educational agenda, practical problems slowed down the policy's implementation. A report published in the newspaper *Visti VUTsVK* regarding school affairs in the Katerynoslav province alarmed Holovsotsvykh so much that in October 1923 it demanded an investigation by the provincial education section.[1] The report claimed that the teachers' standard of living in the Pavlohrad region was nearly desperate. According to one teacher, the majority of schools in the area were not working. Where they remained open, students were using old textbooks, the buildings were in disrepair, and teachers received minimum rations and their salaries a half a year late, if at all.[2] Regional authorities had claimed they would fully support teachers beginning in September 1923, but, in November, announced that they could fund only 10 per cent of the teachers' salaries and encouraged them to seek direct contracts with the local population. Out of desperation, some teachers were leaving the region. Officials had threatened to invoke an emergency court (*troika*) to try those leaving their posts or refusing to work. Teachers faced the dilemma of "whether to hope or scatter."[3]

Although teachers did not confront such dire circumstances everywhere, most eked out a bare existence. Lack of proper funding inevitably affected the quality of education.[4] On the rare occasions when things worked, grateful residents sometimes let central authorities know. In September 1923, twenty-one residents of the village of Tarnoruda in the Podillia province (now in the Khmelnytskyi oblast) wrote VUTsVK, thanking "the powers of the UkrSSR" for appointing a new education inspector, a man named Halii.[5] According to them, Halii had put "school affairs on a higher pedestal all over the world." Until his arrival, they had not known "the truth" of education. Clearly, in the opinion of these villagers, this inspector was an exception to the norm. As will be discussed below, most education inspectors were poorly trained and unwilling or incapable of mustering the resources necessary to make a qualitative change in the level of schooling.

Even those schools that had teachers who knew Ukrainian well and were dedicated to their profession could Ukrainize only cautiously, simply due to the lack of literature available. A Holovsotsvykh plan for Ukrainization cited the insufficient amount, or complete absence, of academic language in Ukrainian as one of the main reasons for the slow development of Ukrainian-language institutions.[6] It called upon VUTsVK and Radnarkom to allot funds to create school libraries with a specific number of children's books, and demanded the publication of new children's textbooks, fiction, and popular scientific works, as well as methodological literature for teachers. It insisted that Derzhvydav (the state publishing house) fully satisfy the need for children's textbooks in Ukrainian by the beginning of the 1923–4 school year. It estimated that giving every school its first 100 books would entail the publication of 1,105,700 books at a cost of 331,710 gold rubles. Plans for the eastern and southern provinces also committed Narkomos to completely furnishing schools with Ukrainian-language textbooks and literature, but allowed that parents might have to contribute to the cost of supplying books.[7]

As early as May, Holovsotsykh had drawn up a list of Ukrainian-language books to be distributed for the 1923–4 school year.[8] Although at first glance the list seems ambitious, the number of copies it prescribed for textbooks and teachers' aids was clearly insufficient. The greatest number of copies Holovsotsvykh planned for any new textbook was 30,000. Given that at the end of the 1922–3 year there were some 779,500 children enrolled in Ukrainian-language schools alone, these target numbers for textbooks fell well short of a full supply.[9] Furthermore, the state publishing house needed to reprint many of the books Holovsotsvykh had designated as essential, and ethnic-minority schools would require copies of Ukrainian-language books as well.

Teachers made do with what they had, reading and translating from Russian-language texts and relying on in-class oral assignments. The children of the Pohozha–Krynytsia Labour School in the Poltava province chose to appeal to the Soviet public in a November 1923 letter they wished to be published: "We have an unshakable hope that the editors of the children's journal *Chervoni kvity* [Red flowers] will stand with the head of our school and aid us with valuable advice and give the children of this village the possibility of obtaining a magical and valuable book."[10] The children pleaded to all "sympathetic institutions and benevolent persons" to provide them with the literature they desperately needed. The school's director likely aided in the drafting of this letter, given its reference to him. Nevertheless, the motivation of the children's appeal seems genuine. It was impossible to truly transfer to Ukrainian-language instruction without the massive publication and distribution of new material.

In a 1924 assessment entitled "The Year of Ukrainization in School Affairs," Deputy Commissar of Education Riappo, an ethnic Estonian, underscored the importance of a transfer to Ukrainian-language instruction to the party as a whole. He wrote that "the complete task [of Ukrainization] of the leading organs of education is such that all this process is directed towards the building of a worker-peasant state and the future Communist society."[11] However, he confirmed many of the problems raised in earlier correspondence to Holovsotsvykh and conceded that this immense task was only in the planning stages: "It is not easy to overturn the inertia of centuries."[12] He believed the greatest problem was that the republic's schools were "extremely weakly equipped with Ukrainian cultural forces," and demanded renewed attention to the training of current teachers and the preparation of new ones. Pedagogical technical colleges (*tekhnikumy*) conducted barely more than half of their instruction in Ukrainian.[13] Although the budget for education had risen over the past two years, it was still well below prerevolutionary levels, and schools struggled to meet the most basic costs.

Riappo saw the greatest problems with progress in Ukrainization in provinces with significant Russian-speaking populations: Kharkiv, Odesa, Chernihiv, Katerynoslav, and Donets. In all of Ukraine, 67 per cent of the schools taught in Ukrainian or in mixed Ukrainian and Russian instruction. However, the proportion of ethnic-Ukrainian children attending school was approximately 75 per cent. Thus, some 8 per cent of the children were not going to school in their native language.[14] He claimed that there was no entirely Ukrainized school in Donets province. The number of Ukrainian teachers in the rural communities, he believed, was extremely small. Furthermore, in Ukraine as a whole, only half of primary-level schools had been supplied with Ukrainian textbooks. Still, he claimed that with the exception of the Donbas, Ukrainization could be largely completed within a year.

This conclusion was overly optimistic. A Chernihiv provincial report from early 1924 suggested that schools in the province still confronted significant challenges in implementing the program. Rural schools lagged behind their urban counterparts. In the city of Chernihiv, six out of seven schools were Ukrainized, but in the Chernihiv region, only 49 out of 197 schools had completed this process.[15] Schools of mixed Ukrainian–Russian instruction continued to operate in this region and others. Ukrainization of these schools would proceed gradually, starting with the youngest groups. The shortage of teachers undoubtedly contributed to this gradual approach. Even in the central provinces, where ethnic Ukrainians formed an overwhelming majority of the population, Ukrainization did not always advance smoothly. The Narkomos Collegium pointed to problems in the Kyiv province in December 1923: "the question of Ukrainization in the city of Kyiv, which has a special significance as the centre of cultural-national life, has not been sufficiently impressed upon the Kyiv Hubsotsvykh [provincial sotsvykh department]."[16] It blamed shortcomings on lack of initiative by the province and lack of funds for children's literature. While the collegium may have seen these problems as understandable elsewhere, it placed special significance on the program's success in Ukraine's cultural and ethnic heartland.

A 1925 article in *Narodnii uchytel* emphasized a greater problem for Ukrainization: the policy's lack of authority in the schools. Kh. Nevira, the author of the article, noted that because of the lack of Ukrainian-language books, sometimes work in the school was reduced to nothing.[17] This standstill naturally created "ambivalence" towards Ukrainization, among both those teachers who relied on books to teach and students who were instructed to privilege published texts. Even worse, according to Nevira, children's activities in the classroom were conducted largely in Russian. In schools just beginning to Ukrainize, like Kharkiv Labour School No. 32, almost all work of the Young Pioneers, the Communist organization for young children, was done in Russian. Nevira attributed this failure to use Ukrainian to poor leadership by the Komsomol: "Very often registered Komsomol do not know the Ukrainian language and Leninist children [Young Pioneers] following after them are ousting the Ukrainian language from their rounds and practical work."[18] Nevira noted that, sadly, children go from the home, where often parents do not speak "pure Ukrainian," to nominally Ukrainian schools, where work is done in Russian.

The situation was little better in fully Ukrainized schools. Nevira reported that the schools' extracurricular use of Ukrainian was limited: "teachers and children (for example during the weeding of the garden, digging of a vegetable plot, game of soccer etc.) employ Ukrainian, but once the Young Leninist exercises, parade practice, meetings, and assemblies begin everything switches to Russian."[19] Schools also published children's newspapers almost exclusively in Russian, even in more ethnic-Ukrainian rural areas. This privileged use of Russian set a dangerous precedent. Children would continue to internalize a hierarchy of languages, accepting Ukrainian as a language for cultural expression but unsuitable for political leadership. Furthermore, the constant use of Russian outside the classroom affected events in the classroom: "The Young Leninist collective is a model and other students operate according to its example. Here it is specially necessary to prioritize this concern so not to negate the time consuming and far from easy work of the pedagogical collective."[20] In other words, Komsomol's refusal to use Ukrainian was having a negative effect on Ukrainization in the classroom. Here, Nevira suggests that Narkomos's demand for teachers to quickly switch to Ukrainian was unrealistic unless the party and its own subsidiary organizations did so.

For true believers in Ukrainization, however, the policy was about much more than changing one's language use. Kaliuzhny, another contributor to *Narodnii uchytel*, argued that Ukrainization was fundamentally about an adjustment of an existence (*buttia*): "It is not just about the formal use of the Ukrainian language or an external re-painting for a Ukrainian appearance."[21] Ukrainization was a comprehensive study of all things that "provide an understanding of 'Ukraine,'" the history, regional cultural growth and traditions, and social– economic life of a population. Kaliuzhny and others who embraced the promise of Ukrainization believed that only this sort of study would provide state leaders with the skills necessary for economic and cultural management and enable union between the proletarian city and the village.

Kaliuzhny conceded that the formal Ukrainization of schools had occurred relatively quickly, with some problems in Donets province and elsewhere. However, teachers would continue to take on great responsibility in Ukrainization, because the schools would supply "workers for the lower state apparat." Thus, while a transfer of the language of instruction had begun, teachers still needed to teach students all things Ukrainian. Ukrainization was not simply de-Russification. Teachers had to deepen their knowledge of the Ukrainian language, aid in orthographic and terminological standardization, and promote broad Ukrainian studies. This was a bold agenda for most rank-and-file teachers.

Teachers' Inadequate Ukrainian Skills Explained

As the example of the Kharkiv schools suggests, all was not right even in fully Ukrainized schools. Teachers illiterate or semi-literate in Ukrainian were doing more harm than good. The pedagogical press is replete with examples. One *Narodnii uchytel* contributor from Pavlohrad, in the Katerynoslav province, wrote that there were still cases in 1925 of teachers who did not know Ukrainian teaching in Ukrainian schools. Children, he said, were speaking with a hard *g*, a phoneme infrequently voiced in Ukrainian but used in Russian.[22] "Why?" he asked in a poem he composed on the subject and then provided the answer: "Those from the instructional personnel, they cannot 'break the tongue.'" Such persons, he insisted, had no place teaching in a Ukrainian school: "When you do not know, do not direct speech. Do not attempt to cripple children too!"

Advocates of Ukrainization were, in effect, making the argument that teachers had a solemn responsibility to ensure the policy was properly implemented. Another writer in *Narodnii uchytel*, M. Makerevych, elaborated on this theme. Also invoking the image of lasting physical harm, he insisted that the poor use or disregard of Ukrainian could impair the development of ethnic-Ukrainian youth: "children must not be crippled [*ne pokalicheni*] by a foreign language. This is critical to the pedagogue."[23] Competent Ukrainian-speaking teachers were rare in Ukrainian schools, he insisted. The majority were Russians, Russified Ukrainians, or "changelings" (*perevertnia*) who used three Russian words for every two Ukrainian words in a sentence. For example, according to Makerevych's assessment, of some 500 teachers working for schools along the Donets railroad line, only 126 knew Ukrainian and only half of them could teach in it properly. Although teachers could enrol in three-month courses for government employees, this was not enough time to learn much. Since the state was too poor to offer longer courses, Makerevych insisted that all teachers had to take responsibility for their own training. Of greatest importance was their participation in requalification seminars in the Ukrainian language: "Each person will understand this, when he accepts that language knowledge in the hands of the pedagogue is a powerful tool of influence on the children's collective." The teachers' own sense of professional and civic duty would motivate them.

Republican Soviet organs saw the cost of Ukrainization as high. In an assessment of the funds necessary for the Ukrainization of its employees, Holovsotsvykh placed the cost of training one group of fifteen to twenty people for two and half months at 120 rubles. It recommended coordination with other commissariats in the capital of Kharkiv and mobilization of fifty teachers to economize.[24] Still, teachers would earn no more than one ruble per hour of instruction. On paper, local authorities gave precedence to the Ukrainization of governmental institutions over schools. The Podillia province allowed teachers six months to receive Ukrainian-language training and local education officials only two.[25] Officials needed to learn Ukrainian so they could speak with "peasants in daily conversation and written correspondence." The level of knowledge the government expected of teachers was, however, considerably greater. They had to not only use Ukrainian properly, but teach children how to as well. The best among them would train bureaucrats of today in Ukrainian. Their common task was to prepare those of tomorrow.

Many teachers, in fact, worried about a formal appraisal of their abilities in Ukrainian. An announcement of an upcoming perevirka in the Ukrainian language appearing in *Narodnii uchytel* reportedly created widespread panic.[26] According to P. Sapukhin, teachers burdened with the already arduous task of switching their lesson plans to Ukrainian resented having their knowledge questioned. The faculty from one school composed a song describing their frustration: "A cloud is approaching again, a perevirka awaits us."[27] Teachers could no longer simply claim to speak Ukrainian and teach in the classroom according to their own innate understanding of the language. State authorities would now hold them more accountable. Sapukhin wrote that this led to a crisis of self-confidence among teachers. What he labelled "Ukrainian arrogance" had led many teachers to assume that they would improve naturally, as if by "impulse." On the contrary, Sapukhin insisted, teachers had to work hard to perfect their language ability.

While the announcement of the 1926 perevirka signalled a call for a broader use of Ukrainian, it also warned those proficient in the language against reliance on historical, romantic notions. Sapukhin singled out teachers who lived according to what he labelled Kobzar "purity [*chystota*]." By this he meant those teachers who saw the language of the national poet Taras Shevchenko as the most correct form and were too enamoured with "primitive" Ukrainian studies. Sapukhin argued that a reworking of Ukrainian was needed in order to respond to current needs. Ukrainian was a tool for class struggle and communism: "Through the national word of Ukrainian workers and peasants we must tell them of the idea of the international unity and brotherhood of toilers, to raise them from the form of a national primitiveness to the international heights of contemporary culture."[28] The schools, and through them the party, would teach lessons about the tasks of socialism to the children of these workers and peasants in Ukrainian. But returning to an essentialized language was impossible and politically dangerous. A Ukrainian rooted in the past risked marginalization and obsolescence.

The perevirka would also test teachers' knowledge of Ukrainian studies, what Sapukhin labelled "the geographic, economic, and historical elements of our country [*nashoho kraiu*], to promote the Marxist-dialectical approach to helpful, practical work, directed at the building of socialism in our country." Failure to learn Ukrainian debilitated the teacher, but language study alone was not enough. Furthermore, Ukrainian speakers had to reject a fixation with Ukrainian lore and study the history of the revolutionary struggle in Ukraine and the republic's potential for economic growth. Sapukhin argued that a perevirka of Ukrainian studies was absolutely necessary: "Without this accounting, we cannot march ahead." If teachers were not held accountable for this sort of knowledge, they could not instruct their students and participate in the development of a Ukrainian socialist culture.

Careful Path Forward: Limiting Priorities, Building Support

In spite of these concerns regarding teachers' low level of Ukrainian knowledge and the slow pace of Ukrainization in some areas, due to the lack of teachers who knew Ukrainian at all, insufficient local funding, or shortages in textbooks and other educational aids, Narkomos remained committed to Ukrainization and the policy did enjoy some early, if qualified, success. The party had implemented Ukrainization in part because it believed that native-language instruction would educate a new generation quickly and effectively. Furthermore, the Soviet government was building in part on a network of Ukrainian-language schools established by Ukraine's short-lived independent governments and championed by a portion of the population. Ukrainian-language schooling was already a reality. The Soviet government broadened and transformed its scope.

An early request by Ukrainian parents and teachers in the Kyiv province to open a new Ukrainian school soon after the Soviet ousting of Ukrainian People's Republic (UNR) forces in 1919 gives some indication of how popular pressure prompted authorities to act where it was easiest to do so. In August, at an assembly of local officials, teachers, union leaders, and workers' club members, a representative of the KP(b)U committee in Kyiv's Podil district introduced a measure to create a Ukrainian gymnasium.[29] He was supported in his proposal by Shmyhovsky, an official from the teachers' municipal union. Shmyhovsky claimed that there were three Ukrainian schools for early grades in the Podil district, but none for the older grades. Those wishing to continue their studies had to do so in Russian schools. Most families did not have the means to relocate from this lower portion of the city or send their children to the central quarter of Old Kyiv, where Ukrainian schools were concentrated. Furthermore, Ukrainian families with children were regularly moving into the Podil from the countryside surrounding the city. Thus, the demand for Ukrainian-language schooling would only increase. Lastly, Shmyhovsky added, a religious school in the district was set for dissolution and the students had nowhere to continue their education. If a student residence was established under the new school, there would be a ready supply of students.

Narkomos insisted upon changing the orientation of the school. Although parents and teachers in the Podil had called for a gymnasium, the representative of the provincial education section, Nahurny, required the school to be organized as a labour school for the upper grades. He submitted a plan for the opening of this school, suggesting that, in time, there might be more than one: "The Podil, which was a greenhouse [*rozsadnykom*] of culture not only in Ukraine, but in Russia [*Moskovshchyna*], should have its own secondary Ukrainian school and not just one."[30] Because of the socio-economic composition of the Podil, he claimed, students attending school in the district would largely come from the labouring population, including unpropertied peasants living in villages across the Dnipro River and near the city. His plan mandated that the school occupy the building of the dissolved religious school, enrol both boys and girls, and maintain a dormitory for village children who had completed the first four years of schooling and showed promise.

Here, then, Narkomos acted not only to satisfy the demands of ethnic Ukrainians, but also to extend its educational mission to as wide a population as possible. This Ukrainian-language school would cater to previously underserved children and replace religious instruction with the progressive pedagogy of the new Soviet school, in a language they could understand. The school's formation was the direct result of a popular petition, and its task was made easier because it did not have to assume the location and student body of an existing Russian-language school.

As has been discussed above, when VUTsVK ordered Narkomos to undertake a more concerted plan of Ukrainization in 1923, local sections had to outline a program for rapid achievement. They were, however, selective regarding where they actually promoted Ukrainization most aggressively. The Odesa Provincial

Education Section compiled a two-tiered program for Ukrainization, dividing schools between those it expected to Ukrainize fully and those that would begin Ukrainization only with the first two grades.[31] In the end, it planned for 53 per cent of primary schools to be ultimately Ukrainized, a proportion correspondent to the size of the ethnic-Ukrainian population in the province. By the end of the 1923–4 school year, the section reported that it expected the plan to be accelerated. This meant that school heads or regional officials had to pursue full Ukrainization in some schools originally designated for a partial approach (gradually increasing the number of Ukrainian-language groups). There was clear enthusiasm among some in the provincial section for the program. It did not rely on Narkomos for a curricular plan, but audaciously worked out its own program for instruction in the Ukrainian language with explanatory notes. It also published 10,000 copies of an alphabet book entitled *Chervona zirka* (Red star) for use in Ukrainian-language schools.

Nevertheless, the section chose to push Ukrainization the hardest where it would reap initial rewards. It reported that in the Kherson region, there were several districts where 80 to 85 per cent of the schools could transfer their instruction "painlessly" (*bezbolezno*) to Ukrainian.[32] It recognized it would have a tougher campaign in the other districts and granted that weekly regional courses in Ukrainian for teachers and Soviet employees were a necessity. In the Odesa region, officials pursued a plan of full Ukrainization in schools where ethnic-Ukrainian children formed a majority and teachers had sufficient knowledge. Elsewhere, only the first two grades would be Ukrainized, and instruction in the remaining groups would be in the language "which is most possible given current conditions." Likewise, although Ukrainian studies was a mandatory subject in all schools beginning in the fourth grade, ethnic-minority schools could choose to study either Russian or Ukrainian as a second language. It was among both Russians and the ethnic-minority populations that local authorities had to tread carefully, although their determined, but gradual, approach in multi-ethnic areas foretold a campaign for the separation and Ukrainization of Russified Ukrainians.

In the Katerynoslav province, Ukrainization also proceeded according to a targeted approach. During the 1922–3 school year, 55.2 per cent of schools were Ukrainized. This figure increased to 69.3 per cent of schools and, in contrast to the Odesa province, Katerynoslav authorities introduced the Ukrainian language as a mandatory subject for all non-Ukrainian children as early as the third grade, and did not offer Russian as an alternative subject of study for ethnic-minority students.[33] They did, however, prioritize the promotion of Ukrainian-language schooling in rural areas, where the ethnic-Ukrainian population was concentrated. This meant the postponement of comprehensive Ukrainization in the predominantly Russian-speaking cities. Similarly, the province cited a lack of funds for its slow Ukrainian-language work among party employees. The same rationale undoubtedly applied to urban schools. Money for teacher training and literature acquisition would be spent first in those areas where the need was most immediate. In these locales, then, Ukrainization was successful. However, this selective approach lent the policy as a whole little authority. Ukrainization of the party was delayed, and the Russian-speaking Ukrainian parents saw little prestige or incentive in switching the language of instruction for their children.

Sometimes, however, Soviet government employees demonstrated greater acceptance of Ukrainization than teachers themselves. Donets, a teacher in the small city of Kremenchuh (Poltava province), wrote a brief account in *Narodnii uchytel* of how city residents viewed Ukrainization. At the post office, a worker did not yet recognize the Ukrainian word for "stamp" when Donets asked for one, but vented his frustration in capable Ukrainian when the stamp stuck to his finger.[34] One employee of the municipal budget office translated the Ukrainian word *sùmma* (cost) into Russian as "bag," by mistakenly picking the definition of the word *sumà* out his dictionary.[35] Her error led everyone in the section to laugh, but Donets downplayed the slip-up, writing that errors are understandable for anyone intent on learning a language. By contrast, at a meeting of Robos, members complained when one teacher made a proposal in Ukrainian and demanded he switch to Russian so they could understand it. According to Donets, they whispered to one another, "Who are these barbarians who wear out all our nerves?" Educators, the very people who were largely responsible for using Ukrainian every day and teaching it to others, displayed the greatest hostility to the policy in Kremenchuh. It could not always be assumed, therefore, that a selective emphasis on Ukrainization in provincial schools would yield favourable results.

If local authorities sought to limit the scope of Ukrainization in their specific province, Narkomos broadened its reach generally. An underlying justification for Ukrainization was that it legitimized the UkrSSR as a protector and advocate for labouring Ukrainians within the Soviet Union and beyond. Thus, Narkomos sought to include Ukrainians from abroad in its work. Scholars who came from Polish-ruled Western Ukraine to work in VUAN laid much of the groundwork integral to the policy of Ukrainization: the development of Ukrainian-studies disciplines, research into new terminology, and sponsorship of new literature. Furthermore, they were closely involved in the standardization of Ukrainian-language orthography to come in 1929.

A remarkable aspect of this policy of inclusion was the schooling of ethnic-Ukrainian children from Czechoslovakia and Poland in the UkrSSR. In December 1924, Kaliuzhny, an officer at the Soviet embassy in Czechoslovakia, requested that Narkomos support the education of a child of Bondar, a prominent Communist senator from Carpathian Rus, in Czechoslovakia.[36] Kaliuzhny claimed that this child could not gain admittance to schools in Czechoslovakia, due to his father's political background, and that, "as for language, it would be easier to teach the boy in Ukraine and, from a political standpoint, [such an education] would give him the best impressions." Kaliuzhny argued that Narkomos should give the boy one of the fifty stipends it had reserved for children of workers and poor peasants in Western Ukraine and even offered to take him with him when he returned to the UkrSSR.

In matters of such political sensitivity, the party itself asserted its leadership role. First Secretary Kviring set the parameters of what could be done for this child in a resolution forwarded to Commissar of Education Shumsky. He resolved that the child be admitted to a vocational school or technical college, but not a party school.[37] The UkrSSR would assume responsibility for the cultural enlightenment of children such as Bondar's, but not, at least at this stage, offer them prestigious leadership training. Bondar's case was not isolated. Kaliuzhny notes that some twenty students had already gathered in Czechoslovakia to await transfer and boarding at educational institutions in the UkrSSR. In July 1925, Lozovy, the head of Holovprofos, the Narkomos Main Administration of Vocational Education (in secondary schools), requested permission from the KP(b)U Agitprop Department to enrol students from the Western Ukrainian regions of Galicia, Bukovyna, and Transcarpathia (in Poland, Romania, and Czechoslovakia, respectively) to schools in the UkrSSR. Lozovy requested thirty spaces in workers' schools (*robfaky*)[38] and eighty in higher educational institutions.[39] The demand for spaces indicates that at least some Ukrainians abroad viewed the Soviet education system positively and believed that it offered an opportunity for their advancement.

There is no evidence of Narkomos's seeking to enrol younger children in the UkrSSR's primary schools, the principal subject of this study. However, its continuing efforts to provide instruction to Western Ukrainian youth do demonstrate a wish to claim a principal role as educator for the Ukrainian nation as a whole.[40] Most likely, only the children of the most pro-Soviet and stalwart Communists were admitted to these schools (or even sought admittance). Even so, the state's guardianship of these children was politically important. The Soviet Ukrainian state would take over where families of Western Ukrainian labourers had left off and provide these children proper proletarian training.

Expanding Objectives: De-Russification and Cultural Aid

While Ukrainization was fundamentally about the promotion of the Ukrainian language, a campaign to eliminate Russian-language predominance in the republic was a central component of the policy. Narkomos strove to make Ukrainian the universal republican language, but it also recognized that the protection and

A demonstration of labour-school pupils in Kyiv, 1924. Courtesy TsDKFFAU.

promotion of ethnic-minority languages could act as a counterbalance to the influence of Russian. It hoped to break the historical authority assigned to Russian in urban centres and thereby offer Ukrainian as a secondary "official" language for ethnic minorities.

Of particular concern was the assimilation of many Ukrainian Jews to Russian. This tendency was particularly common in towns and cities, where middle-class Jews believed Russian-language schooling would ensure advancement for their children. A Kyiv provincial meeting for teachers in March 1925 noted that in the Bila Tserkva region (*okruha*), up to 90 to 95 per cent of children "whose native language is Jewish [Yiddish]" go to Russian schools.[41] The provincial meeting recommended that educational authorities re-examine the need for all Russian-language schools and consider their transfer to "native language instruction" for the 1925–6 school year. In the absence of clear evidence of a strictly ethnic-Russian population, provincial educators saw little reason for Russian schools.

Although Narkomos authorities repeatedly stated they would respect the parents' right to choose the language of instruction for their children, in fact, they regularly worked to convince parents that children learned best in their "native" language. Narkomos directly correlated children's ethnicity with their native language and frowned upon parents who pressed to have their children enrol in non-native schools. In a 1925 report on Ukrainization, dedicated in part to educational institutions for ethnic minorities, Narkomos condemned the "ignorance" (*nesoznatelnost*) of some sections of the population that refused to attend "their" (native) schools.[42] The report specifically emphasized the refusal of Jews to attend Yiddish-language schools, commenting that these schools serve only 14.6 per cent of the Jewish population.[43] Assimilated non-Russians, especially urban Jews, were overwhelmingly enrolling their children in Russian-language schools, a fact that Narkomos noted with displeasure: "Often schools with instruction in Russian are used in these instances by petit-bourgeois groups, who ignorantly oppose the implementation of nationalities policies in the schools." Here, Narkomos linked parents' refusal to send their children to the appropriate school to anti-Soviet behaviour, instigated by classes hostile to proletarian rule. Narkomos held that the privileging of the Russian language by ethnic minorities (together with Russified Ukrainians) constituted a sort of confused chauvinism.[44] The success of Soviet nationalities policy in Ukraine and specifically Ukrainization demanded correction of this behaviour.

Narkomos attempted to remove any rationale for children's refusing to attend their "native" school of instruction. It recognized that schools had failed to open due to a lack of ethnic-minority teachers, and that the generally low level of education among some of those who were teaching reinforced the perception that Russian-language schools were superior. It also blamed poor enrolment on book shortages or, in the case of Bulgarian, Moldovan, or Tatar schools, the near-complete absence in the republic of suitable native-language literature. Although the literature for German, Yiddish, and Polish schools was somewhat better, publication of ethnic-minority textbooks even as late as 1924 was still far below what was needed (only twenty-six titles in ethnic-minority languages as a whole).[45] Those that were published began as translations of Russian or Ukrainian texts. While Narkomos focused on an increase in production, officials in the teachers' union demanded a campaign to retrain ethnic-minority teachers in courses designed to improve both their general knowledge and political training.[46] Like their Ukrainian counterparts in the village, these teachers were the basic representatives of Soviet power and extensions of the party's ideal for the building of socialism in Ukraine. In the minds of Narkomos officials, it was essential that these teachers receive proper training if the Soviet government was to retain authority and the school to earn the community's trust.

By attempting to minimize the use of Russian, Narkomos sought to affirm Ukrainian as the primary language of communication between all nationalities in the republic and grant it increased authority. Narkomos would use the Ukrainian language to recast a new republican identity: supra-ethnic, but universally Ukrainian-speaking. However, it also assumed the role of protector of ethnic Ukrainians abroad, including a large Ukrainian population in the RSFSR (the Russian republic). Language remained a critical identifier of ethnicity. The Ukrainian language connected ethnic Ukrainians abroad to the UkrSSR. Within the republic, ethnic minorities would be linked to their Ukrainian counterparts through their republican identity, expressed by their children's secondary study of Ukrainian. Neither aspect of this policy sat easily with all members of the party.

Narkomos support of Ukrainian-language schools in the RSFSR would increase throughout the late 1920s and early 1930s. As early as 1925, the Narkomos Collegium passed a resolution detailing its backing of these schools. This resolution called for Ukrainian schools in the RSFSR, "where a concentrated Ukrainian population lives."[47] Narkomos stressed that this mandate primarily regarded Ukrainians in villages, although it granted that it was possible to organize Ukrainian skills in the "majority of cultural centres," such as Moscow and Leningrad. Narkomos would help in the establishment of these schools by sending qualified teachers from the UkrSSR, organizing courses in Kyiv and Kharkiv to train teachers from Russia, and supplying Ukrainian-language literature. It recognized that, ultimately, educators would have to draft Ukrainian-language textbooks according to the specific demands of the RSFSR education system (it did not specify how, noting only that Ukrainian textbooks were heavily localized), but, for the time being, these Ukrainian schools abroad could use books published in the UkrSSR. While the Russian Commissariat of Education administered these schools and dictated their curriculum, the schools' tie to Ukraine remained. Narkomos insisted that it was not enough for teachers in the RSFSR Ukrainian schools to know Ukrainian. They had to be experts in Ukrainian literature, history, and geography. This knowledge of a specifically "Ukrainian" republic would be transferred to the children. Just as the UkrSSR offered refuge to radical Western Ukrainians, it assumed guardianship over Ukrainians throughout the broader proletarian homeland of the USSR.

Narkomos's defence of the right to Ukrainian schooling abroad paralleled its promotion of these schools at home. It argued similarly that Ukrainian schools outside the UkrSSR were justified pedagogically, to provide for "the rational ordering of work with children who speak Ukrainian."[48] However, Narkomos also touted these schools for political purposes. In particular, it stressed that Ukrainians might engage in "anti-Soviet agitation on national grounds" if their children were denied the opportunity to study in Ukrainian. It acknowledged that local educational authorities might need to explain the importance of native-language instruction to some parents in the RSFSR, citing teacher-led protests against Ukrainian-language schooling in the UkrSSR as cause for caution. However, it clearly believed that sentiment among ethnic Ukrainians was in favour of Ukrainian-language schooling and that, especially in rural areas, such instruction would enable teachers to best provide for their students' success. If local authorities chose to force Russian-language instruction on ethnic Ukrainians, they would only continue the oppression of their tsarist predecessors and encourage dissent and instability.

Mechanisms for Oversight

Beyond issuing orders for the transfer of schooling to the Ukrainian language, Narkomos required some measure of bureaucratic oversight to ensure that this policy was accomplished. Radnarkom had initially entrusted the Workers' and Peasants' Inspectorate with enforcement of its 1920 decree on the equality of languages and development of a network of Ukrainian-language educational institutions.[49] However, it also gave Narkomos the responsibility both to establish Ukrainian-language schools (and introduce Ukrainian as an obligatory subject in ethnic-minority schools) and to set up courses in Ukrainian studies for all Soviet governmental employees, a category that included teachers and local civil servants. In 1923, when Radnarkom issued formal orders for a concerted campaign of Ukrainization, it had already positioned Narkomos as the primary Soviet organ in charge.

As has already been demonstrated, it was often local education inspectors who monitored the progress of Ukrainization in the schools. They also took a leading role outside the classroom. For example, in late November 1924 the Kyiv Regional Executive Committee ordered the local education inspector to coordinate an assessment of the region's Ukrainian-language courses for government employees.[50] However, not all inspectors knew Ukrainian well. A 1924 report from the Kyiv Provincial Education Section notes that a portion of its inspectors had to enrol in Ukrainian-language courses of the very sort that the regional executive committee had ordered its inspectors to inspect.[51] Although it fell to the education inspectors to report on the progress of Ukrainian-language schools as well, clearly, all were not equipped to do so.

Ultimately, Ukrainization's success depended on teachers. Inspectors held individual educators responsible for failure, but they did not design plans for transfer to Ukrainian-language instruction. In Poltava, for example, in October 1923 the provincial education section entrusted the realization of Ukrainization to its senior inspectors, but it gave its methodological committee the task of working out a program of Ukrainian studies for the schools according to a realistic assessment of the number of teachers it had available.⁵² Inspectors monitored Ukrainization's implementation, but local education sections had to provide training or recruit more teachers if they wanted to remedy the gaps even poorly qualified inspectors inevitably found. Without Ukrainian-speaking teachers, this program would collapse.

It was also teachers who headed the courses in Ukrainian studies for state employees. So, although education inspectors reported on the level of language knowledge among civil servants in the city of Kyiv, it was a representative of the regional campaign to liquidate illiteracy, Liknep, who conducted the testing.⁵³ Teachers were widely expected to perform this role in addition to their teaching duties. In this case, it was work that went uncompensated. The municipal executive commission claimed it had no money to pay the Liknep worker. Progress in Ukrainization, both inside and outside the school, depended on the dedication of individual cultural workers and educators. Unfortunately, as will be discussed, the skill level of even those who volunteered or sought employment as "Ukrainizers" varied.

Central authorities at Narkomos set the broad guidelines for the implementation of Ukrainization and remained interested in the steps taken by local education inspectors, sections, and teachers. It published and disseminated questionnaires (*ankety*) on Ukrainian-language usage. In particular, it asked education authorities whether "obstacles" had occurred in the Ukrainization of their work. In its account of measures taken specifically in the schools, the Odesa Provincial Education Section noted that the situation in outlying regions had not been studied enough.⁵⁴ It expressed concern that, although authorities had planned to Ukrainize 158 schools in the Mykolaiv region, as of 1 January 1924, only 61 had been Ukrainized and 79 were in the process of being Ukrainized. It ordered district cultural sections and regional inspectors to determine what had been accomplished and what still needed to be done.⁵⁵ In its report on the Ukrainization of state institutions, the Kyiv Regional Inspectorate responded that "hostile" employees had avoided Ukrainian-language courses and threatened them with dismissal after "a certain time."⁵⁶ Narkomos, therefore, clearly had information that its ambitious plans were not being fulfilled. It would, in time, look upon reports of quantitative successes by some sections with increasing suspicion.

Although Narkomos remained an important organ with oversight of Ukrainization and the principal agency for its implementation in the schools, the party did not relinquish control. In 1925, the KP(b)U Politburo formed a Central Commission on Ukrainization that would take a more direct role in the Ukrainization of its rank and file and the government. Before the formation of this commission, Narkomos reported its findings on Ukrainization to Agitprop, the Central Committee's propaganda wing. Agitprop's operational plan for December to March

1924 included the following dictate: "Along with this basic task of mass party enlightenment work, before Agitprop the task rises of accounting for achievement of resolutions of the Twelfth Congress regarding the nationality question in party education of the Soviet apparat, cultural work of the unions of Narkomos."[57] Its task was to investigate the degree of Ukrainization at the various levels of education, evaluate all coursework in Ukrainian studies, and determine the extent of party and union involvement in Ukrainian-language study. The plan foresaw the creation of a Central Scientific Methodological Committee under Narkomos to oversee the creation of local committees and confirm a program in Ukrainian studies. It mandated the drafting of Soviet primary-school textbooks adjusted to Ukrainian conditions, and the specific development of an agricultural program for rural schools. Furthermore, it mandated support for the organization of Young Pioneer groups, among Ukrainians and among ethnic minorities, where political and methodological work was scant.

In January 1924, in response to instruction from Deputy Commissar of Education Riappo, the commissariat's administrative section forwarded excerpts of an account on Ukrainization by the Odesa Provincial Education Section to Agitprop.[58] The dispatch is evidence of the Narkomos leadership's continuing concern about the pace of Ukrainization in the South, a concern it communicated to, and shared in common with, Agitprop. In another memorandum, Riappo himself replied to a direct query from Agitprop regarding Ukrainization. He conceded that Narkomos was still investigating the achievements of the policy, and thus he was forced to send incomplete information, much of which had been compiled a year earlier.[59] The text of the Agitprop inquiry, incongruously written in Russian, asked specifically for information on the Ukrainization of business affairs by government institutions, but Narkomos replied with additional information on the Ukrainization of all its "subsidiary" organizations, including the schools. Although there are gaps in the Narkomos information (the material Riappo provided did not go beyond figures collected at the provincial level), its successes were notable in comparison with those of other commissariats and must have been known to Agitprop. Riappo's anticipated audience may have been the wider party leadership, to whom he sought to convey a sense of the work accomplished but also the problems that remained. True Ukrainization would require greater support.

Chapter Five

Learning the New Language of Pedagogy

No longer bound by disciplinary strictures, members of the next Soviet generation would see how the integrative knowledge they had gained through progressive education in the schools might be applied by labourers and stakeholders in a socialist economy. If this was the vision, real teachers were overwhelmed by all the tasks of its realization. Ultimately, and perhaps most critically, a perceived contradiction emerged between the goals of the complex system and the application of Ukrainian-language instruction. This chapter explores the "mechanics of implementation": the tension that emerged between the ideals of this new pedagogical approach, their introduction, and the demands of Ukrainization. Normalization of education in the 1920s meant an end to the chaos and experimentation of the civil war era, but a continued emphasis on the concerted socialist upbringing of the next Soviet generation. Ideological training was the preserve of the Young Pioneers – the Communist children's organization whose linkage with schools later chapters directly address – but schools would develop the politically and economically aware citizen.

The problem with the implementation of the program beyond the ideal models described in chapter 2 was that Narkomos lacked a trained institutional infrastructure to ensure oversight. Most concentrated work on systematizing methodology did not begin until 1923, when social conditions in the country stabilized and Narkomos concurrently undertook the charge of Ukrainization. Narkomos continually emphasized kraieznavstvo as the main approach to make the complex method most relevant, and, therefore, it was local education sections that assumed the greater role in defining what progressive pedagogy meant for the individual teachers. Still, teachers were by and large left to their own devices to ensure implementation of the complex method. This delegation of responsibility concerned education administrators and also made the majority of teachers, inexperienced in progressive pedagogy, uncomfortable.

Teachers, sometimes under the jurisdiction of local education sections, met to discuss the practical implementation of the new methodology. They often complained at these meetings about more mundane responsibilities of daily concern: large class sizes, shortages of basic school supplies, and low pay. Education officials continued to emphasize the critical nature of curricular revision, chiefly the need to integrate regional material into instruction, but the training of conference attendees focused on methods of teacher self-study and planning. Such independent activity invited opportunity for a variety of interpretations of methodology, but leading educational theorists placed greater value on the virtues of decentralized education for young Soviet citizens, a quality equated with the democratic core of Soviet governance.

What was most important in the discussions regarding local studies and progressive pedagogy was the connection to Ukrainization. Educational planners viewed knowledge of the Ukrainian language as a critical tool for the creation and comprehension of complexes. Furthermore, because complexes were locally focused but connected to later studies of the wider republic, educators considered them to be key components of Ukrainian studies. Language proficiency would enable such study, even if, for the educators primarily concerned with progressive pedagogy (and for the political authorities who supported this methodology), language study remained a tool for achieving a larger end. Ukrainization and the complex system were mutually compatible aspects of the central concern of a citizenship project that children would embrace as familiar, active, and meaningful.

By the late 1920s, the emphasis of progressive educators would be even more on the participatory nature of the complexes and increasingly on threats by class enemies, but educators continued to emphasize attention to the local environment and the link to Ukrainian studies. They expressed concern about the students' grasp of formal knowledge, but insisted that the complex system would define this knowledge if properly applied and locally centred. Again, it was teachers whom Narkomos officials held responsible for failure. Teachers often retained a reliance on teaching by subject even if they knew this methodology was out of favour, blaming their own inexperience or overwhelming class size. Outside the teachers' conferences that frequently attracted the most ambitious pedagogues, teachers did not have the time or access to literature for the self-study professional meetings advocated. When forced to adapt, teachers did so without direction. Knowledgeable and trustworthy educators were in short supply. When communities voiced approval of instructors, they were happy just to have ones who were professionally competent, and cared less about their linguistic talents. Rural schools found it hard to attract any well-trained instructor. It was only in the best (urban) schools that teachers were able to meet the dual demands of pedagogical innovation and transfer to the Ukrainian language.

Narkomos officials understood that success in Ukrainization would facilitate the promotion of progressive pedagogy (and vice versa). Study in a student's native language made training by the complex method accessible, and language study could provide some unity to all a complex entailed. (Conceivably, nearly all activities could be subject to a form of language study.) Problems in provision of Ukrainian literature or weaknesses in the teachers' knowledge of Ukrainian could impede the development of a complex and place the larger aim of citizenship training in jeopardy. The experience of a leading Mykolaiv school highlights the difficulties of pushing through Ukrainization concurrently with progressive pedagogy in a mixed-language environment. Although the ethnic makeup of the student body is difficult to determine, there is little doubt that students were accustomed to speaking in Russian in this core urban school in the republic's South. Ukrainization here was said to initially hinder the development of education by the complex method because of the students' failure to comprehend. Yet, the teachers' reports also reveal that children quickly adjusted to the switch in language instruction and their embrace of new instruction improved.

Ukrainizers in Narkomos believed they had little option but to pursue both policies, of Ukrainization and education reform, concurrently. In Ukrainian-speaking areas, such a tactic made pedagogical sense; in non-Ukrainian-speaking historical urban centres, such an approach was a political necessity. Ukrainization had to transform the most prestigious schools if the policy was to have any authority. The issue of sorting out ethnicity (and, to a lesser degree for Narkomos, language preference) would happen later or in concert with this assault on the city. Ukrainizers did not believe the process of Ukrainization was complete until Ukrainian schoolchildren attended Ukrainian-speaking schools in high percentages and the number of full (seven-year) schools expanded. Ideally, this meant a good proportion of the most pedagogically innovative schools would assume a Ukrainian character, and the twin policies of Ukrainization of educational reform would be authoritatively linked. To accomplish this, teachers willing to take on this compound task would need much greater support.

Restoring Order to the New School

The problems inherent in the practical application of the progressive pedagogy were apparent at the First All-Ukrainian Teachers' Congress held in January 1925.[1] The congress underscored the importance of breaking with traditional pedagogy to achieve this end in a resolution it passed on the basis of a report given by People's Commissar Shumsky. It applauded the revolution's destruction of an old system of education based on privileges and the establishment of schools centred "on the principles of national self-determination and labour content."[2] The congress recognized that the civil war led to massive devastation, destroying the economy and any hope of financing its ambitious plans for a complete reworking of education. While it orphaned thousands of children and fractured families, this social dislocation had a positive consequence in the eyes of Narkomos. It created a blank slate for the promotion of *sotsiialne vykhovannia* (*sotsvykh*), the principle of "social upbringing." Defined by the congress as "the state protection and state embrace of all children," this conviction motivated Narkomos to create children's buildings as "universal social–pedagogical centres," in which the state would assume the role of guardian. As chapter 2 argued, the end of the civil war and the introduction of the New Economic Policy (NEP) brought some normalization in educational affairs, but it also meant a decline in the number of children's buildings and what the congress lamented as a reduction in the influence of the state and strengthening of a negative role of the family.

The congress made clear, however, that Narkomos had not given up on its impulse for guided child rearing. It sought to orient schools to the task of social upbringing. They would not be mere places of learning, but places of citizenship training. Ultimately, the congress advised that this task would be accomplished by youth Communist organizations. However, the number of Komsomol organizations was still small, and the number of its subsidiary Young Pioneer troops even smaller. In the city of Myronivka (Kyiv region), for example, the Young Pioneer detachment suffered from weak support from its sponsor, a local sugar refinery. Its activities remained entirely detached from the school.[3] Recognizing shortcomings such as this, the congress urged instructors to place primary emphasis on school curriculum. It directed them to continue the struggle "for the complete rebuilding of a revolutionary pedagogy on a material basis."[4] The essential vehicle for this new pedagogy was instruction by the complex method in the Ukrainian language. The congress envisioned the tying of the complexes to Young Pioneer group activity, where it existed, but, more generally, to issues of production. In the absence of a children's movement, the school would take on its mission: to foster ties with surrounding activity, "with the proletarian and landless peasant society and its productive interests." The congress called upon teachers to innovate, experiment, and make use of hands-on methods associated with productive activities.

This issue of curricular transformation was at the heart of all discussion among pedagogical circles in the 1920s. Ukrainization was a means towards this end. However, a number of practical problems confronted the would-be reformers. The congress detailed several: overburdened teachers, an almost complete absence of funds for instructional training in the schools, shortages of literature, teachers' inability to adapt to the new prescribed methods, and low relative enrolment in rural areas.[5] Funding also remained a problem. Schools relied on local governments for budgetary allotments, and although the congress reported that the amount of money assigned to schools had increased from 19 to 32 million rubles in the 1924–5 school year, more funding was needed for teacher training and the purchase of books and school supplies.

A Holovsotsvykh report on the main tasks for the 1925–6 school year also added to the list of deficiencies that the teachers' congress had raised. For its pedagogical mission to succeed, Narkomos desired universal enrolment of children from eight to eleven years old. For the time being, it concentrated on the enrolment of early school-aged children. At the beginning of the 1925–6 school year, Holovsotsvykh estimated that 457,000 eight-year-old and 300,000 nine-year-old children in the republic were not attending school. To enrol them, schools would have to open 5,000 more groups (classes).[6] This objective required local education sections to build new schools, hire teachers, and procure textbooks. Furthermore, while Holovsotsvykh was primarily concerned with an expansion of the first four years of schooling, ultimately it needed to increase the number of full seven-year schools. In 1925–6, there were approximately thirty groups for every seven-year school. To keep this proportion constant, Narkomos would have to increase the number of these schools too.

The existing state of school affairs was less than ideal. Authorities often housed schools in buildings not meant for instruction, in dilapidated structures or peasant homes. Local education sections were responsible for submitting their own orders to the state publishing house for textbooks, but had little money to pay for new literature.[7] General publication of children's literature was still negligible and school libraries poorly stocked. Schools lacked even the most basic supplies: tables, benches, and desks, to say nothing of "extras" like maps, charts, and writing implements. Holovsotsvykh demanded an account of regional spending to ensure that its sections were providing funds for supply of these items as best as they could. Within the classroom, Holovsotsvykh dictated that teachers instruct no more than forty students. If it was necessary to burden teachers with large numbers of students (as it often was), it was better that they take on one large group rather than two groups that together surpassed this forty-student limit.

Holovsotsvykh also set up auxiliary schools for children who were falling behind. It resolved that Narkomos must provide enough of these remedial schools to meet the needs of approximately 3 per cent of the school-aged children. Without them, it maintained, the work of "normal" children would falter. Holovsotsvykh assumed budgetary responsibility for these schools, as well as schools for juvenile offenders and the blind and the deaf.[8] Holovsotsvykh's primary slogan was the "normalization of work" and, therefore, its operating rationale was to limit distractions away from the schools' chief task: the use of a new, revolutionary pedagogy.

Were schools able to set curricular and methodological affairs in order? Education inspectors' lack of preparation for evaluating Ukrainization has already been discussed. Few were equipped to investigate a school's general activities as well. At a meeting of the Kyiv province's teachers in March 1925, one attendee, Slutsky, argued that the inspectors rarely did their jobs, even if they had the skills to do so.[9] He maintained that some provincial inspectors did not tour village schools or even give instructions to their regional counterparts to do so, but attended only meetings of the inspectorate. Furthermore, many were new graduates of pedagogical schools or occupied positions as heads of schools but had no teaching experience or political training. He suggested that a provincial section employ only former teachers as inspectors and provide them with a readily available form of transportation. Although Holovsotsvykh mandated implementation of its program, it relied upon the initiative of local inspectors to ensure that schools were carrying out its orders. Due to their inexperience, even those who did regularly carry out inspections may have been unable to appreciate the particular challenge of teaching by the new progressive methodology or, more importantly, unable to suggest remedies.

Local authorities also balked at formulating their own applications of the methodology Holovsotsvykh prescribed. Holovsotsvykh intended all teachers to undergo training by the complex method and work out curriculum for their schools. Lypovytsky, another delegate to the Kyiv provincial meeting, reported that directors of the training programs remained dissatisfied with the program for retraining and wanted more detailed and specific plans to pass on to the teachers.[10] Therefore, they waited for instruction from the provincial education section in Kyiv, and the complexes that educators did organize became muddled: "We see from [local teachers'] conferences that while some complexes are organized for the future, others will be stuck in the past. In some districts there may be a complex on the 'February Revolution,' but they will work out something completely different in addition to it."[11] Lypovytsky suggested that it was up to district and school administrators to use the program to "independently revolutionize" their activities. It was, however, this very sort of independence that, ironically, both unnerved teachers and school directors and yet allowed them to resist prescriptions for a progressive pedagogy. Educators requested a neatly defined program, not descriptive directives. They worked out complexes as they understood them, but ones largely bereft of the transformative spirit Holovsotsvykh envisioned.

Notwithstanding the anxiety expressed at these conferences, some exceptional schools did seek to implement a progressive pedagogy. A 1925 report on the state of education in the Bila Tserkva region found that in the Fastiv District Labour School, teachers had instituted a progressive curriculum, but had taken an incremental approach similar to their gradual introduction of Ukrainian-language instruction. They set up an entirely new program in the younger grades, but conceded only partial instruction in the "laboratory method."[12] Similarly, the teachers began full Ukrainian-language instruction only in the first grade. The two aspects of the

Narkomos program were supposed to work in concert with one another. Although teachers at this school demonstrated their commitment to both, they advocated a measured transition, given the difficulty involved in achieving both immediately.

Educators also pushed progressive pedagogy most in the younger grades of the Skvyra District Labour School. Provincial inspectors reported that during a complex on Shevchenko and the February Revolution for the fourth grade, "the group of 64 children was so completely delighted with the work and so thoroughly engaged with the material that, in general, it was evident the leader had skillfully carried out the correct plan." Here too the link between Ukrainization and the complex system is apparent in the successful application of a complex on Shevchenko. This school, like the larger experimental schools in the republic's main cities, served as a model for other schools in the district. At meetings of the district pedagogical council, administrators reported on the school's work and sought to guide that of more rural schools. If progressive pedagogy was going to succeed, schools in the district centres would have to embrace it first and promote its spread. However, it is again noteworthy that even these model schools saw the dual implementation of this pedagogy and Ukrainian-centred instruction as a significant challenge.

Raising Teachers' Qualifications

Building socialism required Narkomos and its subsidiary organs to equip its schools appropriately. A call for pedagogical innovation meant little if teachers were unprepared to accomplish it. They needed to modify the way they taught, and did so only reluctantly. It was not until the summer of 1923 that systematic work on the raising of pedagogical qualifications began in earnest, mostly in the form of conferences and study circles.[13] In 1924, courses on methodology and self-study were held throughout Soviet Ukraine. Partly in response to teachers' demands for publication of pedagogical literature and the establishment of pedagogical libraries, Narkomos began to publish the journal *Radianska osvita* and the teachers' union released the newspaper *Narodnii uchytel*. However, only teachers working in the major cities were able to read these publications with any regularity.

The year 1925 witnessed heightened activity in the drive for teacher preparation. Deputy Commissar of Education Riappo issued orders in April for all provincial sections to oversee more comprehensive summer courses for primary school teachers.[14] Regional sections assumed direct responsibility for the administration of the courses. In addition, Narkomos ordered that the courses take place in the "national language" of the teachers and that regional sections pay for the travel of ethnic-minority teachers to larger, consolidated classes in urban centres.

A local education section's ability to meet Narkomos's mandate depended on a variety of practical considerations. The Chernihiv Provincial Education Section

Delegates from the Kharkiv province at the First All-Ukrainian Teachers' Congress, January 1925. In the centre of the third row, with the goatee, is the Ukrainian People's Commissar of Education Oleksandr Shumsky. To his left is Fedir Uharov (head of the All-Ukrainian Trade Union Council). *Pershyi Vseukraïns's'kyi uchytel's'kyi z'izd* (Kharkiv: Derzhavne vydavnytstvo Ukraïny, 1925), xxx.

formed a bureau for teacher retraining, but its regional sections did not have the money to support regular courses at the lower level.[15] Furthermore, district libraries in the province had almost no pedagogical books for teachers seeking material on their own. Individual initiative counted, of course. Nizhyn regional officials found a way to organize several pedagogical courses, hold conferences, and support the work of teacher study circles. According to the provincial administration, some 286 study circles were active in the whole province, with 18 to 20 participants in each circle. Participants were supposed to read recommended literature, evaluate each other's pedagogical work, and familiarize themselves with local economic questions and agricultural data. However, the Chernihiv report concluded that few had engaged in "planned, systematic, and deep work" and most took the opportunity to complain about their own overwork and poorly supplied libraries. Teachers found little time to significantly engage in these study circles and few resources to help them in their efforts.

Nevertheless, provincial sections continued to design courses that emphasized self-study. The Volyn province organized a congress bringing together district organizers of study groups and teachers undergoing retraining.[16] An April 1925 plan for the congress's work stressed that it would not hold courses specifically for retraining, but would seek to instruct participants in skills necessary for "self-training." Most of the activity of the congress would take place in work groups, with only three summary reports given to the whole congress. Although teachers had some input on the congress's agenda, it would work generally according to a provincial strategy devised by the Zhytomyr education section that gave a central role to "local studies of production" (*vyrobnychne kraieznavstvo*). In the case of the Volyn province, this approach meant an orientation towards agriculture. The congress planners proposed that teachers take part in excursions to observe agricultural work.[17] They believed that schoolchildren should not just study production abstractly, but had to learn about it first-hand. They intended the teachers' trips to the countryside to function as lessons in how to conduct this sort of instruction.

Narkomos officials emphasized kraieznavstvo as the foundation of new instruction. It was, the Volyn provincial congress planners believed, "the most important task in education" and one that they saw at the heart of teacher training. However, their instruction in this critical methodology was decidedly non-specific. They did not mean for the congress to spell out exactly how this instruction would take place, but rather sought to provide teachers with the fundamentals of such an approach. The congress proposed that teachers employ a "shock program," according to which they would adapt the general program to local needs and rapidly transform their work in the schools. For example, in order to teach agriculture, they would draw from their experience in the congress's excursion to oversee their students' cultivation of garden plots and to lead tours in the immediate countryside. The congress also included information on integrating the Communist children's movement into school life and kraieznavstvo. Tying schoolwork to Young Leninist activity would strengthen and broaden the new progressive pedagogy and the push towards the study of "socially productive labour."

Budnov, a speaker at the March 1925 Kyiv provincial teachers' conference, cited comments by Nadezhda Krupskaia (Lenin's widow and a key figure in the field of education) at the First All-Union Conference on Retraining that all teachers must become experts in local studies (Russian – *kraevedy*; Ukrainian – *kraieznavtsi*). The Holovsotsvykh program emphasized the need to localize educational material, but it was up to the teachers themselves to be promoters of kraieznavstvo: "the new program functions as only a skeleton which needs to be given living flesh of local studies material."[18] Teachers needed to connect all complexes to local life. Budnov also cautioned against the study of history and folk customs and lauded an investigation of labour activity. The Holovsotsvykh program demanded this study of labour. The teachers' task was to apply this directive to their own locale. Budnov recommended broadening their study to the whole district, but not beyond. By limiting the study this way, they and their students would focus their observations on what was familiar. Educators had to privilege direct examination above all else. When the students advanced, they would ask them to draw connections to the region and the republic beyond.

There was a danger that educators' emphasis on teacher self-training and independent activity in the schools might have negative consequences. Muzychenko, also a speaker at the Kyiv provincial conference, warned that education sections had to ensure that teachers did not turn kraieznavstvo to ethnography, geography, and the study of olden times.[19] Another participant, Kaminsky, argued that Narkomos must supply teachers with concrete and specific kraieznavstvo material so that teachers would not pick their own disparate materials. He recommended that teachers undergo a full year of instruction in correspondence courses if Narkomos had any hope of setting up instruction in kraieznavstvo complexes. Muzychenko and others added that the number of kraieznavstvo experts outside the city of Kyiv was still small and the success of the program would depend on the cooperation among teachers, ties among central and provincial institutions, and, perhaps most importantly, a revamping of pedagogical training. They insisted that the rationale of all study, whether self-motivated or organized by Narkomos, should be "Soviet building" through kraieznavstvo, not the ethnographic romanticism of the past.

Social Upbringing through Kraieznavstvo

Educators such as Budnov favoured kraieznavstvo so greatly because they claimed it offered a means to ensure that Soviet Ukraine's young citizens participated in the building of socialism. In a remarkable statement that contrasts sharply with the accepted understanding of the command-and-control Stalinism to come, Budnov insisted that kraieznavstvo was "not accidental, not a temporary passion, not a fashion, but rather a natural consequence of the entire internal policy of Soviet power, a policy based and built on decentralization."[20] Teachers, children, and the general public would assume responsibility for surveying the challenges that faced their locality and using the information they gained to suggest solutions to Soviet authorities. Teachers would instruct children in how to conduct kraieznavstvo studies by themselves and form their own circles to coordinate and promote kraieznavstvo.

As has been argued above, advocates of kraieznavstvo believed that the construction of a socialist society and economy required that citizens be fully aware of the republic's revolutionary political history and productive potential. Ukrainian-area studies provided the rationale for a transfer to the complex system. Ukrainization exams for civil servants, trade union members, and party officials not only tested literacy in the Ukrainian language, but also proficiency in Ukrainian studies (knowledge of Ukrainian literature, history of revolutionary movements, geography, economy, etc.). In the schools, Narkomos planned for children to acquire this knowledge at an early age. It firmly linked language study to the study of a school's region and to that of wider Ukraine.

Social studies, as an aspect of kraieznavstvo, constituted the principal discipline involved in this task of training the next generation for the building of socialism. Progressive educators assigned language study a critical but supporting role. In a December 1925 assessment of the state of Ukrainization in the Vasylkiv District Labour School, the school head, Chavdarov, argued that "language is not a goal in itself and therefore the tie with social studies is primary."[21] Children were to study, as much as possible, the "living language." By this, educators meant a language close to that spoken by contemporary Ukrainians, purged of archaisms and artificial constructions.

Again, teachers had to learn how to teach kraieznavstvo properly. A Kyiv regional report on teacher training argued that teachers, aware of Narkomos's emphasis on the complex system, were increasingly interested in retraining. However, the report insisted it was not enough for provincial sections to introduce teachers to models of the new approach. Kraieznavstvo material was necessary for the development of complexes that "children must know about production in our Republic and especially in their own district."[22] It recommended that district education sections, through their methodological committees, oversee the creation of small groups (*kushchi*) of teachers to collect kraieznavstvo material. These groups were to evaluate "territorial specifics" through direct observation, and to consider how they might be integrated into complexes and what sort of "verbal or illustrative" work could be developed. While the district methodological committee would compile a catalogue of the general characteristics of the district with the help of local intelligentsia, each school's faculty would decide what details and subthemes might be used in a given complex.[23] The establishment of the complex system, the new Soviet school in general, depended on the success of Ukrainian studies, localized in the first instance and then broadened to the republican level.

While the Young Pioneer organization offered straightforward political training outside the schools, Narkomos argued that the complex system, infused with local material, would fulfill its vision of "social upbringing" inside the school. Forced to abandon its plans to assume a direct role in parenting through the establishment of children's buildings, the Administration for Social Upbringing (*Upravlinnia sotsiialnoho vykhovannia – Uprsotsvykh*, Narkomos's new abbreviation for its division of primary schooling) held that a school curriculum based on experience, an awareness of local labour and production, and Ukrainian studies would provide children with the civic education necessary for participation in the "building of socialism." For example, planned complexes on Shevchenko and the February Revolution for the 1927–8 academic year offered teachers an opportunity to give children political lessons. First, Uprsotsvykh explicitly linked the two subjects. In its interpretation, the February Revolution fulfilled the vision of Shevchenko's early nineteenth-century struggle against tsarism and the aristocracy. Regarding the February Revolution, Uprsotsvykh recommended that teachers discuss events in Ukraine, including the Ukrainian Central Rada, the revolt against Hetman Skoropadsky's regime, banditry under the UNR Directory, Petliurism, and the relationship between the USSR and UkrSSR.[24] The Uprsotsvykh guide saw the objective of this joint complex as the cultivation of "disgust for social and national subjugation, disgust for national enmities, and a consciousness of the class essence of Shevchenko's works." It suggested that children read Shevchenko's works and biography, as well as works on serfdom, and memoirs and interviews of those who participated in war and the February Revolution. Of course, according to the complex system methodology, work could not be confined just to the classroom. Children were to take excursions to pre-revolutionary landlord estates to witness the history of serfdom first-hand and publish declamations and wall newspapers recounting the events of the revolution in Ukraine and its promise. Above all, Uprsotsvykh emphasized that the "emotional moment" should predominate in all class exercises. Inspiration was primary.

Further instructions sought to make the connection between schoolwork and activity even more explicit. Another program on Shevchenko and the February Revolution directed children to collect stories from their parents about their participation in the war, and determine for whom they fought and for what reason. The purpose of this technique was "to emphasize that the participation of peasants and workers in the war was for the tsar their final subjugation and spoil."[25] Of course, the interviews may well have turned up disquieting material about parents who fought in the tsarist army only to then join Ukrainian nationalist forces or peasant bands opposed to Bolshevik rule. The Uprsotsvykh program gave no advice to school administrators or teachers on how to handle such dangers. Narkomos viewed such political lessons as absolutely necessary, but the very latitude of the complex system presented a dilemma. For the present, educators' trust in the potential of progressive pedagogy displaced these concerns.

A complex on the October Revolution sought to tie instruction to the goals of the revolution. Its prescribed exercises, however, also carried risks. The significance of the complex was obvious. The 1927–8 Uprsotsvykh program insisted that teachers had to use the complex to explain the political meaning of "power in the hands of the workers and peasants" and the role of revolutionary organizations. It also emphasized the importance of the "emotional experience" to instruction, recommending that material for the complex be drawn from local life.²⁶ Elsewhere, it suggested that rural students needed to understand how the October Revolution benefited landless and middle peasants. It proposed having children ask their parents how much land they had prior to the October Revolution and how much they had after the revolution. It assumed that "after having thought about this information in groups, children will very easily understand what the October Revolution gave the peasants and that V. I. Lenin led it."²⁷ Presumably, formerly prosperous parents would have realized the jeopardy involved in answering their children's questions honestly, or teachers would have intervened to limit their children's contribution to class. The boldness of the complex system is, however, striking. Educational planners apparently trusted that the benefits of the October Revolution would be apparent to most and that those who disagreed would take heed.

Local education inspectorates had long been responsible for monitoring the schools' success in making use of locally drafted variants of the central guide for complex instruction. The Kyiv Regional Inspectorate attempted to clarify what complex instruction meant in a 1926 circular it sent out to the heads of all *trudshkoly* (labour schools) under its jurisdiction. Fundamentally, complex instruction meant "study of living items with the assistance of [book] knowledge."²⁸ The best way to provide this sort of training, the inspectorate maintained, was to have children research the environment around them, to do "less talking, more research." Its institution was absolutely necessary because "in the conditions of class war," children had to be equipped with a "class-organizational reflex" to force a change in social relations. The inspectorate, and its more active counterparts across the republic, meant for children to be the activists of the future, to continue the revolution by reordering society. Advocates of the complex system viewed its embrace of applied know-how (*uminnia*) as more beneficial than strict knowledge (*znannia*). Equipped with this training, children would quickly move to their roles as rational organizers of a socialist society. The young researchers of labour would become conscious labourers and managers of labour themselves.

Ideally, the incorporation of local material would orient the school towards the principal fields of production in a given area: for example, wheat cultivation, logging, and coal mining. It was more difficult for schools located in residential and commercial city centres to claim such an orientation than those in industrial or rural areas. The director of Kyiv Labour School No. 1, Durdukivsky, maintained in 1925 that in the absence of appropriate "conditions," his school embraced a generalized "social studies" direction.²⁹ Durdukivsky conceded that the school had not yet set up a comprehensive system, but insisted that teachers were being trained to do so and were leading students on excursions to nearby factories. For the time being, students would mostly study disciplines separately, but social studies, however diluted of its "active" nature, still dominated the school curriculum and guided its direction. Durdukivsky insisted that the "proletarianization" of the school was under way and that the poradnyk was "only a guide, not a dogmatic tool."

Apart from class exercises, Narkomos expected teachers to ensure children's participation in Ukrainian Soviet society. Again, the emphasis of activities supervised by the school was local. The Kharkiv Regional Education Section reported that in the 1926–7 school year, the most successful area of public work was the schools' maintenance of ties with community enterprises.[30] Urban schools also retained direct affiliation with rural schools, simultaneously preserving the smychka and their own cultural leadership. However, beyond the celebration of political holidays, the schools did little. The Kharkiv report evaluated the association of regional schools with a number of public activities, among them participation in Soviet elections, a sowing campaign, and the struggle against saboteurs. Schools had met their "goals" in all by less than 25 per cent.[31] Overall, the report concluded, the schools' work in public activity was sporadic and "isolated from Soviet society and leadership." It pointed to the weakness of the complex system and underscored a need to further localize material. The implicit judgment was that an effective complex system, grounded in local study, would encourage political work, and political work, in turn, would support the complex system.

Reform at the Expense of Formal Knowledge?

The procedure for establishing a complex system of instruction remained vague, and purposefully so. What may have appeared to be a fanciful product of Narkomos ruminations in fact had a firm grounding in Western, progressive, pedagogical theory. However, it had never been applied on the sort of mass scale that Narkomos educators envisioned for Ukraine and, ambiguous or not, it was a task left to local officials to work out the new methodology and cast it in a Soviet mould. In the confusion that followed, parents and individual officials began to point to the system's failure to meet basic educational goals.

Although Narkomos was pushing through a major reform of education, the expectations of parents remained essentially the same. Schools had to provide fundamental knowledge. According to the report of one school director, Pasika, parents were afraid that the overcrowded public schools were not teaching their children the basic skills of reading, writing, and arithmetic. As a result, they were hiring private teachers and forming independent study groups.[32] Pasika warned his audience at a 1925–6 meeting of Kyiv district labour school heads that this practice threatened Narkomos control, and said he hoped that salvation would ultimately be found in the complex system. However, in spite of some discussion of this methodology in teacher conferences, Narkomos had not yet published a new curricular schedule. Pasika conceded that the complex system was mostly a matter of "idle chatter." Even worse, the "ability and knowledge of children in the third and fourth grades in particular do not correspond with the state minimum." According to this report, teachers were providing neither *uminnia* (skill) nor *znavstvo* (knowledge).

While Pasika maintained that only the full transfer to the complex system would increase the Soviet school's authority among the population, his account reveals that teachers had very little idea how to accomplish this. They simply knew that the old methodology was bad. When they tried to implement the complex system, some just worked from the generalized Uprsotsvykh guide or with entirely abstract material. For example, students studied literature on tropical rain forests rather than observe the logging industry in their own districts.[33] Other teachers abandoned methodology altogether or worked only with those students who showed promise. The result was a collapse of discipline and an increase in truancy.

Concerns about children's acquisition of basic skills persisted well into the late 1920s. A 1928 report by the Kharkiv Regional Education Section continued to stress the weak tie between "formal knowledge" and the complexes.[34] Although it found reading in native-language classes (Ukrainian for the majority of schools in the region) to be satisfactory, it concluded that writing was much worse. Very rarely did students, even in the oldest groups, write grammatically. Furthermore, although students did study literature under the complex system, teachers seldom planned work or set defined themes. In any event, students' knowledge of both grammar and analysis of literature did not conform to the minimum set by the Uprsotsvykh guide. On a general level, the Kharkiv authorities estimated, village schools were carrying out only 60 per cent of the official program of study.

In such an environment, parents naturally grew angry. Vasylenko, another district labour school director at the 1925–6 Kyiv regional meeting, cautioned that "the school is not a place for idle talk. When parents are emphasizing that children are not gaining knowledge, then it is necessary to listen."[35] The shortcomings presented by Pasika had to be addressed immediately or schools risked losing the authority they had. Vasylenko similarly did not suggest abandoning the complex method, but rather argued for its acceleration through a re-emphasis on kraieznavstvo study and public work. Again, the children's best education would come through interaction with their surrounding environment and the wider Ukrainian republic.

Even in the area broadly considered kraieznavstvo, there were significant disappointments. In rural schools in the Kharkiv region, children demonstrated some knowledge of general physical geography, but knew very little about the village, district, and region.[36] Their knowledge of the political economy was devoid of historical perspective and context. A report by the Kyiv regional education inspector concluded that in the Ivankivka district (Kyiv region), the four-year school had given little place to the study of the local environment and children were generally not engaged in contemporary life.[37] In another school, students could not name any local bodies of water. When pressed, one student named the Black Sea, but placed it in Japan. They knew about the October holiday, but had no idea that it was to commemorate a revolution, and thought Soviet Commissar of War Mikhail Frunze was a former tsar. The inspector concluded that students needed to spend much more time studying the school's surroundings, and, at the very least, they should be aware of prominent features of the republic, such as the Black Sea and the Dnipro River.[38]

A 1927 inspector's report on the Baryshpil (now Boryspil) district in the Kyiv region criticized one school for expanding kraieznavstvo too greatly: students were studying geographic features of the world, "but they do not know about 'nearby Ukraine.' Local material, the agricultural surroundings, are not studied."[39] In another school, students were studying a geography primer on Ukraine, but understood it poorly. Students' familiarity with their immediate environment shaped their understanding of Ukraine. Each region was a part of a larger, wholly integral Ukrainian land.

Another report by the Kyiv Regional Inspectorate of the Vasylkiv district concluded that the plans for transfer to the complex system were too imprecise and that it was only in the district trudshkoly that teachers incorporated concrete material in their lesson plans for the complexes.[40] A six-day seminar in the district had apparently refined the regional plan, but the regional inspectorate required that schools individualize their own plans, specifically including local material for kraieznavstvo work. According to a 1925 Kyiv provincial report, the Myronivka District Labour School implemented the complex method in the younger groups, but, during the course of the first trimester, teachers of this advanced school switched to instruction by subject area because of the large size of classes and shifts in faculty personnel.[41] School leaders pledged to return to the progressive Dalton Plan in the coming trimester. Other schools observed by the education inspectors in the district used some hybrid of complex and traditional methodology. The Myronivka seven-year school's ambition was exceptional.

It is difficult to see how teachers had time to collect material for a task that already appeared to them ill-defined. One district labour school director complained that the regional inspectorate's expectations were too high, arguing that, at the very least, school directors should be excused from their teaching duties so that they might concentrate on administration of methodology in their schools.[42] Some teachers openly suggested a return to the old school; others made do as best they could. The inspectorate's report on the Vasylkiv district suggests as much.

Schools continued to divide class time by subject area, giving minimal attention to the creation of complexes organized by theme.[43] When they did use complexes, they often retained old methods. Thus, one teacher in a rural school in the district proposed a complex on local agriculture, but the lesson simply consisted of her reading out loud a passage on the cultivation of hemp.[44] The teacher made no provision for the children to observe agricultural activities in the village and apparently did not include possible exercises in writing, arithmetic, and social studies. It was a complex in name alone, void of pedagogical innovation, and – perhaps of greater concern – one that did not allow students to work on basic skills.

Aside from professional conferences, teachers had little opportunity to study the new methodology. At an April 1925 meeting of the teachers' union, Robos, speakers emphasized that teachers were unable to buy pedagogical publications and that concerns for retraining had to be narrowed if teachers were expected to cope.[45] Teachers in the Myronivka District Labour School participated in group training during breaks, but they had to pass around personal copies of new literature to review or borrow publications from the chief employer in the city, the sugar refinery.[46] The amount of new literature in the school library was so small that "really one must speak of 'creating' a library, a teacher and student library."

Therefore, even if schools had well-trained teachers, they needed to equip them properly to succeed. Schools had trouble procuring not only pedagogical publications, but also the textbooks necessary for instruction in class. During 1920–2, there were almost no new publications released in Ukraine, and teachers worked largely with old textbooks. In 1923–4, eighty-two textbooks were released (seventy-nine in the Ukrainian language), but they were primarily old textbooks that were adapted and "only slightly Sovietized."[47] It was only for the 1924–5 school year that Narkomos reworked and partly adjusted textbooks for the complex program of instruction. The DVU, the state publishing house, released 105 textbook titles (62 in Ukrainian) and 37 titles for teacher training. However, the DVU printed a relatively small number of runs for these titles, and, as the Myronivka case illustrates, schools outside large urban centres had difficulty acquiring them.

It fell to teachers and school administrators to perfect the complex system. Narkomos principally blamed teachers for the methodology's failures. The director of the Ivankivka District Labour School, Kryvenko, maintained at the Kyiv regional meeting of school heads that "the teacher does not have a sense of responsibility for his work, no one controls it and [the work] remains dependent upon the unsupervised consciousness of this very worker."[48] He further noted that teachers' work was hampered by an alarming shortage of books, and lamented the fact that students were forced to buy their own. Ironically, it was the very latitude of the complex system that seemed to have troubled him most. Without any direct guidance, and unable to use sanctioned literature, teachers were bound to err. Kryvenko's school is included in a 1926 report of the Kyiv regional inspector. His assessment was generally positive, but it also cited cases where teachers did not allow students to participate in the presentation of material, "thus paralyzing in part the initiative of the children and their self-activity."[49] It is unknown whether this strict style of classroom management was due to Kryvenko's intervention. Regardless, there was little chance of schools' realizing the complex system if teachers kept such an arrangement.

Good Teachers in Short Supply

Finding a teacher well trained in Ukrainian was important, but, for most schools, not as important as finding one with acceptable pedagogical qualifications. Regional inspectors regularly reported on teachers' poor skills, improper behaviour, and public drunkenness, as well as more political concerns, such as their religiosity or affiliation with village kulaks. The Kyiv regional inspector labelled one kraieznavstvo teacher's scolding of students and general laziness in the classroom as "anti-pedagogical behaviour."[50] Such charges carried a definite connotation of something more sinister than just bad teaching. Narkomos considered a poor pedagogue fundamentally un-Soviet, a de facto adversary to its campaign to transform culture. As noted in chapter 2, Narkomos still worried about teachers' political commitment to socialism anyhow, due to their allegiance to counter-revolutionary parties during the civil war. Shumsky had contended that teachers had reformed themselves, yet advised evaluations of their political training and Komsomol oversight of their activities.

Of particular concern to education officials was the situation when a teacher acquired authority in a community and then abused it. An anonymous letter reportedly published in a rural newspaper came to the attention of Uprsotsvykh in 1926. It claimed that peasants in a village in the Ivankivka district (Kyiv region) had recognized the labour school director, Bondarenko, as a community leader. They expected him to uncover "all kinds of lies and evil" in the village; instead, he committed them himself.[51] He allegedly propositioned a widow, drank heavily, and beat and expelled students from the local Liknep program. The letter concluded "it is necessary to say that there is no place for this comrade in the village leadership and teachers' ranks, people who always stand on the side of the victors of October." The then-deputy head of Uprsotsvykh, Vasyl Arnautov, ordered the Kyiv Regional Inspectorate to investigate the matter. Teachers were important representatives of Soviet power in rural Ukraine. Narkomos could not afford to have them further alienate the population.

It was problematic, then, outside of prominent urban and experimental schools, for any teacher to meet the dual challenge of instruction in the Ukrainian language and the institution of the complex system. Even if teachers were not grossly irresponsible, those with a strong commitment to Ukrainization and pedagogical training high enough to realize an ambiguously defined progressive methodology were rare. Indeed, there were few teachers willing to serve in rural Ukraine at all. The Kyiv regional inspector reported in May 1926 that it took a month longer than planned to appoint a new head for the Durdakiv Labour School because of an absence of candidates. Furthermore, it could not find a substitute for a second teacher it wished to fire. Prospective teachers in Kyiv simply had no interest in working in a village for an indefinite period of time.[52] Arnautov also recognized, in a letter he wrote to the editors of the newspaper *Radianske selo,* that "the number of qualified teachers among us is insufficient and that they do not hurry very much to the village, to work in conditions [that are] generally more difficult than in the city."[53] Schools simply often had to make do with incomplete staff.

When communities that believed in the necessity of schooling had good teachers, they tried to hang on to them. In September 1927, parents at Kyiv Labour School No. 47 petitioned Narkomos to keep the head of their school, Ostromensky. The regional education inspector had designated Ostromensky for transfer to the Kyiv Pedagogical Institute two weeks prior to the beginning of the academic year. In the parents' letter, they praised the school head for his considerable skill in grappling with new demands of the Soviet school: "He had displayed a talent in the sotsvykh [primary school] system ... while carrying out individual, difficult responsibilities in the formulation of a program, development and perfection of methods of work, and drafting and publication of textbooks."[54] As evidence of his success, they pointed to the fact that in the previous year, 80 per cent of the graduates of the labour school were accepted into secondary, vocational schools. Not only had Ostromensky reformed the school curriculum, but he had also ensured that the children still acquired the basic skills necessary for advancement. This, of course, was ostensibly the objective of the complex system, but few teachers understood it enough to make it work properly. Apparently, Narkomos recognized this deficiency, because the parents' petition was denied. Ostromensky was needed to train the next generation of teachers.

Conversely, some communities did not appreciate attempts at a reorganization of education. A local party committee in the Chernkhiakhiv district (Volyn region) attempted to transfer the rest day for the schoolchildren from Sunday to another day in the week. According to a May 1929 report by the regional party committee, general attendance at the school quickly dropped 40 to 50 per cent after the shift.[55] Regional party officials intervened and issued orders to suspend the change until the beginning of the next school year. They did not disagree with the premise of the district decision, but rather claimed that district officials needed to undertake proper "agitation and explanatory work." Clearly, a significant portion of the district population, whether out of religiosity or tradition, valued the Sabbath (or its violation) enough to boycott schools. The KP(b)U intended to use the new Soviet school as a vehicle to change such long-held, popular sentiments by beginning the restructuring of society with this institution.

Personal animosities and jealousies sometimes came into play in a community's dealings with teachers. Lower-level officials acted to suppress teachers who became too bold. In the Ripky district (Chernihiv region), the district education inspector and head of the district executive committee presidium issued orders in September 1929 for the dismissal and transfer of a total of seven teachers. According to the regional party committee that investigated the affair, the inspector and presidium head held "unpleasant, bureaucratic, and callous views" towards these teachers.[56] It apparently found the drive of these teachers unsettling, because its orders were "especially directed against teachers who worked for the economic and legal defence of the interests of teachers." Other members of the teachers' union reportedly supported the decision for dismissal of the teachers, hoping to gain something for themselves. The committee alleged that the teachers had made false charges, while at the same time demanding increased apartment space. As a result, the regional party apparat ordered the dismissal of the district inspector and presidium head and reappointment of the teachers.[57] It ultimately judged that activist teachers should be supported within limits and that, at least in this instance, personal rancour should not play a part in the dismissal of teachers who were needed so desperately in rural Soviet Ukraine.

Incomplete Ukrainization as an Impediment to Pedagogical Reform

The switch to Ukrainian-language instruction was supposed to make all this easier. Narkomos administrators maintained that if schools instructed children in their native language, they would produce a more skilled and conscious agricultural or industrial worker capable of entering intermediate leadership positions after secondary vocational schooling or acquiring further training and education. It also held that the new pedagogy would benefit Ukrainian-language study, breaking the boredom of study by rote and allowing children to understand the importance of language expression through a demonstration of its relationship with other disciplines.

In any given complex, language study assumed an important and fundamentally integrating role. In the complex on Shevchenko and the February Revolution discussed above, the Uprsotsvykh program asked students to read original works of Shevchenko and to draft their own interpretations of his work for publication in the school's wall newspaper. Furthermore, the teachers were to write sentences and words drawn from the children's interviews with their parents on the school blackboard for discussion.⁵⁸ Uprsotsvykh intended activity to function as the basis for language analysis and grammar exercises, as well as lessons in social studies, mathematics, and the natural sciences.

As has already been demonstrated, conventional forms of pedagogy often persisted. Teachers continued to look to textbooks for classroom drills, and blamed the lack of Ukrainian-language literature for the failure of "complexes." The head of the Vasylkiv District Labour School complained that among the school library's collection of 2,000 books, there were only 200 Ukrainian lesson books at the end of 1925.⁵⁹ This shortage, he suggested, significantly complicated the school's work, then confined to introducing one complex per semester. Books were less necessary for the complex method, but they still functioned as vital references for active study. Without books, Shevchenko had little significance.

The push to train teachers in complex methodology also coincided with the drive for Ukrainization. The majority of teachers in Ukraine were to teach in the Ukrainian language. Language would be their tool to disseminate new knowledge through complexes to Ukrainian-speaking children, persuade the local population of the school's worth, and involve society as a whole in the lofty task of building socialism. According to the theory propounded by Narkomos officials, knowledge of Ukrainian was one element that would allow teachers to most effectively perform all that was asked of them. Therefore, it was a source of great frustration to planners of the April 1925 Volyn provincial congress for teacher retraining that there was almost no material on the study of language by the complex method.⁶⁰ They recommended the congress seek ways to detail and add to the program. How could Ukrainian children be taught by the complex program if teachers had no instructions on how to refine their language skills under this program? What would new kraieznavstvo knowledge mean, for example, if children could not correctly repeat and articulate it in their native language? Instruction by the complex system demanded the integration of all subject areas into thematic wholes. Language had to be a part of this equation.

Some of the many teachers who actively or passively resisted use of the new pedagogy also resisted teaching in Ukrainian. Instruction in both the complex system and the Ukrainian language meant a fundamental shift in the way they had taught. Prodded by education officials to study and train themselves and threatened with dismissal for failure, these teachers reacted negatively. Their authority had been premised on their strict maintenance of classroom discipline and assignment of high prestige to the fluent use of Russian. The new requirements fundamentally undermined these practices.

Petro Lukashenko, the senior Kyiv provincial inspector, reported at the March 1925 provincial teachers' meeting that in Bila Tserkva, near Kyiv, local authorities had retained the head of a Russian school and a former gymnasium. Lukashenko maintained that this failure to remove him was a serious mistake: indeed, the director was both a supporter of monarchism and an opponent of pedagogical reform.[61] Lukashenko recommended that complexes be introduced into the school without delay and further suggested it might not be necessary to keep Russian as the school's language of instruction. While Lukashenko insisted the provincial section would not follow a policy of forcible Ukrainization, he questioned whether there was, in fact, a true Russian population in Bila Tserkva, arguing that he had evidence only of Russified Ukrainian and Russified Jewish populations. Lukashenko implied that this school director therefore had no place on three grounds: his political orientation, resistance to the complex system, and patronage of Russian-language instruction in a region where there was no sizable Russian population.

In fact, it was unclear to Narkomos planners and local education officials just how much Ukrainization of teachers was needed. It was difficult to accurately gauge their knowledge of Ukrainian or willingness to learn it. Lukashenko criticized the large number of teachers in Bila Tserkva who did not know Ukrainian and maintained that it was difficult to speak of a true Ukrainization of the village school in the region. Another participant at the March 1925 Kyiv provincial conference, Lypovetsky, conceded that "there are truly workers who do not know Ukrainian perfectly. This we know and we are giving them attention."[62] It was not the case, he argued, that over half the teachers in the Bila Tserkva region spoke only Russian. However, even if they all knew Ukrainian, that was not enough: "We say to our workers that you converse in Ukrainian, but you are still not Ukrainized because the majority of you is unfamiliar with the history and economic-geography along with folkways [*pobut*] and these are necessary to know." Teachers had to not only employ Ukrainian, but also master enough Ukrainian studies to create new complexes, integrate new material, and transform their way of teaching. Ukrainization was as much about redefining what was externally Ukrainian and debunking engrained prejudices against Ukrainian culture.

Some teachers viewed Ukrainization as an unnecessary distraction from the difficult task of teaching according to the new methodology. In 1927, the experimental Mykolaiv Labour School No. 28 was in the midst of Ukrainization. At the very same time teachers were attempting to modify the school's curriculum according to the complex system, the regional inspectorate ordered the school to Ukrainize all groups in the school. Although the director complied, he maintained that "such Ukrainization … reflected harmfully in the work and vividly demonstrated that it is possible to Ukrainize the school only gradually, beginning with the first group when children do not use the Ukrainian language in the family."[63]

A series of May 1927 reports from individual teachers at the Mykolaiv school support the director's general conclusion. At issue, but never fully defined, was the ethnic makeup of the school. The teachers' material contained data only on the ethnic composition of the school by group. According to the estimates available, the highest proportion of Ukrainians was in the fourth group, 31.7 per cent, and the lowest in the second group, 9.2 per cent.[64] It is unclear how the teachers were determining ethnicity. The first-group teacher identified speaking ability alone, claiming that it was difficult to use Ukrainian in the classroom because "only 20 per cent of the pupils speak the language."[65] It is uncertain whether the remainder were Russified Ukrainians or ethnic Russians (or, indeed, whether 20 per cent were, in fact, ethnic Ukrainian), and his comments cast some doubt on the data by ethnicity cited by his colleagues. They may well have taken the children's spoken language as a marker of their ethnicity.

The overall concentration of ethnic Ukrainians in Mykolaiv Labour School No. 28, regardless of whether they used Ukrainian, in fact, could have been greater than that of most other schools in the city. The inspectorate may have selected it for Ukrainization for this reason or possibly because of its "experimental" status, hoping that it would quickly transfer to Ukrainian instruction and then attract and serve the Ukrainian population of the city. The uncertainty surrounding this case is indicative of the confusion involved in taking the first steps towards Ukrainization, especially in the largely Russian-speaking environment of the cities. This school, to a greater degree than others, had to meet the added challenge of rapidly switching to the complex system at the very same time.

Regardless of the true ethnic makeup of the school, the teachers clearly state that a majority of students did not speak Ukrainian as their first language. Even with the youngest students, this presented a dilemma for use of Ukrainian in the classroom. The first-group teacher, Lyshenko, wrote that the children regularly had to learn new words, first translating those they did not know into Russian before they could continue their readings: "As a result, energy and time were lost. If instruction were done in the Russian language, the pace would have been much better."[66] The fourth-group teacher maintained that work in native-language instruction should theoretically lend itself easily to instruction by the complex method. However, Ukrainization frustrated application of complexes because students were unable to express their thoughts in Ukrainian. He and the second-group teacher described a gradual shift to Ukrainian instruction, beginning with reading and conversation and progressing to writing and lastly to mathematics.

The consensus among all teachers was that Ukrainization contributed to poor student performance. The oldest students perhaps had the greatest trouble – according to their instructor, Fish – having already studied four years in Russian only to switch to Ukrainian in 1927: "It must be said in general that this Ukrainization bore us much trouble. Our poor children had to make mistakes a lot."[67] The second group lost eight of thirty-five students by year's end, and the fourth-group teacher kept back four of eighteen students, blaming their poor performance partly on Ukrainization. Children had to wait for Lyshenko, the school's methodology specialist, to translate Russian-language texts. Ukrainian texts were in short supply, and the teachers generally considered them to be of poor quality.

Although the school pushed instruction by the complex system in each grade, it also retained classes organized by subject area, supplementing them with "complex material to strengthen work." Here too most of the teachers at Mykolaiv Labour School No. 28 believed that Ukrainization complicated work and limited pedagogical innovation. The social studies teacher, Fish, claimed that because there were few Ukrainian textbooks in the field, "it was necessary to introduce a heuristic form of instruction, and to tell the truth, even the lecture form sometimes."[68] He used complexes, but could not do so in the "active" way Narkomos prescribed. Fish needed to explain material often, lamenting that it was difficult for the children, "due to the fact that they had to write exclusively in Ukrainian and became a little mixed up."[69] When he permitted the students to use Russian-language material, they performed better. Similarly, in the natural science class, the instructor had to teach the children Ukrainian terminology and, consequently, had less time to ensure they met Narkomos requirements.

Even when the school dedicated separate class time to Ukrainian-language study, it found it difficult to meet Narkomos guidelines and expectations prescribed for the 1926–7 academic year. The Ukrainian-language teacher for the fifth group, Buhatska, reported that she spent much of the year introducing the students to basic grammar. She omitted more difficult work from the language program recommended by Uprsotsvykh, divided the class into review groups, and regularly evaluated their progress. Although she formed complexes to incorporate literature into her curriculum, she often excluded material recommended by Narkomos because it was either unavailable or, she believed, too difficult.[70] Buhatska concluded that only students who had studied in Ukrainian since the first grade could follow the Uprsotsvykh program in grammar. This judgment would hold true not only for Russian-speaking students, but also Ukrainian-speaking students who had never been schooled in the language. Some children may well have found the introduction of Ukrainian in the classroom odd, especially in the form presented, but the language itself was not entirely unfamiliar.

Indeed, students appeared to have adjusted relatively quickly to the new language of instruction. This was especially true for the younger groups. After commenting on the difficulties of Ukrainization, the third-group teacher, Martynova, reported that her group's work had entirely transferred to Ukrainian in one trimester and that even during break, hardly any students continued to speak Russian. Furthermore, as children learned Ukrainian, teachers reported a decline in the negative methodological problems associated with Ukrainization.

The fourth-group teacher commented, "From the beginning, Ukrainization introduced horrible disorder, incomprehension on the part of the children ... but as the children mastered the language later, the pace and discipline improved."[71]

Teachers also learned to cope with the lack of literature, supplies, or motivated students. Fish's problematic social studies students had difficulty mastering the terminology of the October Revolution, but responded to his instruction in the history of technology. Improvements in student written and oral work reportedly demonstrated the effectiveness of Buhatska's improved grammar course. The geography teacher similarly cobbled together a course focused on regional and Ukrainian studies without proper school maps. For the theme "Our District," he found a small map included in the brochure "Mykolaivshchyna," and for "UkrSSR and the USSR," he used a map of Europe and Asia. He reported that the geographic material neatly tied into complexes recommended by Uprsotsvykh, and that a majority of the students exhibited favourable progress at the end of each semester. In short, although teachers may have believed Ukrainization hindered education, it did not greatly harm it.

Some schools, in fact, embraced Ukrainization too greatly for the taste of one inspector. Sava Chavdarov, the labour school inspector of the Kyiv region, noted in February 1927 that in one village school in the Baryshpil district, obligatory lessons in Russian were actually conducted in Ukrainian. An article was read in Russian and then worked on in Ukrainian. He further criticized the district labour school for giving insufficient attention to the increased number of children who understood Russian.[72] Even here, teachers substituted a Ukrainian lecture for Russian material. The schools could have been overeager to fulfill Narkomos orders on Ukrainization. Alternatively, they may have been deferring to the children's language strengths, believing that a full program in the Ukrainian language would bring the greatest benefit and least confusion. Schools primarily serving ethnic Ukrainians felt pressure to Ukrainize quickly. Narkomos stressed protection for the Russian ethnic minority, but, outside major urban and industrial centres, local educational authorities issued little guidance on Russian instruction.

Even when teachers and students were ostensibly Ukrainian-speaking, it did not follow that Ukrainization proceeded without incident. Narkomos obligated teachers to use a literary Ukrainian that many teachers did not fully understand and their students did not recognize. According to the Kyiv regional inspector, poor writing was endemic among children in 1926, especially girls, in the Vasilkiv district, but teachers did little to correct their work.[73] The teachers simply did not know how to do that. The writing of children in the Vyshenky Labour School (Baryshpil district) reflected the phonetics of local pronunciation, not standard Ukrainian, and teachers in the Baryshpil District Labour School (the leading school in the district, located in the city of Baryshpil) incorrectly marked the spelling of students, having little awareness of proper writing themselves.[74] Local Baryshpil education authorities recognized that little could be accomplished under such conditions, and resolutions for at least four schools in the district set the elimination of teachers' illiteracy in Ukrainian as an integral objective of their Ukrainization campaigns.[75]

The existence of large numbers of "Russified" Ukrainian children in the eastern and southern regions of the republic raised further questions about the pace of Ukrainization. Holovsotsvykh reported that at the end of the 1924–5 school year, on the republican level, there had been substantial achievement in the Ukrainization of schools. Of the 15,209 schools then operating in the UkrSSR, 77.8 per cent were fully Ukrainized, 4.4 per cent were half-Ukrainized (some classes within these schools continued to use Russian), 10.4 per cent were Russian, and the remainder dedicated to serving ethnic minorities.[76] Holovsotsvykh granted that the 10.4 per cent of schools that operated in Russian should keep that relatively constant, in order to adequately serve "children of Russians." However, Holovsotsvykh demanded that the half-Ukrainized schools transfer immediately to Ukrainian, with Russian kept only as a subject of study.

The drive to enrol all school-age students in heavily Russian-speaking areas had led to the creation of linguistically mixed schools and children's buildings. Holovsotsvykh noted that in Odesa, Katerynoslav, Chernihiv, and Donets provinces, the percentage of half-Ukrainized schools was much larger than the republican average. Children's institutions may have aspired to gradual Ukrainian-language instruction, but the mixing of language speakers often led to the "unacknowledged conquering of one or the other language."[77] More often than not, this victorious language was Russian in the so-called half-Ukrainized school. Holovsotsvykh lamented that among younger children, in preschool institutions, Ukrainization was proceeding very slowly because these younger children "overwhelmingly speak Russian, which appears to them to be native." Given that most schools began Ukrainization with their younger groups, this observation is telling. Although the underlying assumption of Narkomos's policy was that schools should teach all ethnic-Ukrainian children in Ukrainian, the history of Russification in the East frustrated this goal. Holovsotsvykh recommended a more realistic grouping of children by native language, but it held that a child's native language was defined by ethnicity, not competency.

Even elsewhere in Ukraine, where the population was more homogeneously Ukrainian-speaking, the Russian language exercised a heavy influence. Another report on schooling in Bila Tserkva concluded that Russian schools continued to operate in the region in spite of what it viewed as the absence of any need, and that "it is necessary to transfer their language of instruction in future years, depending on the native language of the children," presumably Ukrainian or Yiddish.[78]

The republic-wide account by Holovsotsvykh noted that although the percentage of Ukrainian-language schools (77.8 per cent) was higher than the ethnic-Ukrainian percentage of the UkrSSR population (75.1 per cent), Ukrainian-language schools enrolled a proportionately low percentage of the student population: 62.9 per cent in 1924.[79] According to the report, the phenomenon was explained by the fact that local authorities had Ukrainized schools in the cities much less than in the villages and, similarly, seven-year schools much less than four-year schools. The addition of half-Ukrainized schools would increase the proportion of students significantly (to approximately 73.2 per cent, just slightly lower than the percentage of ethnic Ukrainians). Proponents of Ukrainization used evidence such as this to argue that Ukrainization was incomplete. Narkomos's aim was to provide Ukrainian-language instruction for all ethnic-Ukrainian schoolchildren first and foremost. It gave only secondary, ad hoc consideration to a student's actual spoken language.

In spite of the experience of Mykolaiv Labour School No. 28, Narkomos hoped that by expanding Ukrainian-language schooling in industrial centres and by improving the quality of language instruction throughout the republic, it would fundamentally strengthen the school's chances for pedagogical success. If the number of students attending Ukrainian-language schools were to increase, it would need to employ more, and better, teachers. Narkomos blamed the slow pace of Ukrainization in the Odesa, Katerynsolav, Chernihiv, and Donets provinces on the Russian-language education of most teachers.[80] Donets province further suffered from the almost complete absence of teachers with the most basic skills in Ukrainian.[81] Narkomos recommended that all local organs use the 1925 summer to campaign for the retraining of teachers, not only in the Ukrainian language, but also in the history, geography, and literature of Ukraine. It viewed the supply of Ukrainian pedagogical literature and the newspaper *Narodnii uchytel* as a necessary part of this retraining. The Chernihiv Provincial Education Section reported to Narkomos that it had included work on the Ukrainian language in its operative plan for general pedagogical training. Teachers had organized circles for the study of orthography and literature and were examining other detailed questions individually.[82] However, the Chernihiv section complained, teachers still lacked needed literature for their study. Especially in these more Russian-speaking areas of Ukraine, teachers willing to take on the challenge of Ukrainian-language instruction would need much greater institutional support.

Chapter Six

Limited Urgency

Although schools had formally converted to Ukrainian-language instruction in numbers proximate to the ethnic-Ukrainian proportion of the children's population, the pedagogical press and local education officials expressed concern that teachers were not achieving the sort of change in schooled literacy that Ukrainizers desired. Teachers did not know Ukrainian enough, were not seeking further training (or being told to do so), and quickly lost whatever knowledge they gained in short-term courses. Some administrators suggested that teachers' use of a "flawed" Ukrainian heavily dependent on Russian borrowings was doing more harm than good for the Soviet agenda of uniting the republic's labouring classes under a common Ukrainian national culture. They claimed that it was a language that could not be recognized by Ukrainian speakers (including the peasantry) and implied its use did little to alter the existing linguistic hierarchy, opening up Ukrainian to further ridicule.

Ukrainizing purists contended that the language in its "corrupted" form seemed very much like the unsophisticated dialect of Russian that some opponents to Ukrainization contended it was. Teachers were relaying such prejudices to children, their parents, and to the wider public. Ironically, it was in the republic's rural Ukrainian-speaking areas where skilled Ukrainian teachers were in short supply. Because the language was not taught well, the teachers' critics charged that peasants would take on urban suspicions of Ukrainian as a language that might be spoken but could not be taught. Teachers were undermining the authority of language, the Ukrainian school, and the objectives of Soviet nationalities policy as a whole.

In order for literacy in Ukrainian to have any meaning, Narkomos resorted to testing as a measure of policing and regulating teacher knowledge. In 1927, in distinction from previous efforts, education officials called for a simultaneous republic-wide perevirka of teacher knowledge. The perevirka would test not just basic knowledge of Ukrainian, but also the teachers' command of a national culture, defined according to a now-developed Soviet script. Teachers who failed to perform were threatened with remedial study and, ultimately, dismissal. However, Narkomos officials still left it to local authorities to work out the test content, reporting requirements, and individual punitive action. Local officials expressed exasperation at the number of possible criteria for exception from the necessity to take the exam.

In fact, the number of teachers who actually sat for the exam on time was small, and observers charged that the low testing rate and delays undermined the objectives of Ukrainization in schooling. The failure to enact a comprehensive, well-timed perevirka was connected to larger issues involving the policy of Ukrainization generally. Who would test the teachers? If Narkomos did not assure high-quality Ukrainian-studies knowledge among teachers, who, then, would train and test state employees? The whole policy of Ukrainization depended on a ready supply of experts and – at a local level – the chief source was the schoolhouse.

Meanwhile, the goalposts of Soviet nationalities policy were under dispute. The proposed 1927 perevirka can be regarded fundamentally as pressure on the part of Ukrainizers for a determination of what would constitute schooled literacy in Ukrainian. Who needed to be trained in this form of literacy? Who would be excluded? What political meaning would be associated with this literacy? A larger debate within the KP(b)U and between Commissar of Education Oleksandr Shumsky, Ukrainian First Secretary Lazar Kaganovich, and Stalin focused on the question of ethnicity. That is, should ethnic Ukrainians be in control of political authority in the republic; should the requirement to have a command of Ukrainian studies be extended to all citizens of the republic, specifically workers; and what should the relationship of Ukrainian culture be to the largest category of ethnic Ukrainians by class, the peasantry? In the end, the Communist Party could not concede that Ukrainian literacy should be confined to the peasantry or that rural speakers alone determine its content. Stalin, Shumsky, Kaganovich, and the KP(b)U all conceded that this was a real danger.

The question was how to promote, regulate, and lead the drive towards this new literacy if "Ukrainian elements" in the party and working class were weak. The KP(b)U leadership, with Stalin's concurrence, forbade the use of force for the Ukrainization of the working class. The solution seemed to be a campaign of persuasion and promotion of ethnic elites within the party. Such persuasion would not work, however, if real and symbolic authority remained with the Russian language and career advancement to leadership occurred regardless of language ability. In a way, by making this argument, the party was making the same mistake it had credited to Shumsky: an obsession with ethnicity and an automatic equation among ethnicity, national sensibility, and loyalty to the Ukrainization campaign. To return to the perevirka campaign, the KP(b)U leadership insisted that, in spite of Shumsky's criticisms, the party was making progress, particularly in schooling (ironically under Shumsky's command). However, that failed 1927 perevirka campaign would reveal that teachers were suspicious of oversight, progress was likely not as rapid as hoped, and it was difficult to assess just what was being taught in the schools. School literacy was not neatly reproduced from one school to the next throughout the republic and extended to the working class. The Ukrainian culture that Stalin and the KP(b)U wanted to develop "spontaneously" was, in fact, not under proletarian control and remained the preserve of local regulation, if any regulation existed at all.

Thus, the party faced a dilemma generally. Was the policy of Ukrainization bankrupt without a real growth in Ukrainian culture among the working class? How could the working class (and the party) lead this policy if they did not know the Ukrainian language and were not proficient enough in the basics of Ukrainian studies to direct its content? Schools, for all their problems, were the answer that Narkomos and Ukrainizers within the party looked to as a run against the party's prohibition of Ukrainization of the working class. Schools would teach Ukrainian national culture to the children of Russian-speaking workers. Members of the KP(b)U Politburo Commission on Ukrainization raised specific concerns about the enrolment of ethnic-Russian children (especially children of workers), but education administrators would continue to target children of Russified Ukrainians for Ukrainization.

What "Russified Ukrainians" meant was open to interpretation. Regardless, local education officials stressed that Ukrainian schools must embrace this population, that the need for Ukrainian schools in the "Russified" cities would continue to grow as Ukrainian peasant migrants sought industrial employment. They raised concern that school enrolment (and graduation) of Ukrainian children remained proportionally lower than that of other national groups and that the best schools remained in the hands of Russian speakers, often children of the former bourgeoisie. Parental resistance to Ukrainization was equated with anti-Soviet behaviour and opposition to educational reform. Politically, it was critical that local officials take the Ukrainization campaign to the city core. While acknowledging parental interests, supporters of Ukrainization in the party were willing to override them in order to strengthen the authority of the Ukrainian schoolhouse and tacitly win over the Russified Ukrainian population to their cause (or simply break their resistance if it stemmed from white-collar elements). They conceded the argument of education officials that the working class was beginning to think Ukrainization was just about them. Soviet authorities needed to direct the campaign against the former privileged as well. Ultimately, the Ukrainization of schooling was about shoring up the loyalties of the working class to the objectives of Soviet education and ensuring a calibration of the republic's schooling network to the anticipated growth of Ukrainian elements in this class.

Raising the Bar: Evaluating Teachers' Failures

Teachers in Ukraine faced a daunting task. They had to transfer their instruction to the Ukrainian language, implement a poorly articulated but essentially new methodology, and struggle to achieve authority for themselves and for the school among parents and the wider community. Narkomos considered the first of these tasks – use of the Ukrainian language – to be the principal means for achieving the latter two. However, three years after Ukrainization began in earnest, Ukrainian teachers' knowledge of the language remained poor. Many schools had been Ukrainized in name alone. Narkomos ordered its local sections to make an accurate evaluation (perevirka) of Ukrainization in early 1927 and plan for improvement.

Prior to the beginning of this campaign, regular reports in the teachers' press warned of the poor state of Ukrainization. A January 1927 article in *Narodnii uchytel* argued that claims that schools had been nearly completely Ukrainized were simply false. In fact, "Ukrainian schools are truly much too few and we are very, very far away from 100 percent. In the majority of cases, our schools are hotbeds of Ukrainian semi-literacy."[1] The article insisted the problem was not limited to orthographic mistakes or dialectal variation. Teachers lacked elementary knowledge of the Ukrainian language. Another report maintained that often Ukrainization was doing more harm than good, that schools and other Soviet institutions were sponsoring a distorted form of Ukrainian: "Little by little, but constantly, a so-called 'Ukrainized language' is being pushed into general usage and it is a language that the peasant (that peasant for whom most of the work on Ukrainization is being undertaken) does not want to hear and does not understand."[2] It was difficult, then, to speak of Ukrainization when authorities and teachers alike were using a language that bore little resemblance to the Ukrainian the population recognized and employed.

The pedagogical press spoke often of the "maiming" of the Ukrainian language by teachers. Vasyl Nuzhny, a correspondent for *Narodnii uchytel*, reproduced an excerpt of an official letter by the head of a Dnipropetrovsk railroad school detailing the results of Ukrainian-language study in his school. The excerpt contained numerous borrowings from Russian or slightly Ukrainized forms of Russian words. Nuzhny concluded, "When you read the letter, you ask what language this is in. Language mixing exists among those heads responsible for Ukrainization at the railway."[3] The letter was a lesson in precisely how not to Ukrainize.

Local education sections, then, were desperate not only for qualified teachers who enjoyed the favour and the support of the communities in which they taught and lived, but ones fully proficient in Ukrainian. Remarkably, just as it was easier to find highly trained teachers in urban areas, the pedagogical press and local education sections reported that educators capable, and willing, to teach in Ukrainian were concentrated in the republic's largely Russified cities. *Narodnii uchytel* maintained that, in regard to the Ukrainization of the Dnipropetrovsk railroad schools, there was an overabundance of Ukrainian instructors in large junction centres but that the lack of teachers at small stations severely limited progress.[4] The Odesa Regional Education Section similarly reported in 1926 that a greater proportion of village teachers had no knowledge of Ukrainian compared to city teachers (33 per cent compared to 14 per cent, according to an early perevirka).[5]

Urban areas had greater resources to hire good teachers, as well as to train those they had. However, even this training was limited in scope. The Southwest Railroad administration organized short-term courses in Ukrainian for its various employees, including educators employed in schools along its line. However, the courses were oriented towards the writing of simple letters and business correspondence and offered no job-specific training for teaching. *Narodnii uchytel* lamented this practice, claiming that for teachers, "language is everything, a tool of work."[6] It allowed that teachers of the earliest grades might be able to get by, but not others. They lacked knowledge of orthography, terminology, and the basic literature required to do their job. The books they needed for further study were generally not available in the library, certainly not in outlying areas, and teachers could not afford to buy them themselves. Dnipropetrovsk railway teachers who enrolled in Ukrainian-language courses held in 1924–5 were said to have forgotten what they had learned by the end of 1926.[7] Instruction in the classroom might have been formally in Ukrainian, but daily conversation was in Russian.

In November 1926, Narkomos announced local education sections would hold a series of formal perevirky of Ukrainian knowledge, to begin in January. This announcement caused near-instant anxiety among teachers. According to one account published in *Narodnii uchytel*, a representative of the Bila Tserkva regional education inspectorate announced the upcoming examination at the end of a district teachers' conference. At first, the teachers simply tried to refuse to undergo the perevirka, but the inspectorate representative insisted he would enforce it and dismiss those who failed to demonstrate adequate knowledge.[8] The newspaper detailed how individual schools then formed small, self-study groups (*hurtky*), ostensibly to raise the teachers' qualifications in Ukrainian. In fact, they drew up formal complaints about the lack of Ukrainian literature and the absence of a standard Ukrainian orthography. In response, the regional inspectorate prepared a circular, recommending that teachers actually study, rather than issue protests.

Such sort of passive resistance to the perevirka appears to have been common. The teachers' press acknowledged that although an outline for a preparatory review was widely available, the necessary books and literature were not.[9] Teachers delayed, pleaded for more time and support, or simply claimed that they did not have to study for the exam. *Narodnii uchytel* related a comical story of a Ukrainian teacher who avoided preparing for the perevirka because he was "fully" Ukrainian, with "ancestors stretching back to the Zaporizhzhian Cossacks."[10] He soon learned that the perevirka tested much more than the ability simply to converse or write in Ukrainian. He could not answer any basic pedagogical questions about orthography and pronunciation. The perevirka commission placed him in the lowest category (third) and threatened him with dismissal if he did not raise his qualifications. The next night, Petro Semenovych was haunted by dreams of a demonic representation of the pre-1917 orthography, "in pince-nez eyeglasses with a black beard and black, greasy fleas covering its body." He awoke committed to learning how to pronounce correctly and "not write like a Russian." The newspaper's message was clear. New Ukrainian teachers had to cast away their mimicry of Russian and its tsarist-era standards. The perevirka would test their understanding and embrace of a Ukrainian language defined distinctly by Soviet linguists and reflected in the new revolutionary literature.

Teachers also sought to avoid evaluation by perevirka commissions by demonstrating proficiency through other documentation. A *Narodnii uchytel* reader asked the newspaper's editors if teachers might be exempt from the perevirka if they submitted proof (*dovidka*) they had taken a test in Ukrainian literature previously as part of a short-term pedagogical course. The editors replied that local commissions for Ukrainization could make this determination, but that Narkomos instructions provided for general exemptions.[11] Officially, the following categories of teachers were not required to undergo a perevirka: 1) graduates of Ukrainian-language institutes, *pedtekhnikumy* (pedagogical technical colleges), or secondary schools; 2) those who placed in the first (highest) category in earlier government employee Ukrainization exams; and 3) those who had taught in the Ukrainian language in older groups for at least two years and in younger groups for at least five years. In fact, according to the head of Kyiv Regional Inspectorate, Lukashenko, an overwhelming majority of teachers in the region belonged to one of these three groups.[12] Thus, the reality was that only a small proportion of teachers actually underwent an examination. The *Narodnii uchytel* reader's question was an attempt to diminish this number even more.

Such exemptions weakened the authority of the perevirka before it even began. Lukashenko expressed frustration to Narkomos that his inspectorate could not test many of its teachers, even when it had evidence that "rural school workers are extraordinarily distorting the language, that in 1927 the graduates of post-secondary pedagogical schools [*pedvyshy*] still do not know the language well and those that graduated from 1920–4 absolutely did not know the language."[13] It could do little to force these "new" Soviet teachers to increase their qualifications if they did not have to undergo the perevirka. Ivan Boikiv, an assistant inspector, argued in an

October 1927 report to Lukashenko that no exemption should be given to pedvyshy graduates because their institutes of training had generally given too little attention to writing in Ukrainian, and he further recommended that Narkomos create a special state exam in the Ukrainian language for this category of teachers. He argued that not establishing absolute requirements for Ukrainian-language qualifications was reckless, comparable to allowing a teacher to teach mathematics without knowledge of percentages: "The time has already come to take care of the culture of the native word, to teach the young generation to love it and develop it, but only a person who knows and understands this word can teach it."[14] Inspectors like Boikiv and Lukashenko believed strongly in the task of Ukrainization. They saw little point in holding a perevirka if it could not effect change.

It was a difficult matter to accomplish a perevirka, even in its limited form. A Ukrainization commission in Budaivka (now Boiarka) district (Kyiv region) had earlier chosen not to determine the language level of teachers along with other state employees in 1926, "due to the absence of directives and funds."[15] In Dnipropetrovsk, authorities did not investigate Ukrainization among half the teachers of the railroad as part of a general perevirka of employees. The teachers' union, Robos, had reportedly negotiated an exemption for those teachers attending Ukrainian-language courses.[16] Local officials were undoubtedly financially strapped, but also wary about how to accurately gauge what should be required Ukrainian-language knowledge for a teacher. It was no wonder, then, that local officials approached a republic-wide perevirka of the schools with some trepidation. Teachers had resisted earlier attempts, and Narkomos instructions on how to proceed had been ambiguous.

While some inspectors were worried about the true level of Ukrainian knowledge among teachers, they did not know how to staff the perevirka commissions. One article in *Narodnii uchytel* questioned whether any commission could examine the knowledge of teachers accurately. Inspectorates had to rely on teachers to fill the commissions. These teachers might act to protect their colleagues. Or, worse, "it is no secret that even now there are persons concluding a perevirka of institutions who themselves should be evaluated."[17] The observer recommended that central Narkomos authorities appoint each regional commission with responsible experts. The pool of qualified Ukrainian teachers was too small in the localities. However, it was equally unlikely that Narkomos could have dispatched experts throughout the republic. There were not a great number of so-called experts at its disposal, even in Kyiv. Noting the weak Ukrainization in the city, Boikiv asked Lukashenko, "Why make demands on a province that does not have the ability to use the cultural fruits and achievements of the Ukrainian word, [literature and linguistic material] that is easy to use in Kyiv?"[18] The provinces would, nevertheless, have to find a way.

A delay in the perevirka was perhaps inevitable, then, given the challenges involved. In response to the teachers' demand that they have an additional two months to prepare for the examination, one *Narodnii uchytel* correspondent cautioned, "Almost all teachers believe this and it is necessary to listen to their thoughts."[19] Lukashenko reported that the perevirka in the Kyiv region would take up to two years to complete. As it was, he did not report his concerns about implementation of the perevirka to Narkomos until April 1927, three months after the anticipated date for commencement of the campaign.[20] Faced with the fact that teachers were ill-prepared to undergo a perevirka and that it would likely yield poor and, consequently, demoralizing results, Narkomos allowed individual regional inspectorates to postpone. This suspension reportedly greatly relieved teachers, but *Narodnii uchytel* emphasized that the delay was not intended to remove a "burden," but rather to allow teachers to undertake in-depth study: "The campaign for a perevirka of the Ukrainian language therefore involves systematic study. Short preparation will not bring the anticipated results."[21] The newspaper reminded teachers that the Ukrainian language was "the most essential thing" in their work. Preparation for the perevirka did not mean preparation for a test by rote, but engagement in a cultural struggle.

As will be further discussed, assurance of a high level of Ukrainian knowledge among teachers was also essential to the success of the Ukrainization campaign generally. Teachers not only evaluated other teachers, but also assessed and trained state employees whose knowledge in Ukrainian-language studies was poor. In 1926, the Odesa Regional Ukrainization Commission prepared and requalified some sixty teachers to instruct civil servants in the city: twenty-five for the Ukrainian language, twenty for literature, and fifteen for the history of revolutionary movements in Ukraine.[22] According to the head of the commission, the regional administration regularly monitored these instructors to ensure their Ukrainian knowledge was good and instruction effective.

The Proletariat's Role Debated

The KP(b)U, of course, initiated and determined the course and ultimate future of the Ukrainization campaign. Above all, it was concerned with the development of Ukrainian speakers in the party ranks and state institutions. Two further worries also drove the party's direct intervention: fear that it was losing control over Ukrainization work; and anxiety about how to deal with the Russified and Russian portion of the population, chiefly the "proletariat," the term the party applied to the industrial worker population (although many were recent arrivals to the factories).

The question of Ukrainization of the proletariat had troubled the party since its early debates on nationalities policy and had a fundamental impact on education policy.[23] In March 1923, Dmitrii Lebed, a high-ranking member of the KP(b)U, argued in a well-known article in the journal *Kommunist* that a battle between Russian and Ukrainian cultures was inevitable in Soviet Ukraine. The line between the two cultures was clear: "In Ukraine, due to historical conditions, the culture of the city is the Russian culture and the culture of the village is Ukrainian."[24] Russian, as the "higher," urban culture, would win. In a KP(b)U Central Committee debate that followed the publication of this article, Lebed conceded that Ukrainian might be used for "cultural enlightenment" in the villages, maintaining in a separate report on the nationality question that "it is sometimes necessary for peasants to educate their children in Ukrainian, sometimes necessary to go to the village and answer questions in a language they understand."[25] However, the party absolutely could not promote Ukrainian in the city. The proletariat had no business learning the language of the "backward" peasantry. Lebed strongly opposed the current trend in Ukrainization, because it promised increased use of Ukrainian in the city among the party and the proletariat, emboldened reactionary elements in favour of further nation building ("nationalization"), and, ultimately, was a waste of time. In the end, the peasantry would have to accede to use of Russian. As long as the party remained neutral, the victory of Russian culture was assured.

Most leading members of the party distanced themselves from the theory of a "battle between two cultures," but Lebed himself escaped personal censure. Nevertheless, his contention that Russian culture in Ukraine had become intrinsically urban was a seductive argument for the party's rank and file. It influenced the party's continued caution regarding the city and prohibition against the forced Ukrainization of the proletariat. Yet, a policy of Ukrainization confined to the party and organs of government serving the peasantry had little value in a proletarian state. Future Commissar of Education Shumsky and other strong advocates of an expansion of Ukrainization argued in 1923 that the proletariat was not, by definition, Russian. In response to Lebed, Shumsky claimed in an essay published in the April 10 edition of *Kommunist* that there was no reason that a battle between cultures should take place. Suggesting that the proletariat in the republic was, in fact, of Ukrainian origin and therefore would not permit a struggle against Ukrainian culture, he asked: "From where is the proletariat recruited for industry? Is a battle to take place within the proletariat itself?"[26] The real battle, he suggested, should be about development of the proper language environment for a "single essential culture of worker-peasant industry." He clearly believed that Ukrainian should dominate this setting in the UkrSSR, because it could best secure a union among labourers in Ukraine. For Ukrainization advocates, this union, touted by party propaganda but often ignored in practice, was essential.

Shumsky was unwilling to concede that the proletariat was wholly Russian or even Russified, although he did not deny that Ukrainian speakers were concentrated among the peasantry. He argued that the proletariat was already growing because of Ukrainian membership. The future of industry in the UkrSSR would depend on the productive capacity of these and other workers drawn from the peasantry. Shumsky, in agreement with party doctrine, maintained that the proletariat must lead the peasantry. However, he and other Ukrainizers believed that this charge could not mean neglect of the national question or peasant concerns. The proletariat would guide, not combat, the peasantry.

Ukrainizers maintained that Ukrainization was the key for the merger of a single Ukrainian, but distinctly socialist, nation of labourers. Opponents of Soviet power existed: the bourgeois intelligentsia and kulaks. It was these forces that the proletariat must oppose, by robbing them of any opportunity to stir up national dissent. Shumsky insisted that the bourgeois intelligentsia, both Russian and Ukrainian, were in essence battling for their "daily bread" (*khleb nasushnii*), vying to attract segments of the population to their cause. Proletarian neutrality in the national question would only increase their enemies' chances of success. In the village, if the proletariat permitted a struggle over language, it would "give a reason for the peasants to unite under the kulaks, serve kulak interests of an open battle with the proletariat (not just a cultural one)."[27] Shumsky thus acknowledged the potential of a cultural divide and the peasantry's susceptibility to nationalist influence. However, the solution he saw was in engagement. The proletariat needed to assume leadership of the development of national culture precisely because of its "great meaning" to the peasantry.

What divided Lebed and Shumsky, therefore, was not a difference in belief about the possibility of a struggle between national cultures, but divergent views about its inevitability and the proletariat's relationship with the peasantry. Although Lebed spoke about the need to unite the peasantry with the proletariat, the party would accomplish this alliance through the former's submission. The party, he wrote in response to Shumsky's criticism, had to do away with its previous policy of concessions to the peasantry, "who lead the *petliurovshchina* [anti-Soviet nationalism]."[28] The coming fight over Ukrainization would remain coloured by this judgment. Those who opposed it insisted that there was no need for the proletariat to yield to a language predominantly spoken by a backward and politically suspect population, the peasantry. Those who argued forcefully in favour of it maintained that proletarian mastery of Ukrainian would simultaneously fuse the labouring populations, legitimize and strengthen proletarian leadership, and alter the direction of Ukrainian culture. Ukrainian culture would become fundamentally modern, proletarian, and socialist.

In 1925, the new first secretary of the KP(b)U, Lazar Kaganovich, established a Ukrainization commission under the Politburo in an attempt to reassert the party's authority over the campaign. Kaganovich had grown up in a Jewish family in a Ukrainian village. Upon assuming leadership of the KP(b)U, he polished up his Ukrainian-language skills and demanded that party members learn Ukrainian, use it in official functions, and thereby take on greater leadership of the Ukrainian population. His arrival marked a new campaign for the vigorous Ukrainization of officialdom, yet there was still a limit to the measures he proposed. In March 1926, he suggested that the party reassert its disavowal of the forced Ukrainization of the proletariat in its new theses on nationalities policy. This proposal did not find support by all in the KP(b)U. Shumsky raised strong objections to Kaganovich's management of Ukrainization in a private meeting with Stalin.

According to a letter Stalin wrote to the KP(b)U in April, Shumsky argued that although the intelligentsia was Ukrainizing fast and Ukrainian culture growing, the party and proletariat risked losing influence over the process.[29] In Shumsky's view, one of the greatest "sins" of the party and trade unions was that they had not recruited Communists who had "immediate ties with Ukrainian culture" to leadership positions. Furthermore, the party had permitted incomplete Ukrainization, especially among the working class. He criticized Kaganovich's leadership and urged that the party appoint ethnic Ukrainians to prominent positions in the government and party, recommending, specifically, former Narkmos Commissar Hrynko as head of Radnarkom.

Stalin turned Shumsky's criticisms on their head, agreeing with some of Shumsky's basic contentions but sharply condemning his proposed remedies. Stalin conceded that the party could not allow Ukrainization to fall into foreign hands and that the party needed cadres who both knew Ukrainian culture and understood the importance of the policy. However, he argued that Shumsky's call for greater Ukrainization among the proletariat suggested a policy of forced Ukrainization of Russian-speaking workers. While Stalin allowed that "the population will become nationalized (Ukrainized)" over the long term, he firmly rejected any coercive interference in this "spontaneous" process.[30] Second, he maintained that Shumsky's insistence on ethnic-Ukrainian leadership of Ukrainization had blinded him to the "shady side of this process." Due to the still-weak Ukrainian roots of the party, non-Communist intelligentsia might lead the policy and take on "the character of a struggle against 'Moscow' in general, against Russians in general, against Russian culture and its high achievement – Leninism." He argued that the writings of Ukrainian essayist Mykola Khvylovy demonstrated the real potential of this tendency. Khvylovy's case for the de-Russification of the proletariat and integration of Ukrainian culture with European tradition represented a "run away from Moscow."[31] The party had to struggle against this danger. The development of Ukrainian national culture had to be accomplished within the framework of the Soviet Union, under the leadership of the All-Union Communist Party, the VKP(b).

Even if taken at face value, Stalin's letter to the KP(b)U reveals something about the limits of proposed Ukrainization. The central party leadership intended for the campaign to serve primarily the needs of ethnic Ukrainians. It would not permit any Ukrainization of the Russian population. Furthermore, it would not aggressively Ukrainize the Russified proletariat, and rejected any measure that set the urgent transformation of this group as its target. Second, Stalin regarded the Ukrainian ethnic elite, non-party or not, with great suspicion. He would not sanction any promotion of Hrynko because of his lower "revolutionary and party status." Although Stalin listed other ethnic Ukrainians already prominent in the party leadership, their numbers were comparatively few. The dilemma the party faced, then, was how to Ukrainize if the Ukrainian element in the party was admittedly weak. The party had to rely on non-party intelligentsia to lead Ukrainization in education, but also, as has been suggested, in the training and evaluation of civil servants and party members. In time, it would grow anxious about the intelligentsia's management of this campaign, even as agents of Soviet power.

The KP(b)U Politburo's reply to Stalin conceded some difficulties in Ukrainization, but emphasized that the party had made considerable gains and, under Kaganovich's leadership, was headed in the right direction. For example, from 1924 to 1926, Ukrainian membership in the party had risen from 33 to 44 per cent and in the Komsomol from 50 to 63 per cent. Furthermore, it insisted that others in the party had "just as much right to be called Ukrainians as Shumsky" and that "we think it is not necessary that 100 percent of the higher leadership be Ukrainian by blood."[32] This latter statement suggests the notion of a supra-ethnic-Ukrainian identity. The Politburo did not further define this identity in its letter, but, ethnic Ukrainian or not, the party leadership could not claim to have to large numbers of Ukrainian-speaking cadres to head the largely linguistic campaign of Ukrainization. Its count of Ukrainian membership in the party was based purely on ethnicity and, although there was a rise, the proportion of Ukrainians in the party was still much smaller than their proportion of the republic's population: 80 per cent in 1926.

By the Politburo's own admission, the civil-war legacy of antagonism towards Ukrainian national culture persisted among the party's rank and file. Ethnic Ukrainians such as Shumsky and Hrynko could not join the KP(b)U Central Committee because they "had no influence on the party masses" and still needed to overcome their past "mistakes."[33] The Politburo letter did not specify what their errors were, but suggested that their former membership in the Borotbist party, a Ukrainian communist party that merged with the KP(b)U in 1920, was enough to compromise their authority, although it did not completely exclude the possibility of their eventual advancement. The party had, for a time, sanctioned their management of Narkomos. Yet, even in these positions, the party did not entirely trust Hrynko and Shumsky and acted to remove each, although for very different reasons. For Shumsky, his intervention with Stalin was the beginning of the end; he was ultimately removed from his post as commissar of education in February 1927 for permitting "national deviation" and was replaced by Mykola Skrypnyk.

To compensate for its acknowledgment of low Ukrainian membership in the party, the Politburo offered as evidence of the progress of Ukrainization a description of its greatest success: the expansion of the Ukrainian-language schools. It maintained that primary schools were nearly 80 per cent Ukrainized (consistent with the proportion of ethnic Ukrainians in the republic), secondary schools were Ukrainizing fast, and higher educational institutions had made Ukrainian-language knowledge a requirement for admission. Ironically, then, by the Politburo's own admission, the most dramatic advance of Ukrainization had occurred under Shumsky's watch.

Although the Politburo had sanctioned an increase in Ukrainian education, at the same time, it worried about the development of Ukrainian national culture under party members it did not fully trust. The party had prioritized political consolidation and economic recovery and growth over the educational and cultural fields, but it was in these areas that it found the greatest danger because it did not and could not have complete authority over them. At the same time, education and cultural advancement offered the greatest potential for the party to Ukrainize the proletariat without obvious force. It placed hope in the cultivation of a new generation of Ukrainian-speaking workers. However, the large numbers of Ukrainized schools the party touted also represented a ticking clock. It had to intervene to rein in politically unreliable education administrators, oversee teachers, and ensure the ultimate trustworthiness of school graduates. Otherwise, the party feared, the schools might produce a generation that would undermine its rule in Ukraine.

For the time being, the party attempted to maintain a middle course. A 1926 report given by Secretary of the TsK KP(b)U Fedor Korniushin argued that it was impossible to complete Ukrainization without the active participation of the proletariat. The proletariat and the party needed to head the campaign, completely familiarize themselves with Ukrainian culture, and clean it of its national bourgeois tendency (*pereval*).[34] However, it also recognized that a significant portion of the Ukrainian proletariat was Russified and might react negatively to any ill-considered, hasty campaign. The Ukrainization of the proletariat would take time (the report considered the more than eight years that had passed since the revolution to be brief) and under no circumstances would the party allow the "imposition of Ukrainian culture on workers of other nationalities." Those who argued for an increased pace, the report said, forget "there is not enough strength for this" and make a "fetish" out of national culture. The party had to proceed with careful deliberation, at a rate correspondent with the number of trusted Ukrainian instructors it had at its disposal, and in a manner sensitive to the concerns of the Russian-speaking population.

As a practical matter, this meant the party would push Ukrainization hardest among officials who served the rural population and administered the schools. A proletarian party could not concede that Ukrainian culture was the preserve of the peasantry. Such an acknowledgment would undermine the rationale and intent of the campaign: the liberation of an oppressed national culture and its orientation towards socialism. However, the Ukrainization of the proletariat had to be accomplished gradually. In addition to those at urban academic institutes, the greatest concentration of instructors for the state-run Ukrainization courses was in the schools. It was here, then, that officials hoped to best manage and form a new Ukrainian, proletarian culture.

The party's principal organization for oversight and advancement of Ukrainized education was its youth wing, the Komsomol. The question of the Komsomol's Ukrainization will be discussed in detail in chapter 8. Here, it is enough to say that the party leadership took a direct interest in the Komsomol response to orders to Ukrainize. A March 1926 meeting of the KP(b)U TsK commission emphasized that the Ukrainian Komsomol had to take a leading role in Ukrainization in children's institutions, and that the TsK would hold Komsomol leadership personally responsible for progress in the campaign. The problem was that the commission also found Ukrainization within the Komsomol itself to be unsatisfactory.[35] Although ethnic-Ukrainian membership in the organization generally had risen to 63 per cent, one commission report found that only 43.5 per cent of its sections in industrial areas reportedly carried out their work in Ukrainian (compared to 86.6 per cent of rural sections).[36] An additional report on Ukrainian membership within the Komsomol confirmed these general figures, noting, however, that Ukrainization of the Komsomol apparat was inadequate. Furthermore, a postscript to this report, added in pen, conceded that "a significant portion of those identified in the report as Ukrainian do not know Ukrainian."[37] A Komsomol with few Ukrainian-speaking members had little authority or ability to press schools to rapidly switch their language of instruction.

Not only had the Komsomol failed to Ukrainize, the TsK commission also doubted the commitment of some members to the policy. It concluded that lower-ranking activists in the organization generally had not learned Ukrainian and, in a few instances, had opposed "the political meaning of Ukrainization."[38] The commission found little leadership in the Komsomol for transfer of official functions to Ukrainian, negligence by regional sections regarding Ukrainization, and wide use of Russian by members in all but the most rural areas. Whether by design or not, the Ukrainian Komsomol was resisting the very nationalities policy set by the party.

While the Ukrainization of the Komsomol itself was important, it was necessary because of the supervisory role the organization was supposed to have over Ukrainian youth. First, the TsK commission mandated that all Komsomol activists take part in the organization of Ukrainian-language schools, specifically in industrial districts.[39] Together with the party's propaganda wing, Agitprop, the Komsomol members had to work to ensure "political literacy" in the second level of newly Ukrainized schools. The organization would find it impossible to accomplish both these tasks and lead "Ukrainian cultural life" in the future if the rank and file did not deepen their knowledge of Ukrainian studies and the language. The Komsomol also assumed a direct role over the Communist children's movement, the Young Pioneers. While the schools would provide political training for students, the Pioneers' chief responsibility was to arrange public activity for children outside the school. As will be detailed below, in almost all urban areas and in many of the few villages where the Young Pioneers had sections, work was in Russian.[40] The Politburo Ukrainization Commission considered it an "especially abnormal phenomenon" that Young Pioneer sections operating in fully Ukrainized schools still spoke in Russian regularly at their meetings. The commission placed blame for the failures squarely on the Komsomol. It is little wonder, then, that some in the party worried about the ability of Communists to manage Ukrainization properly.

Re-Ukrainizing Ukrainians

While the Komsomol found it difficult to keep pace with Ukrainization of schools in urban and industrial centres, Narkomos officials continued to worry about the effect the broader Russian-language environment in these areas had on the capacity of schools to fully transfer to Ukrainian. In particular, they pointed to the harmful influence of Russian chauvinism among civil servants, who adamantly refused to send their children to Ukrainian-language schools, even if they were ethnic Ukrainian. Similarly, according to one newspaper account, some older teachers remained hostile to Ukrainization, having, before the revolution, "with the courtesy of inspectors and cultural trainers, painstakingly implanted a foreign language and foreign culture in our children, crippling their living spirit."[41] A 1927 meeting of Kyiv party and school employees identified at least three schools in the city headed by Russian chauvinists like these.[42] Narkomos officials labelled such attitudes "anti-Soviet" and cited their spread as reason for an even more concerted campaign of Ukrainization.

Narkomos had repeatedly set as its target Ukrainian-language schooling for all ethnic-Ukrainian schoolchildren. In a detailed letter addressed to Arnautov, now head of Uprsotsvykh, the Kyiv regional school inspector, Lukashenko, detailed the shortcomings of Ukrainization that persisted as late as 1926–7. He specifically raised concern that the overwhelming majority of children not attending school were of Ukrainian origin and came from what he labelled the most "insecure" portion of the city's population: day labourers and the unemployed.[43] The city's schools had to embrace this population, and continued migration of ethnic Ukrainians into Kyiv would also mandate an increase in the number of Ukrainian-language schools operating at the time. A 1926 report of the Kyiv Regional Education Section had indicated that the proportion of ethnic Ukrainians in the city was likely to rise.[44] At the beginning of the 1925–6 school year, 32.5 per cent of the city's students were studying in Ukrainian-language groups, although the proportion of ethnic-Ukrainian children in school stood at 40.5 per cent as a whole and 44.8 per cent in the first grade alone. Significant numbers of Ukrainian children were not enrolled in Ukrainian-language groups or schools.

Lukashenko placed the blame for this gap squarely on the shoulders of Russified Ukrainian parents who wished to send their children to Russian-language schools because they continued to believe that such schools offer "greater perspectives."[45] In doing so, Lukashenko argued, they ignored the "native language" of the child and made their selection on the basis of which school used to be the privileged gymnasium during tsarist times or had a better administrator or facilities. Lukashenko counselled caution in dealing with these parents. Insensitivity to their wishes might only increase their own chauvinism and hostility towards Ukrainization. District school-enrolment commissions needed to take "an approach of propagandizing and convincing [*shliakh propahuvannia i perekonannia*]" with individual parents. Every increase in the enrolment of Russified Ukrainians in Ukrainian-language schools would strengthen the authority of these schools and the push towards Ukrainization in general. Only when parents could not be convinced otherwise should enrolment commissions assent to their wishes.

However, for Lukashenko, a family's decision to send ethnic-Ukrainian children to Russian-language schools was largely a matter of choice. So, notwithstanding his words of restraint, he condemned the Russophilism he found to be most prevalent among white-collar workers: "In spite of the Ukrainization of the Soviet apparat and his personal work, the Soviet office worker is, en masse, demanding to educate his children in the Russian school."[46] Narkomos officials like Lukashenko must have seen hope in the increasing numbers of working-class children who were attending Ukrainian schools. The KP(b)U and, as a consequence, Narkomos considered the proletariat's embrace of Ukrainization the best determinant of the policy's success or failure. In his letter to the KP(b)U Politburo, Stalin had cautioned against the forced Ukrainization of the proletariat, both ethnic Russian and Russified. The KP(b)U prohibited the Ukrainization of the former. Its approach to the Russified Ukrainian population was more nuanced. Here, Narkomos encouraged, and the party did not contravene, the Ukrainization of the former bourgeoisie. It ultimately decided on a more gradual approach towards the proletariat, whose Ukrainization the party needed, but could not compel.

It was a school's obligatory transfer to Ukrainian-language instruction in the southern city of Mykolaiv, far away from the cultural capital of Kyiv, that raised the question of the Ukrainization of the Russian-speaking population generally for Narkomos and, eventually, the party. In November 1926, TsKNM (the Central Committee for National Minorities, a subsidiary organ of VUTsVK) requested that Narkomos investigate the "abnormal" Ukrainization of Mykolaiv Labour School No. 15. According to a letter subsequently sent to Narkomos by parents of students attending the school, the regional education inspector had Ukrainized the first grade of the school without regard for the predominantly ethnic-Russian composition of the school.[47] The letter further claimed that parents of five children in the Ukrainized group had removed their children from the school and the parents of the other sixty-five were only waiting to remove their children until their case had been reconsidered. The parents who wrote the complaint justified their petition on the basis of a governmental decree protecting the educational rights of ethnic minorities.

In his defence, the Mykolaiv regional education inspector, Yosyp Podolsky, detailed the reasons for the Ukrainization of the school. He argued that the Mykolaiv inspectorate had concentrated its early campaign for the Ukrainization of primary schools in workers' districts, where the Ukrainian population was highest.[48] However, by 1926–7, it turned its attention to the Ukrainization of the lower grades of schools in the central district of the city, where the majority of the population was 'white collar' or artisan. This move was justified first on political grounds, because workers had come to believe that the inspectorate was targeting only their districts for Ukrainization and not the districts of government employees, "who should in fact be the first to demonstrate a model for the implementation of the directives [on Ukrainization] of the central [republican] organs of power and do not read [in Ukrainian]."[49] Second, the national composition of the district demanded some limited opening of Ukrainian schools. Ukrainization had taken place in three schools of the central district, and parents moved quickly to reserve space for their children in them.

According to the Mykolaiv inspector, any school could have been Ukrainized. The inspectorate chose Labour School No. 15, in specific, because it occupied the building of a former gymnasium, owned by the director of the school. The school had used its reputation as a gymnasium among the population and gathered around it a group of supporters. Therefore, Podolsky argued, "In taking the path of Ukrainization, the people's education inspectorate intended to simultaneously and definitively destroy the reputation of this school as a gymnasium and to further change the pedagogical staff of this school, to dismantle any remnants of the olden days of schooling [*shkilnoi starovyny*] in it."[50] Of all the schools Ukrainized in the city, this was the only school parents petitioned to remain Russian.

Podolsky argued that it was primarily parents of older students, whose instruction, in fact, remained in Russian, who protested the school's Ukrainization. An overwhelming majority of parents of the students in the Ukrainized first grade registered their children to stay in the school, and a second group was set up in the school to accommodate the number of students. The inspectorate organized another group in a neighbouring Russian school for those students who wished to transfer. In the final analysis, Podolsky claimed, the parents' protest of the Ukrainization of Labour School No. 15 was reactionary: "The parents were not speaking out to defend 'their children,' but the remnants of the olden days of schooling."[51]

Uprsotsvykh had tried to find the middle ground between the Mykolaiv inspectorate and the parents of Labour School No. 15. It affirmed the general thrust of the inspectorate's Ukrainization policy, but recommended that the inspectorate organize a parallel Russian group for the first grade in this school.[52] Both the parents and the Mykolaiv inspectorate rejected this proposal. In the end, Uprsotsvykh sided with the inspectorate, arguing that the first-grade children in the school had ample opportunity to transfer to Russian groups in other schools, and that children of the parents who mounted the protest were in older groups unaffected by Ukrainization.[53] It recognized that the chief motive of the parents appeared to be an unwillingness to let a Ukrainian-language group use a room in a school renovated out of community funds.

Limits Set

What seemed to be at issue in the Mykolaiv case was the question of whether Russians were an ethnic minority and what sort of protection they deserved. Mykolaiv authorities sought to escape reprimand by arguing that Russian parents still had the option of educating their children in Russian, and that the Ukrainization of Labour School No. 15 served a distinct pedagogical and political aim. However, as Podolsky noted, this school was not the only school Ukrainized in Mykolaiv. Ukrainization proceeded apace in other schools in spite of predominantly Russian student bodies. A December 1926 meeting of the KP(b)U Politburo commission on Ukrainization offered a chance to take stock of the direction of Ukrainization.

The commission met under the veil of criticism mounted by Yurii Larin at an April 1926 session of the All-Union Central Executive Committee (TsIK). At this meeting, Larin addressed the previously taboo question of whether the Ukrainian government should treat Russians as an ethnic minority, arguing forcefully for the affirmative.[54] To support his case, Larin pointed to a series of discriminatory acts against Russian speakers in Ukraine, including the forced instruction of their children in the Ukrainian language.[55] Unlike Larin, however, several representatives at the December meeting of the KP(b)U commission made an effort to separate the question of rights for ethnic Russians versus those of Russified Ukrainians. The problem of what to do about the latter remained open to interpretation.

A June 1926 KP(b)U report by the Left Opposition[56] member and former head of the TsKNM, Mykhailo Lobanov, was an indication of the confusion over what constituted a Ukrainian. He allowed that the party needed to pursue the Ukrainization of its leadership and that of the government and trade unions, but insisted it must reject the forceful Ukrainization of its rank and file. Even Ukrainization of the leadership had to proceed at a rate correspondent with the Ukrainian makeup of the Soviet apparat in general, a figure he insisted must be determined by a survey of language, not "lineage" (*proiskhodzhenie*).[57] The party would not abandon Ukrainization among the general population, but it had to proceed cautiously, supporting Ukrainian cultural institutions in a bid to increase their attractiveness.

Lobanov was trying to walk a fine line. He conceded that the party could simply wait for the gradual re-Ukrainization of the city, yet said it must allow for some amount of coercion: "The Communist Party, having come to power during a revolution, cannot contemplatively, patiently regard the historical process's 'games of power,' observing 'neutrality' towards national relations which are being spontaneously formed." However, the party's "artful forcing of this process" must have limits. Lobanov's report concluded that the present, unbounded policy had allowed for the rise of a competitive struggle among language workers. Its continuation would lead to the growth of Ukrainian nationalism "in some Soviet-protected form" and concealed Russian chauvinism. The party had to act to make the Ukrainian intelligentsia understand the policy had boundaries and to remove any excuse the Russian intelligentsia had to complain of oppression. Lobanov stopped short of demanding "constitutional" recognition of ethnic-minority status for Russians, but demanded that local authorities guarantee access to judicial and cultural services in Russian, especially in workers' districts. The schooling of workers' children was a key element of this requirement. However, Lobanov's stress on language as a marker of ethnicity did not meet with the agreement of current policy.

Mykola Skrypnyk, Shumsky's successor as the Ukrainian People's Commissar of Education, speaks at a meeting of the Communist Children's Movement (Young Pioneers) in Kharkiv, 1930. Courtesy TsDKFFAU.

In the view of many present at the December meeting of the Politburo commission, a certain amount of involuntary Ukrainization of the Russian-speaking population had occurred. Volodymyr Zatonsky, who had previously served as the Soviet Ukrainian state secretary (later commissar) of education during the civil war and then as UkrSSR commissar of education from January 1919 to April 1920 and October 1922 to March 1924, argued that while continued work on Ukrainization was needed among the upper grades of schools, Narkomos had approached the "extreme" of coercive Ukrainization in lower grades.[58] He concluded that continued work in this direction might provoke protest and alluded to the situation in Mykolaiv as an example. The next speaker, Lazovert, was even more specific. He cited the case of Mykolaiv Labour School No. 15 and supported the demands of the parents to reverse the school's Ukrainization, claiming that the large ethnic-Russian population in Mykolaiv needed more Russian schools. Even Mykola Skrypnyk, a defender of Ukrainization and future commissar of education, acknowledged that the policy had sometimes been inappropriately applied: "I personally believe that the dissatisfaction of the population, which does arise, is due to the fact that the requirements of the population are not being met."[59] In effect, he validated the sort of protests mounted in Mykolaiv, if not their specific motivation.

Skrypnyk led the push to recognize the Russian population as an ethnic minority, playing off the more provocative cries of national oppression by speakers such as Lazovert. He conceded that abuses of Russian interests had occurred in individual cases, and recognized openly that the Russian population in Ukraine constituted an ethnic minority and that the party should secure for it corresponding rights.[60] The very success of Ukrainization mandated such action. Other representatives at the meeting echoed this course. Ethnic Russians would be afforded state protection, and the right to educate their children in their native language, previously guaranteed, would be strictly guarded.[61] The Ukrainization commission refrained from calling for an outright constitutional definition of Russian ethnic-minority status. Protection of Russian rights would instead be a matter of rigorous application.

The meeting was decidedly less clear on the question of the Ukrainization of Russified Ukrainian children. Zatonsky made a convincing case that ethnicity did not determine an individual's native language and argued for cautious Ukrainization among the children of railroad workers. For Skrypnyk, the solution to charting a more appropriate course was stricter management of local organs implementing Ukrainization. Particular sensitivity would have to be paid to the demands of the working class, but Skrypnyk, and those who supported his view, maintained that the party must still push fundamental Ukrainization at the primary-school level: Russification continued to influence parental choice, and Ukrainian school attendance was disproportionately low.[62] In short, Ukrainization among children of the proletariat would proceed, but it would have to be carefully calibrated.

Chapter Seven

The Question of the Working Class

Soviet nationalities policy made little sense if it harmed the interests of the political base of Soviet power: industrial workers. However, it could not advance without securing the embrace and promotion of workers. The Communist Party designed the policy to unite the labouring community, but it required leadership by urban-based workers for the policy to be politically palatable in the long term. Thus, even if direct Ukrainization was taboo, education officials and their supporters in the party believed some amount of it was necessary. The route to accomplish this was through the Ukrainization of workers' children. A component of this strategy was to shift the language of instruction and thus the political attitudes of all children of "Russified" Ukrainian parents.

Commissar of Education Mykola Skrypnyk advanced the basic premise of this approach, the idea that the "true" native language of Russified children was Ukrainian. He argued that the "mixed" language they spoke had a linguistic base as Ukrainian. This tack raised essential questions about choice. The state intervened to determine which evolving language standard should predominate among this population: Russian or Ukrainian. Ukrainizers like Skrypnyk and his supporters in Narkomos confronted what they believed to be an essential dilemma: the historically compelling force of Russification for Ukrainians in the city and the general perception among many in the republic that Russian was a more cultured language and should be learned. Ethnicity is a slippery category. If some urban residents chose to identify themselves as Ukrainian, or census takers directed them towards this choice, this correlation did not mean they spoke, or aspired to speak, a language resembling Ukrainian and that they would continue to prefer the label "Ukrainian." Undoubtedly, initial national identification had some durability, but the state's actions were required for it to persist. Education administrators believed that pressure on Ukrainian children to speak Ukrainian would accomplish this. Otherwise, preference for use of Russian for the majority of urban populations would remain. This intervention meant a disregard of individual choice, although, technically, regarding the issue of school enrolment, educators maintained this principle. But parents would need to extend greater effort to overcome the state's presumption.

There could not be a linguistic transformation of the city through schools if Ukrainian children did not attend schools and did not have an opportunity to continue their education in their "native language" beyond the initial primary grades. Education officials looked with disapproval on low attendance rates for Ukrainian children and lamented a shortage in complete (seven-year) schools. They advanced their argument for "full" Ukrainization in the politically appropriate language of class: the proportion of Ukrainian schoolchildren with working-class backgrounds was greater than any other ethnic group in Kyiv, for example. Thus, expansion of the Ukrainian schools would directly benefit the working class. Furthermore, educators needed to plan Ukrainization with an eye towards the future, an anticipated and desired growth in the Ukrainian urban working class and an ambition to provide a path for the uninterrupted education in the Ukrainian language. Educators argued that, for some, a deficiency in the number of schools in their "native language" would give rise to nationalist sentiment and, for others, confirm the Ukrainian language's secondary status. State and party authorities, the documentary record suggests, risked underappreciating the potential to confront and shape the question of schooled literacy at their own peril.

A recurring problem was that the state lacked the ability to train teachers properly for the preparation of workers' children for engaged roles in the socialist state. Narkomos officials instructed teachers in classes (where classes existed) alongside other civil servants and delayed issuing plans for a uniform, profession-specific program, refusing to delegate this responsibility to lower-level authorities. It did issue material for cheaper correspondence courses, but these courses were less rigorous, relying as they did on teachers' own initiative. What seems clear is that teachers felt ill-prepared for further examinations of their knowledge. Education officials claimed that they were willing to exact punishment against those who failed to embrace Ukrainian culture, but they were also unwilling to provide proper support for teachers to meet the targets they, the republican government, and the party set.

Motivated teachers and other members of the intelligentsia stepped in to fill in the gap they perceived in the development of a Ukrainian national culture. However, party authorities expressed concern about the apparent "spontaneity" the state's efforts at Ukrainization had incited. Skrypnyk's predecessor as commissar of education, Shumsky, had argued that the party's failure to capture, direct, and compensate non-party efforts appropriately had, in fact, increased national frustration, a claim repeated in internal party documents. Shumsky used this indictment to call for greater and deeper Ukrainization, but such a charge raised the spectre of nationalism (and was to ultimately contribute to Shumsky's downfall).

Internal KP(b)U Politburo documents discussed in this chapter reveal an early and regular concern over the possibility that Ukrainization had unleashed or provided rein to nationalist forces among the intelligentsia and prosperous peasantry, who were linked in a constructed anti-Soviet conspiracy. This anxiety created vulnerability for teachers who had pursued Ukrainization too energetically in the schools or acted as public Ukrainizers. Unaware of these fears expressed by party authorities, in the mid-1920s, ambitious teachers sought to fulfill this latter role for potential reward. The teachers' press suggests that those who did so without good knowledge of Ukrainian may have actually hurt the campaign by creating a distorted view of the Ukrainian language and sowing the seeds of resentment among public workers required to learn a language that bore little resemblance to that promoted by the state and authoritative Ukrainizers in Narkomos. Furthermore, the teachers were ill-equipped to fulfill the political duties Soviet officials imagined for them.

Nevertheless, the demand for Ukrainian instructors was so high among some governmental departments with budgetary largess that some teachers abandoned their duties in the classroom in order to pursue lucrative (if short-lived) careers as public Ukrainizers. This occupation carried an inherent risk because teachers invited the suspicion of the party if they were too ambitious in their pursuit of Ukrainization. The problem for the Communist Party was that its representation among teachers and intellectuals was weak, however much it claimed to have captured the loyalty of the majority. Party guidance of education could not be guaranteed, especially at the local level. Soviet nationalities policy may have operated largely as soft-line policy, but its potential to change the dynamics of power was considerable, and the party was taking stock of this possibility all along.

Guided Ukrainization of the Proletariat

The party's debate over the status of Russians in Ukraine, provoked by Larin's initial attack, made clear that the party would disallow the Ukrainization of ethnic Russians. Ukrainizers found a solution to the dilemma of the Ukrainization of the proletariat in the younger generation of Russified Ukrainians. They would achieve the gradual Ukrainization of the proletariat through the state's guided, if not coercive, instruction of the proletarian young. Assuming a more interventionist tack than his predecessors, newly appointed Commissar of Education Skrypnyk drafted a report in the summer of 1927 to all regional education inspectors, ordering them to respect parental wishes for a child's language of instruction when considering school enrolment. However, they were to halt Russification by speaking "about reading and writing in the native language, so that further instruction can occur in a language that the child understands."[1] Skrypnyk made clear his developing strategy in a 1931 article in the journal *Bilshovyk Ukrainy* (Ukraine's Bolshevik): Russified Ukrainian children spoke "a mixed and spoken language" whose base was Ukrainian.[2] The true native language of Russified Ukrainians was Ukrainian, and Narkomos needed to recognize this fact in designing educational policy.

More than anything else, for Skrypnyk, if Ukrainization was to continue, school enrolment and the process of switching a school's language of instruction had to appear more transparent. As some of the above examples have made clear, there was considerable public skepticism and hostility towards Ukrainization. Even in Ukraine's cultural capital, Kyiv, parents questioned the motivation for the transfer of their children's schools to Ukrainian-language instruction. Central authorities appeared as confused about the targets of Ukrainization here as they were in Mykolaiv. In response to a 1927 petition by a group of parents, Uprsotsvykh head Arnautov demanded that the Kyiv Regional Inspectorate explain its motivation behind the Ukrainization of city Labour School No. 6.[3] He did not directly criticize the inspectorate, but the uproar the Mykolaiv case created compelled him to take parental complaints seriously and require inquiry.

Narkomos needed to proceed carefully with the Ukrainization of children of the Russified population, but proceed nevertheless. The same 1927 report by Kyiv Regional Inspector Lukashenko to Uprsotsvykh (that had condemned the condescension with which some parents continued to view Ukrainian schools) advised a cautious path, but simultaneously sounded the alarm. Lukashenko maintained that some 1,975 Ukrainian children in the region (together with 9,035 Jewish children) were studying in Russian schools.[4] There were Russians and Jews studying in Ukrainian schools, but their numbers were comparatively small. These discrepancies, Lukashenko suggested, had to be changed. It was only in the rarest of instances that parents could claim that a school did not exist in their district that could provide native-language instruction. Of course, in spite of Skrypnyk's later judgment, the specific "native language" of a child was a matter of dispute.

It is difficult to overestimate the influence urban prejudice against all things Ukrainian had on parental preference. In the minds of some members of the ambitious new proletarian elite and the old intelligentsia, the Ukrainian language was a peasant language, uncultured and parochial. The government's promotion of Ukrainian only increased their antagonism towards it. One Luhansk worker and party member wrote to the KP(b)U TsK that anger towards the Ukrainian language was growing among the proletariat's rank and file due to Ukrainization's rapid advancement "by decree." Workers who had struggled to learn to read Russian now confronted Ukrainian public signage and literacy training: "Semi-literate people prefer to converse or shut up during reading or writing and in place of lessons; one begins to regard the Ukrainian language with hostility."⁵ Even new Ukrainian labourers, recently arrived from the village, may well have been perplexed by the obligation to read and write in Ukrainian if they had acquired basic literacy in Russian. Education in Ukrainian was unwarranted, according to the Luhansk writer, because it only dragged the proletariat behind: "A worker is always ready for labour, if he knows it will bring a more enlightened and better way of life. But he has already failed to understand the Ukrainian language, because his life has no place for it." He allowed that Ukrainization might be begun with the youngest generation, but stressed society's weak support for the policy throughout his letter, even recommending a plebiscite to determine its course. The workers he described would never countenance Ukrainian-language schooling for their own children.

Some white-collar workers looked upon Ukrainization with equal distaste. A December 1926 article that appeared in the wall newspaper of the Petrivka (Podil) polyclinic in Kyiv lampooned Ukrainization. It recounted a conversation between two men (representative state employees), one of whom was enrolled in a Ukrainian-studies course. This man, designated V., complained that Ukrainization had increased his "suffering," taking valuable time away from his professional training by forcing him to memorize tracts of Ukrainian literature and poetry. After a twelve-hour workday, he had little time to study: "I have to read a lot in our field, but instead of this, you have *Aneid*, you caress the works of Shevchenko, how he hounded 'zhydiv' and 'kapatsiv' [Jews and Russians]."⁶ V. clearly believed Shevchenko was a nationalist anti-Semite and yet he risked being labelled a chauvinist himself for holding this opinion. He renamed his institution's Ukrainization commission "the commission for concentration of capital," suggesting that it was opportunistic and akin to the "bourgeois" practice of economic monopoly. This article hung for over a year in the polyclinic secretary's office. Both its publication and display suggest the sentiment the polyclinic's workers had towards Ukrainization. Ukrainian studies were a burden imposed by the state. If Russified Ukrainians could truly exercise free choice in the selection of a school for their children, some undoubtedly would have decided upon Russian.

A year after the article was removed from the Petrivka polyclinic, in March 1929, the regional party committee in Kryvyi Rih reported that the Russified portion of the local intelligentsia was opposed to Ukrainization. Although they maintained a "technically passive relationship" towards Ukrainization measures, in fact, they consciously resisted studying Ukrainian and sometimes even resorted to "demonstrative actions."⁷ The report does not give further details about who pursued what sort of tactics, but its emphasis on the Russified (as opposed to ethnic-Russian) intelligentsia is noteworthy. Ukrainization benefited ethnic-Ukrainian elites most, and yet these Russified Ukrainians were either unable or unwilling to take advantage of the professional advancement the policy afforded them. Like the many teachers described in *Narodnii uchytel* articles, they purportedly lacked confidence in their own Ukrainian abilities and, with the exception of careerist types sensitive to which way the wind was blowing, saw little long-term value in investing in further study. Russian, for them, remained a prestige language that they believed offered the greatest advantage. Whether consciously for them or not, it had become their "native language."

In a draft to his 1927 order advising regional education inspectors to observe parental choice, Skrypnyk suggested a plan on how to properly determine a child's native language. Notably, the procedure he advised did not begin with parental identification of a child's native language. Ideally, schools would create acceptance committees that would decide on the language of instruction for children after an interview. In practice, this method might be seen as coercion. Therefore, he proposed that acceptance commissions converse with prospective students after they received information that the children spoke a language other than "that which the parent considers native."[8] If they found that the language differed, then the commission had to attempt to convince the parents of the "impracticality of teaching a child in a foreign language." The final decision, however, rested with the parents. Skrypnyk's official order directed regional education inspectors to pay attention "to all thoughts of relatives, pupils, and sections of the city soviet" when Ukrainizing the schools.[9] However, it also kept the requirement that they try to convince parents about the importance of reading and writing in a native language. Regardless of the specific method used for determining a language of instruction, it would be the state, through the schools, that would identify a child's "native language." Parents had to refute this affirmation of fact.

Although Skrypnyk was concerned about public cries of forced Ukrainization, he believed that they were mostly the result of a "misunderstanding." In particular, he maintained parents often objected to a change in the language of instruction of a school (and refused to allow the transfer of their children to another school) because they had contributed to the school's betterment. Thus, he advised early notice of a language switch so that education sections might solicit donations for school renovations in good faith. Otherwise, parents might always have the argument: "We repaired the location and you changed the language of study and forced our children to go to another institution and not ours."[10]

While Skrypnyk found this argument credible, he did not believe force was at play. His chief worry was that Ukrainization not "infringe upon the interests of national minorities," a category in which he included Russians since the December 1926 KP(b)U Ukrainization meeting. However, there were enough schools, according to his assessment, for ethnic minorities. The key was to have education sections plan correctly for the formation of schools by national composition and remove any appearance of force or, more specifically, lack of choice. Of course, Russified Ukrainian parents still had to demonstrate that their child's native language was Russian if educators questioned their choice. The paradox, Skrypnyk noted, was that claims of forced Ukrainization were being made at a time when Ukrainization was insufficient in some regions and cities, and "a significant proportion of children who speak Ukrainian study in the Russian language." A large proportion of these were children of urban Russified Ukrainians.

Instructions for local education sections made no allowance for continued Russian instruction of Russified Ukrainians. Contrary to the expectation of Lebed and other like-minded party members, Narkomos officials continued to view a person's assimilation to a "non-native" language as a negative phenomenon. "Nativeness" was determined by ethnicity. Thus, a February 1927 Uprsotsvykh memorandum to regional education inspectors asked: "How is native-language study instruction secured for children of workers? Did it not happen that children of Russian workers were Ukrainized and children of Ukrainian workers were Russified?"[11] Uprsotsvykh's assumption was that, in some instances, schools were altering children's ethnic identity through language. It ordered sections to report such cases and, in particular, incidents of parental complaints.

But, like Skrypnyk's order, Uprsotsvykh was chiefly concerned with process, questioning how local officials determined the language of study for a school. Anticipating the answer, it suggested that the number of true cases of state-sponsored linguistic assimilation were rare, asking if parents faced an entirely different dilemma: "Not to teach children in a school they do not want or not to teach them at all because there is nowhere to send the children." Chiefly, it was soliciting evidence to bolster its presumption that there was an appearance of forced Ukrainization because of parental choice or circumstance: parents did not wish to move their children from a newly Ukrainized school to a school of lesser prestige, or there was a shortage of Russian schools in a given area. Narkomos wanted to ensure ethnic Russians had adequate options for Russian-language schooling, but it generally discounted complaints regarding the Ukrainization of any one school if there was another Russian school in the area. Russified Ukrainians would have to continue to prove that the native language of their children was not Ukrainian, especially if the children were already enrolled in a school chosen for Ukrainization.

At the same time the KP(b)U first began a serious discussion of the issue of "forced Ukrainization," Narkomos continued to push for the expansion of Ukrainian-language schooling. In June 1926, Hordiienko, a representative from its Kyiv section, reported on Ukrainization of trudshkoly to Kyivprofrada, the city's umbrella union organization that included the municipal teachers' union. According to Hordiienko, approximately 30 per cent of children then enrolled in the city's schools were studying in Ukrainian.¹² He proposed that after the designation of nine additional Ukrainian schools, 40 per cent of children in the schools would study in Ukrainian.

This Ukrainization would inevitably cause dislocation for the city's Russian-speaking children, who would have to transfer out of the newly Ukrainized schools. Hordiienko conceded that it would be necessary to establish norms for the number of schools and groups needed for ethnic-Russian children. However, the Ukrainization campaign would also allow children enrolled in Russian schools, but specified by the education section as ethnic Ukrainian, to move to, or remain in, the new Ukrainian schools. According to Hordiienko's numbers, 12.3 per cent of the city's schoolchildren were ethnic Ukrainians attending non-Ukrainian (most likely Russian) schools. These pupils, along with Ukrainian children not attending school and children of anticipated migrants to the city, would fill the Ukrainized schools. When all the groups in these schools had fully transferred to Ukrainian-language instruction, the proportion of children studying in Ukrainian would ultimately rise to 52 per cent, a target Hordiienko expected to correspond with near-term growth of the city's Ukrainian population. He suggested that the education section should specifically target large schools in the centre of the city for Ukrainization. Narkomos needed large schools to contain these increased numbers and central schools to ensure "equal distribution of Ukrainian trudshkoly": to break the monopoly of Russian schools in this area, induce children of Russified elites who lived here to attend school in Ukrainian, and create space for children of new Ukrainian workers.¹³

It should be stressed that many parents readily supported the transfer in language of instruction and most accepted the shift as a matter of course. In response to the above complaint regarding the Ukrainization of Kyiv Labour School No. 6, the school head reported that when parents were told in 1925 that the first groups of the school would transfer to Ukrainian, "there was no dissatisfaction on the part of the parents, with the exception of six persons who transferred their children to other schools."¹⁴ There were apparently so many pupils whose parents wanted them to study in Ukrainian that the following year, the school had to move twenty-seven first-grade pupils to another Ukrainian-language school. One resident of the village of Male Prytske in the Kyiv region wrote to the inspectorate in 1927 to applaud Ukrainization of the schools and ask for the establishment of a Ukrainian-language school.¹⁵ In rural locations, parents who believed in education were desperate for any school; all the better if it was Ukrainian.

As a practical necessity, schools pursued Ukrainization in a piecemeal fashion, beginning the transfer at the youngest grades where children had not yet had extended schooling in Russian. Kyiv Labour School No. 6 may not have had the staff to transfer even the first year entirely to Ukrainian because some Russian groups remained. Furthermore, Russians and Jews continued to attend the school for the time being. They would either complete their schooling in Russian-language groups or transfer to a Russian or Yiddish school when the school had been fully Ukrainized. In fact, the report suggested that some non-Ukrainians at the second- and third-grade levels may have wished to study in Ukrainian, an inclination the school may have been willing to satisfy, if only to make its task easier in the short term. Above the third grade, the preference of the majority of these pupils (and eleven of twenty-nine Ukrainian pupils) was for Russian-language classes or mixed Ukrainian–Russian classes.

Narkomos firmly rejected any claim that Russian was superior to Ukrainian. The push to increase Ukrainian schools in the city was part of a larger campaign to promote Ukrainian as a modern, urban language, equal to Russian. Although a strong belief in the correlation between language and ethnicity motivated Narkomos policy to "re-Ukrainize" Russified children (and thereby bend the general prohibition against Ukrainization of the proletariat), the commissariat did seek to extol Ukrainian among the ethnic-Russian population as well. In Ukraine, all elementary pupils (regardless of ethnicity) were to enrol in Ukrainian-studies classes, and pupils had to demonstrate knowledge of Ukrainian for entry into higher education.[16] While respecting national linguistic rights, Narkomos's hope was that culture in the UkrSSR would have a prevailingly Ukrainian-speaking character. The RSFSR Commissar of Education Anatolii Lunacharsky lent his support to the Ukrainizers' task during a 1928 visit to Kyiv. Criticizing their opponents, he proclaimed, "We, Russian Communists, are outraged at those worthless people [*liudtsiv*] who see in the quickly developing Ukrainian language and Ukrainian culture some kind of unwanted competition."[17] He argued that Russians needed to increase their knowledge of Ukrainian as "an independent part of the world treasury," and proposed the opening of Ukrainian departments in the Russian republic's post-secondary institutions.

Meeting the Needs of the Ukrainian Proletariat

The years 1926 and 1927 saw a heightening of party vigilance against the "excesses" of Ukrainization, but also a renewed commitment to accelerate the campaign. A draft prepared for a June 1926 KP(b)U TsK resolution on the results of Ukrainization noted some shortcomings (*nedochety*) in the "nationalization" of schools and pointed out the absence of Russian schools in some localities where the ethnic-Russian population was significant.[18] On a republican level, it concluded that the number of Ukrainian primary schools was in line with the ethnic-Ukrainian proportion of the population. However, these schools needed to do a better job of attracting Ukrainian children to education. Only 45.95 per cent of Ukrainian children were attending school.[19] Regional education inspectors had maintained that Ukrainization of schools in the cities was helping to increase enrolment, but this Ukrainization had to be implemented responsibly. Ukrainian-language schooling could not be limited to truncated four-year schools or to workers' districts alone.

Educational planners regularly argued that incomplete Ukrainization limited schooling opportunities for working-class Ukrainian children. While respecting the bounds it had set regarding the ethnic-Russian population, the party saw the linguistic Ukrainization of the city as an urgent task. A December 1926 resolution of the Politburo's Ukrainization commission concluded that Narkomos needed to design a plan for the Ukrainization of schools in the growing workers' areas.[20] Under the watchful eye of the party, local education officials would pay attention to the wishes of the population, but their primary aim was to establish a complete network of Ukrainian schools, with full seven-year schools as the base. They were to tie the seven-year schools to a specific plan for the Ukrainization of secondary and post-secondary institutions. Narkomos would not limit Ukrainian-language education to primary schooling, as Lebed and opponents to Ukrainization in the party wished. The Ukrainian population, and particularly the emerging Ukrainian proletariat, had to believe that primary schooling in their native language was the beginning of a path of advancement for its children.

Newly Ukrainized schools were to strengthen their authority by raising the quality of their instruction and doing away with confusing mixed-language instruction. As the example of Kyiv Labour School No. 6 demonstrates, the immediate conversion to Ukrainian might have been more of a wish than an achievable objective. Recognizing that a "native language" was not as innate as the Ukrainizers would have hoped, education inspectors reported that Ukrainian children did not adjust instantly to the switch from Russian. In fully "Ukrainized" schools such as in Komarivka (Kharkiv region), children continued to speak in both Russian and Ukrainian with each other.[21] It did not help, furthermore, that teachers continued to use Russian texts and speak a mixed Ukrainian of their own. Still, Narkomos's argument was that such idiosyncrasies would be temporary. If Ukrainization was accomplished quickly, according to its logic, children and their parents would find classroom activities less perplexing and schools would be more effective in meeting their educational goals.

For Narkomos officials, it was important to retain a proletarian focus to the Ukrainization campaign in schooling. As was suggested briefly above, Kyiv Regional Inspector Lukashenko wrote in his long complaint to the head of Uprsotsvykh that Ukrainian-language groups in the city's schools had a higher proportion of working-class children than any other language group. Workers' children accounted for 44 per cent of the enrolment in Ukrainian groups. The next largest representation of working-class children was a 26 per cent enrolment in Russian groups.[22] Schools, Lukashenko concluded, were increasing their authority among a developing non-Russian proletariat dominated by Ukrainians: "the move to a nationalities policy in the school has led to an interest in education and an elevation of the cultural level of these same culturally backward elements of our society." He considered it critical for schools to increase in this respect.

The problem was that schools still were not adequately serving the Ukrainian population. It has already been mentioned that Lukashenko found the comparatively low Ukrainian attendance rates of Kyiv schools alarming. At the December 1926 meeting of the Politburo's Ukrainization commission, Skrypnyk had placed the proportion of school-age Ukrainian children who did not attend school at 54.4 per cent republic-wide, compared to 46.6 per cent for Russian children.[23] Ironically, Skrypnyk had suggested, Russian dissatisfaction was greater because before the revolution, all urban schools had been Russian, and now education officials had to divide up largely the same number of schools among different language groups. Beyond isolated cases of school realignment to meet "the requirements of the population," Narkomos would have to establish new schools.

Lukashenko clearly argued that school shortages contributed to dissatisfaction and "nationalist sentiments."[24] Classrooms in Kyiv were already stretched to their limit: 40.8 pupils per Ukrainian group and 40.1 per Russian group. Narkomos needed to ensure access to Russian-language schools, as well as expand the network of Ukrainian schools, to attract children of "the unorganized labour population" to school. In Myronivka, regional authorities recommended building a hostel for children from neighbouring villages.[25] Demand for schooling in this city was so great that any further educational progress required an expansion of infrastructure.

Ukrainizers insisted that a failure to pay proper attention to the Ukrainization of the proletariat would mean a weakening of the party's influence in the republic. Thus, although members of the Politburo's Ukrainization commission condemned the forced Ukrainization of the proletariat and acted to protect ethnic Russians as an ethnic minority, the party needed to persuade new Ukrainian labour and Russified Ukrainians to send their children to Ukrainian schools. At the December meeting, the head of Radnarkom, Vlas Chubar, suggested that a detailed study of the ethnic makeup of workers' regions would justify the need for Ukrainian schools. Narkomos had to determine the number of schools based on these data, not an account of initial preference: "To do otherwise would put us on the path urged by Larin, where each person can select the language he wishes, the one he wants to study and emphasize."[26] Chubar argued that if educational authorities did not encourage and plan for "native language" study in the cities, then, in five years' time, Ukrainian students would have nowhere to go for higher education in ethnic-Ukrainian territories except to those in Poland. Mass study in Ukrainian at the primary level would increase demand and strengthen the rationale for this higher education in the UkrSSR. Chubar insisted that Ukrainization was necessary not so much because the proletariat needed to learn Ukrainian, but because the state needed to teach it "so that the proletarian leadership is strengthened and does not slip away, so that the proletariat will build its own state." In a republic of largely Ukrainian-speaking peasants, the proletariat had to show the way. The Ukrainian language offered the means for command.

In spite of the heightened concern that the party demonstrated regarding the Ukrainization of the schools, Narkomos continued to have difficulty in implementing its charge. Just as the party wanted to exercise control over Narkomos, Narkomos wanted to set strict targets for its regional sections. Its expectations were high, but it offered little support on how to achieve them. One persistent problem was that Narkomos had failed to set up a Ukrainization program designed specifically for the demands of teachers, and yet continued to complain that teachers taught poorly. According to Kyiv Regional Inspector Lukashenko, Narkomos promised that a program for teachers' study of Ukrainian would be released in October 1926, repeatedly delayed its publication, and by September 1927 still had not circulated one.[27] He reportedly informed Skrypnyk, who was at a loss to explain the delay. Arnautov, the head of Uprsotsvykh, maintained that Radnarkom's Ukrainization commission was responsible for working out the program and, despite Uprsotsvykh's prodding, he did not expect it until February 1928.[28] He blamed the "bureaucratic process," but, as Lukashenko pointed out, regional sections were forbidden to release their own programs to fill the gap. Whatever the specific reason for the holdup, the Ukrainization commission clearly did not want local authorities taking matters into their own hands. The program had to set standardized norms for all teachers in the republic.

To a certain extent, then, Narkomos's mismanagement contributed to its problems. In the absence of an obligatory program for use in teachers' training courses and faculty groups, Narkomos issued material for a correspondence course. An article in *Narodnii uchytel* explained such an approach was needed because of the high demand for courses in Ukrainian studies among the public (i.e., present and prospective state employees) and teachers alike, but few qualified instructors to teach the material.[29] Ukrliknep designed the courses, not Uprsotsvykh, but geared them to the demands of each professional group. For teachers, Ukrliknep's commission for self-study composed assignments "specific to school duties for the next school year."[30] The commission instructed them to read lectures, complete weekly exercises, send them back to be corrected, and then receive new material. There was a charge for this course, but *Narodnii uchytel* recommended students form groups of five to seven to save on costs and work more effectively. Students were also invited to listen to free lectures on the radio or visit the commission's head office in Kharkiv for consultations.

It is unknown how many teachers enrolled in these courses. However, their incentive to complete them increased with the May 1927 announcement that yet another round of Ukrainian-language examinations would be held at the beginning of the 1927–8 school year, likely targeted for those areas where it had been postponed. The only preparatory work Narkomos organized for the perevirka was correspondence work, which Narkomos published in an addendum to *Narodnii uchytel*. The first lecture appeared in the newspaper in July, and the publication of new lectures continued until the end of the year. Neither the newspaper nor Uprsotsvykh archival record makes mention of where and when the perevirka actually occurred. Preparation must have been difficult. Lukashenko pointed to the continuing "famine" (*holod*) of books and textbooks.[31] The state publishing house was printing pedagogical literature now, but not in the volume needed. This made it difficult not only to teach in the classroom, but also to procure recommended material needed for Ukrainian-language study.

Narkomos's publication of the lectures in Ukrainian studies was a recognition that there was a problem, but it continued to rely on teachers' initiative to first seek out *Narodnii uchytel*, then form a study group and dedicate time to reading and writing out the assignments. The teachers' union, Robos, offered to answer questions on the lectures published in the newspaper, but at a cost: 1.20 rubles for each month's lecture. Few teachers would have been able to spend even this amount of extra money.

Distrust of the Intelligentsia: Early Cries of a Nationalist Threat

The party leadership expected teachers to take up the banner of Ukrainization for the policy to succeed. As Narkomos had argued, an improvement in the quality of Ukrainian instruction would raise the authority of Ukrainian schools, increase attendance, and ensure a more effective education. The party, however, did not entirely trust teachers and non-party intelligentsia to design and implement Ukrainization. In a series of documents beginning in 1926, republican party leaders had pointed to the danger of poor oversight over Ukrainization.

An unsigned Politburo report from 15 March 1926, likely given by Zatonsky at a meeting convened specifically to consider his assessment of the state of Ukrainization, pointed directly to the effect of the campaign on the intelligentsia. In spite of the centralized leadership of Ukrainization, the party had tolerated some "spontaneity" and "uncontrolled elements."[32] Lower organs, particularly in the Right Bank and Poltava regions, had pursued Ukrainization aggressively. Their success had caused a shift in the attitudes of intelligentsia, particularly some teachers. The report suggests that nationalists were seeking to capitalize on the success of Ukrainization and turn the intelligentsia against Soviet power. It cited several reasons for this apparent nationalist infiltration: the increased frustration of low-ranking intelligentsia over their "unendurable, difficult material situation," weakening union influence over the teacher, debts owed by the state press to Ukrainian academics for work they had completed (e.g., Mykhailo Hrushevsky), and the party's neglect of intelligentsia loyal to Soviet power.[33]

Thus, the Politburo report argued, the party had failed on two accounts. First, it failed to address what it considered to be a legitimate issue of the intelligentsia: adequate compensation. Party leaders were fully aware that teachers, in particular, received miserable pay, but their priorities lay elsewhere. What is more surprising is that this report identified a causal link between earnings and national frustration. Perhaps not all party members agreed with this logic, but all must have paid heed to the report's discussion of a disregard of "anti-Soviet elements." Here was the rationale behind Narkomos's insistence, discussed above, that it develop a standardized plan for Ukrainian-language instruction for the whole republic. The party could not trust Right Bank education section administrators, such as Lukashenko, to develop their own. Who knows what they might recommend? The report singled out Kyiv party "higher-ups" in particular for lack of proper leadership, linking this shortcoming with a perceived growth in nationalism and peasant political activity. The party had difficulty combating such tendencies, it explained, because of the "extreme weakness of Marxist forces" among the intelligentsia. In short, the report charged that due to a lack of qualified Communists, Soviet authorities had relied excessively on non-party intellectuals to implement Ukrainization, and some of them were trying to bend the policy to their own design.

Even Shumsky had conceded that anti-Soviet elements had taken advantage of the climate permitted by Ukrainization. He put a definite face on these forces in material he prepared for a Politburo meeting at the end of March 1926, maintaining that one group had coalesced at meetings of the Rukh publishing house. Their platform united "part of the Galician immigrants, some teachers, including teachers of the Ukrainian language, and members of the autocephalous citizenry."[34] He too explained that they were capitalizing on lack of proper government support for Ukrainian cultural affairs. Among several government missteps, he pointed to the nonpayment of honorariums to Hryhorii Ivanytsia (later tried as a member of SVU). Communists also "covered their ears" at what Shumsky suggested was a sincere attempt at a Marxist interpretation of the writings of the famous scholar and revolutionary Mykhailo Drahomanov by Yosyp Hermaize (also arrested as a SVU organizer) and literary scholar Oleksandr Doroshkevych. The party had

A cartoon of a teacher resisting Ukrainization. The caption reads: "Hippopotami. Inoculations for the thick-skinned." On the shot is written the word "Ukrainization." *Narodnii uchytel'* (16 January 1929), 5.

slighted the intelligentsia for no apparent reason and ignored important allies. Some of the Ukrainian intelligentsia, as a result, were demanding a greater role in the administration of culture, and anti-Soviet groups working among them were "winning over the sympathies of the mass of Ukrainian society."

The solution, Shumsky asserted, was in more Ukrainization, not less. First, the party needed to ensure that teachers were properly paid. Teachers' salaries had risen comparatively little versus those of workers, civil servants, and even other higher-ranking intelligentsia. Teachers were overburdened and received no extra compensation for their efforts. "Non-proletarian powers, former counter-revolutionaries, and Petliurists" were inciting discussion of a teachers' strike in twenty-two regions.[35] The party needed to re-examine the question of payment immediately or risk losing political influence. The party also had to increase its authority in trade unions and "fulfill the promises given by Soviet authorities." It was critically important that the party manage the cultural front, prepare workers trained in the nationalities question, and bring sympathetic members of the intelligentsia into the party. However, in making this argument, Shumsky unwisely planted the seed of suspicion and foretold his own downfall. Whom could the party trust?

The republican party leadership could not permit Shumsky's April 1926 protest to Stalin regarding Kaganovich's management of Ukrainization to go unpunished. In that summer, the KP(b)U TsK criticized Shumsky for his defence of "disloyal" Ukrainian intellectuals such as Khvylovy. After a series of such criticisms, in February to March 1927, a plenum of the TsK forced Shumsky to step down from his post as commissar and recommended transferring him outside Ukraine. Karlo Maksymovych, the Western Ukrainian Communist Party (KPZU) delegate to the plenum, spoke against Shumsky's demotion and argued that these measures only harmed the Communist Party's standing among Ukrainians under Polish rule and benefited Ukrainian nationalists and Polish "fascists."[36] Maksymovych's defence of Shumsky led to a split within the KPZU when Maksymovych and his majority faction unsuccessfully protested to the Comintern regarding the KP(b)U's treatment of Shumsky. The Comintern forced a replacement of the entire KPZU leadership in 1928. As Terry Martin writes, "The Shumsky affair then escalated dramatically over the course of the two years from a typical factional struggle in the non-Russian republics to an international scandal and the condemnation of a fascist deviation within the Ukrainian Communist Party [i.e., the KP(b)U]."[37] It confirmed in the minds of many party members an essential suspicion of Ukrainization.

The party's anxiety about Ukrainian nationalism was already high enough in 1926–7. It received regular reports that a Ukrainian nationalist movement was growing. A 1926 KP(b)U TsK assessment entitled "Results of Ukrainization" reminded members of the civil war history of nationalist banditry and linked it to a resurgence of Ukrainian nationalism in the village and in Ukrainian literature.[38] It was careful to note that there was also a parallel rise in Russian chauvinism among government employees who were conducting a campaign against Ukrainization through anonymous letters and other writings. However, even at this early date, the party leadership claimed that Ukrainian nationalism presented a particular threat, for several reasons. First, the KP(b)U's information maintained that nationalism was growing in the countryside, about which the party knew less and which it still viewed as unreceptive if not hostile. Second, whereas the party had made some inroads in Sovietizing government employees, the Ukrainian intelligentsia was largely non-Communist. The likelihood of its turning against the regime was, therefore, viewed as comparatively high.

Another report, prepared for the drafting of the June 1926 KP(b)U TsK plenum theses, pointed to the susceptibility of the rural population to influence by kulaks, who were the supposed custodians of Ukrainian nationalism, according to party belief. The theses stated that the kulak authority was growing largely because "it goes without saying, the continued insufficient satisfactory material position of the basic groups of the rural intelligentsia (teachers, agronomists, and doctors) only favors the growth of kulak influence on them."[39] Nationalism in the city was also reportedly rooted in the village, imported by petit bourgeois and intelligentsia migrants. The report held Ukrainization partly to blame, noting a rise in nationalism among government employees in the Ukrainized Soviet apparat. It stopped well short of criticizing Ukrainization as a whole, but reasoned that the tie between Ukrainian petit bourgeois elements and the newly Ukrainized elite was strong, and that the former would soon try to spread their influence to the proletariat and party.

A previous draft of the report was even more explicit about the peasant origin of Ukrainian nationalism, yet also contended that in the city, the ideology had taken on an even more dangerous bent. It identified nationalism's rise in the village with the increased strength of the kulak under the post-civil war NEP, suggesting it had spread to the city due to an attraction "to the culture of peasant elements," reinforced in part by the Ukrainization of higher education institutes.[40] However, the nationalists also sought to play on the bourgeois and intelligentsia's embrace of modernism. These "modernist nationalists" rejected the romanticization of the peasant: "This group is decidedly sick with the ethnographism of small village kulak Ukrainophilia and provincialism, with the outmoded organic nature of the latter, with the idealization of varenyky [dumplings] and cherry-tinted confinement." The group stood for the industrialization of Ukraine, its opening up to world culture, and, most critically, for the rejection of Russian as an imposition on Ukrainian development. It applauded Ukrainization but wanted even more.

Somehow, these seemingly irreconcilable groups – kulak provincial nationalists and elite urban chauvinists – came to a "deal." The report suggests the possible collusion of a foreign power. It found the latter faction more dangerous because it allegedly included some Soviet specialists, as well as post-secondary instructors and literary critics. Its position was far too seductive: "It holds in its hands a rather serious ideological position, making it possible to influence – with its Europeanism, scholarship, technical level, and formal loyalty – young students, sometimes workers and, finally, even some 'well-shod' Marxist elements inside our party, who have again warmed up the theory of the battle of two cultures and forgot[ten] Lenin's testament."[41]

What mattered, of course, was that the party claimed this union to be the case. A deep-seated distrust of the peasant, represented in his most antagonistic form as the kulak, had developed into a suspicion of all those who promoted the peasant's language too zealously at the expense of Russian. Mykola Khvylovy was the chief representative of the latter view. But the party viewed any gesture away from Moscow as nothing short of heresy. "Khvylovysm," as it came to be called, confirmed the party's distrust of the intelligentsia and allowed it to instinctively question displays of intellectual independence as signs of potential nationalism.

Independence Provokes Suspicion

The reality was that few teachers could be characterized as nationalists. The pedagogical press regularly reported about their unsatisfactory Ukrainian skills. Not only were teachers unable to improve their Ukrainian, some remained openly hostile to the Ukrainization policy. As *Narodnii uchytel* characterized such attitudes, there were school directors "who at every opportune and inopportune occasion attempted to prove their contempt for the Ukrainian language and of Ukrainization in general."[42] Perhaps worse, some teachers had managed to posture themselves as Ukrainizers, but knew little Ukrainian: "They offend the task, lend a hostile attitude to the Ukrainization of employees, and provide material for damaging jokes."[43] In some cases, teachers employed as Ukrainian-studies instructors could teach only the Ukrainian alphabet. Poor instructors in pedagogical institutions were cultivating "semi-literacy" among their graduates.[44] This was not a problem limited to the old guard, then, accustomed to teaching in Russian, but also existed among the lauded next generation of teachers.

The teachers' press maintained that animosity towards Ukrainization was prevalent precisely because teachers such as these did not know how to teach Ukrainian properly. The "spoiling" of the Ukrainian language by teachers emboldened those teachers and members of the intelligentsia who cared about Ukrainization. *Narodnii uchytel* speaks repeatedly of the "profanization" of Ukrainian. Teachers were not simply making mistakes; they were polluting the language and doing lasting harm to its future. Such talk disturbed those party members who saw Ukrainian more as a tool for administration and less as a cultural value.

Of course, the teachers' general poor knowledge of Ukrainian prevented them from accomplishing the very political tasks that the party expected of them. First, teachers could not take on the lead role in explaining Soviet nationalities policy and the importance of studying and using Ukrainian. One *Narodnii uchytel* contributor labelled "hardheaded" (*tverdolobi*) those teachers who refused to improve their Ukrainian and assume a primary role in administering Ukrainization. He described teachers who spoke in Ukrainian only when inspectors visited their schools, and one director who made a cursory attempt at using Ukrainian at a conference and then switched to Russian, apologizing, "You know, after you speak a little in that '*mova*' [language], the jowls hurt."[45] This sort of formal approach to Ukrainization or outright rejection of it reduced the party's own ability to counteract societal prejudice against Ukrainian. For example, one government employee in Dnipropetrovsk refused to undergo a perevirka in Ukrainian because he claimed the language was "doglike."[46] Party assessments of Ukrainization contain several reports of similar anecdotes. One *Narodnii uchytel* comic depicts a hippopotamus receiving a shot marked "Ukrainization." The caption reads: "Hippopotami. Inoculations for the thick-skinned."[47] Such extreme attitudes may not have been wide-ranging, but they were not uncommon.

Teachers who did not know Ukrainian well were also of little use in the party's campaigns to eradicate illiteracy in the countryside and propagandize among the peasantry. Some might have felt comfortable using Ukrainian in the classroom, but still did not know the language well enough to use it for this sort of political work among the general public. They worried about speaking Ukrainian to their students' parents, "fearing compromising themselves in front of the peasantry."[48] Others, who had a better grasp of the language, simply did not believe that Ukrainian should be used for activities outside the school. They procured Russian books for the village reading rooms and thereby both slowed down Ukrainization and reinforced an understanding of Ukrainian as a non-literary language. Vorobiov, a *Narodnii uchytel* contributor, conceded that peasants may have had trouble understanding the sort of standardized Ukrainian being touted by Narkomos, but maintained that teachers still had to forsake their reliance on Russian.[49] Ukrainization would have no meaning otherwise, and peasants would continue to view the teacher as an extension of Soviet power, as fundamentally foreign.

Obviously, the shortage of Ukrainian speakers meant that some who knew the language well had the advantage and could profit. An undated 1926 report to the KP(b)U TsK authored by Arkadii Mykoliuk, assistant head of Ukrliknep, on the "Matter of Ukrainization of the Soviet Apparat" noted that a new type of Ukrainian-language teacher had appeared in the past two years. This teacher was more "developed" (*rozvynutyi*), largely as a result of experience or education in Soviet higher pedagogical institutions.[50] These teachers performed duties for literacy centres, local party cells, and municipal Ukrainization committees, but they also displayed "elements of self-seeking behavior."[51] The report claimed some Kharkiv teachers had abandoned their work in schools altogether for better-paid work as Ukrainian-studies instructors under Ukrliknep. The demand for their skills was so great that they could "slip into positions" and receive even higher, unregulated wages.

This practice undoubtedly increased the party's suspicions of the Ukrainian intelligentsia generally. The majority of the teachers were not party members. Some were former Ukrainian Autocephalous Orthodox priests, whom Ukrliknep attempted to expose and remove from their positions. Ukrliknep made use of the few Communist instructors it had, putting them in workers' clubs and factories and ensuring they had ample opportunity to improve their qualifications.[52] Nevertheless, the report cited twenty-five Communist instructors for the campaign against illiteracy in the whole capital city of Kharkiv. This was not a promising trend. The conclusion the party must have drawn was that Ukrainian cultural forces in the party remained weak and that non-party intelligentsia could not be trusted. The logic party documents suggested was that if Ukrainizers were not nationalists, they were opportunists, seeking to exploit Ukrainization for their own personal gain.

To be sure, there were few options. In effect conceding the culpability of both the party and Narkomos, the report noted that sometimes regional sections employed intelligentsia without a proper understanding of their political orientation: "Willfully or not, Agitprop and organs of Narkomos in localities sometimes used the work of the intelligentsia 'on trust.'"[53] Adherents of Mykola Khvylovy's discredited ideas on Ukrainian autonomy were allegedly particularly strong among the Odesa intelligentsia, although the report did not elaborate.

What appeared to be most vexing to the Ukrliknep report was that members of the intelligentsia were operating outside Narkomos's control. It maintained that they were trying to publish their "own organs" in Kharkiv, Kyiv, and Odesa.[54] A literary circle in Kyiv called Chas had succeeded in putting out an anthology of classical Ukrainian works on its own. Furthermore, some members of the intelligentsia viewed cultural work as apolitical. Professor Oleksa Syniavsky, a member of Narkomos's orthography commission, told an assembly of teachers in 1926 that "political" matters had no bearing on his work.[55] In another context, this perhaps could be considered an admirable sentiment. The orthography commission did strive to establish a standardized Ukrainian that could be recognized by all, doing away with Russian borrowings to the language and integrating Galician variant forms. However, its work was fundamentally political in the sense that the orthography was intended for use in party and government work, for propaganda and administration of Soviet power.

In the absence of competent governmental or party authority, the local intelligentsia had stepped in to administer Ukrainization. For example, the Odesa education section had reported that in 1925, the provincial political education section had organized a scientific commission of Ukrainian activists and intelligentsia. This group attracted dozens of workers to compile a program in Ukrainian language, literature, and embroidery; monitor Ukrainization of Soviet institutions and primary schools; and organize the Ukrainian intelligentsia. Although Odesa officials granted that the efforts of this commission were sincere, the commission operated independently of the regional education section because of lack of supervision and assumed "inappropriate functions."[56] Therefore, the regional executive committee subordinated its activities to a city inspector of Ukrainization, a position provided for by Narkomos instructions, who, in Odesa, also headed a regional Ukrainization commission. Local authorities needed the help of members of the intelligentsia such as teachers, but they could not be permitted to set the agenda for the campaign themselves.

In Kyiv, educators also displayed an excess of initiative that alarmed Soviet authorities. In March 1927, the Kyiv Regional Inspectorate received a memorandum from Kybalchych, the head of Kyiv Labour School No. 38. Kybalchych wrote to honour the tenth anniversary of the establishment of the Taras Shevchenko Kyiv Labour School No. 1, now specified as an experimental school under the patronage of VUAN. He spoke glowingly of its early founding three weeks after the overthrow of the tsar, struggle to survive during Kyiv's occupation by the White general Denikin, and rescue by Soviet power. It had prospered and guided the development of other Ukrainian schools largely due to the efforts of Volodymyr Durdukivsky: "This is ten years of tireless, constant work by its founder and organizer, the current head, 'the soldier of the great army of workers of the Ukrainian school,' comrade V. F. Durdukivsky."[57] Kybalchych made a "secret request" that his school be renamed after Durdukivsky, "the pioneer of the Ukrainian labour school."

The response of Narkomos administrators demonstrated that this petition was too presumptuous. Narkomos named schools after high-ranking party members and acclaimed figures from Ukraine and Russia's revolutionary past, not non-party intelligentsia. Kyiv regional education inspector Lukashenko wrote to the regional Agitprop section, expressing unease about the enthusiasm of teachers for the May celebration of the tenth anniversary of Labour School No. 1: "Considering that without proper leadership from our side, this celebration can acquire an undesired character ... I believe an appeal is necessary to create under Okrnarosvita [regional education section] a commission for the preparation of this anniversary."[58] He asked for directives from the party for the creation of this commission, naming possible members from the regional education section, party committee, and Robos. Among the proposed candidates, Lukashenko included Durdukivsky. His addition possibly represented an attempt to watch over and contain his activity rather than a sign of esteem. A year later, the GPU arrested Durdukivsky for his alleged association with the Union for Liberation of Ukraine (SVU), a fabricated organization, which chapter 10 will discusss in detail. At this earlier date, his growing popularity among Kyiv's national intelligentsia was clearly a matter of concern.

Thus, regardless of whether the members of the intelligentsia were "nationalists" or not, republican party documents reveal that its leadership resented giving control of Ukrainization to them. It viewed independent activity as potentially dangerous because it was incapable of leading the Ukrainization campaign itself. Its language insecurity, coupled with the memory of its struggle against Ukrainian independence during the civil war, only increased its suspicions. It worried that even if the intelligentsia were not involved in political activity directed against Soviet power, intellectuals were not fully committed to its survival. The intelligentsia had to be active propagandists for socialism and not rest content in their scholarship.

The party and Narkomos made a distinction between high intelligentsia: academics, essayists, and pedagogical theorists; and low intelligentsia: teachers. Teachers generally did not know Ukrainian as well as the former group. However, as has been already noted, the party worried that the nationalist intelligentsia might exercise undue influence over teachers and take advantage of teachers' resentment of their poor standard of living. Especially in the cities, teachers who did know Ukrainian joined with more prominent intellectuals in academic circles. Ironically, Narkomos's own recommendations to teachers for Ukrainian study encouraged the very sort of unregulated work that it came to frown upon later. In rural locations, teachers occupied an even more prominent position as representatives of Soviet enlightenment. They led literacy centres, ran reading houses, and, of course, exercised authority over children and their parents. For the party, their potential intellectual autonomy threatened party leadership.

Chapter Eight

Children as Salvation: The Young Pioneers and Komsomol

An institution of a new literacy necessitated the participation of the young for it to succeed. Yet, in the context of the Soviet Union, where this literacy had an explicit political objective, Communist leadership, oversight, and participation were needed. For schools and children, the party delegated this responsibility to the Communist Youth League (Komsomol) and its subsidiary organization for younger children, the Young Pioneers, and it is on their activities that this chapter focuses. It maintains that Komsomol administration over Ukrainization was a critical marker of the viability of Ukrainization. Even if shortcomings in the policy did not immediately affect Communist power in Soviet Ukraine, political authorities in the republic were anxious about the campaign's success, failure, misapprehension, and misapplication. Ukrainization of the Komsomol and Young Pioneers raised essential questions about the implications of popular resistance to the policy, the limits of Communist political authority, and the challenges accompanying the ruralization of Komsomol membership. The Komsomol has been the subject of recent research, but the experience of the Young Pioneers has been written about less, and very little has been said in regard to their relationship to Soviet nationalities policy.[1] This story of these children is critical to a larger understanding of general youth attitudes, generational development, and political integration with the Soviet state.[2] It was upon their shoulders that a Soviet-defined Ukrainian national culture ultimately rested.

Komsomol conversion to Ukrainian-language instruction was slow, according to the organization's own statistical record, and delays and resistance in the Komsomol to Ukrainization had an inevitable effect on the Young Pioneers. Primarily urban-based, the Young Pioneers were a weak link in the policy of Ukrainization generally. When the party began to push the policy hard, Young Pioneers overwhelmingly operated in Russian. Where they used Ukrainian, they did so haltingly, without proper regard to the Ukrainian literacy standard and to the political meaning of their task.

Because Young Pioneer detachments paid little attention to Soviet nationalities policy generally, Komsomol leadership began to suggest that they were unable to articulate lessons in socialism and the objectives of the Soviet state. In some locations, Young Pioneer organizations were losing the battle for the loyalty of non-Russian-speaking children, including Ukrainians and ethnic minorities, because these children saw the Young Pioneer organizations as foreign and their activities lacked relevance to their lives. The Komsomol leadership argued that Young Pioneer organizations overall were in jeopardy because of the corrupting influence of individual Komsomol members. Young Pioneers engaged in "immoral behaviour" because of their own contact with the Komsomol. Importantly, the way out of this mess for both organizations was to dedicate renewed energy to Ukrainization, particularly to expansion of Young Pioneer activity in Ukrainian schools. Ukrainization, in short, was the answer to a more popular, vigorous, and effective children's Communist movement.

The problem was, of course, that the Komsomol did not seem to be taking its own Ukrainization seriously. The key constituency whose attitude Komsomol worried about was working-class youth. On one hand, its motivation was clear. Komsomol documents claimed that the organization faced competition from former youth organizations that played on the national frustration of some young Ukrainian workers, but the Komsomol leadership also raised the persistent question of the prohibition against the Ukrainization of the working class. Here was an analogous situation to what was applied towards schoolchildren. For Komsomol working-class youth, the situation was different from that of the average worker. They had a responsibility to lead Soviet policy. The natural constituency for spearheading and promoting Ukrainian literacy as an authoritative expression of Soviet power was Komsomol members who identified themselves as Ukrainian but spoke, or aspired to speak, Russian; they had to switch to the deliberate and regular use of Ukrainian. Given the contested nature of this effort, the Komsomol opted for a campaign of persuasion or "gentle Ukrainization."

Like Narkomos's policy towards schoolchildren, Komsomol Ukrainizers hoped to avoid a direct assault on working-class interests and yet transform the working class by example and the advancement of the "converted." The transformation of the Komsomol would reinforce the Ukrainization of primary-school-aged children. The Komsomol would ideally work in concert with the Ukrainization of the Young Pioneers, playing off what was imagined as an energetic program of Ukrainization among the youngest. However, the Komsomol also worried about the Ukrainization of youth who had missed or curtailed formal education during the unstable 1920s. Their illiteracy was an essential hindrance to the political acculturation of the working class because of their role as inheritors of the factory floor and sustainers of socialism. What was critical was that the Komsomol approved a plan for literacy training of these youths in Ukrainian, not Russian, in designated literacy schools. The Soviet state would "recapture" these youths for orientation around the newly privileged knowledge of Ukrainian studies. This generation would share a common purpose with young children matriculating through the conventional school system and joining the ranks of the Pioneers.

The Komsomol's grand plans for revival of its own rank and file and the Young Pioneers through Ukrainization, however, faced a significant challenge similar to that of the schools. Children failed to see value in their training in the Young Pioneers, a shortcoming Komsomol documents blamed on a dearth of Ukrainian-specific material. The Komsomol leadership saw such inattention as responsible for large-scale defections of Young Pioneer units. It suggested that Young Pioneer failures in nationalities policy had allowed for the growth in nationalist and religious groups generally. Of particular concern was the failure of Young Pioneer groups attached to a Ukrainian school to transform student attitudes, thus forfeiting a position of command. It was among these groups that Ukrainization should have occurred most quickly.

The question of authority is key to the policy of Ukrainization because it was a policy deemed to be vital to the party's legitimacy, but also one inherently hazardous. An essential dilemma the Komsomol and party leadership faced was growing rural membership. The Komsomol remained distrustful of the peasantry and sought to codify a political education for its youth, but also working-class authority over a new rural majority. This majority could not be permitted to define what constituted Ukrainian language and culture, but if urban youth resisted Ukrainian-language training, this definition by the majority might, in fact, occur by default. The Komsomol leadership feared this phenomenon was already happening in some localities.

Like Narkomos, the Komsomol was also worried about low school enrolment and shortages in teacher staffing as a mark of incomplete Ukrainization and, consequently, a challenge for political education. The Young Pioneers and Komsomol were to work to increase the authority of the schools and use the schools as a base for political activity in the community, but this could not be done without proper language training. An underperforming school was a hindrance to the development of the Young Pioneer movement, but a Young Pioneer detachment incapable of engaging parents, children, and the wider public effectively could also not support the school. The Komsomol leadership saw Ukrainization as key, then, to the intersection between the two.

As the Ukrainization campaign accelerated, Komsomol reports continued to reveal a lack of knowledge of a Ukrainian literary standard among its rank and file. Some reports suggested that some of these workers knew a Ukrainian "vernacular," but refused to speak even this. Some recently arrived rural immigrants wondered why knowledge in Ukrainian was needed at all if their chief duty was

A group of Young Pioneers at a rally in the city of Kyiv, 1930s. Courtesy TsDKFFAU.

the workbench, reinforcing doubts expressed by some in the Komsomol leadership about literacy in Ukrainian for urban workers who functioned largely in Russophone environments. In other words, the Ukrainian language did not hold the command that Ukrainizers expected, and some workers saw the language as irrelevant at best and did not respect knowledge of the vernacular. For the Komsomol and, by extension, the Young Pioneers to succeed at all in this campaign, they needed to effect a fundamental change. They had to turn this population of existing Ukrainian speakers. Otherwise, children would see little reason to hold on to whatever knowledge they had as speakers, or gained and refined, and the Young Pioneers' task would be that much more difficult.

Given the proclaimed critical nature of the campaign, it is perhaps surprising that the Komsomol did so little to offer formal training to its members. Komsomol units habitually chose to encourage members to form their own study groups and clubs rather than fund expensive Ukrainian-studies courses. According to official reports, often few Komsomol members attended these circles. Despite official exhortations, participation in Ukrainization remained a voluntary affair. The language divide between village and city persisted into the late 1920s, with rural units fully Ukrainizing and urban units failing to do so. It is unclear if these rural units were speaking the standard literary Ukrainian codified and sanctioned by the republican authorities. For some, the idea of asking the already stretched workforce to dedicate precious leisure time to overcome this split seemed preposterous.

Not everything needed to be left to whim, however. Some Komsomol members had already enrolled in some formal education. Beyond the schools for literacy, political schools were training Komsomol members explicitly for participation in the state's economic and political campaigns, and this training was expected to occur in Ukrainian. In these schools, the language served as an unadulterated political tool. For the younger generation of children of primary concern here, the Komsomol supported such training at an early age in FZU schools. These seven-year schools were granted by Narkomos as a concession to the interests of trade unions and Komsomol, who fought for an education attuned to the labour culture. Although secondary schooling in Ukraine was much more directed towards the needs of industry than its Russian counterpart, and the primary school embraced elements of this orientation, neither was a vocational school. The FZU school was the closest approximation of such an industrial school; these schools were supposed to offer more vocational and political training than conventional primary schools and were presumably ideal bases of Young Pioneer activity. Progress in Ukrainization among students of these schools was seen as possible (and more beneficial than among traditional primary-school students). The state, in theory, could mould these children to a much greater degree than their seniors in the Komsomol. In reality, the regime made numerous allowances for delay in the FZU school.

And yet, small inklings of progress were apparent. The subscription rate to Ukrainian-language newspapers rose sharply throughout the 1920s. Rural units and some in cities in central Ukraine gradually moved to regular Ukrainian use by the late 1920s. In Kyiv in particular, the Komsomol regional organization reached out beyond its network, ostensibly learning from non-party cultural organizations and thereby increasing its authority. Still, success invited some suspicion that Komsomol members might be learning lessons in nationalism. Conceivably, such a "contagion" might infect Young Pioneers and young children. This sort of rhetoric, mixing praise and opprobrium, became regular and more explicit during the cultural revolution that accompanied the traumatic economic and political campaigns of the later 1920s and early 1930s. In regard to perceptions of success and failure, triumph or danger, place mattered as well, and Kyiv merited the special attention of political authority, as did the multi-ethnic, polyglot port city of Odesa.

National Culture an Organizational Renewal for the Young Pioneers

As has been discussed in brief above, if republican authorities expressed concern about the pace of Ukrainization within the party, they were dismayed at the lack of progress in the Komsomol. Delays in Ukrainization in the Komsomol were to have an inevitable effect on schooling because of the membership of young teachers and pedagogical students in the organization and the Komsomol's responsibility for oversight over the Communist organization for schoolchildren, the Young Pioneers. An early 1927 report issued by the Ukrainian Komsomol TsK argued that the Ukrainization of the Komsomol apparat had "proceeded too carefully" after a TsK plenum had first ordered the program's full-scale implementation in 1925.[3] Prior to a meeting of the TsK plenum in 1926, the Komsomol leadership pursued Ukrainization where it was easiest, in the organization's administrative committees and other places most directly under its control. However, in urban Komsomol cells, "it was very often possible to encounter opposition to all attempts to carry out Ukrainization, to speak in the Ukrainian language."[4] Urban members often failed to understand why Ukrainization was politically necessary or what was the general content of the Communist Party's nationalities policy.

A consequence of this opposition and misapprehension was the weak Ukrainization of Young Pioneer work, especially in the cities. A 1925 order from the KP(b)U Politburo regarding the children's Communist movement posited that "it is necessary to strengthen moments of Ukrainization, transferring [Young Pioneer] detachments made up of Ukrainian children to the Ukrainian language."[5] The decree mandated that Young Pioneer leaders divide up children of ethnic minorities into parallel groups to ensure that they received political training in their native language. It conceded, however, that the final assignment of children to a national detachment be made "while considering the wishes of children." No further detail is offered by the decree as to how authorities might assess these wishes. However, in making this allowance, the decree allowed for the possibility that ambitious parents might make another choice for their children, for a Russian group as well as for a Ukrainian group.

Clearly, the established Young Pioneer detachments, which were already few in number and confined to the cities, operated in Russian, and Ukrainian and ethnic-minority detachments struggled to make headway against this existing predominance. A 1925 Komsomol report on the status of the children's Communist movement in Ukraine claimed that although data were available only for thirty-one regions in the republic, the "vast majority" of Young Pioneer detachments conducted their work in Russian.[6] Because of the weak work in Ukrainization, the report argued, the creation of ethnic-minority detachments was delayed. In other words, whether because of inertia, parental choice and predispositions, or the management of Young Pioneer leaders, few children enrolled in non-Russian detachments of any kind: "Regarding children's relationship with Ukrainization or transfer to work in the native language (Yiddish, etc.), in the cities a passive ... and at times undesirable relationship exists (in Nizhyn, etc.)." Where detachments were carrying out work in Ukrainian, the language Young Pioneers used was "slang" (*zhargon*), reproduced in detachment wall newspapers. As in the schools, one of the principal obstacles was the lack of Ukrainian-language literature, particularly political texts. The KP(b)U Politburo decree recommended Ukrainian Young Pioneer groups make greater use of Ukrainian revolutionary songs, "Red carols," and called for the establishment of a specialized young children's political press in Ukraine.[7]

At this early date, then, the question of Ukrainization of children's political education through the Young Pioneers was intimately tied to the question of de-Russification generally and the moral and organizational development of the Young Pioneers. A memorandum sent from the Komsomol TsK to all regional committees summarized the results of the All-Ukrainian Meeting on the Children's [Communist] Movement in October 1925. Not surprisingly, the meeting found that few Young Pioneer organizations had taken up the task of Ukrainization: "It turned out that the majority of workers do not know Ukrainian, the apparat is not Ukrainized, Russian literature is used, and so on."[8] The TsK ordered Komsomol regional organizations to transfer Young Pioneer detachments, seminars, and study circles with an ethnic-Ukrainian membership to work in the Ukrainian language, and ordered all administrative sections with oversight for the Communist Children's Movement (KDR) to similarly Ukrainize.[9] It also ordered more extensive work among children of ethnic minorities, the transfer of corresponding units to work in ethnic-minority languages, and the appointment of detachment leaders from ethnic-minority membership in the Komsomol.

A clear motivation for the intensification of work among ethnic minorities as well as Ukrainization was a concern about the weakness of Young Pioneer work among predominantly Ukrainian speakers and ethnic minorities. Particularly in regard to ethnic minorities, but arguably among some Ukrainian constituencies, the Komsomol was worried it was losing the battle for political influence: "The question about anti-Communist children's organizations has become a sharp one. Significant growth of such organizations has occurred recently (such as Baptists, Mennonites, Zionists and so on). There have been instances when some Pioneers transfer to these organizations."[10] The Children's Movement meeting claimed that Young Pioneer national groups overwhelmingly conducted work in Russian, consequently limiting its appeal and impact and allowing other, "anti-Communist," children's organizations to compete. In one exception, a Jewish unit conducted its work in Yiddish, but, due to the absence of a parallel German unit, German children were assigned to it, where at least they could "understand something." Thus, as the Komsomol TsK was demanding an increase in attention to ethnic-minority concerns and Ukrainization, it simultaneously called upon regional Komsomol sections to "study methods and forms of work of non-Communist organs."[11] Not only did the Komsomol have to increase the linguistic attraction of its Young Pioneer detachments, it had to learn from (and possibly mimic) its rivals.[12]

Furthermore, the Komsomol TsK believed it had to improve the moral standing of its Young Pioneer members to ensure that detachments continued to develop political maturity. It was in these units that Komsomol leaders would hone the sensibilities of children and ensure their loyalty to the Soviet cause. The problem was that, according to the Children's Movement meeting, the Young Pioneers' association with the Komsomol was having a deleterious effect on children. When Young Pioneers reached eligibility for transfer to Komsomol membership, they failed to understand the "meaning of their transfer," viewing their new status as an opportunity to engage in youthful rebellion. The "Komsomolization" of the Young Pioneer members was equated with what the TsK memorandum calls a loss in "useful habits," or their moral corruption. The former Young Pioneers and new Komsomol members smoked, drank, shirked discipline, and courted Young Pioneer girls. Ann Gorsuch has written at length about the "immorality" of the Komsomol, arguing that, clearly, for some Komsomol members, political education had no effect. She does not discuss the Komsomol–Young Pioneer relationship; an understanding of the linkage offers a fuller account of the leadership's anxiety about this behaviour.[13] The corruption of children could spread, threatening the youngest of children.

The roles of the Komsomol and the Young Pioneers appear to be reversed. Instead of guiding the younger children towards a socialist future, the Komsomol was leading them astray. What appeared to be the Young Pioneers' "useful habits" were their childhood innocence and willingness to take instruction. The TsK memorandum called upon "rank-and-file Pioneers-Komsomolites" to oppose taking up morally suspect habits. The chief concern of the new Komsomol members should be on planning and implementing public work. This was to be done partly with the greater participation of teachers, whose limited role in the children's Communist movement the TsK blamed partly for disorder among Young Pioneer ranks.[14] The organization was to be the "leader essentially of the life in the school," and yet the Komsomol had failed to train leaders to realize this ambition. The solution to the Young Pioneers' own internal dilemma and frustrated purpose was a deepening of Komsomol work in the schools by the creation of new Young Pioneer posts (*forposty*). Older children would focus their energies on the training of younger children; younger children would have little opportunity to adopt the bad habits of their fallen seniors.

Organizational renewal would lead to moral improvement and achievement of sought-after political goals. For schools converting to Ukrainian-language or national-minority instruction, the emergence of politically vibrant Young Pioneer units dedicated to fulfillment of Soviet nationalities policy was to reinforce the political meaning and urgency of this task. The absolute number of Young Pioneer units in the republic remained small as a whole, and the number of detachments genuinely transferring the language of their work was even smaller. In the urban environments where they generally operated, however, they could have a real effect on the success of nationalities policy and, according to the rationale of TsK, give the Young Pioneer groups an advantage in the competition for children's loyalties. Certainly, the resistance of Young Pioneer units to a transfer of language of instruction sent a damaging message for advocates of a de-Russification of the political and educational environment in the republic.

Uncertain Komsomol Leadership and Targets

Having recognized the shortcomings in achieving Ukrainization, the Komsomol TsK sought to work out the mechanics for perfecting the policy's implementation. It formed its own Ukrainization commission in April 1926.[15] It was to meet only once every two weeks, a schedule that seemed out of step with the urgency expressed in the Komsomol's official resolutions. The first meeting dealt with the need to simplify the language of Ukrainian periodicals affiliated with the Komsomol in order to reflect new literary norms. Meetings held that spring considered the use of Ukrainian graduates of party schools for further internal Ukrainization, coordination with the work of the KP(b)U Agitprop, the setting of a three-month deadline for the Ukrainization of the technical apparat of the Komsomol, the assignment of responsibilities for members of the commission, and instructions to regional bureaus.[16] The commission ordered all Komsomol regional secretaries to send reports on the status of Ukrainization within local organizations every three months.

In 1926, Komsomol's progress in Ukrainization was still slow, particularly in the industrial East of the republic. The Komsomol TsK issued a resolution in response to reports of delays in Ukrainization in Dnipropetrovsk region (Katerynoslav up to 1926). It found that the Dnipropetrovsk Regional Komsomol Committee had given little attention to Ukrainization, that not all local Komsomol members understood the policy, and that "there is even a significant subgroup of activists who only mechanically implement Ukrainization, not understanding its political meaning."[17] Again, one of the main motivating points for Ukrainization was the loyalty of Ukrainian youth, but at stake here was the critical category of working-class youth who may or may not have completed schooling but were already employed in the region's factories. The group would have conceivably constituted the core political base of the Komsomol and the Communist Party, but the Komsomol TsK resolution expressed concern that the Ukrainian Communist Workers' Youth Association (*Ukrius – Ukrainska komunistychna robitnycha iunatska spilka*), the youth wing of the Bolsheviks' former rival Ukrainian Communist Party (UKP), had exercised substantial influence among nationally conscious working-class youth in the region until the UKP was forced to merge with the KP(b)U in 1925.[18]

This apparent trend presented the Komsomol with a dilemma. It fully recognized that Ukrainization had to proceed at a quicker pace in order to demonstrate Bolshevik commitment to Ukrainian national interests, but it had to tread carefully so as not to anger ethnic-minority and "Russified youth." The latter group was difficult to define. Important figures in the KP(b)U did not concede Russified Ukrainians' static nature, but instead viewed them as needed candidates for Ukrainization. They enjoyed valued class status and the Communist Party's trust, and could serve as leaders in the creation of a Ukrainian-centred proletarian culture.

The TsK's solution to the Dnipropetrovsk shortcomings was a call for greater Ukrainization, but it was a policy that, in fact, required the participation of ethnic Ukrainians of varying language abilities, but high political loyalty. The Komsomol had to press forward, then, with the gentle Ukrainization of "Russified Ukrainians." Thus, the TsK called for Ukrainian activists in the Komsomol to dedicate themselves anew to language as well as to Ukrainian-area studies. It called for the development of political schools with instruction in the Ukrainian language for Komsomol members who "know Ukrainian, even if not very well." These students would share in the Ukrainization of a whole series of youth activities, from Ukrainian study groups to clubs, the promotion of a Ukrainian-language press, and the Ukrainization of wall newspapers in the workplace. The TsK was particularly concerned with shortcomings in the Ukrainization of Young Pioneers in Dnipropetrovsk. The TsK resolution condemned the region's work on Ukrainization, "which has been pursued too feebly [*kvolo*] until now." In order for a stronger program of Ukrainization to take place, the Komsomol needed to assume a role in training new Young Pioneer leaders who knew Ukrainian, and acquire new Ukrainian-language literature for the Young Pioneer groups. The resolution called, in specific, for the region's detachments to increase their subscriptions to the Young Pioneer newspapers *Bud napohotovi!* (Be alert!) and *Na zminu* (For a change), and required that the Komsomol organization do more to improve the work and publication of the children's writers' group Moloda kuznytsia (Young smithy). In Dnipropetrovsk, the divide between Young Pioneer groups and existing schools was apparent and delayed progress of Ukrainization: "Special attention needs to be paid in order to eliminate conflict among schools of the Ukrainian language and [the] work of detachments that include children of these schools (this work has up until now been carried out in the Russian language)." This tension between the Ukrainized school and the Russian-speaking Young Pioneer unit was a critical concern for the republic-wide Komsomol TsK Ukrainization Commission as well.[19] In Dnipropetrovsk and elsewhere, local Komsomol units sought to recruit Ukrainian youth studying in post-secondary institutions (VUZy) to lead the campaign to reconcile this disagreement at the Young Pioneer level.

The Komsomol risked ignoring children who had missed periods of formal schooling during the chaos of the civil war and the famine-stricken, economically turbulent early 1920s. These now-older youths, generally aged twelve to sixteen (in some cases, fifteen to twenty), sought to complete their education in literacy schools administered by Ukrliknep. Although 99 per cent of rural political schools, according to a report given at a December 1926 meeting of the TsK Ukrainization Commission, conducted their work in Ukrainian or an ethnic-minority language, in the cities and industrial areas, the schools maintained overwhelmingly Russian-language instruction. In the city of Kharkiv, the "Ukrainization of the youth in the city has been horrible [*kepsko*], the Ukrainization of working youth is weak."[20] The reporting member of the commission, Nikoliuk, cited some of the usual reasons or indications for this failure (the shortage of literature, low subscription rates to Ukrainian newspapers, and the expense for working-class youth of attending Ukrainian-language plays), and his comments suggested that Komsomol members had had no greater success in Ukrainization than the general youth population. Elsewhere, the Ukrainian Komsomol TsK called upon the daily *Komsomolets Ukrainy* to assume a greater role in promoting Ukrainization among the rank and file, particularly among youth and the Young Pioneers.[21] In spite of low circulation, the newspaper still needed to inform the small number of activist Ukrainizers to influence the great mass of Komsomol members who continued to assume a passive position towards the policy, in particular in the ranks of the Young Pioneers.

But even for the Ukrainization commission, it was unclear for whom Ukrainization was pursued. Komsomol members, as representatives of political leadership, had an obligation to accept this charge, but illiterate workers in the cities, Ukrainian or not, often privileged literacy training in Russian. Another commission member, identified as Nevidomy, commented upon hearing Nikoliuk's report, "We now have in a series of districts youth of Ukrainian ethnicity [*pokhodzhennia*] who speak Ukrainian, and it is necessary to carry out among them a liquidation of illiteracy in the Ukrainian language, but there is a desire among them for liquidation of illiteracy in the Russian language."[22] He argued for a continued use of the Ukrainian language in the fight against illiteracy among working-class youth, but the original text of the protocol revealed concern that this could not be done. A third member of the commission, Luhivska, had called for only partial Ukrainization of adult literacy schools for peasant employees of the factory, recently arrived from the village. In excised text (crossed out in pen), Nikoliuk lamented, "The Ukrainian nation is turning into [*peretvoriuiet'sia*] a peasant [nation]," remarking in the official record that only establishments in provincial towns (with peasant graduates) were being Ukrainized.[23]

This is a curious phrase and its apparent removal is telling. The Ukrainian-speaking "nation" was, of course, already rooted in the peasantry. Nikoliuk was, in fact, arguing against limiting use of Ukrainian to spaces already inhabited predominantly by peasants; that is, a provincialization or "turning back" of Ukrainian national culture. To claim somehow that this was a possibility revived notions of Lebed's discredited theory of two cultures and probably was unpalatable to the Komsomol leadership. In any case, Nikoliuk's preventative prescription was appropriate. In urban educational establishments (adult literacy schools, primary schools, FZU schools, technical colleges, and post-secondary institutes), Nikoliuk claimed, "the help of the [rank and file] Komsomol" was required to compensate for the shortage of manpower under the Ukrainization commission's command. The commission selected the adult literacy school as a priority institution because it clearly served working-class youth needs (and was thus a politically opportune target) and was an important symbolic link between youths in conventional schooling and those who had failed to complete an elementary education and fallen out of its (and the state's) embrace.

The connection between the Komsomol/Young Pioneer organization and younger youths was still fractured in 1926. A June 1926 resolution of the Central Bureau (TsB) for the Children's Movement in Ukraine reported on the state of children's organizations in the Stalino, Kharkiv, and Kyiv regions. It found that although the children's Communist movement had been growing, especially in public organizations affiliated with city schools, "Zionist" and religious youth groups had been gaining ground in Kyiv and Odesa. Even as Young Pioneer groups seemed to grow in numbers of units, members often continued to leave, and sometimes these departures took an "organized character as a protest versus the unsatisfactory content of work" (in Odesa, Cherkasy, Poltava, etc.).[24] Young Pioneer leaders found undisciplined older children difficult to manage; these children frequently did not last long in their positions with urban Young Pioneer units; and Young Pioneer units had little influence over the content of schoolwork. There were numerous reasons for these failures, including the standard ones: lack of funding and insufficient attention by local Komsomol leaders. More importantly, the resolution blamed the lack of correlation between Young Pioneer work and the "needs of children"; that is, political training that should be of interest to them. In specific, children lacked the most basic information about "our country" (*nasha kraina*, a phrase that usually denoted Ukraine rather than the USSR), important acts of Soviet power, and the situation abroad. Young Pioneer groups had also not successfully linked group activities to the immediate environment, such as the work of adult organizations and worker collectives.

The end result, the TsB memorandum suggested, was that children found participation in the Young Pioneers to be dry and unappealing. It had little to do with their own lives and real conditions in their town or Ukraine. The Komsomol risked losing recruits or members, potentially to the ambiguous non-Soviet youth organizations first specified in the memorandum. Although Ukrainization is not specifically mentioned in the document, the Young Pioneers were supposed to be simultaneously engaging in this campaign, and its influence is clearly present in the TsB's analysis. The TsB recommendation that all future political work inform children about the most important events in "our country" (repeating the phrase), including the "work of factories, villages and organizations with which the Young Pioneers are connected," played upon an established meaning of Ukrainization in the schools: that instruction telescope outwards from the immediately familiar to the republic as a whole. The resolution's censure of Young Pioneer groups that held meetings to discuss "events in the distant past" also reinforced the idea that political instruction, of which Ukrainian studies were necessarily part, should be about present circumstances and needs. If it was expected that some schools would fail in this respect, the Young Pioneers could not. It ultimately fell to them to teach children about contemporary challenges and the Komsomol and party's victories and ongoing tasks.

Another TsK resolution of the same year elaborated more specifically on the danger presented to Komsomol influence in the republic. Although the motivation for the resolution appeared to be the need to demonstrate a united stance against influences of "Trotskyism" in the organization, the emphasis of the document is on the threat represented by forms of nationalism. A report presented to the TsK by Vysochynenko, the head of the Ukrainization commission, insisted that some nationalist organizations such as Ukrius had formally ceased to exist, however, the TsK conceded that there had been a "resuscitation" (*ozhyvlennia*) of groups hostile to Soviet power: religious organizations in the villages (especially among German and Polish youth) and "national-chauvinist elements" who sought influence among village youth, especially those "that are in a difficult material state."[25] Here, the threat was said to stem less from urban youth's disaffection than from the weak influence of the city over the village. The resolution took for granted that the majority of urban youth was loyal to Soviet power. Ukrainization was the key to ensure the "proletarian leadership" of youth and children in Ukraine, especially as the Komsomol expanded to include more rural members: "One difficulty in the implementation of proletarian leadership in the Ukrainian Komsomol is that most working youth do not know the Ukrainian language and this may be overcome only when the line of Ukrainization is carried out in proletarian centers and chiefly by its activists." The TsK criticized some of its members for assuming an apathetic attitude towards Ukrainization, insisting that the study of Ukrainian language, history, and culture needed to be a fundamental feature of "the whole educational work of the organization." In a separate resolution, the Komsomol TsK criticized the editorial board of the Komsomol newspaper *Molodyi Bilshovyk* (Young Bolshevik) for "insufficient treatment [*vysvitlennia*] of the national question," and connected to this a failure to adequately discuss work in the village and publish material that would be of interest to girls.[26] It recommended the promotion of a journal particularly for rural Ukrainian-speaking children, *Bilshovycheniata* (Little Bolshevik), and inclusion of a new heading in the journal, entitled "How to Work as a Pioneer," in order to provide village children with greater guidance on Young Pioneer political campaigns, including Ukrainization.

Still, while it demanded greater recruitment of "Ukrainian forces" (who would most likely be peasants in the first instance), the TsK emphasized the need for vigilance against "nationalist attitudes" as well as "Russophilism."[27] The Komsomol was becoming an institution with a rural majority, and due attention needed to be paid to the needs of poor rural youth and "the specifics of rural and border districts"; it could not be an institution that was defined by rural culture. Matthias Neuman, Isabel Tirado, and Monica Wellman have argued that the Komsomol in the Soviet Union generally sought with some success to integrate rural youth during the NEP era, but that it struggled to keep pace with the rapid expansion of the organization in the periphery.[28] Intertwined in this suspicion of the rural were long-standing Bolshevik beliefs about the anti-modern and petit bourgeois nature of the peasantry, and its status as the primary carrier of nationalist sentiment. The "union [*spaisnist*] of proletarian centers" with the TsK had to be the Komsomol's primary task, and coordination of purpose with working-class youth would ensure working-class leadership of progressive forces in the village, defined primarily by class status. Urban Komsomol members trained broadly in the Ukrainian language and Ukrainian studies would be the best equipped for this role.

A TsK summary of the work of the Ukrainian Komsomol on nationalities policy over the course of 1926 repeated the emphasis of Ukrainization as a tool against the enemies of Soviet power. It cited the Sixth All-Ukrainian Congress of the Komsomol's linkage of the campaign to strengthen the pace of Ukrainization with the "struggle with distortions [*izvrashcheniiami*] in its practical implementation, the struggle with remnants of the Russian and the roots of Ukrainian chauvinism."[29] It focused in particular on failures in the Ukrainization of Young Pioneer units by leaders "who have not embraced the necessity of the Ukrainization of Young Pioneer work." This was the very sort of "distortion" that might lead to increased national frustration and, from the Soviet perspective, give rise to nationalist sentiment. What made matters particularly frustrating for the Komsomol leadership was that in spite of its own resolutions, progress had been slow when it should have been an easy matter, at least formally. As the Fourth All-Ukrainian Meeting on the Communist Children's Movement and the TsK's own plenum's analysis attest, the fact that Ukrainian schools enrolled the majority of Young Pioneer members meant that this work should have been "comparatively easy."

Part of the problem may have stemmed from the fact that the Komsomol apparat as a whole was still far from Ukrainized. A September 1926 report of the Komsomol TsK Ukrainization Commission found that a "significant portion of workers" in the Komsomol administration belonged to the lowest, third category of Ukrainian-language and -studies knowledge and were eligible for dismissal if a planned November examination found that their knowledge had not improved.[30] The commission called for an increase in the number of ethnic Ukrainians working in the Komsomol apparat and noted with concern that the proportion of Ukrainians working in the offices of local Komsomol cells, particularly in industrial regions, continued to decline. This reduction of Ukrainians was occurring as the percentage of Russians employed in the Komsomol apparat continued to rise by 4 to 5 per cent in comparison with other employees. The report explained the rise by citing the migration of Russians from the RSFSR to industrial areas of Soviet Ukraine, where they found quick work and assumed an active role in the Komsomol, but "do not energetically pursue Ukrainization enough and foster an understanding of it in the cells." In rural cells, reported drops in the percentage of Ukrainians were purportedly the result of the formation of ethnic-minority specific cells. The Ukrainization commission considered this latter phenomenon "normal," but the decline in the proportion of Ukrainians in industrial cells and district leadership positions to be "abnormal."

In other words, satisfaction of ethnic-minority interests, particularly in the countryside, where the Ukrainian element safely dominated, was permissible and, in effect, contributed to a general de-Russification of the Komsomol. The Ukrainization commission, however, could not permit cells in politically important industrial cities to become more Russian than they already were. Such a trend would perpetuate the ethnic divide between city and countryside, destabilize Soviet power, and undermine one of the main conditions Ukrainization was meant to alter. The report raised an essential challenge to the creation of a Ukrainian proletarian youth culture. Could the Komsomol expand and still be proletarian? Could it be proletarian and still be Ukrainian? The report concluded that the Komsomol needed to employ Russian activists, but their recruitment could not damage and slow down the work of the promotion of local, working-class Ukrainian activists. This is the essential dilemma of Ukrainization that had an impact on all matters of education, including primary schools. If the power within the Komsomol continued to rest largely with forces passive or hostile to Ukrainization, to what linguistic environment would schoolchildren aspire or enter? What language would teachers and parents believe gave children the most secure future? The Ukrainization commission ordered all local committees to study in detail the approach of all members to official nationalities policy. In the next re-elections to the district committees, the commission needed to decisively increase the number of committee members who were ethnic-Ukrainian workers: farm labourers and poor peasants.

Young Pioneers and School Campaigns

The debate regarding Ukrainization of the Komsomol and Young Pioneer groups took place in the context of a more generalized discussion on the authority of schools and the party's influence over them. If schools were failing in their essential task of training future citizen activists or had little connection to political authority, then the political task of Ukrainization would be fatally undermined. A 1926 draft resolution by the Ukrainian Komsomol TsK school section on general schooling found that a significant number of eight-year-old children were not attending school, a phenomenon that the TsK considered to be "abnormal."[31] The commission blamed Narkomos for this gap, for failing to strictly enforce the age requirement for entry into school. It further cited a need to overcome building shortages by soliciting the support of local populations for the building of new schools, as regional authorities in Kryvyi Rih had apparently successfully done. The TsK underscored the need for local education sections to assume leadership of "work on the popularization of schools" to overcome the perceived lack of public support in rural communities.

A problem that undoubtedly contributed to the school's lack of authority among the population was the shortage of qualified teachers. Because of the expansion of the school network, local education officials were forced to hire teachers with insufficient pedagogical training, and pedagogical *tekhnikumy* and institutes had lowered their educational norms in order to ensure the quick entry of graduates into the workforce. Furthermore, the school commission noted with concern that some graduates of pedagogical institutions did not go into teaching careers, further exacerbating the shortage. New and old teachers alike were confused about how to apply a new methodology of the complex system in the classroom. Here, in short, was the essential problem of Ukrainization and the state's statistics on Ukrainized schools. The state had a clear problem in recruiting qualified teachers at all, let alone any with training in teaching in Ukrainian or the new instructional methodology. How, then, could the political training of children be assured, and how could the state accomplish the replacement of the older generation with "Soviet" teachers? Even if teachers were in Ukrainized schools, they did not necessarily speak Ukrainian well enough to teach at a high level. Even if they knew Ukrainian, it did not mean they had appropriate teaching skills for the demands of the Soviet school.

The Young Pioneers were to reinforce and supplement the political training of schools. If primary schools were to provide children with basic knowledge and a universalized education in the values of citizenship, Young Pioneer instruction was more ideological and applied. However, school curriculum ideally was to maintain a clear tie to practical tasks, and, given the ages of the children involved, both the primary schools and the Young Pioneer organization necessarily emphasized moral training over a strict accounting of Marxist principles. In order for the Young Pioneers to succeed, detachments needed to maintain a link with effectively operating schools. Thus, a Komsomol TsK analysis of the success of the Young Pioneer organization in meeting goals defined by the Fourth All-Ukrainian Meeting on the KDR also viewed the incomplete enrolment of schools as abnormal and stressed the importance of the participation of cooperative organizations (e.g., parental/public) in the administration of schools and efforts to increase its authority.[32] The Komsomol and Young Pioneers were to play critical roles in facilitating such community involvement. The TsK tasked the Young Pioneers with multiple responsibilities, including duties related to the schoolhouse: "Work on hot breakfasts, collective purchases of school equipment, the struggle with those absent or tardy for class, struggle for an attentive relationship with school content [Russian: *imushchestvo*]." They were also asked to engage in activity to change their own behaviour and the culture of their communities; e.g., the promotion of newspaper reading in the village, habits of good hygiene, and the fight against "hooliganism." Part and parcel with this effort was the demand "to entrust the TsB [of the KDR] to work out a specific instruction to localities on the carrying out of Ukrainization of Young Pioneer work." Instructions on the need to increase the Young Pioneer efforts in the development of children's literature and the selection of complex themes for the schools had a specific bearing on the progress of Ukrainization. But, arguably, Ukrainization was fundamental to the entire Young Pioneer mandate, especially as it applied to the activities of rural detachments: the Ukrainized school with high-quality instruction would enjoy greater public support and offer a more stable base for Young Pioneer activity, and the Ukrainized detachment would be more effective in its campaign to alter the views and behaviour of children and the wider community.

The Apathy of Working-Class Youth

The Komsomol TsK continued to investigate the progress of Ukrainization as it regarded youth and children, and its conclusions were unsettling for Ukrainizers within the Komsomol. In an early 1927 observation report, a TsK investigator reported that in Kharkiv's Chervonozavodskyi district, there had been a growth of Ukrainian membership in the Komsomol section, but, on average, members did not know literary Ukrainian, if they knew any level of the language. Those few who could speak in a "simple Ukrainian vernacular" did not use it.[33] Two Ukrainian youths recently arrived from the village were employed in a factory in the district, but assimilated to Russian and resisted recruitment for the Ukrainization campaign. All public meetings' committee work was done in Russian. Although the report claimed there was no antagonism towards Ukrainization among Komsomol workers in the region, there was also no real active desire to participate in the campaign. Komsomol workers often said: "Why Ukrainize us as we are working at our benches? There is no use in this." As an addendum to the report further clarified, those who came to work in the factory were quickly Russified and, as a rule, stopped using the Ukrainian language. The only real progress in Ukrainization appeared to be among Komsomol members who were employed by the state, "but a significant number of Komsomol members do not understand the profoundness of the question [of nationalities policy] and are Ukrainizing without real desire as a 'duty' [*po 'obov'iazku'*] of working in a Soviet institution."[34] This attitude applied to Komsomol "activists" as well as the rank and file.

Other reports from local sections to the Komsomol TsK in January 1927 generally confirm this picture of a passive attitude and uneven progress towards Ukrainization among working youth, even in the face of increased pressure from Komsomol leadership. In Zaporizhzhia, the local section communicated similarly that Ukrainization of the industrial centres was going slowly, whereas the Ukrainization of Komsomol sections in the Soviet government was proceeding "satisfactorily" (at a rate comparable to the Ukrainization of the Soviet apparat generally).[35] The Vinnytsia Regional Committee reported that the Ukrainization of mass public work was at a low level, with youth sections of workers' clubs obstinately refusing to give up use of Russian.[36] The picture presented by the Pryluky committee (also in central Ukraine) was more upbeat in regard to Ukrainization in the factories: "A portion of the Komsomol members are Ukrainized and the other portion writes in Russian still and this is why part of the work in the sections is still taking place in Russian and partly in Ukrainian, but overwhelmingly in Ukrainian."[37] Komsomol sections in the Soviet government were almost entirely Ukrainized.

Progress in conversion to Ukrainian-language use was obviously dependent on local conditions, in particular the history of Russian-language dominance of the principal urban and industrial centres and the extent of peasant in-migration. The situation in Pryluky was not uncommon, as it may have appeared. Peasant migrants may have aspired to use Russian, but, generally, they would have come into the workplace as primarily Ukrainian speakers. The key for Ukrainizers was capturing this moment, making use of a critical mass of Ukrainian speakers to widen the space occupied by the Ukrainian language and to attract Russian speakers to it. The initial effectiveness of recent migrants as surrogate Ukrainizers was debatable, given their lack of knowledge of literary Ukrainian and comparatively low literacy, but the state could conceivably train them quicker, and they could pressure Komsomol cells to satisfy their linguistic interests.

The evidence of the attraction of newly arrived workers to the Russian language appears strong, although this may have been a select group identified in the reports. Those attracted to Komsomol membership were likely more interested in a disassociation from the parochial, rural culture that the Ukrainian language represented. Russian stood for the modern and industrial, and offered a linkage to Moscow, the centre of the party's power and the international socialist movement. These reports say less about sentiments of non-Komsomol membership, although they purported to represent youth working-class sentiment. Of course, it was Komsomol attitudes that the Komsomol ultimately cared about; for this reason, notes of caution regarding what amounted to resistance (active or not) of ethnic Ukrainians to Ukrainization were significant because these were the youths most aligned with Soviet authority. Still, it is important to remember that the proportion of youths enrolled in the Komsomol, even in cities, was a minority of youths in the age group eligible for membership. The Komsomol was supposed to lead youth attitudes, but it was not separate from them, and gains in Ukrainization outside the factory floor could conceivably have had an impact on the rank and file when coupled with the Komsomol leadership's admonitions. Absent from these reports is what trends were like in other professions – of particular importance to this study, the attitudes of young urban teachers and the growing "Soviet" intelligentsia.

Nevertheless, children graduating from primary school in their early to mid-teens faced a youth environment in which disinterest towards Ukrainization was certainly a prominent trend in the cities. The Komsomol had multiple means at its disposal to increase language use. Here again, there was a clear urban–rural divide. According to the Komsomol's statistical bureau, for example, the rural network of schools of political education was almost entirely Ukrainized, whereas in the city, "Ukrainization of political schools has almost not taken place," in spite of the fact that Ukrainian membership in the Komsomol continued to increase.[38] Further growth in urban cells was expected as rural in-migration continued. However, in the city of Dnipropetrovsk, Komsomol members (and party members) attended Ukrainian-studies courses set up by district party committees in early 1926 in such unsatisfactory numbers that the courses ceased operation.[39] These courses were expensive to maintain over any length of time; a less expensive option that was promoted were self-study groups, cultural events, and excursions. An order from the Kharkiv Regional Komsomol Committee is the most detailed regarding the range of cultural activities planned. In addition to formal Ukrainian-studies courses (directly primarily at employees of the Komsomol apparat), the regional committee called for each Komsomol cell to organize Ukrainian-studies circles in the factories and to recruit working youth to attend. Other measures were recommended, among them evening talks in youth sections of workers' clubs on the themes of Ukrainian youth, events in Polish-ruled Western Ukraine, Ukrainian songs, and history; a general city evening meeting to hear a report by Skrypnyk on the Komsomol and national cultural building; a conference on young readers of Ukrainian books in the Metalist union; and excursions to a Ukrainian-language theatre (the Berezil Theater), the Hryhorii Skorovoda Museum of Slobidska Ukraine, and Museum of the Revolution.[40]

This was an ambitious listing of activities meant to transform the linguistic environment for city youth, and in cities around the republic, the Ukrainizing committees met real challenges. To return to Kharkiv's Chervonozavodskyi district, in June 1926, in accordance with a directive from the district committee, one Komsomol cell resolved to organize a Ukrainian-studies circle under the factory committee at the Kharkiv Bicycle Factory (KhVZ). The KhVZ factory committee agreed to sponsor the group because the Komsomol cell reportedly had no money for any such effort. Nothing, however, was done: "Thus a Ukrainian *hurtok* [circle] does not exist, although other *hurtky* carry on work in Russian at the club 'Metalist' outside of the factory."[41] An addendum clarified that a Ukrainian-studies circle was set up in the area and the district committee supplied it with instructional supplies and textbooks, but after two unsuccessful lessons, the district committee was forced to disband it because almost no one attended.[42] In educational circles associated with youth sections in workers' clubs, the question of Ukrainization never came up; only drama and singing groups in the clubs used any level of Ukrainian, but youth took an active part in these. In Zaporizhzhia, circles associated with club work did not exist in 1926, although theatre work was partially in Ukrainian and study circles linked to Ukrainized Komsomol political schools operated.[43] In Vinnytsia, the youth sections of workers' clubs worked in Russian, although there was one Ukrainian dramatic club in the workers' club Rabmolu. Separate Ukrainian-studies circles under the cells did not exist, but Komsomol members took part in the Ukrainian-studies activities organized by the unions.[44] By contrast, in Dnipropetrovsk, workers' clubs established five Ukrainian-studies circles in separate districts of the cities, in which 300 youths reportedly took part.[45] The situation in the Pryluky region was relatively brighter for Ukrainizers as well. As of January 1927, of ninety-three political schools, eighty-eight were operating in Ukrainian, three in Yiddish, and two in Russian.[46] In the villages, all public-work activists had transferred all work to Ukrainian, and the Komsomol had begun work in the cities and factory sections in Ukrainian. The Ukrainization of club work was reportedly almost complete, although there were "rare instances" of exhibitions and reports produced in Russian, and no Ukrainian-studies circles associated with youth sections in the clubs.

Comparative success was likely dependent partly on the ethnic-Ukrainian membership of local sections of the Komsomol. Regional branches provided limited data on the ethnic makeup of the rank and file, and thus it is difficult to offer a detailed analysis. The Dnipropetrovsk Regional Komsomol Committee reported specifically on the Ukrainian representation in district (*raion*) committees and coordinating bureaus. City district committees were 54 per cent "Ukrainized" and village district committees 84 per cent Ukrainized. Below them in the bureau of city cells, there were 223 Ukrainians, or 30.5 per cent, whereas in the bureau of rural cells, there were 443 Ukrainians, or 91.9 per cent.[47] It reasonable to assume the lower-level cell bureaus reflected the rank-and-file membership more, although whether the district committee percentages denoted ethnic-Ukrainian representation or language ability is unclear. Clearly, there was a distinction between pictures of urban and rural membership in the region, as there was throughout Ukraine. The more likely determinant would have been the resolve of local leadership to sponsor Ukrainian programs, and the Dnipropetrovsk region's formal commitment to Ukrainization seemed strong: its regional Komsomol committee had entirely transferred its work to Ukrainian; almost half the members of the committee reportedly knew Ukrainian well; two of its city cells operated entirely in Ukrainian; cells in the region's pedagogical courses were entirely Ukrainized; and correspondence between all cells was almost entirely in Ukrainian. Given the high Ukrainian representation in the leadership of rural cells, the regional committee was likely responding to real pressure to eliminate the clear distinction in linguistic cultures and make the urban environment more hospitable to inevitable transfers in labour force.

What the regional committees found difficult to do was to force Komsomol members to independently pursue Ukrainian studies or internalize the habitual use of the Ukrainian language and an interest in culture. The Komsomol leadership, like the party leadership, was compelled to demonstrate a minimum level of Ukrainian-studies knowledge in state-administered exams, but even its daily use of the language was a matter of duty rather than regulation. Club activity or membership in hurtky were, in the end, voluntary matters, and low rates of participation cast doubt on Komsomol faith in Ukrainization or, at the very least, showed an unwillingness to spend precious leisure time in activity that did not promise any readily apparent gain. The Ukrainizers' task was to convince youth of the advantage of such study, and the tentative progress indicated in the Dnipropetrovsk and Pryluky regions' reports are the results of this effort.

Ukrainian-language periodical readership was another indicator of the sincerity of Komsomol commitment to Ukrainization. According to the Ukrainian Komsomol TsK statistical bureau, there were seven Komsomol newspapers with a general circulation of 27,400 in 1926. Of them, three were in Ukrainian with a circulation of 18,700, and those newspapers in Russian constituted 4,500. The remainder was ethnic-minority newspapers (German, Jewish, and Polish).[48] In Pryluky, authorities reported that were some 309 subscriptions to *Komsomolets Ukrainy*, credited mostly to cell sections. The regional committee dispensed only Ukrainian literature to its members and lower-level units.[49] In the Chervonozavodskyi district of Kharkiv, there were at most thirty subscribers to *Komsomolets Ukrainy*, a fact that the TsK investigator, Fedor Rubinsky, explained was not only as a result of the fact that the newspaper was published in Ukrainian, but because of a perception that it "does not satisfy the needs of the Komsomol members in its content."[50] It is problematic to compare these figures to those of an entire region, but Rubinsky judged them to be insignificant. As a result of the Komsomol perception, a majority of Komsomol members in the district subscribed to the Russian-language *Pravda* or *Komsomolskaia pravda*, and sometimes to the Ukrainian-language *Komunist*. Circulation for *Komsomolets Ukrainy* in Zaporizhzhia in December 1926 was 283 issues and for *Komsomolets ahitator*, it was 200, a respectable combined total.[51] In Vinnytsia, circulation for *Komsomolets Ukrainy* grew from 150 subscribers in October 1926 to 258 in December. Circulation in the region for *Molodyi bilshovyk* stood at 234 subscribers.[52] Dnipropetrovsk authorities reported that subscriptions to the Ukrainian newspaper *Maibutnia zmina* (Future change) had been low, but they had undertaken a campaign to increase the rate. In June 1926, there were some 636 subscribers.[53] Clearly, a public campaign to increase subscriptions could increase the numbers of issues ordered. Rubinsky blamed the Chervonozavodskyi District Committee for failing to do enough to popularize *Komsomolets Ukrainy*. Kharkiv regional authorities, responsible for the Chervonozavodskyi district, put matters more plainly, requiring all activists to read *Komsomolets Ukrainy* and *Molodniak* (Young generation).[54] How this was done is unclear. It was one matter to increase the subscription rate; it was another to ensure that anyone read the newspapers. Given the frankness of the reports regarding lack of attendance of Komsomol members in Ukrainian-studies courses and circles, it is surprising that no mention is made of how frequently the newspapers were opened in the Komsomol and public institutions where the majority of them were received. Because of the low initial rate of subscriptions and the rapid increase reported, there is reason to be skeptical about readership, but the tide was perhaps shifting as the result of pressure from the leadership in some instances.

Komsomol members enrolled in political schools established for the ideological instruction of older youth were also required to read more Ukrainian literature as part of their curriculum. The Komsomol published a journal for city schools entitled *Politnavchannia komsomoltsia*, with a circulation of approximately 7,000 in 1927, and separately distributed a workbook and textbooks in the Ukrainian language.[55] It is safer to presume in this instance that the Ukrainian-language literature was used, although there were Russian-language alternatives already on hand. The Komsomol targeted political schools themselves for Ukrainization; according to an August 1927 order for Ukrainization, industrial sections of the Komsomol should require at least 30 per cent of their political schools to teach exclusively in Ukrainian, with further adjustment by regional party organizations to come. However, as of the beginning of the 1927–8 academic year, major cities in the republic had only one to three fully Ukrainian political schools, or none at all: this included Dnipropetrovsk, Mykolaiv, Odesa, Stalino, and Kharkiv. In Cherkasy, by contrast, sixty-one out of seventy-one political schools were Ukrainized in the city. Nearly all schools in villages throughout the republic were Ukrainized, with the exception of those reserved for ethnic minorities.

It is in such formalized educational spaces that the Komsomol's failings in Ukrainization seemed most apparent. These were sites of Ukrainian studies, but their fundamental purpose was much broader, and they spoke to the basic goal of Soviet nationalities policy: Ukrainization was a prerequisite for the ideological and professional acculturation of youth. Political schools were to offer a stop-gap measure of political instruction for older youths. Ideally, the Soviet state would intervene at an earlier age. Narkomos also maintained the FZU schools described above, a network of seven-year primary schools whose curriculum was to be tied to existing industrial enterprises; it was in these schools that the Komsomol association was most direct. Like the political school, the FZU school under Komsomol oversight appeared institutionally to resist Ukrainization, according to a series of January 1927 reports. In Zaporizhzhia, instruction in FZU schools converted formally, but the policy was "weak." Pupils spoke to each other in Russian, and the extracurricular work was more in Russian than in Ukrainian.[56] Even in the comparatively more rural Pryluky region, where only one FZU school operated, a portion of the students still spoke regularly in Russian, although the school was designated as Ukrainian.[57] In the Vinnytsia region, there were two FZU schools; one had had reportedly "Ukrainized by 50 percent" and the other was in the midst of partial Ukrainization by grade level.[58] The critical subject of social studies in the first grade of the school, for example, maintained instruction in Russian.

None of this is surprising, of course. It would have been a considerable triumph if Ukrainization in any of these places happened as automatically as statistics suggested, and the delays paralleled, in a way, shortcomings in the conventional school system. What was different was that these schools were small in number, and educational authorities and their Komsomol patrons might conceivably have exercised greater authority over the schools' conversion. As in the Komsomol, working-class interests impeded a move away from Russian, especially in areas where the economic agenda seemed most critical. The FZU schools were training the proletariat's children for jobs in the industrial sector, and Ukrainization seemed to have little purpose.

Komsomol Perseverance and the Promise of the Children

The Komsomol regional authorities' extended description of youth apathy towards Ukrainization, especially its repetition of the rationale that Ukrainization was not needed for workers who spent the majority of their time on the factory floor, buttressed the merits of this argument. Delays were undesirable, but understandable. Yet, the Komsomol was unwilling to concede failure in the factory and the FZU school or, perhaps most importantly, among younger youth. Regional committees attempted to stimulate greater activity, energy, and control; for example, in 1926 the Kharkiv region's committee required that its district committees report on Ukrainization activities in each cell after a two-month interval and that its school section monitor progress in the FZU school.[59]

If the challenge to Ukrainization was still significant among older youth, advances might be made among the young. The FZU school occupied a particular position in the educational, political, and administrative landscape that worked to prolong the schedule of Ukrainization. Soviet authorities afforded conventional schools no such latitude; Young Pioneers were to push the agenda forward for themselves and for the schools linked to them. Kharkiv authorities ordered the organization of Ukrainian-studies seminars for Young Pioneer leaders and a review of detachments to determine which further ones could transfer to the Ukrainian language.[60] The distinctions between the urban and rural remained. In city districts of Dnipropetrovsk, only 36.3 per cent of Young Pioneer detachments had converted to the Ukrainian language by 1926, and, in the countryside, 83.4 per cent had.[61] Problems in the Young Pioneers could be blamed on delays among older youths (it was from their ranks that Young Pioneer leaders were to be recruited) and weaknesses in Komsomol oversight, but it was in these detachments that there was perhaps the greatest potential for success, because children carried fewer cultural prejudices regarding language. The very structure of the Young Pioneers promised to bridge the divide between the rural and urban through direct linkages among detachments, common participation in public events, and excursions. Furthermore, a school-aged child's fundamental responsibility was to learn. They did not have to divide their time between employment and learning; they used a smaller set of literature and could be held accountable for its reading. The distancing of symbolic authority from Ukrainian culture was important in determining the perspective of children (older youths and the Komsomol could not continue to privilege Russian-language literacy for Ukrainization to succeed), but here was an opportunity for a shift.

It was in central Ukraine that Komsomol files point to the most striking evidence of success. In February 1928, the Ukrainian Komsomol TsK issued a resolution on the basis of a report heard from the Kyiv Regional Committee's Agitprop section. It praised the Kyiv organization for its work on Ukrainization, particularly for maintaining ties to all Kyiv cultural and literary institutions and unions. This sort of linkage helped inform Komsomol's own work on Ukrainization and allowed the Komsomol to oversee the activity pursued by non-party organizations. For example, the Kyiv Komsomol organized literary evenings by the literary group Molodniak[62] and sponsored excursions to cultural organizations in the surrounding countryside. Thus, Komsomol members benefited from the work of Molodniak, but the group was also brought into Komsomol's fold; trips to village and provincial towns around Kyiv allowed Komsomol members to observe rural Ukrainian culture, but also gave members information necessary for authority over the peasantry. Activists were enrolled in Ukrainization courses throughout the region in ever-greater numbers, participated in Ukrainian theatre, and read Ukrainian-language literature and the periodical press. In the city of Kyiv, the number of subscriptions to Ukrainian newspapers among youth reached 6,000, and whole categories of workers, such as metalworkers, who had never read in Ukrainian began to do so. The TsK resolution argued that the achievements of the Kiev organization were "the beginning of substantive and systematic work regarding the recruitment of youth to the grand process of mastering the creation of Ukrainian proletarian culture."[63] This glowing assessment is almost too good to be believed. It is a purist expression of the intent of Ukrainization, allegedly realized in Ukraine's cultural capital of Kyiv. In the republic's political capital of Kharkiv, the situation was the reverse. The Ukrainian Komsomol TsK judged that the Kharkiv organization "had not until this time practically come to a resolution and realization of the decision of the Ukrainian Komsomol TsK's plenum in the area of Ukrainization and participation in national-cultural building."[64]

The obvious reasons for the difference in results were Kyiv's historical place as a centre of Ukrainian cultural activism and the contemporary concentration of Ukrainian intellectual resources in the city. The Komsomol (and the state and party) placed significant emphasis on the transformation of the linguistic environment of Kharkiv, but the Ukrainization of Kyiv had clearly progressed farther. There was a dark side to this progress: it increased the suspicion of republican party and Komsomol authorities that nationalists might attempt to hijack Ukrainization for their own purposes. With advancement of Soviet nationalities policy, the TsK suggested, came a fight for control, centred on the fate of youth: "When the bourgeois intelligentsia attempts through culture to inculcate in youth political views hostile to the proletariat, it ideologically prepares the groundwork for a restoration of the bourgeois-democratic order." The TsK ordered the Kyiv Komsomol Regional Committee to continue to reveal to youth "the harmful corruptive work on the part of the nationalist opposition in Ukraine, contrasting their work with a Leninist understanding of the development of proletarian culture."[65] The solution was to continue to promote cultural forces drawn from trustworthy, "Sovietized" youth to lead the development of Ukrainian literature and culture, and to send these youths into the countryside in theatre groups to project Soviet ideals and win over the young and youngest. Republican Komsomol authorities, resident in Kharkiv, looked to the Kyiv organization as a model for the development of Ukrainization and a bulwark against the nationalist threat that the policy invited.

Chapter Nine

Ukrainization in a Non-Ukrainian City

For Ukrainization to be successful, Soviet authorities could not shrink from any challenge. They needed to convert the general language environment of public space in the republic. Urban and rural populations alike had to approach all things Ukrainian differently and acquire fundamental skills in the use of the language. Ethnic Ukrainians, it was expected, would take up Ukrainian identity and use this identification to build a modern, national culture. The Komsomol and Young Pioneers were to regulate this effort. Place, however, mattered in the early Soviet period. Local conditions determined how a policy might succeed, if at all. Place refracted central ambitions, shaping them to realities of circumstance. The city and region of Odesa (Russian: Odessa) represented a dilemma to Ukrainizers. It was a multi-ethnic, largely Russophone, and historically cosmopolitan port city, poorly suited for any nation-building project.[1] Yet, it was situated within a largely Ukrainian hinterland and remained a critically important city in spite of its increased isolation in the early Soviet period.

This study has argued that early Soviet policy cannot be understood without an understanding of the local, and has maintained that it was a local understanding that suggested the national. A detailed investigation of Ukrainization of any municipality would offer reward. Ethnic Ukrainians did not constitute a majority in any of Soviet Ukraine's major cities in 1926, and all cities included substantial national-minority populations. Odesa mattered because of its own myth of its own identity: richly local as well as proudly international. Neighbourhood affiliation could hold considerable sway in the city, but these neighbourhoods were under flux because of the migration of Ukrainian peasants to them. Odesa was the least ethnically Ukrainian large city in the republic, yet, under the terms of Ukrainization, Soviet officials could not condone a persistent, non-national, "Odesan" character. As a microcosm and a self-professed particularity, the experience of the city of Odesa is telling for the policy of Ukrainization (Sovietization) overall.

Before a policy labelled "Ukrainization" was pursued in any directed form, a push towards Ukrainian-language schooling coincided with a general campaign to promote an awareness of Ukrainian identity and encourage literacy in Ukrainian among those inhabitants of the region who spoke some vernacular form. The regional education section limited its initial ambition to an increase in prestige for the Ukrainian language, but stopped short of a comprehensive change of the language environment. They assumed gains made in the expansion of Ukrainian schooling for children would have an effect on the attitudes of parents and the general public. Part of this effort was to bring full Ukrainian primary schools into the city. But the number of these schools was limited and they were isolated from the larger educational hierarchy. Secondary and post-secondary education remained largely in Russian.

After 1923, when the republican government named Ukrainization as part of its official policy and applied pressure on regional administrators to conform, the Odesa education section confronted increased hostility towards the Ukrainian language. Some teachers were more willing to change than parents, and local education sections proceeded cautiously, lest they disrupt learning and provoke unnecessary public outcry – confining their attention largely to the abbreviated (four-year) primary schools, ignoring children's buildings under direct state control, and shrinking from a campaign for the expansion of full (seven-year) Ukrainian primary schools that would have served to increase the prestige of the language. Local educators saw such an expansion as inevitable in the long run, as Ukrainian families continued to migrate to the city, but did not want to attack the privileged status of Russian now.

The preferred method to motivate teachers to learn more was the perevirka, or examination, discussed at length by the contributors to the teachers' newspaper *Narodnii uchytel* in chapter 6. The situation in Odesa confirms the picture presented in this newspaper of teachers' passive resistance and some official allowance of delay. Teachers refused to prepare and then froze when education inspectors sprung an exam on them. They were afraid that the examination would reveal their lack of knowledge, but also resented this state-imposed notion of literacy, undermining their authority in the classroom and in the public. However much educational reform and Ukrainization may have relied on teacher initiative, the state (and the party) reserved the role to regulate and redirect. Ukrainization in the schools would provide opportunity for a reminder of state power while at the same time creating space for public participation in an activity deemed vital to governance. Such a perevirka, as vividly expressed by locally derived documents, was the greatest illustration of Collins's claim of the exploitative function of schooled literacy. But here, the objects are not the pupils, but the teachers invested with responsibility of propounding this literacy.

Although teachers complained about the absence of a rigorous program for their training in Ukrainian, what appeared to alarm them most was the lack of clear guidance on the test, and, less universally, a lack of any flexible and authoritative command of the language. Evidence of teacher avoidance of the study of Ukrainian is supplemented by reports of Narkomos employees and administrators failing to attend whatever formal courses the state provided. Writing samples from an actual perevirka reveal, however, some internalization of the political and pedagogical importance of the Ukrainization campaign. When teachers repeated the principles of native-language study and the goal of rural–urban labour solidarity, evaluators judged teacher performance in the examination of Ukrainian studies to be good. Whether teachers would further take up this charge, some clearly understood what environment local authorities expected them to cultivate for the Ukrainian child, whatever the reality of a heterogeneous language environment was in Odesa.

A study of the local reveals further insight into the multiple tools of control and surveillance necessary to push Ukrainization along, and just how much this regulation was entrusted to authorities distant from the initial articulation of the policy. What becomes clear is that education and the institution of Narkomos were at the centre of it all. Teachers and the schoolhouse were key parts of a "network" of nationalities policy. Simply put, the whole Ukrainization campaign would not have made any progress without their active participation.

The Narkomos regional section played a key role in formulating plans for Ukrainization and setting the bar for what should be known in Odesa. Its inspectors certified teacher knowledge of Ukrainian studies, lending an official stamp to a body of newly declared legitimate knowledge. It oversaw state Ukrainization courses for government employees, provided instruction for the region's party and Komsomol cells, promoted public Ukrainization, and supplied training for prospective Ukrainization instructors. Ambitious teachers attended training courses and lectures promoted by Narkomos and found employment as instructors in state institutions.

Narkomos did not always have the amount of control over the education environment that it desired. Subsidiary cultural organizations in Odesa resisted compliance, rejecting the notion that the Ukrainian language might be considered modern. Individual education inspectors refused to use Ukrainian or to study it. For some, it was only because they viewed Ukrainization as politically necessary that they complied. In the mixed, Russian-dominated language environment of the city of Odesa, Ukrainization seemed unnecessary and socially provocative. The objections to it documented by the city's district-level committees on Ukrainization verged on the criminal in the context of the official Soviet nationalities policy and prohibitions against chauvinistic behaviour, but public employees (and certainly Narkomos employees) must have known the regional Ukrainization commission was monitoring them for compliance. They still were relatively brazen. The discourse on Ukrainization was largely open, if not totally transparent.

Within the Odesa regional branch of the Communist Party, resistance also could be found. Of special concern to party reports was the notion that "Russified Ukrainians" resisted using (or learning) Ukrainian, whereas Jewish members were comparatively more flexible. What separated Russified Ukrainians from Russians is unclear, but the party reported that many such individuals had little desire to adjust to a policy that would profit them. In other words, they steadfastly privileged Russophone culture, in spite of their ethnic affiliation. This commitment says something about the emotive power of language and the persistence of cultural norms likely forged by some initial ambition. However, party members were supposed to lead the public in this campaign. This was a considerable objective and one that ostensibly carried with it great responsibility; the regional party leadership grounded an appeal to Ukrainize on a notion of duty. The opposition of some ethnic-Ukrainian party members was undoubtedly reflective of the larger linguistic environment of Odesa, a resistance that was echoed in the attitude of some Narkomos officials, teachers, parents, and children who shared a Russophone orientation. The transformation of the schoolhouse was to be delayed in the absence of party leadership.

Still, it was Narkomos that local authorities charged with remedying matters regarding Ukrainization in the government and party. Its provincial political education department assumed a critical evaluative role. Narkomos was the lead governmental organ responsible for managing tests of Ukrainian-studies knowledge among state employees and designing content for the perevirka. Along with a representative of the Workers' and Peasants' Inspectorate (*Robitnycho-selianska inspeksiia*, RSI) and trade union, a local Narkomos representative formed a three-member exam commission for each institution. In spite of Narkomos's inferior political position, its representative likely drove the proceedings, given its institutional role in defining content for Ukrainian studies in the classroom and public lectures. The regional Ukrainization commission employed teachers and educators as instructors, inspectors, and authors of the local process of Ukrainization, regularly assessed the skill level of educators needed to accomplish this endeavour, and sought to train and refine their knowledge further. The Ukrainization commission also recruited recent post-secondary students to take the campaign to the village, reinforcing the political meaning of Ukrainization. (As products of the Soviet Ukrainian education system, they were relatively more politically reliable and would disseminate a correct version of Ukrainian studies in place of the village teacher in the majority-Ukrainophone countryside.) Hope in the potential of youth (from post-secondary students to schoolchildren) paradoxically existed side by side with a fear of their vulnerability.

In Odesa, like elsewhere in Ukraine, anxiety about the "nationalist past" of teachers persisted. Yet, Soviet authorities still regularly concluded that Odesa teachers were deficient in their knowledge of Ukrainian. Examinations of teacher knowledge (along with those of state employees) tested not only language, then, but also political literacy in Ukrainian. Teachers' need for "legitimate" Ukrainian literacy was higher than that of the average public servant, it was argued, because of the importance and potential volatility of their task. It is in the context of fear of what teachers were perceived to have done or would do that this discussion of literacy makes the most sense.

Thus, by the late 1920s, the emphasis of Narkomos regarding Ukrainization was on the "correctness" of language, rather than on just absolute knowledge and a more controlled process of Ukrainization. In the context of Odesa, Narkomos officials cited the twin challenges of the prevailing "Russianness" of teachers and a tendency of Ukrainizing district sections or individual schools to go too far without concern for the politics of the policy. Incorrect or incomplete Ukrainization undermined the viability of the whole education system. A persistent concern, however, were the social tensions Ukrainization at the primary-school level caused and the delayed overturn of secondary and post-secondary institutions in the city with low Ukrainian enrolment and an overwhelmingly Russophone culture. Ukrainization, if it was to be pursued in Odesa, relied on a certain amount of force.

The future of the policy, in the end, however, hinged on a demographic shift that appeared underway: the migration of ethnic Ukrainians to the city in search of employment. Ukrainizers saw a forward shift in the language environment as necessary to prepare the ground, to ensure that this population too did not aspire to Russian, and, perhaps equally as important, that their knowledge of Ukrainian was directed towards an approved canon. Party interest in the policy failed to rally by the late 1920s, and local authorities reduced budgetary support for the policy. Those activists who did attend courses demanded a basic education in the language only. Party organs delayed payment for Ukrainization instructors, and yet continued to monitor their teaching, especially in non-language subjects of Ukrainian studies.

Ukrainization had some support, however. Many teachers, of course, continued to defy the Ukrainization mandate. They equated the prospect of Ukrainization of the city with its provincialization, occurring simultaneous to the city's withdrawal as a pre-eminent world port. This resistance was a problem in Odesa, but not as big a problem as teachers implementing Ukrainization incorrectly. But the efforts of several energetic teachers pushed policy forward. Individual parents reportedly became enamoured with Ukrainian national culture because of the lessons their children brought home. Others saw opportunity for their children who knew Ukrainian. For Ukrainizers in the local section of Narkomos and in the schools, what mattered most was that the city's tie with the countryside was strengthened. This implied a dramatic reorientation of the city's historical development. The land at its back was more important than the trade offered by the Black Sea it faced. Odesa was to symbolically turn around towards its region, the Ukrainian republic, and Moscow beyond. This circumlocution did not suggest an exclusion of non-Ukrainians (and, indeed, could not happen without their participation, given their majority in the city and strong representation in the countryside); but it did suggest that a Ukrainian national category could be linked to Sovietness. Children, all children, were to be leaders in this process.

The Initial Push: Winning Authority

In the study of Soviet nationalities policy in Ukraine, place is significant. It is only at the level of the local that the mechanisms of administration, as well as the social tensions and promise, produced by the politics of Ukrainization are revealed. In the context of a detailed examination of memory in contemporary Odesa, Tanya Richardson writes, "In Ukraine, location (locality and not just region) matters perhaps more than anything else when it comes to how Ukrainian citizens ask and answer questions about history and identity."[2] It follows that a study of Ukrainization of any location would reveal much about the history of this policy, but Odesa offers a particularly fruitful area of investigation because of the city's location on the border of Soviet Ukraine, external reputation as a multinational port city, and its citizens' own sense of cosmopolitanism. Odesa had undergone significant trauma during the civil war, losing half its population to its devastation and the later flight of many of its residents, and had been considerably reduced in its status as a commercial hub in the early Soviet era.[3] And yet, it was in this era that the "Odessa myth," as Jarrod Tanny calls it, became "firmly entrenched in the city's identity and notoriety."[4] Charles King provides perhaps the most concise description of this myth: "Good-natured criminality, a southern sense of laissez-aller, and a secular, modernized version of Jewishness were part of the city's heritage. To it were added the universal aspirations of Communism, the cult of the workers, and a talent for bending one's ambitions to the dictates of an overweening state."[5] In the 1920s, Soviet citizens inside the UkrSSR and beyond accepted this reputation, particularly because of the activities of Odesan writers, such as Isaac Babel, and the filmmaking of Sergei Eisenstein.[6]

This chapter does not claim to offer a comprehensive investigation of what this myth meant for the period under study; Tanny and King have provided key components of the answer. However, this study does engage the idea of an Odesan construction of distinctiveness and adaptability. Richardson argues, "Odessans

Lenin Street in central Odesa, 1934. Courtesy TsDKFFAU.

appropriated the Soviet language of 'nationality' – a language meant to differentiate and codify discrete nationalities – in order to assert a form of local difference (the Odessan nationality) outside official categories."[7] The reaction of many Odesans to Ukrainization might be categorized generally as one of "national indifference." Tara Zahra cautions historians against the practice of "assuming that other modes of collective action were more authentic, real, compelling, or genuine than nationality."[8] When individuals were not national, it does not necessarily follow that they were "localists" or some other collective group. Still, Richardson's idea of "Odessan nationality" is a compelling one. It suggests that some Odesans were (and are) willing to play with the dominant Soviet narrative of identification in order to describe their own relationship to it. Here, I suggest that at least a portion of Odesans in the 1920s were open to tentative acceptance of national identification because it made their lives easier, and did not view "side-switching" as a strenuous endeavour in an environment where modes of identification were historically dynamic.

As some Odesans today still insist, Odesa is neither Ukrainian nor Russian; it is simply Odesa. According a 1926 census, the Ukrainian population constituted

41.2 per cent of the population of the Odesa province as a whole.[9] However, in the city of Odesa itself, Ukrainians were in the minority at 17.5 per cent of the population in 1926, with Russians and Jews accounting for most of the rest of the inhabitants at 38.7 per cent and 36.4 per cent, respectively.[10] (In the Ukrainian republic generally, Ukrainians stood at nearly three-quarters of the population, but overwhelmingly resided in rural communities.) The Odesa Regional Education Section, in a 1925 plan for Ukrainization of primary schools, conceded that "Odesa conditions" had hampered language transfer to date and would require a further delay.[11] Parents were skeptical of the value of Ukrainization of their children in this most non-Ukrainian of Ukrainian cities. Teachers lacked Ukrainian-language skills and already faced significant challenges in instituting the methodological reform in the classroom required by progressive policy-makers in the republican capital of Kharkiv. Local authorities had to resort to regular exams of the Ukrainian knowledge of government employees and teachers to push the policy forward.

Ukrainization in Odesa would not have happened without this pressure, and its results by 1929 were less than inspiring. Nevertheless, definite achievements were made and evidence suggests that, in spite of continued problems regarding teachers' ability to teach in Ukrainian, some parents were being won over to the idea of the benefits of Ukrainization touted by the government and came to accept a modern, urban, Ukrainian national identity for themselves and their children. Because of this chapter's attention to available archival sources on primary schooling, its conclusions are necessarily partial. Although it suggests broader lessons regarding the significance of early Soviet nationalities policy, it principally seeks to highlight the response to Ukrainization at the most fundamental and influential level: the primary school.

Early information about Ukrainization in the Odesa region is limited. Regional authorities attempted to fulfill early Soviet decrees about the equality of languages, discussed in chapter 4, and ensure a minimum level of Ukrainian-language instruction for the province's largely rural, ethnic-Ukrainian population. Already in March 1920, the Odesa Provincial Education Section ordered the local revolutionary government (*revkom*) to arrange for the publication of 100,000 alphabet books in Ukrainian for use in the schools and a travelling reading program.[12] Here, the education section recognized early on the mutually reinforcing nature of Ukrainization in the schools and public literacy campaign. Ukrainian-language literature and instructional aids were desperately needed for both programs to succeed. Obviously, children who spoke Ukrainian in the home would benefit from study with Ukrainian-language texts. However, if children also learned to value the Ukrainian written word and see it as authoritative, if they brought home literature and written assignments in Ukrainian, they might inspire their own parents to read and write in the language. In 1920, local authorities' sponsorship of Ukrainian was directed primarily at these ethnic-Ukrainian constituencies: children and adults who had not yet acquired full literacy in Russian. They did not seek to overturn Russian dominance of public and administrative space, but rather to ensure that illiteracy was wiped out among the Ukrainian population, a task most quickly accomplished through the "native" language, for children as well as adults.

It must be remembered that at this early date, Ukrainization coincided with Soviet attempts to expand schooling generally and revolutionize education. Thus, the provincial Narkomos branch also authorized the creation of the Ivan Franko First Ukrainian Experimental School, to be enrolled with students already studying in first- and second-year Ukrainian classes. The provincial education section released a building in the central part of the city of Odesa for housing the new school and gave it prestigious status as a seven-year gymnasium.[13] In addition, the provincial education section resolved to create a Ukrainian boarding school/children's colony in the city alongside Russian and Jewish counterparts, and confirmed a "leading pedagogue-instructor" as head of the school.[14] In practice, children's colonies such as these were multi-ethnic, but Soviet authorities revealed here a tendency to lend a national designation to educational institutions and anticipated further distribution of students by ethnicity. Local authorities would not confine Ukrainian-language instruction to the village alone, but rather sought to ensure that Ukrainians and the Ukrainian language had a certain, if comparatively limited, place among the "most Soviet" progressive schools in the province.

Ukrainization began in earnest in 1924, after publication of the Radnarkom decree. Local authorities established an ad hoc provincial-level commission to report on Ukrainization, composed of representatives from the provincial RSI, political education department, military commissions, unions, and the Komsomol, among others. In accordance with RSI instructions from November 1924, this commission compiled a report on the state of Ukrainization within the province and found that state officials were unsatisfactorily implementing the policy, even in the field of education. It specified a need to increase the number of Ukrainian schools as well as the "qualification" (*kvalifikatsiia*) of Ukrainization. There was no guarantee that teachers in schools designated as Ukrainian on paper could actually teach in the language: "The fact is that many of the schools which regional education sections indicated were Ukrainian were only such because the teacher spoke with the children ordinarily in Ukrainian. However, there were not enough Ukrainian books, the teacher did not have enough knowledge of the Ukrainian literary language, Ukrainian culture."[15]

Without real progress in teachers' knowledge of Ukrainian, the whole policy would grind to a halt. Teachers were being trained in Ukrainian and "qualified" for instruction in the language, and the commission mandated that any new teacher must demonstrate competence in the language, although conceded that schools rarely applied this stricture. Its report lamented that the number of competent teachers available for staffing the schools was already small and the number of teachers who could teach in Ukrainian was even smaller. At the secondary and post-secondary level, the pool shrank further, a fact that necessarily constrained the expansion of instruction. Furthermore, according to the commission's report, the 31 per cent of vocational-school (secondary) students in the province who were ethnic Ukrainians were not necessarily capable of learning in Ukrainian at this level: "As a general rule, it is necessary to consider that the designation 'Ukrainian' far from guarantees the possibility of knowledge of the language and furthermore, to such an extent for listening to lectures or for specialized subjects."[16] Primary-school students, then, who wished to matriculate to the vocational school would face an educational environment in which Russian was the default language of instruction, especially in technical courses. Even if children used Ukrainian as their primary language, they likely did not lend it the same sort of cultural authority as Russian.

Adult attitudes towards Ukrainian were critical to children's perceptions. In the Kherson region, three-quarters of the student body of the seven-year school in the district centre of Hola Pristan was ethnic Ukrainian, but the parents (and presumably the children) did not know the Ukrainian language well, viewing it with a "hostile attitude" and protesting against the designation of the school as Ukrainian. The commission's report admitted that "[t]his sort of attitude of parents of pupils towards Ukrainization raises the question of teaching and learning [*vospitaniia i obucheniia*] in extraordinarily difficult conditions."[17] The conversion of the school to Ukrainian-language instruction proceeded regardless, with teachers reportedly proving more willing to adapt than some parents.

Resistance to Ukrainization, whether mounted by parents or teachers, was indicative of more general societal attitudes; perceived "coercive" Ukrainization of schools exacerbated tensions and played into established prejudices. The commission's report identified as the chief obstacles to the expansion of Ukrainization hostile attitudes on the part of the population, the extraordinarily difficult terminology in Ukrainian textbooks, the absence of good Ukrainian textbooks, and the absence of Ukrainian literature in the library and among the population. Only 75 per cent of the older grades in Kherson regional schools had an adequate supply of Ukrainian texts. In the Zinovivske (now Kirovohrad) region, local Narkomos administrators focused exclusively on the Ukrainization of the first four grades and encouraged teachers to take up self-study of the language.[18] For the time being, it seemed, regular use of the language would largely be confined to the youngest population and the teachers who instructed them. Even where Ukrainization was relatively successful, the commission viewed it as disruptive to the educational process. Local authorities proceeded cautiously, refusing to tinker greatly with higher-level education or indiscriminately challenge public sentiment.

Surprisingly, children's buildings for preschool children and children's cities for orphaned or abandoned children remained largely immune to Ukrainization, in spite of the 1920 attempt to set up an exclusively "Ukrainian" colony in the city of Odesa. Inattention to Ukrainization in these institutions was due partly to their predominantly Russian-speaking and multi-ethnic student populations, as well as the language skills of the teachers. These were urban-based institutions, after all, that reflected the background and attitudes of the Russophone urban environments in which they operated. However, in conceding delays to the Ukrainization of the children's buildings, the provincial education section stopped short of altering the language habits of children most directly under the state's control. It may have planned that a portion of these children would eventually transfer to conventional Ukrainized schools. Still, the weak Ukrainization of children's buildings and colonies suggested a lack of firm conviction by Narkomos and the forfeiture of a potentially valuable symbol in its nationalization campaign: the fate of the vulnerable child.

The provincial section of Narkomos continued to report progress, on paper. According to data the provincial education section submitted in a September 1924 report to the Odesa Provincial Commission on the Equality of Languages (the main standing commission at the time that coordinated Ukrainization, overseen by local party authorities) in 1922–3, with a population that was 68.1 per cent Ukrainian and 14.7 per cent Russian, 39.5 per cent of the schools were Ukrainian and 53.7 per cent were Russian. The remaining schools were national-minority schools. As of 1 April 1924, of all schools in the province, 36.0 per cent were Ukrainian schools, 32.3 per cent were in the midst of being Ukrainized, 18.7 per cent were Russian, 4.2 per cent Jewish, 7.2 per cent German, and 7.5 per cent Moldovan.[19] Education administrators thus insisted that all Ukrainian children had an opportunity to study in a Ukrainian or Ukrainizing school.

In keeping with standing policy, Narkomos strove for ethnic consolidation of students, although this aspiration rarely matched reality. Khait, the head of the provincial education section who submitted the report to the commission, did not provide precise data on school attendance by ethnicity, but he conceded that Jews and Moldovans studying in Russian schools created a need for a higher proportion of Russian schools relative to the proportion of ethnic Russians in the province. However, he stopped short of considering that Ukrainian children might well be enrolled in Russian schools as well or that Russians and other ethnic minorities might be enrolled in Ukrainian schools, insisting rather that all 68 per cent of the population that was Ukrainian sent their children to Ukrainian or Ukrainizing schools.[20] This seems unlikely. Parents refused to send their children to Ukrainian schools, or non-Ukrainian children were caught in the midst of a school undergoing Ukrainization. Personal preferences aside, parents had real concerns about the state of instruction in schools where teachers were required to teach in Ukrainian but had insufficient knowledge and were forced to rely on Russian textbooks they haphazardly translated themselves.

Most importantly, although the commission optimistically resolved that all primary schools slated for Ukrainization complete this process by the end of 1924, it allowed for an exception. This requirement applied *only* to lower-level four-year schools. The commission permitted seven-year schools to avoid Ukrainization for the time being, until suitable pedagogical personnel could be trained or recruited. At the same time, it noted that the proportion of Ukrainian schools located in the city of Odesa was inadequate; the commission ordered schools newly opening in the city and province to be designated as Ukrainian and recommended the transfer of teachers and children to these schools, assumingly over the course of the 1924–5 school year. These were contradictory mandates.[21] Most of the seven-year schools (full primary schools) were located in the city of Odesa or smaller towns. Ukrainization in the city of Odesa would be impossible if seven-year schools were exempt. It is unclear which requirement took greater force. By restricting Ukrainization to the lower-level primary school, presumably out of concern for maintenance of instructional quality, Narkomos undermined the very essence and rationale of Ukrainization. It meant that the most advanced primary schools would retain Russian-language instruction, that the Ukrainization of secondary (and post-secondary) institutions would be less critical, and that the Ukrainian language would largely be the preserve of the rural, abbreviated school with diminished cultural authority. It also belied the assertion of nearly complete Ukrainization at this early date. No data are provided on the relative proportion of Ukrainian seven-year schools to Russian (or other ethnic-minority) schools in 1924, but the relatively low enrolment of Ukrainian children in seven-year schools would remain a predominant concern of central and local authorities throughout the 1920s.

Testing Teachers

At the end of the 1924–5 academic year, there were only four Ukrainian schools in the city of Odesa itself. The Odesa Regional Education Section argued that initial attempts at Ukrainization were significantly impeded by the absence of teachers who knew Ukrainian and were available for work in the youngest grades. The Ukrainization process in the city was to be gradual, with only one new school slated for full Ukrainization by the end of the year. Altogether, the plan optimistically anticipated the process would take three years, one year beyond that ordered by republican authorities in Kharkiv. Ultimately, local education planners believed Ukrainian schools would constitute a near majority of schools in the city, as Ukrainian peasants migrated to the city in ever-greater numbers. In the surrounding region, for local Ukrainizers, the situation was more positive in immediate terms. The education section's plan claimed that the majority of rural schools were Ukrainian, and further argued that the existing Russian schools needed to be examined for possible Ukrainization because of the significant number of Ukrainian students in them. The 1925–6 academic year was the critical period for initiating a new drive for Ukrainization. At the centre of this campaign were examinations of teachers' knowledge of the Ukrainian language and subjects, which constituted the primary means to evaluate the progress of Ukrainization as well as motivate the teachers' study of Ukrainian, so that the conversion to native-language study did not just remain "on paper." Technically, teachers were supposed to have advance warning of the examinations, and a three-person commission (*triika*; Russian – *troika*) was to oversee preparations for, and administration of, the test.[22]

The proceedings of the triika for the Ukrainization of Labour School No. 5 in the city of Odesa provide some insight into what were, in the best of circumstances, a commission's expectations. In the commission's report of 21 December 1925, it found that a majority of teachers in the school had joined Ukrainian-language study groups and were generally interested in knowing Ukrainian well. However, there were holdouts in this process. Of the school's twenty employees, five were not participating in the study groups (three teachers and two staff members) because they did not already know Ukrainian, and three others promised to participate at a later time.[23] It is striking that those most in need of instruction in the study groups were not taking part. Nevertheless, the commission believed that most teachers in the school would pass an anticipated Ukrainian-studies examination, likely to be held on 1 January 1926, according to instructions passed to other institutions.

The School No. 5 commission appears remarkable for the confidence it had in the language ability of its teachers and their commitment to study. A report of teacher resistance to the taking of an examination in the Petrovirivka district in April 1926 underscores the apprehension teachers there had about submitting to a test of their Ukrainian-studies knowledge. The district section of the educational workers' union, Robos, held a meeting to investigate why the teachers refused this examination. According to the records of this meeting, the examination was scheduled on the initiative of Zigurd Alvail, an inspector of primary schooling and national minority affairs sent by the Narkomos regional section to investigate the state of Ukrainization in the district. He reportedly did not immediately inform the teachers upon his arrival in the district that he had come to administer an examination. The next day, he called the teachers to assemble at the main district schoolhouse, demanded they sit down, and only then revealed his plans for a Ukrainian-studies examination.[24] The district education inspector, Kiunts, was given the task of explaining the character of the examination.

The announcement of the examination caused immediate panic among the teachers. According to one teacher, Alvail assumed an antagonistic attitude when he confronted initial protestations, saying, "I should carry out the task. You should take the test. Those who refuse will be removed from their position."[25] He threatened to go so far as to close the school and provide no compensation for the days the school remained closed. One teacher was apparently told to leave the school because he was so nervous he could not possibly take the examination. Another was forced to leave the room four times and drink a glass of water to calm down. Others similarly claimed they were so disturbed by the surprise announcement that they could not write. Most of the teachers' accounts repeat that Alvail exacerbated the situation with his behaviour, cutting off the teachers' questions and assuming a rude tone.[26] Ultimately, Alvail was unable to administer the exam because of the degree of teacher resistance.

Alvail represented a general tendency among Ukrainizers at the regional level to use mechanisms of pressure and oversight to accomplish Ukrainization. The establishment of local examination commissions, staffed in part by leading teachers, suggested a transparent, negotiated process, but power still rested with the regional inspector. Teachers could not be trusted, according to this logic, to Ukrainize themselves. Although teachers in this district were willing to formally embrace the task of their Ukrainization, the idea of demonstrating their knowledge clearly scared them. Fundamentally, Alvail's behaviour and his proposed examination called into question the teacher's authority. One preschool teacher, for example, appeared most offended that Alvail had dressed her down in front of her class as the children lined up at the beginning of the day and ordered her to the schoolhouse for the examination.[27] It was one matter to attend study groups for Ukrainian studies regularly; it was another matter to submit to perceived "interference," constituted as external oversight.

The challenge that teachers faced in pursuing Ukrainian studies was significant. An examination commission in the Taras Shevchenko district (now Rozdilna district), northwest of the city of Odesa, found in August 1926 that local authorities had not given enough attention to Ukrainization. They had not organized courses in Ukrainian studies for teachers or ensured that libraries in the district acquired enough books for Ukrainization. Schools had received books only recently and in very small numbers. Teachers were consequently unable to study themselves or ensure that their classrooms truly transferred to Ukrainian-language instruction.[28] The existence of formally constituted Ukrainian-studies courses or study groups, however, did not guarantee that teachers would improve their knowledge.

An internal audit of study groups organized by the regional section revealed that attendance had declined significantly since the section first organized these groups and that administrators participated in these groups only 30 per cent of the time. Like the teachers of the Petrovirivka district, the administrators claimed they were too overworked to engage in serious study, an excuse the section's report rejected.[29]

Yet, in response to pressure from central governmental and Communist Party authorities, the Odesa Regional Administration and Narkomos sections continued to underscore the necessity of Ukrainization, especially of education. Without the Ukrainization of the schools, local officials argued, Ukrainian-speaking children in the region would fail to understand the political meaning of their education, and further Ukrainization of the general population would be impossible.[30] When they submitted to an examination of their Ukrainian-studies knowledge, teachers appeared to have understood the perceived urgency of this mandate. Writing samples, completed by teachers in the city of Odesa as part of an examination held in May 1926, are particularly illustrative of this point.[31] Records such as these writing samples, which reveal the actual content of a portion of the Ukrainization examinations, are rare. They must be read carefully as partly a reflection of teachers' internal thoughts, as well as evidence of the teachers' appreciation of the epistemological and political requirements of the examination.

Several teachers wrote specifically on the topic of the "Meaning of Ukrainization in Political and Pedagogical Relations," although the examination format seemed to have allowed them to select which topic they would pursue. Running throughout the essays are a clear description of the tsarist oppression of the Ukrainian language and culture and an insistence on the liberating nature of the October Revolution, which, as one teacher, Baidura, wrote, "placed before it the task of giving all nations the means to develop and build education in the most familiar, native conditions."[32] The teachers as a whole seemed to accept the idea that an ethnic-Ukrainian child's "natural" language was Ukrainian and, as a consequence, a Ukrainian-language education would be more effective as well as more just. This insistence likely ran counter to the teachers' own personal experience and knowledge of wider language mixing in Odesa. Regardless, as one teacher put it, continued use of Russian (or presumably another "foreign" language) in schools for ethnic Ukrainians would harm children: "Only the native language has secured everything associated with the normative development of the child."[33]

Ukrainization had a definite political purpose, according to these writing samples. The teacher Melnykova explained Ukrainization simply: "Children today have the means to hear in school that language which they hear in their family in order to prepare themselves for a conscious Communist life, to be useful members of the worker-peasant community."[34] Another teacher insisted Ukrainization was a fundamental part of the policy of reaching out to the peasantry and raising culture among them: "Our Ukraine in the current moment and also to a significant extent *in the future* [emphasis in the original] is and remains a peasant, farming state." The teacher went on to maintain that Ukrainization "defeats a nationalist movement that is convinced that the Communist [party] does not undertake nationalities policy."[35] Teachers were critical players in the enactment of this policy, wrote another: the Ukrainization of administrative and cultural centres depended on the Ukrainization of the school, "as the responsible unit" in the village.[36] The most revealing statement was by a teacher named Yefremova: "How funny my youthful desire to go to the Ukrainian village and work for the people in the Russian language now seems to me ... Our direct duty, as the intelligentsia and especially as teachers, is to know the language of the people for whom we are working."[37] Teachers, according to Yefremova, would make little impact in instructing the peasants in the values of the Soviet regime if they continued to use Russian.

A member of the examination commission marked most of these essays in pencil as "good," "satisfactory," or "unsatisfactory." Without information about the criteria the commission used, it is difficult to make a judgment about what the teachers needed to demonstrate in order to achieve a mark of "good." However, spelling and grammar mistakes, occasionally marked by the examiners, did not seem to prevent a grade of "satisfactory" or "good" in essays that included some detailed commentary. Political awareness, it would be fair to conclude, was needed to meet the requirements of the Ukrainization as well. Teachers recognized this fact themselves. Regardless of whether or not they were personally committed to their own disciplined study of Ukrainian, they had internalized the logic of the policy.

The Infrastructure of Ukrainian Studies

Ukrainization required that state and party employees provided employment opportunities for those teachers who could serve as instructors in courses on the Ukrainian language and Ukrainian studies. The state assumed an active role in certifying an instructor's ability to teach in Ukrainian, particularly through the vehicle of the Narkomos apparat. The scientific–methodological committee of the Odesa Provincial Education Section resolved in May 1924 to create a bureau headed by Professor Petro Buzuk to oversee seminars for raising the qualification of instructors in the Ukrainian language.[38] Individual leaders of the seminars/study groups (hurtky) were selected at a general meeting of Ukrainian-language instructors and were required to join the bureau. Buzuk was a language specialist, but he also acted as an agent of the state. It was his responsibility to police what should be taught in Ukrainian, what defined acceptable knowledge. In doing so, he extended the state's authority as mediator in the new national culture. Education inspectors also issued certification to individuals, confirming their qualifications as instructors in the Ukrainian language and further securing a role for state oversight.[39] Leading teachers and Ukrainian intellectuals in the province participated in the shaping of this body of knowledge (partly through their membership in the abovementioned bureau), and, of course, Buzuk assumed the role that he did because of his expertise first. But the state, through appointees like Buzuk and his employer Narkomos, ultimately regulated and sanctioned the new Ukrainian literacy.

Narkomos as an agency was instrumental in setting the agenda for Ukrainization courses. Under the general supervision of Ukrliknep, Narkomos's provincial political education department (Hubpolitosvita) oversaw management of the courses, monitored their success, and set rules for the payment of instructors. For example, in January 1925, Hubpolitosvita assigned one instructor, Herhilevych, for instruction of the Ukrainian language to the suburban territorial commission. He was to teach a three-month course three times a week for two hours each and be paid a sum of 36 *karbonavtsi* per month.[40] Beyond the state and party courses, which were supposed to meet regularly, Hubpolitosvita also arranged for public lectures in Ukrainian studies, as well as courses in trade-union clubs. Lectures were on a variety of topics: the history of the revolutionary movement; the history of Ukraine; and history of Ukrainian literature, art, ethnography, and theatre.[41] As a rule, these lectures employed professors from the Odesa Institute of Public Education (INO, the former university)[42] or research institutes, not primary-school teachers.[43] But teachers and state employees who needed to demonstrate expertise in Ukrainian studies as well as the language undoubtedly attended them. Hubpolitosvita asked the editors of *Visti VUTsVK* to publish the following announcement in 1925: "On January 25 at 3 o'clock in the office of Politosvitnyk (K. Libnekhta 48), a lecture of Professor [Mykhailo] Slabchenko on Ukrainian theater will take place. Tickets [are available] at the entrance at the time of the lecture."[44]

The same desire to regulate courses' language and content knowledge for Ukrainization instructors and Ukrainization courses also compelled the state to oversee the certification of teachers in the Ukrainian language for primary (labour) schools. The Odesa education section's methodological committee issued certificates (*dovidky*) to individuals, certifying their ability to teach in Ukrainian and signed by the commission's main "Instructor for Ukrainization."[45] These certificates allowed teachers to take up their duties in Ukrainian schools, a portion of which were now situated in the prestigious city centre of Odesa. They also permitted teachers to present an official document attesting to their skills for prospective employment as instructors in state Ukrainization courses. If professors were to lead the high-profile lecturers, it was up to teachers and other lower-level intellectuals to serve as the foot soldiers of the campaign.[46]

Employment as an instructor of Ukrainian studies could offer important supplementary income to teachers and other Ukrainian-speaking intellectuals. Some, such as one political worker, Hurmovenko, directly marketed their talents to Hubpolitosvita. Hurmovenko listed the Ukrainian literature he knew and specified that he sought employment in an establishment with "normal conditions."[47] Some establishments asked Hubpolitosvita for any instructor capable of helping their employees meet state-imposed standards for Ukrainian-language knowledge. Others sought out specific individuals who had gained a reputation for their competence (and efficiency). The district office of the All-Russian Textile Consortium and its labour union asked Hubpolitosvita to assign a teacher named Chaikovska to lead courses and study circles in the Ukrainian language, only to then dismiss her in favour of self-study courses after her initial work was complete.[48] It is possible that the consortium viewed Chaikovska as a unnecessary expense once Ukrainization had at least formally begun.

Failure of an establishment to set up courses in Ukrainian studies invited a reprimand early on. The provincial government had to issue such a warning in July 1924 to Proletkult, an organization nominally funded by Narkomos to advance workers' art, literature, and culture, for not organizing any Ukrainian-language courses. It maintained that the Odesa Proletkult organization had less than one month to meet an already-set August 1 deadline for "full Ukrainization," ordered it to turn to Hubpolitosvita for assignment of teachers, and reminded it that all expenses for Ukrainization were the responsibility of the organization.[49] Meeting this very short deadline was entirely unrealistic for Proletkult, as it was anyhow for institutions that had already established Ukrainization courses. The imposition of the deadline applied pressure on state organs, but it also created resentment among administrators and employees. Proletkult's foot-dragging obviously presented Narkomos Ukrainizers with a particular dilemma. Proletkult was ostensibly under Narkomos, yet it was resisting the very policy that Narkomos was supposed to lead. Furthermore, its delay reduced the authority of Ukrainization generally and undermined the political purpose of the policy. If Ukrainization's objective was the development of a modern Ukrainian culture that would bridge the workers' and peasants' worlds, Narkomos could have used Proletkult towards this end. Proletkult's continued use of Russian meant that in its vision, a worker's culture was exclusively Russian. If the parameters of culture were to shift, existing hierarchies of language would remain.

Surveying Compliance

Local authorities also monitored the status of individual attitudes towards Ukrainization. A 1925 report of the Sverdlov district of the city classified sentiment by state institutions and named numerous employees who took a negative view towards the policy. Many of those cited considered the policy coercive. Delylenko, an employee of the Silhospbank (Agricultural Bank), considered Ukrainization "forced according to political circumstances." Employees in the Odesa Regional Administrative Department (Okradminviddil) located in the district refused to study Ukrainian, and the management of the Publishing Union refused to buy textbooks for the study of Ukrainian or pay to maintain study groups. In the district's labour bureau, a representative of the Komsomol, Barzov, argued that Ukrainization would take valuable time away from the office's other responsibilities. Others refused outright to participate in tests, or perevirka, of their Ukrainian knowledge, or claimed they would eventually be transferred to Russia and thus had no need to undergo a perevirka.[50] Whole institutions resisted cooperation with the regional Ukrainization commission. A similar report of attitudes in the Lenin district towards Ukrainization makes this institutional view clear. Thus, for example, the district's customs officers, Soviet commercial fleet, and the regional committee of the Red Cross regarded Ukrainization negatively, and the telephone station simply did not care. The administration of the Chornomorka village (formerly a German colony, Liustdorf, located within the environs of the city) was not interested in Ukrainization and its staff had no knowledge of Ukrainian.[51]

Even the Sverdlov district's education section experienced setbacks in 1925. The report claimed that individual inspectors did not know the language and refused to study it or submit to a test of their knowledge. One education section employee, Seroglazov, knew little Ukrainian, did not attend courses, and did not read any Ukrainian literary or political publications. He did not even know Russian-language literature on the revolutionary movement in Ukrainian. His failures were doubly bad because he taught political lessons (*polithramota*), ostensibly in workers' clubs or reading houses. For him and other Soviet employees like him, "political literacy" could not be achieved through Ukrainian. They weakened the larger project of Ukrainization by refusing to concede that knowledge of even Ukrainian studies constituted a necessary prerequisite of good Soviet citizenship. Another education section employee, Vnukiv, offered a simple rationale for the resistance: "Among the staff Ukrainization is not undertaken because the working masses do not speak in Ukrainian, and industry is still not Ukrainized and there was not enough time set aside for the Ukrainization of the [district's] technical college."[52] Vnukiv claimed that he participated in Ukrainization only because he was a member of the Communist Party opposed in principle to the teaching of Ukrainian in higher education.

Vnukiv's argument raises the question of whether Ukrainization had to be coercive, especially in the Odesa region. For state employees, it clearly was. They were required to study Ukrainian, use it in their work, and submit to examinations of their knowledge. The conversion of the daily speech of the general population, especially of workers, was another matter. Such a project was prohibitive on both political and practical grounds. However, at least for urban communities, their intersection with "Ukrainized" state institutions and political instruction meant, in some sense, a forced engagement with the Ukrainian language. In the city of Odesa, where the public environment was overwhelmingly Russian-speaking, Ukrainization seemed unnecessarily provocative.[53] Here, Ukrainization was an especially tricky endeavour because it overran public sentiment, destabilizing the public space of a multi-ethnic border port. Yet, it is doubtful if Ukrainization could have been accomplished any other way. If one of the principal objectives of the policy was to ensure that the city – the Soviet government, Communist Party, and workers – understood and projected authority in its management of the countryside, even that surrounding Odesa, then knowledge of Ukrainian was a needed tool. In the end, Ukrainization did not anticipate simple bilingualism, but an overturn of the existing language hierarchy, whereby Ukrainian would supplant Russian as the "first" and primary language of public discourse.

To return to the question of schooling, Vnukiv believed that the Ukrainization of secondary, technical schooling was problematic and that of post-secondary education unwarranted. By extension, the Ukrainization of primary schooling would seem to serve little purpose for parents who wanted their children to advance in the education system. Furthermore, Vnukiv's argument regarding the Russian-speaking nature of the working class suggests that he might have viewed the Ukrainization of schools that served this population as improper. Vnukiv was clearly contesting established Narkomos policy. His objections were made more subtly than those of others detailed in the Sverdlov report, but his position as a Narkomos employee made these observations damaging.

There is no mention in the file of authorities punishing any of the employees cited in the report for their failure to learn Ukrainian or for their critical remarks on the language and overall policy. As will be discussed in chapter 10, five years later, the GPU would record similar comments protesting Ukrainization after the announcement of the SVU arrests. Whereas, in the GPU reports, these sentiments appear permissible, in 1925, they are clearly taboo, almost criminal, in the way the district commission lays them out. However, no criminal proceedings followed. The SVU arrests and trial were to make clear the "asymmetric" nature of terror in Ukraine, where alleged Ukrainian nationalists were punished but Russian chauvinists were not. But the Sverdlov district report also revealed something about the nature of discourse in the early Soviet period. As local Ukrainization commissions exhorted Soviet employees to learn Ukrainian and propagandize Soviet national policy among the public, these employees also knew they were being monitored for compliance. Teachers and local education section employees might tout or condemn Ukrainization, but limit their remarks in consideration of state monitoring and in anticipation of shifts in the policy's scope. The full nature of public sentiment is difficult to pinpoint, but, clearly, resistance to Ukrainization was commonplace and it was often not directly rebuffed.

The existence of large numbers of ethnic minorities, as already alluded to, presented a particular challenge for Ukrainizers in Odesa. In the Sverdlov district, one Jewish public employee, Vaisbein, said "he will study the Jewish language [Yiddish] sooner, and Ukrainian [only] when it is demanded of him."[54] It is possible that Vaisbein was invoking the letter of Soviet nationalities policy, whereby each nationality was entitled to receive state services in its "native" language. Clearly, Yiddish was not wholly "native" to Vaisbein, but he was willing to learn it (or improve it) in order to meet what he may have seen as the principal dictate of Soviet nationalities policy. The problem was, Vaisbein was working in an institution that ostensibly did not serve an exclusively Jewish population, since the report viewed his resistance to learning Ukrainian as problematic. Even in institutions designated for ethnic minorities, such as a Bulgarian, German, or Yiddish school, Ukrainization commissions expected a certain minimum knowledge of Ukrainian, although teachers in these schools often delayed compliance.[55]

The Party's Poor Example

A June 1925 meeting of district party committees in the Odesa region, held to discuss the results of tests of Ukrainian-studies knowledge among Komsomol and party activists, suggest that Vaisbein's resistance was not the universal reaction of ethnic minorities. It concluded that "the relationship towards Ukrainization on the part of the Jewish party members can be characterized as a conscious relationship, from an understanding of the necessity and desire to study the Ukrainian language and Ukrainian studies." It further noted that "Ukrainians (Russified) appear this way to a lesser extent and the Russians give entirely little evident attention to this question."[56] Jews, at least in the district party organizations surveyed, were more willing to learn Ukrainian than "ethnic" Ukrainians and, importantly, they understood and had internalized the party's motivation for this policy. The meeting's conclusions also raise the serious question of what it meant to be a Ukrainian. "Russified" Ukrainians in Odesa likely saw little divide between themselves and Russians. Obviously, more recent migrants to the Russophone city might have greater ties to the Ukrainian village, but this fact alone tells us little about an individual's own view of the Ukrainian language. Those Ukrainians who joined the Communist Party, especially at an early date, may well have wished to distance themselves from the Ukrainian language, given its association with the backward peasantry. Ukrainians a generation or more removed from the village may have simply thought of themselves as Russian. Identification as a Ukrainian offered opportunity for career advancement, given preferential promotion and recruitment of ethnic Ukrainians within the KP(b)U, but party members at the district level might not have understood this fact or were unable to overcome their own preference for, and symbolic privileged association with, the Russian language.

Party participation in Ukrainization as a whole was generally weak. A report from 1925 surveying Ukrainization in the Soviet government found that "Ukrainization takes place without sufficient participation in it by members of the party." It called upon party members to increase their work on Ukrainization through involvement in professional commissions and their supervision of work circles within governmental units, as well as the organization of Ukrainian choirs and drama circles in workers' clubs and cells of "Friends of Ukrainian Culture."[57] In other words, the report asked party members to operate through existing institutions, primarily their places of employment and recreation. It was not demanding an internal Ukrainization of the party, but rather ordering members to lead the public face of the campaign, to transform the language of governance and engage society in this campaign. Of course, none of this would be possible if party members did not take an interest in the task and acquire some baseline knowledge of Ukrainian.

Because of the unsatisfactory command of Ukrainian among all levels of the party in the Odesa region, the report recommended that leadership explain to party members that "the study of Ukrainian is a party duty and disregard for Ukrainization should be viewed [as] a break in party discipline."[58] It suggested that the party's control commission hold party members responsible for failure to undertake Ukrainization. Thus, it was a moral imperative for party members to Ukrainize themselves and participate in the wider campaign. The shortcomings in the party's Ukrainization seemed considerable. Knowledge of Ukrainian was limited and the party's commitment to the policy was weak; even party members on the regional Ukrainization commission, the principal driving force for Ukrainization alongside Narkomos, attended meetings irregularly. Questionnaires sent to the regional party committee by local party and Komsomol sections revealed increases in Ukrainian membership, but sporadic use of Ukrainian and little data on the level of knowledge of Ukrainian studies.[59] An August 1925 excerpt of a meeting of the secretariat of the party's Odesa Provincial Committee (Gubkom in Russian; Hubkom in Ukrainian) argued that after the "formal fulfillment of the directives of Gubkom and TsK," such as organization of study circles and courses in Ukrainian studies, little had been done to account for their work. Few in the leadership of district party committees knew Ukrainian, activists were not being trained in Ukrainian, committees were not promoting ethnic Ukrainians, and committees wrote only 5 to 10 per cent of their correspondence in Ukrainian.[60]

While the real application of force seemed needed, the party worked by threat of force instead. So although the report conceded that party employees of state organs could be fired and that the corresponding party organization would institute disciplinary procedures against them, its greatest emphasis was on expressions of duty and responsibility. If party members did actually have to face consequences for their failure, these expressions of a moral imperative left too much to an individual's latitude. Self-Ukrainization might have been just, but many other moral requirements dictated a party member's behaviour. Ultimately, then, in the field of schooling, the party did not lead teachers by example, and its own foot-dragging imperilled true progress. The report's concern for the intersection between party members' behaviour and their role in wider Ukrainization is a telling indication of what was needed to overcome resistance in the schools and what was absent. Odesa regional party and governmental leadership set unrealistic, overly ambitious goals and articulated threats for non-compliance to demonstrate some level of activity to Kharkiv.

Educators at the Centre

At a technical level, in regard to the conversion of paperwork and correspondence to Ukrainian, the situation was already better in governmental institutions by the first part of 1925. The Odesa Provincial Commission on the Equality of Languages, the antecedent of the Odesa Regional Ukrainization Commission, noted that "in [state] establishments the living [*zhyva*] Ukrainian language was lacking, which testifies to the formal, superficial [*poverkhove*] relationship to Ukrainization."[61] Again, a Narkomos department was entrusted with remedying matters. The commission ordered Hubpolitosvita to conduct tests of the Ukrainian language among civil servants, and asked its scientific methodological committee to elaborate a program for study groups. The commission lamented the fact that Ukrainization in state institutions had proceeded without active coordination with Hubpolitosvita's methodological committee, and ordered it to prepare a concrete plan specifically for the Ukrainization of educational institutions.

While, in practice, the provincial sotsvykh department adapted the Holovsotsvykh curriculum for Ukrainian primary schools and oversaw the Ukrainization of their faculty, Hubpolitosvita's methodological committee, in consultation with Ukrliknep, was responsible for the design of courses and testing formats for all state employees in the Odesa province, including teachers and post-secondary instructors. In other words, Narkomos remained the lead institution for Ukrainization, even as other state (e.g., RSI) and party organs were entrusted with general oversight, and it employed "fluent" Ukrainian-speaking teachers to carry out its mission. Furthermore, of primary concern to education, the commission's report made clear that ignorance of Ukrainian "harms the establishment of civic thoughts [*hromadskoi dumky*] among civil servants."⁶² Resistance to Ukrainization in any state institution had an effect on the resolve of all public servants, teachers as well as parents in state employment, to further study Ukrainian and, by extension, the commission's comments suggest, to have the tools for public service.

By the middle of 1925, the Odesa Provincial Commission on the Equality of Languages had been replaced by the Regional Commission on Ukrainization. Each state institution was required to form a commission on Ukrainization, with a perevirka commission above it formed with representatives of the regional executive committee, RSI, trade union organization, and, importantly, Narkomos section. Educators were instrumental to broadening Ukrainization in several concrete ways ordered by the commission. The commission ordered instructors of post-secondary institutions to participate in the organization of a regional seminar in order to familiarize these instructors with terminology being developed by VUAN and ensure uniform instruction. Furthermore, the commission also required a survey "of all local Ukrainian scientific, literary and artistic forces and also an account of instructors for schools of Ukrainian studies" in order to prepare for their possible employment as instructors in state Ukrainian-studies courses.⁶³ It ordered a perevirka of all educational institutions in order to ensure Ukrainian instruction for students, but it was also a valuable tool for assessing the pool of fluent Ukrainian speakers.

Often, the initial efforts of Ukrainizers recruited by the regional commission went to naught. Even when employees acquired training in Ukrainian studies, the rate of recidivism was high. A December 1925 report from the Odesa Regional Commission on Ukrainization noted that a perevirka revealed that many state employees had forgotten their knowledge of Ukrainian and Ukrainian studies after the summer. The commission argued that summer had interrupted the study of state employees and no second-level course had been established. Thus, in August, the commission had set up three-month courses that essentially repeated material and placed second-level courses in only four or five institutions, assigning them the best instructors. A total of 167 study groups in Ukrainian studies enrolled 4,000 employees. It also reviewed the skills of instructors and offered seminars to the instructors in order to refine their skills. Seminars were offered in literature and language, social and economic studies, art, and world studies, and the commission sponsored further lectures on a range of Ukrainian-studies topics in workers' clubs, presumably led by some of the instructors being retrained.⁶⁴

In order to consolidate the gains of 1925, the commission required further testing. It planned a winter perevirka to test the knowledge state employees had acquired over the past three months. Students of the Odesa INO were to observe the districts' progress towards a January 1 target date for Ukrainization and completion of the perevirka.⁶⁵ While the initial Ukrainization relied on established intelligentsia, the commission anticipated a shift in management of the policy. It was in the midst of recruitment of lecturers and translators, a portion of whom included young, skilled schoolteachers, for further staffing of state courses and public activity. It had already ordered the recruitment of students for assignment to the villages in order to prepare for Ukrainization at the local level.⁶⁶ It hoped that products of, and participants in, the Soviet education system would administer the controls necessary to secure the new, modern Ukrainian culture. Soviet authorities intended to turn Ukrainian culture on its head, to direct the village towards the city and ensure that Ukrainian culture was oriented towards an industrialized future, towards the needs and ambitions of youth and the youthful workers' state. It makes sense, then, that Soviet authorities ordered progressive educators, students, and schoolchildren to guard this culture against the rural folklorism of the past. Ironically, youths sent out from the Russophone city were to carry a Ukrainian culture to the village, where it had been historically situated, in order to refashion it.

Whom to Trust?

The Communist Party's trust of pre-revolutionary intelligentsia, especially Ukrainians who had participated in the national movement and supported the UNR government, was always limited. When they could, then, Odesa political authorities turned to graduates of Soviet education, but their training in Ukrainian studies was still not deep by the mid-1920s. A 1927 report compiled by the Regional Inspector of People's Education, presented at a meeting of the Commission on Ukrainization and sent on to local party authorities, revealed past political distrust of teachers and current caution in regard to further Ukrainization in the field of education. It identified Ukrainians, alongside Jews, as "one of the most oppressed nationalities" of the pre-revolutionary era. The creation of national schools was thus a critical element in their "liberation." Individual parents and teachers, largely in rural communities, initiated the establishment of Ukrainian schools, with Odesa authorities becoming involved in planning for these schools only during the 1923–4 school year. The report conceded that Soviet authorities did not and could not form these schools in the aftermath of a civil war, which was "especially bitter" in Ukraine.

There was little that the Soviet government could do to institute control over the establishment of national schools prior to this date, and, practically, it was impossible to stage a more systematic campaign, given very real shortages in teachers, textbooks, infrastructure, and funding. The situation improved slightly after the end of the civil war, but the concern for textbook supplies and textbook forms persisted throughout the 1920s. The report conceded that "it was necessary to undertake a lot of scientific work to create new textbooks, especially in the new Soviet conditions."⁶⁷ The Odesa Regional Education Section needed time to correlate the number of textbooks to the number of Ukrainian schools already established or imagined, but needed to expend even greater effort to ensure that these textbooks taught the "correct lessons." In the case of Ukrainian books, of course, the revision of textbooks was less necessary than the creation of entirely new Soviet ones. The greater risk was that teachers would independently translate pre-revolutionary Russian texts for use in the classroom. However, as has already been made clear above, the introduction of progressive pedagogical methods made teachers' use of textbooks less critical.

Much fell to the individual efforts of teachers to compile work plans that incorporated local material and children's learning aptitude. Thus, Soviet authorities had to have faith in teachers, and this faith was weak in the case of Ukrainian teachers. Generally, according to the report, "It is known that teachers at the time of the beginning of the revolution were infected [*prosiakneno*] with chauvinist, Petliurist carriers [*nosiiamy*], in their political slogans the question of the national Ukrainian school was stressed."⁶⁸ In short, the report claimed that teachers were historically carriers of an anti-Soviet nationalism and thus suspected of still harbouring such sentiments. Ukrainization was meant to undermine the basis of this nationalism, to satisfy the desire to have Ukrainian schools and national culture, but, at the same time, to orient this culture towards the needs of the workers' state. Oddly, however, when "Soviet conditions" called for the creation of Ukrainian schools, the report argues, teachers were unprepared: "a great majority of teachers, even in the villages, at any rate did not know the basic moments of Ukrainian studies: the economy, geography, history, and simply did not know the language to teach children in it." How was this possible? How could teachers be former or potential nationalists, yet ignorant of "national" themes?

On one level, as has been documented throughout this work, teachers' lack of knowledge of both the Ukrainian language and subjects was real. A 1926 perevirka of rural teachers in the Odesa region found that some 33 per cent of teachers did not know any Ukrainian or anything about Ukrainian studies, that they were "simply illiterate people for the Ukrainian school in which they were teaching." It is likely that many of these teachers were "literate" in some language, probably Russian, but they were unable to operate in a Ukrainian-speaking environment. This is a kind of literacy that is functionally defined and likely accounts for a good portion of Narkomos's anxieties. On another level, Narkomos regarded some teachers who were able to speak in Ukrainian and knew something about Ukrainian studies, a portion of whom might have been "Petliurists" or simply nationally minded, as not fully politically "literate." The perevirka demonstrated that only 23 per cent of those tested (148 of 643) had achieved a first-category ranking for state employees: "good knowledge of the language and Ukrainian studies." The regional inspector's report argued that whereas office workers might be able to operate according to second-level skills (satisfactory knowledge of Ukrainian), teachers had to test in the first category to be able to teach in a Ukrainian school.[69] Leaving aside the issue of the objectivity of language standards for now, the Narkomos (Politosvita) designers of the test most certainly had a politically constructed notion of what constituted Ukrainian studies: a history of the revolutionary movement in Ukraine, "red" Ukrainian literature, geography, and economics that emphasized industrial output in the republic. To test into the first category, then, to be fully literate, suggested a different kind of literacy. It is certainly possible by this measure that an "ex-Petliuirst" – indeed, any Ukrainian-speaking teacher – could be categorized as "semi-literate" or even "illiterate."

After the establishment of Ukrainian schools and the *formal* Ukrainization of state establishments, the principal issues for Soviet and party authorities in Odesa became the pace of Ukrainization and what the 1927 education inspector's report to the regional Ukrainization commission defined as "the struggle for the appropriate use of the language." Of course, the two concerns were interrelated. If an unqualified teacher or instructor led Ukrainization in a school or Soviet institution, schoolchildren or state employees would struggle to learn Ukrainian and fail to learn the standardized language being defined by VUAN linguists. It would take that much longer until Ukrainization was complete. Furthermore, "incorrect" Ukrainization risked exacerbating social tensions and heightening resistance by playing to established prejudices against Ukrainian. Parents, teachers, children, and state-course-takers could continue to view Ukrainian as a distorted form of Russian, a peasant dialect without a cultural underpinning. Ukrainization would appear unnecessary and wholly coerced. Thus, of foremost concern to Narkomos was the "problem for literacy [*hramotnist'*], for the quality of the school, that is, the problem for the selection and raising the qualification of the Ukrainian teachers." Standing in the way of a "school of the highest level of quality" was the "psychological Russianness" of parts of the Odesa population. Although the report does not draw a direct causal line, the implication is clear. Russification complicated the practical task of setting up Ukrainian schools and required the Ukrainizers to proceed cautiously but authoritatively ahead.

While Russification was still a problem and it worked to slow down Ukrainization, the report suggests that sometimes the scope of Ukrainization in Odesa was too great. After the revolution, the report argues, once the "difference between the ruling class and peasant language was eliminated," education officials found it easier to establish schools, and resistance to Ukrainization (as well as "Jewishization") waned but did not disappear. The report regards some instances of opposition as legitimate. Authorities were allegedly too aggressive in their haste to establish Ukrainian schools, primarily during the 1925–6 academic year, when the number of Ukrainian schools increased partly through "forced [*prymusova*] Ukrainization" of Russian schools: "It is necessary to say that the process of this Ukrainization was unhealthy because of the existence in places of an intensely expressed unwillingness on the part of parents and a certain number of teachers." While the report condemned this forced or "indiscriminate" (*poholova*) Ukrainization, it also expressed concerned that parents were independently pushing for the "de-Ukrainization" of schools. The report presents a picture of spontaneous Ukrainization and de-Ukrainization, beyond the control of the Odesa Regional Education Section or other state or party oversight. This trend was impermissible, but so was an abandonment of the policy. The report argued that it was necessary to correlate the number of Ukrainian schools with the Ukrainian proportion of the population (a goal already largely achieved on paper) and push for an improvement in instruction. The pace of Ukrainization would not slacken so much as shift. Ever mindful of public sentiment, the definitive achievement of Ukrainization would be high-quality Ukrainian-language instruction and maintenance of the "true Soviet character of the Ukrainized school."[70]

What the "true Soviet character" of a school meant is difficult to precisely identify. The ideal school in Soviet Ukraine in 1927 was engaged in promoting a progressive pedagogical curriculum that was locally derived but attuned to the larger political requirements of the Communist Party. This is a broad description. However, embedded in this statement is an expression of fear of the "non-Soviet" school: nationalistic, reactionary, or simply non-compliant. All, perhaps, were reasons for anxiety, yet, it is this potential for a school to become something undesirable that mattered most. Primary schools were a critical component in the Soviet campaign to orient Ukraine towards a modern, industrialized future. Secondary and post-secondary education may have been where Soviet specialists were being immediately trained, and thus were the focus of the party's attention, but it was in primary schools that an entirely new generation was being cultivated. "Soviet" primary schools were needed to ensure that children were adequately prepared for matriculation to the vocational schools, technical colleges, and institutes. "Non-Soviet" schools suggested a break in this link.

The truly Ukrainized school was conspicuously more rare at the secondary and post-secondary levels. In the city of Odesa, only two vocational schools were entirely Ukrainized in 1927. The inspector's report makes mention of twelve others that were considered Ukrainian, but "are in essence Russian." It allowed that the slow and slipshod Ukrainization of the vocational schools had an effect on the Ukrainization of higher education. Only the Odesa Agricultural Institute and the Odesa INO (the former university) attempted to follow any plan for

Ukrainization. In regard to students, in the city of Odesa, 17 per cent of the vocational-school students were Ukrainian, 19 per cent were Russian, and 54 per cent were Jewish. The proportion was nearly the same for post-secondary schools. Only the city's "workers' faculties" (*robfak* in Ukrainian; *rabfak* in Russian – an educational institution established to supplement the incomplete schooling of workers and to provide career advancement) approached a 50 per cent Ukrainian student body, ostensibly made up of Ukrainian migrants to the city who formed the growing ranks of the working class. Blame for this significant shortcoming, however, was to be found at the primary-school level. According to the inspector's report, the Ukrainian portion of the population was "entirely insufficiently provided for [*obsluhovuietsia*]" because "in the village there is a very small number of seven-year schools which graduate a small contingent of pupils to the profshkoly."[71] Here was a clear formulation of a deficiency in Soviet educational policy and acknowledgment of the interconnected nature of the Ukrainization. A failure to increase the number of seven-year schools for Ukrainians in the countryside meant that secondary schools could not expand into rural communities or recruit boarding students (or anticipate families migrating to the city to have children prepared for further schooling). Ukrainians would remain proportionally less educated, and an essential premise of Ukrainization would be undermined. The recognition of this discrepancy also casts doubt on the report's cited correspondence between the Ukrainian population and primary schools. If the majority of Ukrainian schools were abbreviated four-year primary schools and the majority of Russian schools, for example, were full seven-year primary schools, then "national education" would necessarily remain unequal.

At its heart, this important summary of Ukrainization work to date and work needed claims to be objective and even-handed. It criticizes instances of a formal approach to Ukrainization and calls for a deepening and improvement in Ukrainization, while, in an apparent criticism of overly hasty Ukrainization, argues that "we must further get rid of everything that could be called unhealthy, politically uneven methods of implementation, everything that only harms and discredits Ukrainization itself." It cites as an example of "provocative incidents" an announcement by the head of one Ukrainized school that every pupil who spoke in class in Russian would be fined five kopecks.[72] This comment rings eerily similar to charges made against alleged Ukrainian nationalists during the SVU affair. Conspicuously absent from the report is an equally "provocative" example of Russification or "Great Russian chauvinism," even as it concedes that Russification did persist. Clearly, foremost in the minds of the local Narkomos administrators, given the very real historical place of Russian in Odesa and its demographic mix, was Ukrainization gone awry. And yet, it is difficult to foresee how Ukrainization of the schools could have progressed without force being applied in some limited and transparent way (if not according to the absurd fining policy chosen by the school principal). The institutional inertia of schools and state institutions was often too great, and their compliance with Ukrainization decrees could always be selective. The "asymmetric terror" that the GPU and party would eventually apply against Ukrainizers had its roots in this anxiety about the tensions that Ukrainization caused. Prioritization of this worry over resistance to Ukrainization meant a weakening of the policy's authority and suggested what the 1927 report labelled as the "greatest task of our party in Ukraine" was anything but that.[73]

One year later, the Ukrainization drive already appeared to be on the wane and knowledge of Ukrainian was still cursory, although the Communist Party's demands on its members and state employees, including teachers, remained in effect. A harbinger of the future of the policy in Odesa was its effect on local party activists. A resolution of the Secretariat of the Odesa Regional Party Committee sent to all local Agitprop bureaus from February 1928 noted the "very weak attendance of courses" on Ukrainization for party activists. District party committees had established courses for 300 persons. Although 226 party members had registered for the courses, only 75 attended regularly. Because these party courses were supposed to be self-financing (i.e., students were expected to pay for each course they attended), the courses were in serious financial trouble. The secretariat ordered all district committees to take an account of party members who attended Ukrainization courses and "force" negligent members to attend punctually. District committees were also to monitor the attendance by local propagandists of lectures given by higher-education instructors. However, perhaps in recognition that attendance would continue to be an issue, the resolution called for a reduction in the number of courses available and for stricter budget accounting by the local Politosvita, the Narkomos division responsible for all Ukrainization courses.[74]

In fact, attendance continued to be a problem. The assistant head of the regional Agitprop noted in a November 1928 letter to district party commissions that, in spite of the efforts of Agitprop, new Ukrainization courses that had begun on September 18 of that year were not fully enrolled. He blamed the district commission for telling party members to individually report to courses and for failing to organize equally distributed groups of students. He called on individual party cells to monitor attendance and discipline members who shirked attendance.[75] A report to the regional Agitprop bureau from the local head of the state Ukrainization courses noted that in Odesa's Illich and Stalin districts, ninety-four party activists were registered among a smaller number of groups in September 1928, but less than two-thirds of the registered students attended. Half of those registered were students who had to repeat the course, meaning that they had learned little or nothing during the previous session. Five study groups were left without a regular instructor, although it appears to have been overseen by a course administrator. Instead, they used an instructional program for self-study. The students in these groups appeared to have little regard for elements of Ukrainian studies, specifically "economic geography," which they asked Ukrainization administrators to remove from the course of study. Individual students also introduced a proposal not to study a (historical) sketch of Ukraine. However, they demanded that the number of hours devoted to language study be increased.[76] The report makes no mention of a rationale for this demand. From a functional perspective, this approach made sense. A command of the language was necessary for the practical demands of work as a party activist, and it is possible that students were admitting that it was not so easily acquired. Although students could have been tested in a perevirka on all elements of Ukrainian studies, their proposed revisions may have suggested that allowances be made in the perevirka. Or, they simply believed the minimum of Ukrainian-studies knowledge could be acquired in a different way, maybe through their own reading of Russian-language texts. Regardless, this request to learn "more" language is a notable example of how a select group viewed the demands and potential promise of Ukrainization.

As a result of the overall trend towards non-attendance, the financial crisis of Ukrainization remained unresolved. Furthermore, party members who attended courses were not paying for them: "In spite of the fact that course-takers from the party activists in the first meetings [zboriv] were warned that they needed to bring money, that is, payment for the first lesson, the majority did not bring it." As a result, instructors who were assigned to courses were left unpaid, and the debt Ukrainization administrators owed to instructors from the previous year was carried over. The head of the Ukrainization courses called on higher educational institutions, VUZy, to assume a role in maintaining Ukrainization courses, partly because they provided some of the instructors, and warned that instructors would refuse to lead Ukrainization courses for the party in future if their work conditions remained the same. Besides, the head of courses argued, fees for the courses were already too low and payment was unlikely to increase because attendance would not improve. The administrator suggested that a more direct budgetary allotment be made for Ukrainization courses for party activists.[77] However, a November 1928 letter from the head of the Odesa regional financial section to Agitprop complicated matters, arguing that the current People's Commissariat of Finance budget (1928–9) did not allow for the financing of the Ukrainization of VUZy, specifically of social studies instructors. It would therefore be difficult for the VUZy to assume any role in financing training of party activists. The head of the financial section makes no detailed mention of maintenance of the Ukrainization of state employees generally, but suggests that automatic reimbursement of costs for Ukrainization was foreseen only in the 1925–6 budget.[78] After this time, payment for the requirements of Ukrainization was the responsibility of each individual institution.

Continued Problems and Shifting Parental Sentiment

What did these shortcomings mean for the Ukrainization of schooling? Most importantly, the failure of party members to attend Ukrainization courses and the lack of funding of Ukrainization courses suggested to the Odesa Narkomos administrators that the policy was far from the party's "greatest task." Narkomos was critical to this campaign in two important respects. First, its political department, Politosvita, designed the Ukrainization program that was supposed to be used by party activists and state employees alike. Second, Narkomos provided the instructors for the party courses and lecturers in Agitprop-sponsored clubs. At some level, then, Narkomos understood that if the party was not energetically taking up the Ukrainization campaign and the Ukrainization of VUZy remained at a standstill, the policy as a whole lacked the authority to institute fundamental change even at the basic level of the primary school. Furthermore, Narkomos must have appreciated that funding for a deepening of Ukrainization (e.g., further training of teachers and publication of new texts) would be difficult to procure. In addition, qualified teachers who sought employment as Ukrainization instructors in party courses were likely dissuaded by the party's failure to pay instructors. Employment in Ukrainization courses for state employees remained a possibility (and, for a time, a lucrative one), but teachers must have been concerned about participation in a policy that seemed to lack the support of the determining authority in the region, the regional section of the Communist Party.

Later Ukrainian-studies examinations reveal that progress in knowledge among teachers from the initial push in 1925–6 was uneven. A March 1928 examination in the Komintern district of both government employees and teachers revealed that of the fifteen teachers who appeared for the exam, no teacher scored into the first category ("good"). However, the commission gave exemptions to twelve individuals, including teachers, on multiple grounds: for having earned a first-category ranking in Ukrainian-studies examinations held in 1926; for having taught Ukrainian a long time; or for being a graduate of an INO.[79] This practice of giving exemptions failed to account for loss of language knowledge or to assess the real language ability of practising Ukrainian-language teachers. A report by the Odesa Regional Administration's commission on Ukrainization in late December 1928 argued that the state of Ukrainian knowledge among rural and urban teachers alike was so unsatisfactory that teachers who had earned a second- and third-category ranking needed to be retested at the end of the 1928–9 academic year.[80]

What is most interesting about these examinations of Ukrainian knowledge is that the score teachers earned could shift. The results of an examination of teachers performed in June 1929 in the town of Zhovtneve revealed that several teachers who had previously obtained a second-category ranking were demoted to a third-category ranking. However, they were not dismissed, but rather ordered to study further.[81] In an earlier November 1928 examination of teachers and public workers in the Hrosulove district (northwest of the city of Odesa), the commission had marked down two examinees from a second-category ranking to a third-category ranking, due to their alleged hostility to Ukrainization. Both these examinees were public servants, not teachers (one was a statistician and another an accountant), but the examination concluded that the prevailing attitude in the district towards Ukrainization was apathy. Many of the examinees came late to the examination (there are no separate comments on teachers), and 55 per cent of the examinees as a whole scored into the third category. At a general meeting of teachers and government employees, Bartnykov, the head of the financial section of the Hrosulove District Administration, refused to give a report in Ukrainian, laughing at this prospect.[82] Similarly, in the Leninskyi district of the city of Odesa, teachers reportedly had demonstrated an intolerant attitude towards Ukrainization.[83]

Two years later, little had changed regarding Ukrainization of the party in Odesa. A 1929 protocol of the Odesa Regional Party Committee labelled low attendance by party activists "intolerable" and ordered the party's control commission "to call to party responsibility candidates who are not systematically visiting courses." However, it tasked a local Narkomos official, Pelevin, with the responsibility of developing a budget for the courses and of ensuring payment from course-takers for instruction. This provision is telling. Narkomos was clearly still the lead institution for promoting Ukrainization and yet it clearly lacked the clout of the party to enforce payment for courses that had been chronically not made. Furthermore, the party seemed to lack confidence that Narkomos-appointed instructors were all teaching correctly, ordering its Agitprop department to check (*pereviryty*) the teaching of social studies in Ukrainian.[84] A January 1929 report to the regional Agitprop from the head of the Ukrainization courses reported that enrolment in Ukrainization courses spiked when a perevirka was threatened in state institutions or party committees, but subsequently fell away. Instructors used the plan prescribed by the Narkomos section, but adapted this plan to the needs of their *hromada* (society). Methods of work included lectures and conversations with the students, reading the newspaper, and written work, but the head of courses conceded that the absence of textbooks, even at this late date, impeded work. He claimed that instructors were generally satisfactory, with the exception of one of the instructors, who was dismissed for inattentiveness. In spite of the recurring attendance and budgetary issues, the head of courses insisted that these courses were the required form of Ukrainization. If attendance was more regular and students took the courses seriously, the instructional plan could be instituted in a systematic fashion and Ukrainization would be secured.[85] The problem was that he lacked any real means to ensure a shift in attitudes. Although he appealed to the regional party secretariat to discipline party members, it is difficult to see how this would be accomplished, given its reluctance to assess real penalties.

The archival record on Ukrainization in primary schools in the Odesa region drops off after 1929. (The State Archive of the Odesa Region has no records from the education inspectorates of the 1930s.) However, the poor performance of some teachers in the 1928–9 examinations and the public's general foot-dragging would seem to suggest that considerable improvements in teachers' Ukrainian knowledge were not in the offing. Like the teachers in the Petrovirivka district who resisted taking a "surprise" examination in 1926, at least a significant portion of teachers continued to exhibit hostility to the notion of having their Ukrainian knowledge formally evaluated. Certainly, enough time had passed for them to study adequately, in spite of the constraints of their schedule and shortages of preparatory literature. Wider public Ukrainization continued to be stalled because of the small number of lecturers available from the ranks of teachers who could be assigned to public work. A real shift in the language environment in Odesa could not occur without energetic teacher participation.

And yet, in spite of this evidence, the tide did seem to be shifting for some. In the city of Odesa, the transfer to Ukrainian-language instruction was generally "painless" in Labour School No. 67, according to the records of a meeting of the school's teachers in January 1929. Not all parents were "positively" disposed towards Ukrainization, and the fact that some families of the pupils did not speak Ukrainian at home meant that some children spoke Ukrainian only within the confines of the school. However, the teachers' meeting still concluded that "a rise in national consciousness has been observed [among the parents] that must be attributed to the influence of pupils on family life."[86] In March 1928, parents at Labour School No. 41 voted to petition regional authorities for the gradual but full conversion of the school from Russian- to Ukrainian-language instruction. They were apparently convinced by the school director's argument: "In two years it will already be rare to hear Russian speech … You have children and you are obliged to ensure that they know Ukrainian well, which in Ukraine is the state language without which it will be difficult to receive service and work." As the school director put it, "times were moving ahead" and the school had an obligation to keep pace.[87] This was the sort of recognition persistently sought by the administrators of early Soviet nationalities policy in Ukraine. However, the parents' vote paints a picture of a spontaneous sort of conversion to Ukrainian-language schooling from Russian-language schooling that rarely seemed to occur.

It is unclear what was the precise ethnic makeup of schools No. 67 and No. 41. Strictly speaking, the Ukrainization of schools was supposed to be limited to institutions with homogeneous Ukrainian student bodies, but this was an ambition rather than a reality. Schools targeted or petitioning for Ukrainization were often multi-ethnic. In spite of the minority status of Ukrainians in the city of Odesa, local educational authorities viewed the expansion of Ukrainian schools in the city as essential to strengthen the city's (and, by extension, the Communist Party's) bond with, and authority over, the surrounding Ukrainian-majority countryside.[88] If non-Ukrainian children, specifically Russian or Jewish children, were "temporarily" enrolled in Ukrainian schools, the larger political goals of Ukrainization in general superseded these concerns. Furthermore, Narkomos officials and some Communist Party leaders viewed the creation of Yiddish and other "national-minority" schools alongside Ukrainian schools as an accepted strategy of weakening the assimilation of non-Russians, including Ukrainian peasant migrants, to a historically rooted, urban Russian culture.

The sentiments of the parents of the pupils of schools No. 67 and No. 41 reflect and transform the official rationale for Ukrainization. The policy was a necessary measure to legitimize Communist Party power among the Ukrainian-speaking population, prepare the next generation for their future political and economic roles in an imagined majority Ukrainian-speaking republic, and offer opportunity for professional advancement for those who learned the language, even in decidedly Russophone cities like Odesa. These parents, whether they were ethnic Ukrainian or not, decided that knowledge of Ukrainian was a marker of urban modernity and future prosperity. For those parents who were Ukrainian, the decision to convert these schools to "their" language of instruction may have given them confidence in their newly embraced national identity. Ukrainian was not the tongue of the village alone, but of the socialist city that their children would build.

Chapter Ten

The Correction

By the end of the 1920s, Soviet authorities moved on a long-standing suspicion of non-party educators. Education officials pursued the twin policies of progressive education and Ukrainization in the context of a cultural revolution in the republic: a shakeup of non-party participation in the technical, scientific, and cultural fields. Stalin and his supporters believed this revolution was necessary in order to inspire a new Soviet generation, establish conditions for the replacement of carry-overs from the pre-revolutionary period with Soviet-trained cadres, and create a base of support for Stalin's economic and political agenda. In Ukraine, this policy took on a particular twist because of a persistent concern about the danger of Ukrainian nationalism and the republican Commissariat of Education's lasting commitment to some principles of progressive pedagogy. Both these convictions forced new attention on the field of education, the pursuit of contradictory policies of limitation/alteration, and public calls for expansion. This study has argued that these attitudes were deep-seated, that such a shift had precedence in the very contradictions of these policies. Furthermore, it suggests that education, in spite of the lack of financial investment, was not politically impotent, and the move by the party and security service against educators was evidence of this.

Education had power because of schooling's capacity to shape the attitudes of the young; in the early period of Soviet power, the party leadership saw as crucial education's potential to define the significance of the revolution and consolidate its gains in the imagination of children. If party authorities did not order high investment in education, they kept a watchful eye on the schools and reacted quickly when they identified an undesirable event or trend. A concern about the political orientation of children determined the character of repression and the contours of the cultural revolution in the Ukrainian republic. Schools, teachers, and children were a central component of these campaigns, and Ukrainization and educational reform (in an arguably more nuanced manner) were the subjects of dispute. The teachers' union (Robos) initiated the campaign against its own membership, providing a new emphasis on long-held doubts. Union members decried teachers' failure to instill an awareness of socialism's aims in children through progressive education and their lack of vigilance against enemies within their ranks. Local Soviet authorities pointed to specific instances of infiltration by nationalists who had taken advantage of the conditions created by Ukrainization and distorted pedagogy in the schools. The most widespread failing of teachers was their passivity, their so-called neutrality. What this meant in the context of Ukrainization was difficult to assess. Just how active could Ukrainizing teachers be if the policy itself was under stress? What constituted correct methodology in the schools?

The Soviet press alleged that the nationalists were active in rural schools farther away from the urban bases of Soviet power. Articles clipped by Robos's investigative bureau alleged that rich peasants, or kulaks, were working to undermine the objectives of the Soviet school, to influence the politically vulnerable, passive teachers. A frequent crime cited by newspaper accounts and confirmed by reports issued by purge commissions of Robos was the existence of "national antagonisms" among teachers; in particular, anti-Semitic attitudes. Anti-Semitism was seen as a marker of an anti-Soviet stance and Robos commissions sometimes correlated it to the development of Ukrainian nationalism. As an aggregate, newspaper articles, purge commission reports, and the minutes of Robos meetings questioned the ability of Robos members, teachers, and educators (employed in schools, institutes, and as lecturers and writers of Ukrainian studies) to lead the process of Ukrainization. Robos sought to redeem itself by arguing that most teachers were loyal servants of the Soviet republic, and the Robos leadership investigated controversial cases of teachers whom it judged local commissions had purged without initial conclusive evidence. Robos thus attempted to preserve its status as a representative of teacher interests, but its power and willingness to intervene, especially in criminal cases, were limited. Any taint of past sympathy with the Ukrainian national movement was enough to earn the suspicion of local purge commissions and republican Robos authorities. The answer to mounting charges of suspect loyalty in the teaching profession was demonstration of a firm commitment to the dictates of the cultural revolution and the economic and political campaigns of the early 1930s, and exposure of "enemies" within the teachers' midst.

As of November 1929, a set of these "enemies" had a discernible name: the SVU (*Spilka vyzvolennia Ukrainy* – Union for Liberation of Ukraine). The SVU was a counter-revolutionary Ukrainian nationalist organization fabricated by the GPU. The GPU arrested a high proportion of leading Ukrainian non-party educators, including primary-school teachers, and declared that a school group and a pedagogical group operated as components of the SVU, in conjunction with a subsidiary youth branch. The prosecutor's charges and the "confessions" of the accused suggested that teachers assumed a leading role in disseminating nationalist ideology. The state argued that SVU members were motivated by a fear of the consequences of Ukrainization, the creation of a nationally conscious generation loyal to the Soviet cause, but also maintained that the SVU members had taken advantage of Ukrainization to co-opt the campaign for themselves. In the aftermath of the announcement of the existence of the SVU, teachers had reason to look on the Ukrainization campaign with some trepidation. The efforts of leading Ukrainizers had been condemned, distorted, and criminalized. The Soviet press did not attack Ukrainization directly, and the KP(b)U issued calls to implement correct, Bolshevik, nationalities policy at the very same time the SVU was announced, but the association of Ukrainization with the SVU spoiled the campaign. Party and governmental authorities could and did use the label SVU to paint teachers and children who were not part of the high-profile trial as nationalists.

On the basis of available evidence, it is difficult to say precisely why the GPU and the party chose to move against these individual educators, but the testimony of select accused is revealing. If the definitive motivation was a belief in the untrustworthiness of non-party intelligentsia and an anticipation of their resistance to collectivization and industrialization, it was an uncertainty about what teachers were doing in the classroom and fears regarding their influence on the young that determined the structure of the repression against the intelligentsia. Interrogation files must be carefully read, but they do suggest that there was high intergenerational cohesion between teachers – that young teachers and students who had received some training in Soviet institutions, or were in public work for the Soviet state, did not break from the guidance of their elders who had much deeper roots in the pre-revolutionary past. The GPU was alarmed by this fact, and reimagined this relationship as a united counter-revolutionary network. It reworked dedication to teaching as evidence of plotting in the classroom, and an informal organization of alumni of Kyiv's most prestigious Ukrainian primary school as a nationalist conspiracy hatched by teachers. In the GPU script that emerges from the testimony, much of which must have been forced, teachers were alarmed by the prospect of "losing" children to Soviet ideology and were using the Ukrainization process to "recapture" them. In fact, the GPU's fear, shared by the party leadership, was the reverse: that children were being lost to the nationalist cause. Children were paradoxically vulnerable victims and villainous foot soldiers in the alleged effort to extend nationalist influence. The accused discussed Ukrainization in a contradictory fashion, revealing their own confusion about what they should decry, what should have been permissible, and what was not.

Reports of the SVU affair and eventual trial were no clearer about what constituted "correct" Bolshevik Ukrainization, but the signal the party and the GPU communicated was that "flawed" Ukrainization had produced the SVU. Reports of GPU surveillance of the intelligentsia in Odesa, where the agency identified an SVU cell, suggest that the GPU made the arrests because it was opposed to Ukrainization and wanted to justify its use of coercion against the Ukrainian intelligentsia. Reports of the Russian intellectual community suggest that they understood the essential lesson of the SVU: that Ukrainization had gone too far and affirmed a need for action. The split between the language communities was likely not so stark, but both groups were united by a belief that the policy of Ukrainization was being tested through an exercise of police power. In Odesa, the GPU targeted post-secondary instructors and students for surveillance and reported evidence of anti-Soviet activity, suggesting a concern that post-secondary INO professors were manufacturing such sentiments among the young. This focus had an inevitable effect on primary-school teachers, who maintained ties with INO instructors, participated with them in the public Ukrainization campaign, and were responsible for training pupils for the INO, and who found themselves under suspicion.

In the aftermath of the SVU affair, teachers struggled to make sense of it all. Especially in rural parts of the Ukrainian republic, the tumult of the First Five-Year Plan was to continue, and the Soviet press condemned teachers for non-participation in the state's economic and political campaigns. To do anything else now invited a charge of kulak sympathy and possibly the type of Ukrainian nationalism alleged to have been crafted by SVU members. The teachers' press suggested models of Soviet virtue: martyr teachers whom kulaks injured or killed because of their leadership of collectivization. The Soviet state and Communist Party needed the participation of teachers as representatives of Soviet power in the countryside if the collectivization campaign was to succeed, but these press reports served as reminders of what should have been the teachers' principal concern and of the risks of flawed action. The task of Ukrainization was a distant affair to a profession in which only a portion had ardently taken up the banner. Given the state's assault on a broad stratum of the peasantry, it must have seemed less than necessary to ensure rural/urban union in the republic.

Shifting Contexts

By 1928, the political environment in the Soviet Union had changed significantly. Having defeated the Left Opposition in 1927, Stalin initiated a "revolution from above," designed to rapidly propel the Soviet economy forward. A war crisis, begun with Britain's decision to break relations with the Soviet Union in May 1927, undoubtedly contributed to Stalin's conviction that the party needed to ensure increased production relative to the capitalist world. He encouraged a climate of hysteria that enabled him to demand unity against his critics and advance his plans for rapid industrialization. Confronted with a grain shortage, Stalin moved in early 1928 against the Right Opposition's gradualist program in agriculture and called for the arbitrary confiscation of grain as well as the arrests of peasants who had earlier refused to sell their yield at the artificially low prices set by the Soviet government.[1] The export of grain was desperately needed in order to finance the ambitious plan for industrialization outlined in the country's new economic scheme, set to begin in October 1928: the First Five-Year Plan.

Grain confiscations continued throughout 1929 and, in November, Stalin announced that the mass collectivization of agriculture was required to guarantee an adequate supply of foodstuffs. Although Stalin portrayed the initial collectivization campaign as "voluntary," the VKP(b) TsK made clear to local authorities that they needed to demonstrate widespread "success" in recruitment and meet targets well above those designated in the Five-Year Plan. Concurrent with the collectivization campaign, the party leadership also demanded an assault on kulaks. Officially, the term designated rich peasants, but, in reality, it applied to the broad stratum of middle-income peasants who opposed collectivization. Together, collectivization and dekulakization – the arrest and seizure of peasant property – led to near-civil war conditions in the countryside. After first announcing the campaign's general success, Stalin blamed local authorities for "excesses." Collectivization continued through the early 1930s, but at a slower pace.

In the cultural field, Soviet authorities capitalized on a general resentment among Komsomol members, young party activists, and working-class recruits towards the NEP-era policy[2] of collaborating with bourgeois specialists and intellectuals. The spring 1928 show trial of fifty-three engineers from the Shakhty mining area in the Donbas, on charges of sabotage and collusion with foreign powers, set the stage for the future prosecution of non-party intelligentsia. It also signalled the mobilization of society for the defence and support of the First Five-Year Plan. As part of this campaign, the party leadership permitted and partly encouraged a "cultural revolution," described by Sheila Fitzpatrick as "a political confrontation of 'proletarian' Communists and the 'bourgeois' intelligentsia, in which the Communists sought to overthrow the cultural authorities inherited by the old regime."[3] The transformation of culture, guided by a "proletarian intelligentsia," would enable the behavioural shift required for public participation in the Five-Year Plan. The course of the "cultural revolution" was sometimes spontaneous, but, generally, the social purging demanded by lower-level activists served the short-term needs of central authorities from 1928 to 1932. The "cultural revolution" gave popular sanction to Stalin's "revolution from above" and created space for the assertion of greater party authority after local activists were brought under control.

In the case of Ukrainian primary education, the First Five-Year Plan was to have a number of effects. It placed new demands on teachers to participate in public campaigns beyond the classroom, chiefly collectivization. While he was in Russia, the long-standing RSFSR commissar of education, Anatolii Lunacharsky, was dismissed in 1929 following charges of "bureaucratism" and bourgeois appeasement; Skrypnyk's assumption of the Ukrainian Narkomos delayed a similar shakeup. However, Skrypnyk conceded the need for a radical shift in classroom methodology and structural reorganization. The end result of this effort was a rejection of progressive pedagogy and the subordination of the Ukrainian education system to all-Union norms. Finally, of pre-eminent concern to this study, the party leadership sanctioned a move against what it perceived to be a growing danger in the schools and education system: Ukrainian nationalism.

Teachers Compromised

The identification and suppression of Ukrainian nationalism among educators provided an added dimension to Stalin's revolution in the republic. Fitzpatrick writes that prior to the cultural revolution, central authorities generally treated Soviet teachers lightly because they presented "no potential political threat."[4] Local authorities, however, ignored this restraint. In the case of Ukraine, Stalin and some republican leaders already shared a suspicion of what they believed to be the very real political hazard of Ukrainian nationalism. The cultural revolution provided the vehicle to extinguish it. Furthermore, what was imagined to be at stake was not just "class" leadership, but also the potential corruption of the next generation. Ukrainization would persist, but it would be robbed of the force needed for its realization.

While the KP(b)U Central Committee's reports made generally vague claims about the spread of nationalism, local authorities cited specific cases. A February 1927 meeting of party and Komsomol school staff in the Rakovsky district of Kyiv found that Russians and Ukrainian nationalists had begun to "show their real face."[5] A report by one participant, Klekh, claimed that Russian chauvinist sentiment predominated in at least three of the city's schools. In one of these schools, Labour School No. 67, a former member of the centre-right Kadet party[6] served as director and purportedly fostered an environment marked by nationalist anecdotes, poetry, and drama. Of critical importance to Ukrainization, Klekh singled out the danger represented by Durdukivsky's Labour School No. 1. He maintained that nearly all the teachers at the school were former members of the Ukrainian Social Democratic Workers' Party and the direction of the school remained oriented towards the former national platform of this party. Furthermore, the school administration selected its own employees: "The school is a closed circle. Strangers are not permitted to become acquainted with the circle and its work."⁷ Klekh suggested that local Narkomos authorities were partly at fault for allowing this situation to persist by approving (if not initiating) appointments to the school. He reported that another school, Labour School No. 64, staffed Ukrainian "chauvinist" teachers: the faculty was only 50 per cent "Soviet" and often did not support the activities of the school's reportedly competent head.

The Kyiv meeting blamed the growth of nationalism on the absence of proper local party leadership. A second speaker, Yanyshevska, insisted that Narkomos knew little about actual events in the schools and had not done much to orient teachers towards a labour-based curriculum, and that non-party inspectors and administrators had allowed "deviations" in the schools and were exercising a negative influence over Komsomol members. She cautioned that the danger of this neglect was real, an anti-Soviet mood was spreading, and "the idea is being introduced about the organization of a faction of non-party teachers in order to achieve victory over the Communists." Another city-wide gathering of Communist pedagogues in 1927 confirmed that teachers had joined Russian monarchists and Ukrainian "yellow-azures" (i.e., supporters of the UNR).⁸ The party had been too weak to effect a change in their attitudes to date: "The conditions of work here, as in the periphery, are complicated enough because we cannot politically influence the whole mass of workers with our forces, capabilities, and apparat." Party leadership and growth were needed to combat this perceived nationalism.

If the party's work among educators to date had been insufficient, Robos had also failed. According to Tkach, a contributor to *Narodnii uchytel*, the union had not adequately explained the "ideological essence and social roots of this nationalist deviation."⁹ As a result, even if the majority of educators supported the party, some had fallen victim to the "spontaneous pressure of bourgeois nationalism and remnants of the past." Tkach insisted that Robos needed to explain to teachers the true direction of Soviet nationalities policy, but also the harm committed by Shumsky, Khvylovy, and the economist Mykhailo Volobuiev.¹⁰ He did not criticize Ukrainization directly. On the contrary, he insisted that it enabled recruitment of the peasantry to the socialist cause and permitted a strengthening of its relationship with the proletariat. But Robos's achievements in Ukrainization had largely been formal in character.

A secret GPU report from January 1927 suggested even more ominously that teachers remained hostile towards Soviet power. If they believed in the potential of Ukrainization, they thought the Soviet government's support of the policy was lacklustre. Khrystyna Alchevska,¹¹ a well-known poet and educator, who was monitored by the GPU, allegedly lamented that "the Ukrainian portion of the TsK KP(b)U is destroyed. Stalin is against the entry of Ukrainians into the Soviet apparat of the UkrSSR. What kind of Ukrainization is this?" Teachers as a whole reportedly resented the multiple responsibilities the state required them to fulfill for little pay, including Ukrainization. City teachers were so incensed by their difficult financial situation that they were on the verge of striking. The GPU report specifically claimed that rural teachers felt aggrieved that the party continued to view them as "a narrow-minded and bourgeois element," compelled to participate in the state's public campaigns with little trust or support. They did not have the means to Ukrainize: no literature or opportunity to devote to their own language improvement. In particular, they complained about the obligation to give sparsely attended lectures in village reading rooms: "brainwashing [Russian: *promyvanie mozgov*] peasants takes a lot of time and energy, when one is engaged in education and language [in the school]."[12]

Taken as a whole, these sentiments, as reported by the GPU, did not reveal teachers' rejection of Ukrainization, but rather a belief that it could not be accomplished under the current Soviet leadership in Ukraine (as Shumsky had argued) or, at the very least, under existing work conditions. Missing is an acknowledgment that the whole purpose of Ukrainization was to make public work, like instruction in village reading rooms, more effective. Of course, this was a linkage that the GPU was not going to make. But paradoxically, like Tkach, the document also suggests that the meaning of Ukrainization had not been adequately conveyed.

Teachers needed to actively pursue Ukrainization, but also guard against perversions of the campaign. According to speakers at a June 1928 Robos conference, the teachers' chief failing was passivity. This passivity had led to lax Ukrainization, but it had also permitted enemies of Soviet power to co-opt the campaign for their own use. An educator could not claim to be a Soviet educator, one Robos member insisted, if he remained a "mute witness" to the struggle against nationalism and risked falling under its influence.[13] Teachers needed to take an "enormous role" in explaining the proper meaning of Soviet nationalities policy to the proletariat and peasantry. Failure to do so would mean forfeiture of the policy's very goal, the maintenance of a union between the labouring classes: "Language is the form through which millions of Ukrainian peasants, millions of nationalities oppressed by tsarism, should be tied to the socialist construction of international proletarian culture."[14] Teachers had to commit themselves to the active study of language and convince others of the extreme importance of securing cultural leadership.

Conference speakers argued that the union had failed to safeguard against the distortion of this mandate. Although the majority of teachers had turned away from the Ukrainian counter-revolutionary parties that bid for their allegiance during the civil war, negative influences persisted. During the course of Ukrainization, even "responsible parties fell into the labyrinth of great-state or Ukrainian chauvinism."[15] Some pushed the slogan "Ukraine for Ukrainians," claiming the republic served as a colony of Russia. Teachers remained at risk of joining such a movement because the union's leadership had not been clear. It had promoted knowledge of the Ukrainian language, but had not properly explained its purpose. In the struggle with "*Khvylovysm, Shumskysm,* and *Volobuievshchyna,*" Robos "did not show clear direction and did not come together with the party and Soviet power."[16] How could teachers enlighten the peasantry and proletariat if they did not understand nationalities policy themselves? Conference reports suggest that because teachers had participated in Ukrainization without a proper understanding, they were uniquely susceptible to nationalist influence. A little knowledge was a dangerous thing.

As statements by the Robos leadership made clear, the Ukrainization campaign was intimately tied to broader political campaigns that demanded teacher involvement. Just as teachers could not remain neutral in the Ukrainization campaign, they could not passively regard the growth of enemies of Soviet power. For one thing, according to the party, kulaks and petit bourgeois traders (NEPmen) were, respectively, the carriers of Ukrainian and Russian nationalism. Yet, "there are those teachers that may be nice to workers and to NEPmen, to landless peasants and to kulaks. They want to have authority among one and the other – to serve the Communist guide and please the bourgeois devil."[17] Such appeasement only increased the authority of counter-revolutionary circles and contributed to nationalist attitudes.

Delegates to the Robos conference expressed dismay that earlier slogans by the union regarding "voluntary" public work had allowed some teachers to excuse themselves from public campaigns altogether. Most village teachers were consummate activists, one representative claimed, performing multiple tasks: "The village teacher is, as they say, 'a shoemaker, reaper, and plays the pipe.'"[18] However, there were those who had done so little that other segments of the population took charge of civic and adult education, freeing teachers to walk a "bachelor's walk." Others sunk to the lowest levels of peasant culture, condemning religion publicly but then observing religious customs in their own home. The union could not permit teachers to ignore their responsibilities beyond the school or give them duplicitous attention; they needed to take the lead as "informed" fighters of the revolution.

Teachers who did not assume a role in broader public campaigns and educate the population in their meaning risked political isolation and the taint of nationalism. Skarbek, a Polish teacher, argued that Ukrainian chauvinism was rising among the peasantry in her district in response to the party's grain-requisition campaign: "The Ukrainians say, in regard to the implementation of this campaign, that the grain is being collected by *katsapy* [a derogatory term for Russians]."[19] She claimed that other teachers had not done enough to combat this tendency and protect the interests of non-Ukrainians in the region, including the Polish population. Teacher involvement may not have made any difference in staving off peasant anger over the confiscation of their grain. Yet, the party likely took any teacher absence from the campaign and failure to combat Ukrainian nationalism as signs of anti-Soviet behaviour and, in this context, chauvinist sympathies.

Some teachers tried to demonstrate their commitment to the Soviet cause by their public activism, but they had little specific guidance on appropriate conduct. Starchevska, a representative at the Robos meeting, maintained that the union had failed to offer concrete support for teachers trying to increase their involvement.[20] If they sought to consult the main academic journals for direction, they risked further exposure to nationalist deviation. An August 1926 meeting of the Politburo's Ukrainization commission concluded that the leading Soviet Ukrainian literary journal, *Chervonyi shliakh* (Red path), had "fallen under the surrounding influence of non-class elements." Another important political and cultural journal, *Zhyttia i revoliutsiia* (Life and revolution), had been established in Kyiv to rally the intelligentsia, but was now reportedly being used by "hostile forces." The principal kraieznavstvo organ, *Ukraina* (Ukraine), had dabbled too much in the trivialities of the past and needed to address more contemporary issues proposed by Marxist academics.[21] The commission urged greater Ukrainization, particularly in the Donbas. Yet, in spite of this and Robos's invocations, too much activism on the part of the teachers and other intellectuals was a dangerous thing, particularly in matters concerning Ukrainization. Teachers were doubly damned. Passivity signified political indolence; energy marked assertiveness bordering on counter-revolutionary plotting.

Two brief reports from regional party organizations regarding Komsomol activity in 1929 demonstrate the hazards of lax public activism. In the Luhansk region, the party committee claimed that Komsomol participation in production questions was weak, particularly among young workers in *artels* (communal teams of labourers). In the villages, some Komsomol members resisted collectivization and the grain-requisition campaign; most did nothing. They also failed to appreciate the danger of rightist deviations within the party that favoured some compromise with rural interests and did not push for a renewed campaign of political education: "Parts of the backward worker youth and Komsomol members exhibited destructive attitudes, narrow-mindedness, and were delinquent in their studies."[22] On top of all this, the regional party section's report stressed that Komsomol sections almost entirely avoided work in the "building of Ukrainian national culture" and among ethnic minorities. In short, Luhansk Komsomol organizations were too passive on all fronts. There was little chance of progress on divisive national questions when the Komsomol shrank from engagement on hard-line political issues. Its rural cells were setting a poor example for young teachers and students alike.

In Lubny, the regional party committee suggested that the Komsomol's inattention had led to the growth of kulak membership in the organization. It blamed the organization's passivity and confusion on "defilement" by these foreign elements.[23] Komsomol members had lost "class awareness" and failed to counter the threat embodied by capitalist enemies and deviations in the party. They had neglected recruitment of workers and agricultural labourers, and some had also resisted the party's political and economic campaign; that is, collectivization. The party committee found that the only type of activism prevalent in the Komsomol was "unhealthy." It recommended an immediate purge of the regional organization.

Regional control commissions in 1929 reported that this lack of party and Komsomol discipline endangered pedagogical oversight. In the Kyiv region, party cells at the Prypiat construction site had permitted the appointment of the wife of a priest to a Young Pioneer group (*maidanchyk*). She taught the children to sing "God Save the Tsar."[24] They also had turned a blind eye to bribes offered to the site's administrators by kulaks and children of White Guards seeking employment. In the Dnipropetrovsk region, the secretary of the party section in the village of Khrystoforivka supported the claims of a teacher that agriculture was in decline because of party policy. Under the influence of the teacher and party official, the head of the village council, who was also a party member, failed to mention the size of the community's granaries in his description of taxable property, in an attempt to avoid "a decline of agriculture."[25] The party believed rural authorities were all too susceptible to counter-revolutionary activity it associated with "kulak" teachers.

Occasionally, Soviet officials lent an unambiguous label to the counter-revolutionary, rural activism they described in their accounts: Ukrainian nationalism. A 1928 report from the Obukhiv district education inspector in the Kyiv region found that Cherkasky, a teacher in the village of Khodosivka, was organizing peasants to oppose Soviet power. As early as 1921, he had allegedly distributed Petliurist posters at a secret meeting of prosperous peasants and former members of the defunct Ukrainian cultural association Prosvita. Although Cherkasky presented himself as "a Soviet worker to the eye," he stood with prosperous peasants at meetings, first suggesting that funds raised by taxation would never be spent in the village and then supporting peasant opposition to the head of the school, who was trying to introduce an early school year. According to the account, he had further expressed dissatisfaction with Soviet nationalities policy, claiming that "we do not have our people, they gave us a Lithuanian as head of the RVK [district executive committee], some Pole as an inspector, and so on."[26] His nationalist leanings purportedly fuelled his protection of kulaks. Cherkasky refused to work with the head of the reading house because "he is very Red" and tried to monopolize space in the building for his conspiratorial kulak group. The report claimed that his aim was nothing less than the destruction of peasant trust in Soviet power.

The district inspector's exposure of Cherkasky's intentions was not unusual. Local party officials repeatedly charged educators and students with duplicity in the "cause of the people." In January 1928, the Mykolaiv Regional Party Committee found a group of students had prepared counter-revolutionary propaganda to contest local elections. According to the committee's report, the students sent the most politically active peasants leaflets asking them "to help the people" and resist the proposals of Communists and poor peasants (*bidnota*). At night, they purportedly pasted posters calling on peasants to "Kick out party members from the village soviets."[27] What was alarming to the Mykolaiv party leadership was not just the apparent boldness of this group, but the fact that it counted nine former Komsomol members among its membership. Authorities had deprived the students' parents of their right to vote, presumably due to their identification as kulaks. Another report from April 1929 maintained that teachers and kulaks had apparently organized students for an anti-Soviet demonstration in the Shevchenko (Cherkasy) region, near Kharkiv. An unspecified number of teachers were arrested as a result of the demonstration.[28] Thus, kulak influence had corrupted former Komsomol members and teachers alike, who used their authority to manipulate youth and challenge Soviet power with populist appeals.

The category of kulak was, in fact, a political one, although the party claimed to construct it according to economic criteria. The number of truly "prosperous" peasants was few, with a single head of livestock differentiating them and so-called "middle" peasants. The party's grain-requisition campaign and drive towards collectivization led to widespread social dislocation and popular unrest. A GPU report claimed that some 12,000 peasants had led thirty-seven mass protests across the republic in January 1930 alone.[29] The KP(b)U often identified those who opposed its campaigns as "kulaks," regardless of their actual wealth. Dissatisfaction with these campaigns may have provoked the very sort of demonstrations against Soviet power described by the regional party committees. The Ukrainian peasantry had reason to believe that the party was robbing them of their very means of survival. It is difficult to confirm the accuracy of the specific charges made in the reports, but the likelihood that the peasantry turned to teachers, as representatives of local authority, to protest the grain-requisition campaign seems real.

Regardless, teachers' close association with the peasantry was enough to make the party wary of their influence in besieged rural communities. As has been argued above, teachers earned the party's suspicion if they failed to push the party's programs enough, but also if they appeared overeager, especially regarding Ukrainization. Either they came from kulak, religious, or bourgeois backgrounds themselves, or the party believed they were far too vulnerable to the sway of such hostile forces. The stage was then set for a direct campaign against the Ukrainian intelligentsia, including prominent educators and teachers. They had been the targets of protracted slander. Beginning in May 1929, the GPU rounded up a total of forty-five suspects for alleged membership in a nationalist, counter-revolutionary organization, the SVU.

The Educators' Union as Defendant and Prosecutor

By 1929, the teachers' union began to report a greater incidence of anti-Semitism and Ukrainian nationalism among teachers, or tolerance of "nationalist," counter-revolutionary behaviours. The Robos Investigative Bureau sent several clippings from the newspapers about such anti-Soviet behaviour to the unions presidium. The newspaper *Vinnytsia* reported that in the town of Khmilnyk, local authorities observed the Ukrainian and Yiddish seven-year schools in order to assess how teachers were carrying out lessons in internationalism, and found some disturbing results. Children from the Ukrainian school reportedly taunted and beat Jewish children: "Even when delegates from the Jewish [Yiddish] school were invited to an evening ceremony dedicated to the memory of [Mykhailo] Kotsiubynsky, it ended with them being furtively beaten and thrown down the stairs." More distressing, according to the author of the report, teachers in the Ukrainian school did not believe real anti-Semitism existed in the school, labelling such violence "hooligan pranks."[30] The article blamed such anti-Semitism on the spread of "kulak attitudes" among the students, noting the school's location on the "border between the city and the village" and mixed social composition. It called for the dismissal of Ukrainian teachers who did not identify and fight against anti-Semitism. It also faulted teachers in the Yiddish school for evading this issue, failing to criticize the teachers of the Ukrainian school, and failing to recognize the incident's class origins. The Khmilnyk event, the article concluded, was "evidence of apolitical attitudes, cowardice, lack of self-criticism, avoidance of mutual responsibility."

At the post-secondary level, an article in the republican newspaper *Visti VUTsVK* condemned the existence of anti-Semites among professors at the Kyiv Agricultural Institute, as well as those who refused to teach in Ukrainian. Here, then, faculty was guilty of antagonisms towards both Jewish and Ukrainian national culture. The article also criticized individual faculty members at the institute for opposition to collectivization and other "Right deviationist" attitudes. The article's implicit suggestion was that such chauvinism (anti-Jewish and anti-Ukrainian) was fundamentally tied to a bourgeois antagonism towards Soviet policy. It placed primary blame on the institute's instructors rather than on students who were waging "a determined class struggle for the Leninist line." Still, the worry was that somehow the faculty was perverting young students, some of whom likely came from the village or were destined for careers in small towns like Khmilnyk.

Furthermore, local Soviet authorities recruited educators at all levels – faculty at higher-education institutes such as Kyiv Agricultural Institute, recent graduates, and primary- and secondary-school teachers – for employment as instructors in Ukrainian-studies courses for state employees. A November 1929 article in *Komunist* filed by the Robos presidium noted that a recent perevirka of instructors of the Ukrainian language revealed "foreign elements" among the ranks. One son of a kulak formed superfluous study groups for profit. The students reported that the instructor, Chakalin, was a "self-seeker" (*shkurnyk*) who acquired significant profit from Ukrainization. Another instructor, Silchenko, was condemned as a hypocrite because, as a tsarist-era school inspector, he had ordered all schools to take down portraits of Ukrainian writers. As a result of such examples, a meeting of city instructors resolved to remove seventeen persons as "foreign and unfit" elements, and a contingent argued for their removal from Robos as a whole. They were to be replaced with "young [instructors] who would study in a special course for improvement."[31] The newspaper article explicitly criticized state authorities for allowing such persons to infiltrate the ranks of Ukrainian-language instructors and suggested that Ukrainization itself could easily be corrupted, thus opening up the policy to broader questioning. Action by Robos members, such as the meeting of city instructors, provided a necessary correction, but the findings of the perevirka raised concern about the conduct and authority of the union as a whole. How was it that Robos ever accepted these educators as members? Should Robos be trusted to lead Ukrainization or, more broadly, educate the public in explicit political campaigns (e.g., collectivization, industrialization, continuance of class struggle)? Youth would revive the union and, it was hoped, the prospects for Ukrainization.

The previous generation of educators and cultural workers simply could not be trusted. A December 1929 article in *Narodnii uchytel*, clipped by the Robos press review section, described the trial of two librarians who worked for the Katerynoslav railway. For ten years, the article claimed, the two librarians had distributed counter-revolutionary literature, including Ukrainian nationalist literature (Petliurist songs and a volume allegedly entitled *Soiuz vyzvolennia Ukrainy*, on the recently "exposed" SVU), as well as books on the anti-Semitic Black Hundreds and tsarist-era histories. They explicitly hid Soviet literature: "When workers saw that there was no literature of Lenin or Marx, they gave a book such as the 'Lives of Russian Emperors' and said it was better."[32] The article claimed that the "influence of the [class] enemy" was so great that the cultural section of the railway administration refused to listen to worker complaints, conceding later that only minor problems existed in the library. It condemned one librarian, Staroverov, as a former member of Denikin's army, who sought to foster love towards "great Russia" and the idea of a "tsar-grandfather." The article thus located a centre of counter-revolutionary activity in the library, paradoxically equally disseminating Ukrainian nationalist literature and tsarist literature and undermining legitimate Soviet civic education and cultural advancement among the working class. Ukrainization is not mentioned explicitly (the article labelled the only Ukrainian-language literature disseminated by librarians as "nationalist"), but the railways were the sites of particularly energetic Ukrainization campaigns led by Narkomos. It was in this context that the article must be understood. Ukrainian literature could be dangerous, as dangerous as the most reactionary tsarist-era publications, and the leadership of institutions such as libraries in which Narkomos intended to oversee Ukrainization had to be questioned. By tarring Ukrainian literature with the slander of nationalism, conflating it with counter-revolutionary reaction, the SVU trial and its reporting also undermined the public's faith in Ukrainization and pre-revolutionary cultural elites.

If youth were to direct national culture in the future and replace pre-revolutionary elites, *Narodnii uchytel* claimed, existing children's and youth literature was not up to the task of training the next generation. An October 1929 article in the newspaper claimed that the republic's State Publishing House was not organizing public thought properly: "One gets the impression that plans for production of literature have not been made in the context of the First Five-Year Plan and reconstruction."[33] Particularly missing were accounts of large industrial projects and collectivization ("new life in the village"). Furthermore, the article argued, "biographies of leaders, active participants of the revolutionary movement, especially Ukrainians, that could cultivate in children a revolutionary spirit nearly do not exist." It blamed the lack of authors for children's literature; those who did exist were not party members and did not work on pressing contemporary issues. Ideological errors persisted in existing state-published literature, and a private press, Chas, published old adventure books for children that were "ideologically foreign," such as the Sherlock Holmes mysteries. Overall, the article concluded, due to weak administration, the state press was not living up to its responsibility to provide children with literature that would correctly orient them to the main tasks of the day.

These newspaper clippings all underscored elements of a cultural revolution that had accelerated by the late 1920s. Primary-school teachers as well as post-secondary faculty, librarians, and children's authors faced close scrutiny regarding their activity. They were required to tie their work and cultural production to the economic and political objectives of Stalin's Great Turn: industrialization and collectivization. Failure to do this, or manifestations of other non-normative behaviour, meant that educators and cultural workers had fallen victim to the influence of bourgeois or kulak ideology, or were, in fact, revealing their own class nature. The reports of anti-Semitism among Khmilnyk schoolchildren, according to this logic, meant a violation of Soviet nationalities policy certainly, but also a deepening of class struggle in small-town Ukraine. The newspaper *Vinnytsia* blamed anti-Semitism among children on kulak parents and teachers who had permitted its spread. Anti-Semitism here was a marker of a larger counter-revolutionary antagonism towards the Soviet state. Thus, in the Robos-led purges that occurred simultaneously with the publication of all these articles, teachers were accused of anti-Semitism alongside a host of other counter-revolutionary labels.

The Robos leadership reported that the KP(b)U TsK had charged Robos regional organs in 1929 with the task "of self-purging by us of all hostile elements who had appeared in the course of the strengthening of political differentiation, who affected the educational environment, as a reflection of the sharpening of the class struggle due to the campaign on the remnants of capitalist elements." However, the Robos All-Ukrainian Committee (VUK) plenum reported that the work on the self-purge was inadequate, not enough preparation had been undertaken, and more work needed to be done at the local level, especially in the city. Village primary schools had been affected the most. Local cells did not understand the political importance of the purge and had not received adequate instruction. The Robos leadership stressed the purges were especially necessary for elements "who sow national hostility in the factory, in the union, and in public work and who support the religious movement."[34] There were instances where those people who had been purged had remained in their positions. This had to be corrected. The plenum also conceded that there were instances of members being purged incorrectly for personal reasons, and insisted that the regional Robos sections should be the lead sections to initiate any purge.

Thus, the Robos VUK occasionally intervened to make sure that local authorities had "correctly" purged teachers. In January 1930, it asked for a report from the Mohyliv-Podilskyi section regarding the case of a teacher, Mariia Zaikova. Zaikova wrote in a petition to the committee that she and her husband, Anton, had been unjustly accused of "passivity towards instances of anti-Semitism among the pupils [of their school] and even of an orientation of national enmity in the surroundings." The VUK ordered the regional section to investigate the matter, since it was not clear that the union had taken any role in the matter to date; to defend the teachers if the charges had no grounds; and, "if it is convinced that the teachers are guilty of strengthening nationalist hostility, to step forward as a public [trade] union accuser."[35]

A December 1929 local Robos report claimed that the district commission had charged Mariia and Anton (the head of the school) with violations of the criminal code. The two teachers had permitted a split among Ukrainian students, a portion of whom had been infected with hatred towards Jewish pupils. These students reportedly threatened to beat Jewish students and demanded that Jewish students who exited the school building during break kiss their hands. Furthermore, these Ukrainian students allegedly demanded that the Jewish students teach Ukrainian students Yiddish "dirty words" and forced one Jewish student to smell ammonium chloride spirits until he blacked out. There were shouts during break by the Ukrainian students that they were going to tear apart all Jews. It was reported that the Zaikovs used the word *zhyd* (yid) and quieted children by saying, "be quiet, do not act like a Jewish fair." Mariia allegedly replied to complaints by Jewish children by saying, "Hush! I will not be your nanny."[36] On the basis of this evidence, it was decided to eject Anton out of the union for failing to "liquidate" known anti-Semitism in the schools, and local prosecutors charged him and Mariia with violations of the criminal code for disregarding "national hostility."[37] Interestingly, the regional Robos administration decided to send a representative for defence of the Zaikovs' interests at a review of their case in March 1930 because it judged that charges against them had not been satisfactorily proved when the case was first opened. However, the regional court (Okrsud) ruled against the teachers and required that a censure of the teachers be announced at a school meeting. The regional Robos section now concurred with this judgment because, according to multiple witnesses, Mariia had encouraged anti-Semitic behaviour among the children.

Another teacher, M. Femych-Holovatsky from the village of Vyla-Iaruzki in the Mohyliv-Podilskyi region, also complained to Robos that he had been unjustly dismissed from his teaching position and deprived of his voting rights in May 1930.[38] Officially, the regional executive committee secretary informed him that he was punished because it was believed he had served in the White Army. Femych-Holovatsky claimed that he had never served in the White Army and that, in 1918, he had returned to the village after having studied in an institute (he does not specify which) and serving in the tsarist army during the First World War. He had worked for Soviet power during the revolution to confiscate property from kulaks and redistribute it to the landless. He had also opened a second level in the school and reportedly joined the village soviet, the election commission, the *revkom* (revolutionary committee, a temporary local organ of administration established by the Bolsheviks), and the village cooperative. He instructed villagers on habits of good hygiene and propagandized against religion. In short, he claimed, "no political campaign occurred in the village without my active participation in it," and he had been a model activist and teacher.

Femych-Holovatsky's real problem, he asserted, stemmed from the fact that he had antagonized rich peasants in the village by his active campaigning for Soviet power. He charged that although he had worked in agreement with village soviet and party cell, rich peasants had "distorted the content of my speeches to discredit me in front of local organs and in this way tear me away from the ranks of village activists." For example, in 1928, he worked on the village electoral commission and, on his initiative, it had deprived a former Petliurist volunteer of his rights. This person claimed to the village soviet and Committee of Poor Peasants (*Komitet nezamozhnykh selian* – KNS) that Femych-Holovatsky, as an instructor of the Ukrainian language in a school where this person was studying, had a chauvinistic influence on him and had incited him towards participation in the Petliurist bands. Later, this person submitted forms to the village soviet with forged stamps and was subsequently exiled outside Ukraine; his father, a seller at the cooperative, was dismissed from his position for causing discord.

Femych-Holovatsky claimed that in this way, he had caused trouble for one family twice over and it then sought its revenge against him. Local authorities investigated the complaint of "the Petliurist" that Femych-Holovatsky was a chauvinist instructor and possible volunteer for the Whites (a seeming contradiction in roles), but allegedly made no effort to contact him. Femych-Holovatsky argued that his enemies were rejoicing at his downfall, further tarring his character by arguing to Soviet agents that he had convinced many to abandon the church. Behind their backs, kulaks marshalled peasant anger about collectivization against him as a Soviet activist, and threatened "to shut his mouth."[39] The teacher concluded his petition by lamenting the fact that after over a decade of public work, he was deprived of his right to vote while others he viewed as opposed to Soviet power still enjoyed these rights.

Another teacher, Mykhailo Kalinichenko, appealed to the VUK in December 1930 from jail for a similar intervention. While in police custody, he was charged with participation in Petliurist teachers' conferences, the organization of bands, support for bandits, and recent counter-revolutionary agitation to turn Kryvyi Rih against Soviet power. After further interrogation by the GPU, he was accused of being a member of the SVU. Kalinichenko wrote in his appeal that he considered his arrest to be a horrible misunderstanding. Is it possible, he asked, that he was being punished for being on the side of the Ukrainian national movement in 1917–18, and then working devotedly for Soviet power for ten years? He graduated from the Kherson teachers' seminary in 1916. Beginning in 1917, he attended teachers' conferences, but did not consider them to be Petliurist. At the Kherson *povit* (county) teachers' congress in the spring of 1919, he purportedly defended the Bolshevik line and immediately afterwards took part in a conference on education outside the school, where he was elected a delegate to the All-Ukrainian and All-Russian conferences. Until January 1924, he lived in his native village near Kherson. He then worked briefly in the Kryvyi Rih Regional Branch of Robos and subsequently served as a teacher and assistant head for a seven-year school tied to the Artem Iron Ore Mine in Kryvyi Rih from 1924 to 1930. From August 1930, he was employed as a teacher of the

Ukrainian language at the district school in Zhovtneve, to the east of the city of Kryvyi Rih.

He claimed in his petition that he was never involved in any armed band, but conceded that Soviet authorities had suspected him of participation, and he was arrested in 1921 only to be released after no one came forward to offer evidence against him. He believed he was arrested because in 1917–18, while Ukraine was under German occupation, he fell under the influence of Ukrainian nationalism. Clearly, he felt that his orientation towards the Ukrainian national movement was justified under the conditions of foreign oppression, but undoubtedly this history would have raised the suspicion of Soviet authorities by the late 1920s. Kalinichenko attempted to cover up his previous embrace of nationalism by emphasizing his active participation in public work from the establishment of Soviet power. From 1920 to 1924, he claimed, he served in varous capacities in local units of Robos and Narkomos in Kherson province, worked on the all-Russian census, and periodically read lectures in *selbudy* (village cultural centres), before moving to the city of Kryvyi Rih. He claimed to have always done public work in a voluntary and comradely fashion. Until his arrest in October 1930, he was an officer or member of numerous public organizations, including secretary of the Kultzmychka workers' society and a member of the cultural commission, the Miners' Committee, which assisted brigades of the Unified Union of Miners in the organization of collective farms. From 1920 to 1928, he reportedly participated in all Robos congresses at all local levels, and for more than two years, he was a member of Robos's Kryvyi Rih Regional Administrative Board. After all this, Kalinichenko lamented, he was sitting with kulaks in jail.[40]

Kalinichenko should have been the type of teacher that the Soviet government sought, a publicly active teacher who could demonstrate engagement in Soviet public campaigns outside the schoolhouse: anti-religion education, cultural training for workers, collectivization, and professional engagement. Furthermore, he was a Ukrainizer in a working-class Soviet district. There is no documentary record further detailing the Soviet indictment against him, but there seems little reason to doubt that his civil war-era participation in the Ukrainian national movement later marked him as an unreliable public servant in the heated environment of class warfare of the cultural revolution.

For Kalinichenko, an appeal to his professional organization, Robos, offered at least the possibility of remediation. Robos occasionally responded to petitions from teachers who believed they were wrongly charged, although there is no evidence of such a response in Kalinichenko's case. An April 1930 appeal from the Robos VUK to the RSI reported that Konotop regional officials had purged a teacher named Petrusha from the first category of educational workers because, they claimed, he was a "person who had a foreign psychology and could not supply an internationalist education."[41] The VUK argued that no substantive material existed to support such an accusation, apparently made on the basis of an unspecified incident with a single student in the school's fourth grade. On the contrary, there was ample evidence of Petrusha's dedicated public work, and that the village council and school factory had testified approvingly regarding his positive character. Furthermore, the union argued that the regional education section and inspectorate charged Petrusha with use of physical discipline against the children without grounds. It asked the RSI to re-examine the case, demanded that the regional education section submit evidence of any wrongdoing by Petrusha, and, in the absence of any evidence, hold the person who wrote the charges accountable. In the interim, the union asked that Petrusha to be allowed to return to teaching, but not as head of the school.

What was different about Petrusha's case from that of Kalininchenko was that local authorities had simply dismissed Petrusha from his job. The police had not charged him with any sort of political crime. In fact, the plea contains no mention of Petrusha's class background, only the ambiguous mention of his "foreign psychology." It is noteworthy, however, that the union still took up Petrusha's case, given the broader political climate that accompanied his purge. The members of the VUK must have felt reasonably confident that there were grounds for a dismissal of the charges against him. Petrusha's fate and that of the members of the Konotop education section are unknown. Still, the fact that teachers like Kalininchenko (and most likely Petrusha) appealed to Robos for intervention in their cases is evidence that teachers believed that the union could do something to improve their lot.

Occasionally, further investigation demanded by the union did find mistakes and gain remedy for teachers. The Kyiv regional Robos section sent a June 1930 report to the VUK in which it concluded a local purge commission had made an error in the fate of at least one teacher. The commission had purged teachers from the first category of educational workers because they held anti-Soviet attitudes and maintained ties with kulaks. After receiving an inquiry from the VUK, the Kyiv Robos section and the RSI administration sent their own investigatory commissions to Voronkivka, the town where the teachers had been employed. Ultimately, as a result of these inspections, the RSI decided to deprive three of the four teachers of the right to teach, but to restore this right to one, Karpenko. In an apparent suggestion that the initial purge commission had been unduly influenced by slander, the VUK ordered an investigation into whether "there is not a persecution of a teacher activist by kulaks." The local Robos commission reported that there had been no such persecution in the case of Karpenko.[42]

The Fourth Congress of the Robos Union was held in July 1930. Although the report of the the Robos VUK to the congress was generally positive regarding the public participation of teachers in the collectivization and grain-requisition campaigns, the report conceded that the work of some teachers took on a "formal character." It argued that teachers had not maintained a relationship with the village community where they were assigned, and some local organizations, in fact, merged schools with collective farms, partly due to ignorance regarding how to connect the work of the school to the collectivization of agriculture and partly, the report alleged, due to the influence of leftist sentiments. Although, the report concluded, "the basic mass of educators actively and faithfully is working on public work," other teachers had remained neutral and "there are hostile elements in the ranks of the teachers as the SVU trial indicated."[43] Robos called for greater class vigilance and the deployment of the teachers of appropriate class background in order to protect against the influence of "bourgeois nationalism," attributed to the fabricated SVU, to be discussed in detail below.

A signal and a consequence of the shift towards teachers' active engagement in the political tasks of the Five-Year Plan was the January 1930 changing of the name of Robos's newspaper from *Narodnii uchytel* (People's teacher) to *Za kulturnu revoliutsiiu* (For cultural revolution). The VUK report at the Robos plenum claimed that while *Narodnii uchytel* had been concerned with a narrow collection of interests of the public teacher, *Za kulturnu revoliutsiiu* was "mobilizing rank and file educators for the struggle for the general line of the party in all fields of socialist construction and the cultural revolution," including "the struggle for a Leninist nationalities policy, fighting on two fronts against great-state chauvinism and Ukrainian nationalism."[44] The newspaper was to aid in the "reconstruction" of the Robos's work towards this end by exhorting teachers to fight against class enemies and opportunists within their ranks and for greater quality in their own work.

While the VUK claimed that the political orientation of teachers had improved markedly, significant problems remained among them. Over the past five years, the proportion of teachers trained in the post-revolutionary period had risen to 70 per cent, party membership to 4 per cent, and Komsomol membership to 9 per cent. Although teachers were participating in the tasks of socialist construction in ever-greater numbers, "foreign [class] elements occupied a hostile position, committing hostile actions or hiding their [true] face behind political neutrality."[45] The VUK claimed that in the last three years, class enemies had increased their efforts to discredit, recruit, and terrorize teachers, and cited specific examples of murdered or assaulted teachers.

While teachers were said to have responded to this terror by increasing their participation in public campaigns, the VUK cited several examples of teachers whom it identified as "enemies within the teachers' ranks." For example, at a school in the Chernihiv district, the VUK reported the teacher Khmyrko as an anti-Semite who systematically tormented a Jewish teacher. Two other teachers, who had allegedly helped Ukrainian nationalists or Petliurists, now used their position as members of the editorial commission of the school wall newspaper to promote anti-Soviet poetry on the industrialization campaign. In Odesa, teachers reportedly engaged in "reactionary" talk against Soviet nationalities policy and spread rumours about the state's financial difficulties. In this discussion of "enemies," the report included special mention of the SVU affair: "A vivid indication of the focused harmful work was the Shevchenko school in the city of Kyiv headed by the most active counter-revolutionary from the SVU, Durdukivsky. Approximately ten instructors from this school who now sit on the accused bench (almost all with priestly [family] backgrounds) had for a long time inculcated children in a nationalist perspective and enmity towards Soviet power."[46] The Robos conference conflated the SVU defendants with teachers who stood accused of anti-Semitism and criticism of the state's management of the economy and nationalities policy. As the trial would make clear, prosecutors would charge the SVU defendants with such sentiments as well. Furthermore, any teacher indicted for these more "minor" crimes risked an association with the accusation of high treason engineered for the members of the fabricated SVU.

Specifically in the countryside, nationalist deviation was linked to class background and thus a propensity to commit class-motivated crimes, such as rural teachers' resistance to collectivization. The July 1930 report cited several instances of teachers either encouraging peasants to withhold grain or stealing grain themselves, while maintaining ties with kulaks and hiding their own class backgrounds. In some instances, local Robos organs had reportedly not adequately assisted in the prosecution of such teachers or, conversely, had failed to defend wrongly accused activist teachers against the corruption or ineptitude of local authorities.[47] What was critical was that local authorities could err, and the VUK's intervention brought a correction or the exposure of a perceived wrong. This meant that teachers might have some hope that an appeal could lead to remediation. The VUK ordered a purge of all its organizations in order to ensure that the union and teachers observed correct political behaviour, according to the "Marxist-Leninist spirit," and recommended that the union respond to "invader counter-revolutionaries from the SVU" and other anti-Soviet groups by further developing forms of socialist competition among educators and increasing their participation in the building of socialism. It blamed teachers' failures to embrace public work and to protect their ranks from infiltration by "class enemies" on a lack of Marxist–Leninist training. The report implies that the two failings were necessarily related. Nationalist deviation, as represented by, and credited to, the SVU, could not spread far if teachers remained actively engaged in the tasks of Soviet power.

Of course, the Robos's principal goal was to protect the interests of teachers, but as the collectivization campaign accelerated, the union placed greater emphasis on the personal protection of teachers participating in the campaign rather than on the professional interests of any one teacher. On the one hand, the plenum's report cited, for example, the case of a teacher named Vyshnevska, whom a district executive committee in the Zinovivske region, in agreement with the district Robos organization, wrongly dismissed for "anti-pedagogical methods in work." After an investigation by the regional section of Robos, local authorities were forced to reinstate her after failing to demonstrate sufficient cause. A case like Vyshnevska's showed "the formalism, the unprincipled character that exists in some lower organizations of the union." Presumably, the VUK called the district Robos committee to task for failing to defend Vyshnevska. Yet, in the same report where the VUK cited this case and others that had required remediation by higher-level authorities, it argued that the union's guidance on "defensive work" was deeply flawed. It claimed that a brochure entitled "On the Defensive Work in the Robos Union" had inspired class enemies among the union's ranks and influenced sympathizers to take up opposition to Soviet power. The VUK report charged that Sheremetiev, the author of the brochure, had a clear aim in writing the brochure. He "would incite the essential mass of educators against the Communist Party and Soviet power by artificially picking clearly tendentious facts and imbuing this brochure with content that would disorganize our ranks." [48] Since the exposure of the counter-revolutionary nature of the brochure, Robos had taken measures to purge "the remnants of *Shermetievshchyna*" in the work of the union.

While the VUK continued to reprimand lower-level Robos authorities for not acting to defend teachers wrongly accused of professional (or political) misconduct, it increased its criticism of teachers who had sabotaged the collectivization campaign, and suggested that the union's principal "defensive work" should have been the protection of activist teachers who suffered class-motivated terror. For example, in a village in the Yemilchyne district (Korosten region), a teacher named Chavaniuk was shot and wounded as he gave a speech about the May 1 (International Workers' Day) holiday. Chavaniuk reportedly actively participated in the collectivization of agriculture and exposed corruption in the village's agricultural cooperative, an event that led to the arrest of some members of the cooperative. The VUK report stressed that this and many other examples underscored the central role of educators in the building of socialism and reminded Robos members of one of their main tasks: "Proletarian justice deals and will deal with all severity those who threaten the life of the Soviet teacher." It blamed a sharpening of the class struggle for the "appearance" of the SVU, the Sheremetiev brochure, and the attacks on teachers. In this context, a correction of Soviet nationalities policy was intimately tied to the precarious position of the teacher in the countryside.

The Union for Liberation of Ukraine (SVU)

The SVU was an invention of the party leadership, created to justify its repression of the activities of the Ukrainian intelligentsia, activities that it had long held suspect and could not entirely control. Between 18 May and 18 June 1929, the GPU arrested a group of post-secondary students in Kyiv on the charge of membership in an illegal organization. Among those arrested were youths who had worked with the GPU to establish contact with "nationally minded" persons, and evidence from them was used against the other accused, including Boris Matushevsky and Mykola Pavlushkov, graduates of Taras Shevchenko Kyiv Labour School No. 1. In June 1929, the head of the Ukrainian GPU, Vsevolod Balytsky, reported to the TsK KP(b)U: "An organization has united the anti-Soviet minded intelligentsia, the former prominent participants in the Petliurist movement, activists in the autocephalous church and representatives of the kulaks." Balytsky was evidently in a rush to provide this information because he authored this document before all those initially arrested had provided testimony.[49]

Although the KP(b)U Politburo formally authorized a show trial for a Ukrainian nationalist organization on 3 November 1929, the VKP(b) Politburo issued regular instructions to the Ukrainian central committee on the trial's preparations, including a personal telegram from Stalin ordering doctors to be included among the accused.[50] The Ukrainian GPU subsequently composed a detailed program and administrative structure for the SVU and placed the most prominent nonparty Ukrainian intellectuals at its head. The GPU designated Serhii Yefremov, Pavlushkov's uncle, the vice-president of VUAN and an expert on Ukrainian literature, as the principal leader of the alleged organization. On 5 February 1930, Stalin called a special meeting of the VKP(b) Politburo to confirm members of the court and the prosecution team for the main trial (held from 9 March to 19 April 1930).[51] Of the forty-five people selected for sentencing, twenty-five were professors, teachers, or students. According to a GPU report, some 700 people were arrested across the republic shortly after the trial in connection with the SVU affair, and Voldymyr Prystaiko, Yurii Shapoval, and Vadym Zolotarov estimate that, altogether, 30,000 people were arrested, executed, or exiled during the time of, or after, the official trial on accusations of involvement in the SVU.[52] The GPU officers specifically targeted labour-school teachers and professors for these arrests, but the campaign encompassed the Ukrainian national intelligentsia as a whole: linguists, writers, activists in the Ukrainian autocephalous church, and former officials or employees of the UNR government.[53]

The public show trial of the SVU, held in the Kharkiv opera house, sent a warning to Ukrainian intellectuals everywhere, especially teachers in Ukrainian-language schools. Mere announcement of arrests was enough to incite protestations of

An overhead view of the courtroom in the Kharkiv opera house during the trial of the SVU, 1930. The accused are seated behind the bar, to the right of the GPU guard. Courtesy TsDKFFAU.

loyalty.[54] On 24 November 1929, the Robos leadership and editorial board of *Narodnii uchytel* first publicly reported on the SVU affair, calling on all educators to demand the "most severe" punishment for those charged.[55] Three days later, the Robos presidium insisted that the SVU represented a minority, but conceded that the union needed to renew its efforts to oppose "unfit members of the intelligentsia" lurking in its midst. It ordered teachers "to intensify their work, to have a correct Marxist–Leninist understanding and to strengthen their proletarian-class education in the union and reject those who want to infiltrate it." The best answer to the SVU threat was for educators to take a more active role in the "building of socialism," including the campaigns for industrialization, collectivization, and "Ukrainian culture with national form and international content."[56] If Ukrainization was to proceed, teachers had to accomplish it under the guidance of the party and Komsomol and in concert with the wider political and economic agenda of the First Five-Year Plan.

Local groups of educators similarly pledged their loyalty to Soviet power and committed themselves to fight nationalism at every turn. A Kyiv regional conference of Robos issued telegrams to the VKP(b) TsK and the GPU, condemning the SVU in the name of "an army of 18,000 educators." It also claimed to have organized a popular demonstration against the SVU, after having learned of similar resolutions by district and municipal executive committees. The national question could be resolved only under Soviet power, it insisted, and those enemy elements who sought to rally the population with "national slogans" were hiding their true intention: a return of power to the propertied classes.[57]

Many Robos cells and educational institutions threatened a purge of their own ranks. A Robos meeting in Kamianets (now Kamianets-Podilskyi) boasted it would "use all its strength to expose all class enemies who are hiding under the mask of culture." Kharkiv Labour School No. 30 pledged to submit its workers to a review of the city's executive committee.[58] Educators in the city of Sloviansk (Artemivsk region) pledged to conduct similar internal purges, and the Robos section in Sumy promised to kick "wreckers" out of the ranks of the "red teachers."[59] None of these groups specified the form of these campaigns, but all felt it necessary to announce their commencement, perhaps in order to pre-empt the GPU's own investigations.

Other educators sought to demonstrate their loyalty by fundraising for the Five-Year Plan and Soviet institutions. Instructors at the Izium Pedagogical Technical College (Kharkiv region) pledged money towards a "contract for industrialization" as a sign of protest against the SVU. Some post-secondary students and local scholars vowed to solicit funds for the cost of a new airplane, and schoolteachers promised to raise cash for the Red Army's operations in the Far East. Teachers had to not only display a commitment to Soviet power, but also confirm a central role for education in the construction of socialism. Thus, they needed to build Ukrainian culture and distinguish this task from the activities of the SVU "wreckers." Teachers in Uman pledged to renew their efforts to tie "proletarian education and practice." In the Stalino region, teachers at the Selydove Seven-Year School called on their compatriots to simultaneously build Ukrainian culture, liquidate illiteracy, and collectivize agriculture.[60] Education and Ukrainian culture had to be linked to the primary task of training present and future workers for economic transformation.

Nevertheless, it was in the field of education that authorities located the crucial danger. The UkrSSR chief prosecutor, Lev Akhmatov, warned *Narodnii uchytel* readers about the work of the Scientific Pedagogical Society (*Naukovo-pedahohichne tovarystvo* – NPT). The NPT, Akhmatov argued, allowed for the consolidation of "Petliurists."[61] He charged that members of the society, led by prominent pedagogues Ivanytsia and Doha, regularly criticized the Soviet school in order to foment dissatisfaction among teachers and create distrust in the education system. Akhmatov claimed Ivanytsia advanced the slogan *do svitla* (to the light) in his textbooks, but had found inspiration only among counter-revolutionary circles abroad. He further charged that Doha, then an instructor at a Kyiv Pedagogical Technical College had barred Communist and Komsomol members from his courses to "preserve the purity of the Ukrainian school."[62] The two had allegedly attracted enough anti-Soviet teachers to form a shadow Ministry of Education-in-waiting.

Although the government stressed the threat represented by scholars such as Ivanytsia and Doha, its charges of a counter-revolutionary conspiracy by previously lauded teachers suggested a more insidious source of concern. When *Narodnii uchytel* reported that students and instructors at Ukrainian-studies courses in Kharkiv had criticized the plotting of purported SVU academicians as "a disgraceful and insolent attack on our youth,"[63] it was essentially repeating the official account: the SVU was not just an organization content to band together the remnants of the national bourgeois intelligentsia for the possible overthrow of Soviet rule. Its power depended on the recruitment of the next generation. An effective way to bridge the gap between the duplicitous activity of academicians and the assemblage of a counter-revolutionary movement was to implicate teachers in the SVU conspiracy. The emotive language of a corruption of youth, instigated by scholars but carried out by teachers, lent a sense of urgency to the state's charges. The very future of the revolution was at stake.

Conveniently, the GPU identified a "school group" of the SVU. It charged the well-known pedagogue and advocate of Ukrainian schooling, Durdukivsky, as head of this group. Akhmatov alleged that Durdukivsky, contrary to his published record, was an advocate of the tsarist gymnasium and opposed to the new Soviet school. He and four other teachers at Kyiv Labour School No. 1, who were also arrested, reportedly sought to prevent the admission of children of the proletariat, fearing their influence on the children of "conscious" Ukrainian intelligentsia.[64] As proof of their treachery, Akhmatov claimed, they had read poetry dedicated to Petliura and collected money for a monument to immortalize him. Furthermore, they had admitted only four Jews to the school. Given the Soviet government's own drive towards ethnic consolidation in the schools, this fact, even if true, was unsurprising. Kyiv Labour School No. 1 was designated by Narkomos as a Ukrainian school.

Akhmatov's information was drawn from a set program that SVU members confessed to at trial. An internal GPU report outlined the program, detailing several other functions of the school group, including preventing children from joining Young Pioneer groups.[65] Labour School No. 1 allegedly functioned as an organizational centre for nationalist teachers across the republic. The school group expanded by recruiting provincial teachers who came to Kyiv on excursions, perhaps with their students, as the Narkomos poradnyk recommended. Similarly, the Scientific Pedagogical Society sought to use its public meetings to win over teachers to an anti-Soviet orientation.

Not only had teachers organized, but, even more menacingly, the government claimed, so had the youth. Akhmatov maintained that a fraternal student organization, the Society of Unity and Concord (*Tovarystvo iednannia i zhody* – TIeZ) had secretly created a parallel youth wing to the SVU, the Union of Ukrainian Youth (*Spilka ukrainskoi molodi* – SUM).[66] He named Pavlushkov, Serhii Yefremov's nephew, the Kyiv Komsomol secretary, a member of TIeZ, and a Kyiv INO student, as the organization's head.[67] Under the tutelage of teachers, schoolchildren had also apparently formed counter-revolutionary groups. A GPU document detailing arrests of cultural leaders, professors, and teachers throughout the country for ties to the SVU pointed to one alarming example. In the Pryluky region, a teacher and 1925 graduate of the Kyiv INO had organized a nationalist group, composed primarily of kulak children. The GPU report claimed that the group had read nationalist literature in secret and used Taras Shevchenko's poetry as their inspiration to campaign in surrounding villages for a popular uprising against Soviet power. Authorities arrested six labour-school students as a result of their investigation.[68] Arrests of children appear to have been rare, but the GPU's inclusion of information in its report was an indication of just how far it was willing to go in its operation against the Ukrainian intelligentsia.

The list of the supposed crimes planned by the SVU that was revealed at the trial was long, beginning with proposals for the murder of everyone from Skrypnyk to Stalin and culminating in an elaborate plan for an insurrection against Soviet power and a Polish-aided invasion of the UkrSSR by émigré Ukrainian nationalist forces. The role of youth, Akhmatov made clear, was to incite the population for this uprising and spread nationalist myths, "in defence of Ukrainian culture." The SVU ensured that the revolution was robbed of its heirs, but also made students foot soldiers in a campaign for its overthrow. Reinforcing the image of corrupted youth, Akhmatov lamented that the SVU had planned its treason from the "body of the young socialist republic," deceiving the childlike Soviet society with its blend of national bourgeois historicism and pseudo-Marxism.[69] Elsewhere, Skrypnyk made clear to young cultural activists that the SVU was fighting for control of the preparation of new cadres, a key task of the Five-Year Plan.[70] At stake were the future of the next Soviet generation and the fulfillment of socialism.

The prosecution of "model" teachers and students, themselves products of the Soviet education system, sent a signal to educators. In addition to Akhmatov's warnings and the regular articles in *Narodnii uchytel* and the general press, the government transmitted the court proceedings via radio. The incentive for Robos to make a distinction between the educator/activist and self-indulgent (potentially traitorous) intellectual was high. One Robos section protested that SVU activity had nothing in common with "the work of the broadest stratum of labour intelligentsia and especially teachers, who together with the proletariat and the

Communist Party are carrying out the Five-Year Plan of socialist building."[71] Teachers' critical role in the classroom, coupled with their participation in public work (the fight against illiteracy and the promotion of collectivization), made them suspect, but, at the same time, gave evidence of constructive "action." Scholars had to demonstrate the same.

In November 1929, over seven hundred educators met in the eastern Ukrainian city of Luhansk to consider the SVU conspiracy. The group consisted not only of teachers and vocational education instructors, but also members of the local section of scientific workers. After listening to a report on the SVU by a representative of the regional GPU, the head of the Robos section of scientific workers claimed that local scholars had been too passive: "In the age of socialism it is not possible to just stand on the 'Soviet platform.' We must sit near the engine and help the train travel faster to socialism."[72] The Robos section head conceded that Luhansk scholars had compromised too long with reactionary views of VUAN scholars and therefore were partly to blame. As evidence, he pointed to a 1924 lecture given to graduate students at the Luhansk Marxist–Leninist Academy by Hermaize, a VUAN historian, textbook author, and now-arrested member of the SVU. He suggested that administrators of the academy and local scholars in general had thereby created an environment of reconciliation (*prymyrenstvo*), refusing to see early signs of treason. The meeting denounced the SVU, taking the added step of tying it to a recent attack on a Soviet diplomat in Lwów, Poland, by a Ukrainian student, and resolved to "triple the effort to build the fortress of the socialist homeland of labourers."[73] Scholarly work would have to be justified even more in terms of service to the state.

The SVU arrests and trial did not mean the end of Ukrainization. Instead of attacking Ukrainization, prosecutors argued that the SVU had formed because of the policy's success. Akhmatov himself authored an article in *Narodnii uchytel* in which he maintained that the SVU members viewed Ukrainization as a Soviet "provocation" designed to wrest control of Ukrainian culture from "conscious Ukrainians."[74] While SVU members conceded a practical cooperation with the Soviet government in order to keep the policy "in Ukrainian hands," Akhmatov claimed they worked behind the scenes to bring about its downfall. They exploited the romanticism of some circles of the Ukrainian intelligentsia and managed to convince them that Ukrainization offered a means to simultaneously defend the Ukrainian language and oppose Russian speakers. He again invoked the idea that the SVU was both a counter-revolutionary and anti-Semitic organization premised on the seemingly contradictory idea that the Jewish "nation" was "the carrier of the idea of Russian statehood." Members allegedly taught anti-Semitism in pedagogical institutes, advocated pogroms, and sought to bar Jewish candidates from scientific organizations.[75] Fundamentally, Akhmatov stressed, the SVU sought control over Ukrainization in order to foment nationalist hatred among youth. He repeated that VUAN was the centre of the organization's activity, but it relied on the rural intelligentsia (specifically primary-school teachers) to spread its ideas, disseminate nationalist literature to the young, and combat the work of the Komsomol and Young Pioneers to develop a Soviet generation.

The only way to successfully defend Soviet power, authorities claimed, was to reassert a "pure" understanding of the meaning of the revolution and Leninist nationalities policy. A 1930 Komsomol pamphlet claimed that "Ukrainization will deal a horrible blow to the nation of SUM [Union of Ukrainian Youth] adherents."[76] Nevertheless, while the Komsomol and the party lauded Ukrainization, seeing in its success the motive for the desperate acts of the SVU and SUM, at the same time, the affair deprived the state of committed and capable administrators of a campaign desperate for talent. More ominously, the arrests of alleged Ukrainian nationalists and the SVU show trial sent an unequivocal message to the rank-and-file Ukrainizers: they might be next. One local Robos section's proclamations captured these contradictory sentiments: "The exuberant [*buinyi*] blossoming of Ukrainian proletarian culture testifies that valid national questions are only solved by the working-peasant masses under the leadership of a proletarian-peasant party and its proletarian state." In the same breath, it called for severe punishment of those accused and ordered educators to assist the GPU in exposing "individual scoundrels, who have penetrated the ranks of educators."[77]

The limits of just how much a teacher might add to the "blossoming" of Ukrainian culture were unclear. Few could countenance the crimes with which the state charged SVU members. It was best not to stray into areas that might be considered suspect, and much of Ukrainian culture now was. Martin argues that the party viewed the bulk of the Ukrainian intelligentsia as *smenovekhovtsy*, a term derived from an émigré Russian nationalist organization, Smena vekh (Change of Signposts), which advocated tactical cooperation with the Bolsheviks.[78] From the party's perspective, Ukrainian "bourgeois intellectuals" had made a similar choice. Martin maintains that the party viewed the SVU show trial as a necessary preventive measure because it accepted as a "psychological truth" that the intelligentsia would oppose the Five-Year Plan's cultural revolution, a program for the creation of a new proletarian ethos.[79] Ukrainian historians have tended to argue that the SVU trial was intended to undermine the campaign of Ukrainization.[80] Shapoval, Prystaiko, and Zolotarov contend that "this affair was formulated as a decisive step towards the discrediting of the policy of 'Ukrainization,' which the functionaries of the GPU UkrSSR never considers serious or lasting." Vasyl Danylenko considers the SVU affair a "result of the political investigations of the GPU" that had targeted the intelligentsia, many of whom "were ready to cooperate with the Bolsheviks, especially during the years of 'Ukrainization'."[81]

As chapter 7 discusses, KP(b)U and VKP(b) leaders had very little trust in the non-party educators and the Ukrainian national intelligentsia more generally, and the GPU had none at all. The GPU's predecessor was, after all, a product of the civil war, whose responsibilities included the arrest of pro-UNR elements in areas of Ukraine that came under Red Army control. Vasyl Danylenko describes it as an institution that "from its very beginning developed as a foreign organism for Ukraine in its origin, structure, and appointment."[82] The GPU had planned to deport the accused SVU leader, Yefremov, outside the borders of the USSR as early as 1922, and in 1926, had prepared a report on "rightist" elements among the Ukrainian intelligentsia.[83] Furthermore, the GPU placed the most authoritative new voice in favour of accommodation with the Bolsheviks, Mykhailo Hrushevsky, almost immediately under surveillance upon his arrival in Soviet Ukraine in 1924 after an extended period of self-imposed exile.[84] What is certainly true is that the GPU was one of the fiercest critics of Ukrainization and the least Ukrainized institution in the republic. As a large collection of internal Ukrainian GPU documents edited by Vasyl Danylenko makes clear, the GPU had been preparing through the 1920s for something like the SVU affair, monitoring the activities of the most politically active members of the Ukrainian intelligentsia (including those who would be selected for indictment in the formal trial in Kharkiv) and recruiting a network of informers to provide evidence for their future incrimination.[85]

However, the GPU's antagonism against the Ukrainian intelligentsia does not explain why the KP(b)U, the VKP(b), and Stalin authorized a repression that would damage the very policy of Ukrainization they had defended. Ukrainian historians see a "tight alliance" between GPU and party organs, in which the suspicions of one tended to reinforce the outlook of the other, so that, by December 1929, preparations for the SVU trial were directed by a "party-Chekist tandem."[86] Nevertheless, even if the party leadership in Moscow coordinated details of the trial, Shapoval and Zolotarov grant, "the GPU UkrSSR proposed its own 'drama' for the trial." As Olga Bertelsen's work on the GPU's arrests of Zionists in Ukraine has made clear, the Ukrainian GPU officials could and did set the parameters for an initial campaign of repression –out of ambition, insecurity, or fear – even as they remained subordinate to the directives of central GPU and party organs.[87] Balytsky reported regularly on the dangers of Ukrainian nationalism to the TsK KP(b)U prior to 1929, and, after the KP(b)U Politburo approved the SVU campaign, the GPU arrested not just the "old intelligentsia" as carriers of this nationalism, but members of Ukrainian-studies groups whose creation had been advocated by Soviet authorities (including a "study group of Ukrainizers" organized by teachers in the Luhansk region). Balytsky himself authorized an initial selection of who would appear in the SVU trial, determining the fates of these individuals through a series of annotations to a list of last names. As one GPU investigator repeated in his reports: "We need to put the Ukrainian intelligentsia on its knees."[88]

The Ukrainian GPU's role in setting the initial agenda for the SVU affair is thus critical, although party authorities made final determinations. The GPU's pre-1929 orientation and surveillance operations, selection of arrests, and conduct of interrogations of those accused played into, and consolidated, a KP(b)U anxiety about the management of Ukrainization, even if it did not mean a definitive rejection of this policy. The GPU acted against the Ukrainian intelligentsia not simply because it had always assumed them to be disloyal, but because it and party leaders in Kharkiv and Moscow feared the power of intellectuals to direct education and culture beyond the sphere of the party. It was the uncertainty of the consequences of the intelligentsia's work that troubled all these sides most. Nevertheless, Ukrainian educators were not the calculating opportunists of the GPU's image. Yefremov, Hrushevsky, and others resisted party involvement in academic life and harboured private ambitions to increase the political and economic autonomy of the UkrSSR, and Yefremov's own opinion of Soviet power was less than favourable, especially after assumption of state-directed grain requisitions in 1928.[89] However, the Soviet government put the SVU defendants, Yefremov included, on trial for allegedly doing precisely what it had exhorted them to do: develop Ukrainian culture. This result was the consequence of a "script" that the Ukrainian GPU first drafted and party authorities then produced.

The SVU Interrogation Files

The police interrogation files of the defendants whom Soviet authorities included in the official SVU trial are housed in the State Archive of the Security Service of Ukraine in Kyiv. The files begin with testimony given by the accused immediately after their arrests from May to November 1929 and include interviews/confessions made by the accused until the time of the official trial in the spring of 1930. Although they vary in length and detail, the files provide insight into how Soviet authorities transformed educators from party-endorsed Ukrainizers to counter-revolutionary nationalists, capable of abusing their roles as teachers and mentors. This section focuses on material drawn from files of three individuals: Yurii Trezvynsky (a teacher at Kyiv Labour School No. 1, arrested on July 3), Oleksandr Hrebenetsky (a senior teacher also at Kyiv Labour School No. 1, arrested on July 4), and Mykola Bily (a former primary-school teacher and, at the time of his arrest on November 12, a student at the Dnipropetrovsk INO).[90] Their statements in the GPU files must be read carefully, but their testimony reveals some truths about their own lives and, perhaps even more, about the anxieties of the Soviet leadership about the process of Ukrainization.[91] Highlighting a select group of intellectuals less central to the SVU affair emphasizes the network of nationally minded Ukrainian educated society over the role of any one individual. Professional and personal ties that had proven durable over the course of the tumultuous decade of the 1920s were transformed into anti-Soviet collusion under GPU interrogation.

Fundamentally, as this study has already maintained, the SVU affair was about a fear on the part of the Communist Party leadership about the corruption of youth. This fear concerned the fate of children, but it also concerned the newly emergent intelligentsia, some of whom were trained (or being trained) in Soviet institutions and others of whom were young enough to be less tainted by the "nationalist bourgeois" activity of the pre-revolutionary Ukrainian national movement. This new Soviet Ukrainian intelligentsia was supposed to instinctively question the "romantic" assumptions of their elders, to oppose their leadership, and to forge a modern, urban-oriented culture for a developing Ukrainian working class.

The initial statements of Trezvynsky, Hrebenetsky, and Bily reveal, however, a clear intergenerational cohesion among Ukrainian educators and students. Trezvynsky was born in 1886 in the village of Samoridnia near Kaniv, and had come to Kyiv to study at the theological seminary. After teaching first in a village school, in 1910, he joined the faculty of a city school in Kyiv, which Narkomos converted into a Russian-language "labour school." According to the testimony Trezvynsky gave in his interview with the GPU, he wanted to join a Ukrainian-language school. The district education inspector promised him a place in the school of the Arsenal factory, but the Ukrainization of the school was blocked. Trezvynsky succeeded in gaining employment only through the intervention of Volodymyr Durdukivsky, his former instructor at the theological seminary and then-director of the first Ukrainian-language school in the city, Kyiv Labour School No. 1.

Younger teachers with roots in the countryside, like Trezvynsky, relied on the patronage from more established urban intellectuals for career advancement. Once employed at the school, Trezvynsky joined an apparently close community of teachers. According to Trezvynsky, "I got along well with all the teachers ... V. S. Slutsky was very friendly towards me, [he] often helped me as a poverty-stricken group instructor with advice and defence of my material and professional affairs (a house for rest, etc.)."[92] Hrebenetsky confirmed in his testimony this description of a close, intergenerational teaching community at Labour School No. 1. The teachers regularly visited each other socially, and it was these chats over a "cup of tea" that became the objects of the GPU's interest. According to the later statements of both Trezvynsky and Hrebenetsky, most likely procured under duress, it was at one of these "cup of tea" meetings that Durdukivsky allegedly first proposed organizing a SVU cell in the school. Instead of the older generation's being isolated and out of touch, the ties between them and junior teachers of the school were considerable. The GPU used this reality to paint a picture through coerced testimony of the SVU defendants of a united, counter-revolutionary intelligentsia. According to Hrebenetsky's later statement, at one teacher's meeting, he "also spoke about how the task of the moment required that the Ukrainian intelligentsia unite on the basis of a single national front, doing away with its internal, party, and other objections."[93]

Bily too benefited from the support of elder intellectuals in Dnipropetrovsk (Katerynoslav until 1926). He reportedly maintained a professional and social relationship with Liubov Bidnova, a teacher at Dnipropetrovsk Labour School No. 20, and Petro Yefremov, a professor at the Dnipropetrovsk INO and brother of the academician Serhii Yefremov, whom the GPU identified and Soviet authorities charged as the de facto leader of the SVU. Even in his first statement to the GPU interrogator, perhaps in an attempt to shield them from greater scrutiny, Bily claimed that Bidnova was a woman with an "old manner" and Yefremov was an "individual with an old-world outlook," but one who "always spoke approvingly of the nationalities policy of Soviet power."[94] It seems clear, however, that he maintained a strong professional relationship with Bidnova and spoke to Yefremov regularly, according to his testimony, at the INO or while walking to the INO. Bily's later statements to the GPU interrogator cite Yefremov as the source of his conversion to counter-revolutionary Ukrainian nationalism. Any such statements should be read critically as the products of GPU manipulation, but the following testimony suggests that Bily's respect for Yefremov must contain an element of truth: "He [Yefremov] taught Ukrainian literature with all its wit, in conversations with him after lecture on the street, his pessimism and sad jokes had an effect on my mood."[95] Here, too, intergenerational cohesion persisted. Senior Ukrainian intellectuals continued to exercise great influence.

Yet, the future of Soviet power in Ukraine required the participation of youth in the building of socialism. Soviet authorities structured the SVU affair in the first instance as a battle to "save youth." The Soviets sought to train youth for their future role in Soviet society and the economy; the nationalists, as fabricated by the GPU and made manifest by GPU-directed testimony, sought to "save youth" for their own cause. The GPU chose to target, at least for the official trial, more prominent educators or well-connected educators, teachers, and students. Kyiv Labour School No. 1, where Hrebenetsky and Trezvynsky taught, was the most prestigious Ukrainian-language school in Kyiv. As Hrebenetsky maintained, "all this [prominent issues of pedagogy] was worked out by us and afterwards began to be debated in the pages of the pedagogical press and transferred to life in other schools."[96] The school itself, he initially insisted, was in full accord with Soviet educational policy and was actively involved in its development. He was personally committed to Soviet goals: "I sincerely sympathize with Soviet power and sincerely work for the raising of the Soviet school, giving all my physical and mental strength to school work."[97] Trezvynsky claimed that his devotion was equally ardent.[98] It is remarkable that in Hrebenetsky's later testimonies, even as he was confessing to his participation in an ambiguously defined SVU, he continued to insist he took little interest in its highly ambitious aim of an independent Ukrainian state because he was so preoccupied with teaching.[99]

Bily's own personal history offers insight into how the GPU might question an apparently fresh commitment to Soviet ideals. Bily taught in a rural primary school near Katerynoslav during the early years of Soviet power, until enrolling in the Katerynoslav (Dnipropetrovsk) INO in 1924. He would appear to offer a good model for retraining as a Soviet intellectual. After several years of labouring to raise the cultural level of the village child, Bily sought an education in the INO (in Bily's words, "the Soviet university") in order to further his career as an educator of Soviet youth: "I diligently worked the first two years, concerning myself with the communist outlook, studied Marxism, the revolutionary movement, read the works of Lenin and did not feel at odds with the times that followed."[100] However, his past was suspect, from the perspective of Soviet authorities. Bily had left Katerynoslav after pushing to Ukrainize the university, in order to enrol in the Ukrainian-language university in Kamianets (Kamianets-Podilskyi), served briefly on the editorial board of a local Ukrainian-language pedagogical journal until the arrival of the Red Army, and then returned to Katerynoslav in 1919, only to be arrested by the new Soviet government as a spy for the forces of the anarchist Nestor Makhno. He was released from a jail after a day and half, "due to the absence of guilt in active Petliurist [Ukrainian nationalist] forces."[101] The GPU's 1929 arrest of Bily may have been motivated by the concern that educators like him could use their new Soviet qualifications to reach influential teaching positions, and potentially compromise the next generation with a "hidden" nationalism.

The linchpin in the GPU argument that the Soviet mission to "save youth" was being led astray was TIeZ (*Tovarystvo iednannia i zhody* – Society of Unity and Concord). Hrebenetsky acknowledged the existence of the group early on during his questioning by the GPU, but insisted that group was only a loosely formed alumni association of former graduates of Labour School No. 1, about whom the teachers cared: "We always had very strong ties [*iednannia*] with children, whom we regarded with kindness, and also strong ties between instructors in our work."[102] Hrebenetsky subsequently "confessed" that the aim of TIeZ was something far more sinister. He now claimed that TIeZ's goal was to prevent the "denationalization" of the school's graduates, who faced a Russian environment upon graduation.[103] Trezvynsky, after his initial interrogation by the GPU, stated that Durdukivsky and other teachers claimed that the seven-year labour school could "not satisfy" the Ukrainian population, and that educational authorities were discriminating against Ukrainian children in admissions to secondary vocational schools and disproportionately purging Ukrainians from post-secondary institutions.¹⁰⁴ Hrebenetsky added that teachers in the school were hostile to a class approach to education; his early admission that there was no Young Pioneer organization in the school now seemed to offer evidence of the faculty's sponsorship of a exclusionary, bourgeois, nationalist education.¹⁰⁵ Hrebenetsky disclosed that one of TIeZ's goals was to prevent graduates from joining the Komsomol, from falling victim to Soviet influence, "of which they were terrified of due to impressions from War Communism."¹⁰⁶ In short, through these "confessions," the GPU reworked TIeZ to be an organization meant to "save youth" for the nationalist cause. As such, TIeZ became an outgrowth of the GPU's anxieties regarding Ukrainian-language education.

A careful reading of these GPU-guided testimonies reveals a shift in the imagery of youth from being the object of competing programs of salvation to being the saviours (or demons) of nationalist revolution. Bily insisted at first that the young secondary-school students and Komsomol members whom the GPU had told him were arrested must be "factually innocent" of any charges.¹⁰⁷ Among those arrested was his younger brother, Yevhen Bily. According to Mykola, Yevhen was "an individual of national attitudes, not chauvinistic, but [one] standing on the platform established by party congresses on the national question."¹⁰⁸ True, Yefremov and the INO faculty had taught Mykola (and he taught his brother in turn) to value the Ukrainian language and culture. Hrebenetsky claimed the same for pupils of Labour School No.1.¹⁰⁹ But youth would apply this knowledge in the service of the Soviet state: "From [Yefremov's] lecture ... [I understood] the Ukrainian youth should know the language and literature in order to raise the low cultural level of the peasant masses, in order to perceive Soviet culture."¹¹⁰ This, of course, was one of the principal aims of Ukrainization.

In the eyes of the GPU, such goodwill was suspect. Youth could be corrupted and turned against the state. Hrebenetsky testified that the main task of the SVU was "the education of youth in the national spirit ... to prepare conscious actors in Ukrainian territory [*na ukrainskomu poli*], assistants to us in the struggle for the liberation of Ukraine."¹¹¹ The SVU ostensibly sought to recruit children from the intelligentsia specifically for future roles in the new state.¹¹² In the case of Dnipropetrovsk, Bily confessed to the role of the corrupter of his own brother and his cohort. In his testimony, youth assumed an even more explicit role as leaders of the "liberation" movement. Yefremov allegedly explained to him: "An organization of 'bright,' nationally conscious youth was needed, who would be ready take the place of organizers for this [independent Ukrainian] state."¹¹³ This generation would foster nationalist attitudes among the peasantry and incite it to revolt against Soviet power.¹¹⁴ Bily purportedly left it to his brother Yevhen to initiate what he identified was the first stage in this revolt, national education: "Considering my difficulties of work and that I did not have definite ties with the schools, I could not have carried out this work, [so] I decided to undertake the work through my brother, Yevhen and he created a [pro-independence or SVU] group ... with his comrades."[115] Bily and Hrebenetsky contradicted themselves on the size and ambitions of the SVU groups to which they both professed membership, but both advanced the idea that it was the responsibility of teachers and educators primarily to ensure that children were ready for this role and, when appropriate, extend their circle of influence.

It is difficult for the historian to judge which statements by the SVU defendants were "fed" by the GPU interrogator or represented thoughts that the SVU defendants believed the GPU wanted to hear. The files of Hrebenetsky and Trezvynsky contain minutes of interviews where a defendant testifies in the presence of another in order to "remind" a more reluctant or disoriented defendant of the details of a certain alleged event or statement (*ochnaia stavka* in Russian, or *stavka vich-na-vich* in Ukrainian).[116] However, the voice of the GPU interrogator is most certainly present. The GPU was concerned about what was going on in Ukrainized schools and educational institutions, about the role of non-party intelligentsia in these establishments, and about the distortion of Soviet educational objectives for Ukrainian youth.

If the fate of youth was the overriding anxiety for the GPU, it was ultimately the policy of Ukrainization that these "confessions" question. Trezvynsky, Hrebenetsky, and Bily were all Ukrainizers. Trezvynsky actively sought employment in a Ukrainian school, Hrebenetsky was a leading teacher in the first Ukrainian school in Kyiv, and Bily had sought out an education at a Ukrainian-language university in Kamianets after being frustrated in his struggle to Ukrainize the university in Katerynoslav (Dnipropetrovsk). Each of their testimonies suggests a distorted, "non-Bolshevik" policy of Ukrainization. Trezvynsky testified that the teachers' group spoke confidently of a need for more forceful Ukrainization: "We spoke of Ukrainization – strictly [speaking] about Ukrainizers who were applying pressure on Russians, who were crushing the Ukrainian language."[117] Here, Ukrainization reads like a method of revenge. One of Hrebenetsky's statements suggested that Ukrainization had already gone too far. Among the criticisms of Soviet policy, the teachers' group purportedly objected to "the implementation of Ukrainization in a form that intentionally provokes indignation and enmity towards Ukrainian culture, instead of a purge, non-Ukrainians were being appointed."[118] In a somewhat contradictory fashion, then, the Soviet government was being insensitive (or at least muddled) in its application of Ukrainization, leading to the resentment on the part of non-Ukrainian speakers, but still not doing enough to appoint ethnic Ukrainians to positions of influence.

Of course, some of these sentiments could indicate sincere attitudes whose precise nature cannot be discerned. Bily's own comments regarding Ukrainization are more personalized than that of Trezvynsky and Hrebenetsky. Bily claimed a critical attitude towards one Ukrainizer, Boiakov, who had overreached: "He created a bad impression on me with his relationship to the matter of Ukrainization, with a hostile approach to all weaker, backward elements, mercilessly spoiling their possibility of further overcoming their lack of fluency."[119] Boiakov was reportedly a member of the pedagogical committee of the Dnipropetrovsk Regional Ukrainization Commission. Local authorities set up these commissions at all levels of government to test employees for aptitude in Ukrainian, and recommended, in most cases, further enrolment in Ukrainian-studies classes for those who performed unsatisfactorily. Although commissions ordered dismissal only after employees demonstrated a negative attitude towards Ukrainization or repeatedly failed exams, Boiakov appears to have denied the possibility of retesting for individuals under his review. At what stage he made this judgment is unclear, but, as Bily presents it, Boiakov's attitude may have led to the type of resentment Hrebenetsky described in his testimony.

This incident is specific enough that it would seem unlikely that Bily or the GPU simply made it up. Bily might have had a real problem with how Boiakov approached Ukrainization or simply had a personal grudge with him. Alternatively, he may have thought that if he expressed disagreement with how Ukrainization was being implemented, he might buy some leniency from the GPU. Either way, Bily felt required, or was asked specifically, to talk about Ukrainization, and, as in the accounts of Trezvynsky and Hrebenetsky, the policy comes off in a decidedly negative light. The dilemma that teachers and educators generally faced was how to discern what the limits of Ukrainization were, how much the policy should persuade or compel, how rapid change should occur. Clearly, the individuals studied here knew by the very fact that they had been arrested and then accused of participation in a counter-revolutionary organization that they had overstepped these limits, and guessed or were prompted to identify them. Although coercive Ukrainization was a taboo, it is difficult to escape the conclusion in reading these files that using Ukrainian "to raise the culture level" of the population carried risk.

The SVU Affair in the Provinces: The Case of Odesa

In late 1929, the political environment surrounding Ukrainization in the Odesa region changed fundamentally with the announcement of the initial arrests of members of the Ukrainian intelligentsia for alleged participation in the SVU.[120] The GPU would soon make further arrests in Odesa, but, for the time being, it limited itself to an assessment of the local intelligentsia's reaction to the arrests, including those who would later be arrested. A November report noted that on the evening of November 25, a meeting of scientific workers, including members of the Odesa Scientific Society, met to discuss the arrests and pass a resolution calling for severe punishment for the SVU defendants and praising the activities of the GPU. Prior to the meeting, an INO professor, Andrii Muzychka, reportedly seeded doubt among students about the plausibility of the affairs, saying, "How do we know that this is true? It is not possible to believe only the announcement; it can turn out that today we will protest and tomorrow ask for forgiveness." He did not attend the meeting. Taras Slabchenko, the secretary of the Scientific Society, signed the resolution condemning the SVU, but did not publicly speak at the meeting. Privately, referencing an attack on the Soviet consulate in Lwów (Lviv), he said, "Lviv caused harm for us ... Now, probably they [the GPU] will beat Ukrainians more." His father, the academician Mykhailo Slabchenko, suggested that the SVU was a GPU provocation: "To permit that in Kyiv or in Odesa, or anywhere [there is a SVU] – that is not possible. The announcement about the discovery of some possible counter-revolutionary organization – this is nothing more than a maneuver by the GPU, which wants to prove its value in connection with the mass arrests which have been undertaken recently throughout Ukraine."[121] The academician Volodymyr Lypsky allegedly argued to his colleagues that Lenin had been a "friend to workers, peasants, and the labouring intelligentsia," but that after Lenin's death, elements within the party had encouraged class conflict, thereby cultivating "anti-Soviet attitudes among the intelligentsia." The "*Yefremovshchyna*" [the SVU] was a consequence of this policy of class conflict, which Lypsky clearly refuted, arguing that if those favouring the policy were not removed from positions of party leadership, another anti-Soviet group might form.[122] In other words, if he, in fact, made these statements, Lypsky was arguing that the SVU existed, but that its existence was justified. This was a worse position in many ways.

According to the GPU report, a definite segment of the Ukrainian intelligentsia doubted whether the SVU existed, claiming that the available evidence was not convincing. For example, a lecturer at an unspecified post-secondary institution, Tykulenko, announced, "The 'SVU' is 90 per cent an exaggerated affair. Some idiot now had the idea of liberating Ukraine from the Communists or something else. The GPU has not had a good case for a long time and just as Yefremov returned with his speeches from abroad, well, they seized him. For the campaign they took others. And regarding the creation of a case – the GPU is the master." One Ukrainian-language teacher, Honcharenko, took a different tack, in effect conceding the possible existence of counter-revolutionary nationalists in Ukraine, but suggesting that Soviet authorities would be unlikely to move against "big [*krupnykh*] figures, because of fear of reprisals against Soviet interests abroad."[123] Although the GPU document claims that this statement represented a broader constituency, it offered no further evidence. Regardless, with the exception of the "protest" resolution apparently passed by the Odessa Scientific Society, the GPU document cites no "Ukrainian" intellectual who condemned the SVU. They either doubted its existence or claimed its existence was the result of Soviet miscalculation or, in the case of Honcharenko, powerlessness.

The GPU report identified a category of Odesan citizens labelled the "Russian intelligentsia" as the most vocal in their vilification of the SVU.[124] A portion of this intelligentsia blamed the SVU affair on the machination of Poles. In a comment that perhaps revealed his own "chauvinist" sentiments (although not highlighted as such by the GPU), Professor Georgii Borovikov allegedly said, "The sentencing of Yefremov is an affair at the hands of the Poles … I believe that Russia should be undivided. This autonomy that Ukraine now has is sufficient. The Communists are fed up with the separatists and are shooting Yefremov." Others, such as a Professor Rzhepishevsky, blamed the SVU wholly on Ukrainians: "The Ukrainian counter-revolutionary Yefremov and this campaign [are] very dangerous things because [they have] roots in the prosperous part of the peasantry and Ukrainian intelligentsia."[125] Essentially, these two positions bridged the rationale offered by Soviet prosecutors and "confessed" to by the SVU defendants later at trial. If accurate, the statements suggest two compatible conclusions: on one hand, these intellectuals understood the essential lesson of the SVU affair; and, on the other hand, the GPU case against the SVU defendants was shaped by existing public suspicions.

Some of those "Russian" intellectuals who appeared to doubt the existence of the SVU conceded the existence of Ukrainian nationalism and supported what they viewed as the Communist Party's stance against separatism. Professor Egunov questioned, "Who knows what this affair is about? I do not think that it could be serious. You would have to be an idiot to actively go against the Communists. They are very strong now." However, he also argued that decisive measures must be taken against any nationalist group: "If there was truly a group that wanted the secession of Ukraine, then serious measures, of course, must be taken; if there is a 'Ukraine,' then it will be difficult for Russians." Professor Kipen was willing to accept that a group of Ukrainian separatists existed, even though he stopped short of recognizing a wider SVU conspiracy: "This group is powerless; it consists of the flaccid [*driablaia*], dreamy intelligentsia and they are unable to struggle against the courageous and strong Bolsheviks." He implied that the Bolshevik tolerance (i.e., Soviet nationalities policy) had encouraged this group's boldness: "'Ukrainians' are very small, you know. They are raising their heads because the authorities are flirting with us too much. A blow against the conspiracy and a firm hand will turn these 'Ukrainians' again into citizens of the USSR or Russia."[126] Kipen argued that the GPU move against Yefremov and his compatriots was justified and that the majority of non-party intellectuals sided with the party. Both Egunov and Kipen, in offering their support for what they thought the SVU arrests meant for the party's approach towards Ukraine, in effect criticized Ukrainization and what they viewed as its inevitable outgrowth: Ukrainian nationalism.

It is difficult to measure the selectivity of these comments, but they do reflect the ongoing debate about the desirability of Ukrainization within the party itself. Most importantly, they suggest a possible division in the Odesa intelligentsia, where ethnicity determined an approach towards Ukrainization and "Russian" intellectuals seemed to fear that Ukrainization targeted them. The intellectual world in Odesa was a tight circle. Urban schoolteachers, especially prominent ones, maintained an association with higher education and research institutions through professional organizations such as the Scientific Society and other cultural activity. Honcharenko is the one teacher explicitly cited in this GPU report, but it is reasonable to assume that many of the views articulated here reflected views of teachers or were communicated to teachers. The tie between higher-education students and teachers could have been, in some cases, even more explicit, as former teachers sometimes sought career advancement through enrolment in an INO or pedagogical institute and teachers maintained contact with graduates of seven-year primary schools who matriculated to the INO.

At least in November 1929, the GPU report saw the reaction of INO students to the SVU affair as indifferent or skeptical. The "Soviet portion" of the student body was vocal in its protest against the SVU: "Certain students made speeches in the following spirit: 'Give me a rifle, let's go to fight against the internal counter-revolution.'" However, the GPU report claims this was a minority view. Most said nothing, or complained that they were "being uselessly herded" to demonstrate. One student was reported as saying, "The ongoing protests are insincere. We [students] and school workers will protest, fearing pressure. But if you examine us, the soul of every professor, lecturer, and student, you will see if something is different." What they truly thought is left open to interpretation. By this measure, even the statements of the "Soviet portion" of students could be viewed as insincere. However, the most suspect opinion this report identified was the belief that the SVU affair was a sham, designed to bolster support for the GPU. One student suggested that the uncovering of the SVU affair provided a justification for GPU terror; another argued that it allowed the GPU to clear space for "its people" in VUAN. One INO student, Moisa, proclaimed, "The uncovering of this organization is simply a 'trick.' Simply, authorities want to know the attitude of the masses in this connection. In actuality, there is nothing similar to what is written in the newspaper."[127] That is, the GPU staged the SVU affair in order to gauge public sympathy towards the regime or towards expressions of Ukrainian nationalism.

While these statements were politically dangerous, none suggested an affinity with the proclaimed goals of the SVU. The accounts imply a fundamental lack of faith in the GPU and fear of its repressive powers. They stand in marked contrast to the report's description of worker reaction. Protests were held in Odesa's March Factory, the October Revolution Factory, and the All-Ukrainian Photo-Cinema

Administration's Mechanical Factory. Among the characteristic statements made by workers were the following: "No counter-revolution force will distract us from building the first socialist economy in the world," and "We demand the highest measures of punishment for the organizers of the counter-revolution."[128] Certainly, similar statements were made at protest meetings of professors, teachers, and students, but, clearly, the GPU did not choose to highlight them. The workers' greatest failing was not spreading the word of the SVU arrests, whereas the intelligentsia was discussing the SVU affair in a flawed, almost counter-revolutionary fashion. What is remarkable about the intellectuals' statements as a whole is that they come close to the historical consensus of the SVU affair: it was a conspiracy fabricated by the GPU to undermine the authority of an element of Ukrainian society that the GPU and some in the party had long distrusted: the Ukrainian national intelligentsia, who often served as the practitioners of Ukrainization.

By April 1930, the polemics surrounding the SVU affair heated up. The GPU had arrested Taras and Mykhailo Slabchenko, both of whom the 1929 GPU report had cited for purportedly making remarks criticizing the authoritarian aspects of Soviet power. Mykhailo, the father, suggested that the whole SVU affair was a ruse by the GPU to engage in further repression. Again, the 1929 report did not cite explicit nationalistic statements or suggest involvement by the Slabchenkos (or other intelligentsia) in a nationalist, counter-revolutionary conspiracy. Nevertheless, it is clear from this report that the GPU took a select interest in the Slabchenkos, and their comments, if true, indicated a fundamental aversion to elements of Soviet policy. Yet, the Slabchenkos had also worked for Soviet authorities in Odesa as leading Ukrainizers. In particular, the party documents make numerous references to Mykhailo's role as a public lecturer on Ukrainian history and instructor in state courses on Ukrainian studies. He embodied the fundamental paradox of the SVU affair: Soviet authorities needed highly qualified specialists to lead Ukrainization, particularly in linguistically diverse regions like Odesa, but harboured a distrust of such specialists and their activities in the lecture hall. In regard to educators such as the Slabchenkos, this concern was even more acute because they were responsible for the teaching of youth in their positions as INO instructors, and interacted with a wider pedagogical community.

After the "uncovering" of an SVU section in Odesa, which the Slabchenkos allegedly led, the GPU pointedly exposed the appearance of Ukrainian nationalism among Odesan youth. A GPU telegram sent to the regional party committee noted that a faculty and student meeting was held at the Odesa INO on March 31 to discuss the sentencing of SVU defendants. At this meeting, it was announced that fliers proclaiming nationalist slogans had been pasted in the cloakrooms of the INO. These slogans reportedly declared: "We protest against the trial against the 'SVU'" and "[Serhii] Yefremov is dying, but his cause lives on."[129] The students and professors did not stage an immediate protest upon the discovery of these fliers, but the GPU noted individual students calling for the arrest of those distributing the fliers and one student demanding the execution of the SVU defendants precisely because these fliers had appeared, meaning that he concluded the incident was the result of the SVU's influence in Odesa. Prusakov, another INO student, reportedly singled out a Slabchenko, likely Mykhailo, for specific condemnation: "Firm punishment is needed for that viper [*had*] Slabchenko, who hid under the mask of the Soviet professor."[130] Other students claimed that no INO students could have pasted up the slogans or that the incident was simply a joke: "Someone pulled a stunt [*vykynuv shtuku*] and now is laughing, as the commotion is picking up." Obviously, the GPU did not regard it as such.

Again, it is difficult to ascertain the truth of these statements, but it is striking that the GPU did not record any statements of real support of the SVU defendants from the students. Surely, the reporting of nationalist statements to local party leaders would have bolstered a case for a purging of INO students and faculty. Assuming these "nationalistic" fliers were posted, they suggest some sympathy, perhaps of the INO, for either the plight of the SVU defendants or the fabricated organization's alleged aims. Regardless, the GPU clearly was worried that nationalist sentiment existed among a segment of Odesa's youth, and its arrest of the Slabchenkos provided justification for surveillance within the INO. Because of the discovery of the fliers, the GPU pledged to the party to carry out an investigation of "the political attitudes of professors and students, especially regarding the matter of the 'SVU.'"[131] Of course, this is what it had been doing since the announcement of the SVU arrests; the sentencing of the Slabchenkos and the other SVU defendants meant that Ukrainian nationalism was officially a principal *bête noire* of local Soviet authorities in 1930. The fact that the GPU located Ukrainian nationalism in an institution responsible for training the next Soviet elite placed suspicion on the education system as whole and its Ukrainization. Even those within the regional party leadership who faithfully pushed the Ukrainization campaign must have been asking: what was being taught in Ukrainized establishments, from the elite INO to the primary school? Was a fundamental change in the policy needed?

Simple Priorities

Given the challenges already described in promoting high Ukrainian-language proficiency among teachers, it was unsurprising that many teachers readily abandoned an overt promotion of Ukrainization. Their general activism was another matter altogether. Press reports suggest that some teachers did oppose collectivization. The extent and openness of their resistance are unclear. *Narodnii uchytel* maintained that the number of so-called "kulak sympathizers" among teachers was not great. However, an article in the newspaper listed numerous crimes that teachers had committed. It divided counter-revolutionary teachers into two groups: those who, by landholdings, were kulaks, and others who sided with them by their actions. One teacher's husband allegedly made the dramatic statement at a village meeting: "Do not surrender your grain because the authorities do not give you anything and give only to the workers. When there is war, kill the workers first."[132] It is astonishing that anyone would make such a bold statement in a public forum, although it reveals some insight into the rationale of the requisition campaign. The teacher herself was suspect because of her marriage to this alleged troublemaker.

The article attests that regional Robos meetings further revealed the true attitudes of some teachers towards collectivization. At one such meeting, a teacher suggested the campaign was entirely unrealistic. Others apparently reported that their colleagues confided to the peasantry that they were opposed to the operation, but, nevertheless, had to publicly support it. Some refrained from taking a leadership role, insisting that the peasantry would not listen to them. They logged hours for "civic political work" without any real commitment to the collectivization campaign. The newspaper labelled this approach "kulak" and demanded the dismissal of these "traitors." The teachers' behaviour was, however, reflective of a sentiment shared by the peasantry and teachers who lived among them and depended upon their support: the grain-requisition campaign threatened to cause severe food shortages in the already impoverished countryside. It is reasonable to assume that some teachers took a skeptical, passive, even, as described in the newspaper, duplicitous approach towards a policy that in Ukraine would contribute to the deaths of millions. In the climate of danger introduced by the SVU trial, such a stance was impermissible.

As if to make the line even more clear, at the same time *Narodnii uchytel* was warning of the nefarious activities of SVU educators and cautioning against counter-revolutionary behaviour by rural teachers, it was lauding the bravery of the activist teacher. It thereby provided a model of normative behaviour for teachers to follow and honoured them for their revolutionary heroism. The Soviet press had taken care in the lead-up to the SVU trial to demonstrate the kulak-peasant origins of Ukrainian nationalism. A series of articles on kulak violence against teachers unambiguously exposed the potential of enemies of Soviet power. The newspaper's message was that it was in the teachers' interest to side with public campaigns such as collectivization. To do otherwise meant risking identification with a vilified enemy and the label of "bourgeois nationalism."

Chief Prosecutor Akhmatov again set the stage. In response to the latest in a series of reported murders of teachers, Akhmatov issued a statement to the press in November 1929. He announced that two teachers, Zadorozhny and Beta, had recently been murdered by kulaks in rural eastern Ukraine. They had purportedly been targeted for their active participation in the collectivization and literacy campaigns (involvement in the latter was also strongly identified with Soviet power). Akhmatov took these murders, as well as other acts of kulak "terrorism" (arson, physical assault, and earlier murders), as evidence that the class struggle in the village was sharpening. The majority of teachers, he emphasized, were "on one side of the barricade, together with the poor and hired farmers."[133] Kulaks saw teachers as mortal enemies because they were Soviet workers, critical leaders in the task of building socialism. He promised to make the prosecution of these murders his direct responsibility and to afford teachers all legal protection to defend them against future attacks.

Reports of other acts of violence committed against teachers soon followed. One teacher informed *Narodnii uchytel* readers that kulaks in the Artemivsk region had murdered two poor peasants in connection with their political work and had forced a teacher in one village to flee her post. In another village, kulaks had staged a smear campaign against a teacher, complaining to educational authorities that she was "conducting anti-pedagogical work versus the students."[134] A district commission found the charges baseless. The Robos district section later concluded that the local village did nothing to protect the teacher and oppose the kulaks. Its findings implied that village authorities were firmly in kulak hands and the teachers stood alone against their influence.[135]

The pedagogical press presented teachers in the most positive light possible, in order to repair their public image as well as serve the broader interests of the state. The press touted teachers as defiant heroes, valiantly carrying out collectivization and the demands of the Five-Year Plan in the face of a threat mounted by what it presented as a small but desperate minority. Consequently, when *Narodnii uchytel* reported that the head of a labour school in the Bila Tserkva region had died from eight bullet wounds and four of his colleagues narrowly escaped a similar fate, it also extolled his positive reputation in the community and among his peers.[136] Another, apparently botched, shooting of a teacher and Komsomol member in the Chernihiv region was explained as "kulak revenge for the teacher's active work."[137] In spite of the increase in attacks, teachers refused to back down from their political work. One teacher in the village of Khorostok (Slavuta district, Shepetivka region) who sustained an attack vowed to continue his work for collectivization and Soviet power. Another group of village teachers had contributed to the full realization of the grain-requisition campaign in spite of pressure from kulaks. In this instance, the head of the village soviet had purportedly succumbed to kulak influence and, instead of explaining the importance of the campaign to the village, had blamed it entirely on the teachers.[138] If true, this tactic suggests just how unpopular the grain seizures were. Given the apparent weakness of local authorities, the state relied very much on teacher leadership in this operation. Thus, it followed a complicated strategy of warning educators about traitors in their midst, but exalting those who stood with Soviet power. In the desperate environment introduced by the collectivization campaign, Ukrainization was a negligible concern for rural teachers. They were simply trying to stay alive.

Chapter Eleven

Children Corrupted and Exalted

The GPU, under the direction of the party, undertook the most visible action against prominent educators, including teachers, and sent a signal to the education profession and the wider public about the dangers arising from Ukrainization to the schoolhouse and children. The teachers' union responded to this signal with a condemnation of hidden class enemies in its ranks, calls for energetic participation in Soviet economic and political campaigns, and evaluations and purges of union members. However, the Communist Party entrusted primary responsibility for daily surveillance of educational activity and children to the Komsomol and the Young Pioneers.

For all their problems, these organizations were considered by the KP(b)U more immediately reliable than Robos or the Narkomos administration. Because of their close interaction with schools and younger children, the Young Pioneers are the focus of this chapter. The themes of vigilance, jeopardy, and heroic sacrifice also emerge from a reading of archival material and press reports on the Young Pioneers. However, as a result of the Young Pioneers' political status and reputation as a non-Ukrainized organization, the history of the Communist children's movement in this era suggests a heightened tension. Should Ukrainization continue in the Young Pioneers at all? Were the Young Pioneers the correct organization to oversee the contradictory policies of expansion and restraint? Furthermore, an understanding of the Young Pioneer role at this time provides perspective into Ukrainian primary schools in the 1930s, an era for which the Narkomos archival record is limited, and it returns children to the centre of discussion as objects of political concern. It is the fate of children and youth, as the preceding chapters have argued, that played a critical role in debates over education. In this context, teachers were important insofar as their actions had primary bearing on children's development.

Although Young Pioneers were to safeguard and push Stalin's revolution among children, Komsomol leaders continued to insist that the school remain the primary institution responsible for cultivating the attitudes of children. Schools embraced a far greater population than Young Pioneer units, starting at an earlier age and for a longer period of time. The Young Pioneers could not exist without the school, detachments were tied to particular schools, and Young Pioneer activity ideally worked in concert with the initial agenda schools set. Units would supplement, accentuate, and redirect. As a political organization in union with the Communist Party, the Young Pioneers had to observe stricter ideological accountability in the context of Stalin's revolution from above. They led the campaign for the political and economic marginalization of kulaks and forced kulak children from their ranks. Schools engaged rural realities; Young Pioneers sought a radical break. Both approaches were necessary if revolutionary sensibilities were to spread, yet remain ideologically true.

A principal issue of the early 1930s was the question of enforcing the mandatory enrolment of children. The issue of mandatory enrolment, including kulak children, was intimately tied to Ukrainization because it promised increased opportunity for Ukrainian-language schooling at the same time it suggested potential for "counter-revolutionary," nationalist sabotage. The Young Pioneers were on the front line to protect children from the latter. The Komsomol leadership, however, still found Pioneer vigilance lacking. Reports listed the emergence of anti-Soviet and nationalist groups in specific schools as the overall number of schools expanded. The reports suggest that the Komsomol saw its influence over children as fragile. Whether or not any formal groups existed, children believed that anti-Soviet sentiment and action existed. The Komsomol called on Young Pioneer units to expose such sentiment and break apart any attempt to cover up what Soviet authorities conceptualized as near-criminal behaviour. The Komsomol construed the observations and songs uttered by children, who may or may not have been aware of the context or understood the content of what they said or repeated, as expressions of an organized plot versus Soviet power. The Komsomol understood childhood as a form of junior adulthood, with children capable of making moral choices. Paradoxically, enemies could influence children because of their naïveté, but children were still accountable for their own actions. The Young Pioneers had to do more to ensure that children's activities remained squarely focused on fulfillment of the First Five-Year Plan, that children's loyalties were consolidated by deeds.

A properly directed Soviet schoolhouse was still the solution. For, as much as teachers and the Narkomos apparat were politically inferior to the Komsomol and the Young Pioneers, teachers working under the direction of Narkomos were still the primary educators of children. Their instruction retained inherent power as a result. The Komsomol tasked Narkomos with training leaders for the Young Pioneers and producing material for Young Pioneer activities. Young Pioneer units should not err like schools, but the same governmental organ was responsible for administering the content of separate but linked educational agendas. Their fates were tied. As we shall see in chapter 12, schools reoriented their educational agendas during the cultural revolution to place an even greater emphasis on applied knowledge ("polytechnization"), directed towards children's participation in the fulfillment of the First Five-Year Plan. In a sense, schools were supposed to act like Young Pioneer units, and the clear responsibility of the Young Pioneers was to assist schools in this effort. But schools still defined the educational mission in the classroom and potentially could dispatch greater numbers of "activists" than the Young Pioneers. Teachers continued to play an ad hoc role in a campaign that was imagined as organized, but could not be. Educational goals increasingly privileged urban (and thus established Russophone) schools, but the end result of Young Pioneer coordination with the schools was supposed to be a new rendering of correct, Bolshevik, "internationalist" Ukrainization.

Command of the Young Pioneers continued to be a problem. Ideally, a Komsomol teacher would take on the role of leader of a local Young Pioneer detachment attached to a school. However, Komsomol members trained for this work were scarce, and inexperienced Komsomol members and unaffiliated teachers were required to take charge. Komsomol reports allege that sometimes "class enemies" took advantage of these shortcomings in staff and infiltrated the ranks or exercised a harmful influence. The Komsomol TsK called for a purging of a school's teaching faculty and the proper education of those competent to serve. The Komsomol tie to teachers was viewed as central to the success of the Soviet educational and nationalities policy. Teachers were the subjects of Komsomol criticism, but could also be Komsomol members. These purges (and the stigma attached to a portion of the rural intelligentsia during collectivization) raised the essential question of just who was the good Soviet teacher, Young Pioneer leader, and shepherd of Ukrainization. Who would replace those purged if so few were willing to go to the countryside? (And, as has been suggested, graduates of pedagogical *tekhnikumy* and post-secondary institutes did not know Ukrainian well, were not politically well-versed, or held attitudes inimical to the Soviet regime.) Surveys of teachers and recent Komsomol members were enough to raise concern.

Hope might be found in the youngest. Children became political and economic activists, especially in the countryside, and also became surrogate Ukrainizers as the number of Ukrainian schools continued to grow. As the cultural revolution in education subsided and Narkomos placed greater emphasis on instruction in formal knowledge, this shift promised the state, party, and Komsomol greater control over what was taught in the classroom. The problem was that the Young Pioneer units needed to reinforce this oversight over schools, but continued to operate in Russian when the school they were linked to used Ukrainian. In the aftermath of the SVU affair, the Young Pioneers seemed ill-equipped to undertake the charge of securing Bolshevik Ukrainization.

The "Great Turn" in rural Ukraine unleashed forces of resistance that reportedly turned against Young Pioneer activists who dutifully served in campaigns for collectivization, dekulakization, and public literacy, even as they might have remained apathetic about Ukrainization. The Komsomol and Soviet press heroicized these children in a manner similar to their heroicization of activist teachers, but their applause had even greater significance because of the very vulnerability of children. Child activists represented an unadulterated revolutionary spirit; their injury or death were more tragic. Komsomol reports labelled the children's assailants as kulaks, class enemies, and sometimes unambiguously as nationalists; in the context of early 1930s Ukraine, when kulaks and intellectual class enemies were linked to Ukrainian nationalism, the charge was often implicit. Either way, in the Ukrainophone countryside, Young Pioneer activity was an expression of the direction of Soviet education begun in the cultural revolution, and an element of Bolshevik Ukrainization; Young Pioneers sought to demonstrate their relevance, to definitively prove that they won the battle for children's loyalty against other alleged competitors, including a supposed nationalist camp. The Komsomol TsK harshly condemned teachers who undermined the efforts of the Young Pioneers and local Narkomos, Robos, and Komsomol units who failed to protect them. A rash of suicides of Young Pioneers in rural localities suggested a weakness in one of the basic premises of Ukrainization: it would lead to firmer establishment of Soviet power in the countryside. The Komsomol TsK equated reports of suicide with near murder. The Young Pioneers, as the most basic expressions of Soviet power in the village, were exposed. Children's loyalties would mean little if their efforts were threatened, constrained, and extinguished.

A Threat Identified

By 1930, as Viktor Prylutsky has demonstrated, Komsomol concerns regarding hostile threats to the organization's authority grew more defined, and Komsomol leadership blamed the lack of vigilance by individual cells for the reported rise in the influence of nationalist and other counter-revolutionary forces among the Young Pioneers.[1] According to a November 1930 meeting of children's workers in the Donbas, "In places among the Pioneers there are noticeable instances of a class-enemy influence (kulaks, sects) to which Young Pioneer organizations are not giving a necessary retort."[2] It reported that "opportunistic elements within the Komsomol" undermined the organization of a campaign to increase production of coal, and this failure had a negative effect on children's view of Komsomol authority. Most Komsomol and party organizations (at every level) had neglected work among children, and, consequently, Young Pioneer detachments became detached from Komsomol work, real life, and the state's economic goals. Part of the problem, the delegates to the meeting believed, was that much of the current leadership of Young Pioneer detachments in the Donbas was drawn from civil servants, not workers, and Komsomol and party oversight of this leadership was weak. One of the Komsomol's principal tasks was "to appeal to the key Pioneer detachments, and through them to the children's masses for their participation in the fulfillment of economic-political tasks, especially and most principally in the carrying out of plans in the production of coal in the urgent quarter of the third year of [the] five-year plan." For this to happen, the Komsomol needed to compile new Pioneer literature, issue a children's newspaper directed specifically towards the need of the Donbas, and, most importantly, change the leadership of Komsomol detachments to ensure children's dedication to Soviet aims.

In spite of the concern for development of the Young Pioneers and the Komsomol, then, the school was to remain the most important feature in the lives of children during the "Great Turn." The Donbas meeting insisted that schools "can and must be used as an important force in the struggle of the Donbas Komsomol on the coal front" and criticized the Young Pioneer leaders for neglecting their ties to the school.[3] In 1930 a long Komsomol TsK report on the matter of Communist education argued that "Among all the elements of the system of Communist education in the reconstruction period, the central element must be the school."[4] Schools not only would teach the basic principles of Communism, but would raise children to be the generation that finally establishes Communism. Other forms of educational work, including the Young Pioneer organization, should "deepen, develop, and add to the basic material that the school gives," and the school should unite their activity. Schools embraced the greatest number of children and provided them with the most planned, sustained influence. Ideally, Young Pioneer organizations acted as a supplement and stimulus to the educational activity conducted in the school. They could lead activity that schools found less feasible to lead, due to constraints of time and curricular organization, but they could not exist without schools.

Young Pioneers and the Schools

The ongoing political and economic campaigns of the "Great Turn" had inevitable effects on the school and the Young Pioneer organization. In the countryside, this meant their participation in the struggle for collectivization and dekulakization. A 1930 Komsomol TsK report argued that these campaigns inspired "class enemies" to step up their "struggle for the young generation," to corrupt children with their shameful work.[5] The Komsomol needed to redouble its efforts to strengthen the "Communist upbringing of the children's masses" and require their participation in "socialist construction," including the "liquidation of kulaks as a class." The Komsomol's responsibility was to prepare the Young Pioneers, schoolchildren, and "the unorganized children" for this campaign by raising their class consciousness and vigilance. The project recommended that children assume an active role in conversion of buildings seized from kulaks for use by schools, Young Pioneer clubs, and crèches. City children needed to help detachments and schools in villages by joining Young Pioneer brigades for excursions to areas in the midst of collectivization and sending literature to be discussed by meetings of schoolchildren.

Of central importance was the issue of what to do with the children of kulaks. In regard to membership in the Young Pioneers, the TsK proposed an end to admission of kulak children to Young Pioneer organizations and a purge of those children who were already members but had not participated in "areas of work directed at the liquidation of kulaks as a class and towards a strengthening of the socialist sector in the village." How it was possible for "kulak children" to take a role in "liquidation" of their families is unclear and likely meant little in practice. Children of families designated as "kulak" would find it progressively harder to escape this label, and Young Pioneers leaders saw little reason to retain their membership. What to do about the enrolment of kulak children in schools was more complicated. The TsK project stated that Komsomol and Young Pioneer organizations that argued for the exclusion of these children were wrong. On the contrary, "it was possible to exclude only those children [who] would display an inimical influence on the rest of the children, who cannot be re-educated."[6] The incomplete four-year primary schools needed to accept all children, and, for villages in the midst of collectivization, this type of school was the overwhelming majority. However, the TsK made a qualification in regard to the less numerous, full seven-year schools. In the older concentrations of these schools, children of workers, farm labourers, and poorer and middle-income peasants were to be given priority enrolment, and only if there was space left would schools allow "non-hostile" kulak children into these classes. Lastly, the Komsomol needed to ensure that children from the correct social background were serving in elective leadership positions in schools and the Young Pioneer organization.

The schoolhouse remained, then, the primary institution responsible for shaping children's attitudes and orienting them towards the requirements of the Soviet state. This is not to discount the Young Pioneer role. Even if the membership of Young Pioneer organizations was comparatively small, especially in the countryside, the class war awarded detachments with new meeting houses, heightened their political purpose, and strengthened the leadership of urban units over the village. The Young Pioneers were projections of the Communist Party's authority and needed to maintain a "purer" constituency than the schools, which represented the complexity of the rural population as it was rather than how it might be expected to be. If the party and the Komsomol had any hope of shifting rural attitudes, especially in the context of the violence that accompanied collectivization, then the school had to teach its agenda to as wide a body as possible. The party viewed children's attitudes as more malleable and less prejudicial, and the Soviet state's progressive self-image required it to provide basic services to the entire population, excluding only those whom it believed were dedicated to its downfall.

Schools embraced this mission of educating a wide student body, and the Young Pioneers and Komsomol assumed a supporting role in this drive. In order to operate most effectively, the Komsomol and Young Pioneer organizations needed to be shorn of corruptive influences. A Ukrainian Komsomol TsK proposal written in November 1930 noted that the Komsomol (and Young Pioneers) still was vulnerable to infiltration by "right opportunists" and "class enemies" who sought to undermine the Komsomol's political and educational campaigns. It claimed that Komsomol committees in Kakhovka, Bozhedarivka, and Starobilsk districts and elsewhere "demonstrated a Right-opportunist practice" in their approach to the issue of universal enrolment, and other local committees simply disregarded the political significance of this campaign.[7] The TsK was responding to a November 26, 1930, decision by the KP(b)U TsK regarding the unsatisfactory leadership of the Komsomol of this campaign. Not all children attended school, and attendance by older children was especially unsatisfactory. According to the Komsomol, its subsidiary organizations had not mobilized sufficient numbers to help guarantee enrolment; acquire equipment, buildings, and material help for children of poor peasants; or ensure implementation of party decrees regarding the assignment of teachers and improvements in their qualifications. The Party Control Commission had taken up disciplinary procedures against individual district Komsomol secretaries, and the Komsomol TsK was to review and issue reprimands in the case of those who simply failed to act.

Children as Nationalists

The TsK proposed a number of measures to respond to perceived distortions in its educational mission. It ordered its cultural workers to recruit working youths in order to support the Komsomol's campaign for universal enrolment and provide aid to poor children and teachers. In addition to the assignment of additional Komsomol activists and the patronage of individual schools by Komsomol cells, the TsK was to send a brigade of eighty people who would not return until completion of the campaign. It warned that "Komsomol deserters from the pedagogical front" could be expelled. Young Pioneer units were to assume a critical role in the campaign, alongside their other educational work (general literacy; maintenance of school buildings, property, and books; support of efficient instruction in the classroom and timely student advancement; and supply of hot breakfasts). The Komsomol was to work together with Narkomos to train local Komsomol committee members (and Young Pioneer leaders) to meet this goal of universal primary instruction. As discussed above, instruction in (and outside) the classroom was fundamentally shifting, and the viability of any efforts towards Ukrainization must be called into question. But achievement of Ukrainization was still connected to the issue of school enrolment. Ukrainizers in Narkomos had called attention to the comparatively lower enrolment of Ukrainian children in schools, especially in the growing workers' districts on the outskirts of the republic's majority cities such as Kyiv, and the low number of full seven-year schools in provincial areas dominated by Ukrainians. A campaign to increase enrolment for the entire child-aged population should have benefited Ukrainization. However, this says little about events in the classroom or the quality of Ukrainian instruction. On one hand, the Komsomol document implied that "class enemies," including Ukrainian "bourgeois nationalists," feared the enrolment campaign because any success of Soviet education would counteract the "nationalist influence," but, on the other hand, expansion invited infiltration. The Komsomol and Young Pioneers assumed the position of watchdogs against this possibility.

As the economic and political campaigns accelerated in Ukraine, Komsomol documents begin to characterize incursions by "the class enemy" in much more specific terms. The Komsomol listed vulnerabilities in Young Pioneer detachments alongside those of specific schools, further reinforcing the linkage between the two. Young Pioneer detachments were responsible for safeguarding schools from such corruption and yet, clearly, were failing to protect their own. A 1931 TsK memorandum summarized the findings and instructions of the eighth and ninth Komsomol congresses to Komsomol district committees and cells regarding leadership of the children's movement. The Komsomol memorandum ordered Young Pioneer organizations to step up their participation in the fulfillment of the Five-Year Plan's production goals by tying unit activity to specific factories and collective farms.[8] This sort of engagement had faltered in the face of reported failings by local Komsomol cells. In the Svatove district (Kupiansk region), to give a sense of relative membership, there were 2,600 Young Pioneers and 30 Komsomol members. Several of the latter were semi-literate and politically uninformed, according to the findings of the congresses. The shortage of skilled Komsomol talent was such that the head of the Dzerzhinsky Boarding School in Zaporizhzhia found it impossible to find Komsomol members to lead Young Pioneer detachments for the school.

The memorandum reported that children in some schools revealed "hostile class sentiment," and cited numerous examples. In the Romny district, in the village of Perekopivka, children reportedly declared that "grain procurements have to be fulfilled in order to send [them] to the 'katsapy' [a derogatory term for Russians] in Moscow."[9] In the city of Kremenchuh, children in Labour School No. 1 had organized a "free Cossack community [*kazachestvo*]" and "declared war" on other groups in the school. In this school and the railroad school, children proclaimed the slogan

"Long live the Soviets, Long live the Vipers [*hady*]." Students in Labour School No. 6 repeated the following anecdote: "After the five-year plan a portrait of Lenin, Stalin's directives, and a worker's skeleton will be left." At the instigation of one teacher, students staged a strike to protest the school's shortages of firewood. The Kremenchuh City Komsomol Committee raised concern about these reported incidents, but did not decisively discipline those responsible or strengthen its leadership over Young Pioneer units that might have acted to stem the schoolchildren's conduct. In short, the Kremenchuh Komsomol was guilty of "insufficiently educating the masses of children in the individual interests of the class enemy."

If these reports are to be believed, children undergoing the trauma of grain requisitions expressed their opposition to the campaign in nationalist terms, blaming their families' suffering on Russians. The memorandum's mention of the formation of a "Free Cossack Community" is curious. The children allegedly invoked Ukrainian historical and political tradition to structure their resistance to Soviet policy. There is no further mention in the report of how children understood this Cossack community, and it seems at least likely that teachers were involved in its creation. Regardless, for delegates to the Komsomol congresses, the report must have reminded them about the past threats of the Ukrainian civil war, when Ukrainian nationalists and peasant bands formed "Cossack hosts" to oppose Soviet power or defend local interests. Whether or not schoolchildren understood and embraced a nationalist-inflected agenda (and, clearly, one was not always expressed here), for Soviet authorities, it perhaps mattered less. The children in Kremenchuh and elsewhere viewed Soviet power as alien and harmful.

Komsomol reports were not limited to relaying alleged counter-revolutionary statements and loosely articulated sentiment, but also exposed more discernible hostile groups and actions, including among Young Pioneer detachments. The central Komsomol leadership accused Young Pioneer units in some cases of failing to rebuff these groups. A 1931 report on the children's movement in Ukraine, by the head of the propaganda department of the Ukrainian Komsomol TsK, held that the "class enemy" was not just engaging in rumour and slander, but also "by various means incites stratums of children not only to anti-Soviet agitation against collective farms, grain collections, and so on, but also for the creation of a counter-revolutionary subsidiary children's group and anti-Soviet action by children."[10] In the village of Novoiehorivka (Bashtanka district, Mykolaiv region), children under the reported influence of kulaks allegedly diluted material in the collective farm shed on multiple occasions. The report claimed that kulaks, priests, and other religious activists sought to disorganize Young Pioneer detachments. Rumours spread in another village in the same district, Marianivka, that a war would start soon and all Young Pioneers would be hung by their red kerchiefs.[11] As a result, 90 per cent of the Young Pioneers announced they were quitting, and only after local leaders explained to the contrary at length did the majority of them return to the Young Pioneers. Some teachers and children "are introducing a class-hostile influence and attitude in the schools" in Kharkiv, Poltava, Kyiv, Zaporizhzhia, and Romen. Often, the report claimed, these anti-Soviet attitudes took on explicitly nationalist forms: "anti-Semitism, Ukrainian national chauvinism, Jewish nationalism." It cited the apparent appearance of two groups as examples: Za nenku Ukrainu (For Mother Ukraine), allegedly operating in the Kyiv area under the patronage of teachers tied to the SVU,[12] and Hashomer Hatzair (Youth Guard), supported by Jewish activists in Kremenchuh.[13] It seems unlikely that these groups existed in any formal sense, but the Komsomol was clearly worried that its hold over youth sentiment was tenuous, and, if the report on Marianivka is to be believed, children thought organized anti-Soviet action was a possibility in the countryside, even if not committed by them.

Recasting the Young Pioneers

In general, the Komsomol argued that Young Pioneers reacted heroically when confronted with challenges to their, or general Soviet, authority, but this was not the universal reaction. The propaganda department's report claimed that "there are quite a few vivid examples of children selflessly, heroically fighting against kulak excursions, in defence of collective farmers and in the defence of schools, Soviet teachers, and children who exemplify high ideological-class-proletarian firmness."[14] The Young Pioneers spoke out against the spread of anti-Soviet songs among children and kulak "sabotage" in the schools. Yet, the report was still critical of the failure of individual units to react, especially to instances of "chauvinism" (nationalism) among children: "There are facts regarding a cover-up of instances of national-hostile unit leaders [*vatazhky*] and pedagogues, fearing scandal [*pohovir*] in school or punishment." Young Pioneers themselves displayed anti-Soviet, nationalist attitudes, criticizing food shortages, retelling anti-Soviet anecdotes, and singing jeering songs. The connection between anger over the grain requisition and nationalist outrage was not always plain, but, clearly, within the context of the recent SVU show trial, the Komsomol could blame "chauvinist attitudes" for expressions of discontent. Conspiracy provided a convenient pretext for disciplining authentic disquiet.

Whether it was taking up the charge of Ukrainization in response to the supposed nationalist threat or leading collectivization and dekulakization, Young Pioneers needed to redouble their efforts. A June 1931 resolution by the republican party's leadership, the Orgbiuro TsK KP(b)U, found that although the Young Pioneer organization had increased its efforts to coordinate its activity with state organs and workers after the beginning of the Five-Year Plan, shortcomings remained. Some Young Pioneer units "did not give a decisive retort to appearances of the class enemy."[15] In schools in Poltava, Kharkiv, Kamianets, and elsewhere, Young Pioneer units delayed in

Young Pioneer girls conducting a public reading of Ukrainian-language newspapers in the field camp of the Taras Shevchenko Collective Farm, then in the Kharkiv oblast, 1933. Courtesy TsDKFFAU.

dealing with "setbacks in the schools." Although Young Pioneer membership had grown considerably in Ukraine, from 405,000 in 1928 to more than 900,000 in 1931, new members were "mechanically drawn" to the ranks, without undergoing political education. They had not fought against "remnants of the old way of life" or against "hooliganism," and, importantly for an organization that was supposed to be still engaged in a deepening of Ukrainization, there had been "an insufficient consideration of international work" among Young Pioneers in the schools. From the party's perspective, this meant these children were susceptible to nationalist influence and had privileged work among co-nationals. The report pointed to the failure of Narkomos and Young Pioneers to coordinate their activities. Although the real influence of the Young Pioneers on any given school might have been small (due to a small or inactive membership), the schoolhouse, in the end, remained the chief concern of the movement and the Komsomol.

The irony was that the party now assigned the commissariat most responsible for failings in the schoolhouse with the task of training new staff for the Young Pioneers. Narkomos was to prepare and expand courses for this staff, sponsor scholarly study of Young Pioneer work, and ensure that children's literature, consumed by Young Pioneer members, was oriented towards technological know-how and class struggle. Clearly, the party believed that progress in the children's movement would positively influence the classroom, and Narkomos could still make the best use of children activists. What the Young Pioneers offered, more than any local Narkomos organ, was grassroots pressure for the fulfillment of the party's priorities, and, at least in the early 1930s, the party still trusted central Narkomos officials to appropriately deputize these young activists.

A persistent issue of concern for the party, Komsomol, and Narkomos remained a strengthening of general education through the above-cited issue of universal enrolment and the polytechnization of schools. An April 1931 decree from the First Control Plenum of the TsB KDR (Central Bureau of the Communist Children's Movement) under the Ukrainian Komsomol TsK cited a report given at the meeting on the tasks of the new school year.[16] In the decree, the tie between the government's political needs and primary schooling was made explicit. Narkomos would not just prioritize space in the older concentrations of seven-year schools for workers, but it also specified a proportional allotment for the child-aged population. The TsB KDR ordered upper grades "in the city, industrial districts, and districts of compact collectivization" to take in 100 per cent of graduates of four-year schools. For the remainder of the republic, the proportion was set at 70 per cent. Narkomos officials needed to complete expansion of the republic's specialized schools, the FZU and ShKM (school for the Collective Farm Youth), to full seven-year schools and ensure that these schools offered "productive instruction" for an overwhelming majority of their students. Ordinary schools were to offer "instruction in work for no less than 50 per cent of pupils of the I concentration [first through fourth grades] in the cities and 30 per cent in the villages." These percentages, of course, represent an ideal that was impossible for schools to reproduce precisely. But a number of conclusions can be drawn.

The Komsomol was concerned first and foremost with enrolment in areas of greatest importance to the economy of the Five-Year Plan. It saw the FZU school and ShKM as models for the integration of applied labour instruction (polytechnization), and believed that all levels of primary school needed to orient their teaching in this manner and, importantly, that the Young Pioneers had to ensure this approach. Young Pioneer-led excursions to major industrial centres, like Kharkiv, Stalino, and Dniprobud (the huge dam project on the Dnipro River), would allow urban and rural students alike to prize work in such enterprises.[17] Through the support of Young Pioneer organizations, children were reported to have played a significant part in the polytechnization of schools and the enlistment of absentee children for class.[18] District conferences of schoolchildren were held in February 1931 to discuss ways to push polytechnization of schools, with Young Pioneer patronage.[19] In the context of Ukrainization, such efforts privileged the instruction (and enrolment) of Russian-speaking urban children, but it also required children from all parts of the republic to reconsider their association with one another and participate in the modernization of Ukrainian culture.

The full enrolment of children was an ambitious vision of embracing all children and ensuring their proper Soviet upbringing. In a way, the new methodology embraced by Narkomos in the early 1930s was a continuation of the objective of progressive pedagogy, the training of a self-conscious "builder of socialism," but its lessons were no longer derived from an assessment of a child's individual talent. The state's aspiration was greater control over school-aged children and accountability for their development and political orientation. Full enrolment offered a means of ensuring command, but the requirement that teachers lead classrooms to participate in political campaigns, especially in the countryside, required spontaneity on the parts of the children and teacher. The objective of ordered and directed primary schooling fractured against the reality of a society under stress. It is in this context that it is necessary to understand Ukrainization's continuation in the school and its intersection with the pedagogical aims of the Soviet state in Ukraine.

The Young Pioneers were supposed to counteract any corrosion of education, but its own historical weakness in rural areas worked against it. A document on purges in district Komsomol organizations in the Odesa and Dnipropetrovsk oblasts (territories) held in November 1932 maintained that entire Young Pioneer units had disappeared in the Velyka Lepetykha district (then in the Dnipropetrovsk oblast).[20] In the whole district, there were only five Young Pioneers. In other districts, Young Pioneer units existed only on paper or non-party teachers led them. Komsomol organizations reportedly paid little heed to the children's affairs and the need to employ Young Pioneer units in the grain-requisition campaign. If Komsomol members led Young Pioneer organizations, they gained their positions "by chance" and were "generally untalented," understanding little about their responsibilities or their importance. "Hostile" class elements reportedly had stepped in to fill the gap of this Komsomol inactivity, and had exercised their influence on children's views. A separate report from the Solone district (Dnipropetrovsk oblast) to the Ukrainian Komsomol TsK concluded it could find evidence of operating Young Pioneer groups in three of the district's nineteen schools and that it had no comprehensive information on the makeup of Young Pioneer leadership.[21] A purge of the existing Young Pioneer organizations revealed "foreign" elements, "Mazhura, Slastin and others who caused this chaotic situation of the Young Pioneer organization." The report blamed the district Komsomol for entrusting Young Pioneer work to "non-party, untested teachers" and for failing to do anything to monitor the status of Young Pioneer units.

The Pioneers as Surrogate Instructors

The Komsomol and the party blamed teachers for a whole series of political errors in their work with children. Although the Orgbiuro TsK KP(b)U had found in June 1931 that there had been a "turn of the overwhelming majority of teachers" towards children's participation in the economic plans of the Five-Year Plan, "[as] a consequence of the sharpening of the class struggle, a definite group of teachers has and is actively exerting a hostile influence on the children."[22] It called for Robos and the Komsomol to strengthen the political education of teachers, to enlist teachers for aid to Young Pioneer organizations, and to purge their ranks. The concern was not just the reported hostility of individual teachers, but their non-participation in the class struggle. The Komsomol was tied to the fate of teachers because of their mutual charge over children, the possible appointment of teachers to positions of leadership over the Young Pioneers, and the common interest in the fate of primary-school graduates. But young schoolteachers were also formal Komsomol members. Ideally, it would be Komsomol (and party) teachers who would assume responsibility for the classroom and the activities outside of it, such as the Young Pioneers. Thus, although the party ordered purges of teachers, purges of the Komsomol organization affected teachers as well. Teachers were the external targets of Komsomol outrage, but were also were internal objects of the Komsomol's own political accounting.

The purging of Komsomol teachers raises the important question of who was a good Soviet teacher. The November 1932 purge of Komsomol organizations in the Odesa and Dnipropetrovsk territories offers some important instruction in how Komsomol members were purged. District purge committees focused on teachers who had not been active in the state's economic campaigns or maintained an association with those of an "alien" class background. In the village of Novohryhorivske (then in the Velyka Lepetykha district), the local cell purged a teacher who had reportedly refused to take part in the grain-procurement campaign, had disassociated herself from the Komsomol, and had married the son of a kulak.[23] The purge report identified other teachers in the two territories whom local cells had purged and it now identified as class enemies: Petliurists (Ukrainian nationalists), kulaks, children of clergy, former White Army officers, etc. It concluded that the political level of teachers who were part of the Velyka Lepetykha district organization was "low," and that teachers in general worked independently of their obligations to the Komsomol. In the Snihurivka district (Odesa oblast), the report labelled the teacher Meshkova a "corrupted person" who hosted evening parties, shirking her duties towards children and in the grain-requisition campaign. Not surprisingly, there were even more "enemies" among non-Komsomol young teachers and the rural intelligentsia generally. Although the report insisted that the "overwhelming majority of people [in the villages] are socially close to us," political inactivity plagued even those members of the rural intelligentsia who should have been predisposed to aid Soviet authorities.

The Komsomol's task was to convert rural intellectuals to the leadership of the Komsomol cell. But, as the final summary for this report noted, Komsomol cells had been thoroughly gutted by the purge. The percentage of members purged in local cells reached as high as 38 per cent in the case of the Vasylkivka district (Dnipropetrovsk oblast); this proportion could be considered even higher because more than 200 members on the books were no longer considered active members of the Komsomol (they had left the district and avoided the purge).[24] From the perspective of the report, of course, the Komsomol emerged from the purges stronger, but, clearly, cells viewed it as necessary to sever critical connections to members of the rural intelligentsia, whom the report cast as a whole with an aura of suspicion. It is difficult to see how the Komsomol's authority over teachers and the schoolhouse, which in the Ukrainian village was never great, increased in the immediate term.

Where was the new Soviet teacher who would replace the pre-revolutionary Ukrainian intelligentsia whom the SVU affair had eliminated or cowed? Even teachers not identified as "socially alien" were reportedly not up to the demands of the Komsomol and the Soviet state. A numerically smaller Komsomol, even if more disciplined and directed, must have found it hard to influence an intelligentsia now further separated from it. What change, after all, had the Komsomol accomplished in the Ukrainian school in the nearly fifteen years since the revolution? The separate 1932 purge report from Solone district argued that teachers, even if they were not likely to commit counter-revolutionary activity, were still politically unreliable as Komsomol members. There were forty-three Komsomol teachers in total in the district, at least one in every Komsomol cell: "These people do nothing but work in the school and do not take part in political work in the village, in the grain requisition campaign."[25] Some job-hopped from one school to another, keeping undesirable company and neglecting to pay their yearly Komsomol dues. In some villages, no one knew they were Komsomol members. When queried about their political passivity, "they said that it was not possible to tie the tasks in the village to the school, that as teachers they could not be useful to political campaigns in the village." The report blamed this error on the influence of "foreign elements." Most were not satisfactorily versed in the political knowledge essential to every Komsomol member, especially to those responsible for teaching children. They knew nothing about the history of the Komsomol or party, and revealed a fundamental ignorance of party leadership in Ukraine and outside.

> To the questions we posed: "What is the party?" "What is Soviet power?" "Who is Stalin?" "Who is Skrypnyk?" "Who is Kosior?" and also to a question about who is in charge of the district and a series of other questions prompted from the masses of the kolkhoz members, the Komsomol teachers did not know [the response].[26]

Perhaps equally important regarding their status as educators, the teachers could not explain the difference between the Soviet and tsarist schools. The majority of these Komsomol members joined the organization from 1928 to 1930. In other words, if they were not old Bolsheviks, they were certainly Soviet teachers who joined the Komsomol when the GPU was targeting their professional predecessors, the pre-revolutionary Ukrainian intelligentsia. Yet, they saw their role as fundamentally the same as that of those recently disgraced or worse.

The responsibilities of the Soviet teacher were various. In the village, the primary site of these purges, participation in the grain-requisition campaign was key, as this repeated charge against fallen teachers attests. But teachers also had a privileged charge over children, and the Solone report makes plain that the Komsomol expected teacher-Komsomolites to use this role to extract intelligence from the hearsay of kulak students, to uncover hiding places for stolen grain, and to expose "wreckers" in the village: "While re-educating the family through children, children-pupils came to us during the purge and spoke a lot about kulaks in the village and the tie between them and separate Komsomol members."[27] Teachers could encourage such testimony, but children assumed the responsibility themselves of acting as the vanguard of the Soviet state in conditions of "class hostility."

In the end, this was the principal preoccupation of the school and the Komsomol/Young Pioneers in Ukraine in the early 1930s. As the preceding discussion makes clear, schools emphasized a connection between lessons and the classroom and activism outside the school. This approach built upon an orientation of the progressive pedagogy of the 1920s, but Narkomos no longer emphasized a concern about the children's place in compiling the content of curriculum and structuring lesson plans according to children's own interests and talents. It had been an essential truth for Narkomos that children would innately be more intrigued by the study of the environment surrounding them. Now, Narkomos would require children to go beyond the study of the familiar and serve the state through applied learning in a more directed way. In the countryside, this meant children participating in grain requisitions and dekulakization, and the Komsomol and Young

Pioneers would ensure this involvement. The main preoccupation of Soviet education officials in this period was the full enrolment of children in schools, in order for the state to assume charge over a wide population. This campaign was the prelude to a final shift in pedagogy towards a more conservative turn discussed in chapter 12: an increase in the use of textbooks, an emphasis on formal knowledge, and a strengthening of the authority of the teacher in the classroom (with state oversight). As has been argued, full enrolment offered schools the opportunity to increase the number of children exposed to Ukrainian studies. Although the preference given to children of workers proportionally favoured non-Ukrainian children, it also worked to satisfy a long-standing concern of Narkomos Ukrainizers: the enrolment of children of Ukrainian migrants to the city in full seven-year schools and of more "Russified" Ukrainians in schools formally Ukrainized. The requirement for children to participate in the state's economic and political campaigns ideally allowed for the consolidation of what was termed "Bolshevik Ukrainization"; that is, Ukrainization under firm party and Komsomol control and directed towards party priorities. The shift towards a standardization in the teaching of formal knowledge in theory allowed for more accountable instruction in the Ukrainian language and studies.

This discussion has repeatedly emphasized the reported failures of Komsomol and Young Pioneer organizations to react against threats from the "class enemy," enemies whom the party believed formed the mainstays of support for Ukrainian nationalism. Ukrainian nationalism was sometimes specifically blamed for these threats recounted by Komsomol reports of the early 1930s. Yet, at the same time the Komsomol was pointing the finger at corrosive nationalism in 1931, it noted "there was insufficient recruitment of Young Pioneers and schoolchildren for participation in national cultural building."[28] Ukrainization needed to continue, and children had to take a more prominent role, as long as they understood the essence of "Leninist nationalities policy," and the Young Pioneers and schools promoted an international upbringing as a counterbalance to nationalism's alleged pull. As has been argued above, this proposal required a reworking of the character and leadership of the policy. In the context of a discussion of full enrolment of children in schools, the Ukrainian Komsomol TsK and TsB KDR commented in a September 1931 resolution, "in many instances in the Pioneer units work is undertaken in Russian when [instruction] in the school is in Ukrainian."[29] This disjuncture, long an issue in Komsomol reports, could not be allowed to persist. Now, conceptually, it was seen as a restraint on the campaign to strengthen general education, to increase the authority of schools. Similarly, although Young Pioneers had reportedly been instrumental in the fight against illiteracy, "Pioneer organizations were not conscious of the fact that national cultural building is an inalienable part of the whole front of social construction."[30] It is hard to see how any campaign against illiteracy among the Ukrainian-speaking population could be led by an organization that had proven itself averse to the use of the Ukrainian language. The Komsomol reformulated Ukrainization for the Young Pioneers to more explicitly embrace "the struggle for Ukrainian proletarian national culture."[31] The school's curriculum followed the same course, and its ambition could only be strengthened by a definitive Young Pioneer transformation. Young Pioneer acceptance of work in Ukrainian would allow it to translate "proletarian values" to its struggle against illiteracy in, and other public work among, the Ukrainian-speaking population, promoting the party's presence in socially stressed rural areas.

During the midst of the state's campaign to refashion the Ukrainian countryside, reports of physical violence and emotional harassment directed against Young Pioneers and schoolchildren became more numerous. Increased responsibility for implementation of the "Great Turn" brought with it new vulnerabilities. The state and Komsomol used children and youth as agents of revolution, and, as surrogates for the party, the press and the party heroicized their sacrifice. Odesa oblast party officials reported in July 1934 that multiple youths and children had been murdered, attacked, or threatened as part of "insolent terrorist plots against the Komsomol and Young Pioneer guards of the harvest."[32] One Young Pioneer scout was mugged for his work in locating trap doors hiding "stolen" grain; another was threatened with a knife. In the Chernihiv oblast, the Ichnia district Young Pioneer bureau reported to the organization's newspaper, *Na zminu* (For a change) in January 1934 that kulaks had attempted to murder a Young Pioneer girl, Uliana Skakodub, when she was returning home from a meeting of a political studies group. Two kulaks reportedly beat the girl unconscious and threw her down a well. Although the newspaper received Prosecutor Akhmatov's personal assurance that prosecutors would deal with Skakodub's case quickly, Valentyn Bychko, the editor of the newspaper, travelled to the district and confirmed "the complete lack of accountability regarding the political significance of the kulaks' attempted activity against children." [33]

According to the *Na zminu* editor's report to the Ukrainian Komsomol TsK, the district and oblast prosecutors had failed to appreciate the political importance of the case and delayed its prosecution, playing into "the hands of the class enemy." Bychko cited the analogous, undated case of the murder of Nadia Rynda, another Young Pioneer girl and the daughter of a member of the presidium of a village soviet in Pokrovske in the Artemivsk district (Donets oblast). The investigating commission called the murder an act of hooliganism. The kulak whom the editor claimed had arranged for the girl's murder was released, while the boy who shot Rynda was handed over to the commission for juvenile affairs. It was only after *Na zminu* had conducted its own investigation that the district prosecutor took up the case again and revealed the "class character of the murder." Bychko believed that any attempt to minimize such cases of assault against Young Pioneers only emboldened kulaks: "We already have in Ukraine the repeated assault and murders of Young Pioneers by kulaks. There is no feeling of a quick and strict class hatchet, which perceives as its goal to take revenge for active children-Young Pioneers."[34] It mattered less what these "child activists" were actually accomplishing than that their generation accepted the basic premises of the "revolution from above" and participated in it. Individuals in the countryside who were angered by grain requisitions and collectivization and suffered the effects of famine may have attacked Young Pioneers because they were particularly vulnerable representations of Soviet power. Regardless, this is how the central republican press described the assaults and viewed the existing dangers to children.

Clearly, republican authorities did not trust local officials, either to understand the "true nature" of the threat to children or to do anything about it. If class enemies terrorized the lives of children active outside the classroom, in the school, enemy teachers undermined the development of political awareness necessary for the embrace of this activism. They represented a force opposed to the whole of the shifting Soviet pedagogy, and their reappearance in 1934 party and Komsomol communications signified the pressure that teachers faced when republican party officials publicly condemned high-ranking leaders of linguistic Ukrainization, underscored the pre-eminent danger of "local nationalism," and issued the definitive reorientation (if not dissolution) of the Ukrainization campaign. If the press and party documents did not label the Young Pioneers' assailants outside the classroom and corrupters in it as nationalists, the suggestion was implicit in the repeated identification of kulak and intellectual class enemies. In this context, a report from the Kyiv Oblast Party Committee discussed the suicide of a student named Hanna Shumeiko in January 1934. According to an April resolution of the oblast party section, the suicide of the girl in the village of Domantove (Zolontosha district, then in the Kyiv oblast) was the result of "the systematic destruction and persecution of her by the former head of the school, Zhyrnovy (an anti-Soviet person who systematically corrupted the Soviet school and pressured it with criticism and self-criticism) with the indulgence and support of a segment of teachers."[35] The resolution does not detail how such pressure was administered, but makes clear that this was not a singular event, that oblast authorities had received material about similar suicides of children in other districts in the oblast, and that the party section would act severely against anyone responsible for the "longtime cruel treatment of students" that might have precipitated these and other suicides. It clearly believed "enemy teachers" were chiefly responsible, but so were those who allowed such distortions to happen under their watch.

In regard to the Shumeiko case, the Kyiv Oblast Party Committee resolved that the school director's actions represented a wider method of resistance to Soviet rule. The case signified "a new tactic in the struggle with remnants of class-enemy elements," and the failure of Zolontosha District Committee to expose the class element to this crime was "a consequence of the dulling of Bolshevik vigilance and the ignoring of the political value of work among children and the struggle for securing their ideological upbringing."[36] The oblast party committee censured the district organization as a whole and called for the dismissal and criminal prosecution of the head of the district education section, Vlasenko, for his support of class enemies in the schools and cover-up of the affair. The district party committee was to undertake a campaign to purge enemy elements from the ranks of the teachers, and to strengthen party control of the Young Pioneer organization in the school, as well as to hold a meeting of teachers from the district "to deliberate the political findings from the matter of Shumeiko and rebuild their leadership with the schools, in accordance with the demands of the party." It held the district Komsomol and Robos representatives responsible as well for Shumeiko's suicide, for failure to regularly ensure that the political education of children remained in the hands of teachers loyal to the party. In short, the Shumeiko affair was a collective failure of all players responsible for the girl's development: teachers, Narkomos, Robos, the Komsomol, and the party. The implied argument was that the class enemy sought not just to corrupt children, but also, if it failed to turn them, to destroy them. If accountable authorities failed to prevent this, they were, in turn, seeding the downfall of Soviet power in the Ukrainian village, thereby undermining part of the purpose of "Bolshevik" (correct) Ukrainization: the unification of the Ukrainian-speaking, labouring population to the common task of building socialism in the republic.

Given the previous linkage of Ukrainian nationalist activity with class enemy concerns, the suicides provoked by an ideologically alien teacher suggested that the Komsomol and party believed that nationalists might have been at work. Elsewhere, the Komsomol leadership made this connection plain. A 1934 Ukrainian Komsomol TsK study, undertaken to assess the ideological status of Young Pioneer organizations and schools in the aftermath of the party's decision to label "local nationalism" the chief danger to Soviet power, revealed "a network of factions of counter-revolutionary work of nationalists among the mass of children" and cited the comments of alleged nationalist teachers and students.[37] Children blamed the "katsapy" for Ukraine's trouble; Young Pioneers removed their red kerchiefs and offered no protest.

Chapter Twelve

The Path Ahead

In the aftermath of the SVU affair, the KP(b)U and the Ukrainian republican government remained committed to the growth of Ukrainian national culture, including the development of Ukrainian schooling. The party, however, could no longer permit "bourgeois specialists" to carry out the daily administration of the campaign. One way to make Ukrainization more Bolshevik was to link it to the Young Pioneers; another was to tie it to the lives of the working class. The latter strategy meant taking the campaign to urban centres, growing as a result of the First Five-Year Plan's industrialization push. A central tension in this new emphasis was the long-standing prohibition against the "forced" Ukrainization of the working class, a limitation that the party leadership observed with greater vigilance in the early 1930s because of its warnings of nationalist conspiracies seeking to undermine proletarian control. Nevertheless, party authorities believed trusted activists might inspire worker interest in Ukrainian culture and language among workers.

Broad demonstrations of support, however, seemed to matter more than intensive work. In spite of a mandate to increase the profile of Ukrainian culture in the Donbas, a chief centre of economic activity during the First Five-Year Plan, not much progress was made. Robos union members appeared to care little for advancing the agenda of Ukrainization, and children overwhelmingly attended Russian schools in areas where the Ukrainian population was on the rise due to labour migration. Political pressure was needed for even slight change to occur. It was in these areas, where workers were quite literally building socialism, where Ukrainization needed to appear as a dynamic force, as an expression of the new present. However, even more than before, the picture of Ukrainization that emerges from this time is of a plodding, forced effort in predominantly Russian areas. Ukrainization seemed stalled in established cities too, especially as it was linked to the extension and improvement of elementary schooling. The number of wholly converted, full seven-year Ukrainian schools remained small.

In short, Ukrainization was constrained, and Narkomos had reason to question the quality of instruction in the large number of abbreviated primary schools that, on paper, were designated as Ukrainized. Its primary-school inspectors ordered a new round of examinations of teacher knowledge just as the SVU arrests were announced. The pedagogical press argued strongly that rank-and-file teachers' knowledge of Ukrainian was producing a generation that was functionally illiterate in Russian or Ukrainian, implying that these children would be unfit for the demands of socialist citizenship. Teachers reportedly only studied for the exam, without comprehension or conviction in the value of Ukrainization. The exam revealed unsatisfactory knowledge of Ukrainian studies and pedagogy, linking these two concerns in a formal evaluative structure. Inadequate awareness of one suggested failing in the other, as this study has argued. To be a superior pedagogue in a Ukrainian school meant expert knowledge of Ukrainian; to be an effective Ukrainizer required a grasp of "modern" pedagogical method (which, in 1929–30, was still progressive pedagogy). Whether teachers' failings could be explained away seemed less important than the consequence of their unsatisfactory performance: a teaching cadre illiterate in Ukrainian and incapable of training the majority of the republic's children.

The warnings in the pedagogical press regarding the need of teachers to improve their knowledge were dire. They claimed that a high degree of teacher knowledge was all the more critical in the context of the "cultural revolution," especially in the village, where, it was suggested, enemies lurked to distort and redirect Ukrainian culture to their own purposes. Ukrainization at all levels of the education system was a weapon against those who sought to undo Soviet power. The problem was that no one seemed to be suggesting a solution other than those already tried. In fact, funding for Ukrainization was on the decline. Narkomos did not carry through with threatened dismissals for those who did not improve their knowledge, and the party (and even the RSI) placed no pressure on Narkomos to be more forceful. The GPU had arrested prominent Ukrainizers, and the party, state officials, and the pedagogical and popular press warned of the threat of Ukrainian nationalists, but no such campaign was initiated against those who condemned official nationalities policy and Ukrainization. The spectre of terror was fully directed towards excess or perverted Ukrainization, and teachers were reluctant to take up Ukrainization's banner.

Priorities for the state and party organs lay elsewhere by the turn of the decade. Even as Narkomos inspectors and the pedagogical press were vexed about the lack of progress in the Ukrainization of the schools, Narkomos administrators were engaged in the reworking of the entire education system. Prompted by the economic considerations of the First Five-Year Plan, which set production targets for the entire Soviet Union, Skrypnyk conceded that the Ukrainian republic needed to unify its independent education system with that of the Russian republic and the entire Soviet Union. Such a merger was necessary in order to ensure uniform education for all Soviet citizens, including those of the Ukrainian republic, and transportable training for the labour needs of the socialist economy anticipated by the First Five-Year Plan. Some Ukrainian educators argued that no single system could answer all local labour needs, while others suggested that meeting those needs might happen on the basis of the Ukrainian model; that is, the retention (and reproduction) of Ukraine's linkage between the labour school and a two-year vocational school.

Much of the debate centred on which education system offered a "polytechnical" education favoured by all-Union political authorities; that is, a system that struck the correct balance between technical training and a generalized education (with Ukrainian educators insisting they had it right or simply needed to tweak their existing system). An all-Union conference on education confirmed a commitment to unification, however, that set the stage for a later abandonment of Ukrainian particularities and adoption of a modified system closer to the Russian model. This merger signalled a new attention by the party to educational affairs and provided tools for greater intrusion by central political authorities. The all-Union party leadership always had retained this option, but its decisions could now have a more immediate and direct impact.

The reform and standardization of the education system paved the way for a conservative pedagogy and final abandonment of the sort of progressive pedagogy that Ukrainization was supposed to have enabled and benefited from, and that was arguably a more persistent feature of primary schooling in the republic than elsewhere. Ukraine's distancing from progressive schooling underwent several shifts (Narkomos administrators initially required teachers only to make progressive pedagogy more applied), but, ultimately, polemics in the pedagogical press blamed SVU defendants for using progressive pedagogy to confuse pupils, obfuscate a true understanding of Marxism, and disrupt the achievement of academic goals. Skrypnyk vilified advocates of progressive pedagogy (including prominent Ukrainizers). Because of progressive pedagogy's initial incorporation of local and Ukrainian studies and its lack of dependence on scarce Ukrainian textbooks and literature, this rejection was an attack on the form of Ukrainization as it had been practised. Ukrainization had celebrated the local, and the local mattered increasingly less for education.

As the preceding chapter emphasized, party and Komsomol authorities attached high importance to the schoolhouse in the early 1930s, but not fundamentally to its Ukrainization. In the context of the "class war" unleashed by cultural revolution, schools took on an even greater meaning as a space in which to sort the meaning of this conflict (or "counter-revolutionary activity") for a Soviet generation in the midst of it. In terms of methodology, the years 1928 to 1932 were a time of great tumult when teachers struggled to understand what was authoritative and what was not. Narkomos officials questioned and then overturned the favoured instructional approach; the pedagogical press condemned previously touted literature and theorists. On paper, the number of Ukrainian schools continued to grow, exceeding the ethnic proportion of the population. But education officials enrolled record amounts of children into schools already overcrowded and understaffed, giving reason to question the quality of these schools and the reliability of this data.

While Narkomos administrators clearly saw Ukrainization of primary schools as an unfinished matter and expressed concern about its continued shortcomings, in the economic and political environment of the 1930s, they clearly had other priorities. In the extant archival record, it is the Ukrainization of secondary and post-secondary institutions that received principal attention. However, evidence offered by educational-inspection brigades in the Dnipropetrovsk oblast suggest the children's knowledge of literary Ukrainian in primary schools had not advanced and teachers were not adequately prepared to promote an improvement and remained confused about methodological standards during a time of flux. Young, "more Soviet" teachers in Ukrainian villages and provincial towns still lacked comprehensive secondary or post-secondary training and, in the conditions of an horrific 1932–3 famine, struggled to feed themselves on meagre rations and pay.

A February 1933 meeting of the heads of the oblast education sections suggested that a full-scale shift in the understanding of Ukrainization and a new purge of Narkomos were in the offing. Speakers repeatedly reported on the negative consequences of Ukrainization, specifically the "forced Ukrainization" of national minorities (chiefly ethnic Russians) and the policy's exploitation by Ukrainian nationalists. They argued that the liabilities of Ukrainization had caused a whole host of problems: an incomplete conversion to polytechnical instruction, shortcomings in grain requisitions, and a failure to prepare ethnic-Russian cadres. "Bolshevik Ukrainization" was presented as the opposite of these negatives.

Two weeks later, Skrypnyk was dismissed from his post as commissar of education, subject to internal party criticism for his leadership of education and to public condemnation. A plenum of the TsK KP(b)U that met in the aftermath of his suicide also condemned him as a leader of Ukrainian national deviation, and labelled "local Ukrainian nationalism" the main danger to Soviet power in the republic. Volodymyr Zatonsky, the new commissar of education, oversaw a wide-ranging purge of the commissariat, pedagogical institutions, and the teaching ranks. A 1935 publication of the new Narkomos gives a sense of Ukrainization in the aftermath of this shift. It also linked a growth in Ukrainian nationalism to progressive pedagogy and detailed measures to implement polytechnical instruction and to put the education of children in responsible hands, sidestepping the question of the now-tainted training of these "new pedagogues." Most importantly, it also decried the "forced Ukrainization" of ethnic Russians under Skrypnyk, emphasized Narkomos's corrections to this offence, and made clear that the objectives and character of Ukrainization after 1933 were critically different. A snapshot of Ukrainization in 1934 drawn from local archival records for the city of Odesa, where Ukrainization had been significantly tested in the mid-1920s, provides some clues to its new character. Local authorities were still ordering public servants to comply with standards for linguistic Ukrainization. However, funding for this effort was non-existent, and the city council questioned the qualifications of Ukrainian-studies instructors, the political reliability of the literature they used, and the orthography of the language itself. This was "Bolshevik Ukrainization": localized, regulated, and undoubtedly less attractive to teachers, children, and parents.

Ukrainization and the Five-Year Plan

Inevitably, the heightened political language of the Five-Year Plan had an effect on the classroom itself. The Sumy Regional Party Committee informed the KP(b)U Central Committee that a local newspaper, *Serp i molot*, had reported on class struggle among children in the schools. According to the party section, the newspaper had incorrectly emphasized the battle against children of class enemies and had not adequately discussed the principal tasks of the school within the wider environment of class struggle: the strengthening of instruction, party leadership over education, and the organization of self-reliant Young Pioneer organizations to oppose bourgeois infiltration of the schools.[1] The party did not intend the harassment of children, but rather a full-scale redirection of education.[2] The regional section ordered a purge of the newspaper's editorial board and instructed its Agitprop activists to prepare another article explaining party educational policy. It is not surprising, however, that the newspaper made this "error." Broader pedagogical questions took a decidedly inferior place to daily reports of rural class struggle, kulak violence, and orders for proletarian vigilance.

As discussed above, the party rejected the forced Ukrainization of the Russian-speaking population, but Narkomos continued to favour the gradual Ukrainization of the Russified, but ethnic-Ukrainian, proletariat through their children. Without the Ukrainization of the proletariat, Soviet nationalities policy had little meaning in the republic. In the post-SVU environment, in spite of Narkomos's efforts, the campaign hesitated. Of course, the need for the Ukrainization of the proletariat was officially even greater. Clearly, in the party's eyes, the old national elites could not be trusted to administer the republic's scientific and educational

A group of schoolteachers in the village of Huliaipole in the Kyiv oblast, 1934–5. Courtesy TsDKFFAU.

establishments. If Ukrainian national culture was to survive, Narkomos had to situate it firmly in the proletarian camp. The new emphasis on the use of trusted cadres (ideally, party members) meant the circle of qualified Ukrainian-language instructors was still small. Furthermore, with some of the most prominent Ukrainizers purged, the teachers Narkomos relied upon to move the campaign forward grew even more timid. Ukrainization was supposed to be for and by the proletariat. However, the incentives for educators to realize this strategy seemed few, the practical challenges many, and the risks high.

The attack on bourgeois culture and specialists that defined the "cultural revolution" of the Five-Year Plan generally argued for a shift in Ukrainization strategy. The party began to turn its attention to the concerted "cultivation of modernized, industrial Ukrainian culture."[3] On 23 December 1929, seven months after the first SVU arrest, the KP(b)U published a decree on the state of Ukrainization in the critical industrial centres. It emphasized that the proletariat needed to take a leading role in the building of Ukrainian national culture, but recognized that the government was still battling with "Russophilic talk (*balachka*)" and that the proletariat were indifferent.[4] While the party had some success in the general development of Ukrainian culture, it conceded that lower-party organization in the industrial regions of the Donbas had not responded to the party's calls for an intensification of the campaign, and work remained sporadic. The decrees of the party had proven insufficient, proper checks on implementation did not exist, and many cadres did not even understand the need for the campaign. It blamed part of the failure on the influence of industrial specialists educated during the pre-revolutionary period: "From here arises not only a negative attitude on the part of a significant part of specialists to Ukrainization, but signs of open Russophilic great-state attitude."[5] The party had not done enough to rebuff these attitudes, which were spreading to the working masses.

Importantly, the KP(b)U held the educational bureaucracy responsible. The tempo of Ukrainization, it reported, was particularly weak among local education sections. While recognizing a shortage of Ukrainian-speaking instructors in the Donbas, it recommended a full-scale review of their numbers in order to properly develop and staff a network of Ukrainian schools. Teachers who did not know Ukrainian would have to be quickly trained. The party also assumed a renewed responsibility to Ukrainize and promote Ukrainian speakers within its own ranks. It ordered regional party organizational sections to each produce thirty workers for Ukrainization in the Donbas, Kryvyi Rih, and Dnipropetrovsk in two months' time.[6] It would have to change attitudes towards Ukrainization fast.

In spite of this bold gesture by the party, it remained ill-equipped to prod these industrial areas into action. In the view of one metalworker, who was part of a delegation from the Donbas that met with Skrypnyk, sentiment for Ukrainization in the region was not high among the young. According to him, a group of students from the Kharkiv Agricultural Institute, who had come to the Donbas to evaluate its cultural needs in 1928, informed the local Narkomos section: "The Donbas does not need qualified Ukrainian workers because the Donbas is Russian [*ruskyi*]."[7] The metalworker complained to Skrypnyk that the students had no right to make this determination. Nevertheless, the anecdote's assumption is instructive. These representatives of the new Soviet intelligentsia, who might have been recruited to staff Ukrainian-language schools and propagandize among the unions, collective farmers, or even the party, were doubtful of the program's utility.

Furthermore, attempts to expand a proletarian Ukrainian culture in the Donbas were problematic. A KP(b)U directive had ordered trade unions to organize a month of Ukrainian culture in the Artemivsk, Luhansk, Dnipropetrovsk, and Kryvyi Rih regions for June 1930.[8] It further instructed them to organize brigades of writers to popularize Ukrainian literature and scholarship, award workplaces that organized the best "red corners" on Ukrainian culture, and generally popularize Ukrainian culture. However, one week after the month was supposed to have commenced, little had been accomplished. According to *Narodnii uchytel*, Robos members had been particularly negligent in their responsibility as "the vanguard of the cultural front."[9] When the secretary of the Robos All-Ukrainian Committee was asked what his organization had done for the month, he answered: the entire union was on vacation.

The place of Ukrainian in the eastern Stalino region further illustrates the weakness of Ukrainization in industrial and mining areas, even in spite of a clear influx of ethnic-Ukrainian labourers. The regional executive committee in this region reported that the use of "broken Ukrainian," or language that pretended to be Ukrainian, was commonly used in Soviet institutions. Apparently, local authorities saw little use in studying Ukrainian or promoting its use. In spite of the fact that the worker population was over 30 per cent ethnic Ukrainian, children overwhelmingly attended Russian-language schools in 1930.[10] Of 2,340 Ukrainian children enrolled in school, only 193 studied in the one seven-year Ukrainian school that existed in Stalino. Russian and ethnic-minority schools had even sought to bypass the Narkomos requirement for a separate class in Ukrainian by creating courses in Esperanto.

In mining sites located outside the city, where the ethnic-Ukrainian population constituted a clear majority of the working force, there were no Ukrainian cultural groups and only a smattering of Ukrainian literature available in workers' libraries. In the past year, over 7,000 Komsomol members and 1,200 contractors had come to work in the mines. All of them reportedly spoke Ukrainian, but trade union authorities led cultural work in Russian only. Until fall 1929, there were no Ukrainian-studies courses available to workers throughout the region. Union leaders were either apathetic or openly hostile towards Ukrainization. Only as a result of pressure from Stalino leaders did the local union administration consent to the assignment of Ukrainizers to the region.[11] The challenge for the future, however it was painted, was immense.

The Façade of "Full Ukrainization"

The shortage of Ukrainian schools in Stalino was characteristic of new manufacturing and mining centres in the Donbas. The ethnic-Ukrainian population in this area fluctuated according to the labour demands of expanding industry. It was admittedly more difficult for local authorities to determine the specific educational needs of groups within diverse, growing populations. In more established urban centres, Ukrainization in the schools appeared fine on paper. According to a 1930 report by the Kharkiv regional Narkomos inspector, there were

28 Ukrainian-language schools out of the 63 schools in the city (43.7 per cent) and 488 out of 686 four-year schools in the surrounding districts (85.5 per cent). These figures indicate a slight excess of Ukrainian schools relative to the proportion of the ethnic-Ukrainian population in the city (38.4 per cent) and in the countryside (81.7 per cent).[12] Regional inspectors reported similar successes in formal Ukrainization in Dnipropetrovsk and Chernihiv.[13]

What is surprising is that as late as 1930, inspectors were still reporting on the existence of schools of mixed Ukrainian–Russian instruction.[14] There were ten such schools in the city of Kharkiv, three in the city of Dnipropetrovsk (eleven in the region's countryside), and three in Chernihiv.[15] Although local authorities foresaw the "full Ukrainization" of these schools, the fact that they continued to exist suggests that schools did not have enough qualified Ukrainian speakers to staff all its schools and raises questions about the quality of instruction in the formally Ukrainized schools. If there were competent Ukrainian speakers in surplus Ukrainian schools, why were they not transferred to schools designated for Ukrainization? Why were half-Ukrainized schools needed anyhow if the Narkomos leadership's objective continued to be the formation of monolingual schools comprised entirely of a single ethnicity? In fact, some of the formally Ukrainized schools were schools of mixed instruction. This was especially true for the higher grades. Full seven-year Ukrainian schools were still few in number.

While Skrpynyk boasted that 97.4 per cent of Ukrainian children attended Ukrainian-language school (a figure that must have included Russian-speaking Ukrainians) in 1929–30,[16] Narkomos inspectors recognized that figures regarding full Ukrainization told only part of the truth. The commissariat therefore instituted new perevirky of teachers in the winter of that academic year. Articles in the pedagogical press explained the need for, and requirements of, the examination. Ivan Prysiazhniuk, a contributor to *Narodnii uchytel*, claimed that it was not uncommon to encounter teachers who continued to use the Ukrainian language with Russianisms and that this habit of mixing Ukrainian and Russian was being passed on to the children.[17] The teachers' language was, in some instances, so muddled that children could not understand the lessons. Prysiazhniuk claimed there were instances of local authorities appointing teachers who even deliberately confused children in this manner. He argued some remedy was needed quickly or teachers would continue to "pollute" the Ukrainian language and, significantly, harm the development of the children. They would not be literate in Ukrainian or Russian. News of a coming perevirka again sent teachers into a panic. They scrambled for literature and demanded more detailed instructions. Prysiazhniuk described their desperate, last-minute preparations as behaviour similar to "feeding hounds when they are starving."[18] They did not intend mastery of language, or understand why it was necessary. They simply wanted to survive the process.

Given what has already been discussed about the lack of Ukrainian-language schooling and studies in the Stalino region, it is not surprising that a December 1929 perevirka in this area revealed an utter lack of knowledge of Ukrainian. It disclosed the extent of the ignorance and apathy in detail. Only a minority of the teachers knew anything about Ukrainian culture and history. Even teachers in the higher grades who had some ability in Ukrainian had not read any new writers or engaged in any substantive language study. Even if they had read Ukrainian classics, they did not understand their value and, importantly, failed to provide any Marxist social analysis of these works. The only teachers who purportedly attempted to keep up to date on pedagogy were in the Russian schools.[19] In short, teachers not only had weak Ukrainian skills, but were also ill-equipped to apply any such knowledge to Narkomos's principal goal: the transformation of the school for the building of socialism. Skrypnyk's report that almost all Ukrainian children enrolled in school were attending Ukrainian-language institutions in 1929–30 did not mean that the instruction in the Ukrainized schools had changed greatly. Quantitatively speaking, the Ukrainization of schools was "one of the greatest successes" of the campaign.[20] However, authorities needed to do much more to ensure that these numbers meant anything.

The situation was reportedly no better in Soviet Ukraine's heartland of the Kyiv region. One *Narodnii uchytel* writer, K. Kost, claimed that teachers' understanding of language had declined. Kost reviewed the archive of a tsarist-era higher school (funded by a *zemstvo*, local representative council) and argued that the written work of teachers in this school was superior to that of contemporary teachers: "We are not idealizing the old school, but only underlining that a certain knowledge of grammar (etymology and syntax) was demanded from the teacher. Without this knowledge, a person is not a teacher."[21] He claimed that it was not only Narkomos that required teachers to improve their language skills, but populations served by these teachers. These communities sought punishment for those teachers who continued to "cripple" the Ukrainian language. Kost insisted that teachers needed to recognize their obligations themselves, they had to be "smiths and jewelers" of the word. If they failed in their duty, they would compromise their students' future.

Local authorities sometimes made allowances for shortcomings in the teachers' knowledge. Another *Narodnii uchytel* contributor, Eskiz (pseudonym), claimed that only one teacher formally passed the Ukrainian-language perevirka in the Makariv district (Kyiv region). Most teachers petitioned the examination committee for a postponement of their examination until the spring or summer break; the remainder fell into the lower second or third categories of knowledge.[22] The committee evidently chose either to grant these petitions or "temporarily" place teachers in the above categories and give them the option of repeating the evaluation. Eskiz suggested that the perevirka may have been too demanding. It consisted of written work in Ukrainian literature, an oral quiz in syntax, and dictations. During the oral quizzes, participants were required to talk about the content of some author's work and use proper style and pronunciation. The problem, he maintained, was that teachers rarely received new Soviet literature or a description of the Narkomos program. Narkomos gave them no time to prepare or any indication of the themes that would be covered. It was no wonder, then, that the teachers failed to perform adequately. A postponement in the perevirka for most meant that local authorities recognized the challenges in preparing for the perevirka and had to adjust accordingly.

Another *Narodnii uchytel* article blamed the difficulties teachers encountered in the perevirka on Robos. The author claimed that the problem of Ukrainization was worse in rural schools, but the union had not pressed state publishers to distribute literature across the republic. A "wave of perevirka of Ukrainian studies has swept to distant corners 'blocked by heaps of snow,'" and book deliveries had not broken through to these far-flung locales.[23] Even if teachers managed to get their hands on some literature, it was almost always technical in nature. Literary journals, which reviewed and published the new authors covered in the perevirka, were reportedly impossible to obtain. Although regional education inspectors had promised to organize preparatory courses, they had broken this pledge. Robos officials assumed no accountability themselves. In short, the article concluded, teachers faced "insurmountable difficulties." Ukrainian literacy, according to this understanding, was fundamentally about command of the content and style of new "red" literature, not simply a demonstration of conversational fluency. Teachers had to prove they could participate in the cultural campaigns associated with the Five-Year Plan. The random publications to which rural teachers had access were clearly insufficient.

However, not all in the press were willing to give teachers such latitude. Another correspondent for *Narodnii uchytel*, Samarchenko, reacted to reports of teacher anxiety and complaints with indignation. He questioned why, more than ten years after the revolution, Narkomos still had to raise the question of "Ukrainizing Ukrainian teachers." Ideally, teachers had nothing to fear from a perevirka.

> Teachers should come to the commission in a comradely way and demonstrate that the 'modern teacher' is an unquestionably literate [*pysmenna*] person in regard to Ukrainian studies and that he will not simply cripple [*kalichyty*] the children's language, but rather will raise the language of Ukrainian children to the higher level of a literary language.[24]

Reality, however, was shattering such "rose-coloured dreams." Teachers still did not know Ukrainian well enough and resisted having their knowledge evaluated. Previous perevirky had obviously made little impact.

Samarchenko rejected the notion advanced by Eskiz and others that perevirka commissions were too harsh. Teachers did not have the excuse of not having access to books, he claimed. Those who really wanted to could procure them. At the very least, they should not confuse the literature they had read. Furthermore, their knowledge of basic Ukrainian grammar and syntax was so poor that even the teacher petitions were filled with mistakes. The perevirka was meant to send teachers a signal. However, ultimately, the teachers had to overcome their own apathy. State-run courses in Ukrainian knowledge, Samarchenko implied, could not simply "plant knowledge of Ukrainian studies in the head."[25] Teachers who did not pursue this knowledge themselves had no right to teach in Ukrainian schools. He contended that the "depressed mood" predominant among teachers taking the perevirka would befall Soviet society generally. How could teachers illiterate in Ukrainian advance the cause of socialism in a predominantly Ukrainian-speaking republic? Soviet Ukraine would be the eventual victim of their failings.

In spite of the threat of additional perevirky and even dismissal, Narkomos reports confirm that teachers' Ukrainian knowledge remained poor. The Kryvyi Rih Regional Inspectorate informed Narkomos in 1930 that "schools still do not clearly and intensely undertake lesson[s] in the Ukrainian language."[26] The results of an earlier perevirka found that teachers still made extensive use of slang; 69 passed the examination, 598 failed, 168 did not appear, and 148 were given exemptions. The regional education section did attempt a remedy. District methodological committees organized a total of sixty courses in Ukrainian studies and the state of Ukrainization became a regular subject of discussion in teachers' meetings and in the regional newspaper, *Chervonyi hirnyk* (Red miner). However, a second perevirka in 1929 was delayed. As of the writing of the report in May, authorities had carried out a perevirka only in the city of Kryvyi Rih and in two districts. In the city, 50 per cent of the teachers passed; in the surrounding countryside, only 30 per cent passed. The inspectorate pledged to carry out a perevirka in the districts by the end of the year. However, the continued high failure rate of teachers was alarming. Furthermore, although the inspectorate had promised to expand Ukrainian-language use for children's extracurricular activities, all youth work in the region's principal cities remained in Russian. The chance of dismissal was slight, and few teachers or youth leaders saw real incentive to improve their Ukrainian-language skills.[27] Demonstration of a bare minimum of knowledge provided grounds for a regular delay in an examination and postponement of disciplinary action.

Authorities in Mykolaiv corroborated this picture of the state of Ukrainization in the schools. In April 1930, the Mykolaiv Regional Inspectorate and Robos head sent a letter to teachers in the region. It reported the results of a perevirka held at district teachers' conferences. Only five to ten teachers in each district had met Narkomos's minimum requirement for Ukrainian-language knowledge. Most did not know grammar or orthography well; some were entirely illiterate. If they spoke Ukrainian, they often had mastered only the local peasant dialect.[28] Furthermore, they used archaic expressions in their writing and expressed astonishment that there was anything new in the Ukrainian language, regularly referring to the authority of "[Taras] Shevchenko's language." Regarding Ukrainian studies, they were familiar with only a few names of Ukrainian authors and could repeat excerpts of literature only by rote, without reference to context. Their knowledge of Ukrainian history was similar. They had memorized phrases written by the Ukrainian Marxist historian Matvii Yavorsky, but had little understanding of what they meant. They had ignored kraieznavstvo altogether.

The letter stressed the central role of the Ukrainian language in the Five-Year Plan and called teachers to action. If teachers neglected Ukrainian knowledge, they diminished the influence of Soviet power.

> The matter of Ukrainization has acquired special significance now when the question of a cultural revolution has been broadly posed, [a question] that, in specific conditions of Ukrainian culture, especially in the village, should concern the work of conscious Ukrainian citizens, primarily, of course, the cultural authority in the village – teachers who uphold Ukrainian culture in its essence and in competent work.[29]

Teachers needed to be "armed" with Ukrainian culture for both their pedagogical and public work. Thus, the inspectorate promised to pay special attention to the state of Ukrainization during the course of its regular inspections and threatened Narkomos would "take measures against those who do not achieve the program's minimum." It recommended that teachers form their own study groups for Ukrainian knowledge. In a separate communication to Narkomos, the inspectorate announced it had already enrolled 155 teachers in special courses on Ukrainian studies and promised to hold another perevirka at the end of the academic year.[30] Clearly, it felt the need to demonstrate some sort of progress.

The problem was that the shortcomings educational authorities cited and the solutions they proposed in 1929–30 were little different from those suggested when the Ukrainization campaign began. At the time of the SVU arrests and show trial, few in Narkomos were willing to suggest bold solutions to the vexing problem of Ukrainization, and educators responded to renewed campaigns with as little effort as needed. An April 1929 article in *Narodnii uchytel* on the state of Ukrainization in higher education reveals some of the inherent tensions in the party's nationalities policy at the time of the cultural revolution. It found that many post-secondary administrators took a formal approach to Ukrainization.[31] Professors either did not push Ukrainization or were openly opposed to it.

Students did not understand the policy and some sought to deliberately sabotage it. Education administrators purportedly did little to oppose such "rabble rousers."

It was not enough for educators to rest, content with an improvement in their own language knowledge. They needed to be ever-watchful against "stewing" of groups opposed to Soviet nationalities policy. The article claimed that this danger came from two fronts: Russophilic bureaucrats and the bourgeoisie, who were opposed to Ukrainian culture generally; and Petliurists and kulaks, who sought to co-opt it and incite Ukrainian chauvinism and anti-Semitism. It instructed the post-secondary instructors to see Ukrainization as a call to battle: "He should be an active builder in the construction of a Ukrainian culture in form, but proletarian and internationalist in content."[32]

Martin argues that the SVU show trial established a pattern of "asymmetric terror," where the party framed fighting bourgeois nationalism as a core task and korenizatsiia as a secondary one.[33] Those who resisted Ukrainization did not suffer the same fate as "deviationist" Ukrainizers, in spite of Lazar Kaganovich's attempt to exert greater pressure on them. Although Terry Martin claims that threats of dismissal motivated some higher-education instructors to accept Ukrainization, the above *Narodnii uchytel* report casts doubt on the sincerity or value of their efforts. Certainly, at the primary-school level, teacher avoidance and failure of examinations revealed that resistance was still widespread.

The safest course in 1930 was the principal approach the article in *Narodnii uchytel* had criticized: passivity. Clearly, many post-secondary instructors had already chosen this path. Primary-school teachers were unlikely to turn from their example. Open resistance to Ukrainization invited charges of Russian nationalism; an overzealous embrace raised the flag of Ukrainian nationalism. The warnings associated with Ukrainization stand out in much greater relief than the article's invocation. Few tempted fate by trying to sort out the difference between cultural form and content. It was best to prove one's commitment to Soviet nationalities policy only as much as necessary.

The Subordination of Ukrainian Educational Norms

A fundamental redirection in educational policy would take place in the organization of the Ukrainian system of education. Debate over standardization of educational norms coincided with the commencement of the First Five-Year Plan and presaged a prioritization of all-Union demands over republican interests. Mykola Skrypnyk sanctioned the dismantling of the Ukrainian system largely out of consideration of the VKP(b)'s broad economic goals. This process occurred gradually, overlapping in part with the SVU show trial. Although not directly connected to the educational standardization talks, the SVU affair offered Narkomos an excuse for a redirection once discussion had begun. A consequence of this effort was a framework for increased party control, particularly from the centre, over education. Ultimately, the door was open for a rejection of the progressive pedagogy that Ukrainization was supposed to have enabled.

In October 1928, the subject of centralization of republican education systems assumed centre stage at an All-Ukrainian Teachers' Conference. The head of the conference's commission on unification declared at the outset that he did not believe that standardization was necessary: the Russian and Ukrainian systems of education, the chief competing options, answered the specific needs of each republic, and centralization would "cripple education."[34] Another participant agreed, arguing that the thought of an identical education system throughout the Soviet Union was ridiculous: "It is impossible to put all institutions under one stamp." Much of the debate centred on the meaning of a polytechnical education. The conference attendees criticized the Russian polytechnical school as being too abstract.[35] They defended the link between the Ukrainian labour school and the secondary vocational school. Better coordination between the schools might be needed, but the system enabled children to receive focused vocational training only after they had acquired an education in basic labour ideology at the labour-school level. This system best met the needs of Ukraine's labour-shortage economy and represented a true polytechnical approach.

Discussion at the local level varied. Kyiv regional educational authorities passed a resolution in April 1929 confirming the centralization of the Soviet education system on the basis of the Ukrainian model. It emphasized that the labour school must offer a terminal polytechnical education, but offered little in the way of modifying the current system other than suggesting that an eighth year of primary schooling might be added when economic conditions improved. It even confirmed the continuance of the pre-vocational industrial FZU school and the agrarian ShKM at a level parallel to the labour school's higher grades.

A report by the Odesa Regional Inspectorate indicated considerable debate over the question of centralization in the region. The report claimed that there was a general consensus among the educators for centralization of the education system on the basis of an eight-year school. However, there were a handful of teachers opposed to centralization entirely, as well as those who argued for rigid adherence to the Ukrainian seven-year school and those who wished wholesale replication of the Russian nine-year school.[36] In December 1928, educators confirmed a series of theses on centralization. They insisted on maintenance of the Ukrainian system's nomenclature, a division between social upbringing and vocational education. The labour school, as the basis of this system, was not just a general educational school, but also a "public-political" one, designed to "bring up" (*vykhovaty*) children in the values of socialism. The educators' resolution suggested the labour school had neglected this task, due to an overload of expectations. It thus proposed an additional year of labour-school instruction without an accompanying increase in the school's program.

Skrypnyk argued similarly for centralization based on a reform of the existing Ukrainian system. He had long believed that the republic's vocational secondary schools were too specialized, in spite of his predecessors' insistence on their polytechnical character: "I think that this theory is only a belated attempt at correcting an inopportune theory of monotechnism."[37] He maintained that a compromise between the Ukrainian and Russian systems might be reached if the Ukrainians generalized the curriculum of their vocational secondary school: "Our schools must be vocational-polytechnical. They must dispense knowledge and prepare a worker for a specific qualification, but simultaneously must provide theoretical and practical familiarity with every important field of production."[38] Other republics might then adopt this secondary school.

Skrypnyk linked the task of the centralization of the system of education to the economic priorities of the Five-Year Plan. He stressed that an all-Union scheme for economic coordination required educational unity between the republics. All educational institutions had to be devoted to the common task of training the next generation of labourers. His commissariat had already come under criticism for its failure to produce a large educated workforce.[39] Skrypnyk repeated his commitment to the goal of universal primary schooling and its qualitative improvement, arguing for the replacement of rural four-year schools with seven-year instruction wherever possible. He maintained that the seven-year school offered the best chance of giving the young a comprehensive, labour-oriented education, yet still assuring that they begin "vocational-polytechnical" training by age fifteen in order to participate in the building of socialism in the shortest time frame possible. The demands of industrialization meant that a student's general education in the labour school should not be lengthened. It also could not be shortened. Skrypnyk was sharply critical of the FZU school's recruitment of students who had completed only four grades, and stressed the importance of a complete program of "social upbringing" before any skill training began.[40]

A preliminary step towards unification was the comprehensive reorganization of Narkomos and purge of its apparatus in 1930–1. The Narkomos unit responsible for primary schooling, the Administration for Social Upbringing (Uprsotsvykh), was renamed a "sector" (Sektor sotsvykhu), a change that suggested its integration into a more clearly hierarchical bureaucracy, and the number of inspectors for labour schools under its direct employment was increased to allow for greater oversight. The Narkomos secretariat and collegium were almost entirely replaced and three new deputy commissars of education were appointed by mid-1930:

Vasyl Kuzmenko, Oleksandr Polotsky, and Yevhen Hirchak. Vasyl Marochko and Hillig Götz view this purge as a consequence of the post-SVU climate of political repression (even if was not directly linked to the SVU affair) because Hirchak and others in the new leadership had already been involved with the exposure of "national deviationists" in the late 1920s and could be trusted to clean house.[41] A June 1930 Radnarkom resolution on the Narkomos reorganization made clear that the commissariat needed to ensure that all aspects of education conformed to a "single plan of the cultural revolution." This concern included the "leadership of the implementation of the Ukrainization."[42] The new Narkomos leadership aimed to closely monitor its institutions and prepare for any structural changes required by educational standardization.

The complete centralization of the education systems was not immediate, but, in spite of the public discussion over its possibility and form, the party leadership had already determined it would occur. An all-Union party meeting on education was planned for April 1930 in Moscow, some ten long years after Hryhorii Hrynko defended (and won support for) the Ukrainian system of education at the first meeting in 1920. Although Mykola Skrypnyk and the new RSFSR people's commissar of education, Andrei Bubnov, were scheduled to speak at the meeting, their speeches were cancelled because they had already signed documents setting the stage for a "unified" system of education.[43] When the conference met, it unanimously resolved: "The further existence of different education systems in the union republics cannot now be justified. The specifics of national culture and local conditions must be addressed in a single system of people's education and in a single plan of cultural work for the whole USSR."[44]

The final form of a unified system would not be decided until later. The all-Union party meeting concluded that all schools needed to emphasize a polytechnical approach and ordered Ukrainian vocational schools and the two highest grades of the Russian nine-year school to convert to technical colleges (*tekhnikumy*). In August 1932, the All-Union Central Committee abolished this arrangement and ordered all seven-year schools to convert to ten-year polytechnical schools by the 1932–3 academic year.[45] Union authorities assumed direct control over higher education in the same year. However, scholars widely consider 1930 the end of a separate Ukrainian education system.[46]

The beginning of the 1930s was, then, a time of remarkable confusion for teachers trying to sort out what the new Narkomos expected of them methodologically. The 1929–30 curriculum fundamentally altered the focus of schools. In Russia, an activist pedagogue named Viktor Shulgin had been criticizing schools for their lack of revolutionary zeal. During the midst of the cultural revolution, he became a leading administrator of the RSFSR Commissariat of Education and used his position to exhort teachers to pursue socially useful "projects" with their students, linking activities to factories or collective farms.[47] As Gail Lapidus has written, the party's attempts to mobilize students for work during the Five-Year Plan had already disrupted the work of educational institutions. When Shulgin began to speak of the imminent "withering away" of the school, he was, in fact, offering an "optimistic rationalization of educational chaos."[48]

There has been remarkably little written on Shulgin's influence outside Russia. The Ukrainian Commissariat of Education responded to this pressure from its Russian counterpart by reworking its previous demands for kraieznavstvo production-oriented exercises. On one level, this approach built upon the 1920s experience. Lev Mylovydov, a contributor to the pedagogical journal *Radianska osvita*, noted that the 1929–30 curriculum was similar to the old program in its directives to draw general lessons from local study.[49] Education authorities continued to use progressive language. Skrypnyk stressed that a student needed to acquire "knowledge on his own initiative with his labour and wisdom," but insisted that the Ukrainian Narkomos would not permit the use of child labour by collective farms or factories for labour's sake.[50] He maintained that Ukrainian teachers must always prioritize the pedagogical value of any activity.

However, there was heightened militancy to this brand of methodology that overrode all other concerns. Mylovydov argued that the 1929–30 program placed a new emphasis on direct observation. According to the program, "the school organizes around itself all of society, participates, and gives direction to the life of the district."[51] The program included a whole section of explanatory notes on how to accomplish this task. Skrypnyk argued this sort of activity would train students for leadership.

> Social upbringing, in my opinion, is ideological production, particular to the phase of socialist reconstruction of our country, which has as its task the re-education and upbringing of millions of adults and young generations of labouring humanity to remake and make them capable of the execution of great historical tasks, to have them become a proletarian class before us.[52]

The project method was indoctrination through application. Now, students' activities were linked to concrete tasks: industrialization, collectivization, and class struggle. Although complexes were nominally retained, these themes alone guided instruction.

More research needs to be done on the actual impact of the "project" method at the level of the classroom in Ukraine. Nevertheless, the 1929–30 academic year marked a critical juncture in educational policy. It was at this time that practices that Shulgin had long advocated came to fruition. By 1931, Shulgin's favour among the party leadership was already waning. The commissariats of education did not, however, advocate a return to 1920s progressivism, but rather opted for traditional, subject-oriented methodology, designed to provide students with a set body of knowledge. Although the cultural revolution did not anticipate this turn, Lapidus argues that, in the Russian case:

> By facilitating the short-term economic needs, and by injecting direct, if crude, political criteria into the evaluation of the educational theory and practice, the cultural revolution destroyed the limited autonomy that [the RSFSR] Narkompros had achieved, and its vision of an education that joined social needs to individual development.[53]

Similarly, in Ukraine, Narkomos would exercise stricter control over the field of education. Gone was the complex system's focus on civic instruction through the development of the child's interests and talents.

A survey of pedagogical literature in Ukraine demonstrates this important shift in educational policy during the early 1930s. As already noted the teachers' newspaper *Narodnii uchytel* ceased publication in 1930, having lasted only five years as an advocate of both the complex system and Ukrainization. The largely theoretical journal *Shliakh osvity* was replaced in 1931 by *Komunistychna osvita*, which placed a class understanding of the school's mission at the fore. The journal *Radianska osvita* merged one year later with a new competing journal, *Za politekhnychnu osvitu*, as *Politekhnichna shkola*. These were years of immense flux, and editorial boards were struggling to adapt to a changed environment. But, already by 1930, it was clear that progressive pedagogy, as advocated by non-party theorists and administrators, had been significantly amended.

The SVU show trial helped lend a sense of urgency to the task of educational reform, and the gradual subordination of the Ukrainian system gave authorities powerful tools to control curriculum in the classroom. Skrypnyk explained that Narkomos's chief responsibility now lay in the coordination of methodology, not administrative operations. The existence of "counter-revolutionary ideological saboteurs" in education required new attention.[54] At first, authorities claimed imprisoned SVU members like Durdukivsky had tried to force a return to "formal" instruction in the schools.[55] They had not only tried to implant a nationalist orientation in their students, they had also undermined Soviet pedagogy through an alleged restoration of pre-revolutionary methods of instruction.

By 1932, the pedagogical press targeted the real innovation of 1920s pedagogy: the complex method. One critic, Vasyl Pomahaiba, accused SVU "member" Hryhorii Ivanytsia of intentionally equating the complex method with Marxism in order to confuse teachers.[56] He found numerous counter-revolutionary passages that appeared in the textbooks and pedagogical writings of Ivanytsia and Vasyl

Doha (both arrested as members of SVU). He did not describe specific "nationalist" tracts, but rather the failure of SVU members to acknowledge class struggle and the role of the party. One article edited by Doha, Durdukivsky, and Ivanytsia allegedly excluded the "primary role of the teacher." Of course, progressive pedagogy dictated that the teacher's role was as a facilitator, and Ivanytsia was a leading proponent of exercises favouring child self-activity. In a 1932 report to Robos, Skrypnyk labelled as enemies "all philosophical, idealistic, and theoretical founders of the complex system."[57] The SVU then became a convenient excuse to end such excessive theorizing in pedagogy, as well as teacher and student independence in the schools.

Ukrainian proposals for the standardization of the Soviet education system during the debates of the late 1920s imagined an extension of the heart of Soviet Ukrainian pedagogy: the creation of a new socialist citizen, familiar with all aspects of labour, equipped to learn more, but not locked permanently into any one profession. Centralization, as imposed from above, ultimately meant an end to this progressive zeal. In response to the demands of the party, Narkomos came to stress the importance of discipline in the schools, textbooks, and a traditional hierarchy of institutions.[58] Acquisition of basic knowledge and an emphasis on educational progression superseded pedagogical experimentation. Ukrainization at the primary-school level continued, but remained troubled. The homogenization of education offered reasonable grounds for an adjustment. It demonstrated that power lay in the centre and privileged the transportability of education. Professional advancement would require mastery of the language of the centre: Russian. This reality did not mean the end of Ukrainian schooling, but the beginning of its limitation.

From the perspective of educational policy, then, 1930 was a critical year. The SVU show trial in the spring of 1930 also changed nationalities policy irrevocably. Most importantly, it removed or scared Ukrainization's most committed administrators and suppliers of the "raw material" needed for success. The period following 1930 was a time of an apparently significant expansion of Ukrainian-language schooling. Bohdan Krawchenko labels it the "high point," noting that, by 1932, 87 per cent of general education schools had Ukrainian as their language of instruction and 85 per cent of children enrolled in schools were of Ukrainian nationality.[59] However, as reports of the 1930 perevirky have made clear, additional research needs to be done on the quality of Ukrainian-language instruction and the level of preparation of teachers during this time. Given the chaos provoked by Shulgin's "project method" and the party's abrupt turn against it, teachers were much more concerned with sorting out what teaching method was now permissible than improving their Ukrainian. They would have had few sources to consult. As Krawchenko concedes, a 1931 review of books published between

1928 and 1930 revealed "major ideological errors," and their editorial staffs were purged.[60] In one of its last editions in November 1930, the *Narodnii uchytel* editorial board called for the severe punishment of the manager of its own publishing house for allowing the publication of a "rightist" brochure.[61]

Qualitative Stasis

The archival record for Narkomos in the years that followed 1930 contains no comprehensive files about Ukrainization at the primary-school level. Of preeminent concern for the party during this period were VKP(b) TsK decrees of July and August 1930 ordering universal enrolment of school-aged children.[62] The Ukrainian Commissariat's claim that 98.2 per cent of children aged eight to ten were enrolled during the 1930–1 academic year, compared to 75.2 per cent during 1929–30, seems highly inflated. While the presidium of the VUTsVK declared great success in a September 1931 report, it also acknowledged that not all local authorities had met their targets.[63] Regardless, even if the official figures are somewhat accurate, not enough schools had been built and teachers trained in the intervening time to serve the new students, and students placed in newly "Ukrainized" schools were subject to a poor-quality education. Government statistics may have reflected high Ukrainization, but this meant little more than that schools had been designated as such on paper, and increased numbers of ethnic-Ukrainian students were enrolled in already overcrowded schools.

While it is difficult to accurately gauge the position of Ukrainian-language instruction in primary schools with the extant archival record, it is clear that Narkomos viewed the campaign as incomplete in the early 1930s in spite of statistical success. In March 1930, the Narkomos Collegium addressed the topic "On the Status of Ukrainization in Sotsvykh [Primary] Schools." The minutes of the meeting do not provide insight into what was discussed, but the collegium resolved that, in the absence of available data, Uprsotsvykh (soon to be Sektor sotsvykhu) and Narkomos's main Ukrainization inspector needed to gather material and present a collaborative report in the near future.[64] However, a work plan of the city of Kyiv's education section for the 1931 year made no mention of Ukrainization, instead focusing on targets for universal enrolment of school-age children; requirements for conversion of schools to polytechnical instruction; the integration of Young Pioneers into the school; and promotion of social studies, anti-religious instruction, and an internationalist education. Teachers were not given the same flexibility to create their own instructional plan; the work plan ordered district authorities to maintain oversight with teachers, consult regularly with the Uprsotsvykh, and ensure a "class line" in the schools.[65] A May 1932 instruction from Deputy Commissar of Education

Oleksandr Karpeko to local education sections regarding their educational tasks for the year included brief mention of their duty to "organize and administer the development of Ukrainian proletarian culture, national in form and socialist in content," in a long document dedicated largely to overarching political and methodological concerns.[66] Although the Narkomos Collegium may have worried about progress in Ukrainization, local education officials clearly had more pressing issues to worry about and likely did little in the way of compelling an improvement in Ukrainian instruction at the primary school level, especially when formal targets had been surpassed.

When the existing Narkomos records of the early 1930s mention Ukrainization directly, they reference the campaign in areas outside primary schooling. A series of early 1931 reports from technical colleges, specialized institutes, and the central Narkomos methodological committee show that Narkomos was pressuring secondary and post-secondary instructors to learn Ukrainian quickly and fully Ukrainize instruction.[67] The proceedings of a February 1931 meeting of the Dnipropetrovsk Mining Institute's Testing Commission for the Ukrainian-Language Knowledge suggest that the institute granted some instructors an extension on when they would have to undergo an examination to demonstrate their proficiency in Ukrainian, but not generally to ethnic Ukrainians (as recognized by the commission) and Komsomol and party members.[68] Skrypnyk's Narkomos was clearly interested in the transformation of these higher-level education centres, especially those that offered knowledge and training associated with the achievement of the First Five-Year Plan's industrial goals.[69] These institutions had generally resisted the early demands of Ukrainization, partly due to the absence of Ukrainian technical instructional material and shortages of Ukrainian-speaking instructors, but the expansion of the Ukrainian-language primary schools had little meaning if graduates of these schools subsequently had to pursue an advanced education in a Russophone environment. Symbolically, the Ukrainization of the "commanding heights" of the education system signified a larger shift, and local examination commissions could not give those who might most readily contribute to this move (ethnic Ukrainians) or had to lead it (Komsomol and party members) reason to contribute to a delay.

Although Narkomos reports noted achievements in Ukrainization in the early 1930s, they continued to underscore that significant work remained in educational institutions, even if they did not detail events in primary schools. A July 1932 order from Narkomos Deputy Commissar Oleksandr Karpeko and Ukrainization Inspector Mykhailo Pavlyshyn to all local education sections established the position of an oblast Ukrainization inspector, who would be on the staff of every oblast education section and be paid out of the budget for the state-mandated municipal courses in Ukrainian studies in each oblast centre. The position's payment was to correspond to the payment of an inspector of public (mass) education.[70] In effect, the order was simply confirming the transfer of the position of regional inspector to the oblast level after the dissolution of the *okruha* as an administrative unit in 1932 and its replacement by the larger oblast. However, the instruction also reasserted Narkomos's status as the leading branch of the republic's government responsible for correcting the shortcomings in Ukrainization that clearly remained.

An August 1932 Narkomos report on the status of Ukrainization, compiled in part with the help of local Ukrainization inspectors, conceded that "in spite of the great success in the field of national-cultural construction," many state establishments continued to conduct their public work in Russian. In institutions at every level, there were employees who did not know or study Ukrainian and, perhaps worse, employees who had received certificates in Ukrainian-studies knowledge from a perevirka commission did not speak Ukrainian at work. Many local Ukrainization commissions hardly met, and education sections did not carry out Narkomos instructions regarding the campaign.[71] A September 1932 Narkomos order from Karpeko and Pavlyshyn called on local education sections to organize permanent state courses in Ukrainian studies in each district and oblast centre (with affiliated correspondence courses) and initiate a new press campaign to explain the importance of "building Ukrainian proletarian culture as a component of the construction of socialism" to members of the public who still had not understood the lesson.[72] Primary schools faced a host of challenges in the early 1930s beyond Ukrainization, but, as they struggled to meet them and simultaneously improve the quality of Ukrainian-language instruction, local education sections still must have had trouble in offering them assistance.

In short, the Ukrainization of primary schools in the early 1930s was largely a static process. To the extent that Narkomos officials worked actively for Ukrainization, they directed their attention to other levels and areas of the education system. Narkomos believed that the proportion of Ukrainian primary schools in the republic was equivalent to the ethnic-Ukrainian proportion of the children's population. To repeat, the extant Narkomos records for the 1930s as a whole are sparse and files dedicated wholly to events in primary schools are even fewer.[73] One of the small number of surviving files in the central government archive that directly concerns issues in the classroom regards a survey of schools in the Dnipropetrovsk oblast in March 1933. Brigades, made up of officials from the district party organizations, education sections, and the RSI, who visited primary and secondary schools in the oblast, authored the reports. Their findings suggest there had been little qualitative improvement in knowledge of literary Ukrainian among schoolchildren and teachers were still not qualified or equipped to promote the commissariat's standards. In the Pervozvanivka seven-year school (Zinovievsk district), pupils demonstrated mixed performance in tests in Ukrainian-language knowledge, with only a minority getting a "good" mark at any level. In the fifth grade, 55 per cent of the pupils earned an unsatisfactory grade. The school retained elements of the complex method in their instruction, if they employed any methodology at all, and did little to combat absences in spite of Narkomos's proclamations regarding universal enrolment and polytechnical education.[74] Teachers in the Velykovesele seven-year school (Bradiivka district) had received the program late and did not have enough Ukrainian-language textbooks for all grades. The instructor in the Ukrainian language for the fifth and sixth grades did not use any literature in class because he had little in the way of material. Another teacher, who was teaching the Ukrainian language for the sixth and seventh grades, had no qualifications for this instruction. The inspection brigade blamed uneven pupil performance across the grades on these problems as well as shifts in class attendance.[75]

Schools had trouble teaching any subject, including the Russian language, to the satisfaction of these brigades, but the shortcomings in Ukrainian-language instruction that had persisted from the late 1920s were still clearly present. The economic and political stresses of the early 1930s only exacerbated the material condition of rural teachers and limited the likelihood of any qualitative improvement in Ukrainian instruction. What had changed in the early 1930s was an infusion of younger teachers, trained in Soviet institutions. However, an April 1933 report from a school inspection brigade about the status of young teachers of schools in the Hryshyno district (Donets oblast) details the extreme poverty of teachers in the district. Teachers had received their pay late, if at all, had had reduced flour and milk rations, and worked without textbooks or heat.[76] One teacher from the Vovchansk district (Kharkiv oblast) wrote a letter in March 1933 to Volodymyr Zatonsky, Skrypnyk's successor to the post of commissar of education, complaining of similar hardships and warning that if teachers' poverty persisted, they might leave work entirely "in order to find salvation from hunger."[77] A December 1932 report from the head of the Donbas education section, Vasyl Piven, conceded that education had not been a priority in the Donbas, that industrialization and the struggle for grain had taken precedence, and there had been delays in payment of teachers' salaries. Although the majority of teachers "were heroically overcoming difficulties," some had cried "run to where you can."[78] What is not mentioned in any of these documents is the 1932–3 famine, but its effects on the teaching profession seem plain. Furthermore, even if the teachers had been better off, as a whole they still lacked appropriate training to promote Ukrainian schooling. According to one Narkomos official, in some districts in the Kyiv oblast, 70 per cent to 80 per cent of teachers had completed only a seven-year primary school by 1933, and this low level of training was also true for the young teachers in the Hryshyno district surveyed by the inspection brigade.[79] A January 1933 order from Narkomos to raise the bar on qualifications for the appointment of teachers – for the lower grades of primary schools, only graduates of pedagogical technical colleges or comparable institutions would be eligible – seemed aspirational rather than realistic.[80] New, "more Soviet" teachers had provided no guarantee of advanced qualification or improvement in instruction. The characterization of 1930–3 as the golden age of Ukrainian schooling does not appear apt.

Making a Positive a Negative

The proceedings of the Second All-Ukrainian Meeting of the Heads of Oblast Education Sections, held in Kharkiv, 15 to 18 February 1933, provides critical and rare insight into the state of Ukrainization throughout the republic less than two weeks before Mykola Skrypnyk's dismissal as commissar of education and the KP(b)U's condemnation of his leadership of Ukrainian national culture. What is clear is that members of the Narkomos Collegium (its governing body, directly under Skrypnyk) and oblast leaders were already preparing for a definitive adjustment to Ukrainization in the schools, even if they would not be the ones instituting this shift after a wholescale purge of the commissariat in 1933.[81] Ukrainization of the schools was not a direct topic of concern to the meeting of oblast education sections, but speakers repeatedly reference or suggest matters that concern the campaign. The then-head of Sektor sotsvykhu, Rakhil Barun, set the stage for a discussion of the campaign on Feburary 15, the first day of proceedings, by placing nationalities policy within the context of budgetary concerns. She cited the improper closure of several national-minority schools and groups in the Vinnytsia oblast.[82] In specific, she criticized the closure of the upper grades of a Yiddish school in the Babanka district. She claimed that this decision, justified by local authorities on budgetary grounds (the school needed three more students to rationalize an expenditure of funds for these grades), violated the principle of native-language instruction and argued that oblast sections needed to exercise greater control to ensure that authorities drew up budgets with critical political questions in mind.

The next day, her colleague in the collegium, Deputy Commissar of Education Karpeko, extended this rationale, maintaining that "we can never forget in the formation of our budget ... that we are concerned with the matter of national cultural construction, that we are the people to whom the party has entrusted the entire responsibility to carry out Leninist national policy."[83] Fulfillment of the cultural needs of all national groups, he suggested, should be primary in the consideration of a budget to fund the republic's network of primary schools. In fact, however, "among us there is a gap in supplying the cultural needs of individual national minorities, there is a gap in the implementation of Ukrainization." Karpeko focused in specific on the ethnic-Russian population, conceding that, over the past five years, Narkomos had increased the number of Russian children attending schools, but expressing concern that 9 per cent of Russian children in the UkrSSR still were not able to enrol in Russian-language schools. He stressed that this percentage was higher in parts of the republic, specifically the Kharkiv, Odesa, and Kyiv oblasts (but he noted that the situation was "better" for Russian children in the Donbas, where much of the recent Ukrainization effort had been focused).

Barun and Karpeko made their argument on the grounds of national impartiality. They did not question the existence of any particular Ukrainian school, but rather argued on the basis of well-established Soviet nationalities policy: every national minority group, a category in which they importantly included Russians, had the right to obtain native-language instruction for their children. However, their speeches suggested that Ukrainization that had overreached, and their rhetoric cast a dark shadow on the policy. Karpeko was explicit in his criticism: "we have in the conduct of our school affairs an element of forced Ukrainization, that contradicts party directives, that in no way can be recognized as Bolshevik Ukrainization."[84] Over the next few days, several speakers rose to provide evidence of such "forced Ukrainization." Volodymyr Lobanov, the head of the Vinnytsia Oblast Education Section, using the same phrase, conceded that errors had occurred in the "forced Ukrainization" of some Poles as well as Russians.[85] He provided the most specific anecdotes of such mistakes. For the Polish population, Lobanov argued that shortcomings occurred in areas where the Polish population was not compact enough and resources were scarce; district-level educational authorities placed Polish children in local Ukrainian schools rather than grouping Polish children in boarding schools under the largest seven-year school. However, he suggested the "forced Ukrainization" of Russians was a greater political concern, since the majority of the Russian children were going to Ukrainian schools and, in this fortified border oblast, they were often the sons and daughters of Red Army soldiers.

Other speakers suggested that, somehow, local authorities had failed to correctly account for the present population's needs. Tykhon Vnykov, the Odesa head, conceded that there were not enough Russian schools in the oblast. In the city of Odesa, only 15 per cent (eighteen schools) of the total number of primary schools were Russian when the Russian population was over 40 per cent.[86] Synelov, the Kharkiv head, agreed that education officials had not given enough attention to national-minority concerns because of the absence of an inspector.[87] Russian children in the Kharkiv oblast were reportedly attending schools in lower numbers than Ukrainians, due to this negligence. He acknowledged that, in the city of Zaporizhzhia, the number of Russian groups in schools was dropping and the number of Ukrainian groups was rising, even though the size of the Russian population had evidently not changed. Mixed Russian–Ukrainian schools continued to persist and twenty-one schools were in the midst of Ukrainization. He concluded: "What is this process for? Is the gradual reduction of Russian groups a healthy process or not?" Synelov refrained from offering a definitive judgment, calling for further study, but his question seems rhetorical.

Missing from any of these accounts is a clear description of the size of the Ukrainian population or any attempt to wade into the murky question of Russified Ukrainians or Poles. The phrase "forced Ukrainization" means, of course, that authorities were pressing children into Ukrainian schools against their will, when, in fact, national identities and languages practices were in flux since the 1926 census, and even parents who may have unambiguously considered themselves Russian may have sought out schooling for their children in Ukrainian. Arguing on the grounds of equal national rights, the repeated invocation of the term "forced Ukrainization" tainted the policy by association. Furthermore, the speakers at the meeting appeared much more concerned with the victims of "forced Ukrainization" than those Ukrainians whom the Ukrainization was supposed to assist, but had not. For example, Yurko Kisilov, the assistant head of the Dnipropetrovsk Oblast Education Section, remarked that Ukrainian children were occasionally enrolled in national-minority schools (German and Jewish).[88] According to one district-level official, Ukrainian children learned just as well as Jewish children in Yiddish. Ukrainian children who lived near a German settlement in the Dnipropetrovsk district were enrolled in a German school because the nearest Ukrainian school was twelve to fifteen kilometres away: "they know the German language no worse than the Ukrainian language and were successfully learning in this school." Piven, from the Donets oblast, argued that in the oblast's industrial districts, "Russian children are in Ukrainian schools and Ukrainian children are in Russian [schools]."[89] However, he went on to focus exclusively on the wrong committed on Russian children in Ukrainian schools: "We have facts that Russian children are studying in Ukrainian schools in Stalino, Makiivka, and other districts. In my view, now it is necessary to undertake a deep study of this question and not approach the solution formally."

Assumingly, the oblast officials thought the question of the small number of Ukrainian children enrolled in Russian or other national-minority schools would sort itself out in time. This distinction in rhetoric and the reporting of evidence suggests that already a shift in policy was occurring away from an emphasis on the expansion or value of Ukrainization to a concern that the policy had gone too far. The Ukrainization of schools implied a sense of dynamism and movement that was now stalled. Education officials still attempted to keep the number of Ukrainian schools approximate to the size of the Ukrainian population, but they did not see shortcomings in this effort as grounds for automatic reaction. The cases presented in this meeting were perceived as unremarkable, whereas instances of "forced Ukrainization" called for an immediate response.

A failure to satisfy the needs of national minorities was compromising the full conversion of schools to a polytechnical orientation and, as a consequence, the political and economic campaigns of the Soviet government. Kisilov linked problems in the "construction of polytechnical schools" to "corruption [*perekruchennia*] of nationalities policy."[90] Ilko Profatylov, the Robos VUK representative at the meeting, argued that because not all Russian children were attending Russian polytechnical schools, "we are conceding a whole string of other important political questions in this work."[91] He cited a speech by Skrypnyk to the Narkomos Collegium on February 14, one day before the commencement of the meeting, in which Skrypnyk lauded a graph by the Kyiv Oblast Education Section, highlighting two principal concerns for the section (represented as "curves"): fulfillment of a plan for grain procurement, and success in the polytechnical school. According to Profatylov, Skrypnyk noted that "these two curves nearly merge, that is – where the plan for grain procurement is fully carried out, we have great success in the school." Mykhailo Zhydkoblinov, another speaker from Dnipropetrovsk, criticized the level of "polytechnization," arguing that there continued to be a disconnect in schooling between theoretical instruction and applied work; specifically, instruction in the service of "public-political work."[92] Education, a comprehensive conversion to "true" polytechnical schools, would contribute to political success in the countryside and this was impossible without the "full" enrolment of national-minority children, specifically Russian children. What also seems present here is an anxiety over the displeasure, at least on the part of the Russian population, about shortages in Russian-language schools.

A speech by Pavlo Tytarenko, another representative of the Donets oblast, in the meeting's last session on February 18, is especially revealing regarding the Narkomos understanding of native-language schooling. Tytarenko also criticized the failure of local officials to provide Russians with native-language instruction, insisting that such schooling was a critical policy concern. The complete enrolment of all children, but particularly Russian children, was really a "question for the preparation of socialist cadres, of the development of our national cultural construction."[93] Of course, this had always been true, but Tytarenko's formulation and omission of any mention of the progressive force of Ukrainization suggests an upending of this policy. Ukrainization had been designed to break a Russian and Russophone monopoly of leadership in the republic; now, the training of Russian-language cadres was said to be in jeopardy.

If the school was a site for furthering the aims of the Soviet political and economic goals in 1933, it was also a place where these education officials claimed these objectives could be corrupted. Numerous speakers stood up to argue that weak schools and poorly trained teachers had provided an opportunity for influence of the class enemies to grow. Their charges replicate much of the material already discussed regarding party and Komsomol reports of the early 1930s regarding teachers' lack of class consciousness, misapprehension of the aims of Communist education, and ignorance of the importance of the grain collection. In the Kharkiv and Donets oblasts, children were overheard singing counter-revolutionary songs and repeating anti-Soviet jokes, reportedly spread by kulaks in the village or by anti-Soviet elements among the teachers' ranks.[94] In the Kharkiv oblast, Synelov reported, teachers did nothing to prevent such exchanges; had not engaged in anti-religious, internationalist, or class-oriented instruction; and continued to rely on now-discredited methods favoured by the complex system of allowing student input to drive lesson work. Synelov stressed the importance of social studies to a Communist education and decried the lack of proper attention to this approach. In the oblast's Dykanka district, six instructors of social studies in the schools were party members, but had no qualifications to teach this discipline. One teacher, known as the "best Marxist," in another unspecified district, engaged in "babble" (*lepet*) and demonstrated no knowledge of history or social studies.[95] Earlier in the meeting, Synelov had argued that when social studies were improperly taught, "there was the greatest number of anti-Soviet, kulak incidents."[96]

These charges suggest that as schools were supposedly shifting to disciplinary, formal studies and away from the remnants of the complex system, they, in fact, confronted far greater challenges raised by the political and economic tumult set in motion by the campaigns of the First Five-Year Plan. In 1933, peasant children and parents as well as rural teachers alike faced starvation in the countryside as famine spread. Some teachers were arrested for helping to hide grain from Soviet authorities.[97] In this environment, it is understandable that teachers were failing to meet the pedagogical challenge of the newly mandated shifts in methodology. One of the essential requirements of Ukrainization, the acquisition of knowledge of "Ukrainian studies," furthered by social studies instruction, certainly could not have improved, even in a supposedly altered, "more Marxist" form.

According to the understanding of the oblast Narkomos officials, strong schools were supposed to provide a bulwark against the class enemy and, by implication, the advancement of so-called Bolshevik Ukrainization. However, they often linked the sorts of anti-Soviet activity they described to the activity of alleged Ukrainian nationalists. Profatylov argued that nationalist, kulak influence in the village was sabotaging the aims of the Narkomos and the grain-collection campaigns. Local

Narkomos officials needed to help party organizations to "organize their attention and class vigilance for the struggle with Petliurism, [Nestor] Makhnovism, and other kulak armies who are defeated, but still not finished off, who are raising their heads and beginning to hiss and creep into every cranny, where we have no eyes, where a direct, Bolshevik response is not organized."[98] A lack of Narkomos attention was not only allowing teachers and pupils to speak out and act against the interests of Soviet power, but also allowing this activity to assume a nationalist guise.

In the February 16 session of the meeting, Baleva, an official from the Narkomos Organizational-Instructional Committee, the body that defined and approved methodology for use in the schools, had reported on the results of an inspection she conducted of seventy districts in the republic. She too observed anti-Soviet teachers, children's ignorance about the aims of the grain collection, and conciliatory attitudes on the part of local Narkomos officials. She reported that the singing of counter-revolutionary songs by pupils in one school in the Borzna district (Chernihiv oblast) was a sign of the spread of "Petliurist, hostile" attitudes among children, and that one pupil openly claimed that Soviet officials were seizing Ukraine's grain for the benefit of "Moscow."[99] Baleva suggested teachers of kulak background had inspired or tolerated such alleged nationalist proclamations. Yosyp Pelekh, the Chernihiv oblast representative at the meeting, in a later session, confirmed anti-Soviet activity by teachers in his oblast, including teachers stealing grain. In the Chernihiv district, Pelekh claimed children in a Ukrainian class had beaten children in a Jewish (Yiddish) class, assumingly in a school of mixed-language instruction. The leader of this "instance of national chauvinism" was the son of a teacher.[100] An investigation found that the assault was not the act of a single pupil, but the result of a "general attitude" in the school and lax administration. The head of the school was a party member, but Pelekh claimed he had done little to respond and had been dismissed from his position. Nationalist attitudes, however ill-defined, were thus said to be behind a whole host of counter-revolutionary acts, and the rural schoolhouse was often presented as the nexus of this activity.

Perhaps not surprisingly, Narkomos administrators blamed Ukrainization, distorted and misdirected, for the spread of Ukrainian nationalism. In essence, they were repeating a formulation that consolidated during the time of the SVU trial, if not earlier. But, in the context of the repeated accusations of "forced Ukrainization," absence of any detailed articulation of the benefit of Ukrainization, and the heightened internal political tension of 1933, the identification of the supposedly negative consequences of the policy had an even more damning overtone. Karpeko, after his initial comments on the second day of the meeting condemning the "forced Ukrainization" of Russian children, criticized Narkomos for not understanding the political weight of this question. He linked the failure of Narkomos to provide Russian-language schools to class war with kulaks; shortcomings in nationalities policy impeded "the fraternal cooperation of the peoples of the Soviet Union," ostensibly to fight this battle. In Ukraine, a struggle persisted with "remnants of nationalist chauvinists, Ukrainian elements, Petliurists, Makhnovists, and others." For Karpeko, incorrect implementation of Ukrainization had provided opportunity to these enemies of Soviet power: "Now this line of Ukrainization may not lead to Bolshevik Ukrainization, and as defined by us, but to Petliurization." Not only had "Petliurization" incited resistance to the grain-collection campaign and occasioned the slogan "Do not give grain to the Muscovites," but it had also led to the failure to provide for the "cultural needs of national minorities, especially the Russian nationality."[101] In Karpeko's framing of the question, Ukrainian nationalism was simultaneously a consequence of incorrect Ukrainization and a contributor to the corruption of the policy. One of the ways to combat it was a proper resolution to the "question of support for the Russian nationality."[102] However, Karpeko's comments also clearly demonstrate that the policy of Ukrainization as a whole was under stress.

The onus was on Narkomos employees to stem the supposed growth of Ukrainian nationalism. The head of the Narkomos Organizational-Instructional Committee, Andrii Lykhansky, spoke at length in the last session of the meeting on February 18 of the dangers of implementing Ukrainization incorrectly, and his speech, which came before discussion of the group's future business, offers a conclusion of sorts for the meeting and early 1933 educational and nationalities policy. Lykhansky also underscored the tie between the class war and Ukrainization, calling on education sections to "break apart attempts of the class enemy to penetrate into separate sections of national cultural construction" and assess the ability of Narkomos cadres to fight back. Citing the tensions of the grain-collection campaign, he warned against the "strengthening of class hostile influences on individual groups of children, the activation of Petliurist forms of teachers' and students' class hostile circles and so on." Lykhansky then repeated Karpeko's formulation: because of the inattention of Narkomos officials, class enemies had attempted and succeeded in "using the forms of Ukrainization in many instances, distorting our Bolshevik Ukrainization into Petliurization, [a corruption] which had appeared in the disregard of the cultural needs of national minorities, especially the Russian national minority."[103] In this final, definitive statement of the meeting, Lykhansky held up Ukrainization as a policy with the potential of danger and not promise.

What was the path forward? Lykhansky suggested that the best defence against the class enemy was a Narkomos system engaged in self-criticism, suggesting a purge of Narkomos officials and teachers. He had asked 200 heads of education sections to inform him about "counter-revolutionary activity" in the schools and had received replies from only ten to fifteen heads. To him, this was evidence that few in Narkomos understood the real threat. He criticized Narkomos officials for having an unsatisfactory understanding of Soviet nationalities policy and attacked education inspectors who were trained in the now-discredited complex system and knew nothing about shifts in methodology.[104] In making these charges, he was repeating earlier comments of speakers who criticized the inadequate training of Narkomos officials and low qualifications of teachers.[105] Even if they had not succumbed to nationalism, they were susceptible and had undermined the aims of Soviet education because of their ignorance. A purge of the Narkomos system seemed in the offing.

Ukrainization Altered

Skrypnyk faced significant pressure by early 1933. The editors of his collected works had already been condemned for nationalism, and the KP(b)U Politburo had questioned aspects of his writings on nationalities policy. In a speech to the Narkomos Collegium on February 14, referenced by multiple speakers at the meeting of the Narkomos oblast heads, Skrypnyk sought to stave off any further direct criticism by underscoring the danger of the "forced Ukrainization" of Russian children.[106] However, on 28 February 1933, Mykola Skrypnyk was dismissed from his position as commissar of education and replaced by Volodymyr Zatonsky, who had been a key figure in the establishment of Soviet power in Ukraine and had served previously as commissar of education in 1917–18 and from 1922 to 1924. Under Zatonsky, the new Narkomos Collegium issued a decree on March 22 ordering that an inventory of language of instruction be undertaken for lower-level grades of primary schools in Ukraine. The inventory was a specific response to the findings presented at the February meeting of oblast heads. It was initiated as part of a plan to correct "mechanistic Ukrainization" and ensure strict observance of what a later April Narkomos Collegium decree called "national self-identification [*natsionalne samovyznacheniia*]."[107]

Pavel Postyshev, the newly appointed KP(b)U second secretary, initiated a shakeup of the entire UkrSSR government, a reorientation of the Ukrainization campaign, and an acceleration of grain requisitions in the countryside. The Ukrainian Politburo authorized an open attack on Skrypnyk to be published in the journal *Bilshovyk Ukrainy* just before a KP(b)U TsK plenum was scheduled to meet from June 8 to 11. At the plenum, Skrypnyk acknowledged multiple errors, but Postyshev pressed on with his denunciation, directly accusing Skrypyk of allowing nationalists and counter-revolutionaries to infiltrate Narkomos and to gain control of Ukrainization. The TsK secretary, Panas Liubchenko, who feared that former Borotbists like himself would be targeted next, published a scathing criticism of Skrypnyk in the main government newspaper, *Visti VUTsVK*, condemning him for emphasizing the national struggle over class concerns and blaming him for the spread of Ukrainian nationalism.[108] The public campaign against Skrypnyk's leadership of Narkomos and management of Ukrainization sharpened, and Skrypnyk committed suicide on July 6, likely recognizing his coming fate.

Skrypnyk's fall signalled a fundamental alteration in nationalities policy in Ukraine and in the Ukrainization of the schools. The November 1933 TsK plenum identified Skrypnyk not as a victim of the influence of others, but a leader of "nationalist deviation." In a reversal of existing policy, which stressed the equal dangers of Russian "great power chauvinism" and Ukrainian nationalism to Soviet power in the UkrSSR, the plenum's resolution posited, "the greatest danger is now local Ukrainian nationalism, as it has allied itself with international intervention."[109] This new formulation sanctioned the purge of the Ukrainian educational, academic, and cultural institutions already underway. Zatonsky announced at the plenum that 2,000 Narkomos employees had already been removed; 16,000 new teachers had been rapidly trained to replace those who had died, been fired, or arrested by the GPU; and eleven of twenty-one directors of pedagogical institutions had been dismissed.[110] In a later speech, he estimated that 30 per cent to 40 per cent of the pedagogical ranks in Ukraine contained "hostile class elements."[111] Not surprisingly, Andrii Khvylia, the long-time head of KP(b)U's Agitprop and deputy commissar of education under Zatsonsky, confirmed to teachers in a fall 1933 issue of the pedagogical journal *Komunistychna osvita* what was already plain, that the Ukrainian TsK and Radnarkom had authorized a full-scale reorganization of Narkomos: "The reorganization of the Narkomos apparat, the rebuilt leadership of people's education, – this is an important political matter, a powerful weapon in the struggle against class enemies, against all opportunists on the cultural, school front."[112]

A 1935 book published by the newly constituted Narkomos, entitled *Na fronti kultury*, offered a description of Ukrainization after the November 1933 KP(b)U plenum. The publication repeatedly invoked the spectre of nationalists who had infiltrated Skrypnyk's Narkomos and had operated in all "areas of cultural construction," including the school: "Due to a lack of Bolshevik vigilance by the old leadership of Narkomos nationalist, enemy elements had occupied many of the areas of pedagogical and theoretical work."[113] It blamed Skrypnyk for ignoring party dictates on schooling, allegedly resisting the unification of the Ukrainian schools system with all-Union norms, and advancing "nationalist fascist" pedagogy, including the project method and complex system.[114] In doing so, the publication made clear the association between nationalism and the now-discredited methodologies advocated by Narkomos during the height of

Ukrainization. The book's account of Skrypnyk's objectives in primary schools was unambiguous.

> Skrypnyk gave nationalist directives on all fronts of people's education to teach 'national emotions,' to cultivate 'national energy,' and develop 'national consciousness.' In advancing the theory of 'de-Russification' and 'mixed speech,' he provided the basis for the practice of forced Ukrainization of children of national minorities.[115]

In this rendering, Skrypnyk was accused of a particular nationalist plot, the intentional enrolment of non-Ukrainians in Ukrainian schools through a ruse (the claiming of Ukrainian as the base language of the mixed Ukrainian–Russian dialect of so-called Russified Ukrainians, described in chapter 10) and the denial of native-language schooling to national minorities, including Russians.

Na fronti kultury argued that Ukrainization still had value. It lauded Soviet Ukraine's success in 1933–4 in approaching the objective of universal enrolment of all school-age children, by considerably expanding the number of ten-year schools in the republic and ensuring that 95 per cent of children who completed the first four years of school returned, in spite of the reported sabotage of nationalists and malfeasance of Skrypnyk's Narkomos officials in earlier years. In 1933–4, the publication explained, 84.3 per cent of schoolchildren in the republic were enrolled in Ukrainian schools; this proportion was down from 1932–3, when 88.1 per cent attended Ukrainian schools reportedly as a consequence of "forced Ukrainization" of the Russian population, but it still was slightly more than the ethnic-Ukrainian proportion of the population (80.0 per cent).[116] The book presented this information in contrast to a dramatic decline in the number of Ukrainian schools in Polish Western Ukraine.[117] *Na fronti kultury* thus offered Ukrainization as a success. Ukrainian schools would remain; the institution of a reformed, prescribed, and accountable instructional methodology would guarantee better educational results; and Soviet power would continue to offer the best protection for the national rights of both Ukrainians as well as national minorities in the republic. It forcefully argued against the idea that the struggle against Ukrainian nationalism was a struggle against Ukrainization, and cited KP(b)U Second Secretary Pavel Postyshev's defence of Ukrainian schools as a key element in the "construction of Soviet Ukrainian culture."[118]

However, the framework of *Na fronti kultury* suggested the opposite. It elaborated on the steps Zatonsky's Narkomos had taken to purge the commissariat, its research institutions, and schools.[119] Since 1933, some 200 persons were purged from the central Narkomos apparat and 90 per cent of the leadership of district-level sections and the entire oblast administration were replaced. In the Kharkiv oblast, 701 teachers were dismissed.[120] The book's invocation of Postyshev as the saviour of Ukrainization rang hollow against evidence of Postyshev's role in the repression of the Ukrainian national intelligentsia.[121] It suggested that Narkomos was putting into place new cadres for the leadership of "Bolshevik Ukrainization," but "inadequate work was undertaken in the selection of and education of entirely, tested Bolshevik Ukrainian cadres."[122] Of course, since many of the instructors or teachers who had trained these "new" Ukrainizers had been dismissed or arrested, their repression raised serious questions about the willingness or ability of "Bolshevik Ukrainizers" to fulfill their responsibility.

Furthermore, a positive definition of Bolshevik Ukrainization was not offered; the publication's focus was entirely on the negative: what it was not. Corrections to "forced Ukrainization" emphasized the need to return Russian-language schooling to city centres, insisting that Russian schools had disappeared in the cities of Kherson and Makiivka after the 1928–9 academic year. In Mykolaiv and Kamianets, only 20 per cent of Russian children enjoyed native-language instruction, and in Kharkiv, Kyiv, and Odesa, between 35 and 38 per cent did.[123] In making this claim, the post-1933 Narkomos suggested a reversal of one of the key components of Ukrainization: the claiming of the urban environment and historically privileged urban schools as Ukrainian space. Bound up in the assertion of shortcomings in Russian-language instruction was a dispute about the category of Russified Ukrainian and their language. If children whom Skrypnyk's Narkomos saw as Russified Ukrainians were recategorized as Russian-speaking Russians, these claims about injustice made even more sense. Either way, the boundaries of what constituted Ukrainian-ness had shifted and the protection of Russian culture was to be given special attention.[124] Athough *Na fronti kultury* insisted on the importance of a completely Ukrainian education system, it issued no call for pressure to be placed on secondary and post-secondary institutions to Ukrainize. The best and most prestigious routes for advancement through the education system would increasingly revert to Russian.

This official report was the culmination of political concerns regarding "forced Ukrainization" expressed in the February 1933 meeting of oblast heads and taken up by Zatonsky. Immediately after assuming the post of commissar of education from Skrypnyk, Zatonsky had condemned Skrypnyk's theory regarding the true Ukrainian base of the speech of Russified Ukrainian children as "forced Ukrainization" and "de-Russification." Prior to the publication of *Na fronti kultury*, Zatonsky had ordered a series of investigations into the question of ethnic-Russian enrolment in Ukrainian-language schools in 1933 along with a spring 1933 inventory of the language of instruction of younger grades.[125] The data from these studies were integrated into the book and presented to the public as a justification for corrections to the school system that had already been implemented for the 1933–4 school year. The proportion of students enrolled in Russian-language schools increased from 6.9 per cent in 1932–3 to 8.7 per cent, just less than the percentage of ethnic Russians in the republic (9.2 per cent). A more dramatic change was made in the cities, where the proportion of children in Russian-language schools rose steeply. On the basis of these figures, Terry Martin argues: "Given this officially sponsored rhetoric of [Russian] resentment, the actual revisions made to Ukraine's network of schools in 1933 were strikingly limited."[126]

This is true, to a point. The proportion of Ukrainian schools in the republic remained high, but the impact of linguistic Ukrainization had clearly changed. Giving parents greater choice in the selection of language of instruction for the children, as this new policy suggested, was undoubtedly more fair, but it meant that motivated parents would increasingly select Russian, the historically dominant and prestigious language in urban spaces, now said to be threatened by an expansion of Ukrainian, a language whose very orthography was under assault. *Na fronti kultury* focused on the dilemma of ethnic Russians, avoiding the complex and politically charged question of Russified Ukrainians that Zatonsky had engaged in his criticism of Skrypnyk, but questions regarding their selection of a school likely motivated Narkomos's commitment to a shift in the number of Russian schools, especially in the cities.

Hennadii Yefimenko, the author of several valuable studies on Soviet nationalities policy in Ukraine in the 1930s, argues that primary (and secondary) schooling in Soviet Ukraine from 1933 to 1937 can be characterized as "a period of Bolshevization and unification of the system of school education, in which the role of catalyst for these processes was allotted to the Russian language and literature." In spite of this development, Yefimenko stresses that there was no "fundamental rejection of the policy of 'Ukrainization.'"[127] He notes that even after the spring 1933 inventory of schools was taken, Narkomos administrators prohibited the simultaneous transfer of all grades in a school to a single new language of instruction, and assigned inspectors to monitor the progress of transfer. Sometimes, inspectors reported on unauthorized changes in the language of instruction of the upper grades (initially not supposed to be studied by the spring 1933 inventory or slated for reassignment) to Russian. In other words, Zatonsky's Narkomos did not intend to undo Ukrainization, but rather was proceeding carefully to correct what it labelled the flawed, "mechanistic" form of the policy. Although most national minority schools in Ukraine would disappear by 1938 after a prolonged campaign to "denationalize" their content, Ukrainian schools would survive what Yefimenko labels a "course towards Russification" begun in 1937.[128]

In Yefimenko's final analysis, the adjustment of 1933–4 was a return to the original limited aims of Soviet nationalities policy designed by central party leaders in 1923, which did not imagine increased attention on the national question, the Ukrainization of "partly Russified" Ukrainians, or a separation of the Ukrainian and Russian education systems.[129] This argument has considerable merit, but the Narkomos-led nationalities policy of the early 1930s was not that of 1923; clearly, the party leadership had signalled substantive alteration. Furthermore, Ukrainization was not a static campaign and what may have been imagined by some in 1923 was not neatly determinative. The dismantling of "Skrypnyk Ukrainization" (and the campaign against the Ukrainian national intelligentsia that accompanied the SVU affair in 1929–30) required purges of Narkomos and teachers that critically compromised the party's ability to pursue even limited Ukrainization, regardless of the continued rhetoric of public support. Evidence of continued shortcomings prior to 1933–4 suggests the need for caution regarding any claims of progress achieved thereafter.

Yefimenko acknowledges that Ukrainization ceased to be a priority after Skrypnyk's dismissal, and Martin grants that "comprehensive Ukrainization" was abandoned in 1933. Even if Soviet leaders did not replace it with direct Russification, they laid the groundwork for the gradual constraint or redirection of Ukrainian-language use. Martin suggests that the "modest reforms" of Ukrainian education reflected a growing consensus for "a bilingual public sphere with a strong Russian-language presence in Ukraine's major cities."[130] However, bilingualism in this context was not necessarily equal; choice could be the function of ambition, fear, or genuine will. In any case, Ukrainization's objective to overturn the established authority of Russian was no longer in force.

A suggestion of what this new form of Ukrainization meant in real terms is provided by a September 1934 decree from the presidium of the Odesa city council. Odesan authorities had ordered another round of Ukrainian studies for state workers after a "strengthening of leadership" of Ukrainization courses. Clearly, a decade of Ukrainization had not been enough to considerably improve the knowledge. The decree noted that record numbers of state employees had enrolled in Ukrainian-studies courses in March of that year. However, the presidium expressed concern that the "low-qualified composition of a portion of instructors had complicated the state employees' study."[131] This fact suggests that the initial arrest of leading Ukrainizers and the subsequent republic-wide purging of Narkomos in 1933 had a real effect. Up until 1930, the party and governmental overseers of Ukrainian studies had complained about student attendance or the motives of lecturers, but generally not about the quality of instruction. Clearly, the value of instruction had diminished by 1934, whether due to the withdrawal (or repression) of Ukrainian-studies lecturers or lack of commitment from those employed. For whatever reason, the most skilled were not being recruited from the ranks of Ukrainian teachers and the intelligentsia.

Therefore, it is difficult to conclude that, in spite of the inflated numbers of Ukrainian-studies course takers, the knowledge of these students was improving in any way. Although the Odesa city council attempted to standardize payment of instructors according to class size, that payment remained the budgetary responsibility of the institutions that employed staff taking courses. Progress in Ukrainization would rely on the compliance of individual institutions. The city council's order specified no penalty for failure to pay instructors. As if to confirm a move towards the further decentralization of the policy, the city council ordered that the state courses in Ukrainization be renamed from State Courses in Ukrainian Studies to "courses of Ukrainian language under the City Commission for Ukrainization." In other words, the policy's realization became primarily a local matter and – from the perspective of the city council tasked with overseeing it – a sublocal or institutional matter. This shift in emphasis suggests the state's weaker commitment to achievement in Ukrainization. Although the city council entrusted two of its members to review all the instructors and "permit only highly qualified specialists to work with groups and courses," it is unclear what happened to those judged unfit and where their replacements would be found.[132]

Furthermore, the decree provided greater details on measures to police politically "correct" Ukrainization than on provisions to support instructors in their teaching or aid students in their studies. For example, the city council ordered a detailed review of the libraries attached to the courses, and resolved "to confiscate as harmful literature not needed for courses in literature and give it to the oblast library."[133] The council's resolution did not define what "harmful literature" constituted, but, as *Na fronti kultury* would make clear, the Soviet popular and pedagogical press vilified literature published under Mykola Skrypnyk's leadership of Narkomos as "national-deviationist." It is reasonable to assume some of this literature remained in these libraries, given its association with Ukrainization, and it is even possible that some literature that had been published before the SVU trial also had not yet been removed.

In addition, the city council noted that local authorities continued to post signs and banners with orthographic mistakes. It called for a "massive raid" to examine this "external Ukrainization" and correct errors. A central feature of the 1933–4 crackdown on Skrypnyk and his tenure at Narkomos was a denunciation of the orthography standardized under his leadership. Soviet linguists now labelled it a "treacherous" orthography, intended to drive a wedge between Russian and Ukrainian and bring it closer to the "fascist" Polish language. Its discrediting meant that local authorities had to remove public signage written according to its standards, and it seems likely that this was the Odesa city council's concern. The city council's guidelines for future public signage suggest a sort of linguistic surveillance against a return to the 1929 orthography: "To require [that] all administrators in the establishments and organizations of the city absolutely submit hangings, announcements, advertisements, and posters to be ordered for a perevirka of the text by the Bureau of Examination of the Ukrainian Text of Local Literature and the police." This bureau and the police, then, acted as guardians of the new language environment and, by extension, the new guideposts for national culture. State institutions that wished to pursue the purportedly urgent task of Ukrainization had to procure a seal from these authorities before they could even begin to prepare Ukrainian-language literature for publication or posting. This stricture signalled that a new literacy prevailed, one that required hyper-correct knowledge of a specific form of Ukrainian and its use in a regulated context (including the primary-school classroom). Outside this context – that is, in the informal spaces where decisions were negotiated and evaluated – it was much easier to use the Russian language, which was not subject to the same linguistic limitations and already customary. An addendum to the council's order, noted in pen, warned all administrators of state institutions that "they personally carry responsibility for the Bolshevik Ukrainization of the apparat."[134] Ukrainization technically remained an important task, but state employees who engaged in its pursuit risked censure for straying from its correct "Bolshevik" form. This was the environment that Ukrainian schools now faced.

Chapter Thirteen

Conclusion

In early Soviet Ukraine, the republican and Communist Party leadership asked educators and intellectuals to use language as a tool for the radical transformation of society.[1] This study has sought to unpack what this process meant and demonstrate the union between educational and nationalities policy at the level of the classroom, and to go beyond a discussion of language transfer by decree. The KP(b)U entrusted Narkomos to apply an innovative, progressive pedagogy towards the creation of a new generation of Soviet citizens. Russian educators shared this approach, but their Ukrainian counterparts gave it greater attention because of the distinct vocational orientation of the Ukrainian education system. Narkomos aimed to do away with traditional subject divisions and teacher pedantry by integrating lessons into thematic groupings, or complexes, firmly oriented towards instructing students in the value of labour and the role of production. Students would gain a "labour mentality" by acculturation, and more rapidly take their place in the rebuilding of an economy recovering from the civil war.

Narkomos maintained that instruction in the Ukrainian language was absolutely necessary for teachers to achieve this goal. It judged Ukrainian to be the native language for all ethnic-Ukrainian children, and educators stressed the primary role of language in the new methodology. The commissariat also sought to rationalize education by recommending that teachers develop an awareness of production through the study of the familiar, or "local studies" (kraieznavstvo). The curriculum provided for the gradual broadening of this study to an investigation of a region's tie to all of Ukraine. The Ukrainian language and Ukrainian studies were both at the core of a curriculum that allowed teachers and students considerable freedom to innovate. Narkomos's hope was that children would gain the outlook, self-confidence, and decision-making skills necessary to undertake their public duties as young adults.

However, most teachers were ill-prepared for the dual demands of a progressive pedagogy and Ukrainization. They were inadequately paid, generally had a low level of education, and had little training in how to teach in Ukrainian or design a curriculum on the basis of the complex system touted by Narkomos guides. Schools, on the whole, remained in a state of disrepair, and teachers lacked paper, basic school supplies, and, most importantly, Ukrainian-language textbooks or pedagogical guides. Narkomos had pursued a decentralized process for both Ukrainization and curricular planning, leaving the tasks of school reform to local education sections. The general lack of state and community financial support for education meant that these sections could offer teachers few opportunities for retraining. Some returned to a formalistic approach in the classroom or abandoned methodology altogether.

Importantly, evaluations of teachers' language knowledge revealed that teachers had also not made much qualitative progress in transferring to Ukrainian-language instruction. Narkomos correlated resistance to linguistic and pedagogical reform and viewed instances of both as anti-Soviet behaviour. As the experience of Odesa argued, although local education sections occasionally acted to discipline or dismiss problematic teachers, they also made allowances for delay. There were few incentives for real change. Ultimately, this study has argued, the success of Ukrainization must be judged at this level. An increase in Ukrainian-language schooling did not translate into a rapid transformation of the classroom's language environment.

In spite of the problems associated with Ukrainization, this study maintains that the shift to Ukrainian-language schooling was a fundamental aspect of the party's program for galvanizing republic-wide support for its economic programs and assuring urban authority over the village. If industrial workers and the party were to administer the countryside, they would have to master its language: Ukrainian. The Ukrainization campaign would be ineffectual without the Ukrainization of the proletariat. Nevertheless, protests regarding the "forced" Ukrainization of some labourers (and their children) occasioned the intervention of the party. Narkomos did not (and could not) abandon the Ukrainization of the republic's industrial labourers, but settled on a more indirect formula. Ukrainization of the proletariat would occur gradually through children. Although the KP(b)U absolutely forbade the involuntary schooling of ethnic-Russian children in Ukrainian, it gave Narkomos the freedom to continue to Ukrainize children of "Russified" Ukrainians. In effect, Russified Ukrainian parents had to resist a strong Narkomos campaign of persuasion and disprove the identification of Ukrainian as the native language of their children. Narkomos's final objective was the creation of a Ukrainian-speaking, labour-oriented cadre that would alter the linguistic environment of the cities.

The paradox of both the program for Ukrainization and the new Soviet school was that the Communist Party leadership sought a controlled outcome to education, and yet had little day-to-day management over the classroom and the political costs of its activity. Although the shortcomings of Ukrainization among teachers were widespread, there was a group of educators committed to the policy and its improvement. The person of Ukrainizer and pedagogical innovator was often one and the same. The KP(b)U relied on these individuals greatly for Ukrainization's general success. Consequently, the importance of the field of education, often characterized as a "soft-line" concern, should not be minimized. In some areas, educators were creating centres of authority alternative to Narkomos. The KP(b)U monitored the activity of these figures and grew increasingly worried about their potential power. Non-party educators subscribed to a broad understanding of Ukrainian culture's place in the building of socialism and worked to strengthen this role. They hoped that Ukrainization's ultimate agenda would be shaped by their efforts, and put great faith in the ability of education to define behaviour, a faith that the party leadership ultimately shared.

While focusing on the period of so-called High Stalinism, Serhy Yekelchyk has argued that "Ukrainian culture did not result from Moscow's *diktat* and the suppression of the local intelligentsia's 'natural' national sentiment ... It was their interaction with Moscow, rather than simply the centre's totalizing designs, that produced the official line on non-Russian identities and national patrimonies."[2] As this study has made clear, the centralizing aspirations emphasized in conventional histories of the Stalinist period were considerably absent in the 1920s, but the party/state still mandated that the Ukrainian Soviet education system produce a definite result: a loyal citizen prepared to participate in the new socialist economy. The Ukrainian intelligentsia (educational theorists and teachers) assumed a critical role in determining the process to reach this end. To a significant degree, then, this study provides a helpful prelude to Yekelchyk's argument. As Yekelchyk notes, in the 1920s (and for those whose formative experiences were drawn from this period), socialism and Ukrainian nation building were "potentially compatible projects."[3] Indeed, the high numbers of primary schools Ukrainized stand as evidence of this fact. However, teachers still had significant work to do to meet the standards the Soviet state had set for itself.

While participatory space continued to exist in the Stalinist state and the Soviet Union remained committed to national categories of understanding, this study emphasizes that the repression of a leading segment of the Ukrainian intellectual elite that began in 1930 had an essential effect in setting the limits of negotiation. Thus, although Ukrainian educators like Francine Hirsch's ethnographers adjusted to the realities of Soviet power after the cultural revolution and "learned how to show that their nationalism was the correct 'Soviet' kind, devoid of the 'bourgeois' tendencies and ambitions,"[4] this adjustment was fundamental and not foreseen by the Ukrainizers. Furthermore, this was a decidedly uneven "participatory" process, one already undermined by the Communist Party's suspicions of the Ukrainian intelligentsia. This study has argued that the SVU show trial irrevocably damaged future efforts for Ukrainization and suggested that the oft-cited achievements of 1930 to 1933 must be questioned. The SVU show trial was aimed directly at Ukrainizing and progressive educators. The KP(b)U, guided by Moscow, put forty-five members of the intelligentsia on trial, not just because it had little confidence in non-party intelligentsia, but also because it had misgivings about the real consequences of their work (despite the actual deficiencies of a Ukrainian-language education in 1929–30). This anxiety provided the script for the repression against the intelligentsia, if it was not the sole motivation for this action. The signal that the party intended for teachers was that they must place Ukrainization under the party's leadership and wed it to the public campaigns of the Five-Year Plan. The message teachers understood was that it was best not to burden themselves unnecessarily with the goals of the campaign. Although Narkomos achieved full Ukrainization formally, examinations of teacher knowledge continued to reveal a weak grasp of the Ukrainian language and Ukrainian-studies topics. Few were leading the charge for a policy that the republican leaders continued to tout.

Furthermore, the party's move to rein in Ukrainization corresponded with a protracted move to assume management over classroom methodology. By 1930, it was clear that the complex method had not realized Narkomos's academic goals and had created too much opportunity for variant interpretations of curriculum. Soviet authorities politicized progressive education and linked student activism to the explicit goals of the First Five-Year Plan: collectivization and industrialization. The move to conform the Ukrainian education system to all-Union norms foreshadowed the regimentation of the education system generally. The SVU trial ultimately offered an excuse for a full-scale rejection of the complex system. Several SVU defendants had been prominent sponsors of progressive pedagogy. Now, the complex system as a whole was tainted by association, and the pedagogical press blamed Ukrainian nationalists for confusion in the schools.

Narkomos and the KP(b)U continued to pursue Ukrainization, especially in secondary and post-secondary educational institutions. They had declared significant success at the primary-school level in a generalized sense, but left ambiguous the metrics of what this success meant. The archival material on the classroom in the early 1930s is sparse; still, existing reports suggest that considerable work needed to take place "behind the scenes," at the local level. The "complete" Ukrainization of primary schools had not ceased to be a concern, but the priorities of the KP(b)U and Narkomos were elsewhere, and qualitative improvements in

Ukrainian-language instruction stalled. Meanwhile, reports of Ukrainian nationalist and counter-revolutionary activity in the schools and Young Pioneers detachments, and stories of violence directed against activist children and teachers, continued to mount. By early 1933, when Narkomos administrators discussed the Ukrainization of schools, they increasingly talked about it in a negative sense, as a policy that had violated the rights of ethnic Russians and had led to a rise in Ukrainian nationalism. In 1933–4, when the party finally declared "local nationalism" the chief danger, Soviet authorities purged the Narkomos apparat almost entirely of its existing staff and dismissed thousands of Ukrainian teachers. In the years that followed, the number of Ukrainian schools dropped in major urban centres and Soviet authorities no longer consistently compelled the systematic Ukrainization of higher education, opting instead to permit Russian-language predominance.[5] Both these processes would accelerate after the war. In fact, the die had been cast earlier. The SVU show trial had already fundamentally undermined the potential of Ukrainian-language instruction. Repressions against Ukrainian national elites, in particular educators, ultimately robbed the linguistic component of Ukrainization of its vigour and sent a signal to those who might have too enthusiastically taken up the charge: "Now the Ukrainian language stopped being the basic means for modernization. Those who wanted to win respected social status and gain entry to new information, to contemporary scientific thought and knowledge, had to resort to the Russian language."[6] The examples of Odesa Labour School No. 41 and Labour School No. 67, referenced in chapter 9, evoke an intriguing picture of an acceptance of a Ukrainian national category and the strengthening of national identity in this most non-Ukrainian of cities and regions, and suggest a possible alternative course of how Ukrainization might have proceeded.[7] Perhaps few of the children (or their parents) in these or other Ukrainizing schools privileged concerns about national identity, but they acknowledged that a Ukrainian identity existed, maybe on par with a Russian one.

 Much of the story that is told here is about challenge and failure. A central point of this study is that the Ukrainization of primary schooling, which other scholars have assumed to be automatic, was a demanding, incomplete, and contested campaign. However, Ukrainization's achievements should not be lost on the reader. The problematic route of contemporary Ukrainization is a reminder that perhaps too much was expected in too short a time in the interwar period. Still, given the large, exclusively Ukrainian-speaking population in the republic at that time, the Soviet government might have accomplished more if its trust in the Ukrainizers had been greater. To repeat, the objective of Ukrainization was a levelling of language hierarchy, a reversal of Russification, and the increased use of Ukrainian in the public space. Primarily, the campaign was directed at ethnic Ukrainians, although it required anyone in a position to service Ukrainians as the largest ethnic group in the republic to learn Ukrainian, and assumed a "sorting out" of Ukrainians that was never so neat. The UkrSSR, in fact, took the lead among Soviet republics in promoting ethnic-minority cultures, setting up so-called national districts where its leaders claimed a concentration of a particular ethnic group. Political leaders in the KP(b)U and administrators in Narkomos recognized the ethnic diversity of the republic and strongly supported a network of primary schools to educate ethnic-minority children, so much so that some parents who wished to have their children attend a Russian or Ukrainian school felt their choice was constrained. This particular challenge makes the case of education in Ukraine compelling as an examination of the intersection among education, "national" (Ukrainian, Russian, Polish, Jewish, etc.) interest, citizenship, and parental choice. Although the study privileges the story of Ukrainian-language schooling and its tie to education reform, it is critical to remember that the state pursued these campaigns in the context of a general effort to satisfy all national communities. If any label is to be applied to the linguistic component of educational policy in Ukraine as whole, it should be de-Russification rather than Ukrainization.

Education was not a daily concern of the leadership of the VKP(b) or even the KP(b)U, but challenges regarding schooling could have an impact on political decisions. A study of nationalities and educational policy reveals much about the individual's relationship with the state. Citizens of the UkrSSR were subjects of policies that were still under development. Thus, they were trying to discover what role the state expected of them, what motive they had to participate, and what the limits of their engagement in the policy should be, if any. Both Ukrainization and progressive education required their involvement, and citizen input inevitably influenced the contours of state policy. At the local level, the Soviet Union created space for civic participation, and activities stemming from, and surrounding, the schoolhouse were critical reflections and stimulants of government. As Odesa's story vividly illustrates, the success or failure of Ukrainization of schools hinged on local initiative and, in the end, the compliance of administrators, teachers, parents, and students. Furthermore, the progressive schooling of the 1920s required children to gather information about their local community, information necessary for the fulfillment of the curriculum and of interest to the state. In the end, the party proved itself much more willing to trust children than teachers or even Narkomos administrators, even as it worried about children's vulnerability. Children and youth were a force for change because their views and positions were not static and were capable of implementing change. Some of the very children who were the subjects of Ukrainization and progressive pedagogy in 1923 conceivably took part in the alteration of both by the early 1930s.

This study is a story about nation building, but also an account of urbanization and the development of a modern sensibility.[8] The Soviet state required children and their parents to appreciate the world beyond the village or their city, and offered them an opportunity to identify with a larger construct. Given available sources, it is difficult to specify how children understood what they were being told, but Ukrainization undoubtedly brought the nation into the classroom. The language in which children were taught was the same language spoken in Kyiv, Kharkiv, and Odesa, and excursions and lessons in Ukrainian studies further reinforced this association. The assignment of children to schools by nationality also promoted a sense of national identity, but not exclusively for Ukrainians, since schools were supposed to be established for each concentration of an ethnic minority, including Russians. To select Ukrainian students for one school meant to exclude and redirect students of different ethnic groups. Thus, children of all nationalities were compelled to recognize a Ukrainian national identity as well as a national taxonomy in general. What mattered in the end was the education system's development of these circles of overlapping association and omission.

Moreover, the increased migration of Ukrainians to the cities changed the character of urban life by altering the ethnic picture of cities as well as increasing their "peasantization." The actual or potential future migration of Ukrainian peasants provoked fears of a crisis of authority, and Ukrainizers spoke out strongly of the need to ensure the establishment of "complete" (full seven-year) primary Ukrainian schools for the children of these migrants, even in the most non-Ukrainian city, Odesa. Migration meant that Ukrainization was a necessity because of a real shift in population as well as anticipated future migration. What appeared to be dangerous was not that this shift was occurring (it was desired), but that it might provoke social and political instability. Schooling in Ukrainian was needed to prevent any rise in national frustration and to train children of recently arrived peasants to be politically responsible citizens. They could educate their parents in turn. Narkomos officials also advocated the establishment of Ukrainian schools in city centres, away from where migrants tended to settle. Their aim was to symbolically alter cultural identity; to de-Russify the most valued establishments in a city, including the best schools and former gymnasiums. This effort negatively impacted children who were not Ukrainian or not Ukrainian-speaking and were already enrolled in schools ordered to Ukrainize, but local education officials insisted any temporary dislocation was necessary. Otherwise, urban populations would believe Ukrainization applied only to districts outside the city's heart, and Ukrainian would remain a language solely associated with peasants and the marginalized. Narkomos would pressure Russified Ukrainians to continue their enrolment and, in time, transfer non-Ukrainians to other schools. Narkomos's post-1933 reduction in the number of urban Ukrainian schools because of the "forced Ukrainization" of Russians (and, implicitly, Russian-speakers) meant an abandonment of one of the key aims of the policy: a capture of urban space through the conversion of prestigious city schools to Ukrainian-language instruction.

The transformation of Ukrainian culture into the urban and esteemed was meant to alter children's self-identification regardless of whether they lived in the city, but it was the content of a school's instruction that affirmed children's views of modern citizenship. The education offered in Ukrainian schools was revolutionary in its ambition to train informed, active participants in the building of socialism through instruction driven in the first instance by children themselves. The contradiction in Soviet education generally at this time is that Soviet authorities wanted to create citizens capable of independent, self-motivated action and yet, in the end, they feared children's vulnerability to "foreign" persuasion, as material on the Komsomol and Young Pioneers demonstrates. This study is telling, then, about the Soviet state's aspirations as revealed in its education program and the limitations of its expectations. In progressive pedagogy, Narkomos saw the promise of revolution fulfilled and yet ultimately shifted course towards a new conservatism, partly in recognition of the concerns of some parents and teachers that children were not learning fundamental skills and classrooms were in disorder because of the teacher's diminished authority. Furthermore, the flexible instruction that progressive pedagogy embraced introduced unpredictability and a potential for challenges to Soviet political authority.

The turn to a conservative pedagogy oriented around textbook use and a teacher's leadership diminished the pressure of Ukrainization, in part because of this pedagogy's reliance on literature already in print, much of which still remained in Russian. The accompanying unification of the Ukrainian and Russian education systems also required a uniformity and interchangeability of instruction that Ukrainization, through its instruction in Ukrainian studies as well as the language, complicated. None of this is to say that education in the UkrSSR in the 1930s was "reactionary," but it bears repeating that Ukrainization and the progressive pedagogy of the 1920s were mutually compatible campaigns that were consistent with the revolution's liberating and modernizing goals (and not a retreat). The Communist Party believed Ukrainization was necessary in order correct the tsarist oppression of the past, transmit Soviet values, and transform the workforce of the republic. Tension resulted from the effort to define what the limits of this commitment to the Ukrainian language and culture were and what place non-party intellectuals would have in the campaign. Short of some readily apparent extremes, Ukrainization was initially a negotiated process. The UkrSSR was exceptional among the Soviet republics for being a place where intellectuals and individuals in the republican leadership were willing to push the envelope of nationalities policy beyond that imagined elsewhere.

Chapter Fourteen

Biographical and Informational Sketches

The content for these sketches is mainly drawn from: Volodymyr Kubijovyč, ed., *Encyclopedia of Ukraine*, 6 vols. (Toronto: University of Toronto Press, 1984–). Other key references include the authoritative and recently completed: V. A. Smolii, ed., *Entsyklopediia istoriï Ukraïny*, 9 vols. (Kyïv: Naukova dumka, 2003–2013); or the specialized: V. H. Kremen', ed., *Entsyklopediia osvity* (Kyïv: Iurinkom Inter, 2008).

Petro Buzuk (1891–1943) was a leading Ukrainian linguist and professor at the Odesa INO until 1925 and then at the Belarusian State University in Minsk. A prominent advocate of linguistic geography for the study of the Ukrainian, Belarusian, and Moldovan languages, in 1927, he wrote a major history of the Ukrainian language, *Narys istoriï ukraïns' koï movy*. He was arrested in 1934, and taught at the Vologda Pedagogical Institute in the Russian SFSR after his release.

Liubov Bidnova (1882–?) was a Ukrainian educator and cultural activist of the Katerynoslav region who was arrested in 1929 as an alleged member of the fictional SVU. She was the wife of **Vasyl Bidnov** (1874–1935), a prominent church historian, civic leader, and expert in the history of the Katerynoslav region. From 1918 to 1920, Bidnov was a professor at the Ukrainian State University in Kamianets and served as a member of the UNR Ministry of Religion. He fled abroad after the Bolshevik seizure of the UNR's provisional capital of Kamianets in 1920 and continued his scholarship at posts in Prague and Warsaw.

Borotbists (Borotbisty), or the Ukrainian Party of Socialist-Revolutionaries-Borotbists (Communists), was the left faction of the Ukrainian Party of Socialist

Revolutionaries (UPSR). It advocated a Soviet-style government and cooperation with the Bolsheviks in its newspaper *Borot' ba*. Several of its members participated in the Bolsheviks' Soviet Ukrainian government during the Red Army's occupation of Ukraine at the beginning of 1919. The faction renamed itself the Ukrainian Communist Party (of Borotbists) and merged with other pro-Bolshevik Ukrainian forces. The party dissolved itself and its members joined the KP(b)U in March 1920 after the Comintern denied their application for admission as an independent "national communist" party and they received Bolshevik assurance that a separate UkrSSR would be formed alongside the RSFSR.

Communist Party of Western Ukraine (*Komunistychna partiia Zakhidnoi Ukrainy*, KPZU) was founded by a group of Borotbists in Stanyslaviv (formerly part of the Habsburg Empire) as the Communist Party of Eastern Galicia in February 1919. It was dissolved after the Red Army failed to hold onto Galicia. The party reformed in late 1920 as a coalition for pro-Communist groups in the territory, now under Polish control. The KPZU argued for the incorporation of Western Ukraine into the UkrSSR, rejecting the more limited goal of self-determination within Poland. The Central Committee of the KPZU supported Commissar of Education Oleksandr Shumsky's advocacy of a widening of Ukrainization in the UkrSSR. A pro-Shumsky majority was expelled from the Comintern in February 1928 and its leaders eventually recanted their position. The Comintern dissolved a reformed KPZU in 1938.

Vasyl Doha (1885–?) was a leading pedagogue and researcher at the Scientific-Pedagogical Academy of Sciences. He authored several school textbooks and contributed multiple articles on teaching methodology to the Soviet Ukrainian pedagogical press. He was arrested as an alleged member of the fictional SVU and sentenced to a three-year imprisonment outside the borders of Ukraine. His final fate is unknown.

Volodymyr Durdukivsky (1874–1937) was the director of the Shevchenko First Ukrainian Gymnasium in Kyiv under the UNR, renamed the Taras Shevchenko Labour School No. 1 by Soviet educational authorities. He led the Scientific-Pedagogical Commission of the All-Ukrainian Academy of Sciences until its dissolution in 1930 and was the author of numerous articles that appeared in the pre-revolutionary and Soviet Ukrainian cultural and pedagogical press. He was arrested in 1929 as an alleged member of the fictional SVU and sentenced to an eight-year imprisonment, was released early, but then was subsequently rearrested and executed in 1937.

Yosyp Hermaize (1892–1958) was an historian and political activist. An ethnic Jew, he graduated from Kyiv University, joined the Ukrainian Social Democratic Workers' Party, and served on the Mala Rada, the central executive committee of the UNR Central Rada. He was a professor of the Kyiv INO, secretary of VUAN's historical division, and director of its Archeographic Commission. He authored multiple works on Ukraine's social and political history, including *Narysy z istoriï revolutsiinoho rukhu na Ukraïni* (1926). He was arrested in 1929 as an alleged member of the fictional SVU and sentenced to a five-year imprisonment. After his release in 1934, he was arrested again in 1937 and died in the labour camps after his sentence was extended by another ten years.

Mikhailo Hrushevsky (1866–1934) was Ukraine's most influential historian and a leader of Ukrainian cultural and scholarly activity. He was born in Kholm and completed his undergraduate and graduate studies at Kyiv University. In 1894, he was appointed professor of the new chair of Ukrainian history at Lviv University, then in the Habsburg Empire. He advanced the idea that the Ukrainian nation had, since the founding of Kievan Rus', followed an historical path distinct from that of Russia. After the 1905 revolution, Hrushevsky became increasingly active in politics in Russian-ruled Ukraine. During the Ukrainian Revolution, he was elected the UNR's first president in April 1918, but then emigrated after Pavel Skoropadksy's coup against the UNR. He moved to the UkrSSR in 1924, attracted by the KP(b)U's promotion of Ukrainization. He held the VUAN Chair of Modern Ukrainian History, but was also the object of regular GPU surveillance. In 1931, he was exiled to Moscow and later died in Kislovodsk, Northern Caucasus, where he was undergoing medical treatment.

Hryhorii Hrynko (1890–1938) was a Communist Party figure and the Ukrainian commissar of education. During the Ukrainian Revolution, he sided with the Borotbists and, in 1919, after the Borotbist merger with the Bolsheviks, served as a member of VUTsVK and Radnarkom. He became commissar of education in 1920 and established the foundations of the Soviet Ukrainian education system. He oversaw the introduction of Ukrainian as a separate subject in Soviet Ukrainian schools in September 1920, but his commissariat was much more concerned with setting up a network of schools for training a labour force for the republic's economic recovery. From 1926 to 1929, he served as deputy chairman of the USSR State Planning Commission and then USSR commissar for finance. He was arrested in 1937 and executed the following year, accused of plotting to kill Stalin.

Hryhorii Ivanytsia (1892–1938) was a professor at the Kyiv INO, secretary of the VUAN Pedagogical Commission, and co-editor of *Radians'ka osvita*. He published multiple articles on methodology of teaching Ukrainian language, literature, and orthography as well as textbooks, including a study guide on the Ukrainian language for Russian speakers. He was tried as an alleged member of the fictional SVU in 1930 and died in a labour camp in the Magadan oblast in northeastern Siberia.

Lazar Kaganovich (1893–1991) was a leading Communist and Soviet leader. An ethnic Jew from Kabany, Kyiv province, he joined the Bolshevik Party in 1911 and held key posts in Belarus, Russia, and Turkestan during the revolution and civil war. As first party secretary of the KP(b)U from 1925 to 1928, he promoted Ukrainian national culture, but clashed with Commissar of Education Oleksandr Shumsky over the question of ethnic-Ukrainian leadership of the KP(b)U and the pace and manner of the Ukrainization campaign. As head of the VKP(b) Central Committee's agricultural department in 1933, he helped oversee collectivization in Ukraine through a policy of forced grain requisitions. He was ejected from the Communist Party in 1957 for his role in a failed coup to oust Nikita Khrushchev from Soviet leadership.

Mykola Khvylovy (1893–1933) was a leading Soviet Ukrainian writer and publicist. He joined the KP(b)U in 1919 and was one of the founding members of the proletarian writers' group Hart in 1923. He subsequently left this group, criticized it for prioritizing mass participation in writing over artistic values, and founded a rival group, VAPLITE. Most famously, he wrote a series of 1925–6 polemical pamphlets in the newspaper supplement *Kul'tura i pobut* in which he argued that Ukrainian culture needed to break free of its historical cultural subservience to Russia through an embrace of European progressive values. Although supported by Shumsky, the KP(b)U leadership sharply criticized Khvylovy for his ideas, encapsulated in his slogan, "Away from Moscow." In 1933, he committed suicide during the midst of a new campaign of political and cultural repression in Ukraine.

Dmitrii Lebed (1893–1937) was a prominent Communist Party leader and Soviet official. The son of a Russian unskilled worker from a village in Katerynoslav province, Lebed aligned with the Bolshevik faction of the Russian Social Democratic Labour Party in 1909 and led the Bolshevik organization of the Katerynoslav railway after the February Revolution. He rose to become second secretary of the Central Committee of the KP(b)U, a position he occupied from 1920 to 1924. He was an outspoken opponent of Ukrainization, outlining his theory of the "struggle of two cultures" at a Kyiv party conference in August 1923. He subsequently occupied a series of high-level all-Union and Russian governmental posts. He was arrested in 1937, ironically accused of Ukrainian nationalism, and executed.

Biographical Sketches 353

Karlo Maskymovych (1892–1937). Born as Karlo Savrych in Kukilnyky, Galicia (Habsburg Empire), Maksymovych was a Western Ukrainian Communist activist. One of the founders of the Communist Party of Eastern Galicia, later the KPZU, he was elected party secretary, but fled to Galicia to escape arrest by Polish authorities and to advocate from abroad for the union of Ukrainians under Soviet rule. In 1922, he returned to Poland to work as secretary of the UkrSSR diplomatic mission in Warsaw, but he was subsequently expelled one year later. He moved to Kharkiv and served as the KPZU representative to the Central Committee of the KP(b)U. In spite of support from a majority of the KPZU, Maksymovych was sent to administrative exile in Astrakhan and was arrested and executed in 1937.

Hryhorii Petrovsky (1894–1951) was a key Soviet and Communist Party official. Born in Kharkiv, he served as the RSFSR commissar of internal affairs and then chair of the All-Ukrainian Central Executive Committee (1919–38). As a long-time member of the KP(b)U Politburo (1920 to 1938), he supported the party's official position on Ukrainization, but resisted its expansion as advocated by national-communists. In 1926, Soviet authorities renamed the city of Katerynoslav to Dnipropetrovsk in his honour. He is viewed as one of the chief architects of the 1932–3 famine in Ukraine because of his role in pushing continued grain requisitions in the face of evidence of widespread starvation. After the final purge of the KP(b)U Politburo, he was demoted and reassigned to Moscow as a deputy director of the USSR Museum of the Revolution.

Oleksandr Shumsky (1890–1946) was a Communist Party figure and the Ukrainian commissar of education. Shumsky was a leading member of the Ukrainian Party of Socialist Revolutionaries. In 1918, he aligned himself with the Borotbists and pushed for their merger with the Bolsheviks. He occupied numerous party and government posts in the UkrSSR from 1920 to 1925, including commissar of internal affairs (1920) and head of the KP(b)U's propaganda department, Agitprop (1923 to 1925). He became commissar of education in September 1924, and it was under his tenure that the Ukrainization campaign truly accelerated and progressive pedagogy reached its widest use. Shumsky's defence of "deviationist" Ukrainian intellectuals and his protest to Stalin regarding Kaganovich's leadership raised the ire of the central party's leadership in Moscow. He was forced to resign his post after a party censure in February 1927. He was reassigned outside Ukraine to the directorship of the Institute of the National Economy in Leningrad. He was arrested in 1933 and sentenced to an initial ten-year imprisonment. He committed suicide in 1946 while incarcerated in a concentration camp in the Solovets Islands.

Mykola Skrypnyk (1872–1933) was a Communist Party figure and the Ukrainian commissar of education. Skrypnyk became a member of the Social Democratic Labour Party in 1899, later aligning with its Bolshevik faction. After 1917, he was instrumental in the formation of the first and second Ukrainian Soviet governments. From 1919 to 1927, he served as commissar of state control, commissar of internal affairs, and commissar of justice. In March 1927, he was appointed commissar of education after Shumsky's dismissal. He is widely credited for being a strong defender of Ukrainization and of Ukrainian "state" interest, fighting with central authorities to extend the Ukrainian republic's border and ensure cultural autonomy for ethnic Ukrainians in the RSFSR. However, he was also a vocal critic of Shumsky. Skrypnyk came under fire in 1933 for his work on the linguistic standardization of Ukrainian. He was removed from his post as commissar, accused of separating the Ukrainian language from Russian and protecting nationalists. He committed suicide on 6 July 1933.

Mykhailo Slabchenko (1882–1952) was a leading historian and civic activist. Under Soviet rule, he served as chair of Ukrainian history at the Odesa INO and directed the social-historical section of the Odessa Scientific Society. He also served as a lecturer for State Courses in Ukrainian Studies and was a leading Ukrainizer of the Odesa region in the 1920s. He was arrested along with his son Taras in 1929 as an alleged member of the fictional SVU, served a six-year imprisonment in the Solovets Islands, returned to the UkrSSR, and was then rearrested in 1937. In 1947, he worked as a schoolteacher and municipal education inspector in Pervomaisk in the Mykolaiv oblast. He was exposed at a city teachers' conference in 1949, dismissed, and died penniless.

Oleksa Syniavsky (1887–1937) was a prominent linguist. He graduated from Kharkiv University and, during the 1920s, taught as a professor of the Ukrainian language at the Kharkiv INO, and served as head of the VUAN Dialectological Commission (1928 to 1934). From 1932 to 1937, he served as a lecturer in the Ukrainian language at Kyiv University and Kyiv Pedagogical Institute. Syniavsky played a critical role in the standardization of literary Ukrainian and was editor of the final text of the unified Ukrainian orthography formulated for official use by Soviet and Western Ukrainian linguists in 1929. He was arrested in 1937 and died in prison in Kyiv.

Ukrainian Autocephalous Orthodox Church (*Ukrainska Avtokefalna Pravoslavna Tserkva*, UAPTs or UAOC) is a national Ukrainian Orthodox Church that claimed independence from the Russian Orthodox Church and formed its own structure and hierarchy. A meeting of nationally minded Orthodox clergy from

Ukrainian territory proclaimed the autocephaly or independence of the church in May 1920. In October 1921, Vasyl Lypkivsky was consecrated as the first metropolitan of the church. The church advocated conciliarism, the decentralization of church governance, and regular participation of the laity in church life, and the Ukrainization of the church rite. Soviet authorities sought to weaken the church through intimidation, eventually placing Lypkivsky under house arrest in 1926 and forcing his replacement. In 1929, the UAOC was accused of collaborating with the fictional SVU and many of its leaders were arrested. In January 1930, the church was dissolved. Adherents of Ukrainian Orthodoxy survived in Western Ukraine in the interwar period and in the diaspora; the UAOC has since reconstituted itself in post-Soviet Ukraine.

Ukrainian Communist Party (*Ukrainska komunistychna partiia* or *Ukapisty*) was a Communist party that advocated for Soviet rule of Ukraine but opposed what its members felt was the pro-Russian orientation of the KP(b)U. It was formed in January 1920 out of members from the Independist faction of the Ukrainian Social Democratic Workers' Party, a national communist grouping that initially rejected cooperation that advocated the UNR's transformation into a Soviet-style government. It attracted former Borotbists who resisted incorporation into the KP(b)U as well as other KP(b)U members, and, at its height, had around 3,000 members. The KP(b)U allowed the Ukapisty to operate as an ineffectual legal opposition, seeking first to undermine the group from within by sponsoring factional division. In December 1924, the Comintern ordered all factions of the party to dissolve; its members joined the KP(b)U and became leading advocates of Ukrainization.

Ukrainian People's Republic (*Ukrainska Narodnia Respublika*, UNR) was a Ukrainian state that claimed sovereignty over the central Ukrainian territory of the Russian Empire and, after January 1919, the western Ukrainian territory of the former Habsburg Empire. Its autonomy was first proclaimed on 20 November 1917, by the Central Rada, a Ukrainian national council and then revolutionary parliament established to administer central Ukraine after the February Revolution. Formally, it remained in federation with Russia until it declared complete independence on 25 January 1918, after the Bolsheviks established a rival government in Kharkiv and opened hostilities with the UNR. On 29 April 1918, the Germany army then occupying Ukrainian territory helped engineer a coup against the UNR. Pavel Skoropadsky, a former lieutenant general in the tsarist army, proclaimed himself hetman of the Ukrainian State and dissolved the Central Rada by edict. His government was overthrown in November 1918 by Ukrainian forces led by Symon Petliura, a journalist and political activist turned soldier who had been imprisoned by Skoropadsky. Petliura emerged as leader of the Directorate of the UNR, a temporary, revolutionary government, in February 1919. A failed Polish–UNR campaign to wrest Ukraine from Soviet control led to the final ejection of UNR forces from Ukrainian territory.

Mykhailo Volobuiev (1903–1972) was a lecturer at the Kharkiv Technical College of the National Economy, assistant head of the propaganda department of Holovpolitosvita, and later professor of political economy in the Kharkiv Mechanical Machine Construction Institute. In 1928, he wrote an influential article in *Bil'shovyk Ukraïny*, the leading theoretical journal of the KP(b)U Central Committee. The article argued that Ukraine was an economically distinct space in the Russian Empire and, under Soviet rule, Ukraine had the right to define its own budget and determine its own economic development. He published multiple withdrawals of his argument, but he was arrested in 1933 and exiled to Kazakhstan for five years. He resumed his teaching after the Second World War in Rostov-on-Don and was officially rehabilitated in 1957.

Matvii Yavorksy (1885–1937) was a leading historian. Born in Korchmyn, Galicia, Yavorksy graduated from Lviv University and served in the Ukrainian Galician army, but he remained in Kyiv in 1919 after the army's withdrawal from central Ukraine, joining the KP(b)U in 1920. He led the historical section of the Ukrainian Institute of Marxism-Leninism and Ukrholovnauka, the Narkomos organ responsible for administration of scholarship in the UkrSSR. He authored several comprehensive histories of Ukraine and the revolution in Ukraine, some of which were used in the primary schools in the 1920s. Yavorksy embraced a Marxist interpretation in these texts but, by 1929, was increasingly subject to official censure for "national deviation." He was expelled from the KP(b)U in 1930, arrested in March 1931 for alleged membership in a fabricated national military organization, and executed in a labour camp in the Solovets Islands in 1937.

Serhii Yefremov (1876–1939) was a prominent literary critic, historian of literature, and political activist. Yefremov graduated from Kyiv University and played a key role in pre-revolutionary Ukrainian national politics. He was deputy head of the UNR Central Rada and was a member of its delegation to the Provisional Government in Petrograd. Under Soviet rule, he was elected vice-president of the VUAN governing council and secretary of its historical-philological division. He emerged as a leading figure in literary studies in the pre-revolutionary and Soviet periods, advocating a populist literature that remained connected to the life of the Ukrainian people. He was arrested in 1929 as the alleged leader of the fictional SVU. Yefremov was sentenced to ten years of imprisonment in isolation. He was killed in 1939 in a labour camp.

Volodymyr Zatonsky (1888–1938) was a Communist Party figure and UkrSSR commissar of education. Zatonsky was the sole commissar of education in the 1920s to complete a post-secondary degree, graduating from Kyiv University in 1912. He joined the Bolsheviks in 1917, served twice as state secretary (then commissar) of education in the first Soviet Ukrainian governments of the civil war era, and was instrumental in the formation of the KP(b)U. Zatonsky was again appointed the Ukrainian commissar of education in October 1922 after Hrynko's tenure. Although the reorganization of Ukrainian schools continued under Zatonsky's tenure, Ukrainization of the schools did not accelerate until Shumsky assumed leadership of Narkomos. Zatonsky took over editorial duties of the literary journal *Chervonyi shliakh* in 1926 and worked in this capacity until 1930. He also served as deputy chairman of Radnarkom from 1927 to 1933 and was elected a member of VUAN. He reassumed the position of commissar of education after Mykola Skrypnyk's dismissal in 1933. He was arrested in 1937 and later executed.

Notes

A Note on Administrative Divisions

1 I have relied partly on Robert Magocsi's valuable atlas for this description: Paul Robert Magocsi, *Ukraine: A Historical Atlas* (Toronto: University of Toronto Press, 1985), 21–2. For further discussion of the importance of these administrative changes, see: A. A. Nedukh, "Osnovni zminy v administratyvno-terytorial'noho ustroï URSR u 1919–1978 rr.," *Arkhivy Ukraïny*, no. 5 (1979).

Introduction

1 An important exception to this high-level concern is Kate Brown's *Biography of No Place* that discusses the Soviet attempt to promote national identities in multi-ethnic Volhynia, where rural populations had demonstrated little regard for such affiliations. Her study, however, focuses largely on the Soviet decision to delimit Polish (and German and Jewish) populations and says less about the details of *korenizatsiia* implementation, especially regarding the majority Ukrainian population. Francine Hirsch also emphasizes the role local elites played in crafting Soviet nationalities policy. This study benefits from her identification of a participatory process that "helped to assimilate the Union's disparate parts and strengthen Soviet rule," but it seeks to extend the local lens further, beyond information that all-Union authorities received and solicited, to the carriers of korenizatsiia in the schoolhouse. See: Kate Brown, *A Biography of No Place: From Ethnic Borderland to Soviet Heartland* (Cambridge: Harvard University Press, 2003); Francine Hirsch, *Empire of Nations: Ethnographic Knowledge and the Making of the Soviet Union* (Ithaca: Cornell University Press, 2005), 15. Other examples of recent English-language works that reference the question of local implementation of Soviet nationalities policy outside

Ukraine include: Per Anders Rudling, *The Rise and Fall of Belarusian Nationalism, 1906–1931* (Pittsburgh: University of Pittsburgh Press, 2014); Adrienne Lynn Edgar, *Tribal Nation: The Making of Soviet Turkmenistan* (Princeton: Princeton University Press, 2006).

2 *Tsentral'nyi derzhavnyi arkhiv vyshchykh orhaniv vlady i upravlinnia Ukraïny (TsDAVOU)*, f. 166, op. 4, spr. 129, ark. 110; Narodnyi komisariat osvity USRR, *Na fronti ku'ltury* (Kyïv: Radians'ka shkola, 1935), 28. According to the 1926 census, 80.0 per cent of the UkrSSR's population was ethnic Ukrainian.

3 I use the term "Ukrainizer" throughout this study as a broad category to reference individuals employed as instructors in Ukrainian-studies courses, public advocates of the expansion and deepening of Ukrainian-language use (who sometimes published in the pedagogical press), inspectors, Narkomos section heads and leaders who were tasked with the promotion of Ukrainian-language use, party and Komsomol activists, and their patrons in the KP(b)U leadership.

4 The manuscript draws from research I have published elsewhere. For an abbreviated description of the process of linguistic Ukrainization in the schools, see: Matthew D. Pauly, "Tending to the 'Native Word': Teachers and the Soviet Campaign for Ukrainian-Language Schooling, 1923–1930," *Nationalities Papers* 37, no. 3 (2009): 154–6. For a description of Ukrainian use of progressive pedagogy as it related to instruction in local studies, see: "Teaching Place, Assembling the Nation: Local Studies in Soviet Ukrainian Schools during the 1920s," *History of Education* 39, no. 1 (2010). I have also published a shorter version of the history of Ukrainization in the city of Odesa in German and Ukrainian: "'Odesa-Lektionen': Die Ukrainisierung der Schule, der Behörden und der nationalen Identität in einer nicht-ukrainischen Stadt in den 1920er Jahren," in *Die Ukraine: Prozesse der Nationsbildung*, ed. Andreas Kappeler (Köln, Wien: Böhlau Verlag, 2011); "'Odes'ki lektsiï': ukraïnizatsiia shkoly, ustanov, ta natsional'noï identichnosti v ne-ukraïns'komu misti v 1920-kh rr.," in *Ukraïna: Protsesy natsiotvorennia*, ed. Andreas Kappeler and Volodymyr Masliychuk (Kyïv: K.I.S., 2011).

5 See: John Reshetar, *The Ukrainian Revolution, 1917–1920* (New York: Arno Press, 1972); Felix Schnell, "'Tear Them Apart … And Be Done With It!' The Ataman Leadership of Nestor Makhno as a Culture of Violence," *Ab Imperio*, no. 3 (2008).

6 George Liber, *Soviet Nationality Policy, Urban Growth, and Identity Change in the Ukrainian SSR, 1923–1934* (New York: Cambridge University Press, 1992), 21–2, 107–10.

7 Kate Brown cautions that repeated Soviet invocations of a fight against backwardness in the countryside functioned as a sort of "colonialist narrative" in which rural inhabitants were reduced to "passive subjects of alien forces beyond their comprehension." Brown, *Biography of No Place*, 84–7.

8 Ihor Bondar-Tereshchenko offers an engaging investigation of early twentieth-century Ukrainian understandings of modernity and their expression in the Soviet period through a reading of literature: Bondar-Tereshchenko, *U zadzerkalli 1910–30-ikh rokiv* (Kyïv: Tempora, 2009). See also: *Borys Kosarev: kharkivs'kyi modernizm 1915–1931* (Kyïv: Rodovid, 2011).

9 Lebed conceded that "cultural enlightenment" (for example, primary schooling) might take place in the village in order to prepare the Ukrainian peasantry for assimilation to Russian, but even this was a dangerous proposition because of the risk that nationalists might co-opt this effort. Terry Martin, *The Affirmative Action Empire: Nations and Nationalism in the Soviet Union, 1923–39* (Ithaca: Cornell University Press, 2001), 78–9.

10 Playing off an early formulation by Lenin, Martin labels a Soviet shift to intervention in nationalities affairs "affirmative action." Martin argues, "In this new model, neutrality would inevitably lead to voluntary assimilation due to the historic strength of Russian national culture. Positive action, therefore, was needed to defend non-Russian culture against this unjust fate." Ibid., 16.

11 I differ somewhat from the perspective of Myroslav Shkandrij and Olga Bertelsen, who emphasize early party-authorized police surveillance of the Ukrainian intelligentsia in an important study that questions the sincerity of the Ukrainization policy. I also highlight GPU suspicions of, and party anxieties about, Ukrainization later. However, Narkomos officials and teachers expended significant effort, in the face of regular resistance, to carry out Ukrainization with the support of party leaders who were aware of the GPU's activities. Ukrainization was a contested and often contradictory policy, but its demise was not preordained at its outset even if powerful forces unquestionably sought to undermine it. See: Myroslav Shkandrij and Olga Bertelsen, "The Soviet Regime's National Operations in Ukraine, 1929–1934," *Canadian Slavonic Papers* 55, no. 3–4 (2013). For other views that argue for the strategic nature of Ukrainization, see: Elena Borisenok, *Fenomen sovetskoi ukrainizatsii, 1920–1930-e gody* (Moskva: Izdatel'stvo "Evropa," 2006); Mykola Doroshko, *Nomenklatura kerivna verkhivka radians'koï Ukraïny (1917–1938 rr.)* (Kyïv: Nika-Tsentr, 2012), 285–99. Even Martin argues, "*Korenizatsiia* was in fact an instrumental strategy, but to be effective it had to be presented as an essential goal." Martin, *Affirmative Action Empire*, 222.

12 This study seeks to build upon the work of Ukrainian historians who have been cautious in their evaluation of Ukrainization's achievements by detailing some of the difficulties in the critical area of primary schooling. Serhy Yekelchyk, *Ukraine: Birth of a Modern Nation* (New York: Oxford University Press, 2007), 94. For research by Ukrainian scholars on Ukrainization of education, see: V. A. Smolii, ed., *"Ukraïnizatsiia" 1920–30-kh rokiv: peredumovy, zdobutky, uroky* (Kyïv: Instytut istoriï

Ukraïny NAN Ukraïny, 2003); V. S. Lozyts'kyi, "Polityka ukraïnizatsii v 20–30-kh rokakh: istoriia, problemy, uroky," *Ukraïns'kyi istorychnyi zhurnal*, no. 3 (1989); V. L. Borysov, "Ukraïnizatsiia ta rozvytok zahal'noosvitnoï shkoly v 1921–31 rr.," *Ukraïns'kyi istorychnyi zhurnal*, no. 2 (1999); Konstiantyn Malyi, "Ukraïnizatsiia osvity: 20-ti roky," *Ridna shkola*, no. 11–12 (1996). The Ukrainian Institute of History has also published a guide to sources on korenizatsiia in Ukraine: P. M. Bondarchuk, V. M. Danylenko, and H. Iefimenko, eds., *Polityka korenizatsiï v radians'kii Ukraïni, 1920–1930-i rr.: naukovo-dopomizhnyi bibliohrafichnyi pokazhchyk* (Kyïv: Instytut istoriï Ukraïny NAN Ukraïny, 2003).

13 This book shares Stephen Velychenko's conviction that the authority of the government in Ukraine depended on "socialization" and the actions of lower-level administrative personnel. Ultimately, for the twin policies of Ukrainian-language schooling and progressive pedagogical instruction to have thrived in the Soviet era, education officials, teachers, parents, youth, and children needed to accept the merits of these campaigns. Stephen Velychenko, *State Building in Revolutionary Ukraine: A Comparative Study of Governments and Bureaucrats, 1917–1922* (Toronto: University of Toronto Press, 2011), 5, 14.

14 Francine Hirsch, *Empire of Nations*, 10–11. James Andrews's illuminating work on science in 1920s Soviet Russia similarly explains how pre-revolutionary provincial scientific societies adapted their objectives to the demands of new Soviet state. James T. Andrews, *Science for the Masses: The Bolshevik State, Public Science, and the Popular Imagination in Soviet Russia, 1917–1934* (College Station: Texas A&M University Press, 2003).

15 Like Tracy McDonald's findings, my work contends that local state servitors in Narkomos and teachers applied their own understanding of state policy and were the subjects of anxiety for the centre(s), both Kharkiv and Moscow. In the Ukrainian countryside, teachers, children, and youth in the Komsomol and Young Pioneers occupied a comparable position to McDonald's politically active peasants who simultaneously represented the village and the interests of the state. Tracy McDonald, *Face to the Village: The Riazan Countryside under Soviet Rule, 1921–1930* (Toronto: University of Toronto Press, 2011).

16 James E. Mace, *Communism and the Dilemmas of National Liberation: National Communism in Soviet Ukraine, 1918–1933* (Cambridge: Harvard Ukrainian Research Institute, 1983); Liber, *Soviet Nationality Policy*, 120.

17 Martin, *Affirmative Action Empire*, 122–3.

18 Strictly speaking, these *viddily* were under the administration of local governments (executive committees), but they reported directly to, and received orders from, the central Commissariat of Education, Narkomos. I generally refer to these *viddily* as education sections, but occasionally make their operational status as subunits of Narkomos explicit.

19 Martin uses both descriptors to describe the process. Elsewhere he writes that the Ukrainization of primary education "had been largely accomplished" by June 1925. Similarly, Liber writes that "Ukrainian became the dominant language in the education system ... This was very impressive, since Ukrainian-language schools did not exist before the revolution." Ibid., 86–7, 98; Liber, *Soviet Nationality Policy,* 109.

20 The Soviet drive to create ethnic homogeneous schools (and thereby reify national categories) had a parallel in the Bohemian experience under Habsburg rule, when Czech and German nationalist movements sought "to ensure that children were not 'lost' to the national community because of parents' persistent indifference to nationalist priorities in the home." Tara Zahra, *Kidnapped Souls: National Indifference and the Battle for Children in the Bohemian Lands, 1900–1948* (Ithaca: Cornell University Press, 2008), 52. Kate Brown emphasizes the often contrived nature that this process of national sorting had in the Markhlevsk Polish Autonomous District (*raion*) in interwar western Soviet Ukraine, where Soviet officials "chided local mayors and teachers when they continued to speak Ukrainian although they were counted as Polish." Kate Brown, *Biography of No Place*, 44.

21 As this study will detail, many teachers viewed orders to Ukrainize as a bother and some clearly did not accept the Soviet association of language with fixed national identity. Parental and teacher "indifference" to Ukrainization was often political in the sense that they resented an adjustment to the character of schools in which they had invested considerable social and economic capital. For an in-depth discussion of Zahra's concept of "national indifference," see: Tara Zahra, "Imagined Noncommunities: National Indifference as a Category of Analysis," *Slavic Review* 69, no. 1 (2010).

22 *TsDAVOU*, f. 166, op. 5, spr. 166, ark. 77.

23 Liber, *Soviet Nationality Policy,* 188.

24 This spelling is the correct transliteration of the newspaper's title as it was originally published.

25 Bohdan Krawchenko cites Yosyp Hermaize, a well-known pedagogue and historian, to argue that such a new generation, "organically tied to the Ukrainian language," had already developed. Bohdan Krawchenko, *Social Change and National Consciousness in Twentieth-Century Ukraine* (Edmonton: Canadian Institute of Ukrainian Studies, 1985), 92.

26 This study pays particular attention to the activities of mid-level and lower-level officials tasked with implementing and overseeing Ukrainization and pedagogical reform, as well as teachers and school directors who received the orders to change. For detailed accounts of the Narkomos bureaucracy, see: M. Iu. Vyhovs'kyi, *Nomenklatura systemy osvity v USRR 1920–1930-x rokiv: sotsial'ne pokhodzhennia personal'nyi sklad ta funktsii* (Kyïv: Heneza, 2006); I. L. Likarchuk, *Ministry osvity Ukraïny: u dvokh*

tomakh, vol. 1 (Kyïv: Vydavets' Eshke O.M, 2002). Vasyl Marochko and Hillig Götz also provide sketches of the lives of select Narkomos officials: Vasyl' Marochko and Khillih H'ots, *Represovani pedahohy Ukraïny: zhertvy politychnoho teroru* (Kyïv: Naukovyi svit, 2003). The history of many of others has yet to be written. Wherever possible, I have attempted to determine the full names of the individuals I discuss. Sometimes this is not possible. Archival files often do not include full names and educators occasionally published under pseudonyms in the pedagogical press. *TsDAVOU*, f. 166, op. 12 contains the personal files of Narkomos officials and is an invaluable resource for biographical data.

27 Unlike service in the Ukrainian revolutionary governments of Stephen Velychenko's study, it was not enough for Soviet officials, particularly those employed by Narkomos, to work as capable bureaucrats and remain indifferent to the national question during the height of linguistic Ukrainization. Narkomos employed high numbers of ethnic Ukrainians to pursue what was an explicitly national concern. Velychenko, *State Building in Revolutionary Ukraine*, 247–57.

28 Although this study necessarily highlights the activities the Soviet Ukrainian state undertook for the expansion of Ukrainian schooling for ethnic Ukrainians in Kyiv, the ethnic heterogeneous character of the city highlighted by recent scholarship functions as a backdrop to the story of the Ukrainization of the city's education system. Furthermore, the question of student enrolment raised important questions regarding a dissonance between national identity and language choice in Kyiv. For a wide-ranging discussion of the multi-ethnic contributions to Kyiv's cultural life, see: Irena R. Makaryk and Virlana Tkacz, eds., *Modernism in Kyiv: Jubilant Experimentation* (Toronto: University of Toronto Press, 2010).

29 The term "Russification" is a problematic one. Here, I use it to refer to the legacy of a Russian linguistic monopoly of primary schooling and urban culture in Ukraine. Referencing a larger historiographical debate, Andreas Kappeler writes that historians have used the word to denote a wide "tendency towards swift administrative, social, and cultural integration" in the Russian Empire, but it is a descriptor that should be sensitive to "regional and chronological terms." Andreas Kappeler, *The Russian Empire: A Multiethnic History*, trans. Alfred Cleyton (Harlow: Longman, 2001), 248. See also: Jeremy Smith, *Red Nations: The Nationalities Experience in and after the USSR* (Cambridge: Cambridge University Press, 2013), 16.

1. Primary Lessons

1 Martin, *Affirmative Action Empire*, 119.
2 Michael G. Smith, *Language and Power in the Creation of the USSR, 1917–1953*, ed. Joshua A. Fishman, vol. 80, Contributions to the Sociology of Language (New York: Mouton de Gruyter, 1998), 50.

3 William Fierman, "Language Development in Soviet Uzbekistan," in *Sociolinguistic Perspectives on Soviet National Languages*, ed. Isabelle T. Kreindler, *Contributions to the Sociology of Language* (New York: Mouton de Gruyter, 1985), 40.
4 Pierre Bourdieu, *Language and Symbolic Power*, trans. Gino Raymond and Matthew Adamson (Cambridge, MA: Harvard University Press, 1991), 48.
5 For an illustrative early example, see Aaron Retish's discussion of worker participation in the Week of the Peasant in Viatka, Russia. Aaron Retish, *Russia's Peasants in Revolution and Civil War: Citizenship, Identity, and the Creation of the Soviet State, 1914–1922* (New York: Cambridge University Press, 2008), 216–18. For other recent works on the Soviet government's engagement of the peasantry, see: Hugh D. Hudson, *Peasants, Political Police, and the Early Soviet State: Surveillance and Accommodation under the New Economic Policy* (New York: Palgrave Macmillan, 2012); McDonald, *Face to the Village*; James W. Heinzen, *Inventing a Soviet Countryside: State Power and the Transformation of Rural Russia, 1917–1929* (Pittsburgh: University of Pittsburgh Press, 2004).
6 Smith, *Language and Power*, 7, 80.
7 Bourdieu, *Language and Symbolic Power*, 48.
8 Ibid., 60–61.
9 James Collins, "Literacy and Literacies," *Annual Review of Anthropology* 24 (1995): 79.
10 Prosvita operated first in Habsburg-ruled Galicia before appearing in the Russian Empire after the revolution of 1905. The Soviets viewed Prosvita societies as centres of Ukrainian nationalist activity and sought to convert them to Soviet reading houses or disband them by 1923. For more on the history of Prosvita, see: Volodymyr Herman et al., *"Prosvita" – istoriia ta suchasnist': (1868–1998)* (Kyïv: Vydavnychyi tsentr "Prosvita": "Veselka," 1998).
11 Collins, "Literacy and Literacies," 84.
12 Ibid., 86.
13 James Collins and Richard K. Blot, *Literacy and Literacies: Texts, Power, and Identity* (Cambridge: Cambridge University Press, 2003).
14 Ibid., 96.
15 Stepan Siropolko, *Narodnia osvita na soviets'kii Ukraïni* (Warsaw: Pratsi Ukraïns'koho naukovoho instytutu, 1934). For a brief sketch on the Ukrainian education system, see: I. Krylov, *Systema osvity v Ukraïni: 1917–1930* (Munich: Institute for the Study of the USSR, 1956). Zenon Wasyliw's work on the Soviet countryside in the 1920s is instructive regarding the multiple responsibilities of village teachers, although necessarily limited in focus. Zenon Wasyliw, "Education Policy and Rural Schoolteachers in Soviet Ukraine," *East/West Education* 19, no. 1/2 (1998). Soviet-era surveys reveal less about the true course of educational policy or the acts of individual educators and planners due to their focus on statistical successes. H. I. Iasnyts'kyi, *Rozvytok narodnoï osvity na Ukraïni (1921–1932 rr.)* (Kyïv: Vydavnytstvo Kyïvs'koho

universytetu, 1965); A. H. Bondar et al., eds., *Narodna osvita i pedahohichna nauka v Ukraïns'kii RSR* (Kyïv: Radians'ka shkola, 1967). A 1996 edited volume by Oksana Sukhomlynska presents a broader and more accurate picture, but is concerned foremost with methodology and uses limited archival evidence. O. V. Sukhomlyns'ka, ed., *Narys istoriï ukraïns'koho shkil'nytstva (1905–1933)* (Kyïv: Zapovit, 1996). For similar studies, see also: V. I. Borysenko and I. O. Telehuz, *Natsional'na osvita i formuvannia ukraïns'koï modernoï natsiï u 1921–1934 rokakh: ievropeis'ki tendentsiï ta radians'ki realiï* (Kyïv: Vydavnytstvo NPU im. M. P. Drahomanova, 2012); P. I. Drob'iazko, *Ukraïns'ka natsional'na shkola: vytoky i suchasnist'* (Kyïv: Akademiia, 1997). Hennadii Yefimenko has also published several informative articles and essays on the daily life of teachers in Soviet Ukraine and their public roles beyond the classroom. H. Iefimenko, "Hromads'ka robota iak chynnyk povsiakdennoho zhyttia vchytelia," *Problemy istoriï Ukraïni*, no. 17 (2006); "Sotsial'ne oblychchia vchytel'stva USRR v konteksti transformatsiï suspil'stva (1920-ti roky)," *Problemy istoriï Ukraïni*, no. 17 (2007); "Povsiakdenne zhyttia vchytelia shkoly sotsial'noho vykhovannia," in *Narysy povsiakdennoho zhyttia radians'koï Ukraïny v dobu NEPu (1921–1928 rr.)*, ed. S. V. Kul'chyts'kyi (Kyïv: Instytut istoriï Ukraïny NAN Ukraïny, 2010).

16 Other Ukrainian studies have offered valuable discussion of Ukrainization within the general context of the development of the republican education system, an account of Narkomos administrations, or political repression, but they do not examine the intersection between progressive pedagogy and nationalities policy (neither do they detail the multiple challenges teachers as a whole faced or the role of the Komsomol and Young Pioneers in the schools). For additional surveys of early Soviet Ukrainian education and Narkomos beyond those already mentioned, see: V. V. Lypyns'kyi, "Kontseptsiia ta model' osvity v USRR u 20-ti rr.," *Ukraïns'kyi istorychnyi zhurnal*, no. 5 (1999); V. V. Lypyns'kyi, *Stanovlennia i rozvytok systemy osvity USRR u 20-i roky* (Donets'k: DonDTU, 2000); V. M. Danylenko and M. M. Kuz'menko, *Sotsial'nyi typ ta intelektual'no-osvitnii riven' nomenklatury skrypnykivs'koho narkomosu: biohrafichni narysy* (Sevastopol': Veter, 2003); M. M. Kuz'menko, "Systema osvity v USRR u 1920-x rr.: istoryko-teoretychnyi aspekt," *Ukraïns'kyi istorychnyi zhurnal*, no. 5 (2004); T. Antoniuk, "Rozvytok osvitn'oï systemy v USRR (20-ti-pochatok 30-x rokiv)," *Istorychnyi zhurnal*, no. 6–7 (2004).

17 Thomas E. Ewing, "Ethnicity at School: 'Non-Russian' Education in the Soviet Union during the 1930s," *History of Education* 35, no. 4–5 (2006): 503.

18 Sheila Fitzpatrick, *Education and Social Mobility in the Soviet Union: 1921–1934* (New York: Cambridge University Press, 1979), 18–19.

19 Larry E. Holmes, *The Kremlin and the Schoolhouse: Reforming Education in Soviet Russia, 1917–1931* (Bloomington: Indiana University Press, 1991), 4.

20 Catriona Kelly, *Children's World: Growing Up in Russia, 1890–1991* (New Haven: Yale University Press, 2007), 527, 529. While offering considerable perspective on

the child's view of schooling, Kelly's focus is on schooling for ethnic Russians and says little about education outside Russia for the Soviet period. A recent essay by Ben Eklof is similarly focused on Russia and Russians in its discussion of nationhood and citizenship: Ben Eklof, "Russia and the Soviet Union: Schooling, Citizenship, and the Reach of the State, 1870–1945," in *Mass Education and the Limits of State Building, c. 1870–1930* (New York: Palgrave Macmillan, 2012).

21 William Parlett, "Breaching Cultural Worlds with the Village School: Educational Visions, Local Initiative, and Rural Experience at S. T. Shatskii's Kaluga School System, 1919–1932," *Slavic and East European Review* 82, no. 4 (2004); "The Cultural Revolution in the Village School: S. T. Shatskii's Kaluga School Complex, 1919–1932," *Journal of the Oxford University History Society*, no. 3 (2005); "Bourgeois Ideas in Communist Construction: The Development of Stanislav Shatskii's Teacher Training Methods," *History of Education* 35, no. 4–5 (2006).

22 Parlett, "The Cultural Revolution in the Village School," 4; Parlett, "Breaching Cultural Worlds," 884–5.

23 The accounts of John Dewey and George S. Counts are the most famous American observations of Soviet education. See: John Dewey, *Essays, Reviews, Miscellany, and "Impressions of Soviet Russia,"* ed. Jo Ann Boydston, vol. 3, *The Later Works, 1925–1953* (Carbondale: Southern Illinois University Press, 1981); George S. Counts, *The Soviet Challenge to America* (New York: The John Day Company, 1931). For a description of how progressive pedagogical ideas were instituted elsewhere in Europe, see: Marjorie Lamberti, *The Politics of Education: Teachers and School Reform in Weimar Germany* (New York: Bergham Books, 2002); Laura Lee Downs, *Childhood in the Promised Land: Working-Class Movements and the Colonies de Vacances in France, 1880–1960* (Durham: Duke University Press, 2002). Critics of American "social reconstructionists" charged them with Communist sympathies in the early 1930s, making the association between the Soviet Union and progressive education plain. See: Tracy Lynn Steffes, *School, Society, & State: A New Education to Govern Modern America, 1890–1940* (Chicago: The University of Chicago Press, 2012).

24 James C. Scott, *Seeing Like a State: How Certain Schemes to Improve the Human Condition Have Failed* (New Haven: Yale University Press, 1998).

25 Ernest Gellner's claim that a state's "exo-socialization" of its population is a precondition for nationalism is premised on the idea of a centralized education system. Ernest Gellner, *Nations and Nationalism* (Ithaca, NY: Cornell University Press, 1983), 38. For a classic description of this process, see Eugene Weber, *Peasants into Frenchmen: The Modernization of Rural France, 1870–1914* (Standford: Stanford University Press, 1976), 308–38.

26 Russian provincial education sections recommended that teachers instruct students in local dialects, the "living languages," instead of teaching them formalized grammar, but such ambitions were short-lived. Holmes, *Kremlin and the Schoolhouse*, 10–11.

27 For more on this subject, see: Lisa Kirschenbaum, *Small Comrades: Revolutionizing Childhood in Soviet Russia, 1917–1923* (New York: RoutledgeFalmer, 2001), 50–62.
28 Holmes, *Kremlin and the Schoolhouse*, 44–5.
29 Fitzpatrick argues that the Ukrainian secondary school operated according to "the distant ideal of a smoothly functioning socialist economy, in which all resources including human ones were rationally supplied and distributed according to a central plan." See Fitzpatrick, *Education and Social Mobility*, 45. Ukrainian education officials, however, regularly insisted that these schools were not trade schools. Rather, these schools intended to give students a familiarity with a type of production and its place in the economy as a whole.
30 George Y. Shevelov, *The Ukrainian Language in the First Half of the Twentieth Century (1900–1941): Its State and Status* (Cambridge, MA: Harvard Ukrainian Research Institute, 1989), 11–20. By 1914, 97 per cent of Ukrainian children went to Ukrainian elementary schools in the Habsburg Empire. See also: Paul Robert Magocsi, *The Roots of Ukrainian Nationalism: Galicia as Ukraine's Piedmont* (Toronto: University of Toronto Press, 2002), 83–98.
31 Shevelov, *Ukrainian Language*, 189–90. For more on the Galician role in late nineteenth- and early twentieth-century discussions of language standardization, see: Paul Wexler, *Purism and Language: A Study in Modern Ukrainian and Belorussian Nationalism, 1840–1967* (Bloomington, IN: Indiana University Press, 1974), 39–156.
32 For example, the number of Ukrainian schools declined from 2,510 in Galicia in 1914 to 804 in Poland as a whole in 1928. The Polish government did not permit a Ukrainian pedagogical society, Ridna shkola, to operate outside of Galicia and no Polish state university allowed instruction in Ukrainian. Ibid., 179–81. On Ukrainians in Transcarpathia and Bukovina, see: Paul R. Magocsi, *The Rusyn-Ukrainians of Czechoslovakia: An Historical Survey* (Wien: W. Braumüller 1983); Irina Livezeanu, *Cultural Politics in Greater Romania: Regionalism, Nation Building, and Ethnic Struggle, 1918–1930* (Ithaca: Cornell University Press, 1995).
33 A gymnasium was a pre-Soviet secondary school that prepared its students for entry into a university. During the tsarist era, gymnasiums principally served children of the urban elite. The establishment of the Taras Shevchenko Gymnasium represented an assertion of Ukrainian cultural parity with Russian in the city.
34 Shevelov, *Ukrainian Language*, 102.
35 Ibid., 104.
36 Ibid., 108.
37 Wexler, *Purism and Language*, 113–14.
38 Shevelov, *Ukrainian Language*, 130.
39 Ibid., 131.
40 Shevelov argues that Galicians viewed the new orthography with hostility, and only the 1933 Soviet condemnation of the writing system as "nationalist" (and

replacement of it with a standard closer to Russian) caused Galicians to moderate their opposition. The increasing infrequency of contact between Galician and Soviet Ukrainian linguists contributed to resistance as well. Ibid., 187–90. On Soviet Ukraine as a Piedmont for Ukrainians, see: Martin, *Affirmative Action Empire*, 8–9. On the reaction of Western Ukrainians to Ukrainization in the UkrSSR, see: Smolii, *"Ukraïnizatsiia,"* 299–325.

41 Wexler, *Purism and Language*, 136.
42 For a discussion of the self-perception of "Little Russians," see: Andreas Kappeler, *Great Russians and Little Russians: Russian-Ukrainian Relations and Perceptions in Historical Perpsective* (Seattle, WA: Henry M. Jackson School of International Studies, University of Washington, 2003). Faith Hillis provides an invaluable, detailed study of the nineteenth-century origins of the Little Russian idea and contests over its meaning. Faith Hillis, *Children of Rus': Right-Bank Ukraine and the Invention of a Russian Nation* (Ithaca: Cornell University Press, 2013). The term "Little Russian" need not reference linguistic preference. Oleksandr Shumsky used it as a pejorative to denote a Ukrainian who rejected "things Ukrainian" and remained slavishly beholden to Russian culture (and perhaps Moscow) while playing lip service to Ukrainization. Shumsky's use of this term caused an uproar in the KP(b)U, especially among those Old Bolsheviks who assumed Shumsky meant them. Martin, *Affirmative Action Empire*, 212–20.
43 The Soviets conducted three censuses in the 1920s, an incomplete 1920 census, which did not tabulate large parts of Ukraine, a 1923 census that the government confined to urban areas, and the 1926 first truly all-Union census. Because of the limitations of the two initial censuses, the 1897 census helped determine targets for much of the initial work on Ukrainization, but it was also inherently flawed. Hirsch writes that Ukrainian delegates to a preparatory conference for the 1926 census argued for use of the term *nationality* (*nationalnost'*) to avoid a hierarchical classification of identity, suggesting that the Ukrainians were motivated by the 1897 census that labelled Ukrainians as "Little Russians," a regional subcategory of Russians. Hirsch argues that Soviet planners imagined the 1926 census as an interactive process in which census takers guided respondents towards the appropriate answer. Evidence that this was an imperfect process was suggested by Ukrainian scholars who objected that data on high illiteracy among Ukrainians were inaccurate, "since Ukrainians who attended Russian schools 'understand literacy as literacy in Russian' (and 'do not answer that they are literate in Ukrainian')." Hirsch, *Empire of Nations*, 130.
44 Kate Brown gives a detailed description of how political decisions surrounding census data influenced future results in the multi-ethnic western borderland of Soviet Ukraine. The 1920–2 census "became a highly political affair; it rocked back and forth from region to region, adding and sloughing off Poles." Because the Soviet Ukrainian government sanctioned the identification of Ukrainian-speaking Catholics

as Poles, the overall number of Poles in Ukraine rose sharply by the 1926 census. In the end, scholars must judge census data as a mixture of individual, willful decisions and administrative finesse. Brown, *Biography of No Place*, 38–47.

45 For a detailed study of the early Soviet attempt to foster a secular Yiddish identity in Ukraine and in neighbouring Belarus (and a description of the persistence of pre-revolutionary Yiddish culture), see: Jeffrey Veidlinger, *In the Shadow of the Shtetl: Small-Town Jewish Life in Soviet Ukraine* (Bloomington: Indiana University Press, 2013); Elissa Bemporad, *Becoming Soviet Jews: The Bolshevik Experiment in Minsk* (Bloomington: Indiana University Press, 2013). There is a growing literature on the relationship between Jewish identity, Bolshevism (Soviet communism), as well as Ukrainian national culture: David Shneer, *Yiddish and the Creation of Soviet Jewish Culture, 1918–1930* (New York: Cambridge University Press, 2004); Kenneth B. Moss, *Jewish Renaissance in the Russian Revolution* (Cambridge: Harvard University Press, 2009); Yohanan Petrovsky-Shtern, *The Anti-imperial Choice: The Making of the Ukrainian Jew* (New Haven: Yale University Press, 2009); Myroslav Shkandrij, *Jews in Ukrainian Literature: Representation and Identity* (New Haven: Yale University Press, 2009); Anna Shternshis, *Soviet and Kosher: Jewish Popular Culture in the Soviet Union, 1923–1939* (Bloomington: Indiana University Press, 2006); Yuri Slezkine, *The Jewish Century* (Princeton: Princeton University Press, 2004).

46 Drawing from oral testimonies of surviving Yiddish-speakers in the contemporary Vinnytsia oblast of Ukraine, Veidlinger notes the many Jewish children attended Russian schools, but also cites evidence of some rural Jews opting for Ukrainian-language schools because of the comparative lack of higher education in Yiddish or employment opportunities for graduates of Yiddish schools. Outside of the Vinnytsia oblast's major towns, Ukrainian schools predominated and there were sometimes few other choices for Jewish parents who opted for a non-Yiddish education or were faced with the closure of a Yiddish school beginning in the mid-1930s. Veidlinger, *In the Shadow of the Shtetl*, 87–91.

47 It is difficult to personalize this understanding beyond the lens of surviving archival documents, usually authored by state institutions, party and Komsomol organizations, and official unions, and, of course, preserved by the state. A reading of the 1920s pedagogical press, in particular the teachers' newspaper *Narodnii uchytel'*, offers a less regulated insight into the perspective of non-party stakeholders in Ukrainization. For memoir accounts that reference the policy of Ukrainization generally, see: Ivan Maistrenko, *Istoriia moho pokolinnia: spohady uchasnyka revoliutsiinykh podiï v Ukraïni* (Edmonton: Kanads'kyi instytut ukraïns'kykh studii, 1985); Borys Antonenko-Davydovych, *Zemleiu ukraïns'koiu* (Philadelphia: Kyïv, 1955); Anatolii Boiko, ed., *Dzherela z istoriï pivdennoï Ukrainy: Memuary ta shchodennyky*, vol. 5, pt. 1, bk. 1 (Zaporizhzhia: RA "Tandem-U," 2005), cited in Serhii Plokhy, *Ukraine and Russia: Representations of the Past* (Toronto: University of Toronto Press, 2008).

48 Martin labels the prioritization of the Ukrainian language in the public space "comprehensive Ukrainization," but argues that the continued preference of the working class for mostly Russian-language use weakened the program's force and was leading towards the development of a "territorial Ukrainian identity that was bilingual and open to both ethnic Ukrainians and Russians." Martin, *Affirmative Action Empire*, 105. A preference for Ukrainian-language predominance remained official policy well into the early 1930s, and Narkomos consistently pursued the conversion of the language habits of the working class and their children.
49 Michael David-Fox, *Revolution of the Mind: Higher Learning among the Bolsheviks, 1918–1929* (Ithaca: Cornell University Press, 1997); Larry E. Holmes, *Stalin's School: Moscow's Model School No. 25, 1931–1937* (Pittsburgh: University of Pittsburgh Press, 1999); E. Thomas Ewing, *The Teachers of Stalinism: Policy, Practice, and Power in Soviet Schools of the 1930s* (New York: Peter Lang, 2002); David Brandenberger, *National Bolshevism: Stalinist Mass Culture and the Formation of Modern Russian National Identity, 1931–1956* (Cambridge, MA: Harvard University Press, 2002); Kelly, *Children's World*; Larry E. Holmes, *Grand Theater: Regional Governance in Stalin's Russia, 1931–1941* (Lanham, MD: Lexington Books, 2009); Igal Halfin, *Stalinist Confessions: Messianism and Terror at the Leningrad Communist University* (Pittsburgh: University of Pittsburgh Press, 2009); E. Thomas Ewing, *Separate Schools: Gender, Policy, and Practice in Postwar Soviet Education* (DeKalb: Northern Illinois University Press, 2010).
50 Peter A. Blitstein, "Nation-Building or Russification? Obligatory Russian Instruction in the Soviet Non-Russian School, 1938–1953," in *The State of Nations: Empire and Nation-Making in the Age of Lenin and Stalin*, ed. Ronald Grigor Suny and Terry Martin (Oxford: Oxford University Press, 2001).
51 Yuri Slezkine, "The USSR as a Communal Apartment, or How a Socialist State Promoted Ethnic Particularism," *Slavic Review*, no. 53 (1994).
52 Adeeb Khalid, *The Politics of Muslim Cultural Reform: Jadidism in Central Asia* (Berkeley: University of California Press, 1998), 199. For a discussion of pre-revolutionary education in Central Asia, see: Wayne Dowler, *Classroom and Empire: The Politics of Schooling Russia's Eastern Nationalities, 1860–1917* (Montréal: McGill-Queen's University Press, 2001).
53 Adrienne Lynn Edgar, *Tribal Nation*, 164. David Shneer provides another account of collaboration and subsequent disrupture between Soviet authorities and non-Russian intellectuals, focusing in particular on the production of Yiddish literature and press (including in Ukraine): Shneer, *Yiddish and the Creation of Soviet Jewish Culture*, 122–5.
54 The fate of children features in the authoritative, long, documentary collection published by the Institute of History, but there is no separate study on schooling. See: S.V. Kul'chyts'kyi, ed. *Kolektyvizatsiia i holod na Ukraïni, 1929–1933: zbirnyk*

dokumentiv i materialiv, 2 vols. (Kyïv: Naukova dumka, 1993); *Holodomor 1932–1933 rokiv v Ukraïni za dokumentamy HDA SBU: anatovanyi dovidnyk*, (L'viv: Tsentr doslidzhen' vyzvol'noho rukhu, 2010).

55 Gellner, *Nations and Nationalism*, 29.
56 Martin, *Affirmative Action Empire*, 154–6.
57 Smith, *Language and Power*, 80, 7.
58 For the more pessimistic view, see: Mace, *Communism and the Dilemmas of National Liberation* 264–301; Liber, *Soviet Nationality Policy*, 160–74. Yuri Slezkine famously contended that Soviet nation building continued past the early 1930s and the significant contributions of Martin and Hirsch are generally in accord with Slezkine's argument. See: Slezkine, "The USSR as a Communal Apartment," 362–91; Hirsch, *Empire of Nations*, 231–308.

2. Adapting to Place

1 Celia Applegate, *A Nation of Provincials: The German Idea of Heimat* (Berkeley: University of California Press, 1990), 12.
2 See also: Alon Confino, *The Nation as a Local Metaphor: Württemberg, Imperial Germany, and National Memory, 1871–1918* (Chapel Hill: University of North Carolina Press, 1997), 97–210.
3 Several recent publications on regional history and the Russian practice of *kraevedenie* have informed this work. Unlike these works, however, this chapter concerns a definition of local studies articulated by non-local authorities, rather than investigation of events from one regional perspective or an account of a particular group engaged in the telling of local history. See: Donald J. Raleigh, ed., *Provincial Landscapes: Local Dimensions of Soviet Power, 1917–1953* (Pittsburgh: University of Pittsburgh Press, 2001); Susan Smith-Peter, "How to Write a Region: Local and Regional Historiography," *Kritika: Explorations in Russian and Eurasian History* 5, no. 3 (2004).
4 G. Gryn'ko, "Nash put' na Zapad," *Put' prosveshchennia*, no. 7–8 (1923): 1–19, cited in O. V. Sukhomlyns'ka, "Zarubizhnyi pedahohichnyi dosvid v Ukraïni v 20-ti roky," *Ridna shkola*, no. 2 (1992): 3–7.
5 Ibid., 6.
6 *Narys istoriï ukraïns'koho shkil'nytstva (1905–1933)*, 124.
7 Holmes, *Kremlin and the Schoolhouse*, 35.
8 Ia. P. Riappo, *Narodnia osvita na Ukraïni: za desiat' rokiv revoliutsiï* (Kharkiv: Derzhavne vydavnytstvo Ukrainy, 1927), 31.
9 Ibid.
10 Alan Ball suggests, on the basis of published Soviet statistics, the number of homeless and half-homeless children for Ukraine reached two million. Alan Ball, "The Roots

of Besprizornost' in Soviet Russia's First Decade," *Slavic Review* 51, no. 2 (1992): 247; *And Now My Soul Is Hardened: Abandoned Children in Soviet Russia, 1918–1930* (Berkeley: University of California Press, 1994).
11 Riappo, *Narodnia osvita na Ukraïni: za desiat' rokiv revoliutsiï*, 62.
12 Ninel' Kalenychenko, "Problema sim'ï ta simeinoho vykhovannia," *Shliakh osvity*, no. 4 (1997): 47.
13 Sukhomlyns'ka, *Narys istoriï ukraïns'koho shkil'nytstva (1905–1933)*, 86.
14 Riappo, *Narodnia osvita na Ukraïni: za desiat' rokiv revoliutsiï*, 31.
15 Lypyns'kyi, "Kontseptsiia ta model' osvity v USRR u 20-ti rr.," 5. Lypynsky, like Olha Sukhomlynska, places primary emphasis on Hrynko's role in the formation of this separate Ukrainian education system, but Ihor Likarchuk stresses the importance of Volodymyr Zatonsky in defining the initial organizational structure of this system, citing his signature on several key founding documents on the Narkomos bureaucratic structure. I. L. Likarchuk, *Ministry osvity Ukraïny: u dvokh tomakh*, vol. 1 (Kyïv: Vydavets' Eshke O.M, 2002), 234. For a detailed discussion of the creation of the Ukrainian system, see also: Lypyns'kyi, *Stanovlennia i rozvytok systemy osvity USRR u 20-i roky*, 23–46.
16 Fitzpatrick, *Education and Social Mobility*, 45–6; Holmes, *Kremlin and the Schoolhouse*, 22–3.
17 Holmes, *Kremlin and the Schoolhouse*, 23.
18 Fitzpatrick, *Education and Social Mobility*, 44.
19 Riappo, *Narodnia osvita na Ukraïni: za desiat' rokiv revoliutsiï*, 38.
20 Ibid., 39.
21 Sukhomlyns'ka, *Narys istoriï ukraïns'koho shkil'nytstva (1905–1933)*, 185.
22 Ibid., 176.
23 Vyhovs'kyi, *Nomenklatura systemy osvity v USRR*, 76, 166–7, 195.
24 Holmes, *Kremlin and the Schoolhouse*, 32.
25 A speaker at a December 1925–January 1926 meeting of school directors in the Kyiv region insisted upon this point, claiming the *poradnyk* provided only a "framework" for Soviet Ukrainian schools. The first poradnyk was published in 1921 in Kharkiv, but it was not until 1923–4 that it incorporated complex methodology. *TsDAVOU*, f. 166, op. 6, spr. 1960, ark. 13.
26 *TsDAVOU*, f. 166, op. 4, spr. 888, ark. 18.
27 *TsDAVOU*, f. 166, op. 6, spr. 1960, ark. 2.
28 *TsDAVOU*, f. 166, op. 6, spr. 1960, ark. 7.
29 *TsDAVOU*, f. 166, op. 5, spr. 666, ark. 82.
30 *TsDAVOU*, f. 166, op. 6, spr. 1960, ark. 2.
31 *TsDAVOU*, f. 166, op. 3, spr. 872, ark. 313.
32 See Anatolii Borovyk, *Ukraïnizatsiia zahal'noosvitnikh shkil za chasiv vyboriuvannia derzhavnosti, 1917–1920 rr.* (Chernihiv: KP Vydavnytstvo "Chernihivs'ki oberehy,"

2008). A comprehensive English-language study of Ukrainian pre-revolutionary schools has yet to be published. For an initial description, see: Krawchenko, *Social Change and National Consciousness*, 21–39. For works on schools and teachers in the Russian Empire generally, see: Ben Eklof, *Russian Peasant Schools: Officialdom, Village Culture, and Popular Pedagogy, 1861–1917* (Berkeley: University of California Press, 1986); Scott Seregny, *Russian Teachers and Peasant Revolution: The Politics of Education in 1905* (Bloomington: Indiana University Press, 1989); Christine Ruane, *Gender, Class, and the Professionalization of Russian City Teachers, 1860–1914* (Pittsburgh: University of Pittsburgh Press, 1994).

33 Shums'kyi, O. "Na tret'omu fronti: do uchytel's'koho z"ïzdu." *Shliakh osvity*, no. 11–12 (1924): xiv.
34 *TsDAVOU*, f. 166, op. 5, spr. 666, ark. 179.
35 *TsDAVOU*, f. 166, op. 6, spr. 1960, ark. 92.
36 *TsDAVOU*, f. 166, op. 6, spr. 1960, ark. 4, 13.
37 Riappo, *Narodnia osvita na Ukraïni: za desiat' rokiv revoliutsiï*, 64.
38 Holmes, *The Kremlin and the Schoolhouse*, 76–83.
39 Sukhomlyns'ka, *Narys istoriï ukraïns'koho shkil'nytstva (1905–1933)*, 208.
40 Ibid.
41 A. Lazaris, "Ukraïns'ke kraieznavstvo i perspektyvy ioho rozvytku," *Radians'ka osvita*, no. 5 (1925): 49.
42 Ibid, 209.
43 See, for example: I. S. Vynokur, L. L. Babenko, and P. T. Tron'ko, *Represovane kraieznavstvo (20–30-i roky)* (Kyïv: Ridnyi krai, 1992).
44 For a classic, general history of VUAN (and its successive purges in the 1930s), see: N. D. Polons'ka-Vasylenko, *Ukraïns'ka akademiia nauk* (Kyïv: Naukov dumka, 1993). For documents on the arrest of VUAN academicians, see: Danylenko, *Ukraïns'ka intelihentsiia i vlada: zavedennia sekretnoho viddilu DPU USRR 1927–1929 rr.*
45 A Central (All-Union) Bureau of Local Studies administered contact between the Ukrainian Committee and local studies organizations beyond the UkrSSR, although Ukrainian authorities also set up their own direct ties. P. T. Tron'ko, *Ukraïns'ke kraieznavstvo v XX stolitti: do 75-richchia Vseukraïns'koï spilky kraieznavtsiv* (Kyïv: Instytut istoriï Ukraïny NAN Ukraïny, 2002), 27–9.
46 Sukhomlyns'ka, *Narys istoriï ukraïns'koho shkil'nytstva (1905–1933)*, 216–19.
47 I. Haliun, "Kraieznavstvo i shkola," *Radians'ka osvita*, no. 5 (1925): 56.
48 Ibid., 54.
49 Ibid., 57.
50 *TsDAVOU*, f. 166, op. 7, spr. 675, ark. 43.
51 I. Kopyl, "Sproba vyvchennia kraiu: zolotonoshs'ka okruha na Poltavshchyni," *Radians'ka osvita*, no. 5 (1925): 58–9.
52 Ibid., 59.

53 Slobidska Ukraine (Slobozhanshchyna) was the historical area around Kharkiv in which several Cossack regiments lived. It had no territorial autonomy from Muscovy, unlike the Cossack Hetmanate state to its south, but its location afforded its inhabitants some initial freedom from state control, and systems of land tenure were less onerous than in Muscovy. A major religious educational centre, Kharkiv College, was located on its territory.
54 Sukhomlyns'ka, *Narys istoriï ukraïns'koho shkil'nytstva (1905–1933)*, 211.
55 Ibid., 214.
56 Ibid., 213.
57 Ibid.
58 *TsDAVOU*, f. 166, op. 5, spr. 666, ark. 7.
59 *TsDAVOU*, f. 166, op. 5, spr. 666, ark. 81.
60 Sukhomlyns'ka, *Narys istoriï ukraïns'koho shkil'nytstva (1905–1933)*, 216.
61 Ibid., 219.
62 *TsDAVOU*, f. 166, op. 5, spr. 671, ark. 468.
63 Haliun, "Kraieznavstvo i shkola," 52.
64 Ibid.
65 George G. Grabowicz, *The Poet as Mythmaker: A Study of Symbolic Meaning in Taras Ševčenko* (Cambridge, MA: Harvard Ukrainian Research Institute, 1982), 1.
66 *TsDAVOU*, f. 166, op. 6, spr. 1960, ark. 11zv.
67 V. Durdukivs'kyi, "Shevchenkivs'ka shkola – Shevchenkovi," *Radians'ka osvita*, no. 3–4 (1924): 37–47.
68 Ibid., 37.
69 Iu. T., "Pered Shevchenkivs'kymy dniamy: z zhyttia II hrupy Kyïvs'koï 1-oï trudovoï shkoly im. Shevchenka, za 1924 r.," *Radians'ka osvita*, no. 3–4 (1924): 48–56.
70 Durdukivs'kyi, "Shevchenkivs'ka shkola – Shevchenkovi," 46; Iu. T., "Pered Shevchenkivs'kymy dniamy: z zhyttia II hrupy Kyïvs'koï 1-oï trudovoï shkoly im. Shevchenka, za 1924 r.," 56.
71 The kobzars were wandering musicians who played in the service of Cossack detachments and, after the dissolution of the Ukrainian Cossack host, sang about past Cossack glory. Taras Shevchenko titled his collection of poetry *Kobzar* (1840), and kobzars, their music, and their preferred instrument (the stringed bandura) came to be seen as important representation of Ukrainian national identity.
72 Durdukivs'kyi, "Shevchenkivs'ka shkola – Shevchenkovi," 46.

3. The Conversion

1 *TsDAVOU*, f. 166, op. 3, spr. 872, ark. 65–6.
2 *TsDAVOU*, f. 166, op. 3, spr. 866, ark. 12.
3 *TsDAVOU*, f. 166, op. 3, spr. 862, ark. 102.

4 *TsDAVOU*, f. 166, op. 3, spr. 862, ark. 1.
5 In addition to the recent works already cited on the Soviet engagement with the peasantry, there is a wide literature on the initial Bolshevik *smychka* strategy, the internal party struggle over its direction in the 1920s, and Stalin's interpretation. Especially instructive are: Moshe Lewin, *Russian Peasants and Soviet Power: A Study of Collectivization* (New York: Norton, 1975); Lewis H. Siegelbaum, *Soviet State and Society between Revolutions, 1918–1929* (Cambridge: Cambridge University Press, 1992); Stephen F. Cohen, *Bukharin and the Bolshevik Revolution: A Political Biography, 1888–1938* (Oxford: Oxford University Press, 1980), 123–213, 310–16.
6 Vyhovs'kyi, *Nomenklatura systemy osvity v USRR*, 195–6
7 This support existed in spite of the fact that Shumsky was, in the judgment of Likarchuk, "insufficiently interested in the problems of educational construction." Likarchuk, *Ministry osvity Ukraïny*, 179. Quoted in *Nomenklatura systemy osvity v USRR*, 166.
8 The Radnarkom decree further required the study of the Ukrainian language in all non-Ukrainian schools, but Russian remained an obligatory subject. The decree specified that Russian was "a common state language" that "connects the Ukrainian people to the culture of the Union of Soviet Socialist Republics." Vyhovs'kyi, *Nomenklatura systemy osvity v USRR*, 196.
9 *TsDAVOU*, f. 166, op. 3, spr. 862, ark. 103.
10 Ibid.
11 *TsDAVOU*, f. 166, op. 3, spr. 872, ark. 51–3.
12 Ibid.
13 *TsDAVOU*, f. 166, op. 3, spr. 862, ark. 103.
14 *TsDAVOU*, f. 166, op. 3, spr. 862, ark. 104.
15 *TsDAVOU*, f. 166, op. 3, spr. 862, ark. 65–6.
16 *TsDAVOU*, f. 166, op. 3, spr. 862, ark. 106.
17 Ibid.
18 *TsDAVOU*, f. 166, op. 3, spr. 862, ark. 107–8.
19 *TsDAVOU*, f. 166, op. 3, spr. 866, ark. 104; *TsDAVOU*, f. 166, op. 3, spr. 872, ark. 267.
20 *TsDAVOU*, f. 166, op. 3, spr. 866, ark. 13.
21 *TsDAVOU*, f. 166, op. 3, spr. 866, 10.
22 Ibid.
23 *TsDAVOU*, f. 2717, op. 1, spr. 169, ark. 33.
24 *TsDAVOU*, f. 2717, op. 1, spr. 169, ark. 93.
25 "Kulak" was a label Soviet authorities applied to prosperous peasants, generally those who could afford to hire labour, but, more often than not, those who opposed Soviet power. Even poor peasants hired labour during harvest, and peasant prosperity was usually short-term. During the collectivization campaign of the First Five-Year

Plan, peasants who resisted were condemned as kulaks and were either dispossessed, deported, or executed.
26 *TsDAVOU*, f. 2717, op. 1, spr. 169, ark. 82.
27 *TsDAVOU*, f. 2717, op. 1, spr. 167, ark. 166.
28 *TsDAVOU*, f. 2717, op. 1, spr. 167, ark. 174–6.
29 *TsDAVOU*, f. 2717, op. 1, spr. 167, ark. 43.
30 *TsDAVOU*, f. 2717, op. 1, spr. 169, ark. 6.
31 *TsDAVOU*, f. 2717, op. 1, spr. 169, ark. 6.
32 *TsDAVOU*, f. 2717, op. 1, spr. 169, ark. 52.
33 *TsDAVOU*, f. 2717, op. 1, spr. 169, ark. 102.
34 *TsDAVOU*, f. 2717, op. 1, spr. 169, ark. 29.
35 *TsDAVOU*, f. 166, op. 3, spr. 866, ark. 13.
36 Ibid.
37 Ibid.
38 *TsDAVOU*, f. 166, op. 3, spr. 872, ark. 114. Russian workers in the Donbas reportedly rebelled against the Ukrainization of schools through the importation of teachers from central Ukraine and Galicia. For more on the reaction of the Donbas to Ukrainization, see: Hiroaki Kuromiya, *Freedom and Terror in the Donbas: a Ukrainian-Russian Borderland, 1870s–1990s* (Cambridge: Cambridge University Press, 1998), 196–7.
39 A former Borotbist, Mizernytsky became head of the union for educators and teachers, Robos, in the spring of 1924. He notably defended Commissar of Education Oleksandr Shumsky in a February 1927 meeting of the KP(b)U Politburo that condemned Shumsky for "national deviationism." In 1934, he was arrested after a prolonged campaign of public denunciation and spent fourteen years in a labour camp in Siberia. For more on the life and varied career of Mizernytsky, see: Marochko and H'ots, *Represovani pedahohy Ukraïny: zhertvy politychnoho teroru*, 64–9.
40 *TsDAVOU*, f. 166, op. 3, spr. 872, ark. 121.
41 The Ukrainian Soviet government's attitude towards the employment of Galicians would shift considerably from selective support to hostility. During the height of Ukrainization, Narkomos units employed countless Galician teachers and relied on the expertise of Narkomos bureaucrats and eductors of Galician background, many of whom were later arrested. On the Soviet repression of Galicians, see: Olga Bertelsen and Myroslav Shkandrij, "The Secret Police and the Campaign against Galicians in Soviet Ukraine, 1929–1934," *Nationalities Papers* 42, no. 1 (2014).
42 *TsDAVOU*, f. 166, op. 4, spr. 853, ark. 57, 77.
43 *TsDAVOU*, f. 166, op. 4, spr. 853, ark. 77.
44 *TsDAVOU*, f. 166, op. 3, spr. 872, ark. 122.

45 *TsDAVOU*, f. 166, op. 3, spr. 872, ark. 119.
46 The Black Hundreds were a tsarist-era Russian nationalist organization, known for its staunch support of the autocracy, leadership of pogroms against Jews, and refusal to recognize Ukrainian national separateness. They were active in the Ukrainian provinces of the Russian Empire, especially in Volhynia and Odesa.
47 *TsDAVOU*, f. 166, op. 3, spr. 872, ark. 305.
48 *TsDAVOU*, f. 166, op. 3, spr. 862, ark. 196–7.
49 *TsDAVOU*, f. 166, op. 3, spr. 872, ark. 116–19.
50 *TsDAVOU*, f. 166, op. 4, spr. 853, ark. 10.
51 *TsDAVOU*, f. 166, op. 4, spr. 853, ark. 12.
52 *TsDAVOU*, f. 166, op. 4, spr. 853, ark. 26–7.
53 *TsDAVOU*, f. 166, op. 4, spr. 853, ark. 27.
54 *TsDAVOU*, f. 166, op. 4, spr. 853, ark. 40.
55 *TsDAVOU*, f. 166, op. 3, spr. 862, ark. 150.
56 *TsDAVOU*, f. 166, op. 3, spr. 862, ark. 140.
57 Ibid.
58 *TsDAVOU*, f. 166, op. 4, spr. 853, ark. 36.
59 *TsDAVOU*, f. 166, op. 4, spr. 853, ark. 37.
60 *TsDAVOU*, f. 166, op. 4, spr. 853, ark. 100.
61 *TsDAVOU*, f. 166, op. 4, spr. 853, ark. 119.
62 *TsDAVOU*, f. 166, op. 4, spr. 853, ark. 111.
63 *TsDAVOU*, f. 166, op. 4, spr. 888, ark. 13.
64 *TsDAVOU*, f. 166, op. 4, spr. 888, ark. 18.
65 Ibid.
66 P. Sapukhin, "Ukraïnizatsiia. 'Ikhtiozavry' suchasnoï shkoly," *Narodnii uchytel'*, 10 February 1925, 4. P. Sapukhin was most likely Pavlo Sapukhin (1893–1970), a well-known educator, researcher, and author in Sumy. In 1920, he founded a local studies museum in the Velyka Pysarivka Secondary School, was appointed head of the pedagogical department of the district education section from 1939 to 1941, and served as an education inspector and instructor after the war. "Biohrafiia Sapukhina Pavla Andriiovycha," Sums'ka mis'ka tsentralizovana bibliotechna systema, accessed 19 September 2014, http://library-sumy.com/sumy/people_sumy/historians/sapukhin_p/about/.
67 O. Polubotko, "Plian ukraïns'koï movy za kompleksovoiu systemoiu," *Radians'ka osvita*, no. 4 (1925): 39.
68 Ibid., 44.
69 Ibid.
70 Ibid.
71 *Tsentral'nyi derzhavnyi arkhiv hromads'kykh ob"iednan' Ukraïny (TsDAHOU)*, f. 1, op. 20, spr. 2009, ark. 58.

4. Treading Carefully

1 *TsDAVOU*, f. 166, op. 3, spr. 872, ark. 312.
2 *TsDAVOU*, f. 166, op. 3, spr. 872, ark. 313.
3 Ibid.
4 Holmes underscores that underfunding was a problem in Russia also. The budgetary contraints of NEP forced both commissariats to reintroduce school fees in the early 1920s. Holmes, *Kremlin and the Schoolhouse*, 28.
5 *TsDAVOU*, f. 166, op. 3, spr. 862, ark. 175.
6 *TsDAVOU*, f. 166, op. 3, spr. 862, ark. 103–4.
7 *TsDAVOU*, f. 166, op. 3, spr. 862, ark. 102.
8 *TsDAVOU*, f. 166, op. 3, spr. 862, ark. 115–16.
9 *TsDAVOU*, f. 166, op. 3, spr. 862, ark. 108.
10 *TsDAVOU*, f. 166, op. 3, spr. 872, ark. 345.
11 *TsDAVOU*, f. 166, op. 4, spr. 621, ark. 63.
12 Riappo's emphasis suggests an early example of the hard-line rhetoric of Ukrainization to follow two years later. For Narkomos, Ukrainization was always a revolutionary task.
13 *TsDAVOU*, f. 166, op. 4, spr. 621, ark. 70. Ukraine had two types of post-secondary pedagogical institutions: a three- to four-year technical college (*tekhnikum*) and a four- to five-year institute. By 1929, thirty-five out of forty-three pedagogical technical colleges and six out of thirteen pedagogical institutes in the republic conducted coursework exclusively in Ukrainian. Siropolko, *Narodnia osvita na sovietsʹkii Ukraïni*, 205.
14 *TsDAVOU*, f. 166, op. 4, spr. 621, ark. 65.
15 *TsDAVOU*, f. 166, op. 4, spr. 860, ark. 4.
16 *TsDAVOU*, f. 166, op. 4, spr. 858, ark. 4.
17 Kh. Nevira, "Shcho shche halʹmuie ukraïnizatsiiu shkoly," *Narodnii uchytelʹ*, 5 May 1925, 2.
18 Ibid.
19 Ibid.
20 Ibid.
21 N. Kaliuzhnyi, "Ukraïnizatsiia i narodnii uchytelʹ," *Narodnii uchytelʹ*, 14 July 1925, 1.
22 I. Pevnyi, "Perevodymo ukraïnizatsiiu," *Narodnii uchytelʹ*, 14 April 1925, 3.
23 M. Makerevych, "Ukraïnizatsiia ta vchytelʹ: ukraïnizatsiia vchytelʹstva – nevidkladne zavdannia," *Narodnii uchytelʹ*, 13 October 1925, 2.
24 *TsDAVOU*, f. 166, op. 3, spr. 862, ark. 106.
25 *TsDAVOU*, f. 166, op. 3, spr. 872, ark. 53
26 Local Ukrainization commissions, assisted by the regional education sections, administered the perevirky (examinations), but Ukrliknep oversaw their implementation, defined their general content, and supervised the state courses in Ukrainian

studies for all government employees. They reported on the results of the examinations to the Radnarkom Commission on Ukrainization, whose secretary was A.T. Prykhodko, a former Borotbist and future Narkomos deputy commissar under Skrypnyk. Although perevirka records specific to teacher performance appear not to have been kept in the central Narkomos file collection, the chapter discusses files retained in the Odesa oblast archive. For results of tests administered to state employees in multiple institutions in 1926 and Ukrliknep Ukrainization activity, see: *TsDAVOU*, f. 166, op. 6, spr. 570, ark. 2; *TsDAVOU*, f. 166, op. 6, spr. 571, ark. 2, 5–12, 84, 104–13.

27 P. Sapukhin, "Spravy ukraïnizatsiï. Oblik ukraïnizatsiia vchytel'stva," *Narodnii uchytel'*, 15 December 1925, 3.
28 Ibid.
29 *Derzhavnyi arkhiv Kyïvs'koï oblasti (DAKO)*, f. R-142, op. 1, spr. 66, ark. 86.
30 Ibid.
31 *TsDAVOU*, f. 166, op. 4, spr. 129, ark. 104.
32 Ibid.
33 *TsDAVOU*, f. 166, op. 4, spr. 129, ark. 105.
34 Donets', "Niiak ne ukraïnizuiut'sia," *Narodnii uchytel'*, 10 February 1925, 4.
35 The standard orthography increases the confusion by rendering both words as "*suma.*"
36 *TsDAHOU*, f. 1, op. 20, spr. 2009, ark. 4.
37 *TsDAHOU*, f. 1, op. 20, spr. 2009, ark. 3.
38 Robfaky (Russian: *Rabfaky*), or workers' faculties, were preparatory schools for workers, designed to prepare graduates for entry into higher education and to produce a technological elite drawn from the proletariat's ranks.
39 *TsDAHOU*, f. 1, op. 20, spr. 2009, ark. 161.
40 Under Skrypnyk, the UkrSSR Narkomos performed a critical role in training for employment in Ukrainian schools, particularly in the Kuban region around Krasnodar where there was a large community of ethnic-Ukrainian Cossacks. Martin views Skrypnyk's efforts to extend Ukrainization beyond borders as a critical reason for an adjustment in the policy in the UkrSSR. On the 1931 recruitment of teachers for Ukrainian schools in the RSFSR, see: *TsDAVOU*, f. 166, op. 10, spr. 908, ark. 79–81. On a February 1933 report regarding Ukrainian teachers seeking employment in Odesa after Ukrainization had "ended" in the Kuban, see: *TsDAVOU*, f. 166, op. 11, spr. 19, ark. 20–1. For extended analyses on Narkomos's role in the promotion of Ukrainization in the RSFSR, see: Martin, *Affirmative Action Empire*, 282–302; Smolii, *"Ukraïnizatsiia" 1920–30-kh rokiv: peredumovy, zdobutky, uroky*, 230–99.
41 *TsDAVOU*, f. 166, op. 5, spr. 671, ark. 492. Veidlinger also underscores the problem of low attendance of Jewish children of Yiddish-language schools in the city of Vinnytsia, although a 44 per cent attendance rate suggests a greater achievement than

the teachers' meeting claimed for the Bila Tserkva *okruha*. Veidlinger, *In the Shadow of the Shtetl*, 87.
42 *TsDAVOU*, f. 166, op. 5, spr. 666, ark. 181.
43 In spite of Soviet terminology, Veidlinger reminds us, Yiddish-language schools "were not to be confused with Jewish schools, as they deliberately avoided teaching children anything about the Jewish religion, preferring instead to promote a completely secular de-Judaicized vision of Jewish life." Veidlinger, *In the Shadow of the Shtetl*, 82.
44 As Bemporad writes regarding nationalities policy in the Belorussian SSR, a specific objective of support for the Yiddish language was to "dissuade the Jewish population from using Russian." The support for a Soviet Yiddish culture was even greater in the Belorussian republic, Bemporad suggests, but the Ukrainian Commissariat of Education's patronage of Yiddish was still significant and its goals were similar. Bemporad, *Becoming Soviet Jews*, 82–3.
45 *TsDAVOU*, f. 166, op. 5, spr. 666, ark. 179.
46 *TsDAVOU*, f. 166, op. 5, spr. 680, ark. 60.
47 *TsDAVOU*, f. 166, op. 5, spr. 666, ark. 54.
48 Ibid.
49 *DAKO*, f. R-294, op. 2, spr. 108, ark. 68.
50 *DAKO*, f. R-632, op. 1, spr. 4, ark. 25.
51 *TsDAVOU*, f. 166, op. 4, spr. 858, ark. 5.
52 *TsDAVOU*, f. 166, op. 4, spr. 129, ark. 115.
53 *DAKO*, f. R-632, op. 1, spr. 15, ark. 1.
54 *TsDAVOU*, f. 166, op. 4, spr. 129, ark. 106.
55 *TsDAVOU*, f. 166, op. 4, spr. 129, ark. 106.
56 *DAKO*, f. R-632, op. 1, spr. 15, ark. 1.
57 *TsDAVOU*, f. 166, op. 4, spr. 39, ark. 5–18.
58 *TsDAVOU*, f. 166, op. 4, spr. 39, ark. 23.
59 *TsDAVOU*, f. 166, op. 4, spr. 39, ark. 44, 61.

5. Learning the New language of Pedagogy

1 For the published proceedings of this teachers' conference, see: *Pershyi Vseukraïns'kyi uchytel's'kyi z'izd v Kharkovi vid 5 do 11 sichnia 1925 (zi znimkamy uchasnykiv z'izdu)* (Kharkiv: Derzhavne vydavnytstvo Ukraïny, 1925).
2 *TsDAVOU*, f. 166, op. 5, spr. 666, ark. 26.
3 *TsDAVOU*, f. 166, op. 5, spr. 671, ark. 468.
4 *TsDAVOU*, f. 166, op. 5, spr. 671, ark. 28.
5 *TsDAVOU*, f. 166, op. 5, spr. 671, ark. 27.
6 *TsDAVOU*, f. 166, op. 5, spr. 666, ark. 78.

7 *TsDAVOU*, f. 166, op. 5, spr. 666, ark. 79.
8 *TsDAVOU*, f. 166, op. 5, spr. 666, ark. 5.
9 *TsDAVOU*, f. 166, op. 5, spr. 671, ark. 106.
10 *TsDAVOU*, f. 166, op. 5, spr. 671, ark. 92.
11 Ibid.
12 *TsDAVOU*, f. 166, op. 5, spr. 671, ark. 485.
13 *TsDAVOU*, f. 166, op. 5, spr. 666, ark. 180.
14 *TsDAVOU*, f. 166, op. 5, spr. 680, ark. 117.
15 *TsDAVOU*, f. 166, op. 5, spr. 680, ark. 36.
16 Although Soviet administrators introduced *okruhy* as the primary administrative unit in 1923, they did not abolish provinces or provincial-level Narkomos sections until August 1925. The Volyn *guberniia* was the rump of a tsarist-era *guberniia* of the same name that was divided between Soviet Ukraine and Poland in the 1921 Peace of Riga. Its principal city was Zhytomyr.
17 *TsDAVOU*, f. 166, op. 5, spr. 680, ark. 128.
18 *TsDAVOU*, f. 166, op. 5, spr. 671, ark. 206.
19 *TsDAVOU*, f. 166, op. 5, spr. 671, ark. 224.
20 *TsDAVOU*, f. 166, op. 5, spr. 671, ark. 206.
21 *TsDAVOU*, f. 166, op. 6, spr. 1960, ark. 7.
22 *TsDAVOU*, f. 166, op. 6, spr. 1960, ark. 16.
23 The Kyiv regional inspector specifically noted that it was not necessary for schools to use district plans, but they had to adjust complexes to local needs. See *TsDAVOU*, f. 166, op. 6, spr. 1985, ark. 6.
24 *TsDAVOU*, f. 166, op. 7, spr. 675, ark. 25.
25 *TsDAVOU*, f. 166, op. 7, spr. 675, ark. 60.
26 *TsDAVOU*, f. 166, op. 7, spr. 675, ark. 85.
27 *TsDAVOU*, f. 166, op. 7. spr. 675, ark. 52.
28 *TsDAVOU*, f. 166, op. 6, spr. 1985, ark. 26.
29 *TsDAVOU*, f. 166, op. 6, spr. 1960, ark. 29zv.
30 *TsDAVOU*, f. 166, op. 7, spr. 396, ark. 14.
31 Ibid.
32 *TsDAVOU*, f. 166, op. 6, spr. 1960, ark. 2.
33 *TsDAVOU*, f. 166, op. 6, spr. 1960, ark. 4.
34 *TsDAVOU*, f. 166, op. 7, spr. 396, ark. 12.
35 *TsDAVOU*, f. 166, op. 6, spr. 1960, ark. 5.
36 *TsDAVOU*, f. 166, op. 7, spr. 396, ark. 12.
37 *TsDAVOU*, f. 166, op. 6, spr. 1985, ark. 6.
38 *TsDAVOU*, f. 166, op. 6, spr. 1985, ark. 10–11.
39 *TsDAVOU*, f. 166, op. 6, spr. 1985, ark. 63.
40 *TsDAVOU*, f. 166, op. 6, spr. 1960, ark. 92.

41 *TsDAVOU*, f. 166, op. 5, spr. 671, ark. 468.
42 *TsDAVOU*, f. 166, op. 6, spr. 1960, ark. 2.
43 *TsDAVOU*, f. 166, op. 6, spr. 1960, ark. 92.
44 *TsDAVOU*, f. 166, op. 6, spr. 1985, ark. 6.
45 *TsDAVOU*, f. 166, op. 5, spr. 680, ark. 60.
46 *TsDAVOU*, f. 166, op. 5, spr. 671, ark. 468.
47 *TsDAVOU*, f. 166, op. 5, spr. 666, ark. 179.
48 *TsDAVOU*, f. 166, op. 6, spr. 1960, ark. 2.
49 *TsDAVOU*, f. 166, op. 6, spr. 1985, ark. 6.
50 *DAKO*, f. R-1043, op. 3, spr. 28, ark. 203.
51 *TsDAVOU*, f. 166, op. 6, spr. 1961, ark. 2.
52 *TsDAVOU*, f. 166, op. 6, spr. 1961, ark. 4.
53 *TsDAVOU*, f. 166, op. 6, spr. 1978, ark. 8.
54 *TsDAVOU*, f. 166, op. 6, spr. 1978, ark. 19.
55 *TsDAHOU*, f. 1, op. 20, spr. 3099, ark. 80.
56 *TsDAHOU*, f. 1, op. 20, spr. 3099, ark. 103.
57 Ibid.
58 *TsDAVOU*, f. 166, op. 7, spr. 675, ark. 60.
59 *TsDAVOU*, f. 166, op. 6, spr. 1960, ark. 7.
60 *TsDAVOU*, f. 166, op. 5, spr. 680, ark. 133.
61 *TsDAVOU*, f. 166, op. 5, spr. 671, ark. 113.
62 *TsDAVOU*, f. 166, op. 5, spr. 671, ark. 120.
63 *TsDAVOU*, f. 166, op. 6, spr. 2255, ark. 65.
64 *TsDAVOU*, f. 166, op. 6, spr. 2255, ark. 69, 71.
65 *TsDAVOU*, f. 166, op. 6, spr. 2255, ark. 66.
66 Ibid.
67 *TsDAVOU*, f. 166, op. 6, spr. 2255, ark. 80.
68 *TsDAVOU*, f. 166, op. 6, spr. 2255, ark. 82.
69 *TsDAVOU*, f. 166, op. 6, spr. 2255, ark. 81.
70 *TsDAVOU*, f. 166, op. 6, spr. 2255, ark. 84.
71 *TsDAVOU*, f. 166, op. 6, spr. 2255, ark. 75.
72 *TsDAVOU*, f. 166, op. 6, spr. 1985, ark. 63.
73 *TsDAVOU*, f. 166, op. 6, spr. 1960, ark. 92.
74 *TsDAVOU*, f. 166, op. 6, spr. 1985, ark. 63.
75 *TsDAVOU*, f. 166, op. 6, spr. 1985, ark. 77.
76 *TsDAVOU*, f. 166, op. 5, spr. 666, ark. 117.
77 Ibid.
78 *TsDAVOU*, f. 166, op. 5, spr. 671, ark. 485.
79 The report does not include the percentage for 1925.
80 *TsDAVOU*, f. 166, op. 5, spr. 666, ark. 119.

81 *TsDAVOU*, f. 166, op. 5, spr. 666, ark. 118.
82 *TsDAVOU*, f. 166, op. 5, spr. 680, ark. 36.

6. Limited Urgency

1. V. Sihov, "Het' profanatsiiu," *Narodnii uchytel'*, 12 January 1927, 3.
2. V. S., "Spravy ukraïnizatsiï. Za pidvyshchennia ukraïns'koï hramotnosty," *Narodnii uchytel'*, 12 January 1927, 3.
3. Z. Nuzhnyi, "Iak ne slid ukraïnizuvatysia! (Na Dnipropetrovskii zaliznytsi)," *Narodnii uchytel'*, 12 January 1927, 3.
4. Z. Nuzhnyi, "De-shcho pro ukraïnizatsiiu Dnipropetrovskoï zaliznytsi," *Narodnii uchytel'*, 3 November 1926, 3.
5. *TsDAHOU*, f. 1, op. 20, spr. 2253, ark. 4–9.
6. M. Mashkivs'kyi, "Do spravy ukraïnizatsiï vchytel'stva na Pivd.-zakh. zaliznytsiakh," *Narodnii uchytel'*, 6 October 1926, 2.
7. Z. Nuzhnyi, "De-shcho pro ukraïnizatsiiu Dnipropetrovs'koï zaliznytsi," *Narodnii uchytel'*, 3 November 1926, 3.
8. N. I. K. "Ukraïnizatsiia. Syln'a drama z zhyttia Bilotserkivs'koï okruhy na bahato diï z prolohom ta epilohom," *Narodnii uchytel'*, 30 March 1927, 3.
9. S. Khomenko, "Pro perevirku," *Narodnii uchytel'*, 12 January 1927, 3.
10. Mymra, "Pidmet," *Narodnii uchytel'*, 15 December 1926, 3.
11. "Na vsi zapitannia vidpovidni dovidkovo-konsul'tytsionnoho biura," *Narodnii uchytel'*, 4 May 1928, 4.
12. *DAKO*, f. R-1043, op. 3, spr. 28, ark. 109.
13. Ibid.
14. *DAKO*, f. R-1043, op. 3, spr. 28, ark. 110.
15. *DAKO*, f. R-1212, op. 1, spr. 25, ark. 59.
16. Z. Nuzhnyi, "De-shcho pro ukraïnizatsiiu Dnipropetrovskoï zaliznytsi," *Narodnii uchytel'*, 3 November 1926, 3.
17. "De-shcho pro vykladachiv ta komisii po perevirtsti," *Narodnii uchytel'*, 1 June 1927, 3.
18. *DAKO*, f. R-1043, op. 3, spr. 28, ark. 110.
19. S. Khomenko, "Pro perevirku," *Narodnii uchytel'*, 12 January 1927, 3.
20. *DAKO*, f. R-1043, op. 3, spr. 28, ark. 110.
21. V. S., "Spravy ukraïnizatsiï. Za pidvyshchennia ukraïns'koï hramotnosty," *Narodnii uchytel'*, 12 January 1927, 3.
22. *TsDAHOU*, f. 1, op. 20, spr. 2253, ark. 1–6.
23. For more background on the KP(b)U debate between 1923 and 1926, Stalin's intervention, and Shumsky's later censure and dismissal as commissar of education (the "Shumsky affair"), see: Martin, *Affirmative Action Empire*, 78–79, 212–28;

Mace, *Communism and the Dilemmas of National Liberation*, 87–119; Liber, *Soviet Nationality Policy*, 39–42, 131–40; Jeremy Smith, *Red Nations*, 88–90; Smolii, "Ukraïnizatsiia" *1920–30-kh rokiv: peredumovy, zdobutky, uroky*, 40–60.
24 D. Lebed, "Podgotovka partiinogo s"ezda. Nekotorye voprosy partiinogo s"ezda," *Kommunist*, no. 59 (1923): 1. Quoted in Martin, *Affirmative Action Empire*, 79.
25 *TsDAHOU*, f. 1, op. 20, spr. 2255, ark. 11–12.
26 *TsDAHOU*, f. 1, op. 20, spr. 2255, ark. 13–18.
27 Ibid.
28 *TsDAHOU*, f. 1, op. 20, spr. 2255, ark. 19.
29 *TsDAHOU*, f. 1, op. 20, spr. 2248, 1.
30 Ibid.
31 Ibid. To read Khvylovy's original work and some commentary on the political and literary context surrounding their publication, see: Mykola Khvylovy, *The Cultural Renaissance in Ukraine: Polemical Pamphlets, 1925–1926*, trans., ed., and intro. by Myroslav Shkandrij (Edmonton: Canadian Institute of Ukrainian Studies, 1986); Iurii Shapoval, ed., *Poliuvannia na 'Val'dshnepa': rozserekrechenyi Mykola Khvyl'ovyi* (Kyïv: Tempora, 2009).
32 *TsDAHOU*, f. 1, op. 20, spr. 2248, ark. 8–12.
33 Ibid.
34 *TsDAHOU*, f. 1, op. 20, spr. 2255, ark. 1.
35 *TsDAHOU*, f. 1, op. 20, spr. 2247, ark. 4.
36 *TsDAHOU*, f. 1, op. 20, spr. 2247, ark. 13.
37 *TsDAHOU*, f. 1, op. 20, spr. 2248, ark. 57.
38 *TsDAHOU*, f. 1, op. 20, spr. 2247, ark. 13.
39 *TsDAHOU*, f. 1, op. 20, spr. 2247, ark. 18.
40 *TsDAHOU*, f. 1, op. 20, spr. 2248, ark. 57.
41 "Pereshkody v ukraïnizatsii," *Narodnii uchytel'*, 6 October 1927, 2.
42 *DAKO*, f. R-1043, op. 3, spr. 31, ark. 52
43 *TsDAVOU*, f. 166, op. 6, spr. 1978, ark. 30.
44 *DAKO*, f. R-761, op. 1, spr. 363, ark. 80.
45 *TsDAVOU*, f. 166, op. 6, spr. 1978, ark. 33.
46 *TsDAVOU*, f. 166, op. 6, spr. 1978, ark. 39.
47 *TsDAVOU*, f. 166, op. 6, spr. 2255, ark. 36.
48 *TsDAVOU*, f. 166, op. 6, spr. 2255, ark. 45.
49 Ibid.
50 *TsDAVOU*, f. 166, op. 6, spr. 2255, ark. 46.
51 *TsDAVOU*, f. 166, op. 6, spr. 2255, ark. 48.
52 *TsDAVOU*, f. 166, op. 6, spr. 2255, ark. 21.
53 *TsDAVOU*, f. 166, op. 6, spr. 2255, ark. 44.
54 Martin, *Affirmative Action Empire*, 38–39.

55 Although Larin supported the creation of Jewish soviets, he also objected strongly to the forced enrolment of Jewish children in Yiddish schools regardless of what language they spoke. This issue was discussed along with the question of forced Ukrainization of Russian children by the Politburo Ukrainization Commission. Ibid., 49. *TsDAHOU*, f. 1, op. 20, spr. 2247, ark. 95–112.

56 The Left Opposition of the VKP(b) argued that the industrialization policy of the party leadership in the mid-1920s was too slow and that the peasantry needed to be taxed at a higher rate to ensure resources were available for an increase in pace. They feared the growth of capitalism and thought that rapid industrialization was needed to protect the gains of socialism. After consolidating an alliance with forces on the right, Stalin orchestrated the expulsion of its leaders, Grigory Zinoviev and Lev Kamenev, in 1927–28, subsequently adopting many of their principles during the First Five-Year Plan. Most of the former members of the opposition were arrested and placed on trial in 1936–7.

57 *TsDAHOU*, f. 1, op. 20. spr. 2253, ark. 19–25.
58 *TsDAHOU*, f. 1, op. 20, spr. 2247, ark. 97.
59 *TsDAHOU*, f. 1, op. 20, spr. 2247, ark. 102–3.
60 *TsDAHOU*, f. 1, op. 20, spr. 2247, ark. 104.
61 *TsDAHOU*, f. 1, op. 20, spr. 2247, ark. 96, 107–12.
62 *TsDAHOU*, f. 1, op. 20, spr. 2247, ark. 104; *TsDAVOU*, f. 166, op. 6, spr. 10841, ark. 136.

7. The Question of the Working Class

1 *TsDAVOU*, f. 166, op. 6, spr. 10841, ark. 136. In fact, Skrypnyk was finessing prior policy. In response to additional criticism by Larin that Narkomos administrators were ignoring parental wishes in admitting children to primary schools, Shumksy responded in a January 1927 meeting of the Politburo Commission on Ukrainization that officials took family input as well as the language spoken by a child into account: "To make a different decision, means to rape [*gvaltuvaty*], to maim the child. It is necessary to teach reading and writing in language that he [or she] understands." *TsDAHOU*, f. 1, op. 20, spr. 2456, ark. 22. Cited in Borysov, "Ukraïnizatsiia ta rozvytok zahal'noosvitnoï shkoly," 78.

2 Skrypnyk specifically pointed to the need to offer Ukrainian instruction to the majority of the children of the 1.3 million citizens of the republic who claimed Ukrainian nationality, but Russian as a native language in the 1926 census. Schools were to teach the children of the 200,000 citizens who claimed Russian nationality, but Ukrainian as a native language, in Russian. Mykola Skrypnyk, "Perebudovnymy shliakhamy," *Bil'shovyk Ukraïny*, no. 13–14 (1931): 27–34. Quoted in Martin, *Affirmative Action Empire*, 107; H. Iefimenko, *Natsional'na polityka kerivnytstva*

VKP(b) v Ukraïni 1932–1938 rr. (osvita ta nauka) (Kyïv: Instytut istoriï Ukraïny, 2000), 7–8.
3 *TsDAVOU*, f. 166, op. 6, spr. 1978, ark. 13.
4 *TsDAVOU*, f. 166, op. 6, spr. 1978, ark. 26.
5 *TsDAHOU*, f. 1, op. 20, spr. 2253, ark. 90–2.
6 *DAKO*, f. R-1043, op. 3. spr. 28, ark. 63.
7 *TsDAHOU*, f. 1, op. 20, spr. 3099, ark. 59.
8 *TsDAVOU*, f. 166, op. 6, spr. 10841, ark. 140.
9 *TsDAVOU*, f. 166, op. 6, spr. 10841, ark. 136.
10 Ibid.
11 *DAKO*, f. R-1043, op. 3, spr. 13, ark. 111.
12 *DAKO*, f. R-761, op. 1, spr. 363, ark. 80.
13 Ibid.
14 *DAKO*, f. R-1043, op. 3, spr. 13, ark. 117.
15 *DAKO*, f. R-1043, op. 3, spr. 13, ark. 308.
16 *TsDAHOU*, f. 1, op. 20, spr. 2248, ark. 8.
17 "A. V. Lunachars'kyi pro rozvytok ukraïns'koï kul'tury," *Narodnii uchytel'*, 1 August 1928, 2.
18 *TsDAHOU*, f. 1, op. 20, spr. 2248, ark. 137, 180.
19 The document's preceding comments regarding the Ukrainization of the first concentration of school suggest this percentage of Ukrainian children refers to children old enough to attend the first through fourth grades, ages eight to eleven.
20 *TsDAHOU*, f. 1, op. 20, spr. 2251, ark. 1.
21 *TsDAVOU*, f. 166, op. 6, spr. 281, ark. 92.
22 *TsDAVOU*, f. 166, op. 6, spr. 1978, ark. 38.
23 *TsDAHOU*, f. 1, op. 20, spr. 2247, ark. 103.
24 *TsDAVOU*, f. 166, op. 6, spr. 1978, ark. 33.
25 *TsDAVOU*, f. 166, op. 5, spr. 671, ark. 468.
26 *TsDAHOU*, f. 1, op. 20, spr. 2247, ark. 108.
27 *TsDAVOU*, f. 166, op. 6, spr. 1978, ark. 26.
28 *TsDAVOU*, f. 166, op. 6, spr. 1978, ark. 24.
29 "Zaochni kursi ukraïnoznavstva," *Narodnii uchytel' - dodatok*, 13 April 1927, 3.
30 Ibid.
31 *TsDAVOU*, f. 166, op. 6, spr. 1978, ark. 26.
32 *TsDAHOU*, f. 1, op. 20, spr. 2248, ark. 39.
33 Ibid.
34 *TsDAHOU*, f. 1, op. 20, spr. 2248, ark. 43.
35 *TsDAHOU*, f. 1, op. 20, spr. 2248, ark. 46.
36 Mace, *Communism and the Dilemmas of National Liberation*, 113.
37 Martin, *Affirmative Action Empire*, 219.

38 *TsDAHOU*, f. 1, op. 20, spr. 2248, ark. 86.
39 *TsDAHOU*, f. 1, op. 20, spr. 2248, ark. 97.
40 *TsDAHOU*, f. 1, op. 20, spr. 2248, ark. 139.
41 Ibid. Lenin's testament assumingly refers here to his public advocacy of a worker-peasant alliance and concessions to non-Russian national interests, not Lenin's "last testament," detailing the shortcomings of the members of the VKP(b) Politburo.
42 O., "Dumky pro ukraïnizatsiu nesvidomi," *Narodnii uchytel'*, 1 June 1927, 3.
43 "Pereshkody v ukraïnizatsii," *Narodnii uchytel'*, 6 October 1927, 2.
44 V. Sihov, "Het' profanatsiiu," *Narodnii uchytel'*, 12 January 1927, 3.
45 I., "Pro ukraïns'ku movu ta bil' u shchepliakh," *Narodnii uchytel'*, 1 June 1927, 3.
46 *TsDAHOU*, f. 1, op. 20, spr. 2253, ark. 11.
47 *Narodnii uchytel'*, 16 January 1929.
48 Vorobiov, S. "Ukraïnizatsiia v hromads'kii roboti," *Narodnii uchytel'*, 5 May 1927, 3.
49 Ibid.
50 *TsDAHOU*, f. 1, op. 20, spr. 2253, ark. 12.
51 The challenges for Soviet political educators were still significant even where nationalities policy was not an issue in central Russia. See: Alexandre Sumpf, *Bolcheviks en campagne: paysans et éducation politique dans la Russie des années 1920* (Paris: CNRS, 2010); "Confronting the Countryside: The Training of Political Educators in 1920s Russia," *History of Education* 35, no. 4–5 (2006); Charles E. Clark, *Uprooting Otherness: The Literacy Campaign in NEP-Era Russia* (Selinsgrove, PA: Susquehanna University Press, 2000).
52 For a study of how Soviet authorities used "red clubs" to promote Soviet norms of modern culture in Central Asia, see: Ali F. Igmen, *Speaking Soviet with an Accent: Culture and Power in Kyrgyzstan* (Pittsburgh: University of Pittsburgh Press, 2012).
53 *TsDAHOU*, f. 1, op. 20, spr. 2253, ark. 13.
54 One such journal compiled by instructors for state Ukrainian-studies courses in Kyiv, *Holos ukraïnizatora*, had a short-lived period of publication in 1927.
55 *TsDAHOU*, f. 1, op. 20, spr. 2253, ark. 13zv.
56 Ibid.
57 *DAKO*, f. R-1043, op. 3, spr. 13, ark. 13.
58 *DAKO*, f. R-1043, op. 3, spr. 31, ark. 69.

8. Children as Salvation

1 For key published works that concern the Komsomol and the Young Pioneers, see: Isabel Tirado, *Young Guard! The Communist Youth League, Petrograd 1917–1920* (Westport: Greenwood Press, 1988); Anne Gorsuch, *Youth in Revolutionary Russia: Enthusiasts, Bohemians, Delinquents* (Bloomington: Indiana University Press, 2000); Kirschenbaum, *Small Comrades*; Monica Wellmann, *Zwischen Militanz, Verzweiflung und Disziplinierung. Jugendliche Lebenswelten in Moskau 1920–1930* (Zürich: Pano

Verlag, 2005); Kelly, *Children's World*; Juliane Fürst, *Stalin's Last Generation: Soviet Post-War Youth and the Emergence of Mature Socialism* (New York: Oxford University, 2010); Matthias Neumann, *The Communist Youth League and the Transformation of the Soviet Union, 1917–1932* (New York: Routledge, 2011); Sean Guillory, "The Shattered Self of Komsomol Civil War Memoirs," *Slavic Review* 71, no. 3 (2012). For works on the Komsomol in Ukraine, see: V. I. Pryluts'kyi, *Molod' USRR v period utverdzhennia totalitarnoï systemy, 1928–1933* (Kyïv: Instytut istoriï Ukraïny NAN Ukraïny, 1999); *Molod' Ukraïny v umovakh formuvannia totalitarnoho ladu, 1920–1939* (Kyïv: Instytut istoriï Ukraïny NAN Ukraïny, 2001); "Uchast' studentsva USRR v suspil'no-politychnomu ta kul'turnomu zhytti v 1920-ti roky," *Problemy istoriï Ukraïni*, no. 16 (2007).

2 The Ukrainian Institute of History's edited volume references Ukrainization of the Komsomol in a general discussion of the campaign in state institutions and party organizations, and Viktor Pryluts'kyi discusses support for Ukrainization among some post-secondary students. Smolii, *"Ukraïnizatsiia" 1920–30-kh rokiv: peredumovy, zdobutky, uroky*, 64–83; Pryluts'kyi, "Uchast' studentsva USRR v suspil'no-politychnomu ta kul'turnomu zhytti v 1920-ti roky."

3 *TsDAHOU*, f. 7, op. 1, spr. 195v, ark. 52.
4 *TsDAHOU*, f. 7, op. 1, spr. 195v, ark. 52.
5 *TsDAHOU*, f. 7, op. 1, spr. 74, ark. 33.
6 *TsDAHOU*, f. 7, op. 1, spr. 74, ark. 20.
7 *TsDAHOU*, f. 7, op. 1, spr. 74, ark. 29, 33.
8 *TsDAHOU*, f. 7, op. 1, spr. 74, ark. 48–9.
9 A Central Bureau (TsB) of the KDR was established under the TsK of the Ukrainian Komsomol in January 1923 to administer Young Pioneer units.
10 *TsDAHOU*, f. 7, op. 1, spr. 74, ark. 46.
11 *TsDAHOU*, f. 7, op. 1, spr. 74, ark. 49.
12 For a discussion of Baptist competition to the Komsomol for youth loyalty, see: Heather Coleman, *Russian Baptists and Spiritual Revolution, 1905–1929* (Bloomington: Indiana University Press, 2005), 237–62. See also: Pryluts'kyi, *Molod' Ukraïny v umovakh formuvannia totalitarnoho ladu, 1920–1939*.
13 See Gorsuch, *Youth in Revolutionary Russia*.
14 On teachers' public work, see: Iefimenko, "Hromads'ka robota iak chynnyk povsiakdennoho zhyttia vchytelia."
15 *TsDAHOU*, f. 7, op. 1, spr. 195v, ark. 1–2.
16 *TsDAHOU*, f. 7, op. 1, spr. 195v, ark. 10–11.
17 *TsDAHOU*, f. 7, op. 1, spr. 195a, ark. 1.
18 For more on the UKP and Borotbists, see: Iwan Majstrenko, *Borot'bism: A Chapter in the History of Ukrainian Communism* (New York: Research Program on the USSR, 1954); Mace, *Communism and the Dilemmas of National Liberation*, 53–62.

19 *TsDAHOU*, f. 7, op. 1, spr. 195v, ark. 4.
20 *TsDAHOU*, f. 7, op. 1, spr. 195v, ark. 30.
21 *TsDAHOU*, f. 7, op. 1, spr. 195a, ark. 20.
22 *TsDAHOU*, f. 7, op. 1, spr. 195v, ark. 31.
23 More specifically, Nikoliuk says that rural institutions were graduating peasants, while city schools were putting out Russians and could not easily be Ukrainized. The opposition he highlighted was, therefore, between peasants and Russians. According to this logic, peasants could not be Russians and must be Ukrainian, thus affirming his idea of a peasant Ukrainian national identity.
24 *TsDAHOU*, f. 7, op. 1, spr. 195a, ark. 2.
25 *TsDAHOU*, f. 7, op. 1, spr. 195a, ark. 6.
26 *TsDAHOU*, f. 7, op. 1, spr. 195a, ark. 8.
27 *TsDAHOU*, f. 7, op. 1, spr. 195a, ark. 6.
28 Neumann, *The Communist Youth League*, 143–46, 192–200. See also: Isabel A. Tirado, "The Komsomol and the Young Peasants: The Dilemma of Rural Expansion, 1921–1925," *Slavic Review* 52, no. 3 (1996); Wellmann, *Zwischen Militanz, Verzweiflung und Disziplinierung. Jugendliche Lebenswelten in Moskau 1920–1930*.
29 *TsDAHOU*, f. 7, op. 1, spr. 168, ark. 1.
30 *TsDAHOU*, f. 7, op. 1, spr. 192, ark. 57.
31 *TsDAHOU*, f. 7, op. 1, spr. 192, ark. 102.
32 *TsDAHOU*, f. 7, op. 1, spr. 192, ark. 108.
33 *TsDAHOU*, f. 7, op. 1, spr. 195.2, ark. 60.
34 *TsDAHOU*, f. 7, op. 1, spr. 195.2, ark. 62.
35 *TsDAHOU*, f. 7, op. 1, spr. 284, ark. 8.
36 *TsDAHOU*, f. 7, op. 1, spr. 284, ark. 14.
37 *TsDAHOU*, f. 7, op. 1, spr. 284, ark. 1.
38 *TsDAHOU*, f. 7, op. 1, spr. 284, ark. 23.
39 *TsDAHOU*, f. 7, op. 1, spr. 284, ark. 33.
40 *TsDAHOU*, f. 7, op. 1, spr. 284, ark. 31. Renowned Ukrainian playwright Les Kurbas founded the Berezil theatre in Kyiv in 1922. He moved it to Kharkiv in 1926, and it became a major centre for theatrical experimentation and attracted Soviet Ukraine's leading dramatists. In the early 1930s, it came under scrutiny by party authorities and was purged in 1933. Natalia Iermakova, *Berezil's'ka kul'tura: istoriia, dosvid* (Kyïv: Feniks, 2012); Virlana Tkacz, "Les Kurbas's Early Work at the Berezil: From Bodies in Motion to Performing the Invisible," in *Modernism in Kyiv: Jubilant Experimentation*, ed. Virlana Tkacz and Irena R. Makaryk (Toronto: University of Toronto Press, 2010).
41 *TsDAHOU*, f. 7, op. 1, spr. 195v, ark. 60.
42 *TsDAHOU*, f. 7, op. 1, spr. 195v, ark. 62.
43 *TsDAHOU*, f. 7, op. 1, spr. 284, ark. 8.
44 *TsDAHOU*, f. 7, op. 1, spr. 284, ark. 14.

45 *TsDAHOU*, f. 7, op. 1, spr. 284, ark. 33.
46 *TsDAHOU*, f. 7, op. 1, spr. 284, ark. 1.
47 *TsDAHOU*, f. 7, op. 1, spr. 284, ark. 33.
48 *TsDAHOU*, f. 7, op. 1, spr. 284, ark. 23.
49 *TsDAHOU*, f. 7, op. 1, spr. 284, ark. 1.
50 *TsDAHOU*, f. 7, op. 1, spr. 195v, ark. 62.
51 *TsDAHOU*, f. 7, op. 1, spr. 284, ark. 8.
52 *TsDAHOU*, f. 7, op. 1, spr. 284, ark. 14.
53 *TsDAHOU*, f. 7, op. 1, spr. 284, ark. 33.
54 *TsDAHOU*, f. 7, op. 1, spr. 284, ark. 31.
55 *TsDAHOU*, f. 7, op. 1, spr. 195a, ark. 55.
56 *TsDAHOU*, f. 7, op. 1, spr. 284, ark. 8.
57 *TsDAHOU*, f. 7, op. 1, spr. 284, ark. 1.
58 *TsDAHOU*, f. 7, op. 1, spr. 284, ark. 14.
59 *TsDAHOU*, f. 7, op. 1, spr. 284, ark. 31.
60 *TsDAHOU*, f. 7, op. 1, spr. 284, ark. 31.
61 *TsDAHOU*, f. 7, op. 1, spr. 284, ark. 33.
62 Molodniak was a group of proletarian Ukrainian writers who criticized conventional literary forms as hostile to the working class and published their writing in the new Komsomol journal *Molodniak* (founded in January 1927). They opposed the emphasis on aesthetics advocated by Mykola Khvylovy's VAPLITE (the Free Academy of Proletarian Literature) and labelled it "nationalist." Mykola Khvyl'ovyi and Myroslav Shkandrij, *The Cultural Renaissance in Ukraine: Polemical Pamphlets, 1925–1926* (Edmonton: Canadian Institute of Ukrainian Studies, 1986), 19–20.
63 *TsDAHOU*, f. 7, op. 1, spr. 195a, ark. 37.
64 *TsDAHOU*, f. 7, op. 1, spr. 195a, ark. 39.
65 *TsDAHOU*, f. 7, op. 1, spr. 195a, ark. 37.

9. Ukrainization in a Non-Ukrainian City

1 There have been several recent publications on the history of the city of Odesa, but a comprehensive survey of the Soviet period is still needed. One of the best accounts of Odesa's post-revolutionary Soviet past is not a history, but an ethnographic account by Tanya Richardson of how Odesans' memories of this past influence their understanding of the city's place in independent Ukraine. With the exception of King's narrative history, the bulk of publications concern either the imperial and revolutionary periods or the city's important Jewish culture. See: Tanya Richardson, *Kaleidoscopic Odessa: History and Place in Contemporary Ukraine* (Toronto: University of Toronto Press, 2008); Charles King, *Odessa: Genius and Death in a City of Dreams* (New York: W.W. Norton & Co., 2011); Jarrod Tanny, *City of Rogues and Schnorrers:*

Russia's Jews and the Myth of Old Odessa (Bloomington: Indiana University Press, 2011); Roshanna P. Sylvester, *Tales of Old Odessa: Crime and Civility in a City of Thieves* (DeKalb, IL: Northern Illinois University Press, 2005); Robert A. Rothstein, "How It Was Sung in Odessa: At the Intersection of Russian and Yiddish Folk Culture," *Slavic Review* 60, no. 4 (2001); Tanja Penter, *Odessa 1917: Revolution an der Peripherie* (Köln: Böhlau Verlag, 2000).

2 Richardson, *Kaleidoscopic Odessa*, 21.
3 Steven L. Guthier, "Ukrainian Cities during the Revolution and the Inter-War Era," in *Rethinking Ukrainian History*, ed. Ivan L. Rudnytsky and John-Paul Himka (Edmonton: Canadian Institute of Ukrainian Studies, 1981), 175. Cited in Richardson, *Kaleidoscopic Odessa: History and Place in Contemporary Ukraine*, 16.
4 Tanny, *City of Rogues and Schnorrers*, 80.
5 King, *Odessa*, 188.
6 For recent studies of Babel, see: Rebecca Jane Stanton, *Isaac Babel and the Self-Invention of Odessan Modernism* (Evanston: Northwestern University Press, 2012), 141–69; Amelia Glaser, *Jews and Ukrainians In Russia's Literary Borderlands: From the Shtetl Fair to the Petersburg Bookshop* (Evanston: Northwestern University Press, 2012).
7 Richardson, *Kaleidoscopic Odessa*, 22.
8 Zahra, "Imagined Noncommunities," 111.
9 *Vsesoiuznaia perepis' naseleniia 1926 goda*, vol. 12 (Moskva: Izd. TsSU Soiuza SSR, 1928–35), 29. In 1920, Ukrainians constituted 53.6 per cent of the Odesa *guberniia* (province), which encompassed a larger territory than the Odesa *okruha* (region). *TsDAVOU*, f. 166, op. 3, spr. 862, ark. 107.
10 *Vsesoiuznaia perepis' naseleniia 1926 goda*, vol. 13 (Moskva: Izd. TsSU Soiuza SSR, 1928–35), 27–8; Liber, *Soviet Nationality Policy*, 189.
11 *Derzhavnyi arkhiv Odes'koï oblasti (DAOO)*, f. R-134, op. 1, spr. 1849, ark. 135.
12 *DAOO*, f. P-3, op. 1, spr. 78, ark. 6.
13 *DAOO*, f. P-3, op. 1, spr. 78, ark. 8.
14 *DAOO*, f. P-3, op. 1, spr. 78, ark. 9.
15 *DAOO*, f. P-3, op. 1, spr. 1547, ark. 13.
16 *DAOO*, f. P-3, op. 1, spr. 1547, ark. 18zv.
17 *DAOO*, f. P-3, op. 1, spr. 1547, ark. 24zv.
18 *DAOO*, f. P-3, op. 1, spr. 1547, ark. 24zv, 28zv.
19 *DAOO*, f. P-3, op. 1, spr. 1184, ark. 25.
20 *DAOO*, f. P-3, op. 1, spr. 1184, ark. 25.
21 *DAOO*, f. P-3, op. 1, spr. 1184, ark. 25
22 *DAOO*, f. R-134, op. 1, spr. 1849, ark. 149–50.
23 *DAOO*, f. R-134, op. 1, spr. 1849, ark. 175.
24 *DAOO*, f. R-134, op. 1, spr. 1876, ark. 8–9.

25 *DAOO*, f. R-134, op. 1, spr. 1876, ark. 9.
26 *DAOO*, f. R-134, op. 1, spr. 1876, ark. 9–11.
27 *DAOO*, f. R-134, op. 1, spr. 1876, ark. 10.
28 *DAOO*, f. R-134, op. 1, spr. 1876, ark. 1–5.
29 *DAOO*, f. R-134, op. 1, spr. 1849, ark. 178.
30 *DAOO*, f. R-134, op. 1, spr. 1849, ark. 210, 213–14.
31 *DAOO*, f. R-134, op. 1, spr. 1876, ark. 19–67. The city of Odesa constituted the Odesa district (*Odes'kyi raion*), specified by the regional Narkomos section for review.
32 *DAOO*, f. R-134, op. 1, spr. 1876, ark. 26.
33 *DAOO*, f. R-134, op. 1, spr. 1876, ark. 53.
34 *DAOO*, f. R-134, op. 1, spr. 1876, ark. 21.
35 *DAOO*, f. R-134, op. 1, spr. 1876, ark. 32.
36 *DAOO*, f. R-134, op. 1, spr. 1876, ark. 22.
37 *DAOO*, f. R-134, op. 1, spr. 1876, ark. 67.
38 *DAOO*, f. R-150, op. 1, spr. 814, ark. 70.
39 *DAOO*, f. R-150, op. 1, spr. 816, ark. 1.
40 *DAOO*, f. R-150, op. 1, spr. 816, ark. 281.
41 *DAOO*, f. R-150, op. 1, spr. 816, ark. 223.
42 The INO was the primary Soviet post-secondary education institute. They trained specialists, as well as future teachers for the upper levels of the seven-year labour school and the secondary vocational schools.
43 A Gubpolitosvita list of specialists available for lecturing in Ukrainian to clubs specifies Buzuk as a lecturer for the History of the Ukrainian Language. Lecturers were also available to teach in Ukrainian outside of Ukrainian studies: cooperatives, sanitation and hygiene, Soviet law, world studies and political studies. *DAOO*, f. R-150, op. 1, spr. 816, ark. 285.
44 *DAOO*, f. R-150, op. 1, spr. 816, ark. 204. See the discussion of political repression directed against Mykhailo Slabchenk and his son Taras in chapter 10.
45 *DAOO*, f. R-150, op. 1, spr. 816, ark. 280, 309, 314.
46 Ironically, Odesan professors had a reputation among central authorities for resistance to Ukrainization. One Odesa professor earned Skrypnyk's ire when he called Ukrainization "an act of violence" and condemned those who switched to Ukrainian instruction as "renegades" during a December 1928 visit by Skrypnyk. M. Skrypnyk, *Neprymyrennym shliakhom: dopovid' na okrpartkonferentsii v Odesi 12-ho hrudnia 1928 roku* (Kharkiv: Derzhavne vydavnytstvo Ukraïny, 1929), 82. Cited in Martin, *Affirmative Action Empire*, 112. For other instances of Odesan hostility to Ukrainization that came to the attention of the KP(b)U Politburo Ukrainization Committee and Narkomos administrators, see: ibid., 95–6, 109.
47 *DAOO*, f. R-150, op. 1, spr. 818, ark. 11.
48 *DAOO*, f. R-150, op. 1, spr. 818, ark. 7, 8, 42.

49 *DAOO*, f. R-150, op. 1, spr. 818, ark. 86.
50 *DAOO*, f. P-7, op. 1, spr. 354, ark. 53.
51 *DAOO*, f. P-7, op. 1, spr. 354, ark. 47.
52 *DAOO*, f. P-7, op. 1, spr. 354, ark. 53.
53 As will be detailed below, Ukrainian educators and intellectuals interrogated by the GPU for participation in a fabricated nationalist organization, the SVU, made this charge in their testimony, likely at the behest of the GPU.
54 *DAOO*, f. P-7, op. 1, spr. 354, ark. 53.
55 The Regional Commission on Ukrainization blamed shortcomings in Ukrainization, for example, in the Ovidiopol and Demydivka districts on the areas' multi-ethnic populations. *DAOO*, f. P-7, op. 1, spr. 354, ark. 81.
56 *DAOO*, f. P-3, op. 1, spr. 1547, ark. 34.
57 *DAOO*, f. P-7, op. 1, spr. 354, ark. 58.
58 *DAOO*, f. P-7, op. 1, spr. 354, ark. 58.
59 *DAOO*, f. P-7, op. 1, spr. 354, ark. 40.
60 *DAOO*, f. P-7, op. 1, spr. 354, ark. 11.
61 *DAOO*, f. P-3, op. 1, spr. 1547, ark. 33.
62 *DAOO*, f. P-3, op. 1, spr. 1547, ark. 33.
63 *DAOO*, f. P-3, op. 1, spr. 1547, ark. 39.
64 *DAOO*, f. P-7, op. 1, spr. 354, ark. 80.
65 *DAOO*, f. P-7, op. 1, spr. 354, ark. 82.
66 *DAOO*, f. P-3, op. 1, spr. 1547, ark. 39.
67 *DAOO*, f. P-7, op. 1, spr. 1519, ark. 88.
68 *DAOO*, f. P-7, op. 1, spr. 1519, ark. 88.
69 *DAOO*, f. P-7, op. 1, spr. 1519, ark. 89.
70 *DAOO*, f. P-7, op. 1, spr. 1519, ark. 91.
71 *DAOO*, f. P-7, op. 1, spr. 1519, ark. 92.
72 *DAOO*, f. P-7, op. 1, spr. 1519, ark. 92.
73 *DAOO*, f. P-7, op. 1, spr. 1519, ark. 92
74 *DAOO*, f. P-7, op. 1, spr. 2112, ark. 5.
75 *DAOO*, f. P-7, op. 1, spr. 2112, ark. 38.
76 *DAOO*, f. P-7, op. 1, spr. 2112, ark. 41.
77 Literally, he writes: "As result of these observations, it is necessary to consider an expedient transfer of all courses for party activists to the allowance for costs for Ukrainization." *DAOO*, f. P-7, op. 1, spr. 2112, ark. 41.
78 *DAOO*, f. P-7, op. 1, spr. 2112, ark. 39.
79 *DAOO*, f. R-134, op. 1, spr. 1923, ark. 1.
80 *DAOO*, f. R-134, op. 1, spr. 1884, ark. 3.
81 *DAOO*, f. R-134, op. 1, spr. 1937, ark. 15–16.
82 *DAOO*, f. R-134, op. 1, spr. 1937, ark. 11.

83 *DAOO*, f. R-134, op. 3, spr. 42, ark. 16.
84 *DAOO*, f. P-7, op. 1, spr. 2407, ark. 1.
85 *DAOO*, f. P-7, op. 1, spr. 2407, ark. 2.
86 *DAOO*, f. R-134, op. 1, spr. 1071, ark. 104.
87 *DAOO*, f. R-134, op. 1, spr. 1047, ark. 14–14zv.
88 An August 1929 meeting of the municipal soviet's education section made clear that the Ukrainization of schools would continue in the city centre, designating five more prestigious seven-year schools in the Lenin, Stalin, and Illych districts for a gradual transfer to Ukrainian instruction. *DAOO*, f. R-1234, op. 1, spr. 1002, ark. 26.

10. The Correction

1 The Right Opposition of the VKP(b) was led by Nikolai Bukharin, who had previously allied with Stalin to quell voices on the left that favoured rapid industrialization over concessions to the peasantry. The Right Opposition believed an exploitation of the peasantry would be self-defeating, arguing that increased peasant incomes would provide funds for the development of industry. Bukharin and his allies were isolated after Stalin eliminated his enemies on the left and moved towards grain requisitions and collectivization of peasant land. Most of its members were arrested and tried during the purges of 1936–7.
2 NEP was a post-civil war "New Economic Policy," initially meant to ensure a supply of food for the city. Under the terms of the policy, grain requisitioning was halted and a tax in kind per acre was instituted. By 1921, NEP was widened and the Soviet government restored private ownership to the commercial sector, although it retained control of major industry.
3 Sheila Fitzpatrick, *The Cultural Front: Power and Culture in Revolutionary Russia* (Ithaca: Cornell University Press, 1992), 115.
4 Ibid., 100.
5 *DAKO*, f. R-1043, op. 3, spr. 31, ark. 52.
6 The Kadet or Constitutional Democratic Party had favoured the establishment of a liberal democratic state in the Russian Empire, but, critically, had opposed the increased autonomy for Ukraine as a governing party in the Provisional Government that succeeded tsarist authority after the February Revolution.
7 Ibid.
8 *DAKO*, f. R-1043, op. 3, spr. 31, ark. 61–4.
9 Tkach, "Natsional'ne pytannia i zavdannia spilky," *Narodnii uchytel'*, 30 May 1928, 2.
10 Mykhailo Volobuiev was an ethnic-Russian economist and head of Holovpolitosvita, the Narkomos agency for adult political education. He published two articles in the main KP(b)U journal, in which he suggested that Soviet Russia continued to treat Ukraine as a colony and further argued for greater Ukrainian control over the

republic's economy. The KP(b)U leadership immediately condemned this view. Volobuiev recanted his argument, but was later arrested. For detailed discussions of the debate regarding Volobuiev, see Mace, *Communism and the Dilemmas of National Liberation*,161–90; Liber, *Soviet Nationality Policy*, 126–31.

11 Khrystyna Oleksiivna Alchevska was the daughter of the famous Kharkiv pedagogical theorist and activist Khrystyna Danylivna Alchevska. In the pre-revolutionary era, she taught in a Kharkiv gymnasium and authored several collections of poetry. Under Soviet rule, she continued her educational activity, publishing methodological manuals and poetry, and translating works of Pushkin and others for use in schools. V. A. Smolii, ed. *Entsyklopediia istoriï Ukraïny*, vol. 1 (Kyïv: Naukova dumka, 2003–2013), 69.

12 *Derzhavnyi arkhiv Sluzhby Bezpeky Ukraïny (HDA SBU)*, f. 13, spr. 270, tom 1, ark. 41–56. I am grateful to Olga Bertelsen for bringing this document to my attention.

13 *TsDAVOU*, f. 166, op. 8, spr. 55, ark. 49–50.

14 Ibid.

15 *TsDAVOU*, f. 166, op. 8, spr. 55, ark. 47.

16 *TsDAVOU*, f. 166, op. 8, spr. 55, ark. 50.

17 *TsDAVOU*, f. 166, op. 8, spr. 55, ark. 51.

18 Ibid.

19 *TsDAVOU*, f. 166, op. 8, spr. 55, ark. 120.

20 *TsDAVOU*, f. 166, op. 8, spr. 55, ark. 87.

21 *TsDAHOU*, f. 1, op. 20, spr. 2247, ark. 25.

22 *TsDAHOU*, f. 1, op. 20, spr. 3099, ark. 104.

23 *TsDAHOU*, f. 1, op. 20, spr. 3099, ark. 105.

24 *TsDAHOU*, f. 1, op. 20, spr. 3099, ark. 82.

25 *TsDAHOU*, f. 1, op. 20, spr. 3099, ark. 36.

26 *DAKO*, f. R-1043, op. 3, spr. 28, ark. 169.

27 *TsDAHOU*, f. 1, op. 20, spr. 3099, ark. 38

28 *TsDAHOU*, f. 1, op. 20, spr. 3099, ark. 64.

29 Volodymyr Prystaiko and Iurii Shapoval, *Sprava "Spilky vyzvolennia Ukraïny": nevidomi dokumenty i fakty* (Kyïv: Intel, 1995), 39.

30 Veidlinger's commentary on inter-ethnic tensions in rural Ukraine is helpful in offering further context to this affair: "By removing one of the most important venues of interethnic and intercultural exchange the modern state offered – integrated public schools – Yiddish-language schooling heightened the ethnic division between Jews and Ukrainians." This, of course, was also true for Ukrainian-language schools, even if many Jewish and Ukrainian children developed friendships outside of the classroom or in some cases did not attend their "native-language" school. Veidlinger, *In the Shadow of the Shtetl*, 99.

31 *TsDAVOU*, f. 2717, op. 2, spr. 1638, ark. 34.

32 *TsDAVOU*, f. 2717, op. 2, spr. 1638, ark. 22.
33 *TsDAVOU*, f. 2717, op. 2, spr. 1638, ark. 23.
34 *TsDAVOU*, f. 2717, op. 3, spr. 195, ark. 74. For a general discussion of purges of primary school teachers, see: Marochko and H'ots, *Represovani pedahohy Ukraïny: zhertvy politychnoho teroru*, 246–55.
35 *TsDAVOU*, f. 2717, op. 3, spr. 195, ark. 12.
36 Mariia's defence was that she may have used the word "*zhyd*" in personal conversation because she was from Galicia, where the word meant "Jew" and had a neutral meaning. *TsDAVOU*, f. 2717, op. 3, spr. 195, ark. 38. The word is derogatory in Russian, but is considered to have been the standard word for "Jew" in Ukrainian, similar to the Polish "*żyd*." Soviet authorities had banned its use, however, and had purged the word from reprints of nineteenth-century Ukrainian texts, substituting the word "*ievrei*." Serhii Yefremov had recorded the ban of this word in his diary, subsequently used at the SVU trial. Shkandrij, *Jews in Ukrainian Literature*, 33, 65.
37 *TsDAVOU*, f. 2717, op. 3, spr. 195, ark. 13.
38 *TsDAVOU*, f. 2717, op. 3, spr. 272, ark. 68–70.
39 Ibid.
40 *TsDAVOU*, f. 2717, op. 3, spr. 272, ark. 30–3.
41 *TsDAVOU*, f. 2717, op. 3, spr. 195, ark. 47.
42 *TsDAVOU*, f. 2717, op. 3, spr. 195, ark. 83.
43 *TsDAVOU*, f. 2717, op. 3, spr. 296, ark. 4.
44 *TsDAVOU*, f. 2717, op. 3, spr. 296, ark. 26. The report typifies Ukrainian nationalism in the schools as a book by Vadym Sharko (a specialist at the Institute of the Ukrainian Scientific Language who was prosecuted as an alleged member of the SVU), an article by Mykhailo Volobuiev in *Visnyk refleksolohiï i eksperymental'noï pedahohika*, and the "nationalist theories" of the Kharkiv Printing Institute.
45 *TsDAVOU*, f. 2717, op. 3, spr. 296, ark. 4
46 *TsDAVOU*, f. 2717, op. 3, spr. 296, ark. 7
47 *TsDAVOU*, f. 2717, op. 3, spr. 296, ark. 6–7.
48 *TsDAVOU*, f. 2717, op. 3, spr. 296, ark. 6, 23.
49 Iurii Shapoval, Volodymyr Prystaiko, and Vadym Zolotar'ov, *ChK-GPU-NKVD v Ukraïni* (Kyïv: Abrys, 1997), 39–40; Iurii Shapoval and Vadym Zolotar'ov, *Vsevolod Balyts'kyi: osoba, chas, otochennia* (Kyïv: Stylos, 2002), 133–34, 136.
50 Martin, *Affirmative Action Empire*, 258; Shapoval, Prystaiko, and Zolotar'ov, *ChK-GPU-NKVD v Ukraïni*, 41–2; Shapoval and Zolotar'ov, *Vsevolod Balyts'kyi: osoba, chas, otochennia*, 136–7.
51 Prystaiko and Shapoval, *Sprava "Spilky vyzvolennia Ukraïny": nevidomi dokumenty i fakty*, 48.
52 Ibid., 15, 44; Shapoval, Prystaiko, and Zolotar'ov, *ChK-GPU-NKVD v Ukraïni*, 41; Shapoval and Zolotar'ov, *Vsevolod Balyts'kyi: osoba, chas, otochennia*, 135. For additional

studies of the SVU affair and the work of those arrested, see: Anatolii Bolabol'chenko, *SVU – sud nad perekonanniamy* (Kyïv: Kobzar, 1994); Hiroaki Kuromiya, "Stalin'skii 'velikii perelom' i protses nad 'Souizom osvobozhdeniia Ukrainy'," *Otechestvennaia istoriia*, no. 1 (1994); O. I. Sydorenko and D. V. Tabachnyk, eds., *Represovane "vidrodzhennia"* (Kyïv: Ukraïna, 1993); Vynokur, Babenko, and Tron'ko, *Represovane kraieznavstvo (20–30-i roky)*; Vasyl' Danylenko, ed., *Ukraïns'ka intelihentsiia i vlada: zavedennia sekretnoho viddilu DPU USRR 1927–1929 rr.* (Kyïv: Tempora, 2012).

53 I. V. Bukharieva, ed., *Represovani diiachi Ukraïns'koi Avtokefal'noï Pravoslavnoï Tserkvy (1921–1939): biohrafichnyi dovidnyk* (Kyïv: Smoloskyp, 2011); N. I. Boiko, ed., *Represovani movoznavtsi: zbirnyk naukovykh prats'* (Nizhyn: Nizhyns'kyi derzhavnyi universytet imeni Mykoly Hoholia, 2010).

54 Here, I am borrowing from Terry Martin's concept of terror as a "system of signaling." Martin, *Affirmative Action Empire*, 254–60.

55 "Protest spivrobitnykiv VUK'u ta redaktsiï hazety," *Narodnii uchytel'*, 24 November 1929, 2.

56 "Ne damo zhovto-blakytnym bandytam zavazhaty buduvanniu ukraïns'koï kul'tury," *Narodnii uchytel'*, 27 November 1929, 2.

57 "18,000 osvitnykiv Kyieva hanbliat' zukhvalykh kontr-revoliutsioneriv iz SVU," *Narodnii uchytel'*, 1 December 1929, 3.

58 "Osvitiany vyslovliuiut' svoie hromads'ke oburennia z konterrevoliutsiinykh uchynkiv zmovnyts'koï zhraï z 'SVU'," *Narodnii uchytel'*, 4 December 1929, 3.

59 "Vymahaiemo suvoroï kary," *Narodnii uchytel'*, 1 December 1929, 3.

60 "Osvitiany vyslovliuiut' svoie hromads'ke oburennia z konterrevoliutsiinykh uchynkiv zmovnyts'koï zhraï z 'SVU'," *Narodnii uchytel'*, 4 December 1929, 3.

61 The party took care to recruit two education officials to ensure that the proper message was sent at the trial and Narkomos as a whole was not tainted. Antin Prykhodko, the presiding judge, was then Deputy Commissar of Education. Another member of the court was Ivan Sokolianskyi, head of the Institute for Disability Study and a prominent educator. See Prystaiko and Shapoval, *Sprava "Spilky vyzvolennia Ukraïny": nevidomi dokumenty i fakty*, 50.

62 "Zhovtoblakytna kontrrevoliutsiia pered proletars'kym sudom." *Narodnii uchytel'*, 24 April 1930, 3.

63 "Vymahaiemo suvoroï kary," *Narodnii uchytel'*, 1 December 1929, 3.

64 "Zhovtoblakytna kontrrevoliutsiia pered proletars'kym sudom," *Narodnii uchytel'*, 24 April 1930, 3.

65 Prystaiko and Shapoval, *Sprava "Spilky vyzvolennia Ukraïny": nevidomi dokumenty i fakty*, 210.

66 "Zhovtoblakytna kontrrevoliutsiia pered proletars'kym sudom," *Narodnii uchytel'*, 24 April 1930, 3.

67 Pavlushkov lived with Durdukivsky and Yefremov and revealed the location of Yefremov's diary during his interrogation. Soviet prosecutors made extensive use of Yefremov's diary, which was critical of Soviet power, at trial. Yefremov's diary has since been published in Ukraine: Serhii Iefremov, *Shchodennyky: 1923–1929* (Kyïv: Hazeta "Rada," 1997).
68 Prystaiko and Shapoval, *Sprava "Spilky vyzvolennia Ukraïny": nevidomi dokumenty i fakty*, 159–60.
69 L. Akhmatov, "Sprava pro 'Spilku vyzvolennia Ukraïny.'" *Narodnii uchytel'*, 28 February 1930, 2.
70 Mykola Skrypnyk, *Statti i promovy*, vol. 2 (Kharkiv: Proletar, 1931), 366–7.
71 "Vymahaiemo suvoroï kary," *Narodnii uchytel'*, 1 December 1929, 3.
72 "Han'ba zlochyntsiam z taboru SVU," *Narodnii uchytel'*, 1 December 1929, 3.
73 Ibid.
74 L. Akhmatov, "Sprava pro 'Spilku vyzvolennia Ukrainy'," *Narodnii uchytel'*, 28 February 1930, 2.
75 Prosecutors linked the SVU to anti-Semitism by citing passages from Yefremov's diary where he suggested the Ukrainian national leader Symon Petliura might not have been responsible for pogroms committed during the war by Ukrainian forces.
76 Tsentral'nyi komitet LKSM Ukrainy, *Molodi fashysty ukraïns'koï kontrrevoliutsiï do protsesu SVU* (Kharkiv: Derzhavne vydavnytstvo Ukrainy, 1930), 111.
77 "Vymahaiemo suvoroï kary," *Narodnii uchytel'*, 1 December 1929, 3.
78 Martin, *Affirmative Action Empire*, 222. Vasyl Danylenko argues that GPU reserved the label "*smenovekhovstvo*" mostly for the "pro-Russian intelligentsia" and favoured the category "Ukrainian counter-revolutionary" to describe the activities of the Ukrainian intelligentsia, assuming they must occupy an anti-Soviet stance. Danylenko, *Ukraïns'ka intelihentsiia i vlada: zavedennia sekretnoho viddilu DPU USRR 1927–1929 rr.*, 19.
79 Fitzpatrick notes that the formation of this ethos inevitably involved the elimination of the bourgeois intelligentsia through "class war." Fitzpatrick, *The Cultural Front*, 8.
80 Ukrainian scholars have produced a large body of scholarship on the subject of political repression. The number of titles is too exhaustive to cite here, but an essential source for any reader interested in this question is the journal *Z arkhiviv VUChK-GPU-NKVD-KGB*.
81 Shapoval, Prystaiko, and Zolotar'ov, *ChK-GPU-NKVD v Ukraïni*, 44; Shapoval and Zolotar'ov, *Vsevolod Balyts'kyi: osoba, chas, otochennia*, 138; Danylenko, *Ukraïns'ka intelihentsiia i vlada: zavedennia sekretnoho viddilu DPU USRR 1927–1929 rr.*, 27, 31. For a similar view, see: Myroslav Shkandrij and Olga Bertelsen, "The Soviet Regime's National Operations in Ukraine."
82 *Ukraïns'ka intelihentsiia i vlada: zavedennia sekretnoho viddilu DPU USRR 1927–1929 rr.*, 14.

83 Prystaiko and Shapoval, *Sprava "Spilky vyzvolennia Ukraïny": nevidomi dokumenty i fakty*, 23–4. In fact, the Ukrainian GPU and KP(b)U had drawn up a plan for the exile of leading Ukrainian scholars to elsewhere in the USSR, fearing that Ukrainians abroad would be emboldened in their efforts to undermine Soviet power by the arrival of the deportees. The Communist Party leadership in Moscow had overturned this request, although Soviet authorities initially approved the deportation of Yefremov outside the borders of the USSR. Danylenko, *Ukraïns'ka intelihentsiia i vlada: zavedennia sekretnoho viddilu DPU USRR 1927–1929 rr.*, 19–20.

84 Volodymyr Prystaiko and Iurii Shapoval, *Mykhailo Hrushevs'kyi i GPU-NKVD. Trahichne desiatylittia: 1924–1934* (Kyïv: Ukraïna, 1996), 31–3.

85 Danylenko, *Ukraïns'ka intelihentsiia i vlada: zavedennia sekretnoho viddilu DPU USRR 1927–1929 rr.*

86 Shapoval and Zolotar'ov, *Vsevolod Balyts'kyi: osoba, chas, otochennia*, 136; Shapoval, Prystaiko, and Zolotar'ov, *ChK-GPU-NKVD v Ukraïni*, 11.

87 Olga Bertelsen, "GPU Repressions of Zionists: Ukraine in the 1920s," *Europe-Asia Studies* 65, no. 6 (2013).

88 Shapoval and Zolotar'ov, *Vsevolod Balyts'kyi: osoba, chas, otochennia*, 134, 138–9.

89 Shapoval, Prystaiko, and Zolotar'ov, *ChK-GPU-NKVD v Ukraïni*, 36–7; Shapoval and Zolotar'ov, *Vsevolod Balyts'kyi: osoba, chas, otochennia*, 141–2. Vasyl Danylenko writes, according to the GPU secret communications, that the number of members of the Ukrainian intelligentsia who "stood on a right position" was significant. Danylenko, *Ukraïns'ka intelihentsiia i vlada: zavedennia sekretnoho viddilu DPU USRR 1927–1929 rr.*

90 Viktor Danylenko and Alla Kravchenko detail the contents of files of Volodymyr Durdukivsky, the alleged leader of the school section of the SVU. See V. M. Danylenko and A. A. Kravchenko, *Volodymyr Durdukivs'kyi: pedahoh, krytyk, hromads'kyi diach (1874–1938)* (Kyïv: Nika Tsentr, 2000), 37–51. For a discussion of the diary Durdukivsky kept after being rearrested in December 1938, see: Marochko and H'ots, *Represovani pedahohy Ukraïny: zhertvy politychnoho teroru*, 265–71.

91 This approach coincides with Hiroaki Kuromiya's counsel regarding the reading of interrogation files: "The police files are treacherous sources. The police beat confessions out of the arrested in order to confirm their own preconceptions about their 'enemies' ... However, even such files, if handled with caution and care, throw up valuable clues through which one can uncover the lost voices of the dead." Hiroaki Kuromiya, *The Voices of the Dead: Stalin's Great Terror in the 1930s* (New Haven: Yale University Press, 2007), 11–12. I focus here on the meaning the GPU may have sought to infer and transpose from information gained in interrogation rather than an exposure of objective truth.

92 *HDA SBU*, f. 6, spr. 67098 FP, tom 83, ark. 6.

93 *HDA SBU*, f. 6, spr. 67098 FP, tom 63, ark. 20–1.

94 *HDA SBU*, f. 6, spr. 67098 FP, tom 135, ark. 5.
95 *HDA SBU*, f. 6, spr. 67098 FP, tom 135, ark. 33.
96 *HDA SBU*, f. 6, spr. 67098 FP, tom 63, ark. 7.
97 *HDA SBU*, f. 6, spr. 67098 FP, tom 63, ark. 7.
98 *HDA SBU*, f. 6, spr. 67098 FP, tom 83, ark. 35.
99 *HDA SBU*, f. 6, spr. 67098 FP, tom 63, ark. 31–2.
100 *HDA SBU*, f. 6, spr. 67098 FP, tom 135, ark. 33.
101 *HDA SBU*, f. 6, spr. 67098 FP, tom 135, ark. 16, 32.
102 *HDA SBU*, f. 6, spr. 67098 FP, tom 63, ark. 8.
103 *HDA SBU*, f. 6, spr. 67098 FP, tom 63, ark. 13, 23.
104 *HDA SBU*, f. 6, spr. 67098 FP, tom 83, ark. 11.
105 *HDA SBU*, f. 6, spr. 67098 FP, tom 63, ark. 23.
106 *HDA SBU*, f. 6, spr. 67098 FP, tom 63, ark. 27.
107 *HDA SBU*, f. 6, spr. 67098 FP, tom 135, ark. 5.
108 *HDA SBU*, f. 6, spr. 67098 FP, tom 135, ark. 10.
109 *HDA SBU*, f. 6, spr. 67098 FP, tom 135, ark. 13; *HDA SBU*, f. 6, spr. 67098 FP, tom 63, ark. 31–32.
110 *HDA SBU*, f. 6, spr. 67098 FP, tom 135, ark. 13.
111 *HDA SBU*, f. 6, spr. 67098 FP, tom 63, ark. 19.
112 *HDA SBU*, f. 6, spr. 67098 FP, tom 63, ark. 174.
113 *HDA SBU*, f. 6, spr. 67098 FP, tom 135, ark. 34.
114 *HDA SBU*, f. 6, spr. 67098 FP, tom 135, ark. 83.
115 *HDA SBU*, f. 6, spr. 67098 FP, tom 135, ark. 88.
116 Hrebenetsky played the role of "reminder" to Trezvynsky and another defendant and teacher at Labour School No. 1, Nina Tokarevska. See *HDA SBU*, f. 6, spr. 67098 FP, tom 63, ark. 151–2; *HDA SBU*, f. 6, spr. 67098 FP, tom 83, ark. 24–6.
117 *HDA SBU*, f. 6, spr. 67098 FP, tom 83, ark. 9.
118 *HDA SBU*, f. 6, spr. 67098 FP, tom 63, ark. 30.
119 *HDA SBU*, f. 6, spr. 67098 FP, tom 135, ark. 43.
120 A Ukrainian study that addresses the SVU affair in Odesa, but largely concerns the fate of individual teachers and educators in Odesa during the terror of the late 1930s, is: D. M. Kliuienko and L. I. Fursenko, *Represyvna polityka stalinizmu: arkhivni dokumenty svidchat'* (Odesa: Astroprint, 2006). For another localized view of the "signalling" function of the SVU affair, see: T. Demchenko and N. Klymovych, "Protses 'SVU' kriz' pryzmu propahandysts'kykh zakhodiv na Chernihivshchyni (berezen'–kviten' 1930)," *Problemy istoriï Ukraïni*, no. 15 (2006).
121 For a detailed discussion of the life and work of Mykhailo Slabchenko, see: V. M. Zaruba, *Mykhailo Slabchenko v epistoliarnii ta memuarnii spadshchyni:1882–1952* (Dnipropetrovs'k: Vydavnytstvo Iurydychnoï akademiï MVS Ukraïny, 2004).

122 *DAOO*, f. P-7, op. 1, spr. 2212, ark. 3.
123 *DAOO*, f. P-7, op. 1, spr. 2212, ark. 3.
124 The reaction of Jews and other ethnic minorities appears to have not been recorded.
125 *DAOO*, f. P-7, op. 1, spr. 2212, ark. 4.
126 *DAOO*, f. P-7, op. 1, spr. 2212, ark. 4.
127 *DAOO*, f. P-7, op. 1, spr. 2212, ark. 5.
128 *DAOO*, f. P-7, op. 1, spr. 2212, ark. 6.
129 *DAOO*, f. P-7, op. 1, spr. 2457, ark. 11. Soviet prosecutors alleged that Serhii Yefremov was the leader of the SVU.
130 *DAOO*, f. P-7, op. 1, spr. 2457, ark. 12.
131 *DAOO*, f. P-7, op. 1, spr. 2457, ark. 12.
132 O., "Het' kurkuliv ta kurkul'sku ideolohiiuz lav nashoï spilky, " *Narodnii uchytel'*, 17 June 1929, 6.
133 "Na zakhyst uchyteliv-aktyvistiv," *Narodnii uchytel'*, 13 November 1929, 2.
134 Uchytel', "Na grunti kliasovoï pomsty," *Narodnii uchytel'*, 4 December 1929, 6.
135 For more on the teacher's lonely role as mediator of the collectivization campaign, see Ewing, *The Teachers of Stalinism*, 17–52.
136 Ia. F., "Shche odna zhertva," *Narodnii uchytel'*, 4 December 1929, 6.
137 S., "Novyi napad na vchytelia-hromads'koho robitnyka," *Narodnii uchytel'*, 4 December 1929, 6.
138 "Svoïkh pozytsii my ne zdamo," *Narodnii uchytel'*, 4 December 1929, 6; Myropil's'kyi, "Vchyetli vynni," *Narodnii uchytel'*, 4 December 1929, 6.

11. Children Corrupted and Exalted

1 For comments largely regarding older Komsomol youth, see: Pryluts'kyi, *Molod' USRR v period utverdzhennia totalitarnoï systemy, 1928–1933*.
2 *TsDAHOU*, f. 7, op. 1, spr. 40, ark 19.
3 *TsDAHOU*, f. 7, op. 1, spr. 40, ark 19.
4 *TsDAHOU*, f. 7, op. 1, spr. 40, ark 39.
5 *TsDAHOU*, f. 7, op. 1, spr. 40, ark 44.
6 *TsDAHOU*, f. 7, op. 1, spr. 40, ark 45.
7 *TsDAHOU*, f. 7, op. 1, spr. 588, ark. 27.
8 *TsDAHOU*, f. 7, op. 1, spr. 738, ark. 16.
9 *TsDAHOU*, f. 7, op. 1, spr. 738, ark. 16.
10 *TsDAHOU*, f. 7, op. 1, spr. 738, ark. 54.
11 There were several villages named Marianivka in the UkrSSR in 1931, but the report's mention of this village shortly after Novoiehorivka, Bashtanka district, suggests it was referencing Marianivka, Bashtanka district.

myth of the SVU and its youth organization, the SUM, was either providing motivation for anti-Soviet action by youths or reason for repression of non-sanctioned youth culture. *TsDAHOU*, spr. 3066, f. 1, op. 20, ark. 11–12.
13 *Hashomer Hatzair* was a Socialist-Zionist group that had been founded as a scout group in Polish Galicia and, by the early 1930s, operated primarily in Palestine. See: Ofer Nur, "Hashomer Hatzair Youth Movement, 1918–1924 from Eastern Galicia and Vienna to Palestine: A Cultural History" (PhD diss., University of California, Los Angeles, 2004).
14 *TsDAHOU*, f. 7, op. 1, spr. 738, ark. 54.
15 *TsDAHOU*, f. 7, op. 1, spr. 738, ark. 20.
16 *TsDAHOU*, f. 7, op. 1, spr. 738, ark. 20.
17 *TsDAHOU*, f. 7, op. 1, spr. 588, ark. 8.
18 *TsDAHOU*, f. 7, op. 1, spr. 738, ark. 55.
19 *TsDAHOU*, f. 7, op. 1, spr. 588, ark. 1.
20 *TsDAHOU*, f. 7, op. 1, spr. 668, ark. 28.
21 *TsDAHOU*, f. 7, op. 1, spr. 668, ark. 65.
22 *TsDAHOU*, f. 7, op. 1, spr. 738, ark. 22.
23 *TsDAHOU*, f. 7, op. 1, spr. 668, ark. 7–27.
24 *TsDAHOU*, f. 7, op. 1, spr. 668, ark. 46.
25 *TsDAHOU*, f. 7, op. 1, spr. 668, ark. 64–5.
26 *TsDAHOU*, f. 7, op. 1, spr. 668, ark. 65.
27 *TsDAHOU*, f. 7, op. 1, spr. 668, ark. 65.
28 *TsDAHOU*, f. 7, op. 1, spr. 738, ark. 54.
29 *TsDAHOU*, f. 7, op. 1, spr. 738, ark. 25.
30 *TsDAHOU*, f. 7, op. 1, spr. 738, ark. 55.
31 *TsDAHOU*, f. 7, op. 1, spr. 738, ark. 25.
32 *TsDAHOU*, f. 7, op. 1, spr. 470, ark. 6.
33 *TsDAHOU*, f. 7, op. 1, spr. 470, ark. 8–9.
34 *TsDAHOU*, f. 7, op. 1, spr. 470, ark. 9–10.
35 *TsDAHOU*, f. 7, op. 1, spr. 470, ark. 12.
36 *TsDAHOU*, f. 7, op. 1, spr. 470, ark. 12.
37 *TsDAHOU*, f. 7, op. 1, spr. 115, ark. 13–20.

12. The Path Ahead

1 TsDAHO, f. 1, op. 20, spr. 3099, ark. 140.
2 Skrypnyk argued for the education of children of kulaks in order to prevent the formation of a kulak cadre and "create people who will work on the tasks of the Communist Party." M. Skrypnyk, "Osnovni problemy sotsiial'noho vykhovannia za rekonstruktyvnoï doby," *Radians'ka osvita*, no. 5–6 (1930): 29–30.

3 Martin, *Affirmative Action Empire*, 100.
4 "Stan ukraïnizatsiï v promyslovykh okruhakh," *Narodnii uchytel'*, 11 January 1930, 1.
5 Ibid.
6 Ibid.
7 Rama, "Misiachnyk ukraïns'koï proletar'skoï kul'tury," *Narodnii uchytel'*, 22 June 1930, 3.
8 Ibid.; Terry Martin descibes a wider, three-month campaign beginning in June 1929 in which Mykola Khvyolovy played a role. See Martin, *Affirmative Action Empire*, 100.
9 Rama, "Misiachnyk ukraïns'koï proletar'skoï kul'tury," 3.
10 H. Shvydkyi, "Ukraïnizuiut'sia nadto povil'no," *Narodnii uchytel'*, 11 June 1930, 7.
11 Ibid.
12 *TsDAVOU*, f. 166, op. 6, spr. 10841, ark. 421.
13 *TsDAVOU*, f. 166, op. 6, spr. 10841, ark. 420, 427.
14 A Gosplan report on "cultural construction" in January 1932 (but sent or re-sent to Narkomos in 1934) provides evidence that schools of mixed Ukrainian–Russian, Ukrainian–Polish, and Ukrainian–Yiddish instruction existed well past this date in the Kyiv oblast. TsDAVOU, f. 166, op. 11, spr. 356, ark. 12–13 zv.
15 *TsDAVOU*, f. 166, op. 6, spr. 10841, ark. 421, 420, 427.
16 Mykola Skrypnyk, "Perebudovnymy shliakhamy," 27. Cited in Martin, *Affirmative Action Empire*, 107.
17 Ivan Prysiazhniuk, "Polipshuite nashu movu," *Narodnii uchytel'*, 16 January 1929, 5.
18 Ibid.
19 H. Hulak, "Movoznavtsi," *Narodnii uchytel'*, 16 January 1929, 5.
20 Martin, *Affirmative Action Empire*, 107.
21 K. Kost', "Ukraïnizuvalys'," *Narodnii uchytel'*, 16 January 1929, 5.
22 Eskiz, "Lyshe odna … (Makarivs'kyi raion na Kyïvshchyni)," *Narodnii uchytel'*, 16 January 1929, 5. "Eskiz" is a pseudonym meaning "sketch" or "rough draft."
23 V. L., "Sprava ukraïnizatsiï," *Narodnii uchytel'*, 14 March 1929, 4.
24 Samarchenko, "Ukraïnizatsiiu vchytel'stva shche pro te zhe same," *Narodnii uchytel'*, 16 January 1929, 5.
25 Ibid.
26 *TsDAVOU*, f. 166, op. 6, spr. 10841, ark. 415.
27 The inspectorate had dismissed only five teachers to date for refusing to even attempt to learn Ukrainian.
28 *TsDAVOU*, f. 166, op. 6, spr. 10841, ark. 417.
29 Ibid.
30 *TsDAVOU*, f. 166, op. 6, spr. 10841, ark. 416.
31 "Natsional'ne pytannia," *Narodnii uchytel'*, 10 April 1929, 3.
32 Ibid.

33 Martin, *Affirmative Action Empire*, 258.
34 *TsDAVOU*, f. 166, op. 8, spr. 525, ark. 13–14.
35 Sukhomlyns'ka, *Narys istoriï ukraïns'koho shkil'nytstva (1905–1933)*, 174.
36 *TsDAVOU*, f. 166, op. 8, spr. 525, ark. 4.
37 M. Skrypnyk, "Za iedynu systemu narodn'oï osvity," *Radians'ka osvita*, no. 5–6 (1930): 8.
38 Ibid.
39 Mace, *Communism and the Dilemmas of National Liberation*, 223.
40 Ibid.
41 *TsDAVOU*, f. 539, op. 8, spr. 242, ark. 23zv.; Marochko and H'ots, *Represovani pedahohy Ukraïny: zhertvy politychnoho teroru*, 7.
42 *TsDAVOU*, f. 539, op. 8, spr. 242, ark. 28–8zv.
43 Krylov, *Systema osvity v Ukraïni: 1917–1930*, 84.
44 Bondar et al., *Narodna osvita i pedahohichna nauka v Ukraïns'kii RSR*, 53.
45 Iasnyts'kyi, *Rozvytok narodnoï osvity na Ukraïni (1921–1932 rr.)*, 162.
46 Krylov, *Systema osvity v Ukraïni: 1917–1930*, 78.; Bondar et al., *Narodna osvita i pedahohichna nauka v Ukraïns'kii RSR*, 54.; Sukhomlyns'ka, *Narys istoriï ukraïns'koho shkil'nytstva (1905–1933)*, 173.
47 Fitzpatrick, *Education and Social Mobility*, 139–57.
48 Gail Warshofsky Lapidus, "Educational Strategies and Cultural Revolution: The Politics of Soviet Development," in *Cultural Revolution in Russia, 1928–1931*, ed. Sheila Fitzpatrick (Bloomington: Indiana University Press, 1984), 93. For more on the "cultural revolution" and the problems inherent in invoking this term to describe a narrow time frame between 1928 to 1931, see: Michael David-Fox, "What Is Cultural Revolution?," *Russian Review* 58, no. 2 (1999).
49 L. Mylovydov, "Kraieznavstvo v novykh prohramakh trudshkil I-ho kontsentru," *Radians'ka osvita*, no. 4 (1930): 45.
50 M. Skrypnyk, "Cherhovi pytannia sotsvykhu," *Radians'ka osvita*, no. 2 (1929): 9; "Osnovni problemy sotsiial'noho vykhovannia za rekonstruktyvnoï doby," 19.
51 M. Skrypnyk, "Cherhovi pytannia sotsvykhu," 47.
52 M. Skrypnyk, "Osnovni problemy sotsiial'noho vykhovannia za rekonstruktyvnoï doby," 16.
53 Lapidus, "Educational Strategies and Cultural Revolution," 104.
54 M. Skrypnyk, "Za iedynu systemu narodn'oï osvity," *Radians'ka osvita*, no. 5–6 (1930): 13.
55 M. Skrypnyk, "Osnovni problemy sotsiial'noho vykhovannia za rekonstruktyvnoï doby," 21; "Viddil narodn'oï osvity Kyïvs'koï mis'krady," in *V borot'bi za realizatsiiu ukhval TsK VKP(b) ta Kyïvs'koho MPK pro shkolu ta pionerorhanizatsiï* (Kyiv: Radians'ka shkola, 1932), 27.
56 V. Pomahaiba, "Posylyty vohon' po fashysts'kii pedahohitsi SVU," *Politekhnichna osvita*, no. 3 (1932): 8.

57 Skrypnyk, "Viddil narodn'oï osvity Kyïvs'koï mis'krady," 32.
58 The culmination of the new emphasis on the textbook was a TsK KP(b)U decree in March 1933 issued after Skrypnyk's ousting, mandating the use of standard textbooks in the classroom. Skrypnyk was charged with a failure to impose textbook uniformity as a prelude to a later campaign exposing his lack of vigilance against "national deviation." In fact, Skrypnyk's Narkomos had issued a series of resolutions from 1928 to 1930, ordering increased use of standard workbooks. Hennadii Yefimenko argues that the March 1933 decree allowed for institution of curricular norms on Russian terms because RSFSR textbooks were to serve as the basis for textbook development. H. Iefimenko, *Natsional'na polityka kerivnytstva VKP(b)*, 12–13.
59 Krawchenko, *Social Change*, 135.
60 Ibid., 139–40.
61 "Vykorchuvaty korinnia pravoho ukhylu v spiltsi Robos," *Narodnii uchytel'*, 26 November 1930, 1.
62 Bondar et al., *Narodna osvita i pedahohichna nauka v Ukraïns'kii RSR*, 55.
63 Ibid., 69.
64 *TsDAVOU*, f. 166, op. 9, spr. 762, ark. 9, 13.
65 *TsDAVOU*, f. 166, op. 9, spr. 1256, ark. 20–3.
66 *TsDAVOU*, f. 166, op. 10, spr. 968, ark. 41–8.
67 *TsDAVOU*, f. 166, op. 10, spr. 498, ark. 9, 12, 38, 40.
68 *TsDAVOU*, f. 166, op. 10, spr. 498, ark. 12.
69 Martin, *Affirmative Action Empire*, 108–12. For a description of resistance to Ukrainization in November 1931 (and accompanying worries about the spread of Ukrainian nationalism), see: *TsDAHOU*, f. 1, op. 20, spr. 4172, ark. 36–41, 44. The emphasis of this TsK KP(b)U report and accompanying decree is also on secondary and post-secondary institutions (particularly those with an "all-Union significance"), but it mentions briefly the lack of "organic" Ukrainization at the primary school level, especially in the Donbas.
70 *TsDAVOU*, f. 166, op. 10, spr. 968, ark. 34.
71 *TsDAVOU*, f. 166, op. 10, spr. 968, ark. 31–2.
72 *TsDAVOU*, f. 166, op. 10, spr. 968, ark. 38.
73 For example, there a handful of files on primary schooling for 1934 and no files exist for Narkomos as a whole in 1935. The number of reports for 1930 to 1933 that detail events in the schools themselves is limited; they centre on the victories of the enrolment drive and administrative concerns, leaving significant gaps regarding the real state of affairs in the classroom. See *TsDAVOU*, f. 166, op. 11.
74 *TsDAVOU*, f. 166, op. 10, spr. 161, ark. 7–11. An early 1933 Narkomos proposal from Deputy Commissar Karpeko and Administrator of the Sotsvykh Sector Barun underscored a shortage in paper that constrained the ability of presses to provide textbooks for the large number of schools converting to polytechnical instruction. *TsDAVOU*, f. 166, op. 11, spr. 152, ark. 124.

75 *TsDAVOU*, f. 166, op. 10, spr. 161, ark. 12–18.
76 *TsDAVOU*, f. 166, op. 11, spr. 160, ark. 15–16.
77 *TsDAVOU*, f. 166, op. 11, spr. 152, ark. 130. For another example of such teacher complaints, see: *TsDAVOU*, f. 166, op. 11, spr. 152, ark. 125–6.
78 *TsDAVOU*, f. 166, op. 11, spr. 7, ark. 8.
79 *TsDAVOU*, f. 166, op. 11, spr. 11, ark. 113; *TsDAVOU*, f. 166, op. 11, spr. 160, ark. 11.
80 *TsDAVOU*, f. 166, op. 11, spr. 7, ark. 12.
81 Karpeko, for example, was initially demoted and forced to confess to his "errors" as one of Skrypnyk's deputies. In October 1934 he was held directly responsible for distorting "Leninist nationalities policy" in the schools, was arrested, and died in a labour camp. Marochko and H'ots, *Represovani pedahohy Ukraïny: zhertvy politychnoho teroru*, 9; Vyhovs'kyi, *Nomenklatura systemy osvity v USRR*, 254–6.
82 *TsDAVOU*, f. 166, op. 11, spr. 8, ark. 32.
83 *TsDAVOU*, f. 166, op. 11, spr. 9, ark. 62–3.
84 *TsDAVOU*, f. 166, op. 11, spr. 9, ark. 63.
85 *TsDAVOU*, f. 166, op. 11, spr. 13, ark. 30–5.
86 *TsDAVOU*, f. 166, op. 11, spr. 19, ark. 23.
87 *TsDAVOU*, f. 166, op. 11, spr. 19, ark. 13.
88 *TsDAVOU*, f. 166, op. 11, spr. 13, ark. 45.
89 *TsDAVOU*, f. 166, op. 11, spr. 16, ark. 41.
90 *TsDAVOU*, f. 166, op. 11, spr. 13, ark. 45.
91 *TsDAVOU*, f. 166, op. 11, spr. 15, ark. 1–2.
92 *TsDAVOU*, f. 166, op. 11, spr. 11, ark. 120.
93 *TsDAVOU*, f. 166, op. 11, spr. 18, ark. 8.
94 *TsDAVOU*, f. 166, op. 11, spr. 13, ark. 51, 57–58; *TsDAVOU*, f. 166, op. 11, spr. 19, ark. 5.
95 *TsDAVOU*, f. 166, op. 11, spr. 19, ark. 3–5.
96 *TsDAVOU*, f. 166, op. 11, spr. 13, ark. 45.
97 *TsDAVOU*, f. 166, op. 11, spr. 19, ark. 5.
98 *TsDAVOU*, f. 166, op. 11, spr. 15, ark. 1.
99 *TsDAVOU*, f. 166, op. 11, spr. 11, ark. 112–13.
100 *TsDAVOU*, f. 166, op. 11, spr. 19, ark. 27–30.
101 *TsDAVOU*, f. 166, op. 11, spr. 9, ark. 64.
102 *TsDAVOU*, f. 166, op. 11, spr. 9, ark. 65.
103 *TsDAVOU*, f. 166, op. 11, spr. 18, ark. 22–3. The files spr. 18 and spr. 19 are reversed in terms of content. Spr. 18 contains the minutes of the final evening session of the meeting; spr. 19, the morning session.
104 *TsDAVOU*, f. 166, op. 11, spr. 18, ark. 23–24, 32–3.
105 *TsDAVOU*, f. 166, op. 11, spr. 11, ark. 113; *TsDAVOU*, f. 166, op. 11, spr. 19, ark. 20–2.

106 Mykola Skrypnyk, *Narysy pidsumkiv ukraïnizatsiï ta obsluhuvannia kul'turnhkh potreb natsmenshostei USRR, zokrema rosiis'koï* (Kharkiv: Radians'ka shola, 1933).
107 Iefimenko, *Natsional'na polityka kerivnytstva VKP(b)*, 13–14.
108 Martin, *Affirmative Action Empire*, 347–50; Mace, *Communism and the Dilemmas of National Liberation*, 297–300. Liubchenko had served as a public prosecutor of the accused in the SVU trial in 1930. In 1937, after having been accused of leading a nationalist organization, he shot his wife and committed suicide.
109 Liber, *Soviet Nationality Policy*, 168–69; Martin, *Affirmative Action Empire*, 356.
110 Martin, *Affirmative Action Empire*, 351; Krawchenko, *Social Change*, 135–6; Liber, *Soviet Nationality Policy*, 356.
111 Marochko and H'ots, *Represovani pedahohy Ukraïny: zhertvy politychnoho teroru*, 49.
112 A. Khvylia, "Pro reorhanizatsiu aparatu NKO," *Komunistychna osvita*, no. 9 (1933): 60. Following the publication of this article, numerous essays appeared in the pedagogical press, indicting nationalist "sabotage" in the schools, Narkomos, and pedagogical institutions. For example, see: I. Khait, "Za bil'shovytsku rozchystku na fronti pedahohichnoï teoriï," *Komunistychna osvita*, no. 2 (1934); Sobolev, "Zmitsnimo bil'shovyts'kymy kadramy orhany narodnoï osvity," *Komunistychna osvita*, no. 2 (1934); S. Chavdarov, "Cherhovi zavdannia u vykladanni movy v shkoli," *Komunistychna osvita*, no. 10 (1934).
113 *Na fronti kul'tury*, 9.
114 Ibid., 12–13. The book specifically condemned the methodology of what it labelled "the Kharkiv Pedagogical School," a group of scholars whom the pedagogical press associated with republic's leading pedagogues Ivan Sokoliansky and Oleksandr Zaluzhny at the Ukrainian Scientific Research Institute of Pedagogy (UNDIP) in Kharkiv. On the purge of the UNDIP and work and fate of Sokoliansky and Zaluzhny, see: Marochko and H'ots, *Represovani pedahohy Ukraïny: zhertvy politychnoho teroru*, 80–92, 111–23, 140–6.
115 *Na fronti kul'tury*, 13.
116 Ibid., 6, 28. Analyzing statistical data of the spring 1933 inventory of schools, Yefimenko presents slightly different numbers: 89.4 per cent of schools provided Ukrainian-language instruction in 1932–3 versus 84.5 per cent in 1933–4. Iefimenko, *Natsional'na polityka kerivnytstva VKP(b)*, 15.
117 Ibid., 6–7, 28.
118 Ibid., 18.
119 For Zatonsky's direct view of the tasks of the new Narkomos, see: V. P. Zatons'kyi, *Itogi noiabr'skogo plenuma TsK i TsKK KP(b)U i zadachi rabotnykov prosveshchennia (Kharkiv: Radians'ka shkola, 1934); Natsional'no-kul'turne budivnytstvo i borot'ba proty natsionalizmu dopovid' ta zakliuchne slovo na sichnevii sesiï VUAN* (Kyïv: Vydavnytsvo Vseukrains'koï akademiï nauk, 1934).
120 *Na fronti kul'tury*, 14, 30. Numerous local party reports sent to the TsK from 1933–4 detail the "exposure" of nationalists and other class enemies in state

Ukrainian-studies courses, party schools, pedagogical institutes, primary schools, and libraries. See: *TsDAHOU*, f. 1, op. 20, spr. 6214, ark. 67–70; *TsDAHOU*, f. 1, op. 20, spr. 6424, ark. 1–2; *TsDAHOU*, f. 1, op. 20, spr. 6425, ark. 4–5, 33–8, 61–2, 85–8, 101–6, 109–11.

121 Liber, *Soviet Nationality Policy*, 167–70; Mace, *Communism and the Dilemmas of National Liberation*, 296–301.
122 *Na fronti kul'tury*, 18.
123 Ibid., 28.
124 The publication conceded the existence of nationalist saboteurs among multiple other national-minority populations, but not Russians. *Na fronti kul'tury*, 20.
125 Martin, *The Affirmative Action Empire*, 353–5.
126 Ibid., 354.
127 In 1932–3, the study of the Russian language began in the third grade of non-Russian schools for one hour a week. By 1934–5, the time allotted to study of the Russian language and literature had increased by an hour a week in the third and fourth grades and by two hours in the fifth. Iefimenko, *Natsional'na polityka kerivnytstva VKP(b)*, 26, 34. For a broader discussion of Soviet nationalities policy in Ukraine in the 1930s, see: H. Iefimenko, *Natsional'no-kul'turna polityka VKP(b) shchodo radians'koï Ukraïni (1932–1938)* (Kyïv: Instytut istoriï Ukraïny, 2001).
128 In 1933, the number of national minority schools rose as a consequence of the campaign against "forced Ukrainization," but many rural Polish, German, and Yiddish schools were converted to Ukrainian-language instruction already in 1934–5. In his use of the term "Russsification," Yefimenko parts somewhat with the analysis of Peter Blitstein, but makes clear elsewhere that even formal Russification was only "a means for the centralization of power." H. Iefimenko, "Pytannia natsional'noï polityky kremlia v Ukraïni v persh. pol. 1937 r.," *Problemy istoriï Ukraïni*, no. 12 (2004): 292. On the fate of national minority schools in Ukraine, see also: Brown, *Biography of No Place*, 118–33, 160, 187; Veidlinger, *In the Shadow of the Shtetl*, 89.
129 Iefimenko, *Natsional'na polityka kerivnytstva VKP(b)*, 34.
130 Martin, *Affirmative Action Empire*, 355–56.
131 *DAOO*, f. R-1234, op. 1, spr. 1943, ark. 23.
132 *DAOO*, f. R-1234, op. 1, spr. 1943, ark. 23.
133 *DAOO*, f. R-1234, op. 1, spr. 1943, ark. 24.
134 *DAOO*, f. R-1234, op. 1, spr. 1943, ark. 25.

Conclusion

1 Comparisons between language and educational policy of the 1920s and early 1930s and that of the post-Soviet period cannot be easily drawn; however, the place of language is an oft-debated feature of contemporary Ukrainian public

life. There has been a wealth of scholarship produced on recent Ukrainian language politics (and its intersection with the question of schooling). See: Michael Moser, *Language Policy and Discourse on Languages in Ukraine under President Viktor Yanukovych* (Stuttgart: Ibidem-Verlag, 2013); Laada Bilaniuk, *Contested Tongues: Language Politics and Cultural Correction in Ukraine* (Ithaca: Cornell University Press, 2005), 50–63; Alexandra Hrycak, "Institutional Legacies and Language Revival in Ukraine," in *Rebounding Identities: The Politics of Identity in Russia and Ukraine*, ed. Dominique Arel and Blair Ruble (Washington, DC: Woodrow Wilson Center Press, 2006); Richardson, *Kaleidoscopic Odessa*; Abel Polese, "The Formal and the Informal: Exploring 'Ukrainian' Education in Ukraine, Scenes from Odessa," *Comparative Education*, no. 1 (2010); Lowell Barrington and Regina Faranda, "Reexamining Region, Ethnicity, and Language in Ukraine," *Post-Soviet Affairs* 25, no. 3 (2009); Volodymyr Kulyk, "Constructing Common Sense: Language and Ethnicity in Ukrainian Public Discourse," *Ethnic and Racial Studies* 29, no. 2 (2006); Dominique Arel, "Language Politics in Independent Ukraine: Towards One Or Two State Languages?" *Nationalities Papers* 23, no. 3 (1995); Debra A. Friedman, "Speaking Correctly: Error Correction as a Language Socialization Practice in a Ukrainian Classroom," *Applied Linguistics* 31, no. 3 (2010).

2 Serhy Yekelchyk, *Stalin's Empire of Memory: Russian-Ukrainian Relations in the Soviet Historical Imagination* (Toronto: University of Toronto Press, 2004), 6–7.
3 Ibid., 6.
4 Hirsch, *Empire of Nations*, 12.
5 Although Yefimenko emphasizes that it is too early to speak of Russification as an "organized state policy" in 1933–4, he cites instances of post-secondary instructors switching to Russian-language instruction beginning that year (especially in prestigious educational institutes administered by all-Union authorities) and exclusive use of Russian in extracurricular activities. Party leaders ordered a formal increase in Russian-language post-secondary instruction in 1937–8. Iefimenko, *Natsional'na polityka kerivnytstva VKP(b)*, 36–50.
6 Smolii, *"Ukraïnizatsiia" 1920–30-kh rokiv: peredumovy, zdobutky, uroky*, 183.
7 Serhii Plokhy's reading of autobiographical narratives that discuss the era of Ukrainization in Zaporizhzhia is instructive in this context. The life of Mykola Molodyk, whose memoirs Plokhy examines, is probably most in line with the fates of the numerous schoolchildren referenced in the archival record. Molodyk clearly remembered the role his Ukrainian-language education had on shaping his identity as a Ukrainian, but recognized the value of Russian-language use after the arrests of his fellow local Ukrainizers. Plokhy, *Ukraine and Russia*, 148–62.

8 Liber notably identified this linkage, maintaining that, in the 1920s, Ukrainians "had a vested interest in reaffirming their national origins in light of the rapid urban growth, the huge, unassimilable numbers of compatriots migrating to the cities, the psychological alienation and exhilaration produced by migration, and the party's emphasis on Ukrainianization. Now urban growth and urbanization did not equal Russification." Liber, *Soviet Nationality Policy*, 65.

Bibliography

Primary Sources

ARCHIVES

Haluzevyi derzhavnyi arkhiv Sluzhby bezpeky Ukraïny (HDA SBU). Kyiv, Ukraine.
Fond 6. Kryminal'ni spravy na reabilitovanykh osib.
Fond 13. Dovidkovyi aparat
Tsentral'nyi derzhavnyi arkhiv hromads'kykh ob"iednan' Ukraïny (TsDAHOU). Kyiv, Ukraine.
Fond 1. Tsentral'nyi komitet KP(b)U.
Fond 7. Tsentral'nyi komitet LKSMU.
Fond 263. Kolektsiia posudovykh sprav reabilitovanykh.
Tsentral'nyi derzhavnyi arkhiv vyshchykh orhaniv vlady i upravlinnia Ukraïny (TsDAVOU). Kyiv, Ukraine.
Fond 166. Narodnyi komisariat osvity URSR (Narkomos URSR).
Fond 539. Narodnyi komisariat robitnycho-selians'koï inspektsii URSR.
Fond 2717. Vseukraïns'kyi komitet Vsesoiuznoï profesiinoï spilky robitnykiv osvity.
Derzhavnyi arkhiv Kyïvs'koï oblasti (DAKO). Kyiv, Ukraine.
Fond R-142. Huberns'kyi viddil narodnoï osvity.
Fond R-294. Holovyi prodovol'chyi komitet pivdenno-zakhidnykh zaliznyts'.
Fond R-632. Kyïvs'kyi okruzhnyi finansovyi viddil.
Fond R-761. Kyïvs'kyi dil'nychnyi komitet profesiinoï spilky robitnykiv i sluzhbovtsiv zaliznychnoho transportu.
Fond R-1043. Inspektura narodnoï osvity Kyïvs'koï okruhy.
Fond R-1212. Hatnians'ka sil'ska rada.
Derzhavnyi arkhiv Odes'koï oblasti (DAOO). Odesa, Ukraine.
Fond P-3. Odes'kyi huberns'kyi komitet KP(b)U.
Fond P-7. Odes'kyi okruzhnyi komitet KP(b)U.

Fond R-134. Odes'ka okruzhna inspektura narodnoï osvity.
Fond R-150. Odes'ka huberns'ka inspektura narodnoï osvity.
Fond R-1234. Odes'kyi mis'kyi vykonavchyi komitet.

NEWSPAPER ARTICLES

"18,000 osvitnykiv Kyieva hanbliat' zukhvalykh kontr-revoliutsioneriv iz SVU." *Narodnii uchytel'*, 1 December 1929, 3.
"A. V. Lunachars'kyi pro rozvytok ukraïns'koï kul'tury." *Narodnii uchytel'*, 1 August 1928, 2.
Akhmatov, L. "Sprava pro 'Spilku vyzvolennia Ukraïny'." *Narodnii uchytel'*, 28 February 1930, 2.
Chuzhyi. "Vidklaly z metoiu krashchoï pidhotovky (Liakhovets'kyi raion, na Shepetivshchyni)." *Narodnii uchytel'*, 15 December 1926, 3.
"Delehatsia naukovykh robitnykiv na druhii sesii VUTsVK'u." *Narodnii uchytel'*, 24 November 1929, 2.
"De-shcho pro vykladachiv ta komisiï po perevirtsti." *Narodnii uchytel'*, 1 June 1927, 3.
Donets'. "Niiak ne ukraïnizuiut'sia." *Narodnii uchytel'*, 10 February 1925, 4.
Eskiz. "Lyshe odna … (Makarivs'kyi raion na Kyïvshchyni)." *Narodnii uchytel'*, 16 January 1929, 5.
F. "Het' nehidnykiv iz nashykh lav." *Narodnii uchytel'*, 21 December 1929, 5.
F., Ia. "Shche odna zhertva." *Narodnii uchytel'*, 4 December 1929, 6.
G., A. "Ukraïnizatsiia i uchyteli." *Narodnii uchytel' - dotatok*, 11 May 1927, 3.
Hulak, H. "Movoznavtsi." *Narodnii uchytel'*, 16 January 1929, 5.
I. "Pro ukraïns'ku movu ta bil' u shchepliakh." *Narodnii uchytel'*, 1 June 1927, 3.
K., N. I. "Ukraïnizatsiia. Syln'a dram z zhyttia Bilotserkivs'koï okruhy na bahato diï z prolohom ta epilohom." *Narodnii uchytel'*, 30 March 1927, 3.
Kaliuzhnyi, N. "Ukraïnizatsiia i narodnii uchytel'." *Narodnii uchytel'*, 14 July 1925, 1.
Khomenko, S. "Pro perevirku." *Narodnii uchytel'*, 12 January 1927, 3.
Kost', K. "Ukraïnizuvalys'." *Narodnii uchytel'*, 16 January 1929, 5.
L., V. "Sprava ukraïnizatsiï." *Narodnii uchytel'*, 14 March 1929, 4.
Makerevych, M. "Ukraïnizatsiia ta vchytel': ukraïnizatsiia vchytel'stva—nevidkladne zavdannia." *Narodnii uchytel'*, 13 October 1925, 2.
Mashkivs'kyi, M. "Do spravy ukraïnizatsii vchytel'stva na Pivd.-zakh. zaliznytsiakh." *Narodnii uchytel'*, 6 October 1926, 2.
Mymra. "Pidmet." *Narodnii uchytel'*, 15 December 1926, 3.
Myropil's'kyi. "Vchyetli vynni." *Narodnii uchytel'*, 4 December 1929, 6.
"Na vsi zapitannia vidpovidni dovidkovo-konsul'tytsionnoho biura." *Narodnii uchytel'*, 4 May 1928, 4.
"Na zakhyst uchyteliv-aktyvistiv." *Narodnii uchytel'*, 13 November 1929, 2.
"Natsional'ne pytannia." *Narodnii uchytel'*, 10 April 1929, 3.

"Ne damo zhovto-blakytnym bandytam zavazhaty buduvanniu ukraïns'k kul'tury." *Narodnii uchytel'*, 27 November 1929, 2.
Nevira, Kh. "Shcho shche hal'muie ukraïnizatsiiu shkoly." *Narodnii uchytel'*, 5 May 1925, 2.
Nuzhnyi, Z. "De-shcho pro ukraïnizatsiiu Dnipropetrovskoi zaliznytsi." *Narodnii uchytel'*, 3 November 1926, 3.
- "Iak ne slid ukraïnizuvatysia! (Na Dnipropetrovskii zaliznytsi)." *Narodnii uchytel'*, 12 January 1927, 3.
O. "Dumky pro ukraïnizatsiu nesvidomi." *Narodnii uchytel'*, 1 June 1927, 3.
- "Het' kurkuliv ta kukul'sku ideolohiiu z lav nashoï spilky." *Narodnii uchytel'*, 17 June 1929, 6.
"Osvitiany vyslovliuiut' svoie hromads'ke oburennia z konterrevoliutsiinykh uchynkiv zmovnyts'koï zhraï z 'SVU'." *Narodnii uchytel'*, 4 December 1929, 3.
"Pereshkody v ukraïnizatsii." *Narodnii uchytel'*, 6 October 1927, 2.
Pevnyi, I. "Perevodymo ukraïnizatsiiu." *Narodnii uchytel'*, 14 April 1925, 3.
"Protest spivrobitnykiv VUK'u ta redaktsiï hazety." *Narodnii uchytel'*, 24 November 1929, 2.
Prysiazhniuk, Ivan. "Polipshuite nashu movu." *Narodnii uchytel'*, 16 January 1929, 5.
Rama. "Misiachnyk ukraïns'koï proletar'skoï kul'tury." *Narodnii uchytel'*, 22 June 1930, 3.
S. "Novyi napad na vchytelia-hromads'koho robitnyka." *Narodnii uchytel'*, 4 December 1929, 6.
S., V. "Spravy ukraïnizatsiï. Za pidvyshchennia ukraïns'koï hramotnosty." *Narodnii uchytel'*, 12 January 1927, 3.
Samarchenko. "Ukraïnizatsiiu vchytel'stva shche pro te zhe same." *Narodnii uchytel'*, 16 January 1929, 5.
Sapukhin, P. "Ukraïnizatsiia. 'Ikhtiozavry' suchasnoï shkoly." *Narodnii uchytel'*, 10 February 1925, 4.
- "Spravy ukraïnizatsii. Oblik ukraïnizatsiia vchytel'stva." *Narodnii uchytel'*, 15 December 1925, 3.
Shvydkyi, H. "Ukraïnizuiut'sia nadto povil'no." *Narodnii uchytel'*, 11 June 1930, 7.
Sihov, V. "Het' profanatsiiu." *Narodnii uchytel'*, 12 January 1927, 3.
"Stan ukraïnizatsiï v promyslovykh okruhakh." *Narodnii uchytel'*, 11 January 1930, 1.
"Svoïkh pozytsii my ne zdamo." *Narodnii uchytel'*, 4 December 1929, 6.
Tkach. "Natsional'ne pytannia i zavdannia spilky." *Narodnii uchytel'*, 30 May 1928, 2.
Uchytel'. "Na grunti kliasovoï pomsty." *Narodnii uchytel'*, 4 December 1929, 6.
Velychko, V. "Ukraïnizatsiia shkil ta politosvitnikh ustanov." *Narodnii uchytel'*, 8 November 1926, 3.
"Vykorchuvaty korinnia pravoho ukhylu v spiltsi Robos." *Narodnii uchytel'*, 26 November 1930, 1.
"Vymahaiemo suvoroï kary," *Narodnii uchytel'*, 1 December 1929, 3.
Vorobiov, S. "Ukraïnizatsiia v hromads'kii roboti." *Narodnii uchytel'*, 5 May 1927, 3.
"Vseukrains'ka partiina narada pro narodniu osvitu." *Narodnii uchytel'*, 24 April 1930, 2.

"Zaochni kursi ukraïnoznavstva." *Narodnii uchytel' - dodatok*, 13 April 1927, 3.
"Zhovtoblakytna kontrrevoliutsiia pered proletars'kym sudom." *Narodnii uchytel'*, 24 April 1930, 3.

JOURNAL ARTICLES, BOOKS, DOCUMENT COLLECTIONS

Afraimovych, E. "My zrostaemo internatsionalistamy." *Politekhnichna shkola*, no. 4 (1934): 10–11.
Antonenko-Davydovych, Borys. *Zemleiu ukraïnskoiu*. Philadelphia: Kyiv, 1955.
Bachyns'kyi, P. P., ed. *Dokumenty trahichnoï istoriï Ukraïny*. Kyiv: Zhurnal "Okhorona pratsi," 1999.
Boiko, Anatolii, ed. *Dzherela z istoriï pivdennoï Ukrainy: Memuary ta shchodennyky*. Vol. 5, Pt. 1, Bk. 1. Zaporizhzhia: RA "Tandem-U," 2005.
Chavdarov, S. "Cherhovi zavdannia u vykladanni movy v shkoli." *Komunistychna osvita*, no. 10 (1934): 25–40.
Danylenko, Vasyl', ed. *Ukraïns'ka intelihentsiia i vlada: zavedennia sekretnoho viddilu DPU USRR 1927–1929 rr*. Kyïv: Tempora, 2012.
Denysenko, V. "Do zbyrannia vidomostei iz istoriï derusyfikatsiia." *Holos ukraïnizatora*, no. 3 (1927): 45–6.
Dnipropetrovskyi okruhovyi komitet LKSMU. *Za tsilkovytu ukraïnizatsiiu!* Dnipropetrovsk: Vyd. Dnipropetrovskoho Okruzhnomu LKSMU, 1929.
"Do robitnykiv osvity ta studentiv VPSh." *Radians'ka osvita*, no. 4 (1927): 75–6.
Doha, V., ed. *Nashe zhyttia: knyzhka dlia chytannia v druhii hrupi trudovoï shkoly*. Kharkiv: Derzhavne vydavnytstvo Ukrainy, 1927.
Durdukovs'kyi, V. "Shevchenkivs'ka shkola—Shevchenkovi." *Radians'ka osvita*, no. 3–4 (1924): 37–47.
Gryn'ko, G. "Nash put' na Zapad." *Put' prosveshchennia*, no. 7–8 (1923): 1–19.
Haliun, I. "Kraieznavstvo i shkola." *Radians'ka osvita*, no. 5 (1925): 51–8.
Hodyna, M. *Ekskursii ta turyzm u shkil'nii ta pioners'kii roboti*. Kharkiv: Radianska shkola, 1932.
Holodomor 1932–1933 rokiv v Ukraïni za dokumentamy HDA SBU: anatovanyi dovidnyk. L'viv: Tsentr doslidzhen' vyzvol'noho rukhu, 2010.
Horbuz, T. "Kraieznavstvo i trudova shkola." *Radians'ka osvita*, no. 3 (1925): 46–50.
Hryhor'iev, M. "Problema internatsiona'noho vykhovannia." *Radians'ka osvita*, no. 10 (1930): 35–7.
Iefremov, Serhii. *Shchodennyky: 1923–1929*. Kyïv: Hazeta "Rada," 1997.
Ivanytsia, H. "Do pryntsypiv buduvannia prohramy ukr. movy i literatury dlia starshoho kontsentru trudshkoly." *Radians'ka osvita*, no. 4 (1928): 24–31.
Khait, I. "Za bil'shovytsku rozchystku na fronti pedahohichnoï teoriï." *Komunistychna osvita*, no. 2 (1934): 10–50.

Khvylia, A. "Pro reorhanizatsiu aparatu NKO." *Komunistychna osvita*, no. 9 (1933): 59–70.
Khvyl'ovyi, Mykola. *The Cultural Renaissance in Ukraine: Polemical Pamphlets, 1925–1926*. Translated, edited, and introduced by Myroslav Shkandrij. Edmonton: Canadian Institute of Ukrainian Studies, 1986.
Klapchuk, S. M., ed. *Istoriia ukraïns'koï kul'tury: zbirnyk materialiv i dokumentiv*. Kyiv: Vyshcha shkola, 2000.
Kondufor, Iu. Iu., ed. *Kul'turne budivnytstvo v Ukraïns'kii RSR 1917–1929: zbirnyk dokumentiv*. Kyïv: Naukova dumka, 1979.
Kopyl, I. "Sproba vyvchennia kraiu: zolotonosh's'ka okruha na Poltavshchyni." *Radians'ka osvita*, no. 5 (1925): 58–9.
"Korotkyi bibliohrafichnyi poradnyk uchytelev ukraïns'koï movi." *Radians'ka osvita*, no. 3 (1927): 71–4.
Kosobuts'kom, A. "Po shkolakh." *Radians'ka osvita*, no. 4 (1927): 33–7.
Kostiuchenko, A. "Za korektyvy osvitn'oï systemy." *Shliakh osvity*, no. 12 (1928): 54–7.
Kryvonosov, V. "U shkoli ne vse harazd." *Radians'ka osvita*, no. 5 (1928): 57–8.
Kryvoshchyi, I. "Do pytannia pro maibutne roboty Biuletenia." *Holos ukraïnizatora*, no. 3 (1927): 46–9.
Kul'chyts'kyi, S. V., ed. *Kolektyvizatsiia i holod na Ukraïni, 1929–1933: zbirnyk dokumentiv i materialiv*. 2 vols. Kyïv: Naukova dumka, 1993.
Lazaris, A. "Ukraïns'ke kraieznavstvo i perspektyvy ioho rozvytku." *Radians'ka osvita*, no. 5 (1925): 49–51.
Len', I. "Pro internatsional'nyi zviazok shkil." *Radians'ka osvita*, no. 5–6 (1930): 87–8.
Levchenko, H. *Vykorinyty natsionalistychne shkidnytstvo v pidruchnykakh z movy*. Kharkiv: Radians'ka shkola, 1934.
Maistrenko, Ivan. *Istoriia moho pokolinnia: spohady uchasnyka revoliutsiinykh podiï v Ukraïni*. Edmonton: Kanads'kyi instytut ukraïns'kykh studii, 1985.
Mizernyts'kyi, O. "Na shliakhakh radianizatsiï." *Radians'ka osvita*, no. 11 (1927): 1–15.
Mylovydov, L. "Kraieznavstvo v novykh prohramakh trudshkil I-ho kontsentru." *Radians'ka osvita*, no. 4 (1930): 45–51.
Myroniv, M. "U shkoli ne vse harazd." *Radians'ka osvita*, no. 2 (1928): 38–42.
Narodnii komisariiat osvity USRR. Derzhavnyi naukovo-metodolohichnyi komitet. *Materialy Vseukraïns'koï konferentsii vykladachiv suspil'stvoznavstva*. Kharkiv: Derzh. vyd. Ukrainy, 1926.
Narodnyi komisariat osvity USRR. *Na fronti ku'ltury*. Kyïv: Radians'ka shkola, 1935.
Naukovo-pedahohichna komisiia VUAN. "Do vykladachiv ukraïns'koï movy." *Radians'ka osvita*, no. 6–7 (1927).
Panibud'laska, V. F., ed. *Natsional'ni protsesy v Ukraïni: istoriia i suchasnist': dokumenty i materialy, dovidnyk u dvokh chastynakh*. 2 vols. Kyïv: Vyshcha shkola, 1997.
Pasika, T. "Shche pro unifikatsiu systemy osvity." *Radians'ka osvita*, no. 3 (1929): 59–63.

Pershyi Vseukraïns'kyi uchytel's'kyi z'ïzd v Kharkovi vid 5 do 11 sichnia 1925 (zi znimkamy uchasnykiv z'ïzdu). Kharkiv: Derzhavne vydavnytstvo Ukraïny, 1925.

Polemun, N. M., and L. F. Suravko, eds. *Ukraïnizatsiia na Chernihivshchyni v 20–30-ti roky: zbirka dokumentiv*. Chernihiv: Derzhavnyi arkhiv Chernihivs'koi oblasti, 1997.

Polubotko, O. "Plian ukraïns'koï movy za kompleksovoiu systemoiu." *Radians'ka osvita*, no. 4 (1925): 39–50.

Pomahaiba, V. "Posylyty vohon' po fashysts'kii pedahohitsi SVU." *Politekhnichna osvita*, no. 3 (1932): 3–12.

Ponomarenko, H. "Ne til'ky v shkoli ne vse harazd." *Radian'ska osvita*, no. 5 (1928): 48–55.

Popiv, O. "Shevchenko v dytiachii knihozbirni." *Radians'ka osvita*, no. 3 (1930): 44–51.

Postapenko, H. I. "Zhurnal i uchytel' (bilbliohrafichni zamitky z pytan' pryrodnoznavstva)." *Biuleten' odes'koï okruzhnoï inspektury narodnoi osvity*, no. 3–4 (1928): 132–9.

Prit, Ia. "Pro vidomist'." *Radians'ka osvita*, no. 5 (1928): 56–7.

"Pro nadislannia vidomostiv z ukraïnizatsiï." *Osvita na Kharkivshchyni*, no. 13–14 (1928): 36.

"Prohrama z ukraïns'koï movy dlia samoperepidhotovyky robitnykiv osvity Kharkivs'koï okruhy. Kharkiv, 1927 r." *Holos ukraïnizatora*, no. 3 (1927): 58–61.

Prozorovs'kyi, O. "Suchasni metody vykladannia literaturi v trudshkoli." *Radians'ka osvita*, no. 4 (1928): 36–42.

Prykhod'ko, A. "Ukraïnizatsiia narodn'oï osvity." *Shliakh osvity*, no. 10 (1927): 13–19.

Prystaiko, Volodymyr, and Iurii Shapoval. *Mykhailo Hrushevs'kyi i GPU-NKVD. Trahichne desiatylittia: 1924–1934*. Kyïv: Ukraïna, 1996.

– *Sprava "Spilky vyzvolennia Ukraïny": nevidomi dokumenty i fakty*. Kyïv: Intel, 1995.

Riappo, Ia. P. *Narodnia osvita na Ukraïni: za desiat' rokiv revoliutsiï*. Kharkiv: Derzhavne vydavnytstvo Ukraïny, 1927.

Sabadlyr, H. "Prohrama z ukraïns'koï movy dlia osib, shcho bazhaiut' maty kvalifikatsiiu lektora ukraïns'koï movy na kursakh 1-ho tsyklu ta vykladacha ukraïns'koï movy v trudshkolakh na starshomu kontsentri." *Holos ukraïnizatora*, no. 3 (1927): 34–5.

Shapoval, Iurii, ed. *Poliuvannia na 'Val'dshnepa': rozserekrechenyi Mykola Khvyl'ovyi*. Kyïv: Tempora, 2009.

Shapoval, Iurii, Volodymyr Prystaiko, and Vadym Zolotar'ov. *ChK-GPU-NKVD v Ukraïni*. Kyïv: Abrys, 1997.

Shums'kyi, O. "Na tret'omu fronti: do uchytel's'koho z"zdu." *Shliakh osvity*, no. 11–12 (1924): v–xiv.

Skrypnyk, M. "Cherhovi pytannia sotsvykhu." *Radians'ka osvita*, no. 2 (1929): 1–10.

– *Narysy pidsumkiv ukraïnizatsiï ta obsluhuvannia kul'turnhkh potreb natsmenshostei USRR, zokrema rosiis'koï*. Kharkiv: Radians'ka shola, 1933.

– *Neprymyrennym shliakhom: dopovid' na okrpartkonferentsiï v Odesi 12-ho hrudnia 1928 roku*. Kharkiv: Derzhavne vydavnytstvo Ukraïny, 1929.

- "Osnovni problemy sotsiial'noho vykhovannia za rekonstruktyvnoï doby." *Radians'ka osvita*, no. 5–6 (1930): 13–35.
- *Statti i promovy*. Vol. 2. Kharkhiv: Proletar, 1931.
- "Za iedynu systemu narodn'oï osvity." *Radians'ka osvita*, no. 5–6 (1930): 1–13.

Sobolev. "Zmitsnimo bil'shovyts'kymy kadramy orhany narodnoï osvity." *Komunistychna osvita*, no. 2 (1934): 64–73.

Solodkyi, N. "Z praktyky vykladannia ukrains'koï movy v trudovii shkoli." *Radians'ka osvita*, no. 10 (1927): 41–8.

Sulyma, M. "Z pryvodu nashykh movnykh zlydniv." *Radians'ka osvita*, no. 2 (1927): 25–33.

T., Iu. "Pered Shevchenkivs'kymy dniamy: z zhyttia II hrupy Kyïvs'koï 1-oï trudovoï shkoly im. Shevchenka, za 1924 r." *Radians'ka osvita*, no. 3–4 (1924): 48–56.

Tkachenko, H. "Dosiahnennia v ukraïnizatsiinii roboty Kyïvshchyny na 10-u richnytsiu Zhovtnia ta perpspekyvy roboty na maibutnii rik." *Holos ukraïnizatora*, no. 3 (1927): 2–5.

Trozorovs'kyi, V. "Poshyrenyi Plenum Okrmetodkom." *Biuleten' odes'koï okruzhnoï inspektury narodnoï osvity*, no. 2 (1928): 3–27.

Tsentral'nyi komitet LKSM Ukraïny. *Molodi fashysty ukraïns'koï kontrrevoliutsiï do protsesu SVU*. Kharkiv: Derzhavne vydavnytstvo Ukraïny, 1930.

"Ukraïnizatsiia osvitnoï roboty." *Radians'ka osvita*, no. 1 (1927): 85–6.

Viddil narodn'oï osvity Kyïvs'koi mis'krady. *V borot'bi za realizatsiiu ukhval TsK VKP(b) ta Kyïvs'koho MPK pro shkolu ta pionerorhanizatsii*. Kyiv: Radians'ka shkola, 1932.

Vsesoiuznaia perepis' naseleniia 1926 goda. Moskva: Izd. TsSU Soiuza SSR, 1928–35.

Volyns'kyi, P. "Z pryvou pokhodu t. Myronova na reshtky starorezhymnoï shkoli." *Radians'ka osvita*, no. 5 (1928): 58–62.

Vorobiov, S. "Do pytannia pro unifikatsiiu system narodn'oï osvity." *Shliakh osvity*, no. 12 (1928): 50–4.

Zatons'kyi, V. P. *Itogi noiabr'skogo plenuma TsK i TsKK KP(b)U i zadachi rabotnykov prosveshchennia*. Kharkiv: Radians'ka shkola, 1934.
- *Natsional'no-kul'turne budivnytstvo i borot'ba proty natsionalizmu dopovid' ta zakliuchne slovo na sichnevii sesiï VUAN*. Kyïv: Vydavnytsvo Vseukrains'koï akademiï nauk, 1934.
- *Natsional'na problema na Ukraini*. New York: Ukraïns'ki schodenni visti, 1926.

Zaval'nyi, Ia. K., and D. A. Kovalenko. *Shkil'na pratsiia: robocha knyzhka dlia druhoho roku navchannia*. Krasnodar: Derzhavne vydavnytstvo Ukraïny, 1929.

Secondary Sources

JOURNAL ARTICLES AND BOOKS

Andrews, James T. *Science for the Masses: The Bolshevik State, Public Science, and the Popular Imagination in Soviet Russia, 1917–1934*. College Station: Texas A&M University Press, 2003.

Antoniuk, T. "Rozvytok osvitn'oï systemy v USRR (20-ti-pochatok 30-x rokiv)." *Istorychnyi zhurnal*, no. 6–7 (2004): 90–6.
Applegate, Celia. *A Nation of Provincials: The German Idea of Heimat*. Berkeley: University of California Press, 1990.
Arel, Dominique. "Language Politics in Independent Ukraine: Towards One or Two State Languages?" *Nationalities Papers* 23, no. 3 (1995): 597–622.
Ball, Alan. *And Now My Soul Is Hardened: Abandoned Children in Soviet Russia, 1918–1930*. Berkeley: University of California Press, 1994.
– "The Roots of Besprizornost' in Soviet Russia's First Decade." *Slavic Review* 51, no. 2 (1992): 247–70.
Barrington, Lowell, and Regina Faranda. "Reexamining Region, Ethnicity, and Language in Ukraine." *Post-Soviet Affairs* 25, no. 3 (2009): 232–56.
Bemporad, Elissa. *Becoming Soviet Jews: The Bolshevik Experiment In Minsk*. Bloomington: Indiana University Press, 2013.
Bertelsen, Olga. "GPU Repressions of Zionists: Ukraine in the 1920s." *Europe-Asia Studies* 65, no. 6 (2013): 1080–1111.
Bertelsen, Olga, and Myroslav Shkandrij. "The Secret Police and the Campaign against Galicians in Soviet Ukraine, 1929–1934." *Nationalities Papers* 42, no. 1 (2014): 37–62.
Bilaniuk, Laada. *Contested Tongues: Language Politics and Cultural Correction in Ukraine*. Ithaca: Cornell University Press, 2005.
"Biohrafiia Sapukhina Pavla Andriiovycha." Sums'ka mis'ka tsentralizovana bibliotechna systema. http://library-sumy.com/sumy/people_sumy/historians/sapukhin_p/about/. Accessed 19 September 2014.
Blitstein, Peter A. "Nation-Building or Russification? Obligatory Russian Instruction in the Soviet Non-Russian School, 1938–1953." In *The State of Nations: Empire and Nation-Making in the Age of Lenin and Stalin*, edited by Ronald Grigor Suny and Terry Martin, 253–74. Oxford: Oxford University Press, 2001.
Boiko, N. I., ed. *Represovani movoznavtsi: zbirnyk naukovykh prats'*. Nizhyn: Nizhyns'kyi derzhavnyi universytet imeni Mykoly Hoholia, 2010.
Bolabol'chenko, Anatolii. *SVU—sud nad perekonanniamy*. Kyïv: Kobzar, 1994.
Bondar, A. H., et al., eds. *Narodna osvita i pedahohichna nauka v Ukraïns'kii RSR*. Kyïv: Radians'ka shkola, 1967.
Bondar-Tereshchenko. *U zadzerkalli 1910–30-ikh rokiv*. Kyïv: Tempora, 2009.
Bondarchuk, P. M., V. M. Danylenko, and H. Iefimenko, eds. *Polityka korenizatsii v radians'kii Ukraïni, 1920–1930-i rr.: naukovo-dopomizhnyi bibliohrafichnyi pokazhchyk*. Kyïv: Instytut istoriï Ukraïny NAN Ukraïny, 2003.
Borisenok, Elena. *Fenomen sovetskoi ukrainizatsii, 1920–1930-e gody*. Moskva: Izdatel'stvo "Evropa," 2006
Borovyk, Anatolii. *Ukraïnizatsiia zahal'noosvitnikh shkil za chasiv vyboriuvannia derzhavnosti, 1917–1920 rr.* Chernihiv: KP Vydavnytstvo "Chernihivs'ki oberehy," 2008.
Borys Kosarev: kharkivs'kyi modernizm 1915–1931. Kyïv: Rodovid, 2011.

Borysov, V. L. "Ukraïnizatsiia ta rozvytok zahal'noosvitnoï shkoly v 1921–31 rr." *Ukraïns'kyi istorychnyi zhurnal*, no. 2 (1999): 76–80.
Bourdieu, Pierre. *Language and Symbolic Power*. Translated by Gino Raymond and Matthew Adamson. Cambridge: Harvard University Press, 1991.
Brandenberger, David. *National Bolshevism: Stalinist Mass Culture and the Formation of Modern Russian National Identity, 1931–1956*. Cambridge, MA: Harvard University Press, 2002.
Brown, Kate. *A Biography of No Place: From Ethnic Borderland to Soviet Heartland*. Cambridge, MA: Harvard University Press, 2003.
Bukharieva, I. V., ed. *Represovani diiachi Ukraïns'koi Avtokefal'noï Pravoslavnoï Tserkvy (1921–1939): biohrafichnyi dovidnyk*. Kyïv: Smoloskyp, 2011.
Clark, Charles E. *Uprooting Otherness: The Literacy Campaign in NEP-Era Russia*. Selinsgrove, PA: Susquehanna University Press, 2000.
Cohen, Stephen F. *Bukharin and the Bolshevik Revolution: A Political Biography, 1888–1938*. Oxford: Oxford University Press, 1980.
Coleman, Heather. *Russian Baptists and Spiritual Revolution, 1905–1929*. Bloomington: Indiana University Press, 2005.
Collins, James. "Literacy and Literacies." *Annual Review of Anthropology*, no. 24 (1995): 75–93.
Collins, James, and Richard K. Blot. *Literacy and Literacies: Texts, Power, and Identity*. Cambridge: Cambridge University Press, 2003.
Confino, Alon. *The Nation as a Local Metaphor: Württemberg, Imperial Germany, and National Memory, 1871–1918*. Chapel Hill: University of North Carolina Press, 1997.
Counts, George S. *The Soviet Challenge to America*. New York: The John Day Company, 1931.
Danylenko, V. M., and A. A. Kravchenko. *Volodymyr Durdukivs'kyi: pedahoh, krytyk, hromads'kyi diach (1874–1938)*. Kyïv: Nika Tsentr, 2000.
Danylenko, V. M., and M. M. Kuz'menko. *Sotsial'nyi typ ta inteletkual'no-osvitnii riven' nomenklatury skrypnykivs'koho narkomosu: biohrafichni narysy*. Sevastopol': Veter, 2003.
David-Fox, Michael. *Revolution of the Mind: Higher Learning among the Bolsheviks, 1918–1929*. Ithaca: Cornell University Press, 1997.
– "What Is Cultural Revolution?" *Russian Review* 58, no. 2 (1999): 181–201.
Demchenko, T., and N. Klymovych. "Protses 'SVU' kriz' pryzmu propahandysts'kykh zakhodiv na Chernihivshchyni (berezen'–kviten' 1930)." *Problemy istoriï Ukraïni*, no. 15 (2006): 326–38.
Dewey, John. *Essays, Reviews, Miscellany, and "Impressions of Soviet Russia." The Later Works, 1925–1953*, edited by Jo Ann Boydston. Vol. 3. Carbondale: Southern Illinois University Press, 1981.
Doroshko, Mykola. *Nomenklatura kerivna verkhivka radians'koï Ukraïny (1917–1938 rr.)*. Kyïv: Nika-Tsentr, 2012.
Dowler, Wayne. *Classroom and Empire: The Politics of Schooling Russia's Eastern Nationalities, 1860–1917*. Montréal: McGill-Queen's University Press, 2001.

Downs, Laura Lee. *Childhood in the Promised Land: Working-Class Movements and the Colonies de Vacances in France, 1880–1960*. Durham: Duke University Press, 2002.

Drob'iazko, P. I. *Ukraïns'ka natsional'na shkola: vytoky i suchasnist'*. Kyïv: Akademiia, 1997.

Edgar, Adrienne Lynn. *Tribal Nation: The Making of Soviet Turkmenistan*. Princeton: Princeton University Press, 2004.

Eklof, Ben. "Russia and the Soviet Union: Schooling, Citizenship, and the Reach of the State, 1870–1945." In *Mass Education and the Limits of State Building, c. 1870–1930*, 140–66. New York: Palgrave Macmillan, 2012.

– *Russian Peasant Schools: Officialdom, Village Culture, and Popular Pedagogy, 1861–1917*. Berkeley: University of California Press, 1986.

Ewing, E. Thomas. "Ethnicity at School: 'Non-Russian' Education in the Soviet Union during the 1930s." *History of Education* 35, no. 4–5 (2006): 499–519.

– *Separate Schools: Gender, Policy, and Practice in Postwar Soviet Education*. DeKalb: Northern Illinois University Press, 2010.

– *The Teachers of Stalinism: Policy, Practice, and Power in Soviet Schools of the 1930s*. New York: Peter Lang, 2002.

Fierman, William. "Language Development in Soviet Uzbekistan." In *Sociolinguistic Perspectives on Soviet National Languages*, edited by Isabelle T. Kreindler. Contributions to the Sociology of Language, 205–33. New York: Mouton de Gruyter, 1985.

Fitzpatrick, Sheila. *The Cultural Front: Power and Culture in Revolutionary Russia*. Ithaca: Cornell University Press, 1992.

– *Education and Social Mobility in the Soviet Union: 1921–1934*. New York: Cambridge University Press, 1979.

Friedman, Debra A. "Speaking Correctly: Error Correction as a Language Socialization Practice in a Ukrainian Classroom." *Applied Linguistics* 31, no. 3 (2010): 346–67.

Fürst, Juliane. *Stalin's Last Generation: Soviet Post-War Youth and the Emergence of Mature Socialism*. New York: Oxford University, 2010.

Gellner, Ernest. *Nations and Nationalism*. Ithaca, NY: Cornell University Press, 1983.

Glaser, Amelia. *Jews And Ukrainians in Russia's Literary Borderlands: From the Shtetl Fair to the Petersburg Bookshop*. Evanston: Northwestern University Press, 2012.

Gorsuch, Anne. *Youth in Revolutionary Russia: Enthusiasts, Bohemians, Delinquents*. Bloomington: Indiana University Press, 2000.

Grabowicz, George G. *The Poet as Mythmaker: A Study of Symbolic Meaning in Taras Ševčenko*. Cambridge, MA: Harvard Ukrainian Research Institute, 1982.

Guillory, Sean. "The Shattered Self of Komsomol Civil War Memoirs." *Slavic Review* 71, no. 3 (2012): 546–65.

Guthier, Steven L. "Ukrainian Cities during the Revolution and the Inter-War Era." In *Rethinking Ukrainian History*, edited by Ivan L. Rudnytsky and John-Paul Himka, 156–79. Edmonton: Canadian Institute of Ukrainian Studies, 1981.

Halfin, Igal. *Stalinist Confessions: Messianism and Terror at the Leningrad Communist University*. Pittsburgh: University of Pittsburgh Press, 2009.

Heinzen, James W. *Inventing a Soviet Countryside: State Power and the Transformation of Rural Russia, 1917–1929*. Pittsburgh: University of Pittsburgh Press, 2004.

Herman, Volodymyr, Pavlo Movchan, Vasyl Klichak, and Shevchenka Vseukraïns'ke tovarystvo "Prosvita" imeni Tarasa. *"Prosvita"—istoriia ta suchasnist': (1868–1998)*. Kyïv: Vydavnychyi tsentr "Prosvita": "Veselka," 1998.

Hillis, Faith. *Children of Rus': Right-Bank Ukraine and the Invention of a Russian Nation*. Ithaca: Cornell University Press, 2013.

Hirsch, Francine. *Empire of Nations: Ethnographic Knowledge and the Making of the Soviet Union*. Ithaca: Cornell University Press, 2005.

Holmes, Larry E. *Grand Theater: Regional Governance in Stalin's Russia, 1931–1941*. Lanham, MD: Lexington Books, 2009.

– *The Kremlin and the Schoolhouse: Reforming Education in Soviet Russia, 1917–1931*. Bloomington: Indiana University Press, 1991.

– *Stalin's School: Moscow's Model School No. 25, 1931–1937*. Pittsburgh: University of Pittsburgh Press, 1999.

Hrycak, Alexandra. "Institutional Legacies and Language Revival in Ukraine." In *Rebounding Identities: The Politics of Identity in Russia and Ukraine*, edited by Dominique Arel and Blair Ruble, 62–88. Washington, DC: Woodrow Wilson Center Press, 2006.

Hudson, Hugh D. *Peasants, Political Police, and the Early Soviet State: Surveillance and Accommodation under the New Economic Policy*. New York: Palgrave Macmillan, 2012.

Iasnyts'kyi, H. I. *Rozvytok narodnoï osvity na Ukraïni (1921–1932 rr.)*. Kyïv: Vydavnytstvo Kyïvs'koho universytetu, 1965.

Iefimenko, H. "Hromads'ka robota iak chynnyk povsiakdennoho zhyttia vchytelia." *Problemy istoriï Ukraïni*, no. 17 (2006): 108–31.

– *Natsional'no-kul'turna polityka VKP(b) shchodo radians'koï Ukraïni (1932–1938)*. Kyïv: Instytut istoriï Ukraïny, 2001.

– *Natsional'na polityka kerivnytstva VKP(b) v Ukraïni 1932–1938 rr. (osvita ta nauka)*. Kyïv: Instytut istoriï Ukraïny, 2000.

– "Povsiakdenne zhyttia vchytelia shkoly sotsial'noho vykhovannia." In *Narysy povsiakdennoho zhyttia radians'koï Ukraïny v dobu NEPu (1921–1928 rr.)*, edited by S. V. Kul'chyts'kyi, 5–78. Kyïv: Instytut istoriï Ukraïny NAN Ukraïny, 2010.

– "Pytannia natsional'noï polityky kremlia v Ukraïni v persh. pol. 1937 r." *Problemy istoriï Ukraïni*, no. 12 (2004): 277–94.

– "Sotsial'ne oblychchia vchytel'stva USRR v konteksti transformatsiï suspil'stva (1920-ti roky)." *Problemy istoriï Ukraïni*, no. 17 (2007): 138–61.

Iermakova, Natalia. *Berezil's'ka kul'tura: istoriia, dosvid*. Kyïv: Feniks, 2012.

Igmen, Ali F. *Speaking Soviet with an Accent: Culture and Power in Kyrgyzstan*. Pittsburgh: University of Pittsburgh Press, 2012.

Kalenychenko, Ninel'. "Problema sim'ï ta simeinoho vykhovannia." *Shliakh osvity*, no. 4 (1997): 47–50.

Kappeler, Andreas. *Great Russians and Little Russians: Russian-Ukrainian Relations and Perceptions in Historical Perpsective*. Seattle: Henry M. Jackson School of International Studies, University of Washington, 2003.

Kappeler, Andreas. *The Russian Empire: A Multiethnic History*. Translated by Alfred Cleyton. Harlow: Longman, 2001.

Kelly, Catriona. *Children's World: Growing Up in Russia, 1890–1991*. New Haven: Yale University Press, 2007.

Khalid, Adeeb. *The Politics of Muslim Cultural Reform: Jadidism in Central Asia*. Berkeley: University of California Press, 1998.

King, Charles. *Odessa: Genius and Death in a City of Dreams*. New York: W.W. Norton & Co., 2011.

Kirschenbaum, Lisa. *Small Comrades: Revolutionizing Childhood in Soviet Russia, 1917–1923*. New York: RoutledgeFalmer, 2001.

Kliuienko, D. M., and L. I. Fursenko. *Represyvna polityka stalinizmu: arkhivni dokumenty svidchat'*. Odesa: Astroprint, 2006.

Krawchenko, Bohdan. *Social Change and National Consciousness in Twentieth-Century Ukraine*. Edmonton: Canadian Institute of Ukrainian Studies, 1985.

Kremen', V. H., ed. *Entsyklopediia osvity*. Kyïv: Iurinkom Inter, 2008.

Krylov, I. *Systema osvity v Ukraïni: 1917–1930*. Munich: Institute for the Study of the USSR, 1956.

Kubijovyč, Volodymyr, ed. *Encyclopedia of Ukraine*. 6 vols. Toronto: University of Toronto Press, 1984–.

Kulyk, Volodymyr. "Constructing Common Sense: Language and Ethnicity in Ukrainian Public Discourse." *Ethnic and Racial Studies* 29, no. 2 (2006): 281–314.

Kuromiya, Hiroaki. *Freedom and Terror in the Donbas: a Ukrainian-Russian Borderland, 1870s–1990s*. Cambridge: Cambridge University Press, 1998.

– "Stalin'skii 'velikii perelom' i protses nad 'Souizom osvobozhdeniia Ukrainy'." *Otechestvennaia istoriia*, no. 1 (1994): 190–7.

– *The Voices of the Dead: Stalin's Great Terror in the 1930s*. New Haven: Yale University Press, 2007.

Kuz'menko, M. M. "Systema osvity v USRR u 1920-x rr.: istoryko-teoretychnyi aspekt." *Ukraïns'kyi istorychnyi zhurnal*, no. 5 (2004): 66–80.

Lamberti, Marjorie. *The Politics of Education: Teachers and School Reform in Weimar Germany*. New York: Bergham Books, 2002.

Lapidus, Gail Warshofsky. "Educational Strategies and Cultural Revolution: The Politics of Soviet Development." In *Cultural Revolution in Russia, 1928–1931*, edited by Sheila Fitzpatrick, 78–104. Bloomington: Indiana University Press, 1984.

Lewin, Moshe. *Russian Peasants and Soviet Power: A Study of Collectivization*. New York: Norton, 1975.
Liber, George. *Soviet Nationality Policy, Urban Growth, and Identity Change in the Ukrainian SSR, 1923–1934*. New York: Cambridge University Press, 1992.
Likarchuk, I. L. *Ministry osvity Ukraïny: u dvokh tomakh*. Vol. 1. Kyïv: Vydavets' Eshke O.M, 2002.
Livezeanu, Irina. *Cultural Politics in Greater Romania: Regionalism, Nation Building, and Ethnic Struggle, 1918–1930*. Ithaca: Cornell University Press, 1995.
Lozyts'kyi, V. S. "Polityka ukraïnizatsii v 20–30-kh rokakh: istoriia, problemy, uroky." *Ukraïns'kyi istorychnyi zhurnal*, no. 3 (1989): 50–1.
Lypyns'kyi, V. V. *Stanovlennia i rozvytok systemy osvity USRR u 20-i roky*. Donets'k: DonDTU, 2000.
Lypyns'kyi, V. V. "Kontseptsiia ta model' osvity v USRR u 20-ti rr.". *Ukraïns'kyi istorychnyi zhurnal*, no. 5 (1999): 3–13.
Mace, James E. *Communism and the Dilemmas of National Liberation: National Communism in Soviet Ukraine, 1918–1933*. Cambridge: Harvard Ukrainian Research Institute, 1983.
Magocsi, Paul R. *The Roots of Ukrainian Nationalism: Galicia as Ukraine's Piedmont*. Toronto: University of Toronto Press, 2002.
– *The Rusyn-Ukrainians of Czechoslovakia: An Historical Survey*. Wien: W. Braumüller, 1983.
– *Ukraine: A Historical Atlas*. Toronto: University of Toronto Press, 1985.
Majstrenko, Iwan. *Borot'bism: A Chapter in the History of Ukrainian Communism*. New York: Research Program on the USSR, 1954.
Makaryk, Irena R., and Virlana Tkacz, eds. *Modernism in Kyiv: Jubilant Experimentation*. Toronto: University of Toronto Press, 2010.
Malyi, Konstiantyn. "Ukraïnizatsiia osvity: 20-ti roky." *Ridna shkola*, no. 11–12 (1996): 29–30.
Marochko, Vasyl', and Khillih H'ots. *Represovani pedahohy Ukraïny: zhertvy politychnoho teroru*. Kyïv: Naukovyi svit, 2003.
Martin, Terry. *The Affirmative Action Empire: Nations and Nationalism in the Soviet Union, 1923–39*. Ithaca: Cornell University Press, 2001.
McDonald, Tracy. *Face to the Village: The Riazan Countryside under Soviet Rule, 1921–1930*. Toronto: University of Toronto Press, 2011.
Moser, Michael. *Language Policy and Discourse on Languages in Ukraine under President Viktor Yanukovych*. Stuttgart: Ibidem-Verlag, 2013.
Moss, Kenneth B. *Jewish Renaissance in the Russian Revolution*. Cambridge: Harvard University Press, 2009.
Nedukh, A. A. "Osnovni zminy v administratyvno-terytorial'noho ustroï URSR u 1919–1978 rr." *Arkhivy Ukraïny*, no. 5 (1979): 59–67.

Neumann, Matthias. *The Communist Youth League and the Transformation of the Soviet Union, 1917–1932*. New York: Routledge, 2011.
Nur, Ofer. "Hashomer Hatzair Youth Movement, 1918–1924 from Eastern Galicia and Vienna to Palestine: A Cultural History." PhD diss., University of California, Los Angeles, 2004.
Parlett, William. "Bourgeois Ideas in Communist Construction: The Development of Stanislav Shatskii's Teacher Training Methods." *History of Education* 35, no. 4–5 (2006): 453–74.
- "Breaching Cultural Worlds with the Village School: Educational Visions, Local Initiative, and Rural Experience at S. T. Shatskii's Kaluga School System, 1919–1932." *Slavic and East European Review* 82, no. 4 (2004): 847–85.
- "The Cultural Revolution in the Village School: S. T. Shatskii's Kaluga School Complex, 1919–1932." *Journal of the Oxford University History Society*, no. 3 (2005): 1–27.
Pauly, Matthew D. "'Odes'ki lektsiï': ukraïnizatsiia shkoly, ustanov, ta natsional'noï identichnosti v ne-ukraïns'komu misti v 1920-kh rr." In *Ukraïna: Protsesy natsiotvorennia*, edited by Andreas Kappeler and Volodymyr Masliychuk, 298–306. Kyïv: K.I.S., 2011.
- "'Odesa-Lektionen': Die Ukrainisierung der Schule, der Behörden und der nationalen Identität in einer nicht-ukrainischen Stadt in den 1920er Jahren." In *Die Ukraine: Prozesse der Nationsbildung*, edited by Andreas Kappeler, 309–18. Köln, Wien: Böhlau Verlag, 2011.
- "Teaching Place, Assembling the Nation: Local Studies in Soviet Ukrainian Schools during the 1920s." *History of Education* 39, no. 1 (2010): 75–93.
- "Tending to the 'Native Word': Teachers and the Soviet Campaign for Ukrainian-Language Schooling, 1923–1930." *Nationalities Papers* 37, no. 3 (2009): 251–76.
Penter, Tanja. *Odessa 1917: Revolution an der Peripherie*. Köln: Böhlau Verlag, 2000.
Petrovsky-Shtern, Yohanan. *The Anti-imperial Choice: The Making of the Ukrainian Jew*. New Haven: Yale University Press, 2009.
Plokhy, Serhii. *Ukraine and Russia: Representations of the Past*. Toronto: University of Toronto Press, 2008.
Polese, Abel. "The Formal and the Informal: Exploring 'Ukrainian' Education in Ukraine, Scenes from Odessa." *Comparative Education*, no. 1 (2010): 47–62.
Polons'ka-Vasylenko, N. D. *Ukraïns'ka akademiia nauk*. Kyïv: Naukov dumka, 1993.
Pryluts'kyi, V. I. *Molod' Ukraïny v umovakh formuvannia totalitarnoho ladu, 1920–1939*. Kyïv: Instytut istoriï Ukraïny NAN Ukraïny, 2001.
- *Molod' USRR v period utverdzhennia totalitarnoï systemy, 1928–1933*. Kyïv: Instytut istoriï Ukraïny NAN Ukraïny, 1999.
- "Uchast' studentsva USRR v suspil'no-politychnomu ta kul'turnomu zhytti v 1920-ti roky." *Problemy istoriï Ukraïni*, no. 16 (2007): 147–62.

Raleigh, Donald J., ed. *Provincial Landscapes: Local Dimensions of Soviet Power, 1917–1953*. Pittsburgh: University of Pittsburgh Press, 2001.

Reshetar, John. *The Ukrainian Revolution, 1917–1920*. New York: Arno Press, 1972.

Retish, Aaron. *Russia's Peasants in Revolution and Civil War: Citizenship, Identity, and the Creation of the Soviet State, 1914–1922*. New York: Cambridge University Press, 2008.

Richardson, Tanya. *Kaleidoscopic Odessa: History and Place in Contemporary Ukraine*. Toronto: University of Toronto Press, 2008.

Rothstein, Robert A. "How It Was Sung in Odessa: At the Intersection of Russian and Yiddish Folk Culture." *Slavic Review* 60, no. 4 (Winter 2001): 781.

Ruane, Christine. *Gender, Class, and the Professionalization of Russian City Teachers, 1860–1914*. Pittsburgh: University of Pittsburgh Press, 1994.

Schnell, Felix. "'Tear Them Apart … And Be Done With It!' The Ataman Leadership of Nestor Makhno as a Culture of Violence." *Ab Imperio*, no. 3 (2008): 195–221.

Scott, James C. *Seeing Like a State: How Certain Schemes to Improve the Human Condition Have Failed*. New Haven: Yale University Press, 1998.

Seregny, Scott. *Russian Teachers and Peasant Revolution: The Politics of Education in 1905*. Bloomington: Indiana University Press, 1989.

Shapoval, Iurii, and Vadym Zolotar'ov. *Vsevolod Balyts'kyi: osoba, chas, otochennia*. Kyïv: Stylos, 2002.

Shevelov, George Y. *The Ukrainian Language in the First Half of the Twentieth Century (1900–1941): Its State and Status*. Cambridge, MA: Harvard Ukrainian Research Institute, 1989.

Shkandrij, Myroslav. *Jews in Ukrainian Literature: Representation and Identity*. New Haven: Yale University Press, 2009.

Shkandrij, Myroslav, and Olga Bertelsen. "The Soviet Regime's National Operations in Ukraine, 1929–1934." *Canadian Slavonic Papers* 55, no. 3–4 (2013): 417–47.

Shneer, David. *Yiddish and the Creation of Soviet Jewish Culture 1918–1930*. New York: Cambridge University Press, 2004.

Shternshis, Anna. *Soviet and Kosher: Jewish Popular Culture in the Soviet Union, 1923–1939*. Bloomington: Indiana University Press, 2006.

Siegelbaum, Lewis H. *Soviet State and Society between Revolutions, 1918–1929*. Cambridge: Cambridge University Press, 1992.

Siropolko, Stepan. *Narodnia osvita na soviets'kii Ukraïni*. Warsaw: Pratsi Ukraïns'koho naukovoho instytutu, 1934.

Slezkine, Yuri. *The Jewish Century*. Princeton: Princeton University Press, 2004.

– "The USSR as a Communal Apartment, or How a Socialist State Promoted Ethnic Particularism." *Slavic Review*, no. 53 (1994): 414–52.

Smith, Jeremy. *Red Nations: The Nationalities Experience in and after the USSR*. Cambridge: Cambridge University Press, 2013.

Smith, Michael G. *Language and Power in the Creation of the USSR, 1917–1953.* Contributions to the Sociology of Language, edited by Joshua A. Fishman. Vol. 80. New York: Mouton de Gruyter, 1998.

Smith-Peter, Susan. "How to Write a Region: Local and Regional Historiography." *Kritika: Explorations in Russian and Eurasian History* 5, no. 3 (2004): 527–42.

Smolii, V. A., ed. *Entsyklopediia istoriï Ukraïny.* 9 vols. Kyïv: Naukova dumka, 2003–2013.

– "Ukraïnizatsiia" *1920–30-kh rokiv: peredumovy, zdobutky, uroky.* Kyïv: Instytut istoriï Ukraïny NAN Ukraïny, 2003.

Stanton, Rebecca Jane. *Isaac Babel and the Self-Invention of Odessan Modernism.* Evanston: Northwestern University Press, 2012.

Steffes, Tracy Lynn. *School, Society, & State: A New Education to Govern Modern America, 1890–1940.* Chicago: University of Chicago Press, 2012.

Sukhomlyns'ka, O. V., ed. *Narys istoriï ukraïns'koho shkil'nytstva (1905–1933).* Kyïv: Zapovit, 1996.

– "Zarubizhnyi pedahohichnyi dosvid v Ukraïni v 20-ti roky." *Ridna shkola*, no. 2 (1992): 3–7.

Sumpf, Alexandre. *Bolcheviks en campagne: paysans et éducation politique dans la Russie des années 1920.* Paris: CNRS, 2010.

– "Confronting the Countryside: The Training of Political Educators in 1920s Russia." *History of Education* 35, no. 4–5 (2006): 475–98.

Sydorenko, O. I., and D. V. Tabachnyk, eds. *Represovane "vidrodzhennia."* Kyïv: Ukraïna, 1993.

Sylvester, Roshanna P. *Tales of Old Odessa: Crime and Civility in a City of Thieves.* DeKalb, IL: Northern Illinois University Press, 2005.

Tanny, Jarrod. *City of Rogues and Schnorrers: Russia's Jews and the Myth of Old Odessa.* Bloomington: Indiana University Press, 2011.

Tirado, Isabel. "The Komsomol and the Young Peasants: The Dilemma of Rural Expansion, 1921–1925." *Slavic Review* 52, no. 3 (1996): 460–76.

– *Young Guard! The Communist Youth League, Petrograd 1917–1920.* Westport: Greenwood Press, 1988.

Tkacz, Virlana. "Les Kurbas's Early Work at the Berezil: From Bodies in Motion to Performing the Invisible." In *Modernism in Kyiv: Jubilant Experimentation*, edited by Virlana Tkacz and Irena R. Makaryk, 362–85. Toronto: University of Toronto Press, 2010.

Tron'ko, P. T. *Ukraïns'ke kraieznavstvo v XX stolitti: do 75-richchia Vseukraïns'koï spilky kraieznavtsiv.* Kyïv: Instytut istoriï Ukraïny NAN Ukraïny, 2002.

Veidlinger, Jeffrey. *In the Shadow of the Shtetl: Small-Town Jewish Life in Soviet Ukraine.* Bloomington: Indiana University Press, 2013.

Velychenko, Stephen. *State Building in Revolutionary Ukraine: A Comparative Study of Governments and Bureaucrats, 1917–1922.* Toronto: University of Toronto Press, 2011.

Vyhovs'kyi, M. Iu. *Nomenklatura systemy osvity v USRR 1920–1930-x rokiv: sotsial'ne pokhodzhennia personal'nyi sklad ta funktsii*. Kyïv: Heneza, 2006.

Vynokur, I. S., L. L. Babenko, and P. T. Tron'ko. *Represovane kraieznavstvo (20–30-i roky)*. Kyïv: Ridnyi krai, 1992.

Wasyliw, Zenon. "Education Policy and Rural Schoolteachers in Soviet Ukraine." *East/West Education* 19, no. 1/2 (1998): 36–50.

Weber, Eugene. *Peasants into Frenchmen: The Modernization of Rural France, 1870–1914*. Standford: Stanford University Press, 1976.

Wellmann, Monica. *Zwischen Militanz, Verzweiflung und Disziplinierung. Jugendliche Lebenswelten in Moskau 1920–1930*. Zürich: Pano Verlag, 2005.

Wexler, Paul. *Purism and Language: A Study in Modern Ukrainian and Belorussian Nationalism, 1840–1967*. Bloomington: Indiana University Press, 1974.

Yekelchyk, Serhy. *Stalin's Empire of Memory: Russian-Ukrainian Relations in the Soviet Historical Imagination*. Toronto: University of Toronto Press, 2004.

– *Ukraine: Birth of a Modern Nation*. New York: Oxford University Press, 2007.

Zahra, Tara. "Imagined Noncommunities: National Indifference as a Category of Analysis." *Slavic Review* 69, no. 1 (2010): 93–119.

– *Kidnapped Souls: National Indifference and the Battle for Children in the Bohemian Lands, 1900–1948*. Ithaca: Cornell University Press, 2008.

Zaruba, V. M. *Mykhailo Slabchenko v epistoliarnii ta memuarnii spadshchyni:1882–1952*. Dnipropetrovs'k: Vydavnytstvo Iurydychnoï akademiï MVS Ukraïny, 2004.

Index

Agitprop, 97, 102–3, 145, 182, 229, 305
Akhmatov, Lev, 260–1, 262, 263–4, 279, 298
Alchevska, Khrystyna, 241
Alvail, Zigurd, 212–13
anti-Semitism: against Jewish children, 247, 330; nationalism and, 236, 247; and nationalities policy, 249–50; SVU and, 263, 399n73; teachers and, 250–1, 255–6
Arnautov, Vasyl, 67, 77, 121, 145–6, 155, 163
Artemivsk: peasant murders in, 279; Ukrainian culture month in, 307

Babel, Isaac, 205
Balytsky, Vsevolod, 258, 265
Baran, Mykhailo, 72–3
Barun, Rakhil, 325, 326, 406n74
Baryshpil District Labour School, 128–9
Bekhterev, Vladimir, 45
Bidnov, Vasyl, 349
Bidnova, Liubov, 268, 349
Bila Tserkva: Fastiv District Labour School, 109–10; Jews in Russian-language schools in, 98; *perevirky* in, 135; Russian schools in, 124–5, 129–30; shootings in, 279
bilingualism, 71; mixed Polish–Ukrainian schools, 404n14; mixed Russian–Ukrainian schools, 309, 337; mixed Yiddish–Ukrainian schools, 404n14
Bilshovycheniata, 187
Bily, Mykola, 266, 267, 268, 269, 270–1, 271–2
Bily, Yevhen, 270–1
Boikiv, Ivan, 136–7
Bolshevik Ukrainization, 297, 301, 305, 326, 329, 335, 339
Bondar-Tereshchenko, Ihor, 361n8
Borotbist party, 50, 142–3, 349–50
Borovikov, Georgii, 274
Bourdieu, Pierre, 18, 19, 21
Bubnov, Andrei, 317
Bulgarian schools: enrolment campaigns and, 35; native-language literature in, 99; Ukrainian-language teachers in, 220
Buzuk, Petro, 215–16, 349
Bychko, Valentyn, 298–9

censuses, 28, 369n43–4
Chas, 171, 249

chauvinism. *See* nationalism
Chavdarov, Sava, 128
Chepiha, Yakiv, 45
Chernihiv: anti-Semitism in, 330; shooting of teacher in, 279; teacher retraining in, 110–11; Ukrainian-language schools in, 89; Ukrainian–Russian mixed-language schools in, 309; Ukrainization in, 130, 309
Chervona zirka, 95
Chervoni kvity, 88
Chervonyi shkoliar, 57
Chervonyi shliakh, 244, 357
children: as activists, 283–4, 292, 296–7, 298–9; anti-Soviet activities, 288–9; arrests of, 262; buildings, 46, 69, 80–1, 107, 129, 201, 210; civil war and, 23, 42, 46, 184; colonies, 208; education centred on, 48; famine and, 42, 46, 184; and first Five-Year Plan, 283; and grain requisition, 288–9, 296–7; homes, 23, 42; knowledge of local environment, 118–19; learning aptitude, and education, 45; and nationalism, 237, 240, 289, 291; socialism building by, 74, 75; social upbringing of, 46–7; suicides of, 299–300. *See also* youth
Chubar, Vlas, 162–3
cities: Five-Year Plan and growth of, 301; migration of ethnic Ukrainians to, 204, 297; nationalism and, 168–9; national-minority populations in, 200; rural migration to, 200, 204, 297, 345–7; Russian language in, 8, 126, 152–3; and Russian vs Ukrainian cultures, 139; Ukrainization and, 12. *See also* urban schools
civic education: and building of socialism, 115; at Kyiv Labour School No. 1, 60–1; progressive pedagogy and, 84; Young Pioneers and, 84
civil servants. *See* government employees
civil war: and children, 23, 42, 46, 184; and education, 44–5; Narkomos and, 107; and nationalism, 168; peasantry and, 5, 66; and schools, 44–5, 46, 184; and social upbringing, 107; and teachers, 50, 72–3; and Ukrainian-language schools, 64, 68
class: among Young Pioneers, 284, 289; and assaults against Young Pioneers/schoolchildren, 298–9; categories/identification of, 294–5; and children, 296–7, 300, 305; and grain requisition, 331; Komsomol and, 35, 283, 287, 288, 297; Narkomos and, 331–2; and nationalism, 256, 260, 297, 300; and progressive education, 105; rural intelligentsia and, 295; and schools, 288–90, 303–4, 329; and SVU, 257; teachers and, 249–50, 255, 279, 294, 299; and Ukrainian language/culture, 93, 302; and universal school enrolment, 288; Young Pioneers and, 287, 288, 290–1, 297
collectivization: children's/youth literature and, 249; Komsomol and, 245; kulaks and, 238, 239, 252; Kyiv Agricultural Institute and, 247; rural teachers and, 238, 255, 256, 257, 278, 280; and social dislocation/unrest, 246; Stalin and, 239; Young Pioneers and, 285, 299
Collins, James, 19–20, 201
Commission for Kraieznavstvo of Slobidska Ukraine, 55
Committee of Poor Peasants (KNS), 252
Communist Party: and education, 10, 345; and intelligentsia, 4, 154, 224,

274; and link between language and educational radicalism, 64; and Narkomos, 10; and peasantry, 5, 67; and primary schools, 4; and progressive pedagogy, 227; and Russian language, 30, 86; and teachers, 4–5, 154; and Ukrainian language, 30; and Ukrainization, 5, 66–7, 342, 347. *See also* KP(b)U; VKP(b)

Communist Youth League (Komsomol). *See* Komsomol

complex method: about, 48–9; application of, 117–21; children's participatory role in, 49, 60, 105; and civic training, 60–1; and counter-revolutionaries, 319–20; cultural revolution and, 62; and curricula, 118; dangers of, 62; and excursions, 115; February Revolution complex, 115; and formal knowledge, 83, 105, 117–18; growth of, 49; and independent study, 60, 61; inspectors and, 9–10, 116, 119–20; KP(b)U and, 84; and *kraieznavstvo*, 52, 53, 55, 118–19; and labour culture, 51; and language study, 123–4; local studies and, 43, 114; Narkomos and, 43, 49, 50, 51, 52, 53, 61–2; Narkompros and, 51; native-language instruction and, 83, 106, 126; October Revolution complex, 115–16; production issues complex, 107; progressive pedagogy and, 43, 48–9, 117; in rural schools, 53; and Russian-language instruction, 125; Shevchenko complex, 58, 60–1, 115; and socialism, 51, 116, 117; social studies and, 58, 127; and social upbringing, 114–15; subject area instruction vs, 119, 120, 127; SVU show trial and, 38; teachers and, 43,

49–50, 51, 62, 83, 104, 109, 119–21, 125, 190, 341; and textbooks, 51, 120, 124; and Ukrainian language, 64, 105, 127; and Ukrainian studies, 61, 105, 113–14; Ukrainization and, 110, 125; and vocational training, 51; Young Pioneers and, 107, 191

conservative pedagogy: cultural revolution and, 39, 319; and formal knowledge, 297; progressive pedagogy vs, 303, 347; shift to, 297, 347; and textbooks, 297; and Ukrainization, 347

counter-revolution/-revolutionaries: among educators, 261; anti-Semitism and, 250; and children, 288–9; complex method and, 319–20; educators and nationalism, 266–7; and importance of schools, 303; libraries and, 248–9; mandatory school enrolment and, 282; nationalism and, 245–6; SVU as organization of, 263; teachers and, 244, 278; and youth, 40

cultural revolution: about, 239; acceleration of, 249–50; and complex method, 62; and educational acceleration, 16; and elimination of vocational secondary schools, 9; and formal knowledge, 283; impact on schooling, 10–11; and nationalism, 235, 240; and nationalities policy, 11, 16, 313–14; political orientation of children and, 235; and polytechnization, 283; and progressive pedagogy, 62, 235; and return to conservative education, 39, 319; rhetoric used during, 179; Robos and, 236; and Shakhty engineers show trial, 239; Stalin and, 235; teacher knowledge and, 302; and Ukrainization, 38, 306–7; and

unification of Ukrainian and Russian education, 39; and Young Pioneers, 284; and youth, 38–40
curriculum: centralization of schools and, 317–18; complex method and, 118; cultural revolution and, 283; *kraieznavstvo* in, 53; local character of, 49; progressive education and, 15–16; regional material in, 105; subordination of Ukrainian system, 319; teachers and, 109; transformation of, 107–8; Ukrainian studies in, 52; Ukrainization and, 4; vocational secondary schools and, 24, 48; Young Pioneers and, 190

Dalton Plan, 46, 48, 83, 119
Danylenko, Vasyl, 264, 265, 399n76
Denikin, Anton, 73, 76, 172
Derzhvydav (state publishing house), 88
Dewey, John, 42, 45–6, 48, 61–2
Dnipropetrovsk: Komsomol in, 194–5; Mining Institute Testing Commission for Ukrainian-Language Knowledge, 322; railroad schools, 134, 135, 137; Russian language in, 184, 185; Ukrainian culture month in, 307; Ukrainian language in, 304; Ukrainian–Russian mixed-language schools in, 309; Ukrainian-studies courses in, 194; Ukrainization brigades, 323–4; Ukrainization commission, 272; Ukrainization in, 184–5, 194–5, 307, 309; Ukrainization of Komsomol in, 183–4; Young Pioneers in, 184, 293
Dnipropetrovsk (city): INO, 270–1; Komsomol members in Ukrainian-studies courses, 193; Labour School No. 20, 268; Ukrainian political schools in, 196; Ukrainization of Young Pioneers in, 198
Doha, Vasyl: accusations against, 260–1; biography, 350; counter-revolutionary writings, 319–20; SVU show trial and, 258
Donbas: ethnic-Ukrainian population in, 308–9; industrialization vs education in, 324; national culture in, 301; proletarian Ukrainian culture in, 307–8; Russian children in, 326; Russian language in, 307; Russian workers in, 377n38; teachers' poverty in, 324; Ukrainian-language schools in, 309; Ukrainization in, 301, 307, 377n38; Young Pioneers in, 284–5
Donets: native-language schooling in, 327; Russian-speaking population in, 89; teachers' poverty in, 324; Ukrainian-language schools in, 67, 69, 71, 91; Ukrainian-language teachers in, 69–70; Ukrainization in, 65, 80–1, 89, 130
Doroshkevych, Oleksandr, 165
Drahomanov, Mykhailo, 165
Durdakiv Labour School, 122
Durdukivsky, Volodymyr: arrest, 173; biography, 350; and formal instruction, 319; as head of "school group" of SVU, 261; as head of VUAN orthography division, 25; and seven-year labour school, 269; and SVU, 173, 267; SVU show trial and, 62, 256, 258; and Taras Shevchenko Gymnasium, 25; and Taras Shevchenko Labour School No. 1, 58–61, 116–17, 172, 267; and Trezvynsky, 267
DVU (state publishing house), 120

education: Communist Party and, 10; cultural revolution and, 16; decentralization of, 105; Five-Year Plan and standardization of, 314; flexibility of, 22, 37; and *korenizatsiia*, 17; KP(b)U and, 10; and labour culture, 19, 22, 23, 39; and language, 15, 17–18, 18–19; and nationalities policy, 15; and nation building, 16, 22–3; normalization of, 104; and proletarian culture, 322, 323; in RSFSR vs Ukraine, 46, 47–8; shift to more conservative (*see* conservative pedagogy); and socialism building, 323; and Soviet political agenda, 15; standardization/unification of systems, 11, 315–17, 320

educators. *See* teachers

Eisenstein, Sergei, 205

Ekonomichna heohrafiia Ukrainy (Economic geography of Ukraine; Sukhov, Voblyi), 56

enrolment, school: class enemies and universal, 288; and ethnic minorities, 35; Five-Year Plan and, 292–3; Komsomol and, 282; and number of schools, 189; in rural areas, 189–90; of Russian working-class children, 162; of Russified-Ukrainian children, 297; of Ukrainian children, 133, 153, 161–2, 288; in Ukrainian-language schools, 35, 130, 146; of Ukrainian migrant children, 297; Ukrainization and, 161, 176, 288; universal, 8, 108, 282, 287–8, 292, 297, 321, 324, 334; of working-class Ukrainian children, 162; Young Pioneers and, 190–1, 282, 293

ethnicity: in children's buildings, 81; language and, 20, 86, 99, 100, 125–6, 149, 152, 158, 160; and native language, 129, 151, 158; and numbers of schools, 162; spoken language and, 126; and Ukrainian control, 132; and Ukrainian membership in KP(b)U, 142

ethnic minorities: in cities, 200; enrolment campaigns and, 35; and Komsomol, 181, 183, 188–9; lack of teachers, 99; Narkomos and languages of, 98; and native-language schools, 29; and Russian language, 95, 99; in Russian-language schools, 210; Russian language vs languages of, 32; teachers' education levels/training, 99, 110; textbook shortage, 99; Ukrainian-language instruction for, 63; Ukrainization and, 157, 220; Young Pioneers and, 179–80, 180–1

ethnic-minority schools: assimilation of non-Russians vs, 234; closures, and nationalities policy, 325; ethnic-Ukrainian children in, 327; forced Ukrainization and number of, 409n128; by group, 157–8; and nationalities policy, 363n20; and polytechnization, 328; and Ukrainian studies, 58; Ukrainization in, 95

examinations *(perevirky):* about, 131–3; for civil servants, 222–3, 223–4; commissions, 223; delays/postponements, 138; exemptions from, 136–7; local Ukrainization committees and, 379–80n26; for state employees, 203; for teachers, 135–8, 201–2, 231–3; for teachers in Ukrainian language/studies, 85, 86, 92–3, 212–15, 225–6, 309–13; in Ukrainian knowledge, 207; Ukrliknep and, 379–80n26 famine: and assaults against Young Pioneers, 299; and children, 36, 42, 46, 184; grain requisition and, 278; and rural schools, 24, 184; and rural teachers, 304, 324, 329

Fastiv District Labour School, 109–10

February Revolution: complex on, 110, 115, 123–4; and Ukrainian-language schools, 64

Femych-Holovatsky, M., 251–2

Five-Year Plan: children and, 39, 62, 283, 289; and complex method, 39; and economic conditions, 329; effects on education, 240; and grain requisition, 239; and industrialization, 239, 301, 322; and literature, 249; and repression of intelligentsia, 17; and school enrolment, 292–3; and schools, 62; and standardization/unification of education, 302–3, 314, 316; teachers and, 238, 240, 294, 311; Ukrainian language in, 313; and Ukrainian studies, 329; and Ukrainization, 38, 259, 305–8, 343; Young Pioneers and, 288, 290

forced Ukrainization: Bolshevik Ukrainization vs, 326; in Donets, 327–8; and ethnic-minority children in enrolment campaigns, 35; of ethnic-Russian children, 341; of general population, 218–19; of Jewish children, 149; KP(b)U and, 158–9, 222, 305, 341; meaning of, 327; and number of national-minority schools, 409n128; in Odesa, 204, 218–19, 222; and resistance to Ukrainization, 209; of Russians, 305, 326; of Russian schools, 227; Skrypnyk on, 157–8; and state employees, 218–19; of working class, 132–3, 141, 301, 341

formal knowledge: complex method and, 83, 105, 117–18; Durdukivsky and, 319; parents and, 24; shift to conservative education and, 297; subsidence of cultural revolution and, 283

FZU schools (Factory Apprenticeship Schools): expansion of, 292; Komsomol and, 47–8, 178, 196–7; polytechnization and, 292, 315; and Russian language, 197; Skrypnyk on, 316; and Ukrainization, 197

Galicia: and new Ukrainian orthography, 368–9n40; teachers from, 30, 77, 400n89; Ukrainian culture in, 25

Gellner, Ernest, 36–7, 44, 367n25

German children: enrolment campaigns and, 35; religious organizations, 187; in Ukrainizing school, 29; and Yiddish language, 181

German newspapers, 195

German schools: literature for, 99; percentage of, 210; Ukrainian children enrolled in, 327; Ukrainian-language teachers for, 70, 220

government employees: examinations/*perevirky* for, 207, 222–3, 223–4; in Odesa, 202; and Russian language, 323; and Russian- vs Ukrainian-language schools, 145–6; and Ukrainian language, 102, 138, 204, 222–3, 323, 338; and Ukrainian studies, 86–7, 203, 248, 323; and Ukrainization, 64–5, 66, 92, 96, 156, 168, 218–19, 305; Ukrainization courses for, 202; as Young Pioneer leaders, 285

GPU (State Political Directorate): arrests, 37–8, 62, 173, 247; and intelligentsia, 265, 266, 399–400n81; and nationalism, 277; and Odesa, 13; and SVU, 37, 236, 266, 273, 276; and Ukrainization, 6, 237, 238, 241–2; and youth, 40

grain requisition: children and, 288–9, 296–7; class enemies and, 331; industrialization and, 239; kulaks and, 246; and nationalism, 290; peasantry and, 246, 256; Petliurization and, 331; and polytechnization, 328; rural teachers and, 329; Stalin and, 239; teachers and, 36, 255, 256, 278, 279–80, 296; Young Pioneers and, 36, 293, 299

Great Turn, 249, 284, 285, 298–9

Greens, the, 66

gymnasia: about, 368n33; Ivan Franko First Ukrainian Experimental School as, 208; Mykolaiv Labour School No. 15 and, 147–8; "new school" vs, 44; Taras Shevchenko Gymnasium, 25, 58–61; Ukrainian-language, 94

Haliun, I., 53–4, 57

Hashomer Hatzair, 290

Hermaize, Yosyp, 165, 258, 263, 351, 363n25

higher education. *See* post-secondary education

Hirchak, Yevhen, 317

Hohol, Stepan, 77

Holovnauka, 52–3

Holovsotsvykh: auxiliary schools, 108; and class size, 108; on cost of Ukrainization training, 92; and dismissal of teachers opposed to Ukrainization, 80; and educational deficiencies, 108; and experimental institutions/model schools, 56–7; and *kraieznavstvo*, 112–13; "normalization of work" slogan, 108; Odesa sotsvykh department and curriculum of, 222; and school conditions, 108; and Ukrainian-language literature, 70, 88; Ukrainian-language plan, 68–70; and Ukrainian-language schools, 71, 75–6, 81, 87; and Ukrainian-language teachers, 70; and Ukrainization, 65; and Ukrainization of schools, 129; Ukrainization plan, 87–8. *See also* Sektor sotsvykhu; Uprsotsvykh

Horozhynsky, Ivan, 77

Hrebenetsky, Oleksandr, 266, 267, 268, 269, 270, 271, 272

Hrushevsky, Mikhailo, 56, 165, 265, 266, 351

Hrynko, Hryhorii: biography, 351; on children's buildings, 46–7; as head of Radnarkom, 141; KP(b)U and, 49, 142–3; "Our Path to the West," 45; succeeded by Zatonsky, 49, 357; and Ukrainian system of education, 317; and vocational schools, 47; and VUAN's orthographic standardization, 25–6

industrialization: and growth of urban centres, 301; peasantry and, 140; and socialism, 386n56; Stalin and, 239

INOs (Institutes of People's Education): about, 393n42; Dnipropetrovsk, 268, 270–1; Katerynoslav, 269; Kharkiv, 55; Odesa, 216, 223–4, 227–8, 275, 276–7

inspectors: about, 109; and centralization of education, 315–16; complex method and, 9–10, 116, 119–20, 125, 126; in Kharkiv, 81; knowledge of Ukrainian language, 101, 108–9; in Kyiv, 101, 102, 109, 119–20, 155; and language

vs identity, 27–8; in Mykolaiv, 125, 126, 147–8, 155; in Podillia, 87; in Poltava, 101–2; power of, 213; regional to oblast level, 322–3; and Russian vs Ukrainian languages, 69, 148; and teacher opposition to Ukrainization, 102; and teachers' knowledge of Ukrainian, 11, 30, 69, 78, 135–6, 137–8, 312–13
Institute of the Ukrainian Scientific Language, 26
intelligentsia: and activism, 244; Communist Party and, 4, 154, 224, 274; cultural revolution and, 239; GPU and, 265, 266; high vs low, 173; in Kharkiv, 171; KP(b)U and, 169, 264, 265; in Kyiv, 171; and language, 18; and librarians' trials, 248–9; and national culture, 153; and nationalism, 154, 169, 173, 274, 342–3; "new labour" and, 57; as non-party, 11, 168; in Odesa, 13, 171, 172, 272, 273–4; proletarian, 239; replacement elite for, 38; repression of, 17, 40, 342–3; Robos and, 259; Russian, 274, 275; Shumsky on, 140; and SVU, 258, 272, 273–4; SVU show trial and, 258–9, 276, 295, 343; teachers and, 50, 74, 171; trust in, 265; and Ukrainization, 6–7, 141, 142, 164–7, 172, 173, 224, 263, 342–3, 361n11; as united, 267–8; and working-class development of, 267
Ivan Franko First Ukrainian Experimental School, 208
Ivankivka District Labour School, 120–1
Ivanov, T., 79–80
Ivanytsia, Hryhorii: biography, 351–2; counter-revolutionary writings, 319–20;

Shumsky's accusation regarding, 165; SVU show trial and, 62, 258, 260–1
Izium Pedagogical-Technical College, 260

Jadids, 32
Jewish children: attacked in schools, 247, 330; in Kyiv Labour School No. 6, 160; in Russian schools, 370n46; in Ukrainian-language schools, 370n46; in Yiddish-language schools, 380–1n41, 381n43, 386n55; in Young Pioneers, 181
Jewish newspapers, 195
Jewish schools: literature for, 99; Ukrainian-language teachers for, 70; Yiddish-language schools vs, 381n43. *See also* Yiddish-language schools
Jews: activism, 290; in Kyiv Labour School No. 1, 261; and nationalities policy, 29; in Odesa, 203, 207; and Russian language, 98, 381n44; Russian-language schooling and, 98, 99; as Russified population, 29; and Ukrainian vs Russian languages, 203; and Ukrainization, 203, 220; and Zionism, 181, 186, 265, 290, 403n13

Kaganovich, Lazar: biography, 352; and ethnicity, 132; Stalin's views and, 10; and Ukrainization, 7, 140–1, 142, 314
Kalinichenko, Mykhailo, 252–3, 254
Kamianets: Russian native-language instruction in, 335; Ukrainian-language university in, 269
Karpeko, Oleksandr, 322, 323, 325–6, 330–1, 406n74, 407n81
Katerynoslav: INO, 269; Russian-speaking population in, 89; transfer of teachers, 76; trial of railway librarians in, 248–9; Ukrainian-language schools

in, 65, 67, 69, 71, 95–6; Ukrainian-language teachers in, 70; Ukrainization in, 89, 130. *See also* Dnipropetrovsk
KDR (Communist Children's Movement). *See* Young Pioneers
Kharkiv: education section, 117, 118; Izium Pedagogical-Technical College, 260; Russian-language schooling in, 326; Russian schoolchildren in, 326–7; teachers' poverty in, 324; Ukrainian-language schools in, 67, 69, 71; Ukrainian-language teachers in, 70; Ukrainization of Russian-speaking population in, 89; Ukrainization of schools in, 65
Kharkiv (city): about, 12; Communist instructors in, 171; complex method in, 49; INO, 55; intelligentsia in, 171; Komsomol in, 191, 193–4, 199; KP(b)U and, 12; Labour School No. 30, 260; Labour School No. 32, 90; Pedagogical School, 408n114; Russian language in, 82; Russian native-language instruction in, 335; Ukrainian-language schools in, 82; Ukrainian political schools in, 196; Ukrainian–Russian mixed-language schools in, 309; Ukrainization in, 12, 211–12, 308–9; Young Pioneers in, 198, 290–1; youth Ukrainization in, 184
Kherson, 209
Khmilnyk, anti-Semitism in, 247, 249–50
Kholodny, Hryhoryi, 26
Khvylia, Andrii, 333
Khvylovy, Mykola: biography, 352; and nationalism, 241, 243; and Ukrainian autonomy, 171; on Ukrainian culture and Europe, 141; and Ukrainian language, 38; and Ukrainian vs Russian language, 141, 167, 169
Kobzar (Shevchenko), 375n71

kobzar/*kobzari*, 61, 92–3
Komsomol: about, 33; and children, 282, 284, 296–7, 300; and citizenship training in schools, 107; and class enemies, 35, 283, 287, 288, 297; corruption of members, 181; dangers of influence, 186–7; de-Russification of, 189; and ethnic minorities, 181, 183, 188–9; ethnic Ukrainians in, 142, 188, 194–5; "foreign elements" among, 245; and FZU schools, 178, 197; kulak membership in, 245; leadership shortages, 288; membership as minority within age group, 192–3; and nationalism, 35, 179; and nationalities policy, 33, 35, 174, 179, 188–9; opportunistic elements in, 284, 287; and peasantry, 176; and political schools, 183–4, 196; political training in, 178; and primary schools, 281–2; problems in, 245; public activism, 244–5; purges of, 294, 295; in rural areas, 174, 176, 178, 295; rural–urban relationship and, 193; and rural youth, 176; and Russian language, 144, 175; Russians employed in, 188, 189; and Russified youth, 183; and school enrolment, 176, 282, 287–8; and teachers, 50, 121, 255, 283, 294; teacher shortages, 176; teachers' lack of political knowledge, 295–6; TsK, 179, 180–4, 186–91, 195, 198–9; and Ukrainian language, 175–6, 178, 183–4, 195; and Ukrainian-language instruction, 174; and Ukrainian-language literature, 180, 195–6; and Ukrainian studies, 178, 183–4, 195, 196; and Ukrainian vs Russian languages, 90; and Ukrainization, 16, 174, 182–5, 191, 195, 196–7,

218, 264, 297; Ukrainization commission, 182–5, 188–91, 283, 284; Ukrainization of, 144–5, 175, 176, 178, 179, 188–9; and vocational schools, 47–8; VUAN and, 264; and working-class youth, 175, 183; and Young Pioneers, 33, 175, 179, 181–2, 198, 282, 283, 284, 285, 294; and youth literacy, 174

Komsomolets ahitator, 195

Komsomolets Ukrainy, 184–5, 195, 196

Komunist, 195

Komunistychna osvitu, 319

Kopyl, I., 54–5, 57, 62

korenizatsiia. See nationalities policy

Korniushin, Fedor, 143–4

Korotka istoriia Ukraini (Short history of Ukraine; Yavorsky), 55–6, 57

Kotsiubynsky, Mykhailo, 247

KP(b)U (Communist Party (Bolshevik) of Ukraine): and complex method, 84; and education, 10, 36–7; ethnic Ukrainians in, 220–1; and exile of scholars, 399–400n81; and forced Ukrainization, 33, 132–3, 141, 158–9, 222, 305, 341; and intelligentsia, 169, 264, 265; Kaganovich as leader of, 140–1; and Kharkiv, 12; "kulak" definition of opposers, 246; merger of UKP with, 183; and national culture, 143–4, 301; and nationalism, 10, 167–8; nationalities policy, 138–9; in Odesa, 203, 220–2, 229–30; and proletariat, 138; and Russified Ukrainians, 138, 147, 183; suspicions regarding teachers, 36–7; and SVU show trial, 264, 266; Ukrainian membership in, 142; and Ukrainian studies, 84, 230; and Ukrainization, 5–6, 7, 10, 37, 40, 66–7, 133, 138–9, 165, 220–2, 229–30, 266, 297, 307, 341, 342; and Ukrainization of ethnic Russians, 147, 154; VKP(b) and, 10; and working class, 132–3, 141, 147, 341; and Young Pioneers, 35, 282; and youth, 39–40, 267

KP(b)U Politburo: and ethnic Russians vs Russified Ukrainians, 149; and Hrynko's education reform, 49; report on Ukrainization, 164–5; and Skrypnyk's writings, 332; and SVU show trial, 258, 265; Ukrainization Commission, 11, 102, 133, 140, 142–50, 154, 161, 162, 244

KPZU (Communist Party of Western Ukraine), 167, 350

kraieznavstvo. See local studies

Kremenchuh: Komsomol in, 288–9; Ukrainization in, 96

Krymsky, Agatangel, 26

Kryvyi Rih: accusations against teacher in, 252–3; Ukrainian culture month in, 307; Ukrainian language in schools in, 312; Ukrainization in, 307

kulaks: about, 246, 376–7n25; and anti-Semitism, 247, 250; anti-Soviet demonstrations, 246; and assaults against Young Pioneers/schoolchildren, 298–9; and children, 289, 290, 296; children of, 286, 403n2; and collectivization, 239, 252; cultural revolution and, 236; KP(b)U and, 246; membership in Komsomol, 245; and Narkomos, 329–30; and nationalism, 168, 243, 245, 278; and peasantry, 169, 279; proletariat and, 140; teachers and, 238, 256, 278, 279; Young Pioneers and, 282, 285–6, 289, 298–9

Kuzmenko, Vasyl, 317

Kviring, Emanuel, 65, 84, 97
Kyiv: centralization of Soviet education system in, 315; inspectors in, 101; Party Committee, 299–300; Regional Inspectorate on complex method, 119–20; Russian-language schooling in, 326; teachers and Ukrainization in, 310–12; teacher training in, 324–5; Ukrainian-language schools in, 71
Kyiv (city): about, 12–13; education section plan for 1931, 321; ethnic heterogeneity of, 364n28; ethnic Ukrainians in, 146; intelligentsia in, 171; Kharkiv compared to, 12; Komsomol in, 179, 198–9; nationalism in, 13; poverty in, 61; Russian native-language instruction in, 335; Russian schools in, 159; Russian-speaking children in, 159; school shortages in, 162; Taras Shevchenko Gymnasium, 25, 58–61; transfer of schools to Ukrainian-language instruction, 155; Ukrainian newspaper readership among youth, 198; Ukrainization in, 13, 158–9, 161, 198–9
Kyiv Agricultural Institute, 247
Kyiv Labour Schools: No. 6, 155, 159–60, 161; No. 38, 172; No. 47, 122; No. 64, 241; No. 67, 240; Taras Shevchenko Labour School No. 1, 25, 116–17, 172, 240–1, 258, 261, 267, 268–9, 270

labour culture: complex method and, 51; education and, 19, 22, 23, 39; labour schools and, 315–16; progressive education and, 9, 15, 43; Ukrainian-language instruction and, 123; vocational secondary schools and, 24
labour schools, 98f; about, 56; complex method in, 116; and labour culture, 315–16; polytechnical education in, 315; "public-political" education in, 315–16; religious school changed to, 94; and vocational schools, 303, 315
language: education and, 15, 17–18, 18–19; ethnicity and, 20, 100, 125–6, 149, 151, 152, 158, 160; French Revolution and, 18; intelligentsia and, 18; and international proletarian culture, 242; and national identity, 27–8, 327; and political power, 18; and progressive pedagogy, 340; in Ukrainian public life, 409–10n1
Larin, Yurii, 149, 154, 162, 386n1
Lebed, Dmitrii, 6, 139, 158, 161, 185, 352; "Battle of Two Cultures," 5
Lenin, Vladimir, 47, 66, 116, 273, 388n41
Leninist Young Communist League of Ukraine (LKSMU). *See* Komsomol
Likarchuk, Ihor, 373n15, 376n7
literature: collectivization and, 249; in ethnic-minority schools, 99; Five-Year Plan and, 249; "harmful," 338; industrialization in, 249; for Jewish schools, 99; Komsomol and, 180, 196; pedagogical, 110, 111, 120, 130, 279, 319; in Russian language, 64; shortage of children's, 108; Young Pioneers and, 180, 184, 191, 285, 292, 295. *See also* textbooks
Liubchenko, Panas, 332–3
Lobanov, Mykhailo, 149
Lobanov, Volodymyr, 326
local studies: about, 52; and building socialism, 113–14; Central (All-Union) Bureau of Local Studies, 374n45; complex method and, 43, 52, 53, 55, 114, 118–19; in curriculum, 53; decentralization and, 113; and excursions, 54–5; institutional

oversight of, 55; museums, 57;
Narkomos and, 23, 55, 58, 104,
112–13; and national identity, 44;
and nationalism, 23; native-language
instruction and, 124; and production,
112, 116–17, 340; progressive
pedagogy and, 22; project method in,
318; regional planning commissions,
55; in rural schools, 53–4; school
centres, 57–8; and self-discovery, 52;
and standardization of instructional
content, 55–6; teachers and, 52–3, 57,
112–13, 114, 313; and textbooks, 43,
53, 55–6, 57; and Ukrainization, 58,
105; urban children and, 53
Lubny, Komsomol in, 245
Luhansk: Komsomol in, 244; SVU in,
263; Ukrainian culture month in, 307;
Ukrainization of children's institutions
in, 80–1
Lukashenko, Petro: and books/textbooks,
164; and complex method, 125; and
Durdukivsky, 173; on enrolment in
Russian schools, 155; and *perevirky*,
136–7, 138; and Russian-language
schools, 124–5; and Russian- vs
Ukrainian-language schools, 146; and
teachers' Ukrainian studies, 163; on
Ukrainization of schools, 145–6; and
white-collar Russophilism, 146; on
working-class children, 161–2
Lunacharsky, Anatolii, 82, 160, 240
Lykhansky, Andrii, 331–2
Lypkivsky, Vasyl, 355
Lypsky, Volodymyr, 273

Maibutnia zmina, 195–6
Makerevych, M., 91–2
Makhno, Nestor, 66, 269
Maksymovych, Karlo, 167, 353

Matushevsky, Boris, 258
Matusivka Sugar Refinery Labour
School, 79
methodological committees: local, 53, 57,
101, 114, 312; Narkomos central, 103,
322; in Odesa, 215–16, 222
Mizernytsky, Oleksandr, 76, 377n39
Moldovan children: in Russian schools, 210
Moldovan schools: native-language
literature in, 99; percentage of, 210
Moloda kuznytsia, 184
Molodniak, 198, 391n62
Molodniak, 196
Molodyi Bilshovyk, 187
Molodyk, Mykola, 410n6
Muzychka, Andrii, 273
Mykolaiv: counter-revolutionary activity
in, 246; Labour School No. 15, 147–8,
150–1, 155; Labour School No. 28,
125–8, 130; progressive pedagogy
in, 106; Russian native-language
instruction in, 335; Ukrainian-
language teachers in schools in,
312–13; Ukrainian political schools in,
196; Ukrainization in, 102, 106
Mylovydov, Lev, 318
Myronivka: District Labour School, 57,
119, 120; hostel for children, 162

Na fronti kultury (Narkomos), 333–5,
336, 338
Narkomos: Central Scientific
Methodological Committee, 103;
and children's buildings, 23, 107; and
homeless children, 46; Hubpolitosvita,
216, 217, 222, 226, 229; and
locally centred texts, 43; *Na fronti
kultury*, 333–5, 336, 338; naming of
schools, 172; in Odesa, 202–3, 208,
210; Organizational-Instructional

Committee, 330; purge of, 304, 316–17, 331–2, 334–5, 337; and *Radianska osvita,* 110; records, 4; reorganization of, 316–17, 333, 334–5
Narkomos and Ukrainian language/Ukrainization: and Agitprop, 102–3; census data as guideline for progress, 28; chief responsibility in, 75–6; and correctness/standardization of language, 18, 65, 204; decentralization to local education sections, 341; of employees, 70; and ethnic-Ukrainian children in Ukrainian-language schools, 22, 323–4; goals/targets, 8, 163, 211; instruction in, 63, 80; KP(b)U and, 341; and nationalism, 330–1; network of Ukrainized schools, 67; Odesa commission, 203–4, 211; orthography commission, 30, 171–2; and primary schools, 85; program for teachers, 163–4; Radnarkom and, 68, 101; at secondary/post-secondary levels, 203–4, 322–3; self-identification of Ukrainians and, 29; and socialism, 18; soft- vs hard-line, 17; and state establishments, 323; and teachers, 76–9; and Ukrainian as primary language of communication, 100; and Ukrainian-language schools abroad, 100–101; and Ukrainian-language self-study groups, 70; and Ukrainian studies, 58; and Ukrainian-studies courses, 86–7; and urban–rural union, 18; VUTsVK and aggressive program, 94–5; and working class, 146–7, 161
Narkompros (RSFSR): and civil war children, 24; and complex method, 51; and Russian school system, 47; and vocational schooling, 48

Narodnii uchytel: cessation of publication, 319; change of title to *Za kulturnu revoliutsiuu,* 255; on employee Ukrainian courses, 135; grouping of counter-revolutionary teachers, 278; launch of, 110; Narkomos and, 130; on *perevirky,* 136; punishment of manager for rightist brochure, 321; on teachers' attitudes toward Ukrainian language/Ukrainization, 169, 170
nationalism: and anti-Semitism, 236, 247; anti-Soviet attitudes and, 290; children and, 237, 240, 262, 289, 291; in cities, 168–9; civil war and, 168; class and, 256, 260, 297, 300; cultural revolution and, 235, 240; exo-socialization and, 367n25; GPU and, 277; grain requisition and, 290; growth of, 167–8; intelligentsia and, 154, 169, 173, 274; Komsomol and, 35, 179; KP(b)U and, 10, 167–8; kulaks and, 168, 245, 278; local studies and, 23; mandatory enrolment and, 282; modernist, 168–9; and national identity, 28; and nationalities policy, 297; NEPmen and, 243; peasantry and, 5, 140, 154, 168, 169, 278; progressive education and, 236; Prosvita and, 365n10; Robos and, 241; rural activism and, 245–6; in rural schools, 236; Soviet education vs, 288; SVU affair and, 38, 238, 277; teachers and, 36, 37–8, 169, 204, 225, 236, 237, 240, 242–4, 247, 253, 260, 342–3; Ukrainian language and, 153; Ukrainian-language literature and, 249; Ukrainian orthography and, 368–9n40; Ukrainization and, 154, 168, 225, 304, 330–1, 334; in villages, 168, 169; P. Yefremov and, 268; Young

Pioneers and, 179, 284, 290, 291; youth and, 40, 262, 268, 270, 276–7
nationalities policy: about, 3–4; and affirmative action, 361n10; anti-Semitism and, 249–50; and cultural revolution, 16, 313–14; education and, 15, 17; ethnic homogeneous schools and, 363n20; and industrial workers, 152; Jews and, 29; Komsomol and, 33, 35, 174, 179, 188–9; KP(b)U and Ukrainization of proletariat, 138–9; local aspects of, 3–4, 10; nationalism and, 297; native languages and, 220, 325–6; Odesa and, 205–6, 207; place and, 16, 205; polytechnization and, 328; primary schools and, 4; repression of 1930s and, 32; Robos and, 241, 242–3; schools and, 11; and *smychka*, 66; in Soviet Union, 3–4; SVU and, 37, 237, 320; teachers and, 74, 170, 202, 242–3, 256, 257; Ukrainian objectives, 5–7; Ukrainization and, 336–7, 347; Ukrainization of proletariat and, 305; Young Pioneers and, 33, 35, 174, 175, 176, 182
national minorities. *See* ethnic minorities
native-language instruction: children's right to, 71, 86; and complex method, 83, 106, 126; and grouping in schools, 20; and *kraieznavstvo*, 124; literature shortage, 84, 99; Narkomos and, 9, 99, 328; and national culture, 325–6; and national identity, 346; nationalities policy and, 17–18; percentage of non-attendees, 89; and political ideology, 83–4
Na zminu, 298
Nevira, Kh., 90
New Economic Policy (NEP), 107, 168, 239, 395n2

Nizhyn, teacher retraining in, 111
Nuzhny, Vasyl, 134

Ocherki obschchestvovedeniia (Essays on social studies; Volfson), 55, 56
October Revolution: complex on, 115–16; and education, 44
Odesa: about, 13; Bureau of Examination of the Ukrainian Text of Local Literature, 339; centralization of education in, 315–16; children's buildings in, 201, 210; ethnicity in, 210, 228; ethnic Ukrainians in, 200; government employees in, 202; GPU and, 13; higher-education students in, 275; Hubpolitosvita, 222; identity myth, 200, 205–6; intelligentsia in, 13, 171, 172, 272–7; Jews in, 207; KP(b)U in, 203, 220–2, 229–30; location, 205; Narkomos and, 202–3, 208, 224–8; nationalism in, 171; and nationality, 205–6; parents in, 207, 209, 210–11; peasant migration to, 200; *perevirky* in, 201; professional-school students in, 228; protests in, 275–7; Provincial Commission on the Equality of Languages, 210, 222–3; regional education section, 135, 207, 225; Regional Ukrainization Commission, 138, 172, 218, 221, 222, 223; Russian language in, 201, 202, 210, 219; Russian-language schooling in, 210–11, 233, 326; Russian-speaking population in, 89, 207; Russification in, 228; Scientific Society, 272–3; SVU in, 13, 272–7, 273, 276, 277; teachers and Ukrainian language in, 225–6; teachers' Ukrainian-studies examinations in, 212–13, 214–15, 231–3; Ukrainian-language

literature in, 207–8; Ukrainian language of village vs city teachers in, 135; Ukrainian-language schooling in, 67, 69, 71, 201, 210–12, 227, 228; Ukrainian-language teachers in, 70; Ukrainian-language textbooks in, 224–5; Ukrainian population, 206–7; Ukrainian studies in, 215–17; Ukrainization commissions in, 220; Ukrainization in, 13, 65, 94–5, 102, 103, 130, 172, 200–201, 202–6, 207–31, 233–4, 276, 337–9; VUAN Commission of Kraieznavstvo in, 55; workers' faculties in, 228; Young Pioneers in, 293

Odesa (city): about, 13, 200, 205–6; Agricultural Institute, 227–8; children's colony in, 210; Institute of Public Education (INO), 216, 223–4, 227–8, 275, 276–7; Labour School No. 5, 212–13; Labour School No. 67, 212–13; policy on state Ukrainization courses, 338; Russian native-language instruction in, 335; ties with countryside and region, 205; Ukrainian political schools in, 196

Osmolovsky, Mykola, 77–8

parents: and children's native language, 157; choice of language of instruction, 154–5, 336, 345; and de-Ukrainization of schools, 227; and formal knowledge, 24, 117–18; in Odesa, 207, 209, 210–11; and Russian-language schools, 146, 148; of Russified Ukrainian children, 336, 341; state as, 23–4; and Ukrainian-language schools, 145, 146, 210–11; and Ukrainian national culture, 204–5; and Ukrainization, 133, 147, 148, 207, 209

Parkhurst, Ellen, 46
Pavlov, Ivan, 45
Pavlushkov, Mykola, 258
Pavlyshyn, Mykhailo, 322, 323
peasantry: and Bolsheviks, 66; civil war and, 66; and collectivization, 239, 246; Communist Party and, 5, 67; and grain requisition, 246, 256; and Greens, 66; and industry, 140; Komsomol and, 176; and kulaks, 140, 279; migration to cities, 200, 346–7; and national culture, 144; and nationalism, 5, 140, 154, 168, 278; October Revolution complex and, 116; poor vs rich, 73; proletariat and, 66, 140; and Red Army, 5; and Russian language, 139, 361n9; socialism building by, 75; teachers and, 170, 242, 246; and Ukrainian language, 67, 131, 134, 139–40, 155, 185, 220–1; Ukrainization and, 67, 69, 214–15. *See also* kulaks

pedagogical literature: educational reform in, 319; teachers and, 110, 111, 120, 279; in Ukrainian language, 130

pedagogical technical colleges. *See* technical colleges

Pelekh, Yosyp, 329

perevirky. *See* examinations *(perevirky)*

Petliura, Symon, 73, 261, 355–6, 399n73

Petliurism/*petliurovshchina*, 115, 140, 225, 226, 245, 258, 260, 269, 331

Petrovsky, Hryhorii, 81, 353

Piven, Vasyl, 324, 327

Podillia: inspectors in, 87; teacher transfers in, 77–9; Ukrainian-language schools in, 71; Ukrainian-language teacher training in, 92; Ukrainization of education section in, 69

Podolsky, Josyp, 147–8

Pohozha–Krynytsia Labour School, 88

Polish children: religious organizations, 187; schooling of, 326; in Ukrainian schools, 326; in Ukrainizing school, 29
Polish schools: literature for, 99; Ukrainian-language schools mixed, 404n14; Ukrainian-language teachers for, 70
Politekhnychna shkola, 319
political schools: Komsomol and, 178, 183–4, 196; purpose of, 198; Ukrainization of, 193, 194, 196
Politnavchannia komsomoltsia, 196
Polotsky, Oleksandr, 317
Poltava: inspectors in, 101–2; Pohozha-Krynytsia labour school, 88; teacher transfers, 76; Ukrainization in, 101–2; Young Pioneers in, 290–1
Polubotko, O., 82–4
polytechnization: of education, 303, 304–5; grain requisition and, 328; in labour schools, 315; and nationalities policy, 328; national-minority schools and, 328; Russian, 315; Russian-language students and, 328; of schools, 283, 292–3, 317; and textbooks, 324
Pomahaiba, Vasyl, 319–20
Poradnyk sotsiialnoho vykhovannia (Handbook for social upbringing), 48–9, 56, 117, 261, 373n25
post-secondary education: anti-Semitism in, 247; ethnic Ukrainians in, 269–70; institutions in, 379n13; Narkomos and, 322–3; in Odesa, 227–8; Russian-language instruction in, 201, 344; Ukrainian-language instruction in, 209; Ukrainization in, 304, 313–14, 322; Ukrainized schools in, 227–8; VUZy, 230–1. *See also* INOs; technical colleges
post-secondary students: arrests of, 258; in Odesa, 275; and SVU defendants, 277; taking Ukrainization to villages, 203–4; ties of educators with, 275; in villages, 203–4
Postyshev, Pavel, 332, 334–5
primary schools. *See* labour schools; schools
production: complexes and, 107; in education, 53, 54; *kraieznavstvo* and, 340; and local studies, 112, 116–17; secondary schools and, 368n29
Profatylov, Ilko, 328, 329–30
progressive pedagogy: about, 42–3; Bolsheviks and, 42; centralization of education and, 320; and children as activists, 296; and civic education, 84; class enemies and, 105; Communist Party and, 227; conservative vs, 303, 347; cultural revolution and, 62, 235; and curriculum, 15–16; and excursions, 83; in Fastiv District Labour School, 109–10; and grouping in schools, 20; and labour culture, 9, 15, 43; language and, 340; linguistic Ukrainization and, 45; model schools for, 56–7; and nationalism, 236; political fear of, 38; reasons for support of, 22; religious education vs, 94; and rural–urban divide, 21, 105; in Skvyra District Labour School, 110; and socialism, 236; socialization and, 362n13; Soviet education and, 293; SVU defendants and, 303; teachers and, 4, 104–5, 110, 320; and textbooks, 225; and transformation, 61–2; Ukrainian-language instruction and, 64, 82–3, 123, 190; and Ukrainization, 7–10, 9, 21, 23, 38, 105–6, 302, 303, 315, 341, 347; and vocational schools, 9. *See also* complex method; local studies

project method, 317–18, 320. *See also* complex method
proletariat. *See* working class
Proletkult, 217
Promin, 57
Prosvita, 19
Prykhodko, Antin T., 380n26, 396n61
Pryluky: FZU schools in, 197; Komsomol in, 194; Russian language in, 197; Ukrainization in, 194
Prysiazhniuk, Ivan, 309
public servants. *See* government employees

Radianska osvita, 52, 110
Radnarkom: about, 11; Commission on Ukrainization, 380n26; equality of languages decree, 101; Hrynko as head of, 141; and Narkomos, 101; orthographic commission, 26–7; and Ukrainian-language literature, 70, 88; and Ukrainization, 68, 101, 208; Ukrainization commission, 11, 163; Ukrainization decree, 68, 77; Zatonsky and, 357
Red Army, 5, 66, 265, 326
reflexology, 45
religious education, 94
Revoliutsiia na Ukraini (Revolution in Ukraine; Yavorsky), 56
Riappo, Jan, 46, 47, 48, 49, 51, 103, 110; "The Year of Ukrainization in School Affairs," 88–9
robfaky, 97, 380n38
Robos: about, 63–4; All-Ukrainian Committee (VUK), 250; and anti-Semitism, 236, 247; appeals/petitions from charged teachers, 253–4, 256; blamed for teachers' *perevirky* difficulties, 311; and cultural revolution, 236; educator/activists vs intellectuals in, 262–3; and intelligentsia, 259, 262–3; and *Narodnii uchytel,* 110; and nationalism, 241; and nationalities policy, 241, 242–3; and *perevirky,* 137; self-purging, 250, 260; and SVU, 259, 260; and teacher commitment to socialism, 63–4; and teachers' professional identity, 74; and Ukrainian vs Russian languages, 96; and Ukrainization, 248, 308
RSI (Workers' and Peasants' Inspectorate), 201, 203, 208, 222–3, 253–4, 302, 323
Rubinsky, Fedor, 195
Rudnytsky, Stepan, 56
rural areas: intelligentsia in, 295; Komsomol in, 174, 295; school attendance in, 189–90; Ukrainian language in, 12; Ukrainization in, 12; Young Pioneers in, 293. *See also* peasantry; villages
rural schools/teachers: and collectivization, 238, 255, 256, 257, 278, 280; complex method and, 49, 53; conditions, 50, 304, 324; enrolment and, 8; famine and, 24, 304; GPU on, 242; and grain requisition, 36, 255, 256, 278, 279–80, 296, 329; *kraieznavstvo* and, 53–4; nationalism and, 236; and progressive pedagogy, 105; and Russian language, 170; teacher shortages, 105; textbooks, 84; Ukrainian-language instruction, 89, 95; and Ukrainian-language literature, 89; Ukrainization and, 35–6, 105, 191; and urban schools, 54, 117
rural–urban relationship: and Komsomol, 193; labour solidarity, 202; progressive

pedagogy and, 21; and Ukrainian language in Young Pioneers, 198; Ukrainization and, 5, 12

Russian language: centralization of education and, 320; in children's buildings, 210; in cities, 8, 126, 152–3; Communist Party and, 30, 86; in Donbas, 307; ethnic minorities and, 99; and ethnic-minority children, 95; ethnic-minority languages vs, 32; extracurricular use of, 90, 410n5; FZU schools and, 197; influence of, 129–30; Jews and, 98, 381n44; Komsomol and, 144, 175; migration of ethnic Ukrainians to city and, 204; Narkomos and, 97–8, 100, 145; as native language, 157; and native-language instruction for schoolchildren, 86; in non-Russian schools, 409n127; peasantry and, 139, 361n9; in primary schools, 86, 90; privileging/prestige of, 6, 85, 97–8, 99, 152, 157, 346–7; publications in, 64; reform of, 29; rural teachers and, 170; schoolchildren and, 64, 68, 70–1, 81, 126; schooled literacy and, 15, 19, 131; state employees and, 323; teachers and, 8, 64, 69, 71, 82, 125, 130, 136, 204; Ukrainian language borrowings from, 27, 131; Ukrainian language vs, 18, 20, 29–30, 129, 160, 219, 226; Ukrainization and, 161; urban population and, 152–3; in urban schools, 95–6, 106; working class and, 155–6, 178, 191, 192, 219, 371n48; Young Pioneers and, 8, 90, 145, 174, 180, 181, 184, 283, 297

Russian-language instruction: complexes and, 125; as default, 209; ethnic Russians and, 151; in Odesan schools, 211; in post-secondary education, 201, 344; for Russified Ukrainian children, 158; in secondary education, 201; Ukrainian vs, 126

Russian-language schools: enrolment in, 326–7; ethnic-minority children in, 210; ethnic-Russian children and, 326, 335–6; ethnic-Ukrainian children in, 210, 212, 301, 308, 327; Jewish children in, 98, 99, 155, 370n46; numbers of, 326, 336; numbers of Ukrainian children in, 155; parents and, 146, 148; persistence of, 129–30; polytechnization and, 328; as preference, 133; Ukrainian-language schools mixed, 309; and Ukrainization, 91, 212; white-collar workers and, 146

Russians, ethnic: children, 160, 326, 335–6, 341; forced Ukrainization of, 305; intelligentsia and Ukrainization, 156–7; in Kyiv, 161; and Russian-language instruction, 151; Russified Ukrainians vs, 149, 203, 220; Ukrainization of, 147, 154

Russian State Academic Council, 48

Russification: meaning of, 364n29; as policy, 410n5; and Ukrainization, 226, 228

Russified-Ukrainian children: enrolment of, 297; native language of, 152; and pace of Ukrainization, 129; Russian-language instruction for, 158; Ukrainian-language instruction for, 33, 146, 154–5, 162; Ukrainian-speaking, 158; Ukrainization of, 151, 152, 341

Russified Ukrainians: ethnic Russians vs, 149, 203, 220; intelligentsia, 156–7; Komsomol and youth, 183; KP(b)U and, 183; KP(B)U and, 138; and "Little Russian," 369n42; meaning of, 133; as Russian vs Ukrainian, 28–9; and Ukrainian language, 28, 155, 203; Ukrainization of, 16, 147, 183; working class, 305

Rynda, Nadia, 298

Sapukhin, Pavlo, 92–3; "Ukrainization: 'Ichthyosaurs' of the Modern School," 82

schooled literacy: about, 19; *perevirky* and, 131, 201; and Russian language, 15, 19; teachers and, 131, 132, 201; in Ukrainian, 3, 131, 132; Ukrainization and, 19–20; and working-class children, 153

schools: civil war and, 46; conditions of, 108, 110, 341; day of rest, 122–3; libraries, 108, 120; nationalities policy and, 4, 11; network of, 42; "new," 44–5; polytechnization of, 283, 292–3; structure of, 24, 39, 47, 48, 74; and transformation, 21; in Ukraine vs Russia, 24, 47

Scientific Pedagogical Society (NPT), 260, 261

secondary education/schools: general vs vocational education and, 47; Holovprofos, 97; numbers of Ukrainized, 143; in Odesa, 227–8; Russian-language instruction in, 201; and socialist economy, 368n29; trade schools vs, 368n29; in Ukraine vs Russia, 47–8; Ukrainian-language instruction in, 209; Ukrainization of, 304, 322; Ukrainized schools, 227–8. *See also* vocational schools

Sektor sotsvykhu, 316, 325. *See also* Holovsotsvykh; Uprsotsvykh

Semenovych, Petro, 136

Shatskii, Stanislav, 21

Shevchenko, Taras: complex on, 60–1, 110, 115, 123–4; *Kobzar,* 375n71; nationalism and, 58, 262; and Ukrainian language, 93, 313

Shevchenko Scientific Society, 25

ShKM (School for Collective Farm Youth), 315

Shliakh osvity, 45, 319

Shulgin, Viktor, 317–18, 320

Shumeiko, Hanna, 299–300

Shumsky, Oleksandr, 111f; on anti-Soviet elements in Ukrainization, 165, 167; biography, 353, 357; and ethnicity, 132; KP(b)U and, 142–3; and "Little Russian," 369n42; Mizernytsky and, 377n39; and nationalism, 241, 243; ousting of, 10; on parental wishes regarding education, 386n1; and peasantry, 139–40; and *perevirky,* 132–3; and progressive pedagogy, 106; and proletariat, 139–40; on Radnarkom orthographic commission, 26; and rural teachers, 50; and Stalin, 141, 142–3; and teachers, 121; and Ukrainization, 7, 68, 141, 143, 153–4

Skakodub, Uliana, 298

Skoropadsky, Pavlo, 26, 115, 355–6

Skrypnyk, Mykola, 150f; on attendance of Ukrainian children, 162, 309, 310; biography, 354; on complex method, 320; on determination of child's native language, 157; dismissal as education commisar, 304, 332; fall of, 27, 332–3; and forced Ukrainization, 157–8, 305; on grain procurement and polytechnization, 328; on halting of Russification, 154–5; on kulaks' children's education, 403n2; and

Narkomos program for teachers and Ukrainization, 163; and nationalism, 332, 333, 334, 338; orthography standardization under, 27, 338; and progressive pedagogy, 303; and Radnarkom orthographic commission, 26; and Russian population, 151; as Shumsky's replacement, 143; on social upbringing, 318; Stalin's views and, 10; suicide, 304, 333; on SVU, 262; and textbooks, 406n58; on Ukrainian as language of Russified Ukrainians, 28, 152; and Ukrainian extension beyond borders, 380n40; and Ukrainian Narkomos, 240; and Ukrainization, 7, 17, 38, 357; and Ukrainization in Donbas, 307; and unified all-Union education, 39, 302–3, 314, 316, 317; and universal primary schooling, 316; vilification of, 304

Skvyra District Labour School, 110

Slabchenko, Mykhailo, 273, 276, 277, 354

Slabchenko, Taras, 273, 276, 277

smychka, 18, 66, 67, 117

socialism: children and building of, 74, 75; civic education and building of, 115; complex method and, 116, 117; education and, 293, 323; educators and building of, 257, 259, 260; ethnic-minority teachers and, 99; industrial education and, 62; industrialization and, 386n56; *kraieznavstvo* and, 113–14; national culture and, 3; national identity and, 3; native languages and, 8; normalization of education and, 104; peasantry and building of, 75; progressive education and, 236; schools and, 22, 110; *smychka* and, 18; social studies and, 114; teachers and, 3, 63–4, 73–4, 121, 279, 310; Ukrainian-language schooling and, 9; Ukrainization and, 3, 4, 67, 301; Young Pioneers and, 175; youth and, 268

social studies, 58, 114, 116–17, 127, 128

social upbringing: children's buildings and, 46–7; civil war and, 107; complex method and, 114–15; Narkomos and, 107; and schools, 107; Skrypnyk on, 318

Society of Unity and Concord (TIeZ), 262, 269–70

Sokolianskyi, Ivan, 396n61, 408n114

Stalin, Joseph: and cultural revolution, 9, 10–11, 235; and ethnicity, 132; on forced Ukrainization of proletariat, 146–7; Great Turn, 249; "revolution from above," 238–9; Shumsky and, 141, 143; and SVU show trial, 258; and Ukrainian-ethnic elite, 142; and Ukrainization, 6, 7, 10, 141

Stalino: Selydove school, 260; Ukrainian language/culture in, 308; Ukrainian political schools in, 196

state employees. *See* government employees

Stodolia, Pavlo, 76, 77

subject area instruction, 127, 319

Sukhov, Oleksandr, *Ekonomichna heohrafiia Ukrainy* (Economic geography of Ukraine), 56

SUM (Union of Ukrainian Youth), 262, 264, 403n12

SVU (Union for the Liberation of Ukraine): about, 236–7, 258; and anti-Semitism, 263, 399n73; class struggle and, 257; as counter-revolutionary, 263; creation of, 257, 258, 276; GPU and, 37, 273; intelligentsia and, 10, 258, 272, 273–4; interrogation files, 266–72; in Kyiv Labour School No. 1, 267; and nationalism, 38, 238; in Odesa, 13, 273, 276, 277; Robos condemnation of, 260; "school group" of, 261; SUM and, 40; and Ukrainization, 31, 237–8; Ukrainization and formation of, 263–4; and VUAN, 264; and youth, 261, 262, 267, 270–1

SVU show trial, 259f; about, 258–9; and asymmetric terror, 314; and educational reform, 319; and intelligentsia, 258–9, 276, 295, 343; KP(b)U and, 264, 266; and nationalism, 277; and nationalities policy, 320; in Odesa, 272–7; progressive educators and, 62, 303; purges of teachers after, 36; reasons for, 265–6; Robos and, 259; and Ukrainian-language teachers, 258–9; and Ukrainization, 37–8, 263–4, 271–2, 343; and youth, 268

Syniavsky, Oleksa, 171, 354

teachers: Bolsheviks and, 72; and child activism, 299; civil war and, 72–3; and class, 255, 279, 294, 299; Communist Party and, 4–5, 154; conditions of, 24, 50, 87; earnings, 165, 171, 242; Five-Year Plan and, 294, 311; and intelligentsia, 50, 74, 171; intergenerational cohesion with students, 237; murders of, 279; neutrality/passivity of, 236, 242, 255, 314; pedagogical literature for, 110, 111, 120, 279; political activity, 50, 154, 237, 243–4, 246, 255, 278, 294; public activities/work by, 252, 253, 255–6; qualifications, 84, 92, 121, 190; Robos and, 63–64; rural (*see* rural schools/teachers); and Ukrainian studies, 91, 93, 125, 313

teachers and Ukrainian language/ Ukrainization, 166f; ability/knowledge in, 12, 30, 91, 125, 134–5, 154, 157, 169–70, 190, 225–6, 309–13, 341; examinations/*perevirky* in, 85, 86, 164, 207, 212–13, 214–15, 225–6, 309–13; GPU and, 237, 241–2; and illiteracy eradication, 170; as instructors in Ukrainian language/ studies, 102, 138, 171, 215–16, 217; and lack of literature, 87–8; Narkomos and program for, 163–4; and new pedagogy, 24; in non-Ukrainian-instruction schools, 70; numbers in rural communities, 89; in Odesa, 201, 204, 207, 225–6; opposition to, 79–80, 145, 169; at post-secondary level, 209; progressive pedagogy and, 341; qualifications for, 12, 208–9, 216, 341; relocation of, 76–9; resistance in, 212; responsibility for success of, 3, 8–9, 91, 101–2; in rural vs urban schools, 74; in secondary school, 209; self-study, 153, 163–4; shortage of, 69, 85, 190, 209, 307; and standardization of Ukrainian, 27; study groups, 212; SVU and, 237–8; training/retraining in, 82, 91–2, 109, 110–13, 114, 131, 153, 307, 324–5; and Ukrainian-language schools in RSFSR, 100

technical colleges, 97, 185, 227, 317, 322, 356, 379n13; pedagogical technical colleges, 89, 136, 190, 260–1, 285, 325

Teslenko, Arkhyp, "Shkoliar" (The pupil), 83

textbooks: adaptation of technical works as, 55–6; for city vs rural schools, 84; complex method and, 51, 120, 124;

ethnic-minority, 99; Institute of the Ukrainian Scientific Language and, 26; lack of Ukrainian-language, 50; local studies and, 43, 53, 55–6, 57, 84; paper shortage and, 406n74; progressive pedagogy and, 225; publication abroad, 45; shift to more conservative education and, 297, 406n58; shortages, 55–6, 99, 120; teachers and, 51, 56, 124; and Ukrainian language instruction, 81
trade unions, 141, 149, 307–8. *See also* Robos
Trezvynsky, Yurii, 60–1, 266, 267, 268–70, 271, 272
Tytarenko, Pavlo, 328

UKP (Ukrainian Communist Party), 183, 354–5
Ukraina, 244
Ukrainian Autocephalous Orthodox Church, 165, 171, 258, 355
Ukrainian children, ethnic: from Czechoslovakia, 96–7; enrolment of, 153, 161–2, 288; living outside UkrSSR, 86; in national-minority schools, 327; in non-Ukrainian schools, 159; from Poland, 96–7; in Russian-language schools, 68–9, 210, 212, 308, 327; in secondary vocational schools, 269; Ukrainian as native language for all, 340; Ukrainian-language instruction and, 69, 80, 130; and Ukrainian-language schools, 22, 70–1, 145–6, 323–4; Ukrainization and, 95; working-class backgrounds, 153; Young Pioneers and, 178, 181
Ukrainian language: attitudes toward, 19, 85, 88, 155, 226; borrowings in, 26–7, 30, 131; correctness/purity of, 27, 131, 134, 204, 338–9; dictionaries, 26; funding for use of, 6; higher education institutions and, 143; orthography, 135, 171–2, 338–9; as primary language of communication, 86, 100; resistance to, 202; rural vs urban environments and uses, 7–8, 30–1; Russian language vs, 18, 20, 27, 29–30, 129, 131, 160, 219, 226; Russified Ukrainians and, 203; standardization of, 25–7, 29–30; under tsarism, 66
Ukrainian-language instruction: expansion of, 81; and labour culture, 123; in pedagogical colleges, 89; prioritization of conversion to, 63; in secondary schools, 209; spoken languages vs, 129, 130; and transformation, 64; and writing skills, 128–9
Ukrainian-language literature: alphabet books, 207; instructional, 11; Komsomol and, 196; lack of, 85, 87–8, 135; and nationalism, 249; in Odesa, 207–8; in primary schools, 89; Radnarkom and, 70; shortages, 124, 164, 324; textbooks, 99, 164, 209, 224–5, 324; under tsarism, 66; and Ukrainian-language schools in RSFSR, 100; Young Pioneers and, 180, 184, 191
Ukrainian-language schools/schooling: abroad, 100–101; and academic achievement, 126–7, 130; civil war and, 64, 68; ethnicity and number of, 162; extracurricular use of Ukrainian in, 90; gymnasia, 94; and national identity, 28, 29; numbers of, 4, 143, 208, 304, 336; overcrowding of, 321; Polish-language schools mixed with, 404n14; popular pressure for, 93–4; at post-secondary level, 209;

in primary schools, 68–71; quality of education in, 7–8, 320, 343–4; in RSFSR, 100; rural vs urban, 130; Russian-language schools mixed with, 309, 327; Russification of, 336; secondary, 143; socialization and, 362n13; Yiddish-language schools mixed with, 404n14

Ukrainian Party of Socialist Revolutionaries (SRs), *See* Borotbist party

Ukrainian People's Republic: about, 13, 93; Soviet understanding of, 73, 93; intelligentsia/teachers and 224, 241; GPU repression of former UNR supporters, 258, 265

Ukrainian Social Democratic Workers' Party, 240, 351, 355

Ukrainian studies: about, 32; complex method and, 61, 105, 113–14; and curriculum, 52; in Dnipropetrovsk, 193; and ethnic-minority schools, 58; examinations in, 212–13, 214–15; Five-Year Plan and, 329; full school enrolment and, 297; and government employees, 86–7, 203, 222–3, 248, 323; in Kharkiv, 193–4; Komsomol and, 178, 183–4, 195, 196; KP(b)U and, 84, 230; Narkomos and, 58; in Odesa, 215–17; *perevirky* and, 93; Shevchenko and, 61; teachers and, 91, 93, 125, 212, 213–16, 217, 225–6, 313

Ukrainians, ethnic: in Donbas, 308–9; identification of, 16, 28–9, 220–1; in Komsomol, 188, 194–5; in KP(b)U, 220–1; in Kyiv, 146; migration to cities, 204; and number of Ukrainian primary schools, 160–1; in Odesa, 200, 204, 228; party members and Ukrainian language, 203; percentage of population, 68; in post-secondary institutions, 269–70; in RSFSR, 77–8; teachers and Ukrainian language, 82; Ukrainian language and, 16; Ukrainian-language instruction for, 63, 158–9, 207; and Ukrainization, 156–7, 192, 344–5

Ukrainization: about, 90–1, 125; anti-Soviet elements in, 165; arrests and support for, 302; authority and, 176; Bolshevik, 297, 301, 305, 326, 329, 335, 339; Bolsheviks and, 85; complete vs incomplete, 31, 37, 161, 176, 204, 344; comprehensive, 371n48; and cultural advancement, 67; decentralization of, 7, 64; in early 1930s, 321–5, 347; and legitimacy of UkrSSR, 96; limits of, 6, 68, 142; non-Bolshevik policy of, 271–2; place and, 205; political purpose, 214–15; Radnarkom and, 101, 208; regional context of, 12–13; republican vs local institutions defining, 11; resistance to, 204, 209–10, 217–18, 223, 226–7, 229; selective approach to, 96; and *smychka*, 67; and social transformation, 4–5, 6; soft- vs hard-line, 17, 175; Soviet education and, 293; Stalin and, 6, 7, 10, 141; sucesses of, 334, 344–5; targets for, 95–6, 163; Ukrainians from abroad and, 96. *See also* forced Ukrainization

Ukrliknep: about, 11; design of Ukrainian-studies courses, 216; and Holovsotsvykh curriculum, 222; and Komsomol youth, 184; and *perevirky*, 379–80n26; teachers as Ukrainian-studies teachers under, 171; and teachers' correspondence courses, 163;

Ukrainian-studies courses for state employees, 86–7
Uprsotsvykh: and complex method, 114, 115–16, 118, 123–4, 127, 128; and native-language instruction, 158; renamed Sektor sotsvykhu, 316; and Ukrainization, 148, 321. *See also* Holovsotsvykh; Sektor sotsvykhu
urban–rural relationship. *See* rural–urban relationship
urban schools: affiliation with rural schools, 117; progressive pedagogy in, 105; relationship with city, 75; rural schools and, 54; Russian language in, 95–6, 106; textbooks for, 84; Ukrainization in, 105, 106

Vasylkiv District Labour School, 114, 124
villages: nationalism in, 168, 169; and Russian vs Ukrainian cultures, 139; youth Ukrainization assignments in, 203–4, 224. *See also* rural areas
Vinnytsia: FZU schools in, 197; Jewish children in, 380–1n41; Jewish children in Russian schools, 370n46; Komsomol in, 194; national-minority schools in, 325; Russian language in, 197; Ukrainization in, 192
Vinnytsia, 247, 250
Visti VUTsVK, 87, 216, 247
VKP(b) (All-Union Communist Party), 141; and campaign against non-party educators, 10; and collectivization, 239; and intelligentsia, 7, 265; and KP(b)U, 10; and nationalities policy, 10; Politburo and show trial, 258; and polytechnization of education, 303; and universal enrolment, 321
Vnykov, Tykhon, 326

Voblyi, Konstantin, *Ekonomichna heohrafiia Ukrainy* (Economic geography of Ukraine), 56
vocational schools: about, 47; complex method and, 51; creation of, 24; elimination of, 9; ethnic-Ukrainian children in, 269; and labour culture, 24; labour schools and, 122, 303, 315; primary school curricula and, 48; progressive education and, 9; as technical colleges, 317. *See also* FZU schools
Volfson, Miron: *Ocherki obschchestvovedeniia* (Essays on social studies), 55, 56
Volobuiev, Mykhailo, 241, 243, 317, 356
Volyn: provincial congress for teacher retraining, 124; teacher retraining in, 112; Ukrainian-language schools in, 71
Vovchenko, Ivan, 80
VUAN (All-Ukrainian Academy of Sciences): about, 13; Kraieznavstvo Commission, 55, 56, 96, 172; and orthographic commission, 25–6; and standardization of language, 226; and SVU, 264; and terminology for Ukrainization, 223; and Ukrainian language, 19; and youth, 264
VUTsVK (All-Ukrainian Central Executive Committee): TsKNM (Central Committee for National Minorities), 147, 149; and Ukrainian language, 65; and Ukrainian-language literature/libraries, 88; and Ukrainization, 64–5, 67, 68, 69, 77, 94; and universal enrolment, 321
Vyhovsky, Mykola, 49
Vyshensky Labour School, 128–9

White Army, 251, 252
working class: Bolshevik Ukrainization and, 301; cultural revolution and, 239; forced Ukrainization of, 33, 132–3, 141, 146–7, 301, 341; intelligentsia and, 267; and national culture, 131, 133, 298, 306–7; nationalities policy and, 152; and peasantry, 66, 140; and Russian language, 178, 191, 192, 219, 371n48; as Russian vs Ukrainian, 139; as Russified, 143; Russophilism and, 307; schools *(robfaky)*, 97, 380n38; and Ukrainian language, 133, 139, 141, 178; and Ukrainian vs Russian languages, 155–6; Ukrainization of, 16, 33, 35, 138, 143–4, 151, 152, 161–2, 163, 175, 305–8
working-class children: enrolment of, 288; and *kraieznavstvo*, 53; in Kyiv, 161–2, 261; and labour culture, 51, 60, 62, 321, 323; roles in socialist state, 153; and Ukrainian-language instruction, 33, 153, 156, 341; Ukrainization of, 152, 161, 341; and vocational schools, 47
working-class youth: Komsomol and, 175, 183; and Russian language, 191; and Ukrainian language, 187, 191; Ukrainization of, 191–2
writing skills, 82–3, 128–9

Yakymenko (teacher), 74
Yavorsky, Matvii, 62, 313, 356; *Korotka istoriia Ukraini* (Short history of Ukraine), 55–6; *Revoliutsiia na Ukraini* (Revolution in Ukraine), 56
Yefremov, Petro, 268
Yefremov, Serhii: biography, 356; diary, 398–9n66, 399n73; GPU and, 265, 268, 274; and Soviet power, 40; and SVU, 258, 268; on teachers as revolutionary, 73; and Ukrainian culture/language, 266, 270, 277; and VUAN dictionary, 26
Yiddish language, 194, 220
Yiddish-language schools: anti-Semitism and, 247; assimilation of non-Russians vs, 234; and division between Jews and Ukrainians, 396n30; Jewish children in, 99, 160, 380–1n41, 386n55; Jewish schools vs, 381n43; mixed Ukrainian-language schools, 404n14; in Pryluky, 194. *See also* Jewish schools
Young Pioneers, 177f; about, 33, 35; anti-Soviet youth organizations and, 187; assaults against, 298–9; and Bolshevik Ukrainization, 301; Central Bureau (TsB), 185–6, 191; and child activism, 296–7; children's attitudes toward, 186; and children's literature, 191, 292; and civic education, 84; civil servants as leaders, 285; class and, 284, 287, 288, 289, 290–1, 297, 305; and collectivization, 285; command of, 283; and complexes, 107, 191; cultural revolution and, 284; and ethnic-minority children, 180–1; and Five-Year Plan, 288, 290; Fourth All-Ukrainian Meeting on, 190; and FZU schools, 178; and grain requisition, 36, 293; Great Turn and, 284, 285; growth of, 186; and industrial excursions, 292–3; Jewish children in, 181; Komsomol's relationship with, 33, 175, 179, 181–2, 198, 282, 283, 284, 285, 294; KP(b)U and, 282; kulaks and, 282, 285–6, 289; in Kyiv Labour School No. 1, 261, 269; leadership, 293, 294, 295; literacy campaign, 297–8; membership numbers, 289–90, 291; Narkomos

and, 282, 291, 292; and national culture, 297–8; and nationalism, 179, 284, 290, 291; and nationalities policy, 33, 35, 174, 175, 176, 182; and non-Russian-speaking children, 175; and non-Soviet youth organizations, 186; numbers of, 107; numbers of units, 182, 186; and political training, 104, 114, 179–80, 186, 190–1; and polytechnization of schools, 292–3; in rural areas, 293; and Russian language, 8, 145, 174, 180, 181, 184, 283, 297; and school enrolment, 190–1, 282, 287–8, 293; and schools, 104, 145, 182, 282–3, 285–7; and socialism, 175; teachers and, 284, 294; Ukrainian children and, 178, 181; and Ukrainian language, 174, 180, 298; in Ukrainian-language schools, 175, 176; and Ukrainian vs Russian languages, 90; and Ukrainization, 16, 35, 174, 180–1, 197–8, 283; Ukrainization of, 175, 176, 179–80, 184, 188, 191; urban–rural divide and, 198; VUAN and, 264

youth: assignment to villages for Ukrainization, 224; and building of socialism, 268; corruption of, 261, 267, 269, 270; counter-revolution and, 40; cultural revolution and, 38–40; GPU and, 40; Komsomol and, 176; KP(b)U and, 39–40, 267; membership in Komsomol, 192–3; and nationalism, 40, 262, 268, 270, 276–7; organization of, 262; religious organizations and, 187; suicides of, 299–300; SVU and, 261, 262, 267, 268, 270–1; TLeZ and, 269–70; and Ukrainization, 191, 193, 196–9; VUAN and, 264. *See also* children

Zaikova, Anton, 250–1
Zaikova, Mariia, 250–1
Za kulturnu revoliutsiuu, 255
Zaluzhny, Oleksandr, 408n114
Za nenku Ukrainu, 290
Za politekhnychnu osvitu, 319
Zaporizhzhia: FZU schools in, 197; Komsomol in, 194; Russian language in, 197; Russian-student attendance in, 327; Young Pioneers in, 290–91
Zatonsky, Volodymyr: biography, 357; as education commissar, 46, 49, 68, 150, 304, 332; and ethnicity and native language, 151; and language equality, 68; purge of Narkomos, 333, 334; and Russified-Ukrainian children, 335, 336; and Ukrainization, 68, 150, 164; and vocational schools, 373n15
Zhyttia i revoliutsiia, 244
Zoloratov, Vadym, 258, 264, 265

www.ingramcontent.com/pod-product-compliance
Lightning Source LLC
Chambersburg PA
CBHW020348080526
44584CB00014B/934